MOON HANDBOOKS

COASTAL CAROLINAS

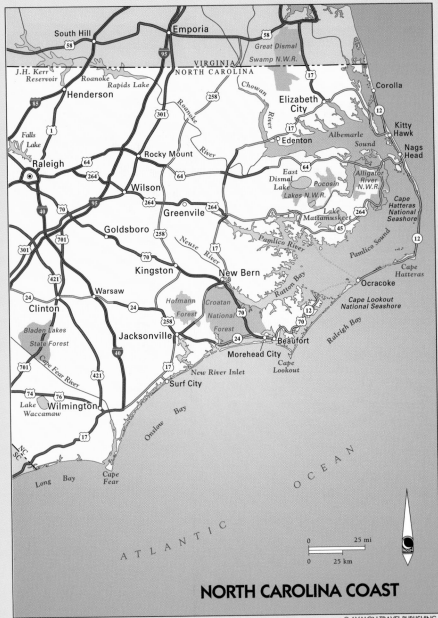

NORTH CAROLINA COAST

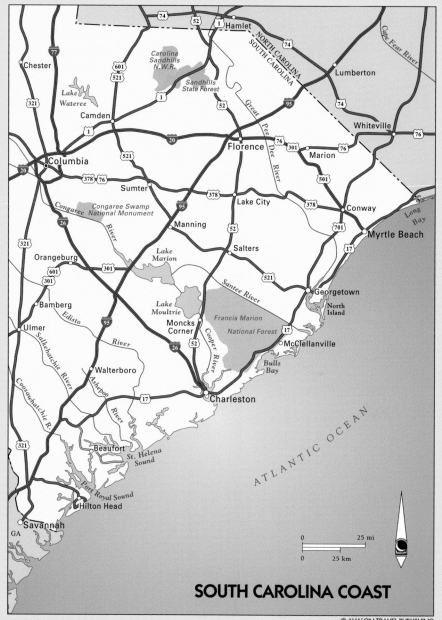

SOUTH CAROLINA COAST

MOON HANDBOOKS

COASTAL CAROLINAS

FIRST EDITION

MIKE SIGALAS

AVALON
TRAVEL

MOON HANDBOOKS:
COASTAL CAROLINAS
FIRST EDITION

Mike Sigalas

Published by
Avalon Travel Publishing
1400 65th Street, Suite 250
Emeryville, CA 94608, USA
Avalon Travel Publishing is a division of Avalon
Publishing Group, Inc.

Printing History
1st edition—May 2001
5 4 3 2

Please send all comments,
corrections, additions,
amendments, and critiques to:

**MOON HANDBOOKS:
COASTAL CAROLINAS
AVALON TRAVEL PUBLISHING
1400 65th Street, Suite 250
EMERYVILLE, CA 94608, USA
email: atpfeedback@avalonpub.com
www.moon.com**

ISBN: 1-56691-267-9
ISSN: 1532-2572

Editor: Marisa Solís
Series Manager: Erin Van Rheenen
Copyeditor: Jean Blomquist
Index: Lynne Lipkind
Graphics Coordinator: Erika Howsare
Production: Marcie McKinley, Kelly Pendragon
Design: Dave Hurst
Map Editor: Naomi Dancis, Mike Ferguson
Cartography: Landis Bennett, Kat Kalamaras, Mike Morgenfeld, Chris Folks

Front cover photo: Beaufort saltwater marsh, © Index Stock Photography, Inc.

All photos by Mike Sigalas unless otherwise noted.
All illustrations by Bob Race unless otherwise noted.

Distributed in the United States and Canada by Publishers Group West

Printed in the United States by Malloy

For Kristin

CONTENTS

SPECIAL TOPICS

NAGS HEAD AND THE OUTER BANKS 86

SPECIAL TOPICS

NEW BERN AND THE CENTRAL COAST. 112

SPECIAL TOPICS

WILMINGTON AND THE SOUTHERN NORTH CAROLINA COAST. 136

SPECIAL TOPICS

MYRTLE BEACH AND THE GRAND STRAND 165

Land; Climate; History

Sights 169
Orientation; Museums and Gardens; Amusement Parks and Other
Adventures; Beaches

Accommodations 178
Resorts; Motels; Guest and Rental Houses and Bed-and-Breakfasts;
Campgrounds

Food 181

Nightlife 185
Clubs and Pubs; Theater and Dance Venues; Movie Theaters

Sports, Recreation, and Shopping 187
On the Water; On Land; Shopping; Best Bookstores

Information and Transportation 190
Information and Services; Getting There; Getting Around

Georgetown and Vicinity 191
History; Sights; Accommodations; Food; Activities; Information; North of
Georgetown: Pawleys Island; To the West: The Chubby Checker
Birthplace; Points South

SPECIAL TOPICS

CHARLESTON AND VICINITY 200

Land; Climate

History 202

Sights 207
Orientation; Plantations, Gardens, and Parks; Museums, Historical
Sights, and Art; Mount Pleasant; Isle of Palms and Sullivan's Island;
Beaches; Colleges

Accommodations 228
Historic District; Bed-and-Breakfasts; East Cooper; West Ashley; Rental
Homes; Campgrounds

Food 235
Charleston Proper; Outlying Areas; Supermarkets

Entertainment and Events 242
Festivals; Concert Venues; Clubs and Bars; Theater and Dance Venues;
Movie Theaters; Coffee Shops and Cafés; More Places to Meet People

Sports, Recreation, and Shopping 247
On the Water; On Land; Professional Sports; Shopping

ABBREVIATIONS

C.S.A.—Confederate States of America
I—Interstate highway (e.g., I-95)
N.C.—North Carolina

NPS—National Park Service
S.C.—South Carolina
SRS—Savannah River Site
UGA—University of Georgia

UNC—University of North Carolina
USC—University of South Carolina
WPA—Works Progress

HELP MAKE THIS A BETTER BOOK

It's unavoidable: between the time this book goes to print and the moment you read this, a handful of the businesses noted in these pages will undoubtedly change prices, move, or close their doors forever. Other worthy attractions will open for the first time. If you see anything that needs updating, clarification, or correction, or if you have a favorite gem you'd like to see included in the next edition, I'd appreciate it if you'd drop me a line.

Address comments to:

Moon Handbooks: Coastal Carolinas, first edition
Avalon Travel Publishing
1400 65th Street, Suite 250
Emeryville, CA 94608
USA

email: atpfeedback@avalonpub.com
(please put "Coastal Carolinas" in
the subject line of your email)

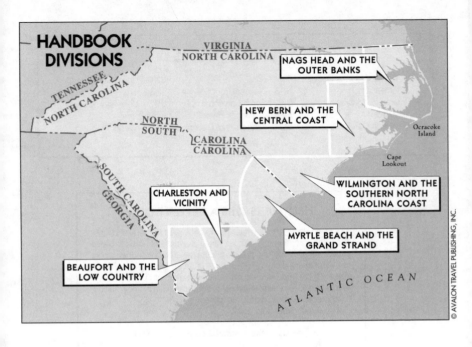

MAPS

MAP SYMBOLS

═══ Superhighway	⬭ Interstate	• Accommodations
══ Primary Road	⬭ U.S. Highway	★ Point of Interest
── Secondary Road	◯ State Highway	▪ Other Location
·········· Ferry	◉ State Capital	▾ Restuarant/Bar
– – – Intracoastal Waterway	○ City	✈ International Airport
┝━━┥ Railroad Tracks	○ Town	✗ Airfield/Airstrip
⸙ Swamp	▲ State Park	▲ Mountain

ACKNOWLEDGMENTS

Thanks to my wife, reader, editor, research assistant, and coach, Kristin, who made this book possible. Thanks also to my sons, Noah and Ben.

Very special thanks to the wonderful folks of the Carolinas and, in particular, to Geoff and Tammy Grafton and family for the van; to Tant and Sharon Ehrhardt for showing us where the key was and learnin' us about hospitality; to Billy and Anita Bryan for the recipe, baby-sitting, and restaurant tips; to Kendall and Meredith Buckendahl for the golf assistance and for giving us the big bed; to Tom and Debbie Caverly and family for the shrimping, swimming, and beach house. Thanks also to my brother, George Sigalas III, horticulturalist, for his help with the flora, and to his wife, Kristin, for the gracious hospitality and photo assistance.

Thanks as well to Connie Nelson of Cape Fear Coast Convention and Visitors Bureau, Quinn E. Capps of the Dare County Tourist Bureau, and to Lisa Hammersley, formerly of the Myrtle Beach Area Chamber of Commerce—all of whom went beyond the call of duty in assisting my research. Thanks also to the helpful folks at the Historical Charleston Chamber; to Megan Jones of Kitty Hawk Kayaks, to Captain Carl Marshburn of the *Henrietta III,* and Rebecca Temples and the rest of the crew at Ripley's; Karen Carter at the Edisto Bookstore; the Wilts at the Rice Museum in Georgetown; the crew at Judy's House of Oldies in Ocean Drive Beach; and to Shagging Czar Barry Thigpen for his research assistance. Thanks also to Angela Brown for sharing stories of her days on St. Helena Island, and to South Carolina hockey expert Stephanie A. Kavanagh.

And to my mother, sister Mary, and Jeanette Pelak, and to Brian and Jen Logue, for the encouragement, flexibility, and child care.

Also to my parents, George and Sue Sigalas, who drove instead of flying.

Avalon Travel Publishing
Thanks to Pauli Galin, Ellen Cavalli, and Marisa Solís for their expert carrot-and-stick work; to Bob Race and Dave Hurst for their skillful job with the visuals; and to the Avalon Cartography Crew, professionals all.

My thanks in advance to those promoting this title, including webmeister Matt Orendorff. And to Ms. Oprah Winfrey, for making this your Book of the Month.

INTRODUCTION

The coasts of North and South Carolina are beautiful in a Carolina way.

Forget the eye-popping, gasp-inducing grandeur of Maine's or California's wave-battered cliffs. Carolina's low, undulating marshes and white, wide beaches cause your breathing to deepen and slow. In its thick, salty air lies a low-key, intangible richness, a gracefulness, a subtlety. It's not a beauty that tips you over in your chair—it hands you a sweet tea, pulls up a rocker, and stays awhile.

This beauty comes from nature, from the growing and dying, the lapping and splashing, the shifting and crumbling and sprouting of the earth, and from the songs and instinctual acts of its creatures. But it's also a world in which people have a place. Standing on Oregon's rocky shore, a person feels like a spectator, an intruder. In Carolina, puttering in a johnboat up a grassy inlet, a pail of shrimp between your knees, you remember, in the deepest part of your being, that humans are indeed indigenous to the earth.

People have traveled Carolina's ocean, sounds, and inlets for centuries. To the first Carolinians, water meant fish, and so early native Carolinians established their villages by the water's edge, fanning out daily in canoes to harvest the bounty of the rivers and sea. The next wave of Carolinians arrived by the sea, and to them, the waterways meant safe harbor, accessibility, and later, profit. Bays, creeks, and inlets were the interstates of colonial America, and these first Euro-Carolina towns bustled as distribution centers for the harvests pulled from the new and fertile lands. Later, when rails and roads replaced water as the preferred medium of economic pursuit, other, landlocked towns became equally or more important than the colonial ports. This slowed, froze, and in some cases, even reversed growth in the port towns, preserving the provincial flavor up and down the coast, from Beaufort, S.C., clear up to Manteo on Roanoke Island.

Traveling the Carolina coasts today, you'll come upon scores of fascinating, timeless water-birthed cities and towns, and you'll enter nearly every one of them by first crossing over a long, sweeping bridge—a steel and concrete homage to the river, bay, or sound whose presence gave life to the town itself.

THE LAND

THE CAROLINA COASTS: BIRTHPLACE OF THE DEEP SOUTH

In some ways, the coasts of South Carolina and North Carolina couldn't be more different. South Carolina, because of its deepwater ports in Beaufort, Georgetown, and most importantly, Charles Town (later Charleston) quickly became one of the wealthiest British colonies in the New World. First lumber, then rice, indigo, and cotton all flowed out of the region, building a powerful aristocracy centered in Charleston, which, until the Civil War, dominated South

Carolina politics and, in fact, the politics of the American South. General William T. Sherman, stationed at nearby Fort Moultrie before the war, recalled the Holy City in the 1840s as a "proud, aristocratic city," which had "assumed a leadership in the public opinion of the South far out of proportion to her population, wealth, or commerce." Long dominated by rice and indigo plantations, this is, of course, the region of the state in which slavery was most prominent. Not coincidentally, this is also the place where you'll find the highest number of remnants of South Carolina's famed antebellum "high" culture. The aristocratic structure of the plantation system, because it condemned many slaves to mind-numbing labor, also freed time—and provided the wealth—for the few fortunates at the top to study arts, architecture, medicine, and poetry; to put on plays, attend school in England, serve as political leaders, and essentially do the things reserved for the "leisure" classes until technology eased the burdens of daily living for the rest of us in the late 19th and 20th centuries. Elite groups tend to perpetuate themselves through governmental control, superior education, and self-promoting literature, and so Charleston's leadership of the region continued even after the soils of the Old South had worn out and the bulk of the South's population and riches had moved Westward into Georgia, Alabama, Louisiana, and Texas.

Today the South Carolina coast features some of the state's foremost attractions: Charleston, Beaufort, Myrtle Beach, and Hilton Head Island.

Along Coastal North Carolina, on the other hand, only the Cape Fear River flowed to the ocean without first threading a gauntlet of coastal islands. At the mouth of the Cape Fear River grew the port town of Wilmington, but north of that the Outer Banks discouraged large cargo and passenger ships from reaching most of the state's three hundred coastal miles. So even though the first English settlements in northeastern Northern Carolina began in the 17th century, that area developed very slowly. Even today towns like New Bern, Edenton, and

---

SIGHT-SEEING HIGHLIGHTS

Outer Banks
• Cape Hatteras National Seashore
• Jockey's Ridge State Park
• Manteo Waterfront
• Ocracoke Village
• Wright Brothers National Landmark

New Bern and Central Coast
• Beaufort Waterfront
• Edenton's Historic District
• Ferry Ride (take your pick)
• New Bern's Historic District

Wilmington and Southern Coast
• Wilmington's Historic District
• Southport

Myrtle Beach
• Brookgreen Gardens
• Huntington Beach State Park

Charleston
• Fort Sumter National Monument
• Historic District
• Magnolia Plantation and Gardens

Beaufort, S.C.
• Historic District

SMALL-TOWN GEMS OF COASTAL CAROLINA

Beaufort, S.C.
A quiet, historic waterfront town made famous in Pat Conroy's *The Great Santini* and *The Prince of Tides*. Lots of historic B&Bs.

Beaufort, N.C.
Beaufort's lively waterfront and closeness to the beach make this a fine vacation destination.

Edenton, N.C.
The Beaufort, S.C., of North Carolina, minus Conroy and the fame.

Georgetown, S.C.
Third-oldest city in the state, Georgetown retains its coastal small-town flavor, while containing ample amenities for tourists.

Manteo, N.C.
Contains a couple of very nice B&Bs and provides lots of dining/shopping opportunities as well as Roanoke Island Festival Park, just across the river.

Ocean Drive Beach, S.C.
Though the high-rises are going up as we speak, North Myrtle Beach's "Old O.D."—ground zero for the shagging subculture—remains a tight-knit beach community devoted to innocent pleasures.

Oriental, N.C.
A favorite stopover from New Bern; great seafood restaurants and a low-key attitude.

Ocracoke Village, N.C.
Sure, it's metacute—a cute village that continues to exist by being a cute village—but for feeling away from it all without formally leaving North America, it's hard to beat Ocracoke.

Southport, N.C.
In a coastline of tourist-driven burgs, Southport stands out as the real thing: a salty fishing town. Nice maritime museum, shops, historic buildings.

Runners-Up: Bath, N.C.; Conway, S.C.; Elizabeth City, N.C.; Folly Beach, S.C.; and Walterboro, S.C.

Possibly in a Few Years: Bluffton, S.C.; Daniel Island, S.C.; Hertford, N.C.; Newpoint (St. Helena Island), S.C.; Port Royal, S.C.; and Washington, N.C.

Other Downtowns Worth Exploring: Market Area, Charleston; New Bern, Old Village (Mount Pleasant); and Wilmington

---

Elizabeth City welcome legions of yachts, but none of the passenger liners and cargo ships you'll find docked at Wilmington.

A state's power tends to reside where its money is made, and in North Carolina, this ended up being inland, in the foothills. While development along most of the North Carolina coast stalled for lack of deepwater ports, the influx of flinty, small-scale farmers from Scotland and Pennsylvania during the 1700s to the state's piedmont and mountain regions quickly shifted the balance of power westward in the state. Wedged between haughty Tidewater Virginia and flamboyant coastal—or "Lowcountry"—South Carolina, North Carolina became, as the saying goes, "a vale of humility between two mountains of conceit;" a state whose psyche was shaped by nose-to-the-plow, Calvinist Presbyterians, not by the high-living, slave-owning cotton- and rice-planting Anglicans of coastal Virginia and South Carolina.

Despite their differences, the Carolina coasts have a lot in common as well. They were both settled originally by small, diverse native tribes. Next came the Spanish (and, in South Carolina, the French,) who poked around, attempted colonization, and departed. And then came the British, who successfully settled the land. Both Carolina coasts contain the oldest towns of their respective states: Charleston, S.C., was founded in 1670 (as Charles Town); Bath, N.C., came along in 1705.

The towns along these coasts generally date from the same period, and the romantic notions that spawned the antebellum excesses of Charleston influenced the wealthy in Wilmington as well, and, to a lesser degree, the wealthy of Albemarle towns like New Bern and Elizabeth

City. All these port towns absorbed the goods and ideas spilling from visiting vessels, creating a uniquely cosmopolitan fabric to the larger waterfront communities.

GEOGRAPHY

Size and Area

Two other things the Carolina Coasts have in common are their abundant beauty and their growing popularity as travel destinations. The coasts of both Carolinas combined contain nearly 500 miles of oceanfront, and the names "Nags Head," "Cape Hatteras," "Myrtle Beach," and "Hilton Head" ring with travelers worldwide, bringing to mind white sands, bathing suits, sand castles, and all the trappings of the traditional American family beach vacation.

Yet here too there's perhaps a difference. The North Carolina Coast—particularly the Outer Banks—seems to roll out a broader towel along the sands of the American consciousness than does the South Carolina Coast. Many non-Southern visitors are surprised to learn that South Carolina perceives itself largely as a coastal state. But it does. South Carolina offers the visitor 185 miles of coastline—twice as much coastline, in fact, as the Hawaiian island of Kauai. Even the official state nickname—the

---

THE TWO CAROLINAS

Because it had no deepwater port and only one river that ran directly to the ocean (most others ran through modern-day South Carolina first), the northern part of Carolina developed quite differently from its southern sister, becoming home primarily to small Welsh and Scottish farmers rather than the type of wealthy English planters found in the Lowcountry. By 1712, the northern half of Carolina was granted its own governor and officially named "North Carolina."

Due to its greater development, South Carolina was the part of Carolina most Europeans meant when they spoke of "Carolina." Even so, the region south of North Carolina came to be known as "South Carolina."

Palmetto State—refers to the tree indigenous to South Carolina's Sea Islands.

This isn't to say that the South Carolina Coast is hurting for visitors. According to the latest statistics, 55 percent of tourists in South Carolina say they come for the beaches. As well they should: from the white sands of North Myrtle Beach to the Gullah Sea Islands at the Georgia border, South Carolina's beaches are a national treasure, and certainly (with the possible exception of central Myrtle Beach) a vast improvement over the overbuilt strips farther south in Florida.

Elevation

The elevation of most of the region is, as you might guess, sea level or slightly higher. With the exception of Wilmington, towns along the coast are notoriously flat. How flat? Years ago locals built a hill on Sullivan's Isle near Charleston, reportedly so that island children might have an idea of what one looked like. The highest spot along both coasts is Jockey Ridge near Nags Head on the Outer Banks. Though the winds and development—which keep new sand from replacing the sand that's blown away—are slowly diminishing its grainy greatness, the highest part of the ridge today towers over the rest of the Carolina Coasts at about 140 feet. But, of course, hotels in Myrtle Beach stand taller than that.

With this lack of horizontal diversity comes a certain dearth of drama. If *Rebel Without a Cause* had been set on the Carolina Coasts, Natalie Wood's boyfriend could never have flown off a cliff to his death. He'd have thudded into a huge barrier dune before he even got to the beach. And if he'd somehow reached the strand, he could have driven easily across the hard-packed sand, and once in the ocean, could have kept driving fifty yards towards Liverpool before the engine ever got wet at all. Then his car would have stalled out, and he could have swum safely back to shore through the pint-size breakers.

No, drama is largely lacking from the geography of the Carolina Coasts—that's where the people come in. But what the coasts lack in eye-popping, jaw-dropping grandeur, they make up for in a low-key, intangible richness, a graciousness, a subtlety.

REGIONS

The Albermarle Region

The first sector of the Carolinas successfully settled by the English was "the Albemarle." In the broadest use of the term, the Albemarle describes all of the northeastern corner of North Carolina. Technically the term describes the mainland inland of the Outer Banks, along the Albemarle Sound. The sound itself, the end of seven different rivers, slices 55 miles into the continent. Those seven rivers intersecting the region create a very watery area, mostly consisting of marsh, maritime forest, wetlands, and bait shops.

Today numerous state- and federally-designated areas, such as the Alligator River National Wildlife Refuge, preserve the area's unique and graceful natural resources.

The Outer Banks

Technically all the coastal islands off the North Carolina shore—all the way down to the Brunswick Isles south of Wilmington—qualify as "outer banks," but in common parlance, the "Outer Banks" refers to the islands from the Virginia border south to Ocracoke Island. Much of this land, fortunately, has been preserved as national and state preserves and parks, including **Mackay Island National Wildlife Refuge,** near the Virginia border; **Currituck National Wildlife Refuge,** near Corolla; **Jockey's Ridge State Park,** near Nags Head; and especially the large **Cape Hatteras National Seashore.** South of Ocracoke, all of Portsmouth, Lookout Island, and the Shackleford Banks have been preserved as the **Lookout Island National Seashore.** This last is perhaps the most pristine of all the preserves. These islands give visitors the chance to visit virtually untouched Atlantic coastline—and they're unreachable except by boat.

The Central Coast

This region has taken to calling itself the "Crystal Coast," but outside of some meth labs that may have been discovered inland, there are no crystals around here. The Core Banks and the Bogue Banks make up most of the central coastline. The Bogue Banks have been developed as a sort of minor league Nags Head, but the Core Banks remain relatively untouched.

The Cape Fear Coast

The Cape Fear Coast, for the purposes of this book, includes all the area from the Wilmington beaches—from Topsail Island southward—to Kure Beach.

Brunswick Isles

The islands south of Wilmington have become increasingly popular in recent years, as Myrtle Beach expands upward and Wilmington expands southward. Inland from the Brunswick Isles, developed but still largely a regional—not national—destination, lies little Calabash, the tiny fishing town near the South Carolina border, that has given its name to a style of seafood.

The Grand Strand

South Carolina's most northern, and most famous, stretch of coastline is the "Grand Strand," a 60-mile stretch reaching from the North Carolina border south to Winyah Bay below Georgetown, paralleled by the Waccamaw River to the north. Some scientists say the strand is built on a 100,000-year-old barrier sand formation.

This region is marked by erosion; despite "beach nourishment" programs, big storms bring out the sandbagging teams, which try to protect oceanfront hotels and other structures.

The Santee Delta

The Santee Delta is a 20-mile zone stretching down the coast from Winyah Harbor south to Cape Romain. The largest delta on the east coast, it has retreated 1,000 or more feet since the 1940s, when Lakes Moultrie and Marion were created upriver, slowing the flow of the mighty river and causing it to drop the bulk of its sedimentary load long before reaching the coast. Newer reservoirs along the river's tributaries and diversions of Santee waters into the Cooper River have further exacerbated the problem.

The Sea Islands

South of the delta, the Sea Islands begin. Biggest is Hilton Head Island, the largest sea island south of New Jersey. Some, such as Sullivan's and Edisto Islands, have been inhabited by European-Americans for centuries; others, including Hilton Head and Kiawah, took on tile-roofed

a Lowcountry salt marsh

condos and putting greens in the 1960s and 1970s; still others, including Seabrook Island and Fripp Island (home of novelist Pat Conroy), are just now being dragged down the path of Disneyfication.

Prime pristine island experiences include Hunting Island and Bull Island—both protected by law from the developers' axes.

RIVERS, SWAMPS, AND LAKES

North Carolina's coast stretches for 300 miles if you fly above it, northeast to southwest, in a straight line. But the true coast has no relation to hypothetical flight paths. Serving as the ocean-end of the Yadkin, Roanoke-Dan, Cape Fear, Neuse, Tar, and Chowan River Basins, the jagged land fingers of the coastal plain touch more than 1,500 miles of waterfront and contain more than 3,000 square miles of water surface. And that's when the region's not flooded.

South Carolina, too, is rich in water. Over 31 billion gallons of water a day flow into the Atlantic Ocean from South Carolina's rivers. South Carolina's three major water systems—the Pee Dee, Santee, and Savannah—all follow the downward northwest-to-southeast slope of their state. They begin in the Upcountry above Greenville as clear, narrow, swift-moving streams and rivers, then widen in the central Midlands region into red, muddy

rivers. As they reach the coastal plain, they begin picking up a tannic acid stain from cypress and other roots, and transform into the legendary slow-moving, blackwater rivers of the Lowcountry.

The **Pee Dee** is the northernmost of the river systems, consisting of the Lynches, Great Pee Dee, and Little Pee Dee Rivers, which join with the Black River and Waccamaw at the head of Winyah Bay near Georgetown. Alone of the major South Carolina rivers, the Pee Dee has not yet been dammed to create hydroelectric power—though this seems about to change. In 1999 the U.S. Army Corps of Engineers announced plans to select the site for a new lake that would allow water to be stored, then released into the Great Pee Dee River during low levels.

Politicos in Dillon County contend that the lake will provide additional water to the Great Pee Dee River, allowing industries to locate there. And industries mean jobs. Unfortunately most experience tells us that it's not the local residents of depressed areas who get the new jobs brought by new industry—normally the jobs go to imported, trained labor. Opponents of the project say it would ruin scenic swamps and encourage increased industrial dumping of pollutants into the river system. The six dams in *North* Carolina are the reason for the Great Pee Dee's water level drop, they argue. However, engineers say that increasing the level of the

Pee Dee could actually help fish and wildlife by diluting the pollutants already in the river and by restoring and extending wetlands.

The fate of the lake on the Pee Dee is anyone's guess. Nonetheless, the Corps is considering 14 different sites, including ones in Cheraw State Park; Spot Mill Creek, near the Chesterfield-Darlington county line; White's Creek, four miles north of Cheraw; Thompson Creek, about two miles south of Cheraw; and Back Swamp, about two miles north of I-95 near Florence. None of these are on the South Carolina Coast, but a dam anywhere along the way will greatly affect the Pee Dee River basin, all the way to the Georgetown region.

The largest of South Carolina's river systems, the **Santee,** is formed by the coming together of the Wateree and the Congaree Rivers. It drains nearly 40 percent of the entire state before finishing its run as a slow-moving black river sliding out between coastal islands into the Atlantic. The **Savannah** river system drains the southwestern reaches of the state as well as northwestern Georgia.

Black Rivers

As opposed to the large rivers draining the Piedmont region, Lowcountry-born black rivers form at a much lower elevation, normally at the foot of the sand hills in the center of the state's coastal plain. As a result, the larger rivers carry sedimentary loads and are often colored a milky reddish-yellow (about the color of coffee with a lot of cream), while the slower, nonsediment-carrying Lowcountry rivers receive their coloring exclusively from the tannic acid that emanates from the decaying coastal plain trees and tree roots along its shores. The color of these rivers is black—about the color of thin, unadulterated coffee.

The **Edisto River** is the longest blackwater river in the world. It combines with other, smaller rivers such as the **Ashley** and **Combahee**, to drain about 20 percent of the state.

The large, sediment-carrying rivers tend to drop their loads right at a river's end, creating river deltas. On the other hand, black rivers, with their slight but steady water flow and very little sediment, dig estuaries and deep embayments,

CAROLINAS' BAYS

No, these oval or elliptically shaped depressions didn't get their name because they look like little self-contained bays, but because of the bay trees that usually grow around them. Look hard enough and you'll find nearly half a million Carolina bays in the coastal plain from Maryland to Florida, but you'll find them most commonly in South and North Carolina. If you drive by one (and you will), you might assume it's just an isolated swamp, but from the air, or on a topographic map, their distinctive shapes make them easy to identify.

So where did they come from? That's what scientists would like to know. Here are the facts: All of South Carolina's bays face in a northwest-southeast direction. Sometimes a sandy ridge will encircle the bay, but almost always only on the southeastern rim.

Is it possible that these bays are the result of a single catastrophic event? Some scientists believe the bays are scars from a meteorite that exploded into thousands of pieces just before hitting the earth. If a meteor hit the earth headed in a northwesterly direction, this would explain the identical direction of the bays and would explain the oblong shape—as meteorite pieces burrowed to a stop in the ground.

It's a fine theory. Unfortunately, no one has found any remnants of a meteor anywhere around the bays, nor have they detected the magnetism normally found around remnant areas.

A second theory, less exciting, argues that the bays' unique shape comes from the area's constant exposure to prevailing southwesterly winds. The ridge of sand around the southeast rim of many of the bays might be the result of occasional strong northwesterly winds from rare winter storms.

Nobody knows for sure. But wherever they come from, the bays are worth visiting. The smallest bays are around four or five acres in area, some serving as private ponds. The largest is **Big Swamp** in the **Manchester State Forest** in Sumter County. The best place to see a picture-postcard bay is probably **Woods Bay State Park,** which preserves a three-mile-long, one-mile-wide bay near the town of Olanta, near where U.S. 378 crosses I-95 in Florence County.

such as Charleston Harbor and Port Royal Sound near Beaufort.

Lakes

The only lakes of any size along the Carolina coasts are **Lake Mattamuskeet, Phelps Lake, Alligator Lake,** and **Pungo Lake,** all south of the Albemarle Sound. In a water-rich area like this, it's easy to see how even the largest natural lake in all of North Carolina—Mattamuskeet—could be taken for granted. Used as the center of an Indian reservation in 1715, local residents drained and used the lakebed for farming twice over the years. Fortunately in 1934, Mattamuskeet became a United States Wildlife Refuge.

Other Waterways

Saddled at the south with "Cape Fear" and at the north with the "Great Dismal Swamp Canal"—and that's not even to mention Bodie (pronounced "body") Island on the Outer Banks—it's a wonder North Carolina's grimly-named coast has ever caught on with vacationers. And yet, despite its self-deprecating name, the Great Dismal Swamp Canal is a favorite of the yachtsy set, who often turn up in Elizabeth City, where, whenever five or more are gathered in the marina, the Rosebuddies will show up, bringing rosebuds, wine, and cheese to the floating visitors. The **Intracoastal Waterway** also slides down the inside of the states, inside of barrier islands, down rivers and through man-made canals. Running from Norfolk, Virginia, to Miami, Florida, the waterway allows boaters to travel up and down the East Coast without worrying about storm waters or the Gulf Stream's prevailing northerly current.

CLIMATE

When to Visit

Most Carolinians will tell you that the best times to see the Carolinas are in the autumn and in the spring. In fact, some Charleston inns consider midsummer and winter to be off-season. And there's some sense to this.

In autumn, the crops are in—meaning roadside stands are packed with fresh fruits and vegetables—and the temperature and humidity are down. In fact, in the Carolinas (as in much of the

> *Carolina is in the spring a paradise, in the summer a hell, and in the autumn a hospital.*
>
> —Colonial American saying

South) most state fairs and county fairs are held in the fall rather than midsummer, to capitalize on the more merciful weather. Of course on the coast, fall is also hurricane season, but—though North Carolina in particular has had more than its share of late—hurricanes generally come along a handful of times each century, while *every* fall features some beautiful cool weather.

In the spring, the dogwood and azalea blossoms are out and the weather is a blessed mix: not too cold, not too hot, but just right.

Even in this age of air-conditioning, South Carolina summers—even on the barrier islands—are just too hot and humid for many people. Temperatures can rise to over 100°F, with humidity above 50 percent (and sometimes much higher). A 100°F temperature with 100 percent humidity is about right for a hot shower, but not a vacation. Count on it being somewhere between 75°F and 88°F on a July day in South Carolina; a little cooler north of Cape Fear.

In truth, though, for people without limitations on their breathing, summer on the Carolina Coasts is not all that bad, and it has its own likable nuances. The ocean waters are warm and swimmable. The kids are out of school and fill the playgrounds at the parks. And there is something to be said for being able to say you've experienced the South's legendary humidity at its high-water mark.

It's also true that a midsummer lightning storm over the Pamlico Sound, or over the salt marshes of the Lowcountry, is an experience not to be missed. And those looking to understand the heart of Carolina culture have only to live through a hot week in August to understand where the slow speech and languid pace of Carolinians comes from. I've woken up plenty of summer mornings with a plateful of goals for the day, but when it's that hot and that humid—when just getting out of bed coats your back with sweat—you don't really feel much like taking on the world. Sitting out on the shady porch with a pitcher of sweet tea sounds like the only reasonable thing to do.

So if you're planning a lot of sight-seeing—as opposed to just lolling by the pool, on the lake, or at the beach—then think twice before visiting between June and September. And this is doubly true if you're planning on camping and hiking, both of which at this time of year become more of a life struggle against the insect kingdom than a time of relaxation. If you're already familiar with the South or come from a place that enjoys a similar climate, then you won't have a problem. But if you're flying in from London or San Francisco and stepping off the plane into the heat of a Carolina August, you're going to need at least a few days (and possibly some grief counseling) to adjust.

Winter in Coastal Carolina is a much milder experience than it is in the eastern parts of the states, where average January temps hover in the mid-40s. Still, a visit at this time of year is a different sort of vacation: the Atlantic will be too cold to swim, though surfers brave it with wet suits. Fortunately the large number of evergreen pines throughout the coastal region keeps the area looking lush even in the winter. If you have the option, you should make an effort to visit Charleston—or many of Coastal Carolina's wonderful small towns—while the Christmas lights are up and the carolers are singing on the street corners. A genuine treat.

Precipitation

First-time visitors to the American South always comment on "how green everything is." The South in general, and the Carolina Coasts in particular, are very damp places. Even the hottest day of the year might have a rain shower. In fact, some parts of Carolina receive as much as 81 inches of rain annually (most of Hawaii gets only 45 inches). The statewide average in both South Carolina and North Carolina is around 49 inches of rain annually.

One thing that many non-Southerners don't realize is that summer is the rainy season in the South. Convectional rain comes on humid days in the summer. As the sun heats the earth, the earth in turn warms the air layers just above it. Pretty soon you've got convection currents—movements of warmed air pushing its way upward through cooler air. Eventually this rising moisture reaches an elevation where it begins to cool and condense, creating cumulus clouds. As the clouds thicken and continue to cool, they create the dark thunderclouds that send picnickers and beach-goers scurrying for cover.

CAROLINAS' SYMBOLS AND EMBLEMS

SOUTH CAROLINA

Animal: white-tailed deer
Beverage: milk
Bird: Carolina wren
Butterfly: tiger swallowtail
Dance: the shag
Dog: Boykin spaniel
Fish: striped bass
Flower: yellow jessamine
Folk dance: square dance
Fruit: peach
Gem: amethyst
Insect: praying mantis
Reptile: loggerhead turtle
Shell: lettered olive
Songs: "Carolina" and "South Carolina on My Mind"
Stone: blue granite
Tree: palmetto
Wild game bird: wild turkey

NORTH CAROLINA

Beverage: milk
Bird: cardinal
Boat: shad boat
Colors: red and blue
Dog: Plott hound
Fish: channel bass
Flower: dogwood
Insect: honey bee
Mammal: gray squirrel
Motto: *Esse quam videri,* "To be, rather than to seem"
Nickname: The Old North State or The Tar Heel State
Reptile: eastern box turtle
Rock: granite
Shell: Scotch bonnet
Song: "The Old North State"
Stone: emerald
Tree: pine
Vegetable: sweet potato

> *After 1893 storm, Colonel Ward take me and Peter Carr, us two and a horse, take that shore to Little River. Search for all them what been drowned. Find a trunk to Myrtle Beach. Have all kinda things in 'em: comb for you hair, thing you put on your wrist. Found a dead horse, cow, ox, turkey, fowl—everything. Gracious God! Don't want to see no more thing like that!*
>
> *Find two them children way down at Dick Pond what drowned to Magnolia Beach ... all that family drown out, because they wouldn't go to this lady's house on higher ground. Wouldn't let none of the rest go. Servants all drowned: Betsy, Kit, Mom Adele. Couldn't identify who lost from who was saved 'til the next morning. Found old Doctor's body by his vest sticking out of the mud. Fetched the Doctor's body to shore and his watch was still a-ticking.*
>
> —1937 WPA interview with
> Ben Horry of Murrells Inlet

In a land this humid, every sunny day holds a chance for "scattered showers." Bring an umbrella; if you're camping, consider tarping your tent and gear before leaving for any long hike—you don't want to return to a soggy sleeping bag and waterlogged supplies. If you get hit by a particularly heavy storm while driving, do what the locals do: pull off under an overpass and wait it out. These types of heavy torrents don't usually last more than a few minutes. As one Carolinian said it, "When God wants to show off like that, I pull over and let Him do it."

As opposed to convectional precipitation—always a warm-weather phenomenon—frontal precipitation nearly always takes place during the winter. Frontal precipitation also differs in its general lack of drama—instead of a rapidly forming and short-lived torrent, it normally takes the form of a steady rain or drizzle, with little or no lightning and thunder. It almost always means chilly and sometimes polar-air masses, but most cold fronts coming down from the north are diverted by the Blue Ridge Mountains. Warm air from the Caribbean often can keep the thermostat at a bearably warm level in the winter.

Frontal precipitation brings what little snow comes to Coastal Carolina. True, Charleston has received snow in the past, but if you're only heading to the Lowcountry, you can feel safe leaving your snowshoes home.

Hurricanes

Floyd. Hugo. Hazel. It seems as if every generation of Coastal Carolinians has its own Day 1, its own hurricane from which to date the events of their lives. As in, "Our Honda's only a couple years old. But we've had that old truck since before Hugo." In 1991 I had the following conversation:

ME: So Hugo really gave you a hard time, eh?

MOUNT PLEASANT SHOP OWNER: Oh no. The fellow down the street, his place got ruined-terrible. Nothing left. But other than losing the roof, we-all here didn't have any damage.

ME: Other than losing the roof?

Hurricanes have undoubtedly struck the Carolina coast ever since there *was* a Carolina coast, but the first one recorded in history books hit in late 1561, when three of four Spanish ships set on settling the Port Royal region were lost. Twenty-six men drowned. North Carolina ranks third, after Florida and Texas, in the number of hurricane strikes since 1899.

In 1686, a hurricane blasted the same section of coastline, just in time to stop a marauding army of Spaniards who had already slaughtered the Scottish settlement in Beaufort and were mauling their way to Charles Town.

Three more hurricanes hit the coast in the first half of the 18th century without causing too much damage, but a 1752 hurricane nailed Charles Town dead center, hurling harbor ships into city streets, flattening homes and trees, and killing at least 28 people.

In 1885, just as South Carolina was shaking off the bonds of Reconstruction and attempting to salvage its economy, a 125-mph hurricane smashed into Charleston, killing 21 people and damaging or destroying nine of every 10 homes in the city.

And then the fun really began. On August 23, 1893, a hurricane swept up from Savannah through Charleston and the Sea Islands, killing at least 1,000 people. Another devastating hurricane followed the same October. Others followed in 1894, 1898, 1906, 1910, and 1911.

Hurricane Hazel of 1954, Hugo of 1989, and Bertha, Fran, Dennis, and Floyd in the late 1990s, are the hurricanes that stick out in the minds of many living Carolinians. Hazel killed 95 people from South Carolina to New York, including 19 in North Carolina, not to mention perhaps as many as 1,000 in Haiti and an additional 78 in Canada. It sent 90-mph winds as far west as Raleigh.

The storm tide at Calabash was boosted by the fact that Hazel came a-calling on the night of the October full moon, the highest lunar tide of the year. On this night, the dotted lines in the centers of island streets normally soak in seawater anyway; with this high tide beneath it, Hazel's storm surges, pushed by 150-mph winds, reached 18 feet at Calabash.

Holden Beach, Little River Inlet, Oak Island, and Wrightsville Beach also took the worst of it. And all the grief wasn't on the barrier islands: Wilmington cowered under near-100 mph winds. The old wooden pavilions what had given birth to the burgeoning shag dancing movement blew down: Roberts Pavilion in Ocean Drive and Spivey's in Myrtle Beach. In fact Hazel destroyed over fifteen thousand homes and structures, and damaged over twice that many, creating $136 million in estimated property losses—in 1954 dollars.

The following year, 1955, Hurricanes Connie, Diane, and Ione all hit North Carolina, causing extensive damage. And then things were relatively quiet—for a while. Most every year came watches, with occasional small strikes. But this lull in Mother Nature's war with Carolinians allowed for large scale development along most of the Carolina Coasts.

The build-up, of course, just set up more pins for Hurricane Hugo to knock over. Hugo blew into the region in 1989, featuring 135-mph winds and a 20-foot storm surge into Bull's Bay, north of Charleston—the highest storm surge in United States history. Hugo claimed 79 people overall (49 in the United States), but—though it slammed through the antiquated, heavily populated Charleston area—only 17 people died in South Carolina. Huge tides and brutal winds tore down electrical lines, wrenched bridges from pilings, and tossed about trawlers and yachts like the Easter Bunny on steroids. Hugo destroyed over

six billion board feet of timber, flattening over 70 percent of the 250,000-acre Francis Marion National Forest, north of Charleston. North Carolina lost another 68,000 acres of timber. Worse, because of the difficulties of transportation and access in post-Hugo days, most of the damaged timber in both states decayed beyond salvaging before foresters could get to it.

Several lesser hurricanes hit the coast between 1989 and 1996, including Emily, which did considerable damage along the Outer Banks in 1994. In July 1996, Bertha hit hard and unexpectedly, turning from a dispersed and dispersing storm into a Category 2 hurricane that blew across Cape Fear. Fran blasted her way through much the same areas in September that same year, tearing down thousands of half-rebuilt structures and razing the morale of the region, before turning west and battering Raleigh to the tune of $1 billion. Bonnie followed in 1998, throttling Carolina Beach and surrounding areas.

But none of this prepared North Carolinians for 1999, when Hurricane Dennis skimmed up the Carolina Coasts and then dropped anchor a few hundred miles from Cape Hatteras, giving Bankers a chance to see what it would feel like to live inside of a car wash for five days. After finally downgrading to a tropical storm, Dennis headed inland to pour out some eight inches of rain in one day, causing widespread flooding.

This would have been all right, as far as natural disasters go, but two weeks later, before the local news shows could even finish up with the heartwarming, post-Dennis human interest stories, Dennis's bigger brother Floyd came barreling in, dropping 20 inches in some areas—and raising flooding to unprecedented heights. The Tar had posted a record crest of 23.9 feet during the rainy March of 1998, but after Floyd, it reached 34–35 feet.

Nearly every year brings two or three hurricane watches, but this doesn't keep people from building expensive multimillion-dollar homes right on the waterfront. And why should it? The Housing and Urban Development Act of 1968 (amended in 1969 and 1972) made federal flood insurance available to homeowners and developers, subsidized by taxpayer money. Thus it is that after each hurricane, homeowners and developers replace the old rambling beach houses of yesteryear with beachfront mansions on stilts.

Earthquakes Too?

It's August 31, 1886, a warm St. Louis evening on the banks of the Mississippi River. You stand on the silent dock, awaiting the whistle of a steamboat, but hear only the sounds of cicadas drifting out over the silent brown water.

And then the surface of the river ripples. The dock quivers, drops you to your knees. What could it be? Then the movement's over and you rise again, thankful the earthquake was minor.

But 1,000 miles away, near the quake's epicenter, all hell has broken loose in Charleston. Buildings 200 years old have crumbled; brick facades topple forward onto passersby in the street.

All those retaining bolts you see in old Charleston buildings aren't there for hurricanes.

The 1886 quake here did more damage than Sherman. After "The Shake," Charleston homeowners inserted long rods between the walls of their houses to brace them. You can still see the unique plates today.

Experts estimate that the 1886 quake ran a 7.7 on the Richter scale and a 10 on the 12-point Mercalli scale of earthquake intensity. It left 60–92 dead (accounts vary) and caused an estimated $23 million in damage. Theoretically at least, another quake is always lurking. Even today, more than 100 years later, South Carolina is rated as a major earthquake risk area, based almost entirely on the 1886 incident and the 351 smaller jolts that followed over the next 27 years.

FLORA AND FAUNA

VEGETATION ZONES

For the following information I owe much to Audubon International; to the fine *Landscape Restoration Handbook* by Donald F. Harker, Gary Libby, Kay Harker, Sherri Evans, and Marc Evans; and to George Sigalas III, horticulturist at Reynolds Plantation resort in Greensboro, Georgia.

LOWCOUNTRY FLORA

Coastal Vegetation

Among the native vegetation you'll see along the coast are the South Carolina state tree, the cabbage palmetto *(Sabal palmetto)*, along with dwarf palmetto *(Sabal minor)* and the groundsel bush *(Baccharis halimifolia)*, covered with what look like tiny white paintbrushes in late summer and fall. You'll also see grand live oak *(Quercus virginica)* and laurel oak *(Quercus laurifolia)* shading the coastal cities.

Many of these trees hang thick with Spanish moss *(Tillandsia usneoides)*, which is not, as many people believe, parasitic. Instead, it's an epiphyte, similar to bromeliads and orchids. These plants attain their nutrients from the air, not from their host plants. Many oaks are also adorned with resurrection fern *(Polypodium polypodioides)*, which looks shriveled up and often blends in with

the bark of the tree it is climbing. When it rains, however, the fern unfolds, and its dark green fronds glisten like green strands of jewels.

Sea oats *(Uniola paniculata)* grow among the sand dunes on the coast. Waving in the ocean breezes, they look like something out of a scenic calendar. Because of their important role in reducing sea erosion, sea oats are protected by state law.

Freshwater Marsh

The Carolina coasts have many freshwater marshes, characteristically thick with rushes, sedges, grasses, and cattails. Many of the marshes and associated swamps were diked, impounded, and converted to rice fields during the 18th and 19th centuries; today many of these impoundments provide habitat for waterfowl. Characteristic plant species include swamp sawgrass *(Cladium mariscus)*, spike-rush, bulrush, duck-potato, cordgrass, cattail, wild rice *(Zizania aquatica)*, southern wax myrtle *(Myrica cerifera)*, and bald cypress *(Taxodium distichum)*.

Southern Floodplain Forest

Southern floodplain forest occurs throughout the coastal plain along large and medium-size rivers. A large part of the floodplain lies saturated during the winter and spring—about 20–30 percent of the year. In these areas you'll find abundant amounts of laurel oak and probably willow oak

(Quercus phellos), sweet gum (Liquidambar sturaciflua), green ash (Fraxinus pennsylvanica), and tulip tree (Liriodendron tulipifera) as well.

In higher areas on the coastal plain, swamp chestnut oak (Quercus michauxii) and cherry-bark oak (Quercus pagoda) dominate; in lower areas, you're more likely to find bald cypress, water tupelo (Nyssa aquatica), and swamp tupelo (Nyssa biflora), along with southern magnolia (Magnolia grandiflora), American beautyberry (Callicarpa americana), common papaw (Asimina triloba), southern wax myrtle, dwarf palmetto, trumpet creeper (Campsis radicans), groundsel bush, Virginia sweetspire (Itea virginica), cinnamon fern (Osmunda cinnamomea), sensitive fern (Onoclea sensibilis), and the carnivorous pitcher plant.

If the last item on that list piques your interest, consider this: the famous **Venus flytrap** is indigenous in only one place in the world—in the area surrounding Wilmington, N.C.

MAMMALS

Scientists have claimed that in ancient days great bison, camels, and even elephants roamed Coastal Carolina, but you won't find any there today. In a few spots, including the Alligator River National Wildlife Refuge, it's possible—but unlikely—that you'll encounter a black bear.

However, you may well see raccoons, badgers, beavers, possums, and a variety of squirrels, though you'll need a flashlight to catch the nocturnal flying squirrel. River otters, beavers, and the seldom-seen bobcat also dwell in the forests, as does the rare red fox, currently being reintroduced into the Francis Marion National Forest north of Charleston.

Ocean mammals include the playful bottlenosed dolphin and the rare, gentle manatee, which attempts to dwell peacefully in the coastal inlets but often ends up playing speed bump to the many leisure craft swarming the waters.

flowering dogwood

AQUATIC LIFE

Featuring everything from clear mountain streams to saltwater marshes and the Atlantic itself, the Carolinas' diverse waters provide a correspondingly wide variety of fish and other sea life.

Coastal and Ocean

The tidal rivers and inlets teem with flounder, sea bass, croaker, drum, and spot. Deep-sea fishing—particularly as you head out toward the Gulf Stream—includes bluefish, striper, flounder, drum, Spanish and king mackerel, cobia, amberjack, shad, and marlin, to name only a few.

Other sealife includes numerous types of jellyfish, starfish, conch (pronounced "conk" hereabouts), sand dollars, sea turtles, numerous species of shark (many of them edible), rays, shrimp, and Atlantic blue crabs. You'll also find oyster beds along the coast, though, due to pollutants, most of these are no longer safe for consumption.

REPTILES AND AMPHIBIANS

The Palmetto and Tar Heel States host a large population of one of the most feared reptiles—the **alligator.** Generally inhabiting the low-lying areas of the coastal plain, alligators prefer fresh water; only very rarely will you find them in the ocean—a fact for which the coastal tourism industry is eminently grateful. Although Carolina alligators are not nearly as large as their counterparts in Florida, they can reach up to six feet or so, plenty big enough to do damage to a human being. While alligator attacks on people are very rare, exercise caution if you see one—these loglike creatures can move mighty quick when food is involved.

Water brown snakes often grow as long as four feet. You'll find them all along the coastal

KUDZU: THE VINE THAT ATE THE SOUTH

Though Asians have harvested kudzu for well over 2,000 years, using it for medicinal teas, cloth, paper, and as a baking starch and thickening agent, the fast-growing vine wasn't introduced to the U.S. until it appeared at the Philadelphia Centennial Exposition of 1876, and Southern farmers really first became acquainted with it when they visited the Japanese pavilion at the New Orleans Exposition of 1884-86. For some 50 years afterward, though some visionaries proclaimed the vine as the long-awaited economic savior of the South, most Southerners thought of it largely as a garden ornamental. They called it "porch vine," since many used it to climb trellises and provide shade for swings.

After the boll weevil infestation of the 1920s wiped out Carolina cotton crops, and as years of single-crop farming began to take their toll on the soils of the South, the U.S. Department of Agriculture under Franklin D. Roosevelt imported vast amounts of kudzu from Japan, and the CCC planted some 50,000 acres of the vine for erosion control and soil restoration. Down-and-out farmers could make as much as $8 an acre planting kudzu, and in the midst of the Depression, few could refuse the offer.

And that was the last time many of those acres saw sunlight. The problem, it seems, is that kudzu's insect nemeses had no interest in immigrating to America along with the vine, so kudzu actually grew better in the U.S. than in Asia—often a foot or more a day. Soon, kudzu had covered fences, old cars, and small houses. It swallowed whole trees, depriving their leaves of sunlight and killing them. And this at about the time that many farmers realized it was loblolly pine timber, not kudzu, that could bring them back to prosperity.

Today, a wiser Department of Agriculture categorizes kudzu as a weed. Millions of dollars are spent each year trying to eradicate the stubborn vine, whose roots survive the South's mild frosts and most available herbicides. Some say it covers more than two million acres across the South, though just over 10,000 acres in South Carolina.

Read any Southern newspaper long enough and you'll run across a dozen varieties of the same story: *Kudzu May Contain Cure for X.* Nobody can believe that the plant could be as annoying as it is without also providing some major benefit to humanity. One thing we do know for sure: as a member of the bean family (Fabaceae), kudzu's roots contain bacteria that fix atmospheric nitrogen and thus help increase soil fertility.

And Carolinians know how to make the best of things. Up in Walhalla, South Carolina, Nancy Basket creates kudzu paper and then uses it in multi-colored collages celebrating rural life and Native American themes. Others weave thick baskets from the mighty vine. Some farmers have experimented with grazing goats and other livestock on kudzu, which not only provides free food for the animals, but also seems to be one of the few dependable ways to constrain the plant.

Though there may be less kudzu in the Carolinas than there was a few years ago, don't worry—you'll still find kudzu all across the Carolina coast, climbing and covering trees, inching toward the edge of the road. It's everywhere. Are you parked on a Carolina roadside as you're reading this? Reach over, open your glove box, and you'll probably find some kudzu.

If you'd like to find out more about the "vine that ate the South," go to the website www.cptr.ua.edu/kudzu.html, which will in turn lead you to a number of other sites dealing with the vine. A documentary, *The Amazing Story of Kudzu,* has been distributed to public TV stations nationwide, so watch your local listings to see when it might be broadcast in your town. Or you can purchase a copy of the video by calling 800/463-8825 (Mon.–Fri. 8 a.m.–5 p.m. central time). Tapes run about $21.

plain. The water brown is also a tree-climbing snake; sometimes you'll see them enjoying the sun on tree limbs overhanging rivers, streams, and swamps. They feed mainly on catfish. In blackwater swamps you'll find **black swamp snakes,** usually just over a foot long.

But these aren't the kinds of snakes most visitors have on their minds when they're hiking in the South. South Carolina, after all, leads the nation in its variety of **poisonous snakes,** containing six different slithering creatures that can bring on trouble with a bite: copperhead, canebrake rattlesnake, eastern diamondback rattlesnake, pigmy rattlesnake, cottonmouth (water moccasin), and the eastern coral snake. Fortunately none of these animals are aggressive toward humans; you'll probably never even see one while in either of the Carolinas. If you do, just stay away from them. Most snakebites occur when someone is picking up or otherwise intentionally disturbing a snake.

brown thrasher

Trail starting in McClellanville; **Magnolia Plantation and Gardens** (near Charleston), **ACE Basin National Wildlife Refuge, Edisto Island State Park,** the National Audubon Society's **Francis Beidler Forest Sanctuary,** the **Pinckney Island National Wildlife Refuge,** near Hilton Head; and the **Savannah National Wildlife Refuge,** near Hardeeville.

INSECTS

The members of the Carolinas' vast insect population that you'll want to know about include **fireflies, mosquitoes,** and **no-see-ums.** The first of these are an exotic sight for those who haven't seen them before; people traveling with kids might want to ask around to find out where they can hope to spot some fireflies come sundown.

Don't worry about where to find mosquitoes and no-see-ums—they'll find you. If you're visiting between spring and late fall and plan to spend any time outdoors, bring insect repellent.

BIRDS

Along the Carolina Coasts, bird-watchers have spotted over 400 different species—over 45 percent of the bird species found on the continent.

Along the coasts, look for various wading birds, shorebirds, the wood stork, swallow-tailed kite, brown pelican, marsh hen, painted bunting, seaside sparrow, migrant ducks and waterfowl, black-necked stilt, white ibis, the marsh wren, the rare reddish egret and Eurasian collared doves, and the yellow-crowned night heron. Popular birding sites include **Pea Island National Wildlife Refuge** and **Cape Hatteras National Seashore, Cape Lookout National Seashore,** the west side of **Sunset Beach,** Fort Caswell on the eastern tip of **Oak Island** near Southport, **Brookgreen Gardens** and **Huntington Beach State Park,** south of Myrtle Beach; **Cape Romain National Wildlife Refuge; Francis Marion National Forest,** including the Swamp Fox section of the Palmetto

ENVIRONMENTAL ISSUES

As opposed to, say, most parts of California, where landscapers must intentionally plant grass and trees—along with artificial watering systems—Coastal Carolina is so fertile that at times it seems that if you don't hack nature back, it might swallow you up. Farmers complain about "wet" summers here. Grass grows to the very edge of the highways. Pine trees grow everywhere they haven't been cut down, and kudzu grows over everything not in motion.

Consequently, while there have always been a number of farsighted environmentalists in the region, many Carolinians have been slow to see a need for conserving natural resources and preserving places of wild scenic beauty. A common Carolina practice when building a home, for instance, is a) clear-cut the entire property of native scrub pine; b) build the home; c) plant a lawn, along with a few nursery-bought oaks or willows for shade.

But this view of nature-as-adversary is slowly changing. With the arrival of so many emigrants and tourists from denuded areas, the Carolinas have of late come to see the beauty that some residents had taken for granted. Of course, some native Carolinians—not uncommonly those who bear long-held deeds to now-developable land—complain that activists so recently arrived from bombed-out northern climes have no business preaching the gospel of conservation in their new home. Fortunately many native Carolinians have noticed the declining quality of life and are just as eager, if not more eager, than the transplants to keep chaos out of the order of nature. The popularity of Adopt-a-Highway programs, the increased traffic to North and South Carolina's excellent state parks, and the huge number of Carolinians from industry, government, and the private sector currently pitching in to build South Carolina's Palmetto Trail—a hike/bike path across the entire state—are all signs boding well for the future of the Carolina's remaining wilderness.

Perhaps the darkest cloud over the coasts is the need to slow suburban sprawl. The population boom of recent years has been one thing. The tendency of migrating Northerners (and inland Southerners) to purchase large lots in cul-de-sac-gnarled "plantations," is another. These huge, upscale developments promise to create an exclusive community for their residents. Not only do these plantations hoard communi-ty interest and activities from residents of the surrounding neighborhoods, but they most commonly are built just outside of town, thus requiring the destruction of free space. They also increase local traffic levels, since people who work in town have to drive to and from their new homes on the outskirts. Around Charleston, S.C., for instance, forecasters estimate that if trends continue, by 2030, developers will have beaten 500 square miles of currently rural land into suburbia. This will create a 247 percent increase in suburban land area to handle a population increase of only 49 percent and destroy the ambience of the Lowcountry forever.

Fortunately, forward-thinking, community-minded North and South Carolinians are taking a stand. Responding to its population surge, Charleston County has moved toward open space zoning (or clustering), which allows development while eliminating as little farmland, timberland, and open space as possible. Communities with open-space zoning allow landowners to subdivide into smaller lots, but only if they permanently protect 50 percent or more of the original parcel from development. Or they allow developers the right to build more houses than normal, but only if they cluster the structures instead of building on the large lots. At press, the East Cooper town of Mount Pleasant was voting on whether or not to reduce its building from an insane 8 percent to 3–4 percent annually.

Residents at Myrtle Beach's Alligator Adventure.

The idea of "clustering" has industrial applications too. In the late 1990s, the South Carolina Coastal Conservation League and Charleston Mayor Joe Riley called for establishing greenbelts around Lowcountry urban areas, and a number of Lowcountry General Plans began to require industry clustering. By locating industries near each other (to preserve natural space), planners hope to encourage plants to use each other's waste products in their own manufacturing whenever possible.

In addition to development regulation, some Carolinians are encouraging outright preservation. In 1997, for instance, South Carolina Senator Arthur Ravenel helped to get acres in Georgetown, Horry, and Marion Counties established as the Waccamaw National Wildlife Refuge.

Another positive sign is the arrival of traditional neighborhood developments (TNDs) all along the coast. On St. Helena Island, Daniel Island, and in Mount Pleasant, Manteo, and elsewhere, builders are recreating the pedestrian-friendly, porch-out-front neighborhoods of the pre–World War II era for a new generation of buyers who have come to appreciate the pleasures of small front yards—the better for porch visiting—community parks, and home designs which treat garages as dirty necessities rather than as the centerpiece of the entire home. Streets are laid out on grids—for easy walks to stores and recreation areas. Best of all, these developments are only going to improve with age.

HISTORY

Because the Carolinas first developed along the coast, much of the early history of the states centers in cities like New Bern, Wilmington, Charleston, and Beaufort. The first European colony in North America nestled, if briefly, near Georgetown, S.C., or Wilmington, N.C. The first attempted English colony—the famed "Lost Colony"—was set on North Carolina's Roanoke Island.

And because the Carolinas—particularly South Carolina before 1865—held especial sway in Southern politics, the coasts witnessed many events of national and even world significance. The War between the States—the Southern term for the Civil War—began in Charleston. The history of propelled human flight began on a sand dune in Kill Devil Hills, on the Outer Banks.

History buffs—or those just looking for enough "cultural value" to justify their beachfront indulgences—will find the Carolina Coasts a rewarding place to visit.

FIRST ARRIVALS

Ethnologists estimate that about 30,000–75,000 indigenous Americans lived in North Carolina at the time of European contact. Another 15,000 lived in present-day South Carolina. By 1715 this number had been halved by European diseases and war, and by the time of the American Revolution, the population was a small fraction of its former size. Two hundred years later, the 1980 census would report only a few thousand unassimilated Native Americans living in South Carolina, mostly in a last-ditch coalition on the Catawba Reservation in the northern part of the state. In North Carolina, most of the Native Americans in North Carolina (less than 1 percent of the total population) were descendants of the Cherokee who, when told to hit the Trail of Tears, had disappeared into the mountains.

The numbers of people claiming indigenous blood is on the rise however. Though still only a tiny minority numerically, Native American Carolinians have recently been lured out of the genetic shadows by the increased celebration of Native American heritage in US popular culture.

Prehistoric Peoples

If these people had only known they'd end up lumped for all eternity into a dimly lit category called "prehistory," they no doubt would have kept better notes for posterity. What many scientists theorize, based on the little existing evidence, is that migrating peoples reached the Carolinas some 15,000 years ago. This was still at the end of the ice age, but they found megafauna such as mammoth, mastodon, and great bison. All we know about these early people is that they made primitive tools and hunted.

THE SPEECH OF SPECKLED SNAKE

The following article was published in the Savannah *Mercury* in 1829. It is rumored to have been written by John Ridge, a young Cherokee named Speckled Snake who had been educated in Connecticut, in protest of Andrew Jackson's proposed moving of the Creeks, Cherokees, and other tribes to the Indian Territory west of the Mississippi. Ten years later, the great removal was completed along the "Trail of Tears." In a grim irony, shortly after the removal Ridge was assassinated by Cherokees for his role in the treaties that gave away their lands.

BROTHERS! We have heard the talk of our great father; it is very kind, he says he loves his red children.

BROTHERS! I have listened to many talks from our great father. When he first came over the wide waters, he was but a little man, and wore a red coat.—Our chiefs met him on the banks of the river Savannah, and smoked with him the pipe of peace. He was then very little. His legs were cramped by sitting long in his big boat, and he begged for a little land to light his fire on. He said he had come over the wide waters to teach Indians new things, and to make them happy. He said he loved his red brothers; he was very kind.

The Muscogees gave the white man land, and kindled him a fire, that he might warm himself; and when his enemies, the pale faces of the south, made war on him, their young men drew the tomahawk, and protected his head from the scalping knife. But when the white man had warmed himself before the Indian's fire, and filled himself with their hominy, he became very large. With a step he bestrode the mountains, and his feet covered the plains and the valleys. His hands grasped the eastern and the western sea, and his head rested on the moon. Then he became our Great Father. He loved his red children, and said, "Get a little further, lest I tread on thee." With one foot he pushed the red man over the Oconee, and with the other he trampled down the graves of his fathers, and the forests where he had so long hunted the deer.—But our Great Father still loved his red children, and he soon made them another talk. He said, "Get a little further; you are too near me." But there were now some bad men among the Muscogees then, as there are now. They lingered around the graves of their ancestors, until they were crushed beneath the heavy tread of our Great Father. Their teeth pierced his feet, and made him angry. Yet he continued to love his red children; and when he found them too slow in moving, he sent his great guns before him to sweep his path.

BROTHERS! I have listened to a great many talks from our great father. But they have always began and ended in this—"Get a little further; you are too near me."

BROTHERS! Our great father says that "where we now are, our white brothers have always claimed the land." He speaks with a strait tongue, and cannot lie. But when he first came over the wide waters, while he was yet small, and stood before the great chief at the council on Yamacraw Bluff, he said—"Give me a little land, which you can spare, and I will pay you for it."

BROTHERS! When our great father made us a talk, on a former occasion, and said, "Get a little further; go beyond the Oconee, the Ocmulgee; there is a pleasant country," he also said, "It shall be yours forever." I have listened to his present talk. HE says the land where you now live is not yours. Go beyond the Mississippi; there is game; and you may remain while the grass grows or the water runs. BROTHERS! Will not our great father come there also? He loves his red children. He speaks with a strait tongue, and will not lie.

BROTHERS! Our great father says that our bad men have made his heart bleed, for the murder of one of his white children. Yet where are the red children which he loves, once as numerous as the leaves of the forest? How many have been murdered by his warriors? How many have been crushed beneath his own footsteps?

BROTHERS! Our great father says we must go beyond the Mississippi. We shall there be under his care, and experience his kindness. He is very good! We have felt it all before.

BROTHERS! I have done.

Toward the end of the Pleistocene epoch, the Paleo-Indian appeared—that is to say, descendants of the same Indians, but with better tools. The culture—primarily defined by its use of Clovis points used on spears—spread apparently from the Great Plains toward the Atlantic. The Paleo-Indians were the first great big-game hunters of the Carolinas. They went after mammoth and mastodon; one of their tricks was to burn the marsh or woods, driving the animals that hid within to slaughter. They may have also added some gathering to their prodigious hunting efforts.

When the ice age finally ended, the Carolinas' physical environment, including flora and fauna, went through some predictably large changes. The early Americans adapted to these changes, creating a society fed on fish, shellfish, small mammals, and fowl. With the greater abundance of game, and the resulting leisure time, you might think that a "high" culture would have developed at this point, but the living was so easy, and apparently the existing philosophies were so comfortable, that little change is noticeable in the artifacts of these cultures, though they're separated by thousands of years.

During this, the Archaic period, Carolinians apparently spent spring and summer near a major body of water—a river, marsh, or the Atlantic; shell middens and shell rings identify these sites. The people would move to higher regions to hunt white-tailed deer in the fall, returning to their waterside digs for the winter. Trade may have also begun during this period: tools made of Piedmont materials have been found along the coast; coastal plain materials have been found at Archaic sites in the mountains.

Pottery some experts date to between 2500 B.C.E. and 1000 B.C.E. first appeared along the Savannah River around the time Moses and the Israelites were waiting for a ferry on the shore of the Red Sea. Archaeologists have found these simple ceramics around the shell middens along the coast.

During the late Archaic period, domestication of such plants as beans, squash, sunflower, and sumpweed began, though apparently corn was not a big crop in the Southeast until much later.

During the Woodland period—1000 B.C.E. to 1000 C.E.—Native Americans began to rely increasingly upon agriculture. Farming both permitted and required a less mobile lifestyle, which in turn gave rise to further development of ceramics (now that nobody had to lug the pots from mountains to sea anymore) and permanent structures. Being tied to one area also meant that hunters needed to be able to kill more of an area's available wildlife instead of moving

on to easier pickings elsewhere; to that end, the bow and arrow—developed around this time—came in handy.

The Mississippian period (named because this type of culture seems to have first appeared in the middle Mississippi Valley region) was a time of great advances. Cultural nuances such as ritual burial practices, platform mounds, and a hierarchical structure organized under village chiefs suggest a sophisticated religio-socio-political system. Just over the South Carolina/Georgia border, near Macon, you can find temple pyramids. Along the Carolinas' fall line, in the decades after 1150 C.E. or so, as the French were constructing Chartres Cathedral, Mississippians were battling their way eastward into the pristine world of the well-established Woodland Indians.

Because the Mississippians were an unwelcome, invading force, their early sites in the state feature encircling palisades—defensive structures for protecting themselves against the hostile Woodland peoples. Eventually, the Mississippians, and the Mississippian way of life, won out.

Mississippians tended to plant their crops in the rich bottomlands beside rivers, building their villages up on the bluffs overlooking them. One of the best—and only—descriptions of one of these "towns" comes from Hernando de Soto. When de Soto explored western South Carolina and North Carolina in 1540 (on his way to discovering the Mississippi River), he encountered Cofitachequi, an important Mississippian town on the banks of the Wateree River in today's Kershaw County. Ruled by a female chief, Cofitachequi consisted of temple mounds and a number of rectangular, wattle-and-daub, thatched-roof houses, with storehouses of clothing, thread, deerskins, and pearls.

The pearls suggest that the good folks of Cofitachequi traded with coastal Indians—an interpretation further bolstered by the fact that they were well versed in the existence of the Spanish, whose only other presence in the region had been established 14 years earlier, on the coast, at the failed colony of San Miguel de Guadalupe.

All the Native Americans who dwelt in the Carolinas at the time of the European invasion derived from Iroquoian, Siouan, Algonquian, and Muskogean language groups. Northeast of the

Catawba-Santee waterway lived the numerous Siouan tribes, the southern portion of the Sioux nation extending to the Potomac River near what would later become Washington, D.C. At the coast, where the living was easy, tribes tended to be small but plentiful: the Croatan, Tuscarora, Combahee, Edisto, Kiawah, Etiwan, Wando, and Waccamaw. The fewer tribes of the Up-country—the Cherokee, Lumbee, and Creek, for instance—were larger and stronger.

For instance, the most powerful tribe, the Cherokee, ruled a 40,000-square-mile region—the northwestern third of modern-day South Carolina and North Carolina—though they were constantly at battle with the more warlike Creeks and the Chickasaws of northern Mississippi and western Tennessee, and the Choctaw in the southern Mississippi region. Only with the Cherokees' help during the Yamassee Wars did the Carolinian colony survive.

Out on the Outer Banks, archaeologists think that 5,000 Native Americans known as the **Croatan** may have populated Hatteras Island from as early as 1000, primarily in the Buxton Woods Maritime Forest on the south end of the island. After European contact, however, the story of the Croatan falls into a familiar pattern: exposure to European diseases and other hardships eliminated all traces of the original Bankers by the 1770s. In the 16th and 17th centuries, two tribes from other regions settled into the Coastal Carolina region. The English in 1584 estimated that some 7,000 Algonquians lived in modern-day North Carolina, but the most powerful group, the **Tuscarora**, were relative newcomers to the Southeast, having recently moved down from New York in a series of migrations. Down in what would become known as South Carolina, the Yamasee Indians, who had had clashes with the Spanish further south in modern-day Georgia, moved up into the Sea Islands around Beaufort after receiving the go-ahead from British colonials in Charleston. The proactivity that caused the tribes to seek out better living places would later cause them to strike out against encroaching settlers, leading to the Tuscarora and Yamassee Wars.

North and South Carolinian Indians contributed many things to the Carolinian way of life, most notably place-names. Whether you're sunning on Edisto Island, surfing off Cape Hat-teras, watching a football game at Wando High School in Mount Pleasant, fishing the Roanoke or Congaree Rivers, or doing time in Pee Dee Federal Penitentiary, take time to reflect on the Native Americans who gave the name to your location. Also, the next time you sit down to a plate of grits or barbecue—*barbacoa*—thank those who first developed them.

BRITISH PROPRIETARY PERIOD

Though the 16th century brought a handful of reconnaissance missions and attempts at colonization by Spain and France, the Spanish and the French had nearly all disappeared by the turn of the following century. Except for a handful of Spanish Jesuit priests, South Carolina was left again to the indigenous Americans—for 83 years. (After a generation or two without them, the tales of armies of marauding white men must have seemed like myths to young Chicoras and Sewees.)

But this didn't mean that Europeans had forgotten about South Carolina. By the second quarter of the 17th century, Spain's power had declined to the point where British monarch Charles I began to assert England's historic claims to the coast, founded on the discoveries of the Cabots. The king was prompted by his need to do something with the French Huguenots who had taken refuge in England. In 1629 he granted his attorney general, Sir Robert Heath, a charter to everything between latitudes 36 and 31 (more or less from the present-day Georgia-Florida line to the North Carolina–Virginia line) and all the way west to the Pacific. In the charter, Charles lists the name of the region as "Carolana," a transmogrification of "Charles." Despite one failed attempt (the famed *Mayflower* miscalculated and landed its French Huguenot passengers in Virginia), no one ever settled in South Carolina under the Heath Charter.

Establishment of the Lords Proprietors

While the Heath Charter was gathering dust, Cromwell and the Puritans beheaded Charles I and took control of England. Upon Cromwell's death, Charles II was restored to the throne, largely due to the efforts of the English nobility.

The king was short of funds but wanted to show his gratitude to his allies, so in 1663 he regranted most of the Heath Charter lands to a group of eight noblemen: his cousin Edward, the Earl of Clarendon; his cousin and counselor George Monck, Duke of Albemarle; William, the Earl of Craven; Lord John Berkeley; Anthony Ashley-Cooper; Sir George Carteret; Sir John Colleton; and Sir William Berkeley. This grant was expanded in 1665 into an even larger swath encompassing everything from 65 miles north of Saint Augustine to the bottom of Virginia.

Of course, the successors of Robert Heath had a legal right to Carolina (Charles II had changed the "a" to an "i"). To mollify them, the king promised future lands, which eventually turned out to be 100,000 acres in interior New York. The original grants were made null and void, and Carolina thereby gained eight lords proprietors.

The term "lords proprietors" does a good job of explaining both the nobles' roles and their motives in the early settlement of Carolina. As "lords," they had penultimate say over what life would be like for settlers in this new land. As "proprietors," they had an almost purely financial interest in the venture. Certainly none of them came to Carolina to live. The weaknesses inherent in this government-by-the-barely-interested were to become apparent before long.

Settlement of the Albemarle Region

Perhaps the first problem the proprietors faced was the defiant attitudes of the settlers who since at least 1657 had been trickling down from the thriving colony at Jamestown, Virginia, and purchasing land from the Native Americans around

the Albemarle Sound at the mouth of the Chowan River. Unlike later settlers, these first Albemarle settlers had lived—and due to fuzzy boundaries between Virginia and Carolina, emigrated believing they would continue to live—under Crown authority. For all its faults, Royal Colonial Rule meant that the colony received the attention of the Crown and his underlings—full-time governing professionals with extensive financial resources. These ex-Virginians tired quickly of the all-too-often amateurish, vascillating, talk-to-me-next-month governing style of the proprietors.

The king himself had his suspicions about the proprietors' ability, and so they set off to prove themselves able governors. First, they divided Carolina into three counties: "Albemarle," "Clarendon," which stretched south from the Chowan river to the Cape Fear Valley, and "Craven," which covered the area south of Cape Romaine, south of present-day Georgetown and including present-day Charleston. The Carolina lands outside these counties—which, on paper, extended westward to the Pacific Ocean—could be settled later, as circumstances permitted.

The Barbadians

After assigning the Albemarle a governor in October 1664, the proprietors went about spurring on the establishment of the two counties to the south. Happily, a number of settlers from the successful British colony of Barbados showed interest in exchanging the West Indies' hurricanes, tropical illnesses, unbearable humidity, and already overcrowded conditions for the chance to settle Carolina. The lords sent the self-named "Barbados Adventurers" an enthusiastic letter promising to assist them "by all way and means" and asking them to spread the word about Carolina among their planter neighbors.

The influence these Barbadians and other planters from the West Indies would eventually have over the structure and flavor of Coastal Carolina culture is hard to overstate. With them they brought the socially stratified European feudalism upon which the Carolina Lowcountry was founded; their experience raising rice largely determined the economy of South Carolina's Lowcountry through the Civil War; and their preference for West African slave labor would shape Carolina society into the 21st century.

WHERE THE BOYS ARE

If any maid or single woman have a desire to go over, they will think themselves in the golden age, when men paid a dowry for their wives; for, if they be but civil and under 50 years of age, some honest man or other will purchase them for their wives.

—From Robert Horne's 1666 pamphlet
Brief Description of Carolina

In 1663 the overeager Barbadians had sent William Hilton sailing along the Carolina coast, looking for a good site for settlement, but other than his discovery and naming of Hilton Head Island, nothing much had come of the expedition. In the fall of 1665, Barbadians established "Charles Town" in the short-lived County of Clarendon at the mouth of the Cape Faire (now "Fear") River. Before long, things in the first "Charles Town" began to resemble a particularly hard-edged episode of *Survivor*. Shipwreck, dissension, Indian trouble, and other problems distressed the settlement, though its population rose to 800 before residents finally abandoned shore and headed for the ships again. Before they did, they sent an exploratory mission captained by Robert Sandford southward to explore the Port Royal area. There Sandford visited with the friendly Edisto Indians. When the ship left to return to Cape Faire, Dr. Henry Woodward stayed behind to explore the interior and study the native languages.

When Sandford returned to the failing settlement at Clarendon, he added to the general discontent with glowing reports of the Port Royal region down in Craven County—as yet unsettled.

The Treacherous First Passage

Port Royal became the new focal point for the proprietors and for their Barbadian clients. Advertisements and pamphlets in England proclaimed the glories of Carolina, and recruitment rolls began to fill with adventurous and sometimes desperate men and women of all circumstances.

After many, many delays, in August 1669 the first three ships (the *Mayflowers* of South Carolina, more or less), named *Carolina, Port Royal,* and *Albemarle,* sailed from England to Barbados, arriving in late fall. Actually the *Albemarle* turned out to be the *Santa Maria* of the journey—it sank off Barbados. After gathering up proprietor-prescribed farming supplies, *Carolina* and *Port Royal* set sail again, with the sloop *Three Brothers* replacing *Albemarle*. Not long afterward, the ships were separated by a storm. *Port Royal* drifted and was lost for six weeks (running out of drinking water in the process) before finally wrecking in the Bahamas. Though 44 persons made it safely to shore, many of them died before the captain was able to build

a new vessel to get them to the nearest settlement. On the new craft, they reached New Providence, where the captain hired another boat that took most of the surviving passengers to Bermuda. There they caught up with the *Carolina*.

In Bermuda, an 80-year-old Puritan Bermudan colonist, Colonel William Sayle, was named governor of the settlement in the south part of Carolina. Under Sayle, the colonists finally reached Port Royal—on March 15, 1670. As Nicholas Carteret reported, the Indians who greeted the settlers on shore made fires and approached them, "whooping in their own tongue and manner, making signs also where we should best land, and when we came ashore they stroked us on the shoulders with their hands, saying 'Bony Conraro, Angles,' knowing us to be English by our color." These Indians spoke broken Spanish, a grim reminder that Spain still considered Carolina its land. The main Spanish base, in St. Augustine, was not all that far away.

Running across overgrown remnants of Spanish forts on Santa Elena Island and remembering the not-so-long-ago Spanish massacre of a French colony there no doubt made the English reconsider the wisdom of settling at the hard-to-defend Port Royal. Neither did the Edistoes seem thrilled to have the English as neighbors. Fortunately for the Brits, the cassique (chief) of the Kiawah Indians, who lived farther north along the coast, arrived to invite them to settle among his people, in exchange for help in beating back the ever-threatening Spanish and their Westo Indian allies.

The settlers agreed to the terms and sailed for the region now called West Ashley, just south of Charleston Peninsula. There, in early April at Albemarle Point on the shores of the Ashley (the site of present-day Charles Towne Landing), they founded Charles Town. The name honored their king.

On May 23 the *Three Brothers* struggled into Charles Town Bay, minus 11 or 12 of its passengers, who had gone ashore for water and provisions at St. Catherine's Island, Georgia, and run into Indians allied with the Spanish. In fact, of all the several hundred who had begun the journey from England or Barbados, only 148 survivors stepped ashore at Charles Town Landing. Three were African slaves.

Carving Out a Home

The settlers immediately set about protecting themselves against the Spanish and their Indian allies, and this was not a moment too soon. In August the Spanish at St. Augustine sent forth Indians to destroy Charles Town. Fortunately Dr. Henry Woodward, who had been left behind by Sandford four years earlier, was now able to help. When the Spanish and Indian aggressors arrived, Woodward had just returned from a diplomatic journey throughout the region, in which he had convinced the Lowcountry's many small tribes to unite with the English into a single, powerful defense league against the hated Spanish.

Facing the united tribes and a British militia well warned of its coming, the arriving Spanish and Westoes decided they didn't really want to attack after all. The Spaniards went back to St. Augustine and decided to get serious about making that a permanent, well-fortified city.

THE SOUTHERN COLONY BLOSSOMS

By the following February, 86 Barbadians had joined the Charles Town settlement. Shortly after that, steady old Governor Sayle died, replaced by the temporary Governor Joseph West, one of the state's most capable Colonial-era leaders. On September 1, 1671, Barbadian Governor Sir John Yeamans showed up with nearly 50 more Barbadians. Yeamans eventually replaced West as governor.

In its earliest days, the economies of both the Albemarle and Charles Town depended largely on trade with the Indians. To coax the continent's furs from the indigenous peoples, traders went deep into the territory—some as far as the Mississippi River—bearing metal tools, weapons, and other things for which the Native Americans were willing to trade pelts.

This same sort of trade was taking place up in Albemarle, but the lack of a deepwater port kept large ships from being able to haul the riches back to England. So while the Albemarle remained small, unprofitable, and unruly, "Carolina"—as the proprietors now referred to the Charles Town region—grew quickly in population and in prosperity. By 1700 it was inar-

Tho' she envies not others, their merited glory,
Say whose name stands the foremost,
  in liberty's story,
Tho' too true to herself e'er to crouch to oppression,
Who can yield to just rule a more loyal submission?

—William Gaston's tortured second verse
to "The Old North State,"
the North Carolina state song

guably the crown jewel of England's North American colonies. However, with so much land and a crop system that required a great amount of labor, the bulk of South Carolina's first immigrants came as indentured servants or slaves to work for those Barbadians already building plantations among the coastal Sea Islands and up the rivers. Since they could legally be kept as slaves for life, and because many of them had experience growing rice back in their native country, West Africans were the preferred import.

Yet while the traders were penetrating the interior as they bartered with the Indians, and the sheer logistics of the growing plantation economy meant that planters had to spread out, in *South Carolina: a Geography,* Charles Kovacik and John Winberry estimate that even as late as 1715, 90 percent of South Carolina's European/African population lived within 30 miles of Charles Town. The danger from the Spanish and Westoes was simply too great for most would-be pioneers to venture farther.

Those whites who did live out on the plantations lived largely among their own slaves, with African-American bond servants outnumbering free persons often as much as 10 to 1 in some districts. The voices of whites who warned that planters were setting themselves up for an insurrection were lost amid the clinking of gold in the planters' coffers. The Barbadians had turned a wild land into a boom economy before, and they were certain that slavery was the way to do it.

The proprietors, who were all for government by the elite, weren't too concerned about the explosion of slavery in Carolina. Neither were the royals, since slavery was yet legal in the British Empire. What concerned them was Carolina's exports: Carolinian rice (and, after 1740, indigo) was extremely valuable to the empire; in the 1730s, England even made a point of settling Georgia to act as a buffer zone between the prized plantations of Carolina and the Spanish at St. Augustine.

By 1680 Charles Town settlers had decided that Albemarle Point was too unhealthy and hard to defend; some settlers began moving north to Oyster Point, site of the present-day Charleston Battery. The white-shell point at the end of a narrow-necked peninsula was much easier to defend—there was no question about which direction a ground attack might come from, and anybody attacking from the harbor would be visible a long way off. In May of 1680, the lords proprietors instructed the governor and his council to resettle Charles Town at Oyster Point.

It really *was* a better spot. Because it was low on the peninsula, coastal planters both north and south of the town could easily transport their goods to Charleston's port using tidal creeks.

Rebellion in Albemarle

Meanwhile, in neglected Albemarle, the crusty old Virginia settlers had had enough. In 1677 they staged the so-called "Culpeper Rebellion," jailing the governor of Albemarle and electing an assembly to carry on the proprietors' business honestly for a change. Historians consider this one of the very first political uprisings in Euro-American history.

For once, the proprietors paid attention to the grievances of the Albemarle settlers and promised to provide a man of justice and integrity to replace the former governor. To find such a man, of course, the proprietors felt they must choose a man of their own social rank, and so they chose Seth Sothel, who had recently bought one of the original proprietors' shares.

Unfortunately, a strange thing happened to Sothel on his way to the governor's seat. A boatload of Turkish pirates captured his ship and took him to North Africa where he was tortured and forced into hauling bricks as a slave.

Sothel escaped the next year and dutifully headed on to Carolina to assume the position. Unfortunately settlers who may have hoped that this spell at the bottom of the social ladder might help Sothel to emphasize with their woes quickly realized that rather than easing their pains, the post-prison Sothel seemed more interested

in spreading his own. He ignored the instructions of the other proprietors, jailed Carolinians who opposed him without benefit of trial, and when asked to help settle some private estates, seized them for himself. By 1689 the Albemarle assembly brought him up on charges and found him guilty. They banished him from the colony for a year and from public office for a lifetime.

Fortunately for the colony, accepted standards for political stability were low in the 17th century, and new colonists continued to arrive, rebellions or no. Boats full of French Huguenot Protestants began arriving in 1680; France's 1685 repeal of religious freedoms for non-Catholics accelerated this process.

By now the Spanish had agreed to stop harassing the English settlement at Charles Town, but they forbade any further encroachment to the south. In 1684 a group of Scottish religious dissenters had tried to start up a community at Port Royal, but the Spanish raided it and slaughtered most of the residents. In 1686, 100 Spanish, free blacks, and Indians landed at Edisto Island and broke into Governor Joseph Morton's house, stealing his valuables and kidnapping and then murdering his brother-in-law. They also kidnapped/liberated/stole 13 of Morton's slaves. Normally the Spanish offered liberty to escaped English slaves. In this case, though, whatever they offered these 13 didn't appeal to two of them; they escaped and returned to their master.

Back in the Albemarle region, the conflicts were still largely internal. The red-faced proprietors had apologized formally for the actions of Governor Sothel and then appointed Phillip Ludwell as governor—and in doing so, made an important distinction. Ludwell's commission described his domain as containing not just Albemarle County, but also the former Clarendon County as well. The concept of the Carolinas as two distinct entities, north and south, and not one or three, had begun to take root.

Unfortunately, after Sothel and some of the scoundrels who had come before him, many Albemarle residents had lost trust in the proprietors' human resources department. Before Ludwell could even get used to the humidity, John Gibbs, who claimed that Sothel had appointed him upon leaving, took two magistrates prisoner, and, with a body of 80 rebels, declared himself the true governor of the Albemarle.

Of course the problem with heading a successful rebellion is that you find yourself trying to govern rebels. Gibbs's government proved to have the staying power of a paper submarine, but the rebels had certainly caught the proprietors' attention. After humoring the yokels, the proprietors now felt certain that the northern part of Carolina was far too undisciplined to exist as a separate political unit. Consequently, beginning in 1691, and continuing through 1705, the northern colony labored under the watchful eye of the governor of South Carolina, who per proprietors' instructions, appointed a deputy governor for Albemarle.

Not that the residents of the southern settlement didn't have their own business to attend to. By 1695 Charles Town's citizens (or rather, their slaves) had built thick stone walls and six bastions, making the city into an armed fortress. By 1702 England was embroiled in Queen Anne's War with France and Spain. Since the French were now in the Mississippi Valley to the west, and the Spanish in Florida to the south, the penned-in Carolinians decided to be proactive and attack the Spanish stronghold of St. Augustine. Unfortunately, though Moore's men were able to clean out smaller Spanish settlements between the rival capitals, the War of Augustino ended in failure—the Spanish would stay in control of Florida until the United States purchased it from them in 1819.

Towns Come to the North

It says something about the different character of the North and South Carolina coasts—and the proprietors' beliefs about their relative potential for profitability—that though North Carolina received its first English settlers 17 years earlier, the state wouldn't have its first permanent town until 35 years after the founding of Charles Town. Nonetheless, in 1705 disgruntled French Huguenots leaving Virginia began bridging the gap between the two colonies by founding the town of Bath south of the Albemarle region on the Pamlico River. In 1710 a Swiss company settled Swiss, English, and German colonists even further south, along the Neuse River. They called the new settlement New Bern, named after the city in Switzerland. The following year brave settlers on the southern side of Charles Town established the

town of Beaufort (now South Carolina), at the location of the massacred Scottish settlement of Stuart Town.

Though settlement continued to accelerate, the first part of the 18th century brought numerous problems to the Carolina coasts—pirates and the Tuscarora and Yamassee Wars principal among them. In each case, when the colonists pleaded with England for help, the proprietors took a deep breath, rolled up their puffy sleeves, and . . . did nothing.

The Carolinians ended up using their own abilities to solve the crises. Consequently, though they certainly didn't mean to do it, it was the proprietors who convinced the Carolinian settlers that they didn't need lords proprietors at all.

"DOWN WITH THE LORDS, UP WITH THE KING": END OF THE PROPRIETORS' ERA

Though North Carolina would continue on under proprietor rule until King George II bought rights to the colony in 1729, by 1719, south of the Cape Fear, it was time for a revolution, South Carolina style.

It was a very polite and orderly revolution. Everyone said "please," "thank you," and "yes, ma'am." No one was killed.

In a sense, the South Carolina Revolution of 1719 was the opposite of the Revolution of 1776. Colonists in 1776 tended to feel some fidelity to the distant King George, even while hating the governors and soldiers he had installed over them. But the revolutionists of 1719—which again, unlike 1776, included just about everyone—very much respected Proprietary Governor Robert Johnson, who had, after all, just saved Charles Town from pirates. But Johnson wasn't popular enough to atone for the sins of the lords proprietors back home. In November 1719, Carolina elected James Moore as governor and sent an emissary to England to ask the king to make Carolina a royal province with a royal governor and direct recourse to the English government.

The royal government—which had interest in Carolina's exports and realized that the lords proprietors were not up to the task of protecting the colony—agreed. While this was all worked out, South Carolina was a self-ruling nation for two years. At the end of this time, Carolinians elected Robert Johnson,the old proprietary governor, as the first royal governor.

Now that the boundaries of South Carolina were more or less defined (though disputes with Georgia over the exact border extended into the 1980s), Johnson set about trying to encourage settlement in the western frontier—both to make Charles Town's shipping more profitable and to provide a buffer against whomever might next want to cause the Carolinians grief. The western frontier at this point meant just about everything beyond the coastal inlets and river mouths.

Settlement continued between the established Carolina colonies too: the first construction in modern-day Edenton began around 1715; the town of Beaufort, N.C., was laid out in 1722, and the town of Brunswick was settled along the Cape Fear in 1725. In 1733 "New Town," later Wilmington, was founded further up the river. In South Carolina, Georgetown came along in 1735.

After the king bought out the proprietors in North Carolina—with the exception of the Albermarle region, which was sold later—North Carolina began a period of prosperity that would carry it through to the American Revolution. Inland settlement began, largely by Scottish Highlanders, who came as early as 1732 and en masse after their defeat at Culloden in 1746. Scots-Irish and Germans also poured down from Pennsylvania looking for fertile land with fewer Indian tensions. Though largely absent until after 1739, by 1760 Scots nearly equaled the number of English, though they didn't have much of a presence on the coast; the vast majority of them settled inland, to the foot of the Blue Ridge Mountains. Pioneer Daniel Boone and future presidents Andrew Jackson and Andrew Johnson would all come from the marriage beds of Scots-Irish pioneers.

The same general mix of peoples was busily populating South Carolina's Midlands and Upcountry as well. Of course, though most of these inland settlers were subsistence farmers, whatever surplus the Upcountry residents did create had to be shipped out through Charles Town Harbor or Georgetown. Consequently the coastal region grew richer and richer.

In fact no other English colony enjoyed the amount of wealth now concentrated in the South Carolina Lowcountry. Plantations generated over one million British pounds annually, allowing planters to hire private tutors for their children and to send their sons to England for further education. It was these well-educated planters' sons—familiar with but not unduly impressed by the subtleties of English law—who would eventually lead the charge for the colony's independence from the mother country.

Of course, if only a handful of elites had wanted revolution, the revolution would never have taken place. But while the wealthy were essentially being raised to lead, the colony's constant battles with Indians, the French, and the Spanish were enhancing the average colonist's feelings of military competence and independence.

"DOWN WITH THE KING, UP WITH 'LIBERTY'": THE AMERICAN REVOLUTION IN SOUTH CAROLINA

Prerevolutionary Agitations

At first glance, most South Carolinians had little reason to want to go to war with England. As a British colony, South Carolina had prospered more than any other. However, the Lowcountry elites had ruled the colony for so long that when an impoverished Crown began taxing the American colonies to raise revenues, the rulers felt put upon. To protest the Stamp Act, South Carolina sent wealthy rice planter Thomas Lynch, 26-year-old lawyer John Rutledge, and Christopher Gadsden to the Stamp Act Congress, held in New York in 1765. Historians commonly group the hot-headed Gadsden—leader of Charles Town's pro-Independence "Liberty Boys" (akin to Boston's Sons of Liberty)—together with Massachusetts's James Otis and Patrick Henry as one of the three prime agitators for American independence. It's Gadsden who designed the famous "Don't Tread on Me" flag, first hoisted on John Paul "I-Have-Not-Yet-Begun-to-Fight" Jones's *Alfred* on December 3, 1775. The flag features a rattlesnake with 13 rattles, each representing an American colony.

When the 1767 Townsend Acts laid new taxes on glass, wine, oil, paper, tea, and other goods, Gadsden led the opposition. Even when the British removed the taxes from everything except tea, Charles Town residents mirrored their Bostonian brethren by holding a tea party, dumping a shipment into the Cooper River. Other shipments, though allowed to land, were left to rot in Charles Town storehouses.

When delegates from the colonies (excepting Georgia, which refused to send any) came together for the First Continental Congress in 1774, five South Carolinians, including the three who had represented the colony in the Stamp Act Congress, headed for Philadelphia; South Carolinian Henry Middleton served as president for part of the Congress. The following January, after being disbanded by Royal Governor William Campbell, the South Carolina colonial assembly re-formed as the extralegal Provincial Congress. During this and subsequent meetings, in June 1775 and March 1776, the South Carolinians created a temporary government to rule until the colony ironed things out with England. Henry Laurens and, later, John Rutledge were voted "president" (de facto governor) of the state.

Unfortunately for the revolutionaries, not all South Carolinians believed it practical or even moral to separate from the British government. Many of these Loyalists, or "Tories," came from the Upcountry, where domination by the elitist Charles Town planter class in an unsupervised new government sounded worse than continued subservience to the British Crown. In order to win over converts to the "American Cause," Judge William Henry Drayton and the Reverend William Tennent were sent into the backcountry to evangelize for the Lowcountry's General Committee and Provincial Congress. They met with limited success.

In September 1775, the Royal Governor William Campbell dissolved what would be South Carolina's last-ever Royal Assembly, and, declaring, "I never will return to Charles Town till I can support the King's authority, and protect his faithful and loyal subjects," was rowed out to the safety of the British warship *Tamar* in Charles Town Harbor.

Violence Erupts

The popular consciousness has so intertwined the American South with the Civil War that it's often forgotten that the Revolution was also fought here. It's said that history is written by

> *Raids, reprisals, and abductions marked the Revolution in the South, one of the most vicious partisan wars ever waged.*
>
> —Kent Britt, *National Geographic,*
> April 1975

the victor, and in an odd way, the North's triumph in the Civil War long gave Northern academia—centered in Boston, the self-proclaimed "Athens of America"—the job of telling the whole American story. And in the Northern version, the Revolutionary battles fought in New England and thereabouts are given all the emphasis. As a result many people are surprised to find out that South Carolina was the site of any Revolutionary action at all. They're even more surprised when (and if) they learn that 137 significant Revolutionary battles were fought within South Carolina's borders—more than in any other state.

On November 19, 1775, revolutionists (or "Whigs") fought Loyalist forces in the old western Cherokee lands at Ninety Six, spilling the first South Carolinian blood of the war. Colonel Richard Richardson rushed a large party of Whigs Upcountry to squelch the uprisings there and to assert the power of the revolutionary General Committee over the entire colony.

The "South First" Strategy, Part I

With war erupting in and around Boston, the British decided that their best strategy was to take advantage of the strong Loyalist support in the Southern colonies. They planned a military drive from Wilmington or Charles Town that might sweep through the South Carolina Upcountry, then on through North Carolina and Virginia, gathering men along the way with whom to attack Washington in the North.

In 1775, most inland Carolinians would probably have been willing to go along with this plan, but Coastal Carolinians threw a conch shell into the middle of England's plans. When Sir Henry Clinton of the British Navy arrived at Wilmington, ready to land troops, he found the port city firmly in the hands of Patriots, who had already vanquished the pro-Crown Highlands Scots, with whom Clinton's troops had hoped to rendezvous. Wisely, Clinton moved on, but not so wisely, in late June 1776 he tried to land the same troops in Charles Town, at Sullivan's Island.

When the South Carolinians under William Moultrie brought the British Navy a stunning defeat at the battle of Sullivan's Island in late June 1776, they gave the American army its first major victory. When the news reached the colonial delegates up in Philadelphia a few days later, it emboldened them to write up and sign a Declaration of Independence from England.

The Sullivan's Island debacle also caused the British to rethink their strategy—and they abandoned the South for nearly three years.

Other Events

The following December, the new state legislature met to complete the state constitution begun the previous October. It de-established the Anglican Church. Meanwhile in the Upcountry, the British had persuaded the Cherokee to fight on their side. The British officer in charge of this operation ordered the Cherokee to attack only organized bodies of patriot soldiers, but the Cherokee employed a more holistic fighting style. Soon murder and cabin burnings plagued the frontier. In response Whigs Andrew Williamson, Andrew Pickens, and James Williams—who for years had been battling the Tories in the Upcountry—launched a successful campaign against the Cherokee. In 1777 the Cherokee ceded their remaining lands in the region to the South Carolina government.

By 1780 the British were back on the Carolinians' doorstep, and the Loyalists and patriots fought the state's first civil war.

The "South First" Strategy, Part II

By 1780 the British had seen enough success up north to attempt the 1776 south-to-north strategy a second time. With George Washington's troops now mired down in the North, the idea was to sandwich them by pushing troops up from the South while Washington tried to defend himself to the North.

British troops moved up from St. Augustine, Florida, landing on John's Island, from where they moved across to James Island and attacked Charles Town. After a two-month siege, General Benjamin Lincoln (who had foolishly allowed his army to get bottled up on the peninsula) was forced to surrender his men, practically every Continental soldier in the Carolinas, to British General Clinton. An army of Continentals under General Gates marched into the state to try to reclaim it for the patriots, but it suffered a devastating defeat at Camden.

This was the low point for the Carolinian revolutionaries. The fence-sitting Carolinians who had finally been persuaded to take the independent government seriously now rubbed their eyes and once again proclaimed allegiance to the King. Even Henry Middleton, one-time president of the First Continental Congress, was forced as a prisoner at Charles Town to take an oath of allegiance to the Crown.

On June 4, 1780, General Henry Clinton gloated,

With the greatest pleasure I further report . . . that the inhabitants form every quarter repair to the detachments of the army, and to this garrison (Charles-town) to declare their allegiance to the King, and to offer their services in arms for the support of the Government. In many instances they have brought in as prisoners their former oppressors or leaders, and I may venture to assert, that there are few men in South Carolina who are not either our prisoners or in arms with us.

Unfortunately for Clinton, South Carolina President John Rutledge was one of the "few men" still on the loose. Lincoln had begged Rutledge and the rest of the state's council to leave Charles Town while there was still time, and they had. Now Rutledge moved to and fro about the state, encouraging the patriots, printing up proclamations and other state papers on a printing press he'd taken with him, and sending letter after letter demanding that the Continental Congress send the Continental Army for the relief of South Carolina.

Clinton's understanding of South Carolina was that it was an essentially Loyalist colony that had been bullied into revolutionary actions by a small minority of rabble-rousers. Certainly this was the way the Loyalists had presented things. Consequently Clinton's idea was to increase the British presence over the entire state and win back the confidence of the moderates so that they too would want to fight for the British in the long-planned northern push.

Clinton's idea of turning the Southern militia into Loyalists willing to shoot their former comrades might have been a bit dubious, but Clinton's public relation skills were even more so. Rather than spending money on extra arms and soldiers, the British would have been wise now to simply hire a few spin doctors. Instead Clinton and his men proceeded to do everything they could to turn the Carolinians against them.

How to Lose Friends and Alienate People

The first thing that made erstwhile Loyalists blink was Clinton's sending Lieutenant Colonel Banastre Tarleton after Colonel Buford and his body of Virginia patriots. Buford had raced south with the intention of defending Charles Town, but turned back when he realized that they had arrived too late. However, Tarleton was unwilling to let the rebels escape back to the North and gave chase. He caught up with them on May 29, near the present town of Lancaster. The Americans were told to surrender but refused. Soon they found themselves attacked furiously by the British. Realizing quickly that they had no chance of victory or escape, the Americans finally threw down their arms and begged for safe quarter, but the British ignored their pleas, butchering the unarmed Americans. Of 350 rebels, only 30 escaped capture, wounding, or death. For the rest of the war, Southern patriots would charge at their British enemies to the cry of "Tarleton's quarter!"—i.e., "Take no prisoners!"

The second major British blunder was Clinton's revocation of the Carolinians' paroles. To gain leverage in the battle for the hearts and minds of the Carolinians, he reneged on the paroles of Carolinians who had surrendered with the understanding that if they did not actively seek to harass the British government, the British would leave them alone. Clinton's June 3 proclamation notified all prisoners of war that they might have to choose between taking arms up against their fellow Americans or being considered traitors to the Crown. This understandably rankled many of the militiamen, whose pride was already bruised by defeat. Many of them reasoned that if they were going to have to take the chance of getting

shot again, they might as well fight for the side they wanted to win.

The third mistake the British made was in harassing the invalid wife and burning the Stateburg home of a rather inconsequential colonel named Thomas Sumter. In his fury at this outrage, Sumpter, known as "The Gamecock," became one of the fiercest and most devastating guerrilla leaders of the war.

Other Carolinian Whigs took matters into their own hands as well. The Lowcountry partisans fighting under Francis "The Swamp Fox" Marion and the Upcountry partisans fighting under Andrew Pickens (whose home had also been burned) plagued British troops with guerrilla warfare in the swamps, woods, and mountains of the state.

The Tide Turns in the Upcountry

At Kings Mountain on October 7, 1780, British Major Patrick Ferguson and his body of American Loyalists were attacked on a hilltop by a body of North and Carolinians under Pickens. This major victory for the patriots—particularly since it was won by militiamen and not trained Continentals—provided a great swing of momentum for the fence-sitting Uplanders who had grown tired of British brutality. Because of this, it is considered by some to be the turning point of the Revolution—especially since it forced General Cornwallis to split his troops, sending Lieutenant Colonel Banastre "No Quarter" Tarleton into the South Carolina Upcountry to win the area back for the British. This division of his forces made it impossible for Cornwallis to move on his plan for a major push north, since that plan required a Loyalist body of troops to stay behind and keep the peace in the Carolinas.

Finally that December, General Nathanael Greene arrived with an army of Continental troops. Once Greene heard of Tarleton's approach, he sent General Daniel Morgan and his backwoodsmen thundering over the Appalachians to stop him. On January 17, 1781, at a natural enclosure used as a cow pen, the two forces met.

Pickens and his guerrillas joined up with Morgan just before the battle. Morgan felt they were still too weak to take on Tarleton's trained troops and, in order to secure a chance of retreat, wanted to cross a river that would have separated them from the British. Pickens convinced him to stay on the British side of the river, so that they'd have to fight it out. And fight they did, in what some military historians consider the best-planned battle of the entire war. The patriots devastated the redcoats, and later victories at Hobkirk's Hill and Eutaw Springs further weakened the Brits. In December 1782 the British evacuated Charles Town. Shortly thereafter jubilant residents changed the name to "Charleston," merely because to their ears it sounded somehow "less British."

One historian notes that some 137 battles, actions, and engagements between the British/Tories/Indians and the American patriots in South Carolina were fought by South Carolinians *alone*. Despite the version presented in United States history textbooks, no other state endured as much bloodshed, sacrifice, and suffering during the Revolution as South Carolina.

THE AMERICAN REVOLUTION IN NORTH CAROLINA

North Carolina agitated less before the war, and when the war came, little of it took place within North Carolina's borders, compared to South Carolina. Nonetheless North Carolinians took part in many of the war's most important battles, and the few incidents that took place within its borders were important ones.

Though Loyalist support was stronger along North Carolina's coast than in its mountains, the Stamp Act drew demonstrations and even armed uprisings in Brunswick and Wilmington; no stamps were ever sold in the state. In 1767 North Carolinas banded together again to boycott a new set of taxes passed by Parliament.

In 1774 Royal Governor William Tryon sent British troops inland to the area around Hillsboro to trounce the Regulators, a militia composed of inlanders who had tired of being abused and ignored by the East-run colonial government. But soon after this, the capable Tryon left Carolina (he'd never much liked it) and became governor of New York. At this point the British might have looked for an able governor who could help quell the general resistance to Parliament control, but instead, as they'd done so often before in North Carolina, the British sent a petty tyrant to do a statesman's work. Josiah Martin, the 34-year-old new governor, paid precious little respect to the elected legislature, fueling the Carolinians' worst fears about the Crown's dismissive attitude toward their attempts at self-government.

Disgruntled North Carolinians flocked to New Bern—then the colony's capital—to attend a convention and elect delegates to attend the Continental Congress. When the Revolution broke out in April 1775, the governor headed north and a provisional government established itself and prepared for war with the British.

Of course, as in South Carolina, not all North Carolinians wanted to go to war. This was particularly true in the Western part of the state, where many of the Scottish Highlanders, devout Presbyterians, had signed an oath before emigrating never to again take up arms against the British government. True to their word, most of these men refused to fight on the American side, and many served as Loyalist (Tory) troops.

Nonetheless the Loyalists were badly outnumbered, particularly close to the coast. Governor Martin began mulling over the idea of arming the coast's huge slave population, but the audacity of this pushed the patriots to the limit. In May 1775, as minutemen marched on the governor's palace in New Bern, Governor Martin fled to Fort Johnston at the mouth of the Cape Fear River. This didn't stop the minutemen however. Five hundred of them marched to see the governor at the fort, but he slipped away onto a British war sloop anchored off shore.

With no governor left to disobey, the Whigs got serious about governing themselves. At the August 1775 congress in Hillsborough, leaders from around the colony formed a provisional government and began organizing an army to defend colonial interests from the British. That December over 700 North Carolinians marched off to western South Carolina to put down the Loyalists there. Others headed north to establish Continental rule in Norfolk, Virginia.

But Governor Martin was not through yet. He recruited Loyalists throughout the colony, including the Highland Scots of the West; the Black Pioneers, a group of free African-Americans; and slaves promised their freedom for service to the Crown.

The Battle for North Carolina

Martin's plan was for the Highland Scots to march eastward in February and rendezvous with British General Cornwallis, who would be coming south by ship to begin his conquest of the South. Unfortunately for Martin's plan, the Scots got there too early, and the Brits got there too late. When General Donald MacDonald's 1,600 Highlanders marched toward Wilmington in February 1776, the minutemen were waiting for them. When the Scots came within twenty miles of the city, patriots sneaked down to the Moore's Creek Bridge at night and removed the bottom of the bridge. Now the Highlanders would have to walk across the bridge's runners. These, the patriots waxed and soaped.

The following morning, an hour before sunrise, patriot sharpshooters lay in wait across the creek as the first Highlanders reached the bridge in the early morning fog. They tried to walk across the slippery runners, but sure enough, most fell into the creek. With the creek filled with drowning and floundering Scotsmen, the sharpshooters opened fire, slaughtering thirty of them and causing the drowning of even more. They took 850 prisoners, guns, wagons, and medical supplies.

The Black Pioneers sat duly upon their assigned ship, the *Scorpion,* no doubt wondering where all the action was.

Cornwallis finally showed up with his 2,000 troops in June. He sent scouts ashore to size up the situation and was told that Wilmington had been lost completely to British rule. They likely found this easy to believe, as Governor Josiah Martin asked (and received) asylum aboard Cornwallis's vessel. And so the Brits headed southward toward what would surely be the simple task of taking Sullivan's Island at Charleston. But you know that story.

Next for North Carolina came the Fourth Provinical Congress, on April 12, 1776, at Halifax. Here patriot leaders authorized their delegates to the Continental Congress to "concur with the delegates of other Colonies in declaring Independency. . . ." According to many historians, though many Americans had been talking about outright independence from Britain in conversation, this was the first time it had been formally and explicitly called for by any colony. Later in the year, the Fifth Provincial Congress approved the first State constitution, which in-

cluded a bill of rights, three branches of government, voting rights for free blacks, and provision for public education.

In 1777 the new State Legislature began to systematically confiscate Tory property. This had the desired effect, causing half-hearted Tories to consider their other ventricles, and sending diehards out of the colony altogether.

After Moore's Creek, North Carolina didn't see much Revolutionary action until 1781, when North Carolinians helped thin out Cornwallis's men—fresh from King's Mountain—at Guilford Courthouse. North Carolinian men, however, served all throughout the war. Many of the men who spent the bitter winter of 1777 with Washington at Valley Forge were North Carolinians. The war did come to North Carolina in 1780 and 1781, when Cornwallis, having gained control of South Carolina at last, headed to Charlotte. While there he received word that over-mountain men—North Carolinians and Tennesseans, mainly—had poured down into South Carolina to destroy his left flank at Kings Mountain, S.C. Now with South Carolina back in the throes of rebellion, and his men encountering bitter resistance in Charlotte ("The hornets' nest" of Revolution, Cornwallis called the Queen City), Cornwallis set after the Continentals, now under the newly arrived Rhode Islander, General Nathanael Greene. The British chased them clear across the state and up into Virginia, which was precisely Greene's plan—he hoped to separate Cornwallis's men from their supply lines. While Greene gathered new recruits ready to take on the invading British, Cornwallis's troops were disappearing one by one into the villages along the way, tired of fighting and ready to make a life in the colonies. Consequently, by the time Cornwallis finally encountereed Greene directly at Guilford County courthouse on March 15, 1781, he had only 2,253 men, while Greene had 4,400. What Cornwallis's men had on their side was experience, and they managed to take a brutal toll on the Continentals; but they also received devastating losses. When Greene finally pulled his men from the field, Cornwallis stood among the dead and dying of his army and realized that this "victory" had likely caused him to lose the war.

Cornwallis marched across the state to Wilmington, which was in British hands. From there he decided to give up trying to take the Carolinas and headed north. Before he left, however, he proclaimed all of North Carolina back under Royal authority and handed over the reins to the dogged Josiah Martin. But if Cornwallis was deluded enough to believe his own proclamation, Martin clearly wasn't. Not long after Cornwallis marched away, he boarded a ship to England and said good-bye to Southern hospitality forever. Cornwallis, meanwhile, with the Carolinas to thank for his army's anemic condition, marched up to Yorktown, where Washington sunk his ivory teeth into the redcoat army's withered remains and effectively ended the American Revolution.

Writing the United States Constitution

In all of those famous paintings of the Founding Fathers, South Carolinians make up a lot of the faces you see behind Washington, Jefferson, Franklin, and the other big names. In 1787 John Rutledge, Charles Pinckney, Charles Cotesworth Pinckney, and Pierce Butler headed up to Philadelphia, where the Constitutional Convention was cobbling together the Constitution. Just 30 years old, Charles Pinckney had long been a critic of the weak Articles of Confederation. Though wealthy by birth and quite the epicurean, Pinckney became the leader of democracy in the state; he was even considered something of a turncoat to his fellow elites. On May 29, 1787, he presented the convention with a detailed outline that ended up as perhaps the primary template for the U.S. Constitution. John Rutledge also gave valuable input. Ominously Pierce Butler's sole contribution was the clause for the return of fugitive slaves.

North Carolinians contributed too. Convention delegate Hugh Williamson suggested, for instance, that the president should be removable by impeachment. He proposed that a two-thirds vote—and not a three-fourths vote—should be sufficient for successful impeachment. Ironically it was North Carolina-born Andrew Johnson who would be the first president impeached under this provision.

The federal (and Federalist-leaning) Constitution was ratified by South Carolina in 1787, as was the new state constitution in 1790, without the support of the Upcountry. Lowcountry elite, controlling three-quarters of the South Car-

olina's wealth, still ruled the state, even though the region held only a quarter of the state's white inhabitants.

The fight to ratify the federal Constitution was even more heated in North Carolina. As in South Carolina, it was small backcountry farmers who valued freedom and autonomy by nature who largely opposed the document, while Easterners, who saw profits in the stability a strong central government could bring, favored it. When the vote came in August of 1788, the anti-Federalists won out, by a vote of 184 to 84. The convention recommended a bill of rights, and proposed twenty-five amendments. Together with Rhode Island, North Carolina stayed outside the new Union of States. Pro-Federalists sent out pamphlets to help people understand the document better, but it was only when it became clear a bill of rights would soon be added that North Carolina agreed to ratify the Constitution on November 16, 1789. Rhode Island waited another five months before signing.

EARLY ANTEBELLUM OLD SOUTH (1790–1827)

In 1786 the rulers of the South Carolina Lowcountry (or enough of them, anyway) agreed that to ease the tensions between Upcountry residents and Lowcountry denizens, it made sense to move the state capital from Charleston to a more convenient spot for everyone concerned. With the capital in Charleston, Upcountry citizens had had to travel two days to reach government offices and courts.

The town of Columbia (the first city in America to take that name) was planned and erected. In 1790 the state's politicians moved in, and nobody's been able to dislodge them since. But Charleston didn't let go of all of its power that easily; some state offices remained in the Holy City until 1865. The Lowcountry and Upcountry even had separate treasury offices, with separate treasurers.

North Carolinians reached a similar compromise. In 1788, the state purchased 1,000 acres near the Wake County courthouse and plotted the town of Raleigh, named after the English investor who had first attempted to colonize the state. In 1793, the state laid the cornerstone of the first building of what would become the University of North Carolina, Chapel Hill. It was the first state-run university in the new nation.

In 1800 South Carolina's Santee Canal, connecting the Santee and Cooper Rivers, was completed, making it possible to transport people and goods directly from the new capital to Charleston. In 1801 Columbia's South Carolina College (now the University of South Carolina) was chartered.

It was after the 1793 invention of the cotton gin, however, that a different series of events caused the Upcountry and Lowcountry to see eye to eye. Though the Lowcountry had grown long staple cotton, the short staple cotton supportable by Upcountry soils took too much time to separate by hand. Eli Whitney's invention of the gin (in Georgia, just over the state line) changed all that. Now short staple cotton couldn't be grown quickly enough.

For the first time, Upcountry landowners had the chance to escape subsistence-level farming and make their fortunes. Unfortunately cotton plantations required great numbers of workers, so Upcountry planters began importing large numbers of African and African-American men and women as slaves. Now with its own wealthy planter class, and with a common interest in protecting the institution of slavery against Northern "do-gooders," the Upcountry

Master had three kinds of punishment for those who disobeyed him. One was the sweat box. That was made the height of the person and no larger. Just large enough so the person didn't have to be squeezed in. The box is nailed, and in summer is put in the hot sun; in winter it is put in the coldest, dampest place. The next is the stock. Wood is nailed on or with the person lying on his back with hands and feet tied with a heavy weight on chest. The third is the Bilbao [or bilbo: foot shackles]. You are placed on a high scaffold for so many hours, and you don't try to keep a level head, you'll fall and you will surely hurt yourself, if your neck isn't broken. Most of the time they were put there so they could break their necks.

—Prince Smith, Wadmalaw Island, WPA interview

began to work alongside the Lowcountry more than it had before. Nonetheless, slaveholding in the Upcountry never reached anything like the level in the Lowcountry. (And since it received three-fifths of a vote for each slave, the South Carolina Lowcountry still managed to politically dominate the state.)

In North Carolina too, the increase in cotton's profitability led to an increase of slaveholding throughout the state. Slaves also made tobacco harvesting more profitable. Predictably though, this race for wealth caused planters to be reckless with their lands. During the winters, they used slaves to tear out woods and prepare new lands for planting more, more, more . . . rather than fertilizing and thus preserving the quality of the land they'd already planted. Soon, in both North and South Carolina, the inevitable happened; lands were destroyed and planters found they needed to move westward to new lands in Alabama, Arkansas, Texas, and Louisiana. Combined with the general depression following the panic of 1819, soil depletion caused a third of North Carolina's population to flee the state between 1815 and 1850. At the same time the coastal counties of North Carolina clung to their rule of state politics, though by 1840 over half the state's population lived west of Raleigh.

Resentment of the North

In 1811 British ships plundered American ships, inspiring the Carolinas' outraged "War Hawk" representatives to push Congress into declaring the War of 1812. During the war, tariffs on exported goods were raised to support America's military efforts, but afterward Northern lawmakers continued to vote for higher and higher levies on exports and imports. These surcharges mainly punished the South for selling its goods in Europe instead of in the North. Not surprisingly laws also forced the South to buy its manufactured goods from the North.

Concluding that they were at the hot end of the poker, many South Carolinians began to talk of seceding from the union to operate as an independent state with trade laws tailored to its own best interests. Even South Carolina–born vice president John C. Calhoun, who had begun as a Federalist favoring a strong centralized government, began to doubt the wisdom of this vision as he saw the rights of his home state trampled for the "good" of the more powerful North. However, he also saw the political dangers in dissolving South Carolina's union with the other states.

The Nullification Crisis

In 1828 Calhoun decided upon the doctrine he would espouse for the rest of his life—the primacy of "states' rights." He believed that constitutionally, the state government of each state had more power within that state than the federal government. Consequently, if a state deemed it necessary, it had the right to "nullify" any federal law within its state boundaries.

To most South Carolinians, this sounded like a sensible compromise. Some in the state, however—such as Joel R. Poinsett (for whom, coincidentally, the poinsettia and Poinsett State Park are named), novelist William Gilmore Simms, and James L. Petigru—believed that while a state had the full right to secede from the Union if it chose, it had no right, as long as it remained a part of the Union, to nullify a federal law. (This same theory has been codified by millions of parents of teenagers as the "As Long as You're Sleeping Under My Roof" Law.)

Not surprisingly the federal government saw the whole idea of nullification as an attack upon its powers, and when in 1832 South Carolina's houses quickly "nullified" the hated federally mandated tariffs, President Andrew Jackson (ironically, South Carolina's only native-born president) declared this an act of rebellion and ordered U.S. warships to South Carolina to enforce the law.

In December 1832 Calhoun resigned as Jackson's vice president (making him the only vice president to resign until Spiro Agnew, some 150 years later) so that he could become a senator and stop South Carolina's destructive run toward secession, while solving the problems that had so inflamed his fellow Carolinians.

Fortunately, before federal forces arrived at Charleston, Calhoun and Henry Clay agreed upon a compromise tariff that would lower rates over 10 years. The passage of this tariff pacified everyone just enough to prevent immediate armed conflict. But the debate between the relative importance of states' rights versus federal power became a dividing line between the North—whose majority position gave it power over federal decisions-and the South—which, because it featured a different economy and social structure from the North, knew that it would rarely be in the majority opinion on a federal vote.

> *I've always respected a white Southerner more than a white Northerner. A white Northerner is one who says openly that he has no prejudice and yet practices it every day of his life. The white Southerner is the one who says, "I am prejudiced, but I have certain friends I would do anything in the world for." In other words, one is a hypocrite and the other is bluntly honest.*
>
> —African-American New York Congressman Adam Clayton Powell

The Abolitionist Movement and Southern Response

By this time the fact that most of the slaves in the Northern states had been freed made it much easier for Northerners to be intolerant toward the sins of their Southern neighbors. Most abolitionists were Christians who saw the protection of African-Americans, along with any other unfortunates, as a God-given responsibility. Southern slaveholders—most of them at least nominally Christian, and many quite devout—generally saw their opponents as dangerous, self-righteous meddlers who would be better off tending to their own sins than passing judgment on the choices of others.

The journal of Mary Boykin Chesnut, native of Camden, S.C., and the daughter, granddaughter, and great-granddaughter of plantation slave owners, shows how one Southern woman perceived the similarities and differences between abolitionists and slave owners. Except for a small group of Southern extremists, both sides agreed that the slave trade was immoral and should remain illegal. The question then was how best to treat the African-Americans already in the country. On one side of the issue, she writes, lay the abolitionists, in "[n]ice New England homes . . . shut up in libraries," writing books or editing newspapers for profit—abolitionist books and tracts sold extremely well in the 1850s and early 1860s. "What self-denial do they practice?" she asks her journal. "It is the cheapest philanthropy trade in the world—easy. Easy as setting John Brown to come down here and cut our throats in Christ's name."

As for Southerners, she argues, "We [are] not as much of heathens down here as our enlightened enemies think. Their philanthropy is cheap. There are as noble, pure lives here as there—and a great deal more of self-sacrifice." Plantation masters and mistresses, she points out, had been "educated at Northern schools mostly—read the same books as their Northern contemners, the same daily newspapers, the same Bible—have the same ideas of right and wrong—are highbred, lovely, good, pious—doing their duty as they conceive it."

Many pro-slavery apologists argued that Northerners had no place in the debate over the morality of slavery, because they could not own slaves and would therefore not suffer the societal impacts that manumission would mean to the South.

The crux of the slavery debate lay in the debate over the extent of the humanity of slaves. Slaveholders contented themselves that Africans, while admittedly sharing many traits of human beings, were somehow less than fully human, which made the slaves' own views about their enslavement unworthy of consideration. Many believed that blacks were on their *way* to becoming "elevated" as a race but needed close interaction with whites (even at gunpoint) to help them along. Hence Columbia-area plantation mistress Keziah Goodwyn Hopkins Brevard could, on the brink of the War between the States, write, "Those who have come & have had kind masters have been blest—had they been left to this day on Afric's sands there would have been one trouble after another for them—it is only in favoured spots *now* that they are safe from war & slavery in their own country."

The effect of bloody slave rebellions, such as the Vesey revolt of 1822 and John Brown's massacre at Harper's Ferry in 1859, embarrassed more moderate abolitionists into silence—particularly in the South—and pro-slavery Southerners perceived these isolated incidents as indicative of the "true" ends and means of all abolitionists, inflaming and galvanizing Southerners into a reactionary anti-abolitionist stance that effectively ended reasoned debate on the issue. To most abolitionists the question was one of man's duty to respect other human beings as children of God; to many Southerners, it was a question of—to use modern terminology, "choice": slave owner or not, they didn't want anybody taking away their legal right to own slaves. They feared that "somebody" would be the U.S. government, ruled by a majority of non-slaveholding states. Gradually as the 19th century pressed on, Southerners realized that as a perennial minority faction, their only hope for self-determination on the slavery issue was to ensure continued state autonomy, hence the "states' rights" argument: defending a state's right to determine what was best for its own people.

Brevard wrote in her journal, "cut throat Abolitionists—I will not call them neighbours—not [sic] they are the selfish & envious . . . not a grain of Christ's charity in their whole body."

The Cult of Slavery:
Slavery as Intrinsically Good

Carolinians had earlier tolerated slavery more or less as a necessary evil. But largely in reaction to the continual sparring with abolitionists, in the last decades before the Civil War many people in the Carolinas reached a new height of sophistry, proclaiming slavery a positive good: a benefit to the enslaved, and a proper response to the "natural" differences between whites and blacks. Apologists such as Thomas Harper argued that the wage-employee system of the North was irresponsible—and more exploitive than slavery itself. The Southern slaveholder, after all, paid room and board for a slave even when the slave was too young, too sick, or too old to work. Meanwhile the Northern capitalist paid his wage earners only for the hours they worked; when they were sick, or

> *If ever [the slaves'] emancipation be effected, it must be through the Divine agency of the light of reason, not by the sword, bloodshed, and rapine.*
>
> —Camden, New Jersey, *Star*, 1822, after exposure of the Vesey conspiracy

when they got too old, or when a new technology came along that they were not trained for, the wage payer could fire the employees, and his responsibility for their welfare was considered finished. (Some historians argue that the average slave was actually paid 90 percent of his or her life's earnings by the time of death.) Virginian George Fitzhugh, in such 1850s titles as *Sociology for the South* and *Cannibals All!*, argued that slavery, being the most humane and efficient system, was destined to regain its popularity throughout the world.

So avid had this defense of the indefensible become that by 1856 Governor James Hopkins Adams recommended a resumption of the foreign slave trade. And a powerful minority of slaveholders always looking for ways to get the rest of the state behind them had begun arguing that every white man should be legally required to become the owner of at least one slave—a measure that would give every male citizen an interest in the issue as well as instilling the sense of responsibility that they believed slave owning engendered in a man.

However, even the Charleston *Mercury,* which had long agitated for secession, denounced the return to the slave trade as cruel and divisive. Nonetheless Carolinians were embittered by the North's refusal to enforce the Fugitive Slave Law. Consequently, in 1858 and 1859, a number of newly captured slaves were imported into the state at Charleston—in violation of federal law. Federal officials in Charleston, Southerners themselves, looked the other way.

Free Blacks and the Vesey Plot

Since colonial times South Carolina had always been home to a sizable population of free blacks, many of them descended from mulattoes freed by their white father/owners. Others had been freed because of faithful service or by buying themselves free with portions of their earnings they had been allowed to keep. As long as there had been free blacks, free blacks had made the white population nervous.

In 1822 free black craftsman and preacher Denmark Vesey was convicted and hanged for having masterminded a plan for slaves and free blacks to overthrow Charlestonian whites. Afterward whites established curfews and forbade assembly of large numbers of African-

Americans. Forbidden, too, was the education of slaves, though this seems to have been widely flouted.

Since the mere presence of free blacks was seen as dangerous, South Carolina leaders also made it illegal for slaveholders to free their slaves without a special decree from the state legislature.

Like Denmark Vesey, many of South Carolina's free blacks lived in Charleston, where their own subculture—with its own caste system—had developed. Charleston free blacks performed over 50 different occupations, including working as artisans. Some African-Americans, such as Sumter cotton-gin maker William Ellison, amassed great fortunes—and did so in the same fashion that most wealthy whites had: through the labor of black slaves. In fact historian Richard Rollins estimates that a full 25 percent of all free Southern blacks legally owned slaves. Some were family members purchased by free blacks, but most were purchased to act as the owners' servants or workers. Opinions vary as to whether slaves could normally expect better treatment from a black owner than from a white one. Some free blacks, wanting to demonstrate their fitness to join "white" society, probably felt a special pressure to exert their authority over their slaves. Doubtless, the relative happiness of a slave owned by an African-American was dependent upon the character of the individual owner.

The Mexican War (1846)

The war with Mexico affected the Carolinas considerably. For Coastal Carolinians, what was at stake was the acquisition of additional lands open to slavery—and hence more representation in the U.S. Congress by slaveholding states. Though North Carolina contributed only one regiment, which saw no significant action, South Carolina's enthusiastic involvement in the undertaking reflected both her regional leadership and her military self-assuredness. Under Pierce M. Butler, J. P. Dickinson, and A. H. Gladden, the Palmetto Regiment's palmetto flag entered Mexico City before any other flag. South Carolina's fighting prowess was once again proven in battle, but, largely due to disease, of 1,100 South Carolinian volunteers who fought in the war only 300 returned alive.

Even with its much smaller population, the South as a whole, in fact, sent and suffered the loss of more soldiers, furnishing 43,232 men in the Mexican War while the North, whose pundits had disapproved of the effort, sent along only 22,136 troops. Hence the Wilmot Proviso, a proposal by a Pennsylvanian legislator to ban slavery within all territory acquired as a result of the Mexican War, struck Carolinians as extremely unjust: Southerners who had risked their lives to win over the new Southwest were now being told they could not expect to bring their "property" with them if they settled there. John C. Calhoun attempted to rally the rest of the slaveholding states to oppose Wilmot's plan as yet another effort to tighten the noose around slavery's neck. The Southern-led Senate blocked the bill.

But the question of how to handle the issue of slavery in the new and future acquisitions of an expanding nation was now out in the open. The issues raised by the acquisition of the American West in the Mexican War made plain to Northerners and Southerners their different visions of America's future, and hence accelerated the nation's tailspin toward civil war. In the North many of those willing to tolerate the cancer of slavery in those states who already practiced it could not with good conscience watch it spread to new lands beneath the shadow of the Stars and Stripes. The South, which had held a hope that territorial expansion and the spread of slavery might allow the South to ascend again to equality or even dominance in national politics, finally had to confront the fact that the North would never willingly allow this to happen. As long as the South remained in the Union, it would always be the oppressed agricultural (and hence to Southern perceptions, slaveholding) region, its interests continually overlooked for the interests of the industrialized North.

South Carolinians had been telling the rest of the South this since the Nullification Crisis 20 years before.

Eruption of Secessionism and the Descent into War

Few Carolina whites saw general emancipation as an option. If blacks—the vast numerical majority in most parts of the state—were freed, whites feared the "Africanization" of their cherished society and culture, as they had seen happen after slave revolutions in some areas of the West Indies.

Carolinian leaders had long divided up between devoted Unionists, who opposed any sort of secession, and those who believed that secession was a state's right. Calhoun proposed that Congress could not exclude slavery from the territories and that a territory, when it became a state, should be allowed to choose which type of economy it wanted—free labor or slave. But after Calhoun's death in 1850, South Carolina was left without a leader great enough, both in character and in national standing, to stave off the more militant Carolinian factions' desire to secede immediately.

"THE WAR FOR SOUTHERN INDEPENDENCE"

In 1850 and 1851 South Carolina nearly seceded from the Union all by its lonesome. Andrew Pickens Butler, considered by historian Nathaniel Stephenson as "perhaps the ablest South Carolinian then living," argued against fiery Charleston publisher Robert Barnwell Rhett, who advocated immediate and, if necessary, independent secession. Butler won that battle, but Rhett outlived him. By 1860 no strong personality in South Carolina was Rhett's equal.

The South, the poor South!
—John C. Calhoun, last words, 1850

Several historians argue that South Carolina's "states' rights" demand to be recognized as an independent, autonomous entity was not simply a rationalization for slavery but rather a protest integral to its nature and understanding of itself. As Stephenson wrote:

In South Carolina all things conspired to uphold and strengthen the sense of the State as an object of veneration, as something over and above the mere social order, as the sacred embodiment of the ideals of the community. Thus it is fair to say that what has animated the heroic little countries of the Old World—Switzerland and Serbia and ever-glorious Belgium—with their passion to remain themselves, animated South Carolina in 1861. Just as Serbia was willing to fight to the death rather than merge her identity in the mosaic of the Austrian Empire, so this little American community saw nothing of happiness in any future that did not secure its virtual independence.

When Lincoln was elected, a number of conventions around the Deep South organized to discuss their options. South Carolina's assembly met first, at Columbia on December 17, 1860. States with strong pro-secession movements like Alabama and Mississippi sent delegates to the convention, where they advised the Carolinians to "take the lead and secede at once."

Thus it was that on December 20, 1860, South Carolinians in Charleston (where the convention had moved following an outbreak of smallpox in Columbia) voted to secede from the Union. The hot-blooded delegate from Edisto Island declared that if South Carolina didn't secede, Edisto Island would secede all by itself.

Six days later, on the day after Christmas, Major Robert Anderson, commander of the U.S. garrisons in Charleston, withdrew his men against orders into the island fortress of Fort Sumter in the midst of Charleston Harbor. South Carolina militia swarmed over the abandoned mainland batteries and trained their guns on the island. Sumter was the key position to preventing a sea invasion of Charleston, so Carolina could not afford to allow the Federals to remain there indefinitely. Rumors spread that Yankee forces were on their way down to seize the port city, making the locals even itchier to get their own troops behind Sumter's guns.

Meanwhile the secessionists' plan worked. Mississippi seceded only a few weeks after South Carolina, and the rest of the lower South followed. On February 4, a congress of southern states met in Montgomery, Alabama, and approved a new constitution—which, among other things, prohibited the African slave trade.

So excited was Florence-born bard Henry Timrod that he was moved to write what many consider his greatest poem, "Ethnogenesis," in honor of the convention, which includes the hopeful lines:

HATH not the morning dawned with added light?
And shall not evening call another star
Out of the infinite regions of the night,
To mark this day in Heaven? At last, we are
A nation among nations; and thee world
Shall soon behold in many a distant port
Another flag unfurled!

Unfortunately for Timrod, Lincoln argued that the United States were "one nation, *indivisible*," and denied the Southern states' right to secede. It looked as if a war were imminent. Virginia, which had not yet seceded, called for a peace conference, and North Carolina, similarly uncommitted, sent delegates. But it didn't matter anyway; Washington ignored the suggestions the conference came up with. Even the best efforts of reasonable minds couldn't pierce the accumulated bitterness on both sides of the Mason-Dixon line.

Anticipating the battles to come, Timrod wrote:

We shall not shrink, my brothers, but go forth
To meet them, marshalled by the Lord of Hosts,
And overshadowed by the mighty ghosts
Of Moultrie and of Eutaw—who shall foil
Auxiliars such as these?

When, on January 9, 1861, the U.S. ship *Star of the West* approached to reprovision the soldiers in Ft. Sumter, two Citadel cadets fired what was arguably the first shot of the War between the States in Charleston Harbor—a cannon shot meant to warn the vessel off. One of the ship's officers quipped, "The people of Charleston pride themselves on their hospitality. They gave us several balls before we landed."

Then, for the rest of the month, nothing happened. Finally Virginian orator Roger Pryor barreled into Charleston, proclaiming that the only way to get Old Dominion to join the Confederacy—and thus bring along the other border states—was for South Carolina to instigate war with the United States. The obvious place to start was right in the midst of Charleston Harbor.

On April 10 the *Mercury* reprinted stories from New York papers that told of a naval expedition sent southward toward Charleston. The Carolinians could wait no longer if they hoped to take the fort without having to take on the U.S. Navy at the same time. Some 6,000 men were now stationed around the rim of the harbor, ready to take on the 60 men in Fort Sumter. At 4:30 A.M. on April 12, after days of intense negotiations, and with Union ships just outside the harbor, the firing began. Thirty-four hours later, Anderson's men raised the white flag and were allowed to leave the fort with colors flying and drums beating, saluting the U.S. flag with a 50-gun salute before taking it down. During this salute one of the guns exploded, killing a young soldier—the only casualty of the bombardment and the first casualty of the war.

Again South Carolina's instigation persuaded others to join the Confederacy: Virginia, Arkansas, and North Carolina, and Tennessee—now certain that Lincoln meant to use force to keep their fellow Southern states under federal rule—seceded, one by one.

Of these Johnny-Reb-Come-Latelies, North Carolina came nearly last of all. In fact, though she would lose more men than any other Southern state to Yankee bullets, North Carolina was always divided in its feelings. The west had long been a hotbed of abolitionism and a thoroughfare for the Underground Railroad, which was itself or-

---

The Truth is the whole army is burning with an insatiable desire to wreak vengeance upon South Carolina. I almost tremble at her fate, but feel that she deserves all that is in store for her.

—Gen. William T. Sherman, December 24, 1864, writing to another Union general

---

ganized largely by Levi Coffin, a Guilford County Quaker. The very inflammatory and influential 1857 book, *The Impending Crisis of the South: How to Meet It,* which Republicans circulated as an antislavery tract during the election of 1860, had been penned by Davie County–native Rowan Helper. And whereas South Carolina's coastal residents, ruled by its large plantation owners, led the charge into the fray, the independent folks of the Outer Banks, at least, saw no benefit in protecting the rights of wealthy slave-owning mainlanders.

All told, North Carolina in 1860 had just 34,658 slave owners out of a white and free-black population of over 660,000. Those 34,658 owned over 330,000 slaves, and each slave counted for three-fifths of a vote, but even this didn't give them a majority in the Tar Heel State. Nonetheless most North Carolinians subscribed to the "states' rights" doctrine, and on general principle resented the intrusion of the federal government into state affairs. Though Governor John Ellis waited to see whether or not Lincoln would send troops to try to hold the more-radical Deep Southern states in the Union, North Carolinians would not stand to see Federals march through their state to fight their Southern brethren.

On January 8, 1861, a day before the firing on Fort Sumter, over-eager North Carolinas disobeyed their governor and seized Fort Caswell and Fort Johnston at the mouth of the Cape Fear River. Ellis, not wanting to provoke the Union to violence, ordered the rebels to return the forts to Federal hands.

On March 15th, North Carolina Senator Thomas L. Clingman and Senator Stephen A. Douglas proposed evacuating nearly all the forts in the seceded states, including Forts Johnston and Caswell, and Ft. Sumter in Charleston. They thought rightly that this would defuse the most obvious flashpoints for confrontation between Federals and local secessionists, allowing time for peaceable discussion of the issues. It was rumored that Lincoln planned to carry out this idea, despite the fact that his old Illinois enemy Douglas had proposed it. Then, unexpectedly, Lincoln sent federal ships to Charleston to re-provision the soldiers in Fort Sumter, which led Charlestonians to fire the first shot of the war.

In truth the outgunned, outmanned, and virtually navy-less South had no chance against

> *In sacred memorials to those who gave their lives in the Confederate cause we find central expressions of the unofficial state religion.*
> —Kevin Lewis, "Religion in South Carolina Addresses the Public Order," in *Religion in South Carolina*, 1993

the North. Federal ships sailed south, sealing off one important port after another.

After the weakly defended Fort Hatteras fell to federal troops in August 1861, the Union-leaning locals held a convention proclaiming secession null and void, and declaring the village of Hatteras itself the capital of "the true and faithful State of North Carolina." In November they elected Marble Nash Taylor as their governor. Like the western Virginians, the Bankers sent delegates to Washington, D.C. with hopes of being seated in the U.S. Congress. Unlike the Virginians, whose region became the state of West Virginia, the Banker delegation never convinced the right people to take them seriously, and they were never seated or recognized.

After capturing Fort Hatteras, the Federals took Roanoke Island in February 1862, New Bern and Washington in March.

The same systematic closing of ports and taking of port towns took place in South Carolina. As early as November 1861, Union troops occupied the Sea Islands in the Beaufort area, establishing an important base for the ships and men who would stymie the important ports at Charleston and Savannah. When the plantation owners—many of them already off with the Confederate Army elsewhere—fled the area, the Sea Island slaves became the first "freedmen" of the war, and the Sea Islands became the laboratory for Northern plans to educate the African-Americans for their eventual role as full American citizens. What the Federals *couldn't* do was take Wilmington or Charleston, and this fact allowed blockade runners to bring in needed supplies to the Southern armies, protracting America's bloodiest war by several years.

Despite South Carolina's important role in the start of the war, and the long, unsuccessful attempt by Federals to take Charleston from 1863 onward, few military engagements occurred within the Palmetto State's borders until 1865, when

Sherman's Army, having already completed its infamous March to the Sea in Savannah, marched north to Columbia and leveled most of the town, as well as a number of towns along the way and beyond.

South Carolina lost 12,922 men to the war—23 percent of its white male population of fighting age, and the highest percentage of any state in the nation. North Carolina lost more men in sheer numbers than any other state: 19,673 killed in battle, a full one-fourth of all Confederate battle deaths. It also lost more men to desertion (23,000) than any other state—as well it should have, given the way the North Carolinians felt the Confederate government mistreated them.

A major complaint of North Carolina Governor Zebulon B. Vance, himself a Unionist before secession, was that the Confederacy kept conscripting his men to fight in other states, carelessly leaving North Carolina's mammoth coastline vulnerable to attack. Vance also protested that a glass ceiling in the Confederate Army—anchored in Jefferson Davis's resentment and distrust of North Carolinians for their slowness at seceding—kept worthy Tar Heel officers from receiving the general's commissions they deserved, thus depriving Tar Heel soldiers of serving under Tar Heel generals. Given the high death rate of North Carolinians on the battlefields of Virginia and Pennsylvania, it's easy to understand Vance's concern.

Sherman's 1865 march through the Carolinas resulted in the burning of Columbia and numerous other towns. As a result, poverty would mark the states for generations to come.

On February 21, 1865, with the Confederate forces finally evacuated from Charleston, the black 55th Massachusetts Regiment marched through the city. To most of the white citizens—those few who hadn't fled—this must have looked like Armageddon. To the African-Americans of the city, however, it was the Day of Jubilee. As one of the regiment's colonels recalled:

Men and women crowded to shake hands with men and officers. . . . On through the streets of the rebel city passed the column, on through the chief seat of that slave power, tottering to fall. Its walls rung to the chorus of manly voices singing "John Brown," "Babylon is Falling," and the "Battle-Cry of

*Freedom." It's hard to conceive of how un-
believable Emancipation must have seemed
for these men and women people born into
slavery.*

At a ceremony at which the U.S. flag was
once again raised over Fort Sumter, former fort
commander Robert Anderson was joined on the
platform by two men: Robert Smalls, escaped
Beaufort slave and African-American Union hero,
and the son of Denmark Vesey.

RECONSTRUCTION

Though they had long made up the majority of
the Carolinas' population, African-Americans
played a prominent role in governing the Carolinas for the first time when federal troops occupied the states from 1866 to 1877.

In South Carolina, despite the anti-Northern
fury of their prewar and wartime politics, most
Carolinians—including South Carolina's opinion maker, Wade Hampton III—believed that
white Carolinians would do well to accept President Andrew Johnson's terms for reentry to full
participation in the Union. However when the
powerful "radical" anti-Southern Congress seized
control of the Reconstruction process, things
got harder for white Carolinians. The idea of
these Republicans was to establish a solidly Republican South by convincing blacks to vote Republican and then keeping former Confederates
from voting for as long as possible.

Both North and South Carolina's federally
mandated new constitutions of 1868 brought democratic reforms, but by now most whites viewed
the Republican government as representative of
black interests only and were largely unsupport-
ive. Laws forbidding former Confederates (virtually the entire native white-male population) from
bearing arms only exacerbated the tensions, especially in South Carolina, as rifle-bearing black
militia units began drilling in the streets.

Added to the brewing interracial animosity
was many whites' sense that their former slaves
had betrayed them. Before the war most slaveholders had convinced themselves that they
were treating their slaves well and had thus
earned their slaves' loyalty. Understandably
most slaves had been happy to give their mas-

ters the impression that they were indeed devoted to the household. Hence, when the Union
Army rolled in and slaves deserted by the thousands (though many did not), slaveholders took
it as a personal affront.

And thus went Reconstruction in the Carolinas: the black population scrambled to enjoy
and preserve its new rights while the white population attempted to claw its way back to the top
of the social ladder by denying blacks those
same rights.

Perhaps predictably, Ku Klux Klan raids began
shortly thereafter, terrorizing blacks and black
sympathizers in an attempt to reestablish white
supremacy. Most of the state's "better element"
showed little tolerance for such violence, especially when undertaken anonymously, and largely squelched the movement locally after a few
years. In 1876 South Carolina Piedmont towns
were the site of numerous demonstrations by
the Red Shirts, white Democrats determined to
win the upcoming elections through any means
possible. Named for their trademark red shirts
(worn to mock the histrionic "waving of the bloody
shirt" of the radical Republicans), the Red Shirts
turned the tide in South Carolina, convincing
whites that, after 11 years of military rule, this
could indeed be the year they could regain control. Before the election, concerned Republican
Governor Chamberlain asked Washington for
assistance and was sent 1,100 federal troops
by President Ulysses S. Grant to keep order
and ensure a "fair" election.

Even so, the hard-fought and bitter political
campaign of 1876 ended in a deadlock, as Hampton won the official vote but Chamberlain and his
followers claimed—accurately, the record seems

---

*Their lives are not worth the powder that will
blow them out of existence. . . . Their slaveholding
Sodom will perish for the lack of five just men,
or a single just idea. It must be razed and got out
of the way, like any other obstacle to the progress of
humanity.*

—New Englander John William Deforest,
*Miss Ravenel's Conversion from Secession
to Loyalty,* 1867 (written while Deforest was
a Union officer working for the
Reconstruction-era Freedmen's
Bureau in South Carolina)

to show—that the Democrats' "victory" was the result of massive voter fraud and coercion by the Red Shirts. In Edgefield and Laurens Counties, for instance, Hampton and other Democratic candidates received more votes than the total number of registered voters in both parties.

Both parties claimed victory, and for a while two separate state assemblies did business side by side on the floor of the state house (their Speakers shared the Speaker's desk, but each had his own gavel) until the Democrats moved to another building, where they continued to pass resolutions and hold forth with the state's business, just as the Republicans were doing. The Republican State Assembly tossed out the results of the tainted election and reelected Chamberlain governor. A week later General Wade Hampton III took the oath of office for the De-

mocrats. Finally, after months of this nonsense—not to mention a couple of near shootouts—in April 1877, President Rutherford B. Hayes—in return for the South's support in his own convoluted presidential "victory" over Samuel Tilden—withdrew federal troops from Columbia, at which point the Republican government dissolved, and Governor Chamberlain headed back north.

The white elites were back in charge of South Carolina, in the person of General Wade Hampton III. Hampton's election marked the establishment of a 99-year hold on the State House by the Democrats; the next Republican governor of South Carolina was James Burrows Edwards, in 1975. The normal American two-party system was thrown off balance because the Democratic Party, in those years, was the "white"

THE RED SHIRTS' *PLAN FOR THE CAMPAIGN OF 1876*

The Red Shirts were founded by General Martin W. Gary of Edgefield, who distributed his *Plan for the Campaign of 1876* to various counties around South Carolina. The plan featured a number of fairly predictable political tactics—encouraging Democrats to get weak or incapacitated Democrats to the ballot box and to prevent nonvalid Republican voters from voting and valid ones from voting more than once, but it also included the following:

12. Every Democrat must feel honor bound to control the vote of at least one negro, by intimidation, purchase, keeping him away or as each individual may determine, [sic] how he may best accomplish it.

13. We must attend every Radical meeting that we hear of. . . . Democrats must go in as large numbers as they can get together, and well armed, behave at *first* with great courtesy and assure the ignorant negroes that you mean them no harm and so soon as their *leaders* or speakers begin to speak and make false statements of facts, tell them *then* and *there* to their faces that they are liars, thieves and rascals and are only trying to mislead the ignorant negroes and if you get a chance get upon the platform and address the negroes.

14. In speeches to negroes you must remember that argument has no effect upon them: they can only be influenced by their *fears,* superstition and cupidity. . . . Treat them so as to show them, you are the superior race, and that their natural position is that of subordination to the white man.

and, finally, ominiously:

15. Let it be generally known that if any blood is shed, houses burnt, votes repeated, ballot boxes stuffed, false counting of votes, or any acts on their part that are in violation of *Law* and *Order!* that we will hold the leaders of the *Radical Party personally responsible,* whether they were present at the time of the commission of the offense or crime or not; beginning first with the white men, second the mulatto men and third with the black leaders. . . .

The draft Gary gave to his secretary contained several items he had reconsidered and marked "omit," including number 16: "Never threaten a man individually if he deserves to be threatened. The necessities of the times require that he should die."

> *The Negro in the country districts must be made to understand what he has already been taught in the city, that freedom does not mean idleness. On the other hand, the late master should specially be made to understand that the spirit of slavery must go to the grave with the thing itself. It will not be an easy work to teach either class its chief lesson. We must have patience.*
>
> —New Yorker Sidney Andrews,
> *The South Since the War,* 1886

party in South Carolina, and whites successfully kept blacks away from the ballot boxes through various Jim Crow laws.

But this by no means resulted in unanimity among South Carolina's fiery electorate. Hampton and other wealthy former Confederate officers, known as "Bourbons," ruled the state, but the farmers of the Upcountry were in no mood to return to the aristocratic leadership that had led them into destruction. Finally at the 1890 election of the great populist and advocate of agriculture, Edgefield's Ben "Pitchfork" Tillman, the Upcountry made its long-awaited ascent to state leadership. But Tillman realized that the divided white electorate made it possible that a united black electorate could again gain control of the state. Therefore in 1892 after his reelection as governor, Tillman led the charge to hold a new state constitutional convention to draw up a new constitution that would disenfranchise blacks.

He succeeded.

At the same time, up in the Wilmington area, a new version of the Red Shirts appeared just before the 1898 elections. Some of them had come from South Carolina. They appeared in Wilmington and stirred up whites and frightened blacks, though at first there was no violence. Just before the election, the chairman of the state Democratic party issued an appeal to white Tar Heels to turn out for the vote, vowing that "North Carolina is a WHITE MAN'S STATE, and WHITE MEN will rule it." Begrudging the continued Republican rule in the black-majority region, and inflamed by alleged dispersions cast upon white women by the editorials of a local black newspaper, some 600–2000 armed whites burned the newspaper offices. Though reports varied, rioters killed some 14 blacks, jailed ten others, and ran the "negro political leaders," including the white Republican mayor, out of town. Some reports claimed that at least one white man was killed as well. This coup d'etat ended with the establishment of a Democratic former Confederate officer as mayor. The following year the triumphant leaders of the Wilmington riot led the movement for the establishment of the Grandfather Clause, which effectively disenfranchised the black population of North Carolina-ensuring Democratic rule for the next sixty years.

THE NEW SOUTH

In 1886 Atlanta newspaper publisher Henry W. Grady, speaking before a New York audience, proclaimed his vision of a "New South"—a South, that is, based on the Northern economic model. By now the idea had already struck some enterprising Carolinians that all that cotton they were sending north at cut rates could be processed just as well down in the Carolinas. By the end of the 19th century, the textile industry was exploding across the state—but particularly upstate, with its powerful turbine-turning rivers—at last bringing relief from the depressed sharecropper economy.

For whites anyway, things were looking up. In 1902, South Carolina hosted the Charleston Exposition, drawing visitors from around the world, hoping to impress on them the idea that the state was on the rebound. On April 9, President Theodore Roosevelt, whose mother had attended school in Columbia, even made an appearance, smoothing over the still simmering animosities between North and South by declaring:

> *The wounds left by the great Civil War... have healed... The devotion, the self-sacrifice, the steadfast resolution and lofty daring, the high devotion to the right as each man saw it... all these qualities of the men and women of the early sixties now shine luminous and brilliant before our eyes, while the mists of anger and hatred that once dimmed them have passed away forever.*

Northerners had long made this kind of reconciliatory talk—the sort of easy generosity possible to the victor, especially if the victor needs the loser's cooperation to have a successful economy. But now—in economics, if not in civil liberties—the Carolinas truly did seem to be improving.

Unfortunately, the invasion of the boll weevil, beginning in 1919, destroyed the cotton crop, which, though it hadn't paid well since before the Civil War, was nonetheless North and South Carolina's primary crop. Thus, just as they were coming out of their post-Civil War slump, the Carolinas and other cotton states toppled into their own Depression ten years before the rest of the nation. Blacks and low-income whites left the states in droves for better jobs up north. Only the establishment and expansion of military bases during World War II, as well as domestic and foreign investment in manufacturing in more recent decades, have revitalized the states.

DESEGREGATION

Compared to hot spots such as Mississippi and Alabama, desegregation went relatively smoothly during the 1950s and 1960s in North and South Carolina. The first sit-in of the Civil Rights era took place in Greensboro, N.C., in February 1960. The tragic shooting at Orangeburg in 1968 made one great exception: three students were killed and more than 30 others were shot by police overreacting to the students' violence. Up in Rock Hill in 1961, nine black Friendship College students took seats at the whites-only lunch counter at McCrory's (now Vantell Variety, on Main St.) and refused to leave. When police arrested them, the students were given the choice of paying $200 fines or serving 30 days of hard labor in the York County jail. The "Friendship Nine" chose the latter, becoming the first sit-in protesters of the Civil Rights movement to suffer imprisonment.

The Carolinas' universities began integrating in the early 60s. When Clemson was forced to allow Harvey Gantt into its classes in 1962, making it the first public college in South Carolina to be integrated, word went out from influential whites that no violence or otherwise unseemly behavior would be tolerated. Gantt's entrance into school there went without incident. Gantt himself had his own explanation for this: "If you can't appeal to the morals of a South Carolinian," he said, "you can appeal to his manners."

Another front of the Civil Rights battle revolved around voting rights, which had been largely denied blacks in both Carolinas since the 1890s. In North Carolina in 1958, for instance, a full 90 percent of all voters were white. Throughout the 1960s, restrictions were lifted and blacks began to vote in larger numbers. However, the flight of African-Americans to the north during the Jim Crow era left few counties with black majorities. Nonetheless African-American legislators, mayors, and judges began to win elections.

Blacks, who tended to be poorer than whites, favored the Democratic Party, with its greater funding of social programs. Whereas the Southern Democratic party had long been the "white man's" party, during the Kennedy/Johnson years, conservative Southern Democrats found themselves unwelcome in their own party. In 1964 Barry Goldwater's platform galvanized South Carolina's "Dixiecrats" and led to major defections into the Grand Old Party, most notably Senator Strom Thurmond. By 1973 North Carolina was ready to elect its first Republican senator in several decades—Jesse Helms. Both Thurmond and Helms of course have become fixed in the Washington firmament, no matter what artillery Democrats might use to try to bring them down. In 1990 and 1996, North Carolinian liberals nearly succeeded in unseating Helms with the black former mayor of Charlotte, Harvey Gantt, who, some 30 years earlier, had been the first black to attend Clemson.

Since the early 1970s, more and more Northerners have discovered the Carolina coasts, and many of them have chosen to move down permanently, especially as the nation's collective memories of race riots and lynchings in the South continue to dim. Even some descendants of black Carolinians who moved out of the South during the Jim Crow years have moved back.

THE PEOPLE

Despite all its physical beauty, despite its music, its food, and the salty scent of the coastal marshes, the very best thing about the Carolinas is its people. Remove Carolinians from the Carolina Coasts, replace them with New Yorkers, give it five years, and what would you have? Florida.

Make no mistake: it's Carolinians who make Coastal Carolina the unique place it is. Despite Charlestonians' legendary pride, by and large Carolinians are a meek lot, humbled by the mistakes of their past in a way that Northerners and Westerners are not.

Unless they leave home, Carolinians cannot escape their past: a white Middleton may well share a classroom with two black Middletons, likely descendants of his great-great-great-grandfather's slaves—and possibly distant cousins.

A lot of Southerners see Northerners as the finger-pointing husbands who quit cheating on their wives and immediately became crusaders against adultery. Westerners are the husbands who ditched their wives and kids and headed to the coast with their secretaries. Southerners are the husbands who have been caught in the act, been half-forgiven, and now live on in a town where—no matter what other accomplishments they may muster—their sin will never be forgotten. And it is because of this that white Carolinians tend to evince an odd mixture of defensiveness, good nature, and perhaps a little more understanding of human nature than other folks. And perhaps because so much of their history has been spent withstanding the tugs and blows of other regions that commanded them to change, Carolinians are none too quick to equate change with progress. This, granted, can make them a bit slow to acknowledge even a good change when it comes about. South Carolina only formally ratified the 19th Amendment, allowing women the vote, in 1969.

This understanding of people as intrinsically flawed creatures also makes Carolinians value traditions and manners more than many—for in a culture where human nature is seen as inherently flawed, "self-expression" and "doing what you feel" are not necessarily good things. To Carolinians some parts of the self are . . . well . . . just selfish. Hence Carolinians use ritualized courtesies copiously to smooth the rough edges of humanity. Carolinians are taught to say "yes, ma'am," "no, sir," "please," and "thank you," whether or not their inner children feel like it.

One of the most charming things about Carolinians is how they're nearly always genuinely surprised to hear that non-Southerners have bothered to come all this way just to see their lit-

a Lowcountry basketmaker

tle state. They know that South Carolina is a gem but won't know how you found out about it. Most Carolinians are proud of where they live and usually quite happy to show you around.

Language

One of the things outsiders often notice about Southerners is the Southern way with figurative language. To some degree this is derived from the strong Biblical tradition of the region; for centuries Southern evangelical Christians have naturally striven to illustrate the intangibles of life with easy-to-visualize parables, following the example of Jesus, who used illustrations drawn from situations familiar to his unschooled 1st-century audiences (a shepherd's concern for his sheep, wheat planted amongst briars, a disobedient son returning home) to explain complex theological doctrines.

Hence if you're butting into a conflict between two Carolinians, you may be reminded that "y'all don't have a dog in this fight." If you

GULLAH CULTURE OF THE SEA ISLANDS

On the quiet Sea Islands south of Charleston, a centuries-old culture is passing away. Like most African-Americans in the state, the Gullah people are descendants of West Africans who made the horrific passage to South Carolina as slaves. (The name of both the people and their language, "Gullah," was long thought to be a derivation of "Angola." Today many believe it evolved from the words Gola and Gora, both tribal names in modern-day Liberia.) Yet even from the first, the Sea Islander slaves lived notably different from those of their enslaved contemporaries. For one thing, most Sea Islanders lived on isolated plantations where one could commonly find 100 or more Africans for every white person; a Gullah field worker might go months without coming into contact with a European. Consequently Sea Islanders retained their West African language, culture, and crafts much more coherently than on the mainland.

After the outbreak of the Civil War, Federal ships swept down upon the Sea Islands, establishing the area as a base of operations as they set about shutting down Southern ports. Sea Island slave owners fled, leaving their rice, cotton, and indigo plantations to their slaves. Though President Andrew Johnson nullified General William T. Sherman's order setting aside the Lowcountry for former slaves, many former white planters did not reclaim their lands, and after a number of deadly hurricanes in the late 1890s, many remaining whites left the islands. Few black Sea Islanders interacted at all with whites, and many had never even been to the mainland in their lifetimes. The truth was, despite the hardships their isolation brought them, the Sea Islanders knew they had a good thing.

Things might have stayed like this indefinitely if mainlanders hadn't woken up to the fact that the islands featured some of the best beaches on the East Coast. The Fraser family from Georgia had bought up much of Hilton Head Island for logging, but then one of them got the idea of turning some of the cheap farmland into golf courses. Snowbirds from places like Jersey and Pennsylvania—as sick of Florida as they were of flurries—flocked to the "new" paradise. As quickly as you could say "Please remove your golf shoes," Hilton Head Island became a Northern beachhead in the area—for the second time in a century.

Land prices for the remaining Sea Islanders on Hilton Head and surrounding islands shot up from around $100 an acre in the 1940s to over $100,000 for some oceanfront acres today. In the intervening years, many of those who didn't want to move have found they can't keep up with the higher property taxes and have been forced to sell. Many of those who have somehow remained have discovered that they aren't adequately trained for the higher-paying jobs the resorts had brought to the islands. Consequently, while mainlanders from around the country move in to take many of the managerial and technical positions, the lower-paid service positions have fallen to the Sea Islanders. For many these become life-long jobs.

And yet, while native Gullah islanders are losing much of their physical and spiritual world to encroaching resorts, network television, and the public schools, the culture lives on, preserved in the still-strong extended families and church-based community.

Culture

Perhaps the best-known craft to the casual Carolina visitor is **basket weaving.** In the Charleston Market and along U.S. 17 north of Mount Pleasant, Gullah women sit in their stands making and selling their wares, the products of a tradition passed down from African ancestors and carried across the Atlantic in the minds and hands of women locked in the holds of slave ships. Most of the baskets you'll see for sale bear European influences as well—the relatively lightweight baskets found for sale are for show, not for carrying clothing, food, or babies, as are the heavier "work" baskets, which are more uniformly African in origin.

Both the "show" and "work" baskets, woven from the Lowcountry's sweet grass, pine straw, bulrushes, and palmetto leaves, contain patterns and designs similar to those found in Nigeria, Ghana, Togo, and Benin. Both boys and girls learn basket making at a young age, though primarily women continue weaving as adults.

Another celebrated element of the Gullah culture is the **storytelling** tradition passed down from time eternal. Many of the traditional Gullah stories (still told today) appear to have African parallels. One popular series features "Brer Rabbit," a wily rabbit who stays one step ahead of those who are physically bigger than him through his quick wits. A lot of historians have theorized that this reflects the slaves' own strategies for outwitting the dominant white class during antebellum times, but as scholar Patricia Jones-Jackson points out in *When Roots Die: Endangered Traditions on the Sea Islands,* Brer Rabbit-like characters abound in West African cultures, suggesting that though slaves may well have found it easy to identify with the Brer Rabbit character, the character itself predates American slavery.

Other common Gullah stories feature Jesus as a character, and always contain some sort of moral lesson. Call-and-response relationships between storyteller and audience, in fact, resemble the ones between Gullah preachers and their congregations. Most Sea Island churches tend toward emotive Baptist and Methodist services with the call-and-response forms found in many African-American cultures. One interesting Gullah belief—progressively less common—perceives the human as divided into body, soul, *and* spirit. At death, the body dies, the soul travels to heaven or hell, but the spirit is left behind to do either good or harm to people here on earth.

Language

Technically speaking the Gullah tongue is considered a creole rather than a dialect like inland Black English or American Southern English. Linguists consider a dialect a variant of standard English particular to a specific region or social environment, whereas a true creole descends from a "pidgin," a combination language created by people speaking different languages who wish to communicate with one another. Technically a pidgin has no native speakers; when because of isolation the pidgin is allowed to become the dominant tongue in a region (as has Gullah on the Sea Islands), the tongue is considered a creole.

While the vast majority of Gullah words come from English, a number of words (one linguist estimates 4,000) derive from African languages, including *gula* for "pig," *cush* for "bread" or "cake," *nansi* for "spider," and *buckra* for "white man."

Jones-Jackson points out a number of grammatical elements to listen for when conversing with a Gullah speaker; they include premarked verbs ("I don shell em" instead of "I shelled them"), verb serialization ("I hear tell say he knows," instead of "I hear it said that he knows"; and adverb-adjective

duplication for emphasis ("clean clean" rather than "very clean"). All of these characteristics seem to have roots in African languages.

Where to Experience Gullah Culture

Near Beaufort, S.C.: The 49-acre, 16-building Penn Center on St. Helena Island stands as perhaps the world's foremost center of information on Gullah culture and on the connections between West Africa and the Sea Islands. The first place to visit is the **York W. Bailey Museum,** 843/838-8562, on the right side of Land's End Road as you come in from U.S. 21. Admission runs $2. Museum hours run Tues.–Fri. 11 A.M.–4 P.M., Saturday 10 A.M.–4 P.M.

If you can make it here in November you may get to take part in the **Heritage Days Celebration,** a three-day festival celebrating African-American Sea Islands culture. Call 843/838-8563 for information.

Right at the intersection of U.S. 21 and Land's End Road, you'll find the **Red Piano Too,** 843/838-2241, an old plank grocery store on the National Register of Historic Places, which has reopened as an art gallery for Gullah artists. A great place to pick up a one-of-a-kind (literally) souvenir, including painted furniture, mobiles, regional landscapes, and books written in Gullah. You'll also notice the **Gullah House Restaurant,** next door, 843/838-2402, with items like "Hot Ya Mout Swimps," and "Uncle Woolie's Crab Cake Dinner," along with meat dishes.

For Beaufort-area tours focused specifically on the Gullah culture, call **Gullah-n-Geechie Mahn Tours,** 843/838-7516 or 843/838-3758.

In May Beaufort hosts a **Gullah Festival** with traditional storytelling, music, and other events. Call 843/525-0628 for information.

Charleston Area: You'll find Gullah basket weavers selling their baskets along U.S. 17 north of Mount Pleasant, around the Market area, and sometimes at other known tourist haunts like the visitors center or at Patriots Point—though prices at the latter tend to be more expensive. The **Avery Research Center for African-American History and Culture,** at the College of Charleston, 125 Bull St., 843/727-2009, features a reading room and archives dedicated to documenting and preserving the cultural history of Lowcountry African-Americans. **Gallery Chuma/African American Art Gallery,** 43 John St., 843/722-7568, email: Chuman@galleryChuma.com, features Gullah artist Jonathan Green's works as a permanent fixture,

(continues on next page)

GULLAH CULTURE OF THE SEA ISLANDS
(continued)

along with those of several other renowned African-American artists. Open Mon.–Sat. 10 A.M.–6 P.M. or by appointment. **Gullah Tours** of Charleston leave from the gallery daily. Call for information. For authentic Sea Island cooking, try **Gullah Cuisine,** 1717 U.S. 17 N, 843/881-9076.

Media
Well-regarded books on Sea Island culture and the Gullah tongue include the very informative *When Roots Die: Endangered Traditions on the Sea Is-* *lands* by Patricia Jones-Jackson (Athens, GA: UGA, 1987), which is highlighted by the inclusion of several transcribed Gullah folk tales, sermons, and prayers. South Carolina Educational Television (SCETV), 800/553-7752, website: www.scetv.org/scetv/mk-thome.html, offers a number of video titles that touch on Gullah and Sea Island subjects.

The bookstore in the museum at the Penn Center is one of the best places in the state (and the world) to find books, music, and videotapes relating to Sea Island culture.

---

think a person is smart just because he went to school, you're forgetting that "livin' in a garage don't make you a Ford." My personal favorite, though I only heard it once, describes a thoughtful person who apparently was "sweeter than sugar cubes in syrup." Makes you want to brush your teeth just hearing it.

Carolinians don't think or figure, they "reckon." They don't get ready, they "fix," as in, "I'm fixing to head down to Charleston." They don't push buttons, they "mash" them. They "cut" lights on and off, "carry" people around in their cars, accomplish urgent tasks in a "skinny minute," and push shopping "buggies" around the Winn-Dixie. If a Carolinian is a stranger to a subject, she "doesn't know 'boo'" about it. If she's never met you before, she doesn't know you from "Adam's house cat." If she *does* know you and sees you, she won't just hug you, she'll "hug your neck." And if a Carolinian says he really needs to "take a powder," it probably just means he has a headache and is taking a dose of Goody's powder (a regional remedy—essentially crushed aspirin). If he tells you he's "like to pass out," it means he's very tired, not drunk.

Carolinians never pop in to say "hello" or "hi"—they stop by to say "hey." In fact you'll rarely hear "hi" in public—it's usually "hey."

Fairly well known is the preference for "y'all," or the more formal "you-all." (Some Carolinians argue that "y'all" is actually more politically correct than the Yankee "you guys," since it's not gender-exclusive.) It's usually the first linguistic nuance you'll pick up when you're in the state, and it's one of the hardest for displaced Carolinians to mask when they're outside of Dixie. It just sounds friendlier. If you meet more than one person walking together on the street, it's proper and friendly to say, "Hey, you-all."

You may also hear (usually) white South Carolinian males call each other "Bo," the way males in other American subcultures might call one another "Homes" or "Dude": "Hey, Bo—can I borrow your johnboat?" "Sure, Bo."

Pronunciation counts too. Though there's not the space to go into all the regional variations, just remember that no one watches television in South Carolina; they watch "the TEE-vee." And cautious Carolinians buy "IN-surance" on their house, which will pay for the family to stay in a "HO-tel" if the house burns down.

In the Upcountry particularly, the "s" on the ends of plurals is often dropped, as in, "That Co-Cola is sixty-five cent."

Terms of Address
One of the most admirable qualities of Southern culture is its resistance to the Cult of Youth. Although perhaps less so along the coastline, Carolina is in general a place where it's not against the law to get old (see Senators Thurmond and Helms). Here age is generally still respected, and one way of showing and reinforcing this respect is the customary respectful way of referring to elders as "ma'am" and "sir." For example:

"Excuse me, ma'am, but could you tell me where to find the trailhead?"

"Didn't y'all see the sign back away? Where the two magnolia used to be?"

"No, ma'am."

Granted, there is some classism involved. Bosses and the wealthy tend to hear themselves addressed as "sir" or "ma'am" more often than, say, gardeners or house cleaners. "Aunt" and "uncle" are familiar terms used by whites toward elder African-Americans, although almost completely absent in all but the oldest generations.

Note that visitors don't *have* to say "ma'am" and "sir"—Southerners expect non-Southerners to be ill-mannered anyway—but doing so might help you blend in a little better.

Children address adults normally with "Mr.," "Miss," or "Mrs." attached to either the adult's first name or last name. Family friends or other adult friends are often addressed by the first name, preceded by either Mr. or Miss—whether or not the woman in question is married. Hence to our friends' children my wife and I became "Miss Kristin and Mr. Mike." It's much more genuine than the automatic uncle or aunt status some parents elsewhere are always trying to confer upon you. It's a typically Carolinian compromise, reinforcing societal roles and responsibilities by keeping the generations separate, yet also encouraging intimacy with first names.

Note too that if a large age difference exists between you and another (older) person, it's still

---

FAMOUS COASTAL CAROLINIANS

ARTS AND LITERATURE

Hervey Allen (Charleston), author of *Anthony Adverse*

Washington Allston (Waccamaw Neck), early American painter

Pat Conroy (Beaufort), best-selling author of *The Prince of Tides, Beach Music, The Great Santini, Lords of Discipline,* and others

Minnie Evans (Wilmington), folk artist

Dubose Heyward (Charleston), author of *Porgy* (basis of subsequent Gershwin opera *Porgy and Bess*)

Julia Mood Peterkin (Waccamaw Neck), Pulitzer Prize–winning novelist

Archibald Rutledge (Waccamaw Neck), author

MUSIC

Chubby Checker (Spring Gully); his "The Twist" is one of the biggest records ever

Charlie Daniels (Wilmington); country fiddler/vocalist, of "Uneasy Rider" and "Devil Went Down to Georgia" fame

SCIENCE

Alexander Garden (Charleston), Colonial-era botanist (the gardenia is named in his honor)

Joel Poinsett (Charleston), former U.S. ambassador to Mexico (the poinsettia is named in his honor)

SPORTS

Joe Frazier (Beaufort, S.C.), former heavyweight boxing champion

Roman Gabriel (Wilmington), former NFL quarterback

Michael Jordan (Wilmington), former basketball superstar

Sugar Ray Leonard (Wilmington), former welterweight boxing champion, Olympic champion

MOVIES AND TELEVISION

Helen Chandler (Charleston), actress, Bela Lugosi's *Dracula*

Stanley Donen (Charleston), director, *Singin' in the Rain* and many other films

Charles Kuralt (Wilmington), *On the Road* host

Chris Rock (Georgetown), comedian, actor

Vanna White (North Charleston), letter turner, *Wheel of Fortune*

Kevin Williamson (Oriental), TV and film writer/producer

POLITICS

Virginia Dare (Roanoke Island), first English child born in North America

Henry Martyn Robert (Roberts), protocol expert, author of *Robert's Rules of Order*

Woodrow Wilson (Wilmington), U.S. president

A PRONOUNCING GAZETTEER OF COASTAL CAROLINA NAMES

Beaufort, S.C.	BYOO-fort
Beaufort, N.C.	BOU-ferd
Blenheim	BLEN-um
Colleton	COL-ton
Congaree	CON-guh-REE
Corolla	Cu-RAWL-uh
Kiawah	KEE-a-wuh
New Bern	NEWburn
Pee Dee	PEE-dee
Pocotaligo	POKE-uh-tuh-LEE-go
Saluda	suh-LOO-duh
Santee	san-TEE
Savannah	suh-VAN-uh
Sherman	SAY-tun
St. Helena	saint HELL-en-uh
Wadmalaw	wahd-MALL-ah
Wando	WAHN-doh
Westo	WEST-oh
Yamasee (tribe)	YAM-uh-see
Yamassee (war)	YAM-uh-see
Yemasee (town)	YEM-uh-see

proper to address an elder as Mr., Ms., Mrs., or Miss; among the 20 fairly Bohemian graduate English students in James Dickey's Poetry Work-shop at USC, I never heard one of us address him (even in private) as anything but "Mr. Dickey."

Southern Subtleties:
How to Read through Southern Manners
You and your travel companion meet a nice Carolinian couple, who invite you to their home for dinner. You eat, you adjourn to the porch for beverages, and then you sit around talking. It gets a little late, but your hosts seem so eager to continue the conversation that you linger. It gets later. You really *should* go, but as you rise, your hosts offer another round of drinks. Finally you decide you must go. You leave, while your hosts openly grieve your departure. You're begged to return again when "y'all can stay a little longer."

What the average unsuspecting non-Southerners don't realize is that they have just committed a major faux pas. Though you of course had no way of knowing, your hosts were ready for you to leave right after dessert, but offered drinks on the porch only because you showed no signs of leaving, and they wanted to be polite.

So what's the rule of thumb when visiting with South Carolinians you don't know very well? Leave about when you first suspect you should, only an hour earlier.

ON THE ROAD

I remember when I first moved from inland South Carolina to the Carolina Coast. The first thing my wife, Kristin, and I noticed were the in-line skaters. Back in Orangeburg and Columbia, the only place we saw people jogging was around the track at the local high school. On a hot day the streets were empty and we'd walk past empty porch after empty porch, the abandoned swings hanging still in the thick heat while the air-conditioners hummed in the background. But then we moved out to Isle of Palms. Suddenly everybody was outside, windsurfing, bicycling, jogging, in-line skating. The coastal types were a different breed.

And yet the Carolina coasts have a reputation, whether down in Beaufort, S.C., or up on the Outer Banks, for a certain languidity. And this sort of graciousness (and, okay, slowness) of living does certainly still exist along the coast. All the water around here, however, has also attracted a lot of active types from other areas—people who didn't just happen to be born here, but who have chosen to live here and who are paying far too much for their house-with-private-boatramp-access-and-a-jogging-path to just sit in the screened porch sipping sweet tea and looking at the view. They're anxious to paddle, windsurf, water-ski, scuba dive, bike, skate, and fish every last inch of Coastal Carolina.

These work hard–play hard sorts, and their time-on-my-hands snowbird brethren, have created a massive entertainment/recreation industry in Coastal Carolina, providing far more recreational opportunities than you'll find anywhere else in the state.

OUTDOOR ACTIVITIES

OCEAN SPORTS

Surfing

Yes, Carolinians surf. What's even more startling to some first-time visitors is that the Carolinas host a full-blown surf subculture as well. The enthusiasm for the sport runs high along the coasts—much higher than the waves in fact. The Outer Banks have a long and distinguished history of surfing, dating back to the 1960s. Stellar local surf shops include **Corolla Surf Shop,** in the Corolla Light Village Shops, 252/453-9283, website: www.corollasurfshop.com, which includes a Surfing Museum inside the store. Down on Hatteras you'll find **Ocean Roots,** across from the Avon Pier, 252/995-3369.

The Southern North Carolina Coast enjoys pretty decent surf for this side of the country, and a very active surf scene. The Wilmington area alone boasts well over a dozen surf shops. East Coast surfers congregate hereabout for surf contests each summer. The best spot in the region is arguably the Crystal Pier, but it's also often the most crowded spot because of this. Good spots include the north end of Wrightsville Beach in front of Shell Island Resort; I've seen some great surf off Fort Fisher, and Maryland Avenue Carolina Beach, and Kure Beach can all be good under the right conditions. So can Bald Head Island, though it's a pain to get there. As anywhere, stop by a surf shop, strike up a conversation with some local surfers, and find out where they're breaking the day you're there. Check out www.sncsurf.com before you come out; it's a great website for planning your Wilmington area surfing.

Down over the border in Myrtle Beach, you'll find the best surf between 20th Avenue N and 20th Avenue S, but that's not saying much; 29th Avenue S and 38th Avenue N are especially popular. Surf shops are good spots to pick up tips on where the "big" ones are breaking and/or to rent boards or wet suits. These include **Surf City Surfboards,** with three locations, 1103 N. Kings Hwy., 843/626-7919; Myrtle Square Mall, 843/626-5412; and N. Myrtle Beach, 843/272-1090. **Village Surf Shoppe,** 30 years old and an institution on the Strand, offers rentals from two locations: 500 Atlantic Ave., Garden City, 843/651-6396; and 2016 N. Kings Hwy., Myrtle Beach, 843/626-8176. Finally, **Xtreme Surf and Skateboard Co.** over at 515 E. U.S. 501, 843/626-2262, makes custom surfboards and skateboards, as well as renting sticks to the visiting gremmies.

When you hit the surf in the Myrtle Beach area, make sure you wear your leash and stay at least 400 feet away from all piers—in Horry County, it's the law.

The single best, most dependable surf spot in the Charleston area, if not in the entire state, is **The Washout,** at the end of E. Ashley Avenue in Folly Beach. If the waves are small everywhere else, they may still be decent here. If they're good everywhere else, here they'll be pounding. Of course, if the swell's good, it's also going to be crowded here, and while the localism among area surfers is nowhere near Hawaii or California levels, you might want to let the tube-starved locals enjoy themselves. The Washout hosts the state's surfing championships every year. To get there, take U.S. 17 south of Charleston, then S.C. 171 until it dead-ends at the Holiday Inn. Turn left at East Ashley and keep going.

Another popular spot at Folly is **10th Street,** where you can count on smaller, but often cleaner and less-crowded, waves than you'll find up at The Washout. The **Folly Beach Pier,** beside the Holiday Inn at E. Atlantic Avenue, sometimes offers cleaner waves and longer rides than The Washout, but keep an eye out for The Law: though not always enforced, it's illegal to surf within 200 feet of the pier.

Over in East Cooper, a lot of folks enjoy surfing at the **Sea Cabins Pier,** right at 21st and Palm Boulevard on Isle of Palms. If the wind's blowing out of the northeast, you may want to head over here, or to **Bert's** at Station 22, Sullivan's Island. Named in honor of the venerable bar out on Middle Street, this is one of the best places to surf at low tide.

McKevlin's Surf Shop offers a 24-hour surf report on Charleston-area beaches, 843/588-2261. It's updated several times throughout the day. The Charleston *Post and Courier* offers its own **InfoLine Surf Report,** updated a minimum of three times a day, 843/937-6000, ext. 7873.

Recently a website opened up featuring South Carolina surfing updates: www.angelfire.com/sc/surfextreme2/index.html.

Other Water Sports

Sailing, parasailing, and **windsurfing,** are all popular along the Carolina coasts. On the Outer Banks, they're legendary. For information on outfitters for all of these sports, see the listings under individual destinations.

Diving

The Carolinas' long history of shipwrecks makes the waters offshore a virtual wonderland for divers. However, if you're here in the winter, rough, cold waters can make offshore diving pretty inhospitable between October and May.

But people dive in the historic rivers and sounds year-round; one Lowcountry favorite is the Cooper River, filled with fossilized giant shark's teeth, bones, and mammal teeth, as well as colonial and prehistoric artifacts. Expect water temperatures in the 50s. See individual destination chapters for dive locations and outfitters.

CANOEING/KAYAKING

The Carolina coasts are a paddler's paradise, lacking only challenging mountain whitewater to complement the peaceful blackwater rivers, swamps, sounds and inlets teaming with wildlife, and challenging Atlantic beach paddles. On the Outer Banks, outfitters run a variety of creative, quality paddling excursions and sea island overnights through such pristine areas as Pea Island National Wildlife Refuge, Alligator River National Wildlife Refuge, Cape Hatteras National Seashore, and the Kitty Hawk Maritime. On the Central Coast, people paddle the Rachel Carson Reserve, Cape Lookout, and the Shackleford Banks.

Ocean kayakers challenge the waves at Myrtle Beach, and paddle the waters of Little River and Murrells Inlet. Outfitters in Mount Pleasant can set up a sea-kayak trip to the uninhabited, well-regulated **Bull Island,** just north of Charleston. If you're a nature lover, it may well be the best experience of your Lowcountry life. Fantastic scenery and birding.

In the Lowcountry between Charleston and Hilton Head you'll find the **Edisto River Trail,** which takes in some 56 peaceful Lowcountry miles along the Edisto River. You'll find guided canoe and kayak tours of the ACE Basin National Wildlife Refuge and the Edisto River Canoe and Kayak Trail.

kayaking the Roanoke Sound

FISHING

The person who invents the all-in-one driving iron and fishing pole will make a quick fortune in the Carolinas. Beyond golfing, Carolinians like most to fish.

The Carolina Coasts feature Gulf Stream fishing for amberjack, marlin, sailfish, tuna, dolphin, and wahoo. Closer in, you can still hope to land mackerel, blackfin tuna, cobia, and shark. Surf, pier, and jetty fishing includes channel bass, Spanish mackerel, shark, flounder, croakers, and whiting. You'll find over 30 public and private piers jutting from Coastal Carolina into the waters of the Atlantic.

SHRIMPING

How To
For shrimping you'll need a cast net and an ice chest or some saltwater. A cast net is round, with weights all along the rim; you throw a cast net somewhat the way you'd throw a Frisbee, though in truth it flies closer to the way an uncooked pizza would, which is one way of saying this might take you a little practice. But what's a half hour or hour's practice when it teaches you how to catch shrimp?

After you've thrown a perfect loop—so that the net hits the water as a circle, its weights bringing the net down in a perfect dome over the unsuspecting shrimp—wait for the weights to hit the bottom. This is something you just have to sense, since you can't see or feel it. Now jerk on the center line that draws the weights together, closing the bottom of the dome into a sphere and trapping the shrimp.

You can rent a small johnboat or outboard, or you can throw from some inlet bridges; it's up to you, but most people seem to feel that ebb tide is the time to throw, since this is when the shrimp, who spend high tide spread out and frolicking in the marsh grasses, are the most concentrated in the creek beds. Cast your net toward the side of a waterway, just on the edge of the grasses, and you may well snag a number of these mobile crustaceans.

CRABBING

How To
Crabbing has to be one of the easiest ways to catch some of the best food found in the ocean. Oh, you can charter your boats far out to sea, slaphappy on Dramamine, but you'll find *me* in the shallows with a bucket, a string, a sinker, a net, and some ripe chicken backs. That's pretty much all you need to land a good supper's worth of **blue crab** in South Carolina. Here's how you do it:

1. Tie the string to a piece of chicken and the sinker.
2. Wade out in the water about waist high.
3. Hold onto one end of the string, and drop the chicken and sinker into the water.
4. Wait for the crabs to come scuttling over for supper.
5. When you feel a tug on the chicken, pull up on the string and swoop beneath the crab with your net.
6. Take a look at the crabs. If:
   • a crab has yellow eggs (roe) on the underside, the law requires you to toss it back.
   • a crab is less than five inches wide across its back, you'll need to toss it back too.

Drop the "lucky" ones who pass these two tests into an ice chest and keep them cold until you cook them. When the ice chest is full of blue crabs, only one step remains:
7. Call me and invite me over for dinner.

HUNTING

For many Carolinians a crisp fall day just isn't complete without the blast of a rifle and the "thunk" of metal tearing flesh.

And who can blame them?

Granted, the only animal I ever shot was tin and had a bull's-eye painted between its forepaws. And granted, irresponsible hunters who kill something as beautiful as a buck only to strap a new pair of antlers to their Blazer should be forced to wear the antlers and a fur coat to the next PETA convention. But few instincts seem to be as ingrained in humans as the instinct to hunt prey, and the activity ("sport" seems somewhat misleading—as if the animals had to kick in a league fee to join the fun) has a long history in the South, and in the cultures from which modern-day Southerners descend.

You'll find white-tailed deer, wild turkey, ruffed grouse, quail, squirrels, and other small mammals just a-beggin' to be gunned down across the Coasts in national and state forests, national wildlife refuges, and wildlife management areas.

Get the specifics from the South Carolina Department of Natural Resources, P.O. Box 167, Columbia, SC 29202-0167, 803/734-3938. For North Carolina hunting, contact the Wildlife Resources Commission at 512 Salisbury St., Raleigh, 919/733-7291.

HIKING AND BIKING

The coasts of North and South Carolina feature a number of excellent hiking trails.

Though it won't help your wildlife-viewing any, during hunting season, try to wear some fluorescent orange. Better yet, you'll find plenty of great trails in hunting-free state parks and nature preserves to keep you busy until the smoke clears at the end of hunting season. Just to be safe, however, it won't hurt to wear some orange here also—to keep safe against poachers.

If you're hiking with a dog, make sure Fido's wearing some orange too.

Some Notable Trails

Northernmost of the great trails is the **Tracks in the Sand Trail** at Jockey's Ridge State Park, a self-guided, 1.5-mile trek past over a dozen interpretive stations which point out the local ecosystems. The **Cape Hatteras Beach Trail** is the most oceanward trail you'll encounter, and the easiest to follow. From Whalebone Junction south of Nags Head, turn right, stick to the shoreline, and head south 75 miles (one-way), through the length of Hatteras and Ocracoke Islands. You'll need to cross some bridges and take a ferry, but this is the best possible way to get a thorough Banks experience. For something much less ambitious, south of New Bern in Croatan National Forest, the 1.4-mile **Cedar Point Tideland**

Trail, makes a loop through hardwood and pine-laced estuary and tidal marsh areas. You can hide behind wildlife viewing blinds along the way and take some great nature shots. Even shorter, but memorable, the **Flytrap Trail** at Carolina Beach State Park near Wilmington carries you through a rare growth of Venus flytraps. Go online to www.sctrails.net/Trails for a very helpful searchable database of nearly 200 South Carolina trails. Go on to the links area for a great listing of trails and outdoor resources on the Internet. Down in South Carolina, you'll find the **Swamp Fox Trail** north of Charleston. Passing through the former gator-infested haunts of Revolutionary guerilla leader Francis Marion (the area is now part of Francis Marion National Forest), the Swamp Fox is also the easternmost leg of the Lowcountry-to-Upcountry **Palmetto Trail.** South of Charleston, the **Edisto Nature Trail** on Edisto Island provides a short (1-mile) walk through cypress swamp and a former barge canal. A spur trail leads to a prehistoric Native American shell mound. Finally, down near Beaufort, the **Hunting Island State Park Trails** provide some 6.5 miles of hiking through pine and palmetto-forested island land. Lots of wildlife viewing.

Biking

North Carolina has taken the lead in providing nine different State Bicycling Highways, several of which at least partially run along the North Carolina Coast. The **Virginia to Florida Bicycle Route** is perhaps the most ambitious. It enters the eastern part of the state on N.C. 32 near Corapeake, travels mostly flat two-lane roads along the Coastal Plain, threading New Bern and Edenton before ending in Wilmington. You can find more information on the route from the folks at Bikecentennial, P.O. Box 8308, Missoula, MT 59807. Another route, the **Ocracoke Option,** covers 175 miles from Wilson in the center of the state, to Cape Hatteras National Seashore. A third traces the Cape Fear River, ending in Southport. For information on these or any of the other North Carolina State Bicycling Highways, contact The Bicycle Program at North Carolina Department of Transportation in Raleigh, 919/733-2804.

Down in South Carolina, by the year 2002, the 21-mile **Waccamaw Neck Trail** will connect Murrells Inlet, Litchfield, Pawley's Island, and historic Georgetown with a buffered eight-foot wide path, providing safe bicycling, walking, jogging, and rollerblading between the communities. See the folks at website www.chronon.com/bike for more information.

A very dependable ride anywhere on the Coasts is to simply take your bike along the hard-packed sand on the beach. See individual chapters for specifics.

TENNIS

The top spots for tennis along the Carolina Coasts would have to be Hilton Head and Myrtle Beach, both of which are world class tennis resorts. See individual regional chapters for specific resorts.

As for watching tennis, the **Family Circle Magazine Cup,** one of the country's top professional women's tennis tournaments on the Corel WTA Tour, takes place in late March or early April on Hilton Head Island. Call 800/677-2293 for information.

GOLF

Both of the Carolinas feature hundreds of opportunities for golfing, but the South Carolina Coast is clearly center stage. With the help of veteran duffer Kendall Buckendahl of Mount Pleasant, here's a rundown of Carolina's finest:

Classic Courses
In the 2000 Course Rankings, *Golf* magazine ranked seven different Coastal Carolina courses to its Top 100; all seven were within South Carolina: Harbour Town Golf Links at Hilton Head Island (#47); Yeamans Hall in Hanahan (#64), Long Cove Club Hilton Head Island, (#66); Kiawah Island (Ocean) (#74),Colleton River Plantation Country Club Hilton Head Island, (95): Bluffton's Colleton River, Bluffton (#99), and The Dunes Golf & Beach Club, Myrtle Beach; #100.

In a separate poll, *Golf* readers named **Sea Pines Resort** on Hilton Head, **Ocean Course** on Kiawah Island Resort, and **Wild Dunes Resort,** among the top 20 golf resorts in the country.

Back in 1998 when *Golf* magazine put out a list of the top 100 courses the average person can play in the United States, **Harbour Town Links** (Hilton Head) and **Ocean Course** (Charleston) ranked in the top 10. **Wild Dunes' Links Course** (Charleston), **The Dunes** (Myrtle Beach), and **Tidewater** (Myrtle Beach) all ranked in the top 40.

Caladonia in Pawleys Island came in at a very respectable No. 85.

Other Stellar Courses
Kiawah Island's refurbished **Cougar Point** is getting a lot of praise. In Charleston, **Charleston National** is a great one that is relatively moderate in price, and the ocean course is the tops by far for ocean scenery.

Values
If you want to golf inexpensively, keep a couple of things in mind. One is the time of year. Spring and fall are high season, and "high season" equals "high prices."

Head to Myrtle Beach in the winter and dead of summer for great price specials. The Grand Strand offers the highest concentration of golf courses in the country. It is really *the* golf destination of the South, if not the nation.

Other values come from areas that have resorts close by, such as Hilton Head and Charleston. The well-cared-for courses at the resorts force the public courses in the surrounding area to upgrade their grounds for competition's sake; the value comes from not having to pay the resort's high prices for a resort-grade course.

In Charleston, **Charleston National** as well as **Dunes West, Coosaw Creek,** and **Crowfield** all have great layouts and cost under $100 to play, even in the high season. At Hilton Head, a couple of names that stand out value-wise include: **Palmetto Dunes, Shipyard,** and **Whispering Pines.**

To Find Out More
South Carolina offers an excellent booklet, the *South Carolina Golf Guide,* published annually; pick one up at one of the state's visitors centers, or call 800/682-5553 for a copy. For North Carolina's, call 800/8474862, or see website www.visitnc.com.

SPECTATOR SPORTS

Football

Though the NFL's Carolina Panthers, based up in border town Charlotte, North Carolina, were carefully named to represent (and, thus, draw) fans from both Carolinas, it's *college* football that still dominates South Carolina. Even people who never got around to completing eighth grade take intercollegiate ball very seriously.

How seriously? Consider South Carolina. If football is a religion, then South Carolina is Northern Ireland. The chief denominations? USC Gamecockism vs. Clemson Tigerism. True believers of either faith can live anywhere in the state, though loyalties grow predictably more fierce near the home coliseums. Signs of devotion can include anything from class rings and ball caps to 40-foot motor homes painted with tiger paws. Yes, other South Carolina colleges have notable football programs (the Citadel Bulldogs are perhaps the third-largest "denomination" available—and the state is home, too, to a number of dissenters who support North Carolina's Duke), but that doesn't mean you can answer "Wofford" when asked who you're *for* on USC/Clemson game day. On that day, in either Columbia or Clemson (it alternates yearly), caravans of color-coordinated trucks, cars, and RVs pour into the game town bearing hordes of the opposing team's faithful. If the game's on a Sunday, sermons end early. Streets are deserted, and an eerie silence pervades the town, broken only by synchronized cheers erupting from a thousand bars and living rooms whenever the home team scores. Up in North Carolina, Duke and Chapel Hill excite similar loyalties.

The biggest, most competitive football played on the Carolina coasts is probably down at **The Citadel,** though **Charleston Southern** has been building its program as of late, and **UNC Wilmington** draws big crowds as well. Getting tickets to a Citadel contest—with its small stadium and ferociously active alumni base—can be a challenge, but check the sports page in whatever town you're in and if it's pigskin season you'll find a college playing somewhere nearby.

Minor League Baseball

It's hard for a lot of fans to take major league baseball seriously these days; it's hard to see much drama in a game when you're looking out at a diamond full of players who, win or lose, are cumulatively worth more than the GM board of directors. If you've grown weary of high ticket prices and multimillionaire players, be sure to catch a minor league game while you're in state. Watching these 18- and 19-year-olds, who are being paid less than a middle manager at Hardee's, battle it out for a chance at the bigs just might help you remember why you fell in love with the game in the first place.

Coastal Carolina is blessed with *three* single-A baseball teams. Northernmost are the **Kinston Indians** 400 East Grainger Ave., 252/527-9111, website: www.kinstonindians.com. The "K-Tribe" is the entry-level team under the Cleveland Indians, and though Kinston's inland, the team serves as the home nine of the Outer Banks. Listen to their games at WRNS-AM 960. Over the years scores of future major leaguers have played home games at Kinston, including Curt Flood, Leon Wagner, Willie McCovey, Rusty Staub, Ron Guidry, Albert Belle, Charles Nagy, Pete Rose, Jr., and Jim Thome. Tickets run $4–6. Small-town baseball at its best.

The newest team along the coast, the Myrtle Beach Pelicans play in the brand-new, $16 million Coastal Federal Field across from Broadway at the Beach, 843/918-6000. They're the single-A Carolina League farm team for Atlanta—an enviable designation hereabouts, since most of Myrtle Beach's visitors are Southerners, and

> *The titanic clashes of annual football rivals in huge stadiums, drawing as they do legions of pilgrim followers garbed in totemic tribal colors to these holy sites, pouring out libations to the gods at ritual tailgating activities, screaming anathemas at their evil opponents while imploring the spotless host of their own team, praying for redemption—all this has the aspect of a public religious observance, perhaps an exorcism, perhaps a collective pursuit of spirit-filled ecstatic trance. In South Carolina such recurring rites are difficult to ignore or to avoid.*
>
> —Kevin Lewis, "Religion in South Carolina Addresses the Public Order," in *Religion in South Carolina,* 1993

most Southerners grew up rooting for the Braves. In their inaugural year the Pelicans drew 240,000 fans to the park, averaging over 3,000 a game. Even more fortunately the Pelicans are *good*. In their first two years of existence, 1999–2000, they won the Carolina League championship back-to-back. You can buy tickets ($3–7.50) in person, by phone, or online at www.myrtlebeachpelicans.com. You can hear their games online as well, at www.broadcast.com.

Furthest south are the **Charleston River Dogs,** who compete in the venerable South Atlantic (or "Sallie") League. They play in Joseph P. Riley Stadium, 360 Fishburne St., 843/577-3647, website: www.riverdogs.com, colloquially known as "The Joe," and named after Charleston's long-time and, as of this writing, current mayor. Overlooking the Ashley River, this is a very classy ballpark by the same people who created nostalgic Camden Yards in Baltimore. The 5,904 seats, legion for a single-A field, go for $4–8.

Professional Soccer
The **Wilmington Hammerheads** play USISL D-3 Pro League soccer at Legion Stadium, 2221 Carolina Beach Road, 910/796-0076 or 910/796-0502; website: www.wilmingtonhammerheads.com. Tickets run $4–7.

The **Charleston Battery** has played in the Holy City since 1993 when the team joined the neophyte USISL, now a conglomeration of nearly 150 teams in five separate leagues. The Battery has placed toward the top of their division every year since 1994, including winning the USISL finals in 1996. After that they moved to the newly forming A-League, where they've remained competitive, winning the Atlantic Division in 2000. Very popular among Charlestonians, the team plays about 20 games a year in the new 5,600-seat stadium on Daniel Island, located right off the Mark Clark Expressway (I-126), 843/740-7787. Tickets run $8–10 for adults, less for kids. Be sure to bring the kids (under 16 years) up to an hour before game time, when the Fun Zone, an "interactive soccer theme park" (which overstates it a bit) is open, including a soccer bounce, various games, a playground for the kids, and a picnic area for kids. See the Battery online at www.charleston battery.com.

Minor League Hockey
Charleston's **Stingrays,** affiliated with the Buffalo Sabres in the NHL and the Rochester Americans in the AHL, have done battle at the North Charleston Coliseum, 3107 Firestone Road, North Charleston, 843/744-2248, website: www.stingrayshockey.com, since first skating their way into the hearts of Charlestonians in 1993.

ENTERTAINMENT AND EVENTS

MUSEUMS

The Carolina Coasts offer a number of stellar museums to peruse. Below I've discussed some of the most noteworthy, but note that these do not count the many small museums found at the states' myriad historic sites.

Historical/Cultural
Nearly every town in the region features a local museum of some sort. Often these are little more than collections of historic objects, with very little interpretation involved. The interpreting usually comes from the volunteer seated by the door.

That said, Coastal Carolina features some of the finest contemporary museums in the South. Here I'll list a handful to give you an idea of highlights and breadth of diverse choices. See the appropriate destination chapters for more choices and more details on the museums listed here. In the Outer Banks the town of Manteo hosts **Roanoke Island Festival Park,** across from the Manteo waterfront, 252/475-1506 or 252/475-1500, which includes a great Roanoke Adventure museum in addition to full scale historic recreations around the park. Down on Hatteras Island the tiny **Frisco Native American Museum and Natural History Center,** 53536 N.C. 12, 252/995-4440, is a homegrown but heartfelt and profound collection of Native

American artifacts and exhibits. Further down Hatteras Island is the new **Graveyard of the Atlantic Museum,** beside the Hatteras-Ocracoke Ferry landing in Hatteras, 252/986-2995; a 19,000 sq. ft. museum (set to open in 2002) features interactive displays on European colonization of the Banks, lighthouses and lifesaving corps, pirates, Civil War blockade runners, and local mysteries.

New Bern is also home to the impressive reconstructed **Tryon Palace Historic Sites and Gardens,** 800/767-1560 or 252/514-4900, with costumed reenactors who help bring New Bern's brief colonial capital period to life. New Bern also holds a small **Birthplace of Pepsi-Cola,** 256 Middle St., 252/636-5898, as well as the **Firemen's Museum,** 408 Hancock St., 252/636-4087, which celebrates the history of one of the nation's oldest continually-operating fire companies—and firefighting in general. Over in Elizabeth City you'll find the **Museum of the Albemarle,** currently at 1116 U.S. 17 S, 252/335-1453, though it should move sometime in 2002. It features exhibits interpreting the human stories of the Albemarle, from the Native Americans on through the first English colonists, and the subsequent farmers and fishermen. Beaufort's **North Carolina Maritime Museum,** 315 Front St., 252/728-7317, website: www.ah.dcr.state.nc.us/maritime/default.htm, presents in-depth and hands-on exhibits that give visitors a good sense of the region's maritime history, and includes relics from what seems to be *Queen Anne's Revenge,* Blackbeard's flagship.

Down in Wilmington, you'll want to make the **Cape Fear Museum,** 814 Market St., 910/341-4350, your first stop upon arriving in the town. It features a scale model of the Wilmington waterfront, circa 1862, as well as the diorama of the battles for Fort Fisher, and the interactive Michael Jordan Discovery Gallery. Train fans will want to head over to the **Wilmington Railroad Museum,** 501 Nutt St. (corner of Red Cross and Water Streets), 910/763-2634, where the old freight traffic office now plays home to dozens of displays honoring the area's railroad history, and celebrating railroads in general. Outside you'll find a steam engine and caboose for the climbing and viewing, always a favorite with kids. Inside the museum they've got a wonderful, massive model railroad diorama upstairs, which kids and not a few adults will enjoy getting a chance to operate. Downstairs you'll find a recreation of a railroad depot office and other interactive exhibits that help bring to life the golden age of rail travel.

The **Charleston Museum,** the oldest museum in the United States, interprets the natural and cultural history of the Lowcountry. **African-American National Heritage Museum**—actually, a collection of sites in the Charleston area, with its hub at the **Slave Mart Museum** on Chalmers Street—is one of the nation's premier museums exploring the origins and contributions of African-American culture in the United States. For the other side of the story, visit the **Daughters of the Confederacy Museum** upstairs above the Old City Market. One of my favorite smaller museums, featuring the "Hurricane Hugo Revisited" exhibit, is the **Museum on the Common** over in Mount Pleasant. Nearby, off U.S. 17, you'll find **Patriots Point Naval and Maritime Museum,** which includes as one of its exhibits a little thing called the aircraft carrier **USS *Yorktown.*** Those fascinated by things nautical can also tour a submarine, a destroyer, and a recreation of a Vietnam naval support base. (Up in Wilmington the **USS *North Carolina* Battleship Memorial** gives you the chance to tour a second warship.)

Brookgreen Gardens, south of Myrtle Beach, is the world's largest outdoor sculpture showcase, containing 550 19th- and 20th-century pieces, landscaped with 2,000 species of plants.

Botanical Gardens, Zoos, and Aquariums

If you want to visit the best zoo in this region, you really ought to drive northwest from Charleston along I-26 to the Columbia and visit the nationally-ranked **Riverbanks Zoo and Botanical Gardens,** a double whammy to those interested in carbon-based life forms.

Wilmington's small, folksy **Tote-Em-In Zoo** is the only notable collection of "exotic" critters along the Tar Heel Coast. Where North Carolina shines is in its chain of small-but-effective state aquariums, which include locations on Roanoke Island, Pine Knoll Shores (near Atlantic Beach), Fort Fisher (near Wilmington), in addition to the **North Carolina Estuarium** (in Washington).

In the past few years South Carolina has sprouted two huge aquariums of its own—each of them larger and more ambitious than any of the ones on the North Carolina coast: Myrtle Beach's entertainment-oriented but still educational **Ripley's Aquarium** and Charleston's educational but still entertaining **South Carolina Aquarium.** For entertainment value Ripley's hard to beat, but its focus is global, not local. If you want a deeper knowledge of Carolinian sealife, try the South Carolina Aquarium, or one of North Carolina's.

If you're looking for alligators, **Alligator Adventure** in Myrtle Beach is a classy, eco-friendly spot. And you'll see more alligators than you can count.

PLANTATIONS

Most non-Southerners don't really feel that they've visited the South until they tour a real plantation. Well, if it's antebellum splendor you're seeking, you'll find it along the Carolina Coasts—particularly starting at Wilmington and working south. In the whole region probably the most outstanding examples of plantation grounds are **Magnolia Plantation and Gardens** and **Middleton Place,** though in both cases the main house has been Shermanized. At Magnolia you'll find acres and acres of beautiful gardens to explore on foot or by boat, and the Audubon Swamp Garden, where the famous wildlife artist himself once wandered about, sketch pad in hand, as a guest of the Drayton family. At Middleton an adjoining guest house survived Sherman; it's where the Middletons lived after the war. Remarkable gardens—the oldest formal gardens in North America—here as well.

Drayton Hall, off Ashley River Rd. in North Charleston, still boasts its original main house, a famous example of early Georgian architecture. Though its main plantation house is a 1935 reconstruction of the original, **Boone Hall Plantation** near Mount Pleasant is worth visiting because 1) it allows you to see what a plantation looked like when it was relatively new; 2) it contains nine original slave cabins, which tell more about slave conditions than all the interpretive exhibits in the world; 3) if you're looking for the type of plantation you saw on TV's *North and South,* Boone Hall Plantation *is* precisely that plantation; it's where that minis-

eries, and several others, were filmed; and 4) rumor has it that Margaret Mitchell's *Tara* (she finished *Gone with The Wind* in 1936) is modeled after the place—down to the gauntlet of moss-dripping oaks at the entrance. Battle reenactments are performed here in the summer, filling the grounds and mansion with period-dressed soldiers and belles (though oddly, nobody seems to want to come dressed as a slave). For the Civil War buff, there's nothing like it.

Farther north along the coast, the **Hampton Plantation State Park** and **Hopsewee Plantation** are excellently preserved properties rich with historical import.

South of Wilmington off N.C. 133 to Southport, you'll find **Orton Plantation Gardens** in Winnabow, featuring 20 acres of gardens with a variety of annuals, perennials, huge oaks, azaleas, and camellias. In North Wilmington **Poplar Grove Plantation** provides a good example of a plantation built in the Greek Revival style at the peak of the antebellum period (1850).

MUSIC

Carolina Beach Music

Outside of the South, beach music is one of the least known and least understood musical genres in America. Part of the confusion lies with those who assume that the term beach music refers to the California vocal surf music of the Beach Boys and Jan and Dean. Carolina beach music is a whole different animal, popular on a whole different coast.One main difference is that it is not primarily music featuring lyrics about the beach or developed to capture the rhythms of the ocean (as instrumental West Coast surf music was), nor is it music that is necessarily written and performed by Carolinian or even Southern artists. Some of beach music's greatest stars have probably never known that they were making "beach music" at all.

Beach music is blues music; most of the early performers of beach music were black. All that was needed was an easy-flowing song with four beats to the measure, about 120 beats per minute. Songs like the Drifters' "Under the Boardwalk," the Tams' "What Kinda Fool Do You Think I Am?," and Maurice Williams and the Zodiacs'

"Stay" became beach classics. Perhaps the "Johnny B. Goode" for beach music is the Dominoes "Sixty-Minute Man."

If people found that a jukebox song was good to shag to—even if recorded and/or lyrically set hundreds of miles from the Strand,such as Bob and Earl's "Harlem Shuffle," for instance—it quickly became absorbed as part of the canon of beach music. Later, in the late 1960s, '70s, and '80s, a few regional groups began to record songs that lyrically celebrated the beach music/shagging subculture, including The Embers' anthemic "I Love Beach Music," and General Johnson and Chairmen of the Board's "Carolina Girls."

Of all of the beach-specific songs, the most popular outside the beach music subculture has been the Tams' "There Ain't Nothing Like Shagging," which surprised everyone when it raced up into the top 20 on the British pop charts in the mid-'80s. And then everyone remembered what "shagging" means in British English and got over their surprise.

Today any song with the right beat—whether it's country and western, gospel, blues, or rock—can make the beach music charts. Such diverse acts as The Cherry Poppin' Daddies, John Fogerty, Tracy Chapman, Alabama, and Patty LaBelle have shared the charts.

You'll find shagging nightclubs in almost any good-sized coastal town.

Other
You'll find most every kind of live music on the coasts of the Carolinas, from church bell choirs to reggae. Check the local listings in whatever town you're visiting.

SHOPPING

Antiques
Because the Carolina coasts were some of the first regions in America settled by Europeans and because it was such a relatively wealthy region in antebellum years, it's not surprising that this is a great area for antique hunters. Charleston's **King Street** is probably the top stretch along both coasts for antique shopping, but you'll find better prices in smaller towns.

Factory Outlets
With all the interstates crossing through the region, Coastal Carolina has more than its share of freeway-close outlet shops. You'll find factory outlet stores near and at the Outer Banks, at Myrtle Beach, and down by Hilton Head.

ACCOMMODATIONS

HOTELS AND MOTELS

The differences between hotels and motels are basically matters of price, amenities, and, in some cases, location. Hotels are usually more expensive than motels, but the increased price is usually—though not always—represented by better facilities. In addition to the pool, ice machine, and soda machine that you'll usually find at a motel, hotels often offer a restaurant or bar, an exercise room, valet parking, and greater proximity to shopping and places of cultural interest.

Another useful distinction for accommodations is proximity to freeways and highways. Sometimes hotels, sometimes motels, these places cater mostly to overnight travelers who

need a place to stay while driving to somewhere else, rather than to extended-stay vacationers who want a relaxing place to spend a week or more. Spend the night at a Motel 6, for instance, and you'll find the parking lot nearly deserted at 9 A.M.

By absolutely no means do these descriptions fit in all, or even most, cases. No class of businesses has a copyright on the words "hotel" or "motel," and any business owner in the country has the right to call an establishment whatever he or she wants, and a lot of motels are confusing the issue by calling themselves inns, lodges, and so on. If you're already in town, it never hurts to just pull into the parking lot and take a look around.

If you are unsure about staying at a motel because you are afraid it will lack the features you want, or about staying at a hotel because you are afraid it will be too expensive, call ahead. You'll probably call anyway for prices and room availability. Consider also what you are looking for in an accommodation. Do you plan to stay more than two nights? Are you in a hurry to get somewhere else, and just need a place to sleep overnight? Do you want a place where you can "get away from it all" for weeks at a time? If you correctly assess your expectations you should have no problem finding a satisfactory accommodation, from $25-a-night roadside motels to $300-a-night luxury hotels.

Some well-known hotel/motel chains include:

- **Best Western**—a chain with no consistent style; most are clean but strictly stick-to-the-freeway type accommodations, but others offer luxurious rooms and prime locations. Call 800/528-1234 in the United States and Canada.
- **Days Inn**—offers clean rooms, low prices ($29–79, depending on location). Call 800/329-7466 in the United States and Canada. Often a continental breakfast buffet is served downstairs in the morning. Visit online at www.daysinn.com.
- **Econo Lodge**—usually close to the freeways, Econo Lodges offer average low-priced accommodations. Call 800/553-2666 in the United States
- **Hilton**—luxurious rooms, numerous amenities, and great locations, 800/445-8667 in the United States, 800/268-9275 in Canada.
- **Holiday Inn**—spacious rooms, quality dining; some offer entertainment, but there is no consistent level of amenities. The phone number is 800/465-4329 in the United States and Canada. See them online at www.holiday-inn.com.
- **Howard Johnson**—aka "HoJo's"—offers spacious rooms close to the freeways; ask about special prices for seniors and families. The toll-free number is 800/446-4656 in the United States and Canada.
- **Jameson Inn**—offers over a dozen locations in the Carolinas, including a nicely situated one in Georgetown, offering a view of the water. Based out of Calhoun, Georgia, they feature work stations, fitness centers, computer-compatible telephone jacks, and continental breakfasts, as well as a Southern colonial theme. Rooms run $50–60 and up. Call 800/526-3766,

or check the website www.jamesoninns.com for information.

- **Motel 6**—close to the freeways, often in the $20s for a single, kids stay free, 800/466-8356 in the United States. The upside is that this is the cheapest chain available. The downside is that, well, this is the cheapest chain available. As you check in late to an urban Motel 6, sliding your money in a tray beneath the bulletproof window to the 24-hour front desk clerk, you may wish you'd spent another $10 to get into a more upscale environment. In most smaller towns, there's nothing to be concerned about. If you're staying in a city with more than one Motel 6, you may find that the one by the local airport (as opposed to the one downtown) is less intriguing, safety-wise.
- **Ramada Inn**—sometimes upscale, sometimes just another hotel. Call 800/228-9898 in the United States, 800/854-7854 in Canada.

BED-AND-BREAKFASTS

Bed-and-breakfasts are usually someone's house or a portion of their house opened as a guest accommodation. The Carolinas have a worthy selection of these, mostly used as weekend getaways but not inappropriate for longer stays. The proprietors provide breakfast in the mornings (hence the name), and some offer lunch and dinner as well. As with hotels and motels, the name is not always indicative of the features. Sometimes older, smaller, rustic hotels call themselves bed-and-breakfasts to attract a wealthier clientele.

Bed-and-breakfasts usually offer personal hospitality and atmospheric, often historic, homes to stay in. Perhaps because the Carolinas are so rich in both of these, their B&B room rates are cheaper than in a lot of other areas, where the hospitality has to be flown in daily. In many smaller towns rooms can dip down into the $50 range, which, considering you'll probably spend the same or more for a sanitized, midrange chain out on the highway, is quite a bargain.

Many B&Bs offer one or two different meal plans included with the price. They may offer the European-style continental breakfast, a light meal including coffee and orange juice; some combination of toast, English muffin, or Danish; and sometimes fruit. On the other hand, if you're lucky, you may be offered a Southern-style breakfast and dinner. Expect coffee, eggs or pancakes, grits, biscuits, bacon or ham, and potatoes for breakfast, and fried chicken, steaks, and salads for dinner.

If you've never stayed at a B&B, one thing to keep in mind is the privacy factor. At some you'll be given a separate cottage or a room with an exterior entrance, which means you won't have to see the proprietors and other guests except at meals, unless you want to. At other lodgings you may share a bathroom with other guests. Or the homeowner may have a curfew, after which you will not be allowed back into the house for the night.

CABINS

Edisto Beach and **Myrtle Beach State Parks** in South Carolina feature rental cabins, which are a great economical stay if you can get one. Reservation season begins for the following calendar year beginning the first Monday following January 1. First priority is given to reservation requests made by phone. None of North Carolina's coastal state parks have vacation cabins.

Another option is check with the local KOA campground to see if they have any of their "Kamping Kabins," which can be really quite nice. Along the Carolina Coasts, you'll find KOAs with Kamping Cabins (usually $35–50 a night) in Rodanthe on Hatteras Island, at Myrtle Beach, outside Charleston (two locations), and close to Hilton Head and Beaufort along I-95 at Point South. Call 800/562-5268 or see website www.koa.com to make reservations.

CAMPING AND RV PARKS

State Parks

North Carolina has some 16 state parks along its coastal plain. Call 919/733-4181 or visit website ils.unc.edu/parkproject/ncparks.html for information on the amenities of a specific park. South Carolina offers over 3,000 campsites at some 50 state parks in its fine state parks system.

Unless specified as a "tent site," all of the sites have electric hookups. Some tenters pack a portable fan and extension cord with the Coleman gear in the summer. If you've camped in the American West, you'll find most of South Carolina's parks relatively "resorty"—meaning rental cabins, snack shops, general stores, monitored swimming beaches, putt putt (miniature golf), and sometimes a full-size 9- or 18-hole golf course or tennis courts as well.

Things are changing, however, as environmentalists push for "less-improved" parks that allow public access to pristine areas without paving it (or sodding it) in the process. Standout state parks of the old school include **Edisto Island State Park** and **Hunting Island State Park.** For a complete listing of state parks, call any state park listed in this book.

One recent development is that many of South Carolina's popular parks have recently taken to accepting reservations for some—but not all—of their campsites. You can reserve your spot as early as 11 months in advance, and no later than 24 hours prior to occupancy. To make a reservation, call, write, or visit the park where you'd like to camp. You can reserve a site for a minimum of two nights and a maximum of 14 consecutive nights. You'll pay an additional $1 a night fee for a reserved campsite, and you'll need to pay your camping fee in full within 10 working days of the date you make your request. No reservation will be confirmed until payment in full is received. The maximum number of sites you may reserve is three; however, each site must be reserved in the name of the individual occupying each site. Requests for adjoining or adjacent campsites will be honored subject to availability. Checkout time is no later than 2 P.M. Cancellations must be made in writing 24 hours in advance and may be subject to a handling fee.

South Carolina parks taking reservations at press time are **Edisto Beach, Hunting Island, Huntington Beach,** and **Myrtle Beach.**

Private Campgrounds and RV Parks

For a listing of North Carolina's privately owned campgrounds and RV parks, contact the North Carolina Association of RV Parks and Campgrounds at 893 U.S. 70 W, Suite 202, Garner, NC, 27529, 919/779-5709, website: www.kiz.com/campnet/html/cluborgs/nccoa/. For a listing of South Carolina's privately owned campgrounds and RV parks, contact the South Carolina Campground Owners Association at Point South KOA, P.O. Box 1760, Yemasee, SC 29945, 843/726-5733.

To camp in the Grand Strand area, call 800/356-3016 for a pamphlet extolling the virtues of camping at Myrtle Beach, *The Camping Capital of the World.*

FOOD AND DRINK

SEAFOOD

Along the coast, seafood is king. Carolina **shrimp** are everywhere; you can catch them yourself or buy them right off the boats or nearly as fresh from coastal supermarkets. Ditto for the **Carolina soft-shell crab** used mainly for crab cakes and She Crab Soup (along the coast, you'll find lots of places serving crab legs, but these are from imported Alaskan king and Dungeness crabs). Up around Myrtle Beach you'll find a lot of "Calabash seafood," lightly battered and deep-fried. The name comes from the tiny port town of Calabash in the very tip of the southeastern corner of North Carolina, where fishing and shrimping crews used to quickly deep-fry some meals at the end of a long day on the boats. Visitors who came down to the docks to purchase fresh fish from the boats got hungry smelling all this crunchy goodness, and soon they were buying it from quick-thinking vendors, who dubbed the fresh-and-fried style "Calabash." Today most Calabash seafood restaurants ironically are not in Calabash, but rather along Restaurant Row in Myrtle Beach.

MEATS

Barbecue

My brother George, who lives not far over the border in Athens, Georgia, told me recently that he and his wife had become vegetarians. I asked him if he was going to have a hard time giving up barbecue. He reminded me that in the South, barbecue is a vegetable.

People have various theories as to how to spot a good barbecue joint. Some say that the presence of a pig anywhere on the sign is a good omen. Others claim that anyplace open more than three days a week (normally Thursday through Saturday) should be avoided like a Danish pizza parlor. I would add only the following amendment: the fewer windows, the better.

The ideal barbecue joint is built of bricks or cinder blocks, usually on a country road where police cruise-bys are weekly events (unless it's mealtime) and where security alarms would only irritate the possums. Hence most barbecue owners seem to figure, no windows, no hassle. And who needs windows anyway? Eating barbecue is a serious business—you're not here to admire the scenery.

There are exceptions to the rule. I have even once or twice been into a decent barbecue with both windows *and* central air-conditioning, but somehow it felt like camping on Astroturf.

Now the question comes: what is barbecue? The answer varies across the country: in the West, "barbecue" is something you do, not something you eat. You barbecue some ribs or steaks. To tell a Nevadan you're going to eat some "barbecue" is like telling them you're going to eat

---

ANITA'S BANANA PUDDING

1 14 oz. can sweetened condensed milk
1 1/2 cups cold water
1 pkg. instant banana-flavored pudding
1 pint heavy whipping cream
2 tablespoons sugar
36 vanilla wafers
3 large bananas
lemon juice to taste

Whisk condensed milk and water. Add pudding mix. Beat. Chill 15 minutes. Whip whipping cream until stiff. Add sugar and whip 30 seconds more. Fold into chilled pudding. Layer 12 wafers, one banana, and one-third of the pudding. Repeat twice more. Chill 4–6 hours minimum.

some "fried." In the Midwest—and Texas—"barbecued" is an adjective and usually comes before "ribs." Most parts of the Deep South agree that "barbecue" (the noun) refers to smoked shredded or pulled pork. Where they can't agree is on how that pork should be dressed.

There are three main camps on this issue in the Carolinas: the vinegar-based camp, the tomato-based camp, and the mustard-based camp. If you hear someone talking about "traditional North Carolina barbecue," they're talking about the vinegar-based variety, and this is probably the most common along the South Carolina coast too. However, the coast has served as a vacation spot for so many inland Carolinians for so long that you'll find a good mix of styles along both coasts. My own preference is for the mustard-based sauces you'll find in the various Dukes and Bessenger-family barbecues along the South Carolina coast, but you'll find some great barbecues of every denomination (and some that have mastered more than one style) from the Outer Banks to Hilton Head.

OTHER CLASSIC CAROLINA EATS

You'll want to try **slaw burgers** and **pimento cheeseburgers,** regional variations on the American artery-clogging favorite. **Slaw dogs** are simply hot dogs with coleslaw on top; you'll also find chili slaw dogs offered at many stands. **Fried chicken** is sold everywhere, from gas stations to Chinese restaurants to drive-up car-hop restaurants. And most of it's good.

Fried **chicken livers** are offered at most places that sell fried chicken. If you've always publicly admired Native Americans for using every bit of the animals they killed, here's a chance to walk your talk.

And of course **chitlins** will give you another such chance. These are the deep-fried small intestines of a pig.

Side Dishes

Of course **biscuits** are an important ingredient in Carolina country cooking. One surprising place where you'll find good biscuits is at Hardee's, but maybe that shouldn't be surprising, since Hardee's was founded in the Carolinas.

Folks trying to eat healthy in the region are sometimes stymied by the tendency of Carolinians toward **stewed vegetables,** including spinach, okra, and collard greens, throwing in a slab of fatback for good flavor, and **fried vegetables,** which again seems to miss the point of eating vegetables entirely. But in the case of okra, perhaps it's an improvement.

Grits have become something like the official food of the South (if you eat at Denny's, you'll know you're in the South when they start including grits on the menu). So strong was the association of Southerners and grits that back in 1980, Bob Hope suggested that Georgia's Jimmy Carter and Walter "Fritz" Mondale should run for reelection as "Grits and Fritz." Grits are made from corn or hominy. Most Northerners would mistake them for Cream of Wheat, but don't put sugar and cinnamon on them. While this doesn't taste too bad, the proper way to eat this plain-tasting food is with butter and salt and pepper—or Texas Pete's hot sauce—and/or mixed in with eggs, ham, and whatever else is on your plate.

Finally no trip to the South would be complete without a helping of **black-eyed peas.** These are actually beans, not peas—they're called cowpeas in other parts of the country—and they're not particularly tasty. If they were, you wouldn't have to come to the South (or to a northern "soul food" restaurant) to eat them. They became popular Southern food items because, like collards, they were easy to grow and cheap to buy down here, in a region that only recently has recovered from the Civil War.

Hot Boiled Peanuts

Take raw, unshelled peanuts. Add water and salt. Boil for about a decade. Now you have hot boiled peanuts, often spelled "hot boil p-nuts" on roadside signs and pronounced "hot bowled peanuts" by most South Carolinians. If you've never heard of them, they sound almost unimaginable. If you've never eaten them before, they taste a little bit like salted peas. But if you've eaten a handful of them, you're probably hooked for life.

You can find hot boiled peanuts for sale in many convenience stores—usually in a brown paper bag enclosed in a Ziploc resealable bag—outside many Wal-Marts, in front of a flea market, or—best of all—at roadside, and at minor league baseball games.

ALTERNATIVES

Soul Food
With African-Americans making up nearly 50 percent of the population in many sections of the Carolina Coasts, you might think there'd be more "soul food" or African-American restaurants. The truth of course is that much of the food you'll find in a soul food restaurant up in New York City is called "country cooking" down here.

Mexican Food
Used to be that the average Mexican restaurant in Carolina would have to feature phonetic spellings and explanations of its items: "*Burrito:* bur-EE-toe: beans, shredded beef, and cheese, wrapped in a flour *tortilla* (see above)." But over the past 5–10 years, coinciding with an increase in the number of Mexican immigrants, numerous Mexican restaurants have opened up in the Carolinas. The influx of people from the south has been much happier for everyone involved than that other invasion from the north a while back. And amazingly, to some degree we have Taco Bell to thank for all this good new spicy food; in many small towns, Taco Bell was the first Mexican food South Carolinians had ever eaten. Fortunately this whetted folks' appetites and has opened the way for more extensive and authentic Mexican restaurants to open, many run by first-generation Mexican immigrants. In other towns chains like Chevy's and Don Pablo's have opened, bringing their experienced Mexican restauranteering into towns that didn't know their *flautas* from a chicken dumpling in 1989.

More International Cuisine
Asian restaurants, particularly Chinese ones, have a long history in most Carolinian towns, partly a result of the Pacific Theater duty many of the state's men saw in World War II. In bigger cities with tourist districts or large transplant populations—Hilton Head, Charleston, Myrtle Beach, Wilmington, Nags Head—you'll find Indian food, Thai food, just about anything you could want.

Health Food/Vegetarian
If you're dedicated to a low-fat, low-cholesterol diet, you really ought to consider going off it while you're in the Carolinas. Otherwise you'll miss most of the most authentic local cuisine. However, even the most dedicated cultural submersionist may have to come up for some unfried air while in Carolina on an extended visit. You'll find health food stores and restaurants in all the sizeable cities, and wherever non-Southerners have come to live, study, or visit en masse. If nothing else, you can find a Subway or Blimpie's in most every town of any size; these can turn out a pretty good vegetarian sandwich in a pinch.

BEVERAGES

Tea
The terms "sweet tea" and "ice tea" (no *d*) are nearly synonymous here. At some restaurants it's served as a matter of course, like coffee at a truck stop diner. The sugar in sweet tea is added while the water's still hot, which allows the sugar to melt and blend more fully into the drink.

If you're at a restaurant, particularly in the country, and you want unsweetened tea, ask for it (quietly) and hope they have it.

Alcohol
The minimum legal age for drinking in both North and South Carolina is 21. Alcoholic beverages can't be served after midnight Saturday and all day Sunday, except in establishments with special permits in Charleston, Edisto Beach, Hilton Head, the Myrtle Beach area, and the I-95 town of Santee.

In South Carolina "hard" alcoholic beverages aren't sold in supermarkets; to buy anything beyond wine and beer, you'll need to visit a package store (also called an "ABC" or "red dot" store), where sales are permitted Monday through Saturday 9 A.M.–7 P.M. You'll notice that the stores do not have the word "alcohol" or "liquor" displayed on the outside—they are marked by the red dot alone, so that only people in the know will frequent them. It also helps make certain that even the illiterate can find the package stores.

It's illegal to have an open container of alcohol in a moving vehicle on North Carolina or South Carolina roads.

SOUTHERN RESTAURANT CHAINS

Waffle House

Each location of this chain is nearly identical—stools, bright yellow and imitation wood Formica, appalling coffee, a sizzling grill, an order-shouting staff, and a jukebox. A patron of the Waffle House in Orangeburg could easily walk into one in Biloxi, Mississippi, blindfolded, sit down, order, play the jukebox and pay the bill without taking the blindfold off. But the Waffle House serves the needs of Southerners so perfectly that it somehow transcends its chain status.

Founded in an Atlanta suburb in 1955—the same year Disneyland opened—the Waffle House calls itself "America's Place to Eat, America's Place to Work." I've never worked at a Waffle House, other than doing some writing at one, but it does seem to be the one inescapable dining experience in the South. Because it's so common (more than 1,000 locations, seemingly off every other highway exit in the South), and because it's so *available* (open 24 hours every day except Thanksgiving and Christmas), it's become an icon of the South.

The chain boasts of being the world's leading server of waffles, omelettes, raisin toast, grits, and apple butter. It's also the only place in the world where the jukeboxes play such specially recorded songs as "Waffle Doo-Wop" and "Good Food Fast"—along with standard oldies and country selections.

Try the pork chops and eggs with hash browns and raisin toast. Bert's Chili is also pretty good. Or just order some hash browns with tomatoes, "Scattered, Smothered, Covered, Chunked, Topped and Diced."

Cracker Barrel

Don't let it keep you away from the mom and pop restaurants in town, but if you're out on the interstate and in a hurry, or in dire need of a pullover, this chain is a safe bet for good country cooking along the interstate. With rocking chairs out front, a fireplace burning, and old-timey photos on the wall, Cracker Barrels feature a warm ambience that makes an hour's meal seem like a genuine break away from the highway.

Founded in 1969 in Lebanon, Tennessee, each restaurant contains a little gift shop fea-

---

ESSENTIAL COASTAL CAROLINA DINING EXPERIENCES

I could easily add 10 or 20 more wonderful dining stops to this list, but here's a representative selection of some of the most interesting and tasty spots in the region. You'll find details on each in the appropriate destination chapters.

Outer Banks
• Etheridge's Seafood
• Pigman's Barbecue
• Weeping Radish Brewery

Central Coast
• Sanitary Restaurant, Morehead City

Wilmington
• The Oceanic Restaurant

Calabash
• Anyplace advertising "Calabash-Style Seafood" will do.

Charleston
• Hyman's
• Poogan's Porch
• Robert's of Charleston
• Melvin's Barbecue (Mt. Pleasant)

Hilton Head
• Old Fort Pub

Beaufort, S.C.
• Shrimp Shack (outside of town)

Hilton Head Island
• Old Fort Pub

---

turing regional knickknacks reflecting the South in general and often the restaurant's location in particular. Before long I imagine these will spread to every state in the Lower 48, but for now they haven't penetrated the West Coast yet.

Hardee's

Hardee's was founded in Greenville, North Carolina, and today the chain has over 2,900 hundred locations in 39 other states. Hardee's is usually the first chain restaurant to infect a small Southern town, opening the way for Ronald Mc-Donald and the rest of the coven.

Some time back, the folks at a consumer magazine rated the fast-food mongers of America and named Hardee's food No. 2 among all major fast-food chains, but it's hard to see what all the fuss is about. The two things that are worth getting here are the breakfast sandwiches made with fresh biscuits and the seasonal peach shakes.

They seem (with some exceptions) to hire some of the most insolent workers you'll find in America. In 1998 Hardee's was purchased by Carl Karcher Enterprises, owner of the Carl's Jr. chain on the West Coast.

Chick-Fil-A

Don't call it "Chick Feela"—it's pronounced "chick fih-LAY." This is the largest privately owned restaurant chain in America. Georgia's Truett Cathy founded his first restaurant back in 1946; today the company operates nearly 600 restaurants. More than 400 of these are in malls, which means you'll see one in nearly every mall in South Carolina (Cathy pioneered the idea of fast-food restaurants in malls). The main thing to get here is a seasoned boneless chicken breast sandwich. Kids love the Chicken Fingers. The food doesn't do much for me, but obviously somebody likes it. Closed on Sunday to allow workers to go to church and spend time with their families, Chick-Fil-A re-

mains a true Southern phenomenon. See them online at www.chickfila.com.

Bojangles

The dirty rice and Cajun chicken make this Tennessee-based chain a cut above the rest.

Shoneys

Food for people who don't care what they eat, cooked by those who don't care what they cook. Some people praise the breakfast buffet, but there's no dearth of good breakfast places on the Carolina Coasts.

BUYING GROCERIES

Farmers' Markets

With all the agriculture in the area, most towns in the Coastal Carolinas have some sort of farmers' market. If you have a certain town in mind, call its chamber of commerce.

For small-town charm, it's hard to beat the **Chowan Farmers' Market** at North Granville Street and Virginia Road in Edenton, North Carolina. Open Tuesday, Friday, and Saturday in season. Call 252/482-8431 for information. Of course, the **Pasquotank County Farmers' Market** on Pritchard Street in Elizabeth City, 252/338-3954, can give it a run for its money. Open Friday and Saturday in season.

Local farmers, canners, bakers, herbalists, and artisans do business down on the New Bern

the Community Store, Ocracoke

waterfront at the **Farmers' Market,** 421 S. Front Street, 252/633-0043. Open Friday, 8 A.M.–5 P.M., Saturday 6 A.M.–2 P.M. You'll find the more food-focused **New Bern/Craven County Farmers' Market,** at Tryon Palace Drive, 252/633-1477, on Tuesday, Saturday and Sunday in season.

The **Old Wilmington City Market,** 120-124 South Front Street on Tuesday, Friday, Saturday, and Sunday in season, is hard to beat for location.

So too is the **Charleston's Farmers' Market** takes place every Saturday at the Maritime Center on Concord St., down by the South Carolina Aquarium, April 18–Oct. 31.

Pretty little Beaufort, S.C., has the **Beaufort Farmers' Market** at Bay & Charles Streets, 843/726-6360, on Saturdays only, in season.

Supermarket Chains

You have your **Piggly Wiggly,** the world's first true self-service grocery store, founded in 1916 by a Memphis, Tennessee, entrepreneur named Clarence Saunders, who later went on to pioneer (unsuccessfully) the world's first completely automated store. Where did the name "Piggly Wiggly" come from? Nobody knows. When people used to ask Saunders, he would answer, "So people will ask that very question."

Do note that though the Piggly Wiggly logo looks a lot like Porky Pig wearing a butcher's hat, Piggly predates Porky by 20 years or so. Today there are more than 700 Piggly Wiggly stores stretching from Texas north to Minnesota, south to Florida, and north to Virginia. You'll find one or two in every decent-sized Carolina town. The Piggly Wiggly store brand is usually a good way to save money—especially their barbecue sauces and peanut butter.

Yes, **Winn-Dixie** sounds like a political statement, but the name actually refers to the 1955 merger of the Winn & Lovett stores from Florida and Georgia, and the Dixie Home Stores of the Carolinas. Now with 12,000 stores in 14 states in the Bahamas, the Sunbelt, and on up to Ohio, Winn-Dixie is building a number of Marketplace Stores, with delis and ATM machines and such.

The new kid on the Southern grocery chain block, North Carolina's **Food Lion** got a lot of bad press a few years back when ABC's television newsmagazine *20/20* sent an undercover reporter to work at one of their stores and exposed some shoddy food-handling practices, including a tendency to relabel outdated meats. Despite successful counter suits that challenged the network's methods, the chain has been troubled since then, though individual locations can be quite good. I don't recommend the Food Lion brand foods, however—they're nothing special.

Kroger stores are a part of a Cincinnati-based chain, but since they're so plentiful in larger South Carolina cities, and because their superstores are often the most comprehensive supermarkets available (including, in many cases, ATM machines), you might want to use them if you're shopping for food while on the road, or while staying at a rental.

If you find a **Publix** in your travels, you've likely stumbled upon a clean, well-lighted place with good produce and fish.

Harris Teeter is probably the high-end choice for groceries. There's a great one located in an old warehouse on East Bay Street in Charleston; for seeing how even chain stores can blend successfully into their environment, it's worth checking out.

GETTING THERE AND AROUND

BY CAR

Several interstates crisscross the Carolinas, making the states quite easy to get to from most anywhere east of the Mississippi, but the coasts have always been just a bit trickier, especially North Carolina's. Nowadays I-40 deadends in Wilmington, making that town—and through a judicious use of U.S. 17, regions north and south— much more accessible than a few years back.

Of course from New York and other parts north, just head south on I-95 (following the historic Fort Lauderdale Trail blazed by generations of spring breakers) until you hit N.C. 158, then head east to reach the Outer Banks, the Albemarle, and the Central Coast (though U.S. 70 will do well for the latter two). For Wilmington continue south until you hit I-40, then head east. For Myrtle Beach you can either follow the Wilmington route and then head south on 17, or you can wait until you hit U.S. 501. If you do this, you'll have the chance to see the infamous South of the Border on I-95 in Dillon. The signs will lead you there.

From Atlanta just head either northeast on I-85 until you cross I-40, then head east. Or head west on I-20 until you get to Columbia, S.C., then head east to Charleston. Another worthwhile route from Atlanta—though infinitely more time-consuming—is to take the Atlanta Highway (U.S. 29) due east through the scenic Piedmont towns of northeast Georgia, including Athens, where if you're lucky you'll run across a member of R.E.M. or the B-52s. If you're really lucky, you'll run across one of my brothers, who live there as well. But as I say, this is the slower, two-lane route, which stops numerous times in small towns all the way across the Piedmont. It's scenic, but don't say I didn't warn you.

If you're up in Charlotte either catch I-85 and head east until you hit I-40, then head to Wilmington, or take I-77 due south to Columbia, and then on to Charleston on I-26. Unless you're planning to hole up in downtown Charleston or Wilmington, or in a resort like Hilton Head that bustles with hotel trams, you'll want a car. Despite all its development, Coastal Carolina remains rural enough that the best way to explore it is still by automobile.

Rentals
You'll find locations for all the major car rental chains throughout Coastal Carolina, and especially around its airports. Call Alamo at 800/327-9633, Avis at 800/831-2847, Budget at 800/353-0600, Enterprise at 800/325-8007, and Hertz at 800/654-3131, website: www.hertz.com.

Rules of the Road
Americans drive on the right side of the road, the way God intended. If you forget and drive on the left side of the road, other drivers will remind you by driving straight toward you and blaring their horns. A driver's license serves as indispensable identification. In America you need a driver's license for everything from cashing a check to renting movies.

A driver must be 25 years old and have a valid driver's license to rent a car. You will have the chance to buy insurance coverage for the car and yourself; unless your policy back home covers you, you'll want to go ahead and get some now. It's illegal to drive without at least liability coverage in the United States.

Travelers from outside the United States must carry an International Driver's Permit as well as a current valid license from their home country.

Note: It's illegal in both North and South Carolina to drive while drinking alcoholic beverages or while under the influence of alcohol.

BY AIR

Charleston, Myrtle Beach, and Wilmington all have fairly large airports. The **Myrtle Beach International Airport** serves as the commercial airport for the Grand Strand and includes scheduled service from USAir, Atlantic Southeast Airlines, COMAir (for Delta connections), Jet Express, Air Canada, Midway Connection,

Spirit, and GP Express/Continental. If you're hunting for cheap tickets and don't mind a few extra miles on the rental car, check out flights into Columbia, S.C.; Greenville, S.C.; Charlotte, N.C.; Raleigh, N.C.; Atlanta or Savannah, Georgia; or Norfolk, Virginia.

BY TRAIN

Most sizable towns in South Carolina are served by Amtrak. For reservations and schedule information, call 800/872-7245.

BY BUS

Most towns, sizable or not, are served by Greyhound Bus Lines. For reservations and schedule information, call 800/231-2222.

BY BOAT

For the nautically endowed—those who own boats—the Carolinas are very accessible. The Atlantic Intracoastal Waterway, a 1,095-mile nautical pathway from Norfolk, Virginia, south to Miami, Florida, passes behind the coastal islands of North and South Carolina. Contact the **South Carolina Marina Association,** P.O. Box 24156, Hilton Head Island, SC 29925, 843/837-9525, for information.

VISAS AND OFFICIALDOM

Entry Requirements

Non-U.S. citizens will need the following for entry to the country:
- Valid passport from a recognized country *or* valid visa
- Round-trip or return ticket, or proof of sufficient funds to support yourself during your visit and to afford a return ticket. You may be required to purchase a return ticket at the airport before you are given a visa, or you may have to show proof of a return ticket when you are actually applying.
- $13.95 in fees for the services of the immigration, customs, and agricultural inspectors

Passports

Passports are the most common type of travel document used as proof of identity when crossing an international border. A passport is required for travel into the United States and even for air travel within the country.

It is always easier to travel with a passport than to try to get by with some other type of photo identification.

If you don't already have a passport, you should start the process for acquiring one as soon as possible. Make sure that it is valid for at least six months, preferably a year, after you plan to return home. If the passport issued to you by the government in your country expires while you are in the United States, you will have to contact an embassy or consulate of your home country to renew it. U.S. passport offices do not provide services to holders of non-U.S. passports.

For extended stays, bring your birth certificate, extra passport photos, and even a photocopy of the original passport. This will help speed the process of replacing a lost or expired passport. If your passport is stolen, report it the police immediately and get a copy of the police report, or at least record the important details contained in it (name and title of the officer, the police precinct number, the file number, etc.). This should also help in replacing your passport.

Visas

Visas are documents, usually a stamp in your passport, that are issued by the government of the country you want to visit. Visas are a precondition for being admitted to a country, but they are not a guarantee of entry. The rules for acquiring a visa are arbitrary and occasionally very strict, but if you plan ahead and follow the rules to the letter, you shouldn't run into any problems.

A very few countries in the world participate with the United States in the Visa Waiver Pilot Program. Check with a U.S. embassy or consulate to find out if your country is included in the program. Otherwise you are required to have a visa. You should always be courteous and respectful to consular, immigration, and customs authorities. If you are applying for a tourist visa to the United States, you will be required to appear in person at a U.S. consulate or embassy for an interview, as well as meet certain

NORTH CAROLINA PUBLIC FERRIES

North Carolina's ferries are uncomplicated to use, either free or inexpensive, and a scenic, memorable alternative to taking the (often longer) land route, especially since they allow everyone in your car—even the driver—a chance to get out, stretch, feed the seagulls, socialize with other visitors, or maybe catch a few winks. Though they vary in size (the longer the journey, the bigger the boat), they all have bathrooms and some semblance of a lounge, usually with a candy machine, soft drink machine, and road coffee. They can handle just about any kind of vehicle you might be driving; if you're not sure, give them a call ahead of time and ask.

You'll need reservations if your ferry leaves from Cedar Island (919/225-3551); Ocracoke (919/928-3841), or Swan Quarter (919/926-1111). Stop by most any tourist-oriented business and ask for a current schedule of departure times and prices, or call 800/BY-FERRY (800/293-3779) for information.

Departure times vary from season to season. Ferries may close due to inclement weather. Try to arrive 15 minutes early to make sure you've got a spot on board, even if you've got a reservation. Below is a list of the state's ferries, with approximate passage times.

Aurora–Bayview Ferry, 30 minutes

Cedar Island–Ocracoke Ferry, 2 hours, 15 minutes; $10 per car

Cherry Branch–Minnesott Ferry, 20 minutes

Currituck–Knotts Island Ferry, 40 minutes

Hatteras–Ocracoke Ferry, 40 minutes

Southport–Fort Fisher Ferry, 30 minutes

Swan Quarter–Ocracoke Ferry, 2 hours, 30 minutes; $10 per car

---

other requirements, including proof that you have a return ticket.

Make sure to find out what the current visa requirements are for travel, or if your country is "officially recognized" by the U.S. government. Visa requirements can change at any time without notice. If you have already bought nonrefundable air tickets and are denied entry, you'll be out of luck.

The United States charges $13.95 in arrival fees to pay for the services of the customs, immigration, and agricultural inspectors.

State Border Crossings
Part of the evidence that the Carolinas and the rest of the Confederacy lost the argument over state sovereignty is the ease with which one can travel between American states. The only restrictions you're likely to encounter involve transporting certain plants or produce across state lines, or transporting illegal substances or guns across state lines.

Border authorities sometimes forbid produce and plants from entering a state because the flora may contain pests or diseases harmful to the native plants or agricultural products of the state. In some cases, if you are carrying produce in your car and are stopped at a state border, you will be asked to dispose of the produce.

Generally forbidden substances include illegal drugs, explosives, or dangerous chemicals. In most states transporting illegal drugs across the state line increases the legal penalty for possession from a misdemeanor to a felony.

Many counties also have laws governing the amount of alcohol and number of cartons of cigarettes you can bring across their border. If a county border is also a state border and you are carrying alcohol or cigarettes into that county, check its laws concerning alcohol and cigarettes. A pack of cigarettes and a bottle of beer are not cause for legal action, unless the beer is open. A carton of cigarettes and a bottle of whiskey might raise a few eyebrows, but shouldn't cause you any trouble. Twenty cartons of cigarettes and a case of whiskey will get you into trouble in many counties.

If you are carrying a gun, you must have a valid permit. Check with the embassy or consulate where you got your passport if you plan to buy and carry a gun while traveling in the United States, and understand that foreign visitors requesting information regarding firearms will be viewed with some suspicion.

Note: in 1996 it became legal in South Carolina for a citizen who has taken a safety course to carry a concealed weapon. Consequently, as you a pass through many business doorways, you'll see signs forbidding concealed weapons while on the owner's private property. Don't let these signs make you think that everyone in South Carolina is packing heat. The number of people requesting such permits is low indeed. But if you are carrying a concealed weapon, you'll need to unpack it—remove the cartridges and put it somewhere where it can't be stolen.

SPECIAL INTERESTS

Travel with Children
The Carolinas are very much family-oriented states. Many parks feature wide, family-size swings; nearly every community event includes children's activities, and most resorts provide thorough programs for youngsters. The only places where children are unwelcome is in nightclubs and bars (obviously), in South Carolina gambling parlors (no big loss), and in many bed-and-breakfasts. Still, the Carolinas seem to have a higher percentage of "children welcome" B&Bs than most other states. Where possible I've noted whenever establishments have stated a preference.

One nice thing about automobile travel in the Carolinas is that everything in the region is so close together that it's rare you'll find yourself driving very long without the opportunity to stop and let the kids get out and burn off some energy. The enclosed playgrounds now popular at McDonald's and some of its competitors make pretty handy pit stops, even on a rainy day.

Women Travelers
I've never been a woman, despite what my football coach used to yell, so I've asked my wife, Kristin, to help with this section:

Most women find themselves treated especially politely in the Carolinas. Doors will be opened, bus seats offered. There are, however, areas still considered male domains—the same places, generally, considered male domains throughout most of the Western world: honky-tonk bars, hunting clubs, golf clubs (some of them), sports bars. A woman is in no particular danger in most of these places, but her presence there may be interpreted as a desire for male companionship.

Women traveling alone should be aware of their surroundings. When you head for your car, carry your keys in hand and get to and into the car quickly. Drive with your doors locked and your windows rolled up.

If possible, carry a cellular phone—otherwise, a breakdown on the highway will leave you waiting and hoping the first motorist to stop for assistance has good motives.

A sizable number of crimes each year are committed by people impersonating police officers. If you're pulled over—especially at night—don't open your car door or window more than a crack, and then only to demand that a marked patrol car be called. This is well within your rights. No matter how authentic the uniform looks, demand to see the marked car. If the officer can't produce a black and white, move on. Don't hand over your license, which gives your name and address.

If you feel suspicious, ask the officer to follow you to a more-populated, better-lighted area.

Gay/Lesbian Travelers
In recent decades American gays and lesbians have begun to enjoy an increase in tolerance toward same-sex couples. In Coastal Carolina

larger cities like Charleston and Wilmington have their share of gay hangouts and night-clubs, many of them private clubs that require a nominal "membership fee" for admittance. In other areas gay and lesbian travelers not wanting to draw attention to themselves generally respect the local mores and avoid public displays of affection.

Travelers with Disabilities

Though all of the Carolinas' new public buildings provide facilities and access for the physically disabled, many of the state's historic structures and sites have been hard-pressed to do the same. Throughout this book I've tried to note attractions that may pose special difficulties for the disabled, as well as those that specifically define themselves as wheelchair accessible. If you're uncertain about the accessibility of a specific attraction, be sure to call ahead.

AA, Al-Anon, and Other Recovery Groups

Chapters of Alcoholics Anonymous hold meetings throughout the Palmetto and Tar Heel States, and most welcome visitors. In North Carolina, call 252/261-1681 in Kitty Hawk, 252/338-1849 in Elizabeth City, 910/794-1840 in Wilmington for information and help, 24 hours a day. In South Carolina, call 803/254-5301, for information and help, 24 hours a day.

Narcotics Anonymous, 800/922-5305, specializes in helping those with other drug addictions. Al-Anon specializes in providing help for the families of alcoholics. It, too, has a 24-hour phone service, 803/735-9944. You'll find an automated information alcoholism resource at 803/612-1666, ext. 8030 or 8031.

Churches

Visiting the Carolinas without attending a church service is like going to Thailand and not visiting a temple. Church life and the spiritual life (and sometimes the two intersect) are of major importance to most South Carolinians, and it would be hard to get any real grasp on the culture without passing between the white pillars and taking a spot in the pew.

If it's a representative experience you seek, then in the Lowcountry you might want to visit one of Charleston's enormous Episcopalian cathedrals or attend synagogue at America's first reformed temple. Or visit the state's fastest-growing church, Seacoast Community Church in Mount Pleasant, a "seeker" church that began with a marketing survey of the affluent East Cooper area and today packs in several thousand young go-getters each Sunday. Up in Wilmington, the beautiful First Presbyterian Church downtown not only features sonorous bells, but it was once pastored by Woodrow Wilson's father. And up in the Outer Banks, there's The Outer Banks Worship Center, a nondenominational church so devoted to evangelizing Banks visitors that they've built their roadside church in the shape of a huge ark to attract passerby. And then there's the eye-catching Nags Head Baptist Church, a little white church standing in the shadow of a huge sand dune south of Jockeys Ridge State Park.

Of course, for every large, celebrity church, a couple hundred humble congregations of every stripe meet each Sunday. To get a truly representative feel for the spiritual tempo of Coastal Carolina, you might be best off pulling out a Yellow Pages, picking a church that catches your eye, and attending a service.

Compared to most parts of the country, Carolinian churches are still fairly dressy: most women wear dresses or pantsuits (most Carolinian women, visiting a new church, wear a dress or skirt just to play it safe); men wear slacks, shirts, and ties, and often jackets. The general philosophy behind all this finery runs something like this: "You'd dress up to go ask some fellow at the bank for a loan. Doesn't God deserve the same respect?" (Whether it's respectful to treat God as though he thinks as superficially as the average loan officer is another question.) Fortunately dress is generally more casual along the coasts, and even more so in nondenominational churches.

With the exception of most Pentecostal and charismatic congregations, very few services are significantly integrated—reminding one of Martin Luther King's quote about Sunday morning being the most segregated hours in America. However, very, very few congregations will object to the presence of friendly, respectful visitors of a different race, and most will be quite happy to have you there.

HEALTH MAINTENANCE

Insect Repellent

Unless you're planning to spend all of your time on city streets, you'll want insect repellent while you're here. The two critters that will trouble you most are no-see-ums (particularly at the coast) and mosquitoes. "No-see-ums" are tiny gnats that bite as if it's personal. The best way to fight them seems to be with Avon's Skin-So-Soft cream. Wear a hat—they'll bite your scalp as well.

Mosquitoes are pleasant companions by comparison, but in swamps and salt marshes they can quickly turn a day hike into a personal purgatory. Skin-So-Soft works with them as well, and so does Deep Woods Off and most Cutter products.

Sunscreen

Carolina summers can be particularly deceiving; though it's hot, the gray sky overhead can lull you into thinking that your skin's not taking a beating from ultraviolet rays—but it is. To ward off skin cancer, premature wrinkles, and sunburn, use sunscreens with an SPF rating of 15 or more—igher for those with fair skin.

ALLIGATORS VS. SHARKS

If you're from a area free of sharks and alligators, you may wonder about the wisdom of sharing the Carolinas' coastal waters with them.

Consider the facts: from 1976 to 1995, of the millions who flocked to the Carolinas' surf and sounds, alligators attacked just six of them, and sharks sunk their teeth into nine others.

So which is worse—a gator attack or a shark attack? Based on statistics compiled on attacks in six states, neither is as lethal as you might expect. If you get attacked by an alligator, you've still got a 96.6 percent chance of walking away—or at least hopping away—from the encounter. And a full 98 percent of shark attack victims live to tell the tale.

Of course, surviving a shark or alligator bite is a lot like buying real estate. It's all a matter of location, location, location.

Adjusting to the Humidity

Stepping off a plane into the middle of a Carolina summer can just about knock you out. If you live in a less humid area and your plans in Carolina include a lot of physical activity, try to give yourself a day or two to acclimate.

LOCAL DOCTORS

The Carolina's have no dearth of qualified physicians for those with the money to pay for them. Neither are these states short of walk-in medical clinics where you can stop in without an appointment. Check the local phone book under "Physicians" to find the address and phone number of physicians in your area, or stop into a shop, explain your situation to a clerk, and ask for a recommendation.

NATURAL HAZARDS

For all its natural beauty, the South does seem to have more than its share of natural hazards—from alligators and poisonous snakes to hurricanes and jellyfish. But 99 percent of the time these hazards can be avoided with a little foresight and caution.

Lightning Storms

Sociologists throw around a lot of reasons for the fervent spirituality of many Carolinians, but one overlooked cause may be the prayer-inspiring lightning storms. When the sheet lightning flares across the sky like a flickering fluorescent bar, and the bolts are blasting transformers to either side of the road, even a trip to the local package store can quickly turn into a religious experience.

In the 31-year stretch from 1959–1990, 228 Carolinians met their maker via lightning—one person zapped to Beulah Land every month and a half. And this is only counting fatalities—859 people took a bolt during that same 31-year stretch, to varying effect.

It really does happen. So if you're out on the trail or the golf course when a storm rolls in, seek shelter—though not under a tree, since the tree is likely to get hit, in which case you don't want to be anywhere around it. Electrocution is rarely worth risking, especially since the average summer convectional storm will be over in less than an hour anyway. Go find a cup of coffee somewhere and enjoy the show from safety.

If you're indoors, do as most Carolinians do—they won't talk on a phone (though cordless phones are okay) or use plumbing when a storm is striking around them, since both phone lines and water can serve as conduits. There are a number of urban legends revolving around a man/woman using the toilet during a lightning storm; ask almost any Carolinian and he or she can fill in the details.

Hurricanes

Hurricanes—and, more commonly, the threat of hurricanes—are simply a factor of life in Coastal Carolina. Annually the Charleston *Post and Courier* includes a prehurricane season insert, providing informative articles that help Carolinians to understand and survive these storms. Local news teams run ads boasting of their prophetic capabilities, and supermarkets like Piggly Wiggly buy full pages to proclaim themselves "Your Hurricane Stock-Up Store."

Pay attention to the public warnings on the radio and television when you're in the state, especially June–October, the hurricane season. The mildest warning is a **Small Craft Advisory,** issued when strong winds—up to 38 mph—strike the coastal waters. This is not the day to rent or charter a fishing boat. Next up is a **Gale Warning,** issued when winds reach 39–54 mph. A **Storm Warning** means winds 55–73 mph. **Hurricane Watches** are issued when hurricane conditions are a real possibility and may threaten coastal or inland areas within 36 hours. A **Hurricane Warning** means a hurricane is expected to hit an area within 24 hours. If you're visiting the coast and a Hurricane Warning is issued, it's time to consider visiting the Carolinas' historic interior for a few days. One way to stay ahead of the game—or to put off a visit if you haven't left home yet—is to check www.stormalert.com, a website run by one of the local news stations.

The two things you *don't* want to do are panic or ignore the warnings. If an evacuation is called, you'll hear about it on the radio and TV. But by this point, you as a traveler should be gone already. Save the spot in the relief shelter for a local resident. Get thee to the Upcountry.

Snakes

No other state offers the variety of poisonous snakes found in the Carolinas. A full six different snakes can make your life complicated here, but even the most outdoorsy visitor is unlikely to come across any of them on a visit.

The **copperhead** averages around two to three feet long and normally lives in damp woods, mountainous regions, or in the high ground in swampy areas—which is to say you'll find it all through Coastal Carolina.

Canebrake, or **timber rattlesnakes,** are also found throughout the state, usually in deciduous forests or swamps on high ground. These snakes average three to four feet in length and can even reach five.

The **eastern diamondback rattlesnake** runs 3–6 feet and up, with a basic dark brown color and brown/yellow diamonds. They mostly keep to the woods of the Lowcountry.

The **pigmy rattlesnake** is rare and only reaches a bit over a foot long. You'll find them in all but the highest lands of the Carolinas. They're dull gray with brown splotches on the back and sides.

The **cottonmouth,** or **water moccasin,** thrives in wetland areas of the coastal plain.

The beautiful black, red, and yellow **eastern coral snake** is rare, found in woods and fields.

Bring a **snake kit,** wear leather boots to protect your ankles, and watch where you step. Here's the good news: several thousand people are bitten by poisonous snakes each year, but less than 10 die in the United States annually.

More good news: in most cases, snakebite is preventable. Over 50 percent of poisonous snakebites take place after the victim has seen the snake and had the chance to get away. In fact most victims are bitten in the attempt to pick up a poisonous snake, harass it, or kill it. The point is simple enough: keep your eyes open when in the woods and stay away from any snake that you're not absolutely certain is non-poisonous.

If you or somebody in your party is bitten by a snake, try not to panic. Even if the snake is poisonous, odds are nearly even that it was a "dry" bite—meaning that no poison was injected into the victim. Nonetheless, don't allow the victim to engage in strenuous physical activity, since this will get the heart pumping faster, thus spreading the poison quicker. Try to safely identify the breed of snake if it's possible, and if it doesn't take too long to do it. Get the victim to the nearest hospital or emergency medical facility as soon as possible.

If local doctors are unsure of the correct snakebite serum to use to treat the bite, tell them to contact the regional Poison Information Center.

Yellowjackets

To avoid most stinging insects, the place to start is in your clothing—bright colors attract, dark ones don't. If you notice yellowjackets about and you're drinking or eating something, be sure to keep checking the food or drink (soda cans are notorious) to make sure no yellowjacket has sneaked aboard.

Yellowjacket stings are painful—not unlike being burned by a just-extinguished match. The danger comes in when people have allergic reactions.

How can you tell if it's an allergic reaction? A good rule of thumb is that as long as the reaction is around the site of the bite, you can assume it's a local reaction and needs to be treated with something like an antihistamine and maybe a little topical steroid, if anything. But if you get bitten or stung by an insect and you develop symptoms elsewhere on your body, those are signs of an allergic reaction; you need to get in and see a doctor.

Some of the signs of an allergic reaction are hives; swelling of the lips, tongue, eyelids, internal organs; blocked airways; shock; and low blood pressure.

If you're headed in this direction, your doctor will probably administer epipens, which contain epinephrine, and quickly reduce the symptoms of an allergic reaction.

Fire Ants

These ants are extremely aggressive when protecting their nests; if you inadvertently knock over a mound, don't stand around apologizing too long or you may soon find yourself covered with stinging ants. Stings can cause a severe reaction and even death. Watch for their domed mounds, commonly at least 15 inches wide at the base and about six inches high, usually found in damp areas—which includes most all of the American South—particularly under trees, in lawns, or in flower beds.

Winged fire ants originated in South America and first appeared on U.S. soil in Mobile, Alabama, in 1918. Since then they've spread like the kudzu of the animal kingdom to 11 Southern states, including the Carolinas, and in the last half of the 1990s made their appearance in Southern California—about the same time as Krispy Kreme doughnuts.

You'll find numerous chemical treatments for ant mounds in any grocery store or hardware store. Some swear that pouring boiling water into the top of an ant mound will do the trick, without harming the local water supply.

Fire ant bites leave a sterile pustule. The urge to scratch or pop the pustule is very tempting, but try not to do it. Scratching or picking at a bite until it becomes open allows it to get infected.

If you're allergic to fire ants, wear shoes and socks; don't go outside barefoot or in sandals.

Jellyfish

If stung by a jellyfish, clean the area carefully. If you have tentacles still stuck to the wound area, don't just pull them off with your hand—they may still have venom sacs attached. Instead, use a credit card to scrape parallel with the skin, pushing the tentacles off sideways. Try not to break any of the venom sacs.

For pain relief, try meat tenderizer, a baking soda and water paste, or vinegar.

Jellyfish stings very rarely cause allergic reactions, but when they do, they can include hives, itching, and swelling on parts of the body that weren't stung. If any of these symptoms occurs, get to an emergency room.

Stingrays

Stingray wounds are much more rare than jellyfish stings, but they happen. To avoid them, shuffle your feet as you walk in the water.

If you do happen to step on a stingray, it will let you know—it'll swing its mace of a tail around and send you hopping back to shore. Most stingray victims get it on the foot or ankle.

One treatment is to submerge the wound in the hottest water you can stand for 20 or 30 minutes. This seems to neutralize the poison. Most people enjoy noticeable relief within minutes.

Even so, if you've danced with a stingray and come away stung, you should still see a doctor—you may need an antibiotic.

Sharks

Usually one to three people get attacked by sharks in Carolina waters each year. A few years back the number shot up above 10, mostly in the Grand Strand—which should put to rest those charges of Myrtle Beach visitors having bad taste.

The odds of being bitten are still incredibly low. To make them lower, the experts say:

- Swim in groups, preferably composed of people better-tasting than you are.
- Don't swim too far out. If you see sharks, you want to be close to shore so you can get out fast.
- Avoid swimming in the late afternoon, at night, or in the early morning. This is when sharks feed the most.
- Lose the flashy jewelry. Sharks can't see well in South Carolina's murky waters, but they'll see the glitter from that belly ring of yours.

Another thing to remember is that sharks don't watch movies, so they don't know that they're supposed to stick their dorsal fins up out of the water as they cruise toward the beach. Most sharks near the shore usually swim on the bottom, so their victims have no advance warning.

Though the whole U.S. East Coast may only see 40 shark attacks a year (and few if any of these fatal), the number of incidents has been increasing over the past decade and a half—presumably because more folks are hitting the surf than ever. Along the East Coast, practically all shark attacks are "hit and run strikes" by black-tipped or spinner sharks, usually no more than six feet long. The shark bites, realizes that the victim tastes bad, and releases. Most bite victims bleed but don't lose any actual tissue.

Of course, sometimes they do kill people—in 1998, a nine-year-old boy died in Florida from a shark attack. But vengeance is certainly ours: while sharks kill about 100 people a year worldwide, humans annually kill some 100 million sharks.

Poison Ivy

If you've been exposed to poison ivy, you have two or three hours to wash it off and avoid a breakout. If you are out and about and can't take a shower, rubbing the skin with alcohol—even beer—will often help. What you *don't* want to do is touch the unwashed, exposed part of your body with any other part, thus spreading the irritating serum.

Giardia

Ironically, one of the smallest critters in the state causes much more cumulative discomfort across the state than any other. While a lake or stream may appear clean, think twice before taking a sip. You're risking a debilitating sickness by drinking untreated water. The protozoan *Giardia duodenalis* is found in fresh water throughout the state, spread by both humans and animals. Although curable with prescription drugs, giardia's no fun—unless bloating, cramps, and diarrhea are your idea of a good time. Carry safe drinking water on any trip. If your canteen's dry, boiling creek or lake water will kill giardia and other harmful organisms. Some hikers prefer to use water filters made by companies like Mountain Safety Research and Pur, about $50 at most backpacking stores. However, cheaper filters may allow the tiny giardia protozoan (as small as 0.2 microns) to pass through; even the best filters may not always filter out other, smaller organisms. Traditional purifying chemicals like chlorine and iodine are unreliable, taste foul, and can be unhealthy. Boiling's really your best bet.

Unfortunately it's also possible to get giardia while bathing; be careful not to swallow water while swimming in fresh water; men with mustaches should carefully dry them after leaving the water.

Lyme Disease

Lyme disease is caused by a bacteria transmitted to humans through the bite of the deer tick. Not all ticks carry the disease, but infection rates in certain areas can be quite high. Don't assume that because you are not in a high-infection area you cannot get Lyme disease. Most cases have been reported in the Northeast and upper Midwest, but an increasing number of cases are being seen in Southeastern states. If you are bitten by a tick anywhere in the United States, you should get checked for Lyme disease. The disease can be detected by a blood test, and early treatment can cure the disease or lessen the severity of later symptoms.

An early symptom of Lyme disease is a red, circular rash in the area of the bite that usually develops a few days to a few weeks after being bitten. Other symptoms can include flu-like symptoms, headache, stiff neck, fever, and muscle aches. Sometimes these symptoms will not show up for months. If any of these symptoms appear, even if you don't remember being bitten by a tick, have a doctor check you. Early detection of Lyme disease provides excellent opportunity for treatment (largely with antibiotics).

The three types of ticks known to carry Lyme disease (not necessarily every individual) are the deer tick (most common) in the Northeast and North-central United States, the lone star tick in the South, and the California black-legged tick in the West. If you are bitten by any tick, save the body for later identification if at all possible.

Remove a tick as soon as possible after being bitten. The best way is to grab the tick as close to your skin as possible with a pair of tweezers. The longer a tick has been on your body, the deeper it will bite you to find more blood. The closer to its head you can grab it, the less chance that its mouth parts or head will break off in the wound. If you can't get the whole thing out, go see a doctor. Clean the wound with antiseptic and cover it to avoid infection.

CRIME

Coastal Carolina's crime statistics aren't overly high, relative to some other regions in the United States, but of course, when it's late at night and you're on a dicey side of town, this doesn't mean much. A friend of mine from Orangeburg says his daddy gave him three rules for staying safe, and they seem worth repeating:

- Nothing good ever happened after 1 A.M.
- Don't carry more than you're willing to lose.
- There's safety in numbers.

Most bars in the Carolinas close at 1 A.M., after which the streets become populated with drunk folk and those who prey upon them. Rule No. 2 is an important one. If you can't immediately hand over your wallet to a robber and know you'll be all right, then you need to go through your wallet and remove the "valuable" contents. Rule No. 3 also makes sense. Single people get robbed more often than couples, who get robbed more often than trios, who get robbed more often than quartets, and so on. The bigger the crowd, the better the odds.

In Charleston a few years back, a Georgia tourist walking with a woman was held up at gunpoint by a trio of young men on bicycles. It was after 1 A.M. The man refused to give his wallet to the kids, and one of them shot him dead before they rode off into the darkness.

Police who responded to the scene found several thousand dollars in the victim's wallet.

How to Protect Yourself

- **Don't carry too much money.** How much is too much? Too much is so much that you won't gladly give over your wallet to get a robber to leave you and your travel companions alone.
- **Don't give carjackers time to size you up.** Walk to your car quickly, with your keys in your hand; get in, lock the doors, start up, and drive off. Fix your hair and/or makeup while you're at a *stoplight,* like a good American.
- **When driving—particularly in urban areas—keep your doors locked and your windows rolled up.** Carjackers are generally not the hardest-working individuals you'll ever run across—they're watching for an *easy* mark.
- **Keep your wallet or purse out of sight when you're driving.**
- **If you're involved in an accident that seems suspicious, signal to the other driver to follow you and then drive to a better-lit, more populated area.** A common ploy for carjackers is to bump their victims from behind and then rob them as they get out to inspect the damage to their car.
- **If you're traveling with children and get carjacked, tell the carjacker you've got a child in back and ask if you can take him or her out.** Many times the carjacker, who doesn't want to add a kidnapping charge to all the others he's racking up, will let you get the child out.
- **Park in a central, well-lit area.** In downtown Charleston, for instance, you might consider using one of the paid lots, which normally have some sort of supervision. Be aware, though: Sometimes the attendant leaves at sunset, which might leave your car unattended in a dark, deserted parking lot until 2 A.M. Ask the attendant how late the car will be supervised.

- **When in public, wear your money and/or purse close to your body—and wallets in your front pocket.** This will make it harder for pickpockets/purse snatchers to rob you undetected.
- **If you're driving a rental car, make sure there are no identifying markers.** Travelers have, in some places in the United States—Florida, most famously—become targets. If there are items that indicate your car is rented—license-plate frames emblazoned with the name of the company, for instance—ask the folks at the rental office if you can remove them while you have the car in your possession.

OTHER ISSUES

Racism

People have found a number of excuses for not loving each other throughout the centuries; one of the most common is racism.

Members of every imaginable race and combination of races live in the Carolinas, but the vast majority—well over 95 percent—consider themselves either "white" or "black." And of course, it is between these two groups that most of the racial tension in the Carolinas has traditionally existed.

Most of what passes for racism in the Carolinas is, instead, largely "classism." What appears as white/black animosity is instead disguised class hatred: in the most common scenario, "racist" whites attribute to blacks all the traits historically attributed to anyone at the bottom of the social ladder—laziness, low intelligence, dishonesty, envy, criminal habits, and reproductive irresponsibility. "Racist" blacks on the other hand, attribute to whites all the traits underclasses generally hang on an upper class: greed, snobbery, condescension, lack of compassion, hedonism, shallowness, spiritual vacuousness, clubbishness. In each case, the "racist" person is probably right to oppose the values they attribute to people they dislike. Where they err is in attributing these values to members of a given race.

If you're "white" or "black," it's possible you'll feel some hostility from "the other" while visiting the Carolinas. If you are part of an interracial couple, you'll possibly experience some disapproving looks from members of both races, especially as you venture into the country or into the more homogeneous neighborhoods of the major cities. (If you're a non-black person of color, and far from any large town, you may find people scratching their heads, wondering how you ever ended up in South Carolina.)

To an amazing degree, a smile and eye contact break down the walls that most people put up between strangers and the "other" and their better selves. Your goal is to show them that you're an exception, that you don't carry the attitudes they expect to find in someone with your pigmentation.

If this doesn't work, the best thing to do is to cut your losses and move on.

Drugs

Neither South nor North Carolina is known for its tolerant attitude toward illicit drugs, or for the comfortable nature of its jails. Possession and sale of marijuana are illegal here, as are all the usual mind-altering substances.

Sexually Transmitted Diseases

AIDS is alive and well in the Carolinas, as are numerous other debilitating sexually transmitted diseases (STDs), including a couple flavors of hepatitis and genital herpes. The safest thing to do is to not share hypodermic needles and not have sex with anyone you haven't screened first. If a person tells you he or she is HIV-negative, make sure the person hasn't had sex with another partner since that last screening. And since there's a six-month window during which someone who has contracted HIV may still show negative in a HIV test, to be safe you need to know that a person didn't have sex for six months *before* the screening (although some people with HIV have tested negative as late as five years after contracting the virus).

If, given the irresistible attractiveness of most Carolinians, celibacy seems an impossible task, you should at least reduce the risk by using a latex condom, though these tear easily.

INFORMATION AND SERVICES

POSTAL SERVICES

Sending mail from the United States to any-where in the world is pretty easy. Almost every town and city in the United States that you are likely to visit has at least one post office, or a local business that acts as the local post office. In larger cities you'll also find the major international delivery companies (UPS, Federal Express, and so on). The U.S. Postal Service and the delivery companies will also ship packages for you to many foreign countries.

Charges are based on weight. At publication, a standard U.S. postage stamp costs 34 cents.

The delivery companies and the postal service offer next-day and two-day service to almost anywhere in the world.

If you plan to receive mail in the United States, make sure that the person sending mail addresses the envelope with your name exactly as it appears on your passport. This will help to avoid any questions as to whether the mail is yours. You can also have mail delivered to your hotel. Make sure to provide the person sending you mail with the correct address. Also request that the person sending you mail print or type your address on the envelope to avoid any confusion that might arise because of worldwide differences in writing styles.

Always attach postage yourself to ensure that the proper amount is used.

When shipping large parcels overseas, it's best to pack the item(s) yourself or oversee the job. There are many packaging stores in the United States, offering boxes in various sizes, as well as tape and other packaging material. Many of these stores double as a post office or pickup/dropoff spot for the large delivery companies.

Unfortunately, though the U.S. Postal Service likes to cite Herodotus's quote, "Neither snow, nor rain, nor heat, nor night stays these couriers from the swift completion of their appointed rounds," you'll find that just about any old bank holiday—even Columbus Day—will stay these couriers. Post offices will also close, and any mail you've already sent off will sit for a full day—so be prepared.

TELEPHONE

Public

Public phones are widely available on street corners and outside convenience stores and gas stations. They are maintained by a variety of private companies, which may sometimes charge more than the usual fee of 35 cents. Use any combination of coins; however, in the case of a 35-cent local call, if you use two quarters, change will not be provided. Dialing directions are usually provided on the face of the phone, but when in doubt simply dial "0" for an operator who will direct your call for an added charge of one to three dollars. To place a local or long distance call, simply dial the number and an automated voice will tell you how much money to deposit. When using a calling card billed to your home account, dial "0" plus the number (including area code) you're calling. You'll hear a tone, then often a voice prompting you to enter your calling card number and personal identification number (PIN). For universal calling cards, follow the instructions provided on the back of the card or dial "0" for operator assistance.

Emergency

In an emergency when an ambulance, firefighters, or police are required, you can dial 911 and be instantly connected with an emergency switchboard; otherwise dial "0" for operator. When you dial 911, your number and address are displayed on a viewing screen, enabling the authorities to locate you, even if you yourself don't know where exactly you are.

Long-Distance

Prepaid calling cards are the most hassle-free method of making long-distance calls, short of carrying around a cell phone. If you purchase a $10 card, you are given $10 of long-distance credit to spend. You can spend it all on one call, or—more likely—on a series of calls. throughout your trip. Best of all, if you lose your card—unlike some other calling cards that give access to your account with your phone company—you can't lose more than the $10 you spent on it. Stores like Kroger and Wal-Mart sell prepaid calling cards.

Phone books are generally available at public phone booths and normally cover everything within the local area code, though frequently they are vandalized. Besides containing phone listings, phone books also carry maps to the local area, zip codes and post offices, information on public transportation systems, and a listing of community services and events.

Area Codes
The North Carolina coast has two different area codes: the 252 area code includes the Outer Banks and the Albemarle. The Wilmington region is the 910 area code. For now, the area code for the entire South Carolina Lowcountry is 843.

INTERNET ACCESS

Internet access has spread through the Carolinas just as it has everywhere else. Internet cafés seem to be rebounding after nearly disappearing from view—you'll find them listed the appropriate destination chapters. Some public libraries boast Internet access, and most business hotels (and not a few B&Bs) offer separate modem lines, or at least modem hookups that use your room phone line.

NEWSPAPERS

Nearly any Coastal Carolina town of any size has its own newspaper; reading these can give you a good feel for the pace of life in a town. The major paper in the Outer Banks region is the *Outer Banks Sentinel,* website: www.outerbanks.nc.us/Sentinel. A major paper in the Central Albemarle region is the New Bern *Sun Journal,* website: www.newbernsunjournal.com. The *New York Times*–owned *Wilmington Star-News* dominates the Cape Fear region, website: www.wilmington.net/starnews. Along the South Carolina Coast, the Charleston *Post and Courier* is well thought of and well read, as is the Myrtle Beach *Sun News.* You can find them online at www.charlestonnet.com and www.thesunnews.com.

You'll also find *USA Today* all around the region. The *New York Times* is available in the business districts of major cities.

RADIO

In most of Coastal Carolina, you'll find a wide variety of music, with a heavy emphasis on country but liberal dosings of urban, metal, and pop stations. Contemporary Christian rock music stations have popped up in a couple of the bigger cities. As usual nearly everywhere in the state, the left end of the FM dial is where you'll find gospel stations (including the new K-LOVE network affiliate), and the South Carolina Public Radio/NPR affiliate, where faithful listeners will find *All Things Considered, Prairie Home Companion,* and *Car Talk,* along with local shows, a few of which highlight regional music.

The AM dial contains gospel music and preaching, country music, some local news and talk shows, and the sonic strip mall that is American syndicated talk radio today.

Classic Radio Stations
WGQR 105.7 FM, Elizabethtown: This "Oldies and Beach" station is probably my favorite station in the United States today. Playing a unique combination of (usually nonstandard) oldies and beach hits, with disc jockeys high on personality and low on attitude, this great little station has won the Small Market Beach Station of the Year award for a number of years—and little wonder. Saturday afternoons feature a beach countdown; every hour of every day includes a "beach break"—three beach favorites, back to back. With all of this, they also sandwich in small-town commercials and live broadcasts of local events. Best of all, you can listen to them before you get to Carolina, at their website: www.wgqr-1057.com/aircheck.htm.

WAVF 96 ("WAVE") FM, Charleston: This may not be the state's most-listened-to station, but you'll probably see more bumper stickers for this station on cars (and skateboards, and traffic signs, and park benches) than any other. WAVE is the prime alternative rock station in the state. It features regional bands.

WTMA 1250 AM: Listen to this Charleston standby in the mornings (before the station goes satellite for Rush Limbaugh and the usual talk offerings) to hear Dan Moon, a local celebrity and a Charleston institution for over a decade, and get a sense of the workings of the city, as he broadcasts live from store openings, flea markets, and just about any event with room for a mobile unit. From 1:00– 4:00 P.M., Nancy Wolf talks South Carolina politics. Listen online at www.wtma.com.

WKCL 91.5 FM: WKCL boasts "100,000 Watts of the Lord's Power, 24 Hours a Day." It's a good place to take a peek into the large evangelical Christian subculture in the state. Musically most of the songs, with different lyrics, would be considered adult contemporary.

WPAL 730 AM, 100.9 FM: Bills itself as "The Soul of Charleston," featuring black gospel preaching and music, and electrifying combinations of both.

Up in the Outer Banks, **Dixie 105.7 (WRSF-FM)** rules the country ranks, and **WORB, 105.7 "The Rock"** provides the Banks with its alternative rock station. Good place to keep up on who's playing where locally.

TOURIST INFORMATION

Statewide Offices

In North Carolina contact the North Carolina Division of Tourism, Film and Sports Development, 301 N. Wilmington St., 4324 Mail Service Center, Raleigh, NC 27699-4324, 800/847-4862 or 919/733-8372, website: www.visitnc.com. In South Carolina call the South Carolina Department of Parks, Recreation and Tourism at 803/734-1700 or fax 803/734-0138 to request a copy of the very helpful and up-to-date *South Carolina Travel Guide,* a travel map of the state, and other materials. Or write to P.O. Box 71, Columbia, SC 29202. Visit the department online at www.travelsc.com.

International visitors from the U.K. can contact the South Carolina Tourism Office at 20 Barclay Rd., Croydon CRO 1JN, United Kingdom, tel. 181/688-1141, fax 181/666-0365, email: 100447.657@compuserve.com. Other Europeans should contact the South Carolina Tourism Office, Simensstrasse 9, 63263 Neu-Isenburg, Germany, tel. 6102/722-752, fax 6102/722-409, email: 100753.500@compuserve.com.

International visitors from other regions should contact the **International Marketing Office,** South Carolina Department of Parks, Recreation and Tourism, 1205 Pendleton St., Columbia, SC 29201, 803/734-0129, fax 803/734-1163.

Welcome Centers

If you're driving into the Carolinas, be sure to stop at one of North Carolina's eight welcome centers, and/or South Carolina's 10 welcome centers along the major highways at the state borders, as well as one in the middle of South Carolina on I-95 in Santee. The folks at these offices are generally very knowledgeable and helpful about the states' recreational opportunities and can help you plan to get the most possible from your stay on the Carolina coasts. They also dispense free maps and about a zillion pamphlets from every region of the state. They can even help you set up tee times.

MONEY

The U.S. dollar is divided into 100 cents. Paper notes include $1, $2, $5, $10, $20, and $100; the $2 bill is rarely seen but perfectly legal. Coin denominations are one cent (penny), five cents (nickel), 10 cents (dime), 25 cents (quarter), 50 cents (the rare half dollar), and the $1 coin (even more rare). Unfortunately there are many counterfeit bills in circulation, usually hundreds or twenties.

In the late 1990s, the old $100, $50, and $20 bills were replaced with new bills featuring much larger portraits on the front side. Tens and fives soon followed. If you're handed one of the earlier forms of bills, rest assured that they're still accepted as legal tender.

Banks

It's best to carry traveler's checks in U.S. dollar denominations. Most businesses and tourist-related services accept traveler's checks. Only in very small towns will you run into problems with traveler's checks, or exchanging foreign money. The solution? Drive to a larger town. It's not a very big state.

Most major banks in big cities are open 9 A.M.–5 P.M. Hours for branches in smaller towns vary. Banks are usually closed on Saturday, Sunday, and most national and some religious holidays. However some larger banks open for limited hours on Saturday, frequently 9 A.M.–1 P.M. Branch offices are becoming more omnipresent in the United States, popping up in grocery stores and shopping malls across the state. But typically only major commercial banks have the ability to exchange foreign currency. Though banks are your best bet, other good places to obtain U.S. dollars include international airports and American Express offices. Check the local phone book Yellow Pages for addresses and phone numbers. Many banks have toll-free numbers answered by an automated voice, which gives options for various numbers. Stay on the line or press the appropriate number to speak to a human.

Most businesses accept major credit cards—MasterCard, Visa, and American Express. On occasion, in very small towns and rural areas, cash (US$) will be the only accepted form of money. It's also possible to get cash advances from your credit card at designated automated-teller machines (ATMs). ATM machines are omnipresent in the United States. You'll see them in grocery stores, shopping malls, sometimes at festivals or fairs, sporting events, street corners, and, of course, at most banks. In Charleston the police department got proactive about the number of incidents occurring around ATM machines and installed one inside the lobby of the police building.

In many supermarkets it's now possible to pay for your groceries with a credit card or a debit card, which deducts the amount directly from your checking or savings account. Often this method incurs a small transaction fee; check with your bank for details. For you to use ATMs and debit cards, your bank must be affiliated with one of the several ATM networks. The most common affiliations are Star, Cirrus, Plus, and Interlink.

Taxes

Expect to pay 6 percent sales tax on anything you buy, except food at the grocery store. You'll also pay a room tax at lodging establishments.

Tipping

It's standard in the Carolinas to tip your waitperson 15 percent of the bill for acceptable service. If you're at a breakfast place, where the bills are lower but the staff is often just as hardworking as those at more expensive dinner spots, you may wish to tip at least 20 percent. Never tip the regular amount to reward rude or inattentive service—it only encourages more of the same.

Tip airport skycaps $1 a bag; the same for hotel bellhops.

READING

You'll find either a college or public library in most every good-sized town along the Carolina coasts. The Main Charleston County Library at 68 Calhoun Street has a fine selection. Probably the coolest little library in the region is the Edgar Allan Poe Library, built into the old fort works on Sullivan's Island.

You'll find all of these libraries listed in the appropriate destination chapters.

ODDS AND ENDS

Photo Etiquette

You will see quaint homes in Carolina. You will want to take pictures of them.

If you're in downtown Charleston, and the house is one of the famous old Charleston houses along the Battery or on Rainbow Row, then go ahead and snap away. If you're up in a tiny Albemarle town and you want to take a picture of a private citizen's house, then you might try to get permission first. It's not really a legal requirement, just a courtesy. And courtesy goes a long way in Carolina.

Some of the savvy basketweaving Gullah women you'll see in Charleston and along U.S. 17 north of Mount Pleasant will charge you $5 or more to take their picture.

Camping Gear

With rain showers so unpredictable, particularly in summer, you'll want a tarp over your tent as well as beneath it. If you're car-camping, consider a screen canopy, inside of which you'll be able to sip your hot cocoa without enduring mosquito and no-see-um bites. If you'll be hiking long distances from a car that can get you to a doctor, then bring a snakebite kit.

WEIGHTS AND MEASURES

The Carolinas, like all other states in the United States, do not use the metric system. For help converting weights, distances, and temperatures, see the table at the back of this book.

Electricity
Despite what Hollywood may have led you to believe, it's rare to find anywhere in the South that doesn't vibrate with electrical power. Electrical outlets in the United States run on a 110 or 120V AC. Most plugs are either two flat prongs or two flat and one round. Adapters for 220V appliances are available in hardware or electronic stores.

Time Zone
The Carolinas rest within eastern time zone, the same one used by New York City, Boston, and Florida. It is three hours ahead of Los Angeles.

VACCINATIONS

The United States currently has no vaccination requirements for any international traveler. Check with the U.S. embassy or consulate in your country and request an update on this information before you leave.

The International Health Regulations (IHR) adopted by the World Health Organization (WHO) state that countries may require an International Certificate of Vaccination (ICV) against yellow fever. An ICV can also be required if you are traveling from an infected area. For current information look up the website for WHO at www.who.ch, or the Centers for Disease Control and Prevention at www.cdc.gov.travel/travel.html.

NAGS HEAD AND THE OUTER BANKS

Few stretches of American coastline hold the mystique of North Carolina's Outer Banks. What traveler of America hasn't looked at a map of the East Coast and wanted to drive the Outer Banks? The long tail of land swoops down from the Virginia line, swerving erratically east, sloppily missing the coast's right turn at Sandy Point, veering out into the ocean as North America's thin shadow, miles and miles from shore, only gradually bending back inland after Cape Hatteras. What would life be like out there on America's thin shadow, to look to either side of the road, and see water? *Surely,* we think, *things would be different.* In an over-complicated age, the Outer Banks, way out there in the Atlantic, seem to offer a scaled down, simpler world. So does the tiny burg of Shamrock, Texas, but it doesn't also offer sandy white beaches and world-renowned outdoor recreation.

And yet, as with most of the Carolina Coast, those who loved the Banks first loved them for reasons other than physical beauty. The aborig-inal Croatan on Hatteras and the British settler who later settled on these stormy banks came because access to the ocean meant access to fish. And while the Bankers, the traditional name for the area's independent, rough-and-tumble residents, have often been described as a people who face the ocean, they repeatedly built their villages on the sound side of the islands, doors turned west toward the markets where they'd sell their catches. According to Roger L. Payne's engaging *Place Names of the Outer Banks,* so strong was this inland orientation that if a Banker made reference to the "back of the beach" he or she was clearly referring to the ocean side of the beach, as though the "front" side of the island was obviously the landward side.

After the tourist trade began in the 1920s, Bankers came to value their sandy beaches as money makers, and the term's definition reversed meanings. Now the ocean side of the island, with its million dollar homes and pricey hotels, is considered the front of the beach.

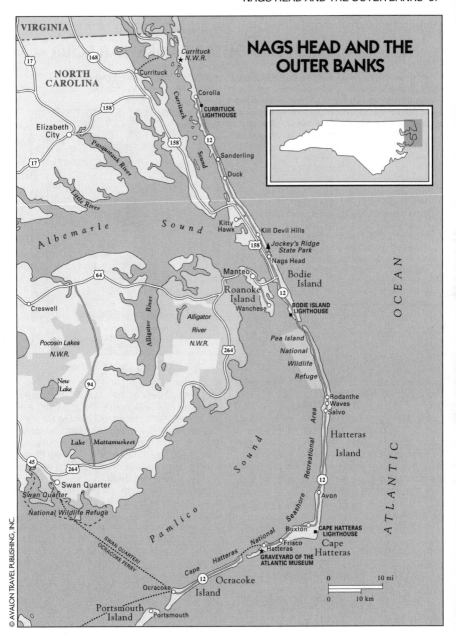

NAGS HEAD AND THE OUTER BANKS

VIRGINIA

NORTH CAROLINA

Currituck N.W.R.

Currituck

Corolla

CURRITUCK LIGHTHOUSE

Elizabeth City

Sanderling

Duck

Pasquotank River

Little River

Albemarle Sound

Kitty Hawk

Kill Devil Hills

Jockey's Ridge State Park

Nags Head

Manteo

Bodie Island

Roanoke Island

Wanchese

BODIE ISLAND LIGHTHOUSE

Creswell

Alligator River

Alligator River N.W.R.

Pea Island

National

Wildlife

Refuge

Pocosin Lakes N.W.R.

New Lake

Rodanthe

Waves

Salvo

Lake Mattamuskeet

Hatteras Island

Pamlico Sound

National Seashore Recreational Area

Avon

Swan Quarter

Swan Quarter National Wildlife Refuge

SWAN QUARTER/ OCRACOKE FERRY

Buxton

CAPE HATTERAS LIGHTHOUSE

Frisco

Hatteras

Cape Hatteras

GRAVEYARD OF THE ATLANTIC MUSEUM

Cape Hatteras National

Ocracoke

Ocracoke Island

Portsmouth Island

Portsmouth

OCEAN

ATLANTIC

ATLANTIC

0   10 mi

0   10 km

© AVALON TRAVEL PUBLISHING, INC.

LIGHTHOUSES: THE OUTER BANKS' FAB FOUR

Of all the lighthouses along the Carolina Coasts, the most famous are the four most easily accessible to motorists on the Outer Banks: **Corolla Lighthouse, Bodie Island Lighthouse, Cape Hatteras Lighthouse,** and **Ocracoke Lighthouse.**

It can be hard to remember which is which, but not for Beatles fans: Cape Hatteras is clearly the Paul McCartney of the bunch—the cute, popular, romantic one, the lighthouse made for the cover of magazines. Ocracoke (John Lennon) is the oldest, quite bright, but also visually mellower. No flashy stripes here. Bodie Island Lighthouse (Ringo) is the most social of the bunch, located as it is just south of bustling Nags Head. And the current structure replaces an earlier, pre-Civil War lighthouse (read: Pete Best). Unpainted Corolla Light (George), long an icon of asceticism far beyond the reach of the paved road, nowadays finds itself very much in the midst of high-dollar developments.

Whether Cape Lookout Lighthouse is Stu Sutcliffe, Billy Preston, or Murry the K, is beyond me.

Hatteras Light

The Outer Banks were not an easy place to settle. Sir Walter Raleigh certainly didn't have any luck on Roanoke Island. And though human life here traces back to aboriginal times, so do violent hurricanes. Ironically one of the early aids to the Banks' settlement came from shipwreck survivors who swam to shore and decided to stay. Still, lifesaving station crews and lighthouse keepers were the only people living along stretches of this brutal coast for many years. Though tourism began in force even in the 1840s, not until roads—and then paved roads—came did the Banks become accessible enough to warrant serious development.

Orientation

The Outer Banks are really not all that long: only 107 miles separate the Banks' northernmost and southernmost landmarks, Currituck Light at Corolla from Ocracoke Light at Ocracoke—less than the distance between Los Angeles and San Diego.

But neither is driving the Banks just any spin on the interstate. You'll follow two-lane N.C. 12 all the way, take one forty-minute ferry ride (to get off Ocracoke you'll take a second), and pass through over a dozen towns and villages. In between the settlements, the state and federal governments protect much of the Banks—most of Ocracoke Island, all of undeveloped Hatteras, and a good bit of the Northern Banks. Though you could conceivably drive the Banks in half a day, you could easily spend a week or two just discovering them.

Starting at the north, the first widely-recognized section of the Banks are the **Northern Beaches,** which include Carova, Corolla, Duck, and Southern Shores—all high-end bedroom communities. Sometimes also included in the "Northern Beaches" designation, but often classified on their own (often simply as "the Nag's Head Area") are the three highly developed, touristy towns of Kitty Hawk, Kill Devil Hills, and Nags Head. Due west of Nags Head is Roanoke Island, quieter, more rural, and more historic. South of this—and separated by Oregon Inlet—is **Hatteras Island,** less developed but developed earlier. South of the little village of Hatteras is the northern tip of Ocracoke Island, which is totally undeveloped except for Ocracoke Village at the island's southern end.

NAGS HEAD AND VICINITY

One thing visitors to the Northern Banks notice is the use of milepost designations in denoting locations from the Kitty Hawk Pier(Milepost 1) south through Kill Devil Hills and Nags Head. The higher the number, the further south you are.

Nags Head
Of all the place names associated with the Outer Banks, perhaps "Nags Head" most spurs the imagination. From what heinous act could this Coppolaesque name possibly derive? Among locals you'll hear a number of name creation myths. Here's the one I wish were true:

OUTER BANKS HIGHLIGHTS

- **Cape Hatteras National Seashore,** Hatteras and Ocracoke Islands

- **Elizabethan Gardens,** Roanoke Island

- **Jockey's Ridge State Park**, Nags Head

- *The Lost Colony* Outdoor Drama, Roanoke Island

- **Manteo Waterfront,** Roanoke Island

- **Nags Head Woods Ecological Preserve,** Kill Devil Hills

- **Ocracoke Village,** Ocracoke

- **Roanoke Festival Park,** Manteo

- **Scarborough Faire, Scarborough Lane, The Waterfront Shops,** Duck

- **Weeping Radish Brewery and Bavarian Restaurant,** Roanoke Island

- **Wright Brothers National Memorial,** Kill Devil Hills

---

in days of old, local "Bankers" used to hang burning lanterns around horses' necks on dark nights and allow the horses to mill about on the shore. These bobbing lights, to the eyes of sailors at sea, would resemble the bobbing lights of boats at harbor. Lured to a harbor that was not, the ships would wreck, enabling the rapacious Bankers to practice their homegrown brand of piracy.

Unfortunately most serious students of local history call this story doubtful. No contemporary accounts or archaeological evidence supports the charge that Bankers, though a rough lot, ever practiced such treachery, and anyway, *just you try to hang a searing, smoking lantern around the neck of a nag,* they say.

More mundane but likelier theories have it that sailors viewing the area from sea thought Nags Head resembled the head of a horse. Yawn. Or that an Englishman who settled in the area called his spread "Nags Head" because the region reminded him of Nags Head on England's Scilly Islands—the last bit of England westbound sailors often saw before heading for the Americas.

Maybe so, but I'm still rooting for the story about the lanterns.

Whether they did in the past or not, these days many industrious Bankers certainly do hang out lights—of the electric variety—along the bypass and the Beach Road, hoping to lure travelers from afar.

Nags Head is bigger and less quaint than most of us would like to imagine, but still smaller and less busy than you may have heard. Its development reaches nowhere near the level of, say, Myrtle Beach. Population through the winter months still runs around 1,800, though that increases manifold during summer.

Kitty Hawk
North of both Nags Head and Kill Devil Hills, Kitty Hawk is most famous to school children of the world as the place where the Wright Brothers

> *"Planters, merchants, and professional men usually have a snug cottage at Nag's Head, to which they remove their families, with the plainer and more common articles of household furniture, one or more horses, a cow, and such vehicles as are fitted for use on sandy roads. . . . One, two, three, sometimes half a dozen servants accompany the family. . . . Gentlemen who are fond of foxhunting bring their horse and hounds, and go galloping over the treacherous sands, much to the hazard of both horse and rider."*
>
> —George Higby Throop, *Nags Head, or, Two Months among the 'Bankers'*, 1849

started the aeronautical age—though of course, they really did it over at Kill Devil Hills. This was just the nearest local settlement and post office. The origin of Kitty Hawk's name is disputed; most likely it's the result of English tongues wrestling with Native American words: specifically, "Chickehauk," the name of a local Indian settlement, or "Etacrewac," the name for the general region. Today Kitty Hawk seems just a bit more worn than the other towns. Hurricane Fran did a good bit of damage here. The Kitty Hawk Fishing Pier has recently been rebuilt.

Kill Devil Hills

The word "kill" isn't a real positive one to find in a place-name; fortunately, the word "devil" immediately afterward seems to make it okay. ("Kill People Hills," for instance, might not really draw the tourists). So where'd the name come from? As usual the most interesting explanations are the least likely to be true. One theory has it that 1) in yet another soul-for-gold-deal-gone-bad, a Banker dug a hole to the bottom of (then unnamed) Kill Devil Hill and tricked Old Scratch into falling into the hole, where the Banker quickly buried him. A second theory concerns the disappearance of several casks of rum from a shipment beached hereabouts. According to this theory, 2) a Banker named Ike offered to spend the night guarding the rum. When he caught the guilty neighbor returning to steal some more, he chased him off, but (to save his neighbor from prosecution) explained previous thefts as having been performed by the devil himself, whom Ike had dutifully killed. Yet another theory has it that 3) the rum made here-

abouts during colonial times was so nasty that people used to say it could "kill the devil," hence the name; and yet another suggests that 4) mariners thought the land mass itself was so treacherous to sail around that the trip itself could "kill the devil." A little more likely theory references the fact that both 5) "kill" and "devil" are Dutch terms referring to, respectively, "stream" and "sand spout," which given the geography makes a kind of sense, but unfortunately there's no evidence that the Dutch had anything to do with naming the area. (They probably stayed away, what with all the satanic apparitions). The dullest and likely most accurate theory has it that 6) the name references the common shorebird popularly called the "killdeer." "Killdeer Hills" was one of the early names for Kill Devil Hills.

Other than Satan being buried here, the most notable event in local history was one of humanity's most important: here, in 1903, Orville Wright became the first person to fly a propelled craft.

SIGHTS

Wright Brothers National Memorial

This 60-foot monument, 800 Colington Rd., 252/441-7430, stands atop the (now) grass-covered 90-foot Kill Devil Hill, from which the Wright Brothers began the world's first controlled (more-or-less) flight, a wobbly jaunt into 20 mph winds that covered 120 feet in the course of twelve seconds. Meaning that as Orville sputtered his way into history, even the slowest sprinter on a weak junior high track squad could have outpaced him. For that matter, since he flew at an elevation of about twelve feet, a good high school pole-vaulter could have vaulted over him.

From aviation's humble beginnings, the rapidity with which we human beings took to the sky after the Wright Brothers provided the initial boost takes one's breath away: only 66 years after Orville lifted off this dune, Neil Armstrong set his foot on the moon. Within twelve years of Kill Devil Hills, men were using airplanes to shoot and bomb each other from the sky.

The monument is really bigger and more impressive in person than in is in pictures, and it's also eye-catching when illuminated at night. A couple times a year it is even opened up and you can walk the stairs inside to the top. Built during the Depression in 1932 of granite from Andy Griffith's hometown in Mt. Airy, the obelisk stands far higher than the Wrights ever flew while here. For that matter, so does the roof of the 1960s-styled museum down at the bottom of the hill. The monument's inspiring inscription reads:*In commemoration of the conquest of the air by the brothers Wilbur and Orville Wright conceived by Genius, achieved by Dauntless Resolution and Unconquerable Faith.* The "Genius" line sounds like it's describing Wilbur and Orville's mother, but it's inspiring nonetheless.

For me though, the visitors center and the markers at the bottom of the hill are what really bring the historic flight to life. The visitors center (which from the outside resembles a miniature LAX, circa 1969) features various exhibits on early aviation and the Wright Brothers, and a model of the first plane—the Smithsonian holds the original. There are marble markers at the bottom of the hill, between the visitors center and the monument, just after you pass the reconstructed Wright Brothers workshop and living quarters on the way up. The markers note the take-off and landing spots of the Wrights' four flights December 17, 1903, the longest (and last) of which was Wilbur's 59-second flight, covering 852 feet. After that a wind gust totaled the world's first airplane, and the two dauntlessly resolute preacher's kids from Dayton packed up and headed home for the holidays. Admission to the park runs $2 per person or $4 a vehicle.

Bodie Island Lighthouse, N.C. 12, 252/441-5711, is named after an island that is no longer an island proper. North of Oregon Inlet (and before Oregon Inlet was cut by a storm), it used to be you'd run across Gunt Inlet. And north of that, at the next narrow spot on the island (south of Washington Baum Bridge), was Roanoke Inlet. Nowadays folks use "Bodie Island" (pronounced "body" or "bawdy", if you will) to refer to various stretches of land, sometimes from Oregon Inlet north to Kitty Hawk, but usually just from Oregon Inlet north to the site of the old Roanoke inlet—near the site of the modern-day bridge to Roanoke Island.

The Bodie Island Lighthouse was built in 1872, just after (and by the same designer of) Cape Hatteras Lighthouse. It stands 156 feet and is only open for climbing some of the time. Call for details.

If you want to see what Kill Devil Hill looked like in the Wrights' day, before it was planted over with grasses to keep it from blowing away, **Jockey's Ridge State Park,** U.S. 158, Milepost 12, 252/441-7132 gives you a chance. The name sounds like a saddle malady, and some say it comes from the fact that this would have been a great place to sit and watch the local horse races in days of yore. But early maps refer to the place as Jackey Ridge, meaning it was named after the man who owned the ridge and surrounding land. The ridge was doomed for improvement in 1973, when the feisty Carolista Baum planted herself in front of a bulldozer and stopped the march of progress in its Caterpillar tracks. In 1975 the dune—the East Coast's highest, rising some 140 feet above the ocean and sound (both of which you can see from the ridge top)—officially became a state park. Though it's nothing compared to, say, Death Valley, in

END OF 1st FLIGHT
TIME: 12 SECONDS
DISTANCE: 120 FT
DEC. 17. 1903
PILOT: ORVILLE

Wright Brothers National Memorial

Death Valley all you can see is other dunes, whereas here you can see the water, sailboats, and many, many rental homes. It's a fun place to take up hang-gliding (Kitty Hawk Kites operates a flight school here) and fun to tumble down. Check out the visitors center, then head over to the dunes. Take off your shoes and enjoy yourself. Summer nights at 8 P.M., head up to the top of the ridge for the ranger-led "Sunset on the Ridge" program. You'll hear about local history and legends, and get to see a beautiful sunset in the west. Also here is the 1.5-mile **Tracks in the Sand Trail,** which begins in the visitors center parking lot and carries you through clumps of live oak, loblolly pine, wax myrtles, and various wildflowers and marsh grasses to the Roanoke Sound.

The Nature Conservancy manages over 1400 acres of maritime forest known as the **Nags Head Woods Ecological Preserve,** 701 W. Ocean Acres Dr., 252/441-2525. It's a fine place to disappear from the traffic and crowds at the beaches. Here you'll see ponds, swamps, beech, hickory, oak and pine, and you couldn't throw a rock without hitting a songbird—which, incidentally, would be frowned upon. Call for hours, and to hear about the various paddling trips the folks here are always putting together.

To get there, turn west at milepost 9.5, Ocean Acres Drive, off of U.S. 158 in Kill Devil Hills. Follow the road until you reach the preserve. After you do, you'll find, canoe trips, a gift shop and visitors center, where you can pick up a trail map, more than five miles of trails to hike. The longest trail, the two mile-long Sweetgum Swamp Trail, climbs a number of ridges and takes you though a variety of plant life. The shortest, a quarter-mile loop starting at the deck of the visitor center, comes with a separate trail pamphlet interpreting 10 different points of interest. One word of advice: bring insect repellent and boots, if possible, to ward off mosquitoes and deer ticks.

ACCOMMODATIONS

Hotels and Motels

On the low end you have **Travelers Inn Motor Lodge,** Milepost 16.5 on Beach Road, Nags Head, 252/441-5242, with a combination of rooms, efficiencies, and cottages, whose rates dip as low as $21 during the off-season. Perhaps cheapest on the oceanfront is **Sandspur Motel & Cottage Court,** on Milepost 15.75, in Nags Head, 800/522-8486 or 252/441-6993, website: www.sandspur@outerbanks.com, with rates as low as $28 during the off-season. Down on the same stretch of beach stands **Beach Haven Motel,** 4104 Virginia Dare Trail, 888/559-0506 or 252/261-4785, website: www.beach-havenmotel.com, offers six efficiencies, a restaurant, a pier, canoes, boats, rafts, open mid-March through November. $47–144. The **Owens' Motel,** Beach Rd., Milepost 16.5, 252/441-6361, website: www.owensmotel.com, offers 17 rooms, 8 efficiencies, a pool, and a restaurant. Closed winters—call for availability. $55–$95, $100–120 for efficiencies. Steady and chain-regular is the **Days Inn Oceanfront,** 1801 North Virginia Dare Trail, $50–200.

Holiday Inn–Nag's Head, 1601 Virginia Dare Trail, 800/843-1249 or 252/441-6333, is hard to beat for location or view. As you choose your floor, keep in mind that it's hard to beat a sliding door leading directly to the sand, and you'll find these only on the first-floor oceanfront rooms. However, the higher floors provide an ocean view unobstructed by the sand dune between the ocean and the inn. Located within walking distance of a handful of good restaurants. $46–200.

Next door you'll find **Miller's Oceanfront Motel** (aka M.O.M.), 1509 S. Virginia Dare Trail, 252/441-7404, is a recently renovated 1950s family motel with 38 rooms, a cottage, 28 efficiencies, and six suites. It's right next across from **Miller's Steak and Seafood,** 252/441-7674, which is a good selling point. Open February–December. $59–89-175, Co-owner Eddie Miller has worked here since the 1950s and bought the place in the 1970s. Ask the manager (Eddie's sister) and maybe you'll hear the story of when a young Eddie backed his car into the motel swimming pool.

On the far side of the Holiday Inn stands the dune-side **Ramada Inn,** 1701 S. Virginia Dare Trail, 800/635-1824 or 252/441-2151, offering 172 rooms, $53–209.

Bed-and-Breakfasts, Inns

First Colony Inn, 6720 South Virginia Dare Trail, Nags Head, 800/368-9390 or 252/441-2343, website: www.firstcolonyinn.com. This

National Register of Historic Places landmark inn was built as a big beach hotel in 1932. Reopened in 1991, it has received four diamonds from AAA. The 26 rooms (private baths) and public areas are furnished with antiques. Breakfast buffet, wraparound porches, dune-top gazebo, afternoon tea, heated towel racks(!), and use of the pool all come for the $75–265 room charge. In high season especially, the prices here will set you back some, but they're not that much more than what you'll pay at, say, the Ramada, and the stay here is so perfectly "Nags Head" that you'll remember it forever. Nonsmoking, no pets. Children are welcome.

The traditional two-story Nags Head house with a picket fence, the **Cypress House Inn,** 500 N. Virgina Dare Trail, 800/554-2764 or 252/441-6127, has six rooms open year-round. Built as a private hunting and fishing lodge in the 1940s, Karen Roos and Leon Faso's inn stands only 150 yards from the Atlantic Ocean, and offers six guest rooms with queen-size beds, private shower baths, and ceiling fans. Outside you'll find a rocker-rich wraparound porch. Full breakfast included. Bicycles, beach towels, and chairs available. Smoking is forbidden, as are children 13 and under, and pets (smoking or non-) of any age.

Greg Hamby's **The Cypress Moon Inn,** 1206 Harbor Court, Kitty Hawk 877/905-5060, website: www.cypressmooninn.com, $125–175, stands within maritime forest on the soundfront; a two-story porch outside the bedrooms offers private access. Not exactly "Old Nags Head," but a nice retreat from the hubbub of the main strip.

Three Seasons Bed and Breakfast, 4628 Seascape Dr., 800/847-3373 or 252/261-4791, offers four rooms, golf privileges, fireplace, tennis privileges. Open April–November. $89–120.

Newer is the **The White Egret B&B,** 1045 Colington Rd., 888/387-7719, website: www.whiteegret.com, $85–110. Three rooms, all with a view of the bay, private baths and Jacuzzis, TV, VCR, and a private phone with Internet hook-up.

Cottage/Condo Rentals

The traditional way to stay in Nags Head is in a cottage, usually rented by the week. **Nags Head Fishing Pier Cottages,** Milepost 12, Beach Road, website: www.nagsheadpier.com, 252/441-5141, rents to happy anglers and their fam-

ilies. Depending on the time and the particular cottage you choose, rates can vary anywhere from $350 a week to $1100. They'll often rent for shorter periods too. **Coleman's Cottages** rents a number of locations all the way from Kitty Hawk to Hatteras; rates vary from $395 to over $2000 a week.

Over 30 rental agencies operate in the North Beach area alone. A couple of the bigger ones are **Ocean Vacations,** 2501 N. Croatan Hwy., 252/441-3127 or 800/548-2033, website: www.oceanfun.com, has 200 cottages, 75 condos to rent. **Sun Realty,** 800/334-4745, website: www.sunrealtync.com., offers over 1,100 stays on the Outer Banks. See website: www.outerbanks.org for more information. At **www.carolinadesigns.com, www.resortrealty.com** and **www.seasiderealty.com,** among others, you can reserve a rental home online, 24 hours a day.

FOOD

Seafood and Steaks

Etheridge's Seafood, Milepost 9.5, Kill Devil Hills, 252/441-2645, is a place where it seems as if everybody I know who stopped into Nags Head stumbled across the place (usually by asking a local for the best local seafood) and raves about it. Very fresh . . . order something you think you've ordered a hundred times before and you'll be surprised how much better it is at Etheridge's. Items on the menu are named after various members of the Etheridge family, three generations of which serve and have served the restaurant over the years. Entrées start at $9.95. Full bar too. If you're here early in the day, stop by for the Early Bird Feast from 3:30–5:30 P.M., featuring a seafood cheese crock and crackers, a cup of bouillabaisse or the soup of the day, a salad, and a choice of seafood entrées, as well as dessert—including a good key lime pie.

While we're in the family way, I'd best mention the restaurants owned by the Miller dynasty, the same family that owns Miller's Oceanfront Motel. The spot with the better location is **Miller's Waterfront Restaurant,** Milepost 16, at the U.S. 158 Bypass, Nags Head, 252/441-6151, a fine place for breakfast overlooking the sound ($.99

specials), and an even better place for a sunset dinner. Also with the $.99 breakfasts is the original Miller restaurant (since 1978) is **Miller's Steak and Seafood,** Milepost 9.5, 252/441-7674, just across from the motel, and a convenient walk from the Holiday Inn or Ramada as well. Along these same lines is **Owens' Restaurant,** Milepost 16.5 Beach Road, 252/441-7309, founded in 1946, offers dinners, mostly in the high teens. **Awful Arthur's,** Milepost 6, Beach Road, Kill Devil Hills, 252/441-5955, is the Hussong's Cantina or Salty Dog Café of the Outer Banks. It features an Endless-Spring-Break atmosphere, lots of T-shirts for sale, and some of the funniest commercials you'll ever see. The food's not bad either. Burgers run $3.95–6.95, dinners—heavy on the seafood but including steaks, pasta, and BBQ, run in the low teens. For a near identical experience at Milepost 13, Nags Head, go to Awful Arthur's spin-off restaurant, **Bad Barracuda's.** A hip spot with a tropical theme, the **Rundown Café,** Milepost 1, Beach Road, Kitty Hawk, 252/255-0026, features sandwiches ($6 and up) and full dinners like jerk chicken, Jamaican pork, St. Martin shrimp, and a fish burrito, running in price from $8.95 to $11.95, and served with black beans, rice, and salsa. Along the same lines, **Tortugas' Lie** Milepost 11, Beach Rd., Nags Head, 252/441-7299, website: www.tortugaslie.com, is a friendly little place across the street from the beach, which features some creative chow including a wonderful coconut shrimp, grilled fish and black bean burrito ($6.95), and Coco Loco Chicken—chicken breast rolling coconut and fried with lime curry dipping sauce ($5.95). You'e welcome to join in the pick-up volleyball games on the court outside.

The Wharf, Milepost 11.5, Beach Road, Nags Head, 252/441-7457, offers a very popular seafood buffet for $15.95. And finally, while I normally stay away from recommending chain restaurants, the folks at the **Western Sizzlin Restaurant,** Milepost 8.75, 804 S. Croatan Hwy., Kill Devil Hills, 252/441-4594, have really gone out of their way to bring a local feel to their restaurant. They offer up a strong buffet as well. And the quaint **Old Nags Head General Store,** where you'll pay your bill, offers some genuinely engaging items for reasonable prices. Breakfast buffet and Outer Banks seafood buffet. The Friday/Saturday seafood buffet runs $14.99 for

adults; the dinner buffet other nights (which usually includes some seafood) runs $8.99. The popular breakfast buffet runs $5.99.

Barbecue
Who'd think you'd find great barbecue on the Outer Banks? You will, though—in two spots: **Bubba's BBQ** soundside in Frisco, 252/995-5421, and **Pigman's Bar-B-Que,** Milepost 9.5, 1606 S. Croatan Hwy., Kill Devil Hills, 252/441-6803, website: www.pigman.com. Of these, Bubba's is the tried and true, small town barbecue joint with the bored teenage help (at least, the times I was there), the great smoked pulled pork, ribs, (also beef and turkey), and the Mason jars full of sauce by the cash register. It's added a second strip-mall location in Avon, 252/995-4385. Sandwiches run around $3.50; most dinners run just under $10. Beer available. Pigman, on the other hand, is much more—it's a barbecue joint on steroids and maybe some other banned substances. It's less an example than a *celebration* of barbecue, the result of a mind that takes barbecue to its logical (and not) conclusion, featuring some fascinating takeoffs on this purest of foods: in addition to the Pork BBQ and the Beef BBQ, Pigman also serves up Turkey BBQ (pretty rare), Tuna-Que, and Catfish-Que. And they all taste great. Sandwiches of the various Ques will run you $3.29–$4.29, add $1.70 for french fries, hush puppies, and slaw. In further implementation of its Rainbow Coalition of Barbecue-attitude, Pigman also serves barbecued "St. Louie Ribs." They'll sell you anything you want (included whole hams) to go, but try to eat here so you can enjoy the fun atmosphere and watch some of the looped (and loopy) Pigman commercials, which play constantly. More upscale but also featuring homemade barbecue, **Jockeys Ribs,** Milepost 13, Beach Road, 252/441-1141, is a little pricier and more of a sit-down place closer to the beach. Great wings. Up in Duck, **Duck's Deli** serves up some pretty good North Carolna and Kansas City Barbecue as well.

Organic Food
Down in Avon on N.C. 12, **The Good Food Store,** 252/995-6986, sells organic foods, herbal supplements, wine, and gifts.

Other Food

If it's late at night, one of the best—and one of the only—alternatives on the Banks is to swing by **Grits 24 Hr Grill,** Outer Banks Mall, Nags Head, 252/449-2888. To some it's just a wannabe small town greasy spoon in a shiny shopping center—and one without great food at that. But it's a (mostly) clean, well-lit place out on the Banks late at night, with a surprising array of options including fresh baked breads and rolls, frozen Caravel Ice Cream items, and (trucked-in) Krispy Kreme donuts. At two in the morning, many miles out into the Atlantic, you can't ask for much more than that. When the sun's out, however, you can ask for a better view than Grits provides, and for this you might head over to the **Kitty Hawk Pier Restaurant,** Milepost 1, 252/261-3151, where the food and decor aren't fancy, but you can eat a good basic breakfast (or lunch or dinner) while sitting over (and looking out on) the Atlantic. Open 6 A.M.–9 P.M. every day. No credit cards. Down at the Nags Head Fishing Pier, Milepost 12, the **Pier House Restaurant** 252/441-5141, is a bit fancier (wood chairs, not vinyl). If you're fishing out on the pier, you can take advantage of their "You Hook 'em—We Cook 'em" special ($4.50 for lunch, $5.95 for dinner).

One thing Grits Grill has going for it is a cool name, and you can say the same thing of **Waffle World,** Milepost 9.5 Bypass, 1504 S. Croatan Hwy., 252/449-6973, open 24 hours in summer. The waffles really are fine, as is the "Texas Size" French Toast. They also serve lunch.

NIGHTLIFE

The best way to find out who's playing where when you get to the Banks is to pick up a free copy of **Coast** and check out their "Club Hoppin'" section. But here's a brief, necessarily incomplete overview of your nightlife options. If you still primarily consider the word "party" to be a verb, you'll probably like **Awful Arthur's,** Milepost 6 on Beach Road, Kill Devil Hills, 252/441-5955, for its drink specials, bar food, and second story, ocean-view lounge. Along the same lines is **Carolinian Oceanfront Hotel Restaurant** Milepost 10.5, Beach Road, Nags Head, 252/441-7171, which also features a deck bar.

The Carolinian offers live entertainment, including comedy acts. **Frisco's Iguana Lounge,** Milepost 4, Kitty Hawk, 252/441-7833, offers dance music, lounge specials, sports on the TV, and even a van to take you home when you've overindulged. **George's Junction,** Milepost 11, Beach Road, Nags Head, 252/441-0606, features national country acts, beach music, and oldies, and a full-service bar. **Jolly Roger Restaurant,** Milepost 6.75, Beach Road, Kill Devil Hills, 252/441-6530, features nightly entertainment, whether that means hearing a local band, or a free-for-all around the karaoke machine. Open year-round.

Madelines, at the Holiday Inn, Milepost 9.5, Beach Road, features a number of different acts, sometimes including Carolina beach music and shagging. **Mama Kwan's Grill and Tiki Bar,** Milepost 9.5 on the bypass, 252/480-0967, is a cozy spot (once you get inside) that features live music and a dance floor until 2 A.M. **Port O'Call Gaslight Saloon,** Milepost 8.5 Beach Road, 252/441-7484, in Kill Devil Hills, features reggae and rock acts, and usually hits you with a cover charge if a band's playing. **Red Drum Tap House,** 2412 S. Virginia Dare Trail, Nags Head, 252/480-1095, offers 18 microbrews on tap, along pub grub and live entertainment. Open year-round. **Rundown Café,** Milepost 1, Beach Road, Kitty Hawk. 252/255-0026, features blues and jazz.

Comedy Club at The Ramada, Milepost 9.5, Beach Road, 252/441-7232, features stand-up on Friday, Saturday, and Sunday at 10 P.M. Eat dinner there before the show, and you'll receive preferred seating. If you find that a good fictitious homicide enhances your dining, call for information about their popular **Murder Mystery Dinner Theatre.**

Kelly's Restaurant & Tavern, Milepost 10, bypass, Nags Head, 252/441-4116, has received the Wine Spectator Award of Excellence. Their tavern doors swing open at 4:30 P.M. Live entertainment. Open all year.

Pool

Shucker's Pub and Billiards at Milepost 8.5, Beach Road (Oceanside Plaza), in Kill Devil Hills, 252/480-1010. 12 pool tables and a whole lot of TVs. **Paradise Billards,** at the Dare Center, Milepost 7, Kill Devil Hills, 252/441-9225, offers Foosball, pool, and big-screen TV.

Movie Theaters

The coolest theater on the Outer Banks is Manteo's little **Pioneer Theatre,** 113 Budleigh Street, 252/473-2216. It's one of the oldest family-owned theaters in America, and it shows one movie, once a day—for three dollars. Other than this, the Outer Banks offers a handful of theaters including, at the north in Corolla, **Corolla Movies 4,** Monterey Plaza Shopping Center, 252/453-2999. Down in Kitty Hawk you'll find the **Kitty Hawk Twin,** Milepost 5, bypass, 252/441-1808, **Cineplex Four,** Milepost 10, on the bypass in Nags Head, 252/441-1808, and the **Avon-Hatteras Four,** in the big Food Lion Shopping Center, Avon, 252/995-9060.

SPORTS, RECREATION, AND SHOPPING

Surfing

The Banks have a long and distinquished history of surfing, dating back to the 1960s. Stellar local surf shops include **Corolla Surf Shop,** in the Corolla Light Village Shops, 252/453-9283, website: www.corollasurfshop.com, which includes a surfing museum inside the store. Down on Hatteras you'll find **Ocean Roots,** across from the Avon Pier, 252/995-3369.

Paddling

Kitty Hawk Sports 3933 S. Croatan Hwy., 252/441-6800, website: www.info@khsports.com, has been in business here since 1981 and runs a variety of creative, quality paddling excursions. From March to December they'll take you out into Pea Island National Wildlife Refuge, Alligator River National Wildlife Refuge, Cape Hatteras National Seashore, and the Kitty Hawk Maritime Forest on two-hour, four-hour, all-day, or overnight tours that explore the salt marshes, sounds, tidal creeks, and ocean. Megan Jones and the rest of the guides for these trips know their wildlife and can help you see—depending on the particular trip—black bear, red wolves, deer, otter, dolphins, osprey, heron, ducks, swans, snakes, turtles, crabs, and more.

Their most popular tour is the Kitty Hawk Woods Maritime Forest Wildlife Tour, which departs from their kayak center in Kitty Hawk, and takes you through a landscape thriving with the critters I mentioned above. You'll even pass by a covered bridge deep in the woods and now accessible only from the water. Costs $35 for 2.5 hours ($19 for children 11 and under who share a double boat with adult). Families often favor the mellow and scenic Sunset Tour, and if that's not dark enough for you, if you're here around a full moon, you can sign up for a full moon tour wherein you paddle by moonlight. Available several nights before and on the full moon. Call for times and prices.

Kitty Hawk Kites, 877/359-8447, also runs a number of interesting tours. Their sea kayaking and surf kayaking classes generally run $35 for beginners classes (two hours) and $49 for three-hour advanced classes. An interesting class perfect for the Outer Banks, the three-hour kayak scuba diving trip ($60), allows you to not only paddle but explore some the local shipwrecks. You'll need your c-card, and you'll need to pay for any dive gear, tanks, or weights. They offer special adaptive paddling classes ($30 hour, $125 a day) for disabled paddlers (available by preregistration only). They also rent kayaks and canoes starting at $10 an hour and $99 a week.

Windsurfing

The Outer Banks are the Promised Land for windsurfers; if you'd like to give it a try, call the folks at Kitty Hawk Sports, 252/441-2756. For $49 they promise to have you skimming like a crooked accountant within three hours. If you have the know-how but not the equipment, they also rent boards with rigs for as low as $20 an hour. In season, meet at their Kitty Hawk Watersports Milepost 16 location at 10 A.M. or 2 P.M., and let the wind blow.

Hang Gliding

The dunes at Jockey's Ridge are the largest migratory sand dunes in North America, ranging in height from 80 to 140 feet. They're pretty much the sort of place Wilbur and Orville Wright were looking for (and found) in Kill Devil Hill (back before it was planted over with grasses): high enough and windy enough to launch from, and soft enough in case the landing doesn't go too well. So it's no surprise perhaps that all the aeronautic ambience in the place where humanity learned to fly would also entice people, even today, to give it a try. Hang gliding has been taught out here for over twenty years. Kitty Hawk Kites has made a special arrangement with the U.S. Park Service, allowing them to hold hang gliding classes on the dunes. Classes run $55 (lessons plus three flights) and up.

Shopping

Duck has some of the best shopping. **Scarborough Lane,** and **Scarborough Faire,** on your right as you drive into the village, have around 30 combined boutiques, shops, and eateries in a pleasant outdoor setting. Faire also includes possibly the Banks' top bookstore, **Island Bookstore,** 252/261-8981. Children's storytime at 4 P.M. on Thursdays. Across the road on the soundfront, **The Waterfront Shops,** feature Duck's General Store (a good place to purchase something with the name "Duck" on it) and the aptly-named **Sunset Ice Cream,** along with a handful of other shops. You'll see plenty of ducks here; stop in the General Store and you can buy a bag of corn to toss their way. The pretty mock-historic **Buccaneer's Walk** at Milepost 4.5 on the bypass in Kitty Hawk, features a number of fun stores including **Voyage Books and Treasures,** 252/261-3667, a toy store, and gift shops.

INFORMATION AND TRANSPORTATION

In an emergency on the Outer Banks, call 911. The number for the Poison Control Center is 800/672-1697.

Getting There

Most people drive to the Outer Banks, either coming over on U.S. 158 through Point Harbor and into Kitty Hawk, or across through Manteo on U.S. 64/264. Yet another way is to access the Banks from the south is to drive north on N.C. 12 from Beaufort until you reach the Cedar Island Ferry. The two-hour ferry ride takes you into the town of Ocracoke. If you want to continue north onto Hatteras Island, you'll need to take a second, shorter ferry. There's a fee for the two-hour Cedar Island Ferry, but the forty-minute Ocracoke/Hatteras ferry is free.

If getting to the Banks for you will include flying, note that by far the closest major airport to the Outer Banks is **Norfolk International Airport,** Norfolk, Virginia, 804/855-7845. From there you can rent a car and drive down to the Outer Banks.

If you don't want to spend the money for a rental car, consider taking **The Connection,** 252/473-2777, website: www.calltheconnection.com, a shuttle service that will get you from the Norfolk Airport to anywhere on the Outer Banks. Prices vary depending on the date and your destination, but it'll cost around $90 to get to Nags Head and around $120 to get to Corolla, $178 for Hatteras. Ocracoke, dead-end trip that it is, runs the most by far: upwards of $250. The good news is that it only costs $10 per additional passenger, so if there's three or four of you splitting the fare, things can get downright reasonable. Travel between 6 A.M. and 6 P.M. and you can ask for their discount rates, which should save you upwards of $10.

Getting Around

If you're going to rent a car, presumably you'll rent it in Norfolk or at whatever airport your use to access the Outer Banks. However, if you find yourself on the Banks and looking for a rental car, consider **Enterprise Rent-a-Car** in Manteo at 252/480-1838. If you want a 4x4 for some off-road driving, you might try Junior Suttle's **Outer Banks Jeep,** Milepost 5.5, Route 158 bypass, Kill Devil Hills 252/441-1146, ext. 7, website: www.outerbanksjeeep.com. Junior will rent you a Jeep or Dodge Caravan for $100 or $50 a day, respectively, plus 25 cents a mile after 75 miles. You can also rent a Dodge Stratus or Plymouth Breeze four-door for $39.95, plus mileage. For a little less you can rent from **U-Save Auto Rental,** located at Midgette Auto Sales, 252/491-8500, just over the bridge in Point Harbor. If you're going to be down in Hatteras Island, **Buxton Under the Sun** 47188 N.C. 12, Buxton, 252/995-6047, rents cars and 4x4s, and provides service to all airports within 250 miles radius, which includes the one up in Norfolk, Virginia.

NORTH OF NAGS HEAD

The further north you go out of Kitty Hawk (the low point on the Outer Banks, price-wise), the less shabby things become and the more the homes cost. Houses in Kitty Hawk in early 2000 averaged $118,000 each; Southern Shores' averaged $279,000, Duck's averaged $322,000, and Corolla's averaged $412,000. In a not-un-related incident in 2000, just 16 years after the dusty little fishing village of Corolla received its first paved road, the town's first full-service stretch limousine company opened for business, serving the needs of vacationing mainlanders who come to the Banks, by all accounts, to enjoy the simple things in life. Life has changed everywhere on the Banks over the past twenty years, but perhaps nowhere as much as it has north of Kitty Hawk.

DUCK

Now here's one name that's easy to figure out: Duck was named after all the ducks who frequented the area, though one suspects that if the town was renamed today it'd be called "Snowbird."

Up until 1984 Duck was the end of the line for N.C. 12, which north of town turned dirt all the way up the distant village of Corolla. In 1984 however, when the state paved the road clean up to Corolla, the roof ripped off of the Northern Banks' real estate market, and Duck went high-end with a fury. Fortunately the change came late enough that the village's quaint personality had become part of its draw—hence those building developments had an interest in preserving some semblance of an Old Beach village in Duck.

Nonetheless the piles of cash haven't exactly rolled off Duck's back. It's lost some of its regional color. One of the village's new condo developments is named "Nantucket Village," and this is perhaps instructive: in some ways Duck's become just another take on the "laid-back beach village" motif of Hilton Head, Kiawah, Bald Head Island, Cape Cod, and most of Eastern

Maine, just another generic stop on the vacation circuit for the upper classes, with epicurean restaurants and expensive gift shops all out of proportion to the size of the "village."

But if Duck has gone from a sleepy, laid-back village to an expensive, exclusive, re-creation of a sleepy, laid-back village, it's still one of the increasingly rare places where visitors can experience even a Disneyfied vision of what the Outer Banks were like thirty or forty years ago. Mansions aside, it's still a cute town.

And with the shrewdness of its namesake, it's fighting to stay cute. In spring 1999, when a huge Food Lion tried to lumber into town, Duck attacked. The town's 500 residents passed a law limiting future buildings in the area to just 10,000 square feet. The Food Lion stalked away, looking for other prey.

Accommodations

Donna Black and Nancy Caviness' **Advice 5 Cents, A Bed and Breakfast,** 111 Scarborough Lane, 252/255-1050 or 800/258-4235, sits in the midst of Duck, in walking distance of Scarborough Faire and most restaurants. Casual, home-baked goodies. Five rooms, each with a private bath, $95–175. Open February–November.

Outside of town, **Sanderling Inn Resort,** 1461 Duck Rd., 800/701-4111 or 252/261-4111, website: www.sanderlinginn.com, offers 77 rooms, three cottages, 10 suites, golf and tennis, canoes, boats, rafts, a jogging/nature trail, a top-notch restaurant, a full spa and fitness center, and access to the 3,400-acre Audubon Preserve next door. Rates run from around $120 for a room in the off-season to nearly $500 a night, in-season, for a villa.

Food

One of the most casual and niftiest spots in town is **Tullio's Pastry Shop,** upstairs in the Scarborough Shops, 252/261-7111, website: tullios@beachlink.com, provides some mouth-watering and mouth-dropping desserts, whipped up by award-winning, Culinary Institute of America chef Walter T. Viegelmann. In addition to breakfast treats and desserts that may well qualify as narcotics, Walter and crew whip up some mean mini-pizzas. Also in the same area is the acclaimed **Fishbone's Raw Bar & Restaurant,** 252/261-6991, email: fishbone@pinn.net, offering local seafood, pork, chicken, pasta, and daily specials, and proud winners of the Outer Banks' Chowder Cook-Off a few years back. Good chance to dine with a view of the sound.

Red Sky Café, actually a part of the Village Wine Shop in the Village Square Shops, 1197 Duck Road, 252/261-8646, email: redsky@interpath.com, sells wood-fired pizzas, soups, sandwiches, and a full dinner menu.

Some argue that the **Sanderling Inn Restaurant,** 252/261-3021, is the very top rung of Outer Banks dining. But vying mightily for that rung is **Elizabeth's Café and Winery,** Scarborough Faire Shops, 252/261-6145, ranked as one of America's Top 100 Restaurants of the 20th Century with 10 or more years of service by the International Restaurant and Hospitality Rating Bureau; it was also conferred with the Best of Award of Excellence by *The Wine Spectator.* As at the Sanderling, call ahead for reservations and bring your bravest credit card (the seven-course wine dinner, served at the second seating, runs $125 a person; the six-course wine dinner runs $80). Lunch and à la carte dinners can be more reasonable. Sample items, though they change nightly, include such complicated appetizers as the "Leaning Tower of Duck," which is stacked sliced roasted duck breast, grilled sweet potatoes and asparagus over organic greens with bacon balsamic reduction ($8); a scallop and brie bisque with diced Granny Smith apples ($8). Entrées include oven-baked semiboneless duck with a dark cherry, merlot, and mango chambord sauce ($22). A friendly warning: try to save money by ordering an appetizer as an entrée and you'll incur a $12.50 "plate charge." Bring in your own wine, and you'll pay $15.00 for a "corkage fee." (As of yet, there's no extra charge if you bring your own date, but you might call ahead about a possible "escort charge.")

For my money, I'll take the barbecue at north-of-town **Duck's Deli** 252/261-3354, anytime. Nice outdoor deck.

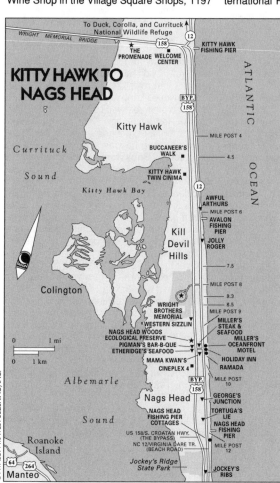

© AVALON TRAVEL PUBLISHING, INC.

For Duck after dark, try the **Barrier Island Inn Restaurant and Tavern,** Duck Rd. 252/261-8700, which sometimes offers live entertainment (including comedy) and always has dartboards and a pool table.

COROLLA

Locally pronounced "Cuh-RAWL-uh," the once tiny, roadless village of Corolla is now a more exclusive version of Duck, but with a lighthouse. The paved road ends here at the start of **Currituck National Wildlife Refuge,** but even this hasn't stopped development north of town—homeowners in newly developing Carova north of the refuge merely shift their Broncos into four-wheel-drive and plunge onward.

The red-brick 158-foot **Currituck Beach Lighthouse,** on the corner of N.C. 12 and Corolla Village Rd., 252/453-4939, may be my favorite. It first lit up surrounding waters on December 1, 1875. You can climb it for $5, which also gives you admittance to the museum in the keeper's house below. Open 10 A.M.–6 P.M. daily. While the other Banks lighthouses were painted different patterns to help sailors to differentiate them from sea, the Currituck light was left unpainted brick for the same reason. Beautiful.

Historic Corolla, 877/287-7488, includes three historic buildings from the late 19th century, including a schoolhouse and a post office/general store. The 1885 Corolla Chapel has become a popular spot for weddings; folks from as far away as Russia and Nigeria have come here to tie the knot, nautical-style. **Ice Cold Corolla,** also located in the village, sells drinks and North Carolina–style BBQ. All in all, this is a nice, shaded walk that gives folks something else to do after taking in the lighthouse, and before heading back on the long drive back to Nag's Head or Hatteras. Just beyond the shadow of the lighthouse stands the **Whalehead Club,** N.C. 12, 252/453-9040. The old building has been under restoration for a while, but the idea is to eventually use the grand old 1920s hunt club as the **Currituck Wildlife**

> *"All of the people had blackout shades on their houses and could have only one light per family. We also were not allowed to have headlights on our cars when driving the beach . . . so that the German subs would not see silhouettes of the ships passing by the coast. . . . The [Nazi] subs would get a ship fairly often, and you could see explosions and the sky lit up from the ship burning. . . . After a ship was hit, the Coast Guard told us not to go out on the beach until they picked up the bodies."*
>
> —Norris Austin, former Corolla postmaster,
> *Whalehead: Tales of Corolla, N.C.*

Museum. Call for tours. Outside you'll see a very pretty (and National Historic Register) footbridge. Just over behind the lighthouse on School House Lane and Corolla Village Road you'll find other restored buildings like the 1895 Lewark Residence, now **The Cottage Collection,** a furniture, antiques, and art boutique. An outbuilding houses a woman's clothing shop. **Island Bookstore** stands where an old general store used to stand. **The Lighthouse Garden** is set in a 1920 residence. Here you'll also find an old 1878 life-saving station turned into a tourists shop; a barbecue place, a restored schoolhouse, chapel, and boathouse. The walk out to the soundside gazebo is a pleasant one, and it's a good spot to get shots of the lighthouse over the marsh.

Over in the Corolla Village Light Shops, a small but pleasant surprise is the **Nalu Kai Surf Museum** in the Corolla Surf Shop, 252/453-9283. The museum features relics and great old pictures that pay tribute to the early days of surfing. No admission—it's just part of the surf shop.

The Inn at Corolla Light, 1066 Ocean Trail, 800/215-0772 or 252/453-3340, offers 43 rooms, tennis privileges, a hot tub, canoes and boats, and a trail for hiking and jogging. **B&B on the Beach,** 1023 Ocean Trail, 800/962-0201 or 252/453-3033, sounds like a quaint little inn, but it's actually a large realty company specializing in rentals. See their website www.bandbonthe-beach.com for photos of rentals.

SOUTH OF NAGS HEAD

HATTERAS ISLAND

The 5,915-acre **Pea Island National Wildlife Refuge,** sits south of the fishing-crazed Oregon Inlet on N.C. 12, 708 N. U.S. 64, 252/987-2394. You'll find the Pea Island visitors center 6 miles south of the inlet. It's a nice on-the-way spot for wildlife displays and a pleasant self-guided walk—the Charles Kuralt Trail—for wildlife viewing the center is open 9 A.M.–4 P.M.

Northern Villages

Just south of the refuge, you'll find the three little villages of Rodanthe, Waves, and Salvo—none of them likely to inspire a *Southern Living* spread anytime soon, but all of them pleasant-enough spots to rent a house and enjoy abundant nature in all directions. In Rodanthe a great, all-in-one spot to do just this is **Hatteras Island Resort,** Atlantic Drive, 800/331-6541 or 252/987-2345, which offers 34 cottages, 34 rooms, and eight efficiencies at the foot of a fishing pier. Open April 1–November 15, or until the weather turns bleak. Rooms run $55–80; two-bedroom cottages run $475–725 a week; three and four-bedroom cottages are also available. On the pier (or, more properly, beneath it), stands **Down Under Restaurant,** N.C. 12, 252/987-2277, which is another unexpected Outer Banks dining experience: an Australia-themed seafood and steak spot founded by an Aussie, and still featuring some great Roo Stew, made with real, imported (obviously) kangaroo, and including a long list of imported beer—presumably many best-described as "hoppy." Its famous for its 10-cent shrimp. Open for breakfast, lunch, and dinner. On the ocean side of N.C. 12 you'll find the **Chicamacomico Lifesaving Station,** founded here in 1874 and under restoration. During the summer reenactors run a "beach apparatus drill," which captures some of the exciting and daring of that time and place. These men, precursors to the Coast Guard, routinely went out in open boats in stormy seas to try to rescue victims of shipwreck. The station is in the midst of refur-

bishment at publication. Call the Chicamacomico Historical Association at 252/987-2626 for more information on its present status—or ask just about anyone in Rodanthe. They'll know.

Incidentally, the origin of the name Rodanthe is hazy; all anybody knows is it was attached to the

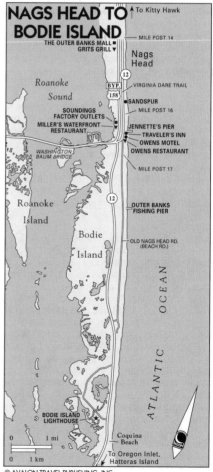

© AVALON TRAVEL PUBLISHING, INC.

place after the U.S. Postal Service rejected the village's first choice—Chicamacomico—as being too hard to spell. Rodanthe's other claim to fame is the fact that it is one of the few communities in the county that still celebrates "Old Christmas," on January 5, a throwback to the days before 1752, when Britain and the American colonies adopted the Gregorian calendar. Certain groups of Protestants, including those in Rodanthe, apparently couldn't accept the change to December 25.

South of Rodanthe comes **Waves,** which also wanted to call itself "Chicamacomico" but was turned down by the U.S. Postal Service. The name apparently refers to the waves at the beach. Waves is home to a lot of vacation homes as well as **Cecil's Cottages,** on the East and West Sides of N.C. 12, 252/987-2673, offering five cottages. Open May–Sept.

Salvo

Salvo, so far as anyone knows, never wanted to call itself Chicamacomico. In fact the village here had no name at all until a Federal ship passed during the Civil War and fired a "salvo" at it. The captain then jotted down "Salvo" on a chart to remind himself of the location of the town.

Salvo Inn Motel, 252/987-2240, nine rooms, three cottages, seven efficiencies, two cabins, playground, canoes. Open Apr.–Nov.

Avon

Little Avon was called "Kinnakeet" until 1873, when people got tired of arguing about how to spell it correctly (I'm serious) and changed the name to Avon, presumably after the river in England, though nobody really knows. One thing we do know for sure: this town is now the busiest on the island. A huge Food Lion pounced upon the island a few years back and now dwells on the bypass near the village, the peaceful village.

If you'd like to stay in town a night or two, soak up some peace and rays, and try your luck with the shore fishing, you might want to stay at the **Avon Cottages,** located on the ocean side of N.C. 12 at 40279 Younce Rd., 252/995-4123, website: www.avoncottages.com. They offer 26 mostly oceanfront cottages that vary from around $640 to $1,300 per week. Those that rent daily vary from $42 to $85 per night. Bring your own linens or be prepared to rent them. **Avon Motel,** N.C. 12, 800/243-5774 or

Chicamacomico Lifesaving Station, Hatteras

252/995-5774, has 14 rooms, 29 efficiencies, laundry, and fishing pier; it's open March–mid-December. **Castaway Oceanfront Inn,** N.C. 12, 800/845-6070 or 252/995-4444, website: www.lfw.corp.com, has 66 rooms, a restaurant and pool, and is open February–November. Call **Hatteras Realty,** N.C. 12, 800/428-8372 or 252/995-5466, website: www.hatterasrealty.com, for information on 300 cottages and 12 condos.

To listen to some (possibly live) music and maybe meet yourself a real-live Avon lady (or gentleman,) head over to **Lily Pad Lounge,** 252/995-4106, or **Bones Island Bar,** 252/995-7751.

Buxton

Buxton sets at the broadest point of Hatteras Island and serves as a hub of sorts. Most famous as being the town closest to the Cape Hatteras Lighthouse, this is also the place where, in 1902, Swedish scientist Reginald Fessenden first broadcast wireless radio to a receiver set on Roanoke Island, over forty miles away. The impressed and fascinated Thomas Edison and Guglielmo Marconi came here to Buxton to investigate. Nine years later a wireless operator working the late shift in Buxton was the only land operator to receive the *Titantic's* distress calls. According to legend the Buxton operator radioed New York but was not believed (the ship was unsinkable, after all) until it was too late. Buxton itself mainly keeps to the soundside of its stretch of island, leaving the beach side to **Cape Hatteras National Seashore.**

Buxton is where Hatteras Island children come to attend the island's one school; this is where many of the island's restaurants, hotels, and stores are. But all in all, it's still a good site less busy than Kitty Hawk.

The **Cape Hatteras Lighthouse,** 252/995-4474, built in 1870, is the tallest of the bunch at 208 feet. This is the light that grabbed a lot of headlines in 1999 (and was the subject of at least one book) by being moved back from the rapidly eroding shore. And a good thing, too. Within a couple of months a couple serious hurricanes had powered through here.

Buxton's other attraction is **Buxton Woods,** home of 500-acres of maritime forest, the largest such preserve in the state. From here you can hike the **Buxton Woods Nature Trail,** all the way down to Frisco.

Cape Hatteras Motel, N.C. 12, 800/995-0711 or 252/995-5611, offers six rooms, seven efficiencies, five condos, 18 suites, a pool, all on the waterfront. The rooms run $52–130 a night. The **Comfort Inn–Buxton,** on N.C. 12 at Old Lighthouse Rd., 800/432-1441 or 252/995-6100, offers 60 rooms, with a pool. **Lighthouse View Motel,** N.C. 12, 800/225-7651 or 252/995-5680, website: www.lighthouseview.com, offers 24 rooms and 23 cottages, along with some efficiency apartments and 22 condos. On the waterfront. $325–650 a week.

As far as Buxton B&Bs go, **Cape Hatteras Bed & Breakfast,** run by Cathy Moir on Old Lighthouse Road, P.O. Box 490, 252/995-6004 or 800/252-3316 sits close to the Cape Hatteras Lighthouse, features a full breakfast and seven rooms, all with private baths, and one suite, for $59–99. Open Apr.–Nov. only.

The Pamlico Inn, run by Scott and Brenda Johnson, 49684 N.C. 12 South, P.O. Box 550, 888/862-7547 or 252/995-6980, offers waterfront rooms facing the inlet. Open year-round. Four rooms, private baths. $75–125 a night.

But perhaps one of the true joys of Buxton is **Uncle Eddy's Frozen Custard,** on N.C. 12, 252/995-4059, set in an old home that the owners turned into a commercial enterprise after the town grew up around it, and featuring, out front, a classy little miniature golf course, and some fine homemade frozen custard (which you can buy as a cone, in a sundae, or by the pint). The miniature golf runs $6 for adults, $3 for kids.

Frisco

Residents of San Francisco, California, regularly wince whenever somebody uses the contraction "Frisco" to describe the City by the Bay, but there's nothing they can do about the town of Frisco, whose name preserves this linguistic heresy for all time. Frisco was originally named Trent, but an inland village carried the same name. So in 1898 the island village's first postmaster suggested

---

UNDER THE FLOOR

A traditional "Hatteras-style" cottage consists of a small clapboard house perched high atop stilts to keep it out of storm surfs, with floorboards spaced just far enough apart to allow in a nice breeze. Usually the large area beneath the house is enclosed in lattice.

Lattice became the trend back back when people first started building vacation homes on the oceanfront side of Hatteras Island. In the days before ferries, with few amenities out on the Banks, the normally wealthy vacationers would bring along their livestock to provide them and their servants with food and milk through the summer. The livestock roamed the island freely, but on the sandy shore, without any trees to provide shade, the animals tended to huddle in the cool dimness beneath the houses. Before long, fleas, ticks, and other critters would infest the homes, so bite-weary vacationers enclosed the stilts in lattice to keep the livestock out.

With the horses and cows long gone these days, the lattice remains as an ornament, though often only on three sides of the undercottage: land prices and lot sizes being what they are, many folks have reclaimed the space beneath their homes for parking.

the name "San Francisco," based on his affection for the California city where he'd spent time before being shipwrecked upon and settling on Hatteras Island. But the Postal Service, which had been rejecting Indian name after Indian name as being too difficult to spell, would have none of this new (Spanish!) candidate. They apparently had no problem with "Frisco."

Set (in part) in what was once Frisco's general store, the **Frisco Native American Museum and Natural History Center,** 53536 N.C. 12, 252/995-4440, is a homegrown but heartfelt and profound collection of Native American artifacts and exhibits. Outside a short trail leads through the woods and past some recreated Native American structures. Price runs $5 for a whole family, or $2 for adults.

The natural-grass **Frisco Mini Golf and Go Karts,** N.C. 12, 252/995-6325, may just be the prettiest miniature golf course you'll ever see. It's a fun place on a quiet Hatteras summer night. The buzzing Go Karts of course cut through the quiet a bit, but most kids won't mind. Golf runs $6 for everyone over six years of age. Go Karts run $5 a ride. Inside you'll find soft-serve ice cream and other fun foods, and a very popular pool room. For a more proper dinner, **Channel Bass,** on N.C. 12, open for dinner, and on the pricy side ($15.95 and up), is very popular seafood and steak spot down on the south side of the island. Nice waterfront view.

Hatteras
Graveyard of the Atlantic Museum, beside the Hatteras–Ocracoke Ferry landing in Hatteras, 252/986-2995, this 19,000 sq. ft. museum (scheduled to open in 2002) features interactive displays on exploration, transportation, and commerce, attempts at colonization, the development of the Labrador and Gulf Stream shipping lanes, the role of the lighthouse and lifesaving services, and mysteries. The Piracy and Warfare display will survey the pirates who camped on our shores and roved our seas while plundering ships of every nationality. Tales of Civil War blockade-runners, the loss of Forts Hatteras and Clark, and the historic sinking of the USS Monitor, will be recounted.

The **Lee Robinson General Store,** founded in 1948 (though the current building was built in 1988), is truly a Hatteras tradition.

"Cape Hatteras is a possible site for nuclear tests. It is relatively accessible by water, yet could be easily placed 'out of bounds' for security control."

—Findings of a secret Atomic Energy Commission report on stateside test sites, 1949. Fortunately the deserts of the Nevada were easier to acquire, and the Banks were saved.

Some folks can't be around all this water and fish without wanting to get out on the former and start pulling out the latter. If you're one of these people, you may want to talk to **Teach's Lair,** 252/986-2460, which books charters.

If you'd like to stay around Hatteras, **Austin's "1908" Guesthouse,** 57698 N.C. 12, 252/986-2695, offers five efficiencies, with kitchens and bike privileges, for $50–90. **Seaside Inn at Hatteras,** N.C. 12, 252/986-2700, website: www.seasidebb.com, has 10 rooms, a lounge, and offers a shuttle to guests. $75–125 a night.

On the high end is **Cochran's Way,** 54470 N.C. 12, 252/986-1406, website: www.cochransway.com, overlooks the Pamlico Sound, features great sunsets, kayaks, and a big porch. Three rooms, each with private bath: $125–145. Open Apr.–Oct.

If camping's an option, **Hatteras Sands Camping Resort,** 252/986-2422, offers over 100 sites, many with full hookups, including cable TV, for $27–34. They also offer six cabins (sleeping four people) for $37–52.

Recreation
If you're looking to get out in the water for pure fun, talk to the folks from **Adventure Center: Hatteras Wind 'n' Surf,** on N.C. 12, across from the Avon Pier, 800/946-37873—they can set you up. For tours, Brian Patteson leads pelagic birding trips off of Hatteras; contact him at www.patteson.com or 252/986-1363.

OCRACOKE ISLAND

Ocracoke Island is the place where, it's generally agreed, the Outer Banks of the popular imagination—a laid-back, unhurried, largely undeveloped utopia—still draws breath. It has only one town, and that town has only two streets running its length: Front Street and the Back Road. In a consumer-run, choice-venerating world, Ocracoke provides an invigorating lack of options—like a theme park based on Anne Morrow Lindbergh's *A Gift from the Sea.*

But like Duck, Ocracoke isn't stupid. It knows it's cute. But somehow Ocracoke carries it off better than other parts of the Banks. It's home to the smallest school in North Carolina (around 75 students, K–12), and it's the sort of place that people come back to every year—if they remember to make reservations well in advance.

The 1895 David Williams House is now home of the **Ocracoke Preservation Society Muse-**

um, 252/928-7375. Set in a former Coast Guard captain's home, the museum features a number of exhibits on the local dialect, the Confederate Fort Ocracoke, fishing boats, and more. Open Monday–Friday, 10 A.M. to 5 P.M., shorter hours on the weekend. Admission free.

Given the name, a lot of people assume that the **British Cemetery,** British Cemetery Rd., 888/493-3826 or 252/925-5201, website: www.ocracoke-nc.com/cemetery, dates to the colonial era, but in truth it's younger than Elvis. It contains the remains from the HMS *Bedfordshire,* torpedoed off Hatteras by the Germans' U-558 on May 11, 1942. The cemetery flies a British flag, furnished annually by the Queen

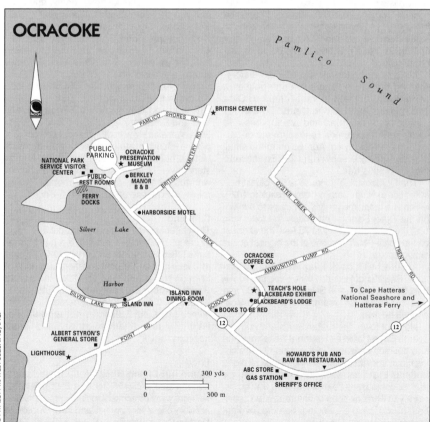

© AVALON TRAVEL PUBLISHING, INC.

herself. An inscription of poet Rupert Brooke, himself killed in World War I, reads, "If I should die think only this of me that there's some forever corner of a foreign field that is forever England."

Teach's Hole Blackbeard Exhibit, Back Road, 252/928-1718, website: www.teachshole.com, is a unique blending of theater, museum, and gift shop. Several nights a week, old Blackbeard himself—or, a local actor portraying him—performs "Blackbeard Lives," a short one-man show delineating the history of local piracy, including the fate of Edward "Blackbeard" Teach himself, who robbed, plundered, extorted, and (indirectly, at least) killed along the Carolina Coasts before being decapitated in a sword fight off Ocracoke in 1718. Afterward audience members can have their pictures taken with the rogue (head still attached) both before and after spilling out into a gift shop crammed full of faux pirate gear.

It's a unique stop alive with local history. And yet the whole thing gives one pause: in centuries to come, will vacationers to Olde Los Angeles and Historic Detroit Towne buy their kids plastic guns and crack pipes and enjoy period-costumed reenactments of carjackings? Probably so. Admission to the small museum and the show runs $3. Entrance to the gift shop is free.

The Ocracoke Light House is the oldest one still in use in North Carolina, dating back to 1823, which is a long time for any structure to survive on the Outer Banks. Fortunately the folks who built the lighthouse—at just 75 feet, the shortest on the coast—built it on one of the highest points on Ocracoke.

About a half a block away you'll see the National Register of Historic Places–registered **Albert Styron's General Store,** built in 1920 and featuring coffee, ice cream, gifts, beer and wine, and gift baskets.

North of town, the rest of the island is given over to **Cape Hatteras National Seashore,** the first national seashore in the country. Stretching clean from just south of Nags Head all along Hatteras Island and south to Ocracoke Inlet, the park encompasses 75 miles, and 30,000 acres. Here you'll find all sorts of nature-related activities: hiking, biking, camping, boating, birding, fishing, surfing, and shelling.

Accommodations

Built in 1936, **Blackbeard's Lodge,** 111 Back Rd., 800/892-5314 or 252/928-1101, website: www.blackbeardslodge.com, is the oldest extant hotel in Ocracoke, and the probably the kind of old place you'd think of when you think of a lodge on Ocracoke. The 37 rooms are clean and airy, and the use of the bikes and pool (and the option of renting one of six efficiency apartments) makes this a great choice. It is under a gradual plan of refurbishment by the owners, Buffy and Ann Warner. The historic **Island Inn,** N.C. 12 and Lighthouse Road, 877/456-3466 or 252/928-4351, website: www.ocracokeislandinn.com, is set inside a 1901 house, features dining, traditional hotel rooms, and one- and two-bedroom condos. Open year-round. $79–89, two-night minimum. Dining.

Harborside Motel, Silver Lake Rd., 252/928-4141, offers 14 rooms right across the street from the waterfront. Also offers a meal plan, a shuttle, and a kitchen if you'd like, $55–80. Continental breakfast served, featuring baked goods the owner makes herself.

Robert and Amy Attaway's **Berkley Manor Bed and Breakfast,** 800/832-1223 or 252/928-5911, website: www.berkleymanor.com, offers a private island estate on three private acres, a historic hunting and fishing lodge with a four-story tower. Now a nonsmoking establishment with full breakfast, open year-round. Twelve rooms with private baths, $75–175 a night.

Camping

The cheapest way to stay on Ocracoke island is to camp. Most scenic is the $15 a night **Ocracoke Island Campground,** 919/473-2111, part of Cape Hatteras National Seashore, just north of town on N.C. 12. In town you'll find the private **Beachcomber Campground,** 252/928-4031. It costs $20 a night and sits behind a convenience store, but it also has hot showers. For RVers, it also offers electricity and water hookups.

Food

Island Inn Dining Room, N.C. 12 and Lighthouse Road, 877/456-3466 or 252/928-4351, website: www.ocracokeislandinn.com, offers reasonable prices for hearty island fare. **Ocracoke Coffee Co.** on the Back Road, 252/928-7473, opens at 7 A.M., pumping out caffeine to a population of laid-back islanders and lying-back vacationers who, you'd think, wouldn't really need it. Nonetheless visiting travel writers are always very grateful to climb up the porch and order a cup of consciousness. Smoothies here as well.

Nightlife
Howard's Pub & Raw Bar, 1175 Irvin Garrish Hwy., 252/928-4441, website: www.howard spub.com, is owned by Buffy and Ann Warner, a former West Virginia state senator and his wife, who moved down here in the early 1990s and quickly became forces to be reckoned with; they also own Blackbeard's Lodge. Howard's offers jazz and blues on the weekends, karaoke some other nights, and a big ol' TV for watching the game. Plus an ocean view rooftop deck, a screened porch, pool table, foosball, and darts.

If you're serious about your beer drinking you'll want to head over to **Pie in the Sky,** 252/928-7766, where some claim you'll find the best choice of beers on Ocracoke.

It'd be a crime to be caught on Ocracoke for any length of time without a good book to read. **Books to Be Red,** N.C. 12 & School Rd., 252/928-3936, though it sounds like the name of a Communist reading course, provides a selection of new and used books for word-hungry Ocracoke residents and visitors. You can buy journals and other items here as well.

PORTSMOUTH ISLAND

Now home to a deserted village and some houses you can rent from the National Park Service, Portsmouth Island is one of the rarest of battlegrounds in the war between humans and nature: here, nature won. At one time the town was home to over 1000 people; the last of them moved off in the early 1970s, worn out by having to rebuild after every massive storm. The only way to get here is by private or charter boat. For information on the latter, call 252/928-1111.

ROANOKE ISLAND

MANTEO

Manteo is a quaint little oceanfront town that reminds you of New England, probably because the original British settlers in this area considered this New England. And of course the trend toward Elizabethan themes for every motel and B&B hasn't hurt any. On the whole the town is as pleasant a stay as you'll find on the Outer Banks.

Settlers in the area originally called this Shallowbag Bay, but the town upgraded to its current name during Reconstruction, when the U.S. Postal Service established an office here. The name comes from the Croatan Indian who, along with the Roanoke Indian Wanchese, was taken from Roanoke to England in 1584 to be presented to Queen Elizabeth I and stir up interest in the colonization of the "New World." Later Manteo was named "Lord of Roanoke" by Sir Walter Raleigh and baptized in the first Protestant baptismal service in American history. To the English at least, he was now the ruler of all Native Americans, though of course under the authority of Her Highness. He also served as middle-man between settlers and his none-too-happy Native American brethren, including Wanchese, more conservative and unwilling to see his culture and people changed by the new arrivals and their ways. One theory as to the colonists' disappearance suggests that they may have left the safety of Fort Raleigh to follow Manteo to live among his people on Croatan (now Hatteras). Whether they made it or not is anyone's guess, though some say they were attacked in-transit by a force led by Wanchese and decimated, with only a few survivors.

Manteo, laid low throughout most of the rest of history as a sleepy fishing town, but since the arrival of *The Lost Colony* Outdoor Drama in 1937, the town has experienced a thematic adjustment toward all things Elizabethan. The Garden Club of North Carolina helped out in 1951 by building the Elizabethan Gardens to capitalize on tourists drawn to the area's early colonial history. More recently the opening of Roanoke Island Festival Park across the bridge gives folks who might have flown through here on the way to

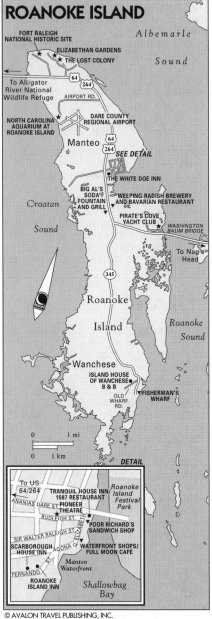

ROANOKE ISLAND

FORT RALEIGH
NATIONAL HISTORIC SITE

Albemarle

ELIZABETHAN GARDENS
THE LOST COLONY

Sound

64
264

To Alligator
River National
Wildlife Refuge   AIRPORT RD.

DARE COUNTY
REGIONAL AIRPORT

NORTH CAROLINA
AQUARIUM AT
ROANOKE ISLAND

Manteo   64
264   *SEE DETAIL*

THE WHITE DOE INN

BIG AL'S
SODA
FOUNTAIN
AND GRILL   WEEPING RADISH BREWERY
AND BAVARIAN RESTAURANT

Croatan   PIRATE'S COVE
YACHT CLUB
WASHINGTON
BAUM BRIDGE

Sound

To Nag's
Head

345

Roanoke

Island

Roanoke
Sound

Wanchese

ISLAND HOUSE
OF WANCHESE
B & B

OLD
WHARF
RD.   FISHERMAN'S
WHARF

0   1 mi
0   1 km

DETAIL

To US
64/264   TRANQUIL HOUSE INN/
1587 RESTAURANT   Roanoke
Island
Festival
Park
ANANIAS DARE ST PIONEER
THEATRE

BUDLEIGH ST.

SIR WALTER RALEIGH ST.   POOR RICHARD'S
SANDWICH SHOP

SCARBOROUGH
HOUSE INN   AGONA   WATERFRONT SHOPS/
FULL MOON CAFÉ

FERNANDO   Manteo
Waterfront

ROANOKE
ISLAND INN   *Shallowbag*
Bay

© AVALON TRAVEL PUBLISHING, INC.

Nags Head another reason to pull over and walk around town awhile. The waterfront's a fine place to spend a morning, afternoon, or evening.

Manteo Area Sights

Roanoke Island Festival Park, across from the waterfront in downtown Manteo, 252/475-1506 or 252/475-1500 (24-hr information line), can be seen as a healthy cross between a national historical site and Disney World. The well-tended park includes the top-notch, interactive Roanoke Adventure Museum, which features a gregarious audio-animatronic pirate, among other Disney-inspired wonders. Before entering the museum, note the rack of Elizabethan garb in the lobby. If you like, you can pick up a costume to wear while on the property. Across the lobby you'll find a theater showing a (no additional charge) short film, *Legend of Two Path,* throughout the day. It tells the story of three local Native Americans—Wanchese, Manteo, and Skyco—who were on the frontlines when the Old and New Worlds collided, and suffered accordingly. It tells the story completely from the Native American point of view, an interesting counterbalance to the mostly Eurocentric focus of *The Lost Colony.*

Another highlight of the park is its intelligent living history interpretations. Be sure to visit the Settlement Site, a re-creation of a 16th-century British landing, complete with reenactors who demonstrate crafts and may even challenge you to a game of ninepins. The Festival Park also includes extensive boardwalks, a fossil pit, a strong museum, an art gallery, and occasional concerts.

The park's undeniable star, however, is the *Elizabeth II,* designed after the ships that sailed under Sir Walter Raleigh in the 1500s. A climb aboard (and below) a ship like this is worth many books'-worth of reading for impressing a visitor with the sheer grit of America's first European settlers. The reenactors who work the ship tell me that the most common question they hear from visitors down in the claustrophobic galley is, "Were the real ships bigger?" No, they weren't. Who would have believed that only four hundred years after the first Europeans crossed the Atlantic to a treacherous life in a strange land in ships smaller than a Greyhound bus, their ancestors would be hurtling back and forth thirty thousand feet above the same ocean in padded chairs watching second-rate movies, listening to Chopin, and complaining that their chicken teriyaki is overdone?

A two-day pass runs $8 for adults and $5 for students. Children under 6 are free.

The **North Carolina Aquarium at Roanoke Island,** Airport Road, 252/473-3494, recently reopened in expanded form and featuring a 285,000-gallon tank wherein fish and sharks swim around and through a one-third scale model of the USS *Monitor.* Among all the things you'd expect, here you'll find a portrait gallery of U.S. Life Saving Services heroes from the past. Prices run $4 for adults, $2 for children 6–12 years old.

Elizabethan Gardens, 1411 U.S. 64/264, 252/473-3234, hasn't been here all that long, but thanks to the good work of the Garden Club of North Carolina, who created it in 1951, it seems as though it has. The ten acres of grounds include statuary, impatiens, roses, gardenias, hydrangeas, and the sorts of herbs

Virginia Dare statue in the Elizabethan Gardens

grown by the original English settlers. You'll enter by passing through the beautiful circular Gate House, and then move out to visit the Sunken Garden, the Queen's Rose Garden, Shakespeare's Herb Garden, and a number of other plantings, all accented by fountains and statues. One of the most famed (and oft-photographed) of the latter is an interpretation of Virginia Dare as a grown woman, dressed in a fishing net. Sculpted before the Civil War by an American expatriate living in Rome, the statue was shipped to America but the ship carrying it sank. The statue spent a couple of years at the bottom of the ocean before it was salvaged and brought to Boston. A New Yorker bought it from the artist and placed it in his studio, but the studio burned, killing the short-lived art collector. Since the New Yorker hadn't paid for the statue yet, the artist, Maria Louisa Ander, got the statue back. In her will she gave the statue to the state of North Carolina where, presumably, the Tarheels would appreciate it. But not long after art supporters placed the statue in Raleigh's Hall of History, the artistic interpretation of the state's best-loved infant as a nude adult drew fire, and Virginia disappeared into a basement for a spell. The state gave Paul Green the hot potato statue after he wrote *The Lost Colony* for them in 1935. When the North Carolina Garden Club created the Elizabethan Gardens in 1951, Green unloaded the statue on them. So here it is, awaiting its next tribulation. Admission runs $5 for adults, $1 for kids over 5. Open daily, 9 A.M.–6 P.M.

If you've been captivated by the story of the Lost Colony, you'll want to be sure to visit the **Fort Raleigh National Historic Site,** U.S. 64, 252/473-5772. The park offers a visitors center, interpretive programs, and a nature trail. The fort was reconstructed for tourists years ago but has since been deconstructed. What you'll see now are berms of grass, the foundations of the original fort. Here too you'll find the Waterside Theatre, home of **The Lost Colony Theatre Under the Stars,** 1409 U.S. 64, 800/488-5012 or 252/473-2127, website: www.thelostcolony.org. This is one of those unique American institutions. *The Lost Colony* has been performed here on this stage since the 1930s. Paul Green's Pulitzer prize–winning Depression-era script presents the unstoppable

the Elizabeth II

determination of the settlers to "civilize" the "untamed" land as encouragement to the poverty-weary audiences of his time. The show features a cast and crew of some 125 and runs $16 for adults and about half that for children. Shows Monday–Saturday.

Across Croatan Sound on U.S. 64/264 you'll find the undeveloped 151,000 acre **Alligator River National Wildlife Refuge,** where you may see black bears or a red wolf, recently reintroduced by the Fish and Wildlife Service.

Hotels and Motels
Duke of Dare Motor Lodge, 100 U.S. 64/264, 252/473-2175, is a 57-room motel out on the main road that won't exactly keep you in the Elizabethan ambience of Manteo. $35–75. The 80-room **Elizabethan Inn,** 814 U.S. 64, 800/346-2466 or 252/473-2101, website: www.elizabethaninn.com, runs $49–135, but includes a breakfast, bicycles, an indoor and outdoor pool, racquetball court, whirlpool, and gym.

Bed-and-Breafasts, Inns
The **Roanoke Island Inn,** 305 Fernando Street, 877/473-5511 or 252/473-5511, is a B&B's B&B. It's pretty, pleasant, within walking distance of the shops and restaurants, offers bikes for riding around town, and features a water view. Eight rooms, open Easter–Thanksgiving. **Scarborough House Inn,** 323 Fernando, 252/473-3849, website: www.bbonline.com/nc/scarborough, $55–85, has a good location just down from the Roanoke. Though the building itself is new, it's built along traditional lines, is furnished in part with antiques. The four-room inn is run by Sally and Phil Scarborough. **Scarborough Inn,** out on the highway at 524 U.S. 64/264, 252/473-3979, email: scarinn@aol.com, offers 12 rooms for $35–65. **Tranquil House Inn,** (800/458-7069, website:www.1587.com) sits right on the Waterfront in the midst of the (mild) waterfront bustle and has 25 rooms, a meal plan, a restaurant, and bikes, $79–169.

The **White Doe Inn,** Bebe & Bob Woody, 319 Sir Walter Raleigh St., 800/473-6091 or 252/473-9851, website: www.whitedoeinn.com, charges $120–225 a night for its seven rooms with bedside fireplaces, a full breakfast, and private baths.

Food
Manteo's cup runneth over as far as great dining goes. **Poor Richard's Sandwich Shop,** on the waterfront, 252/473-3333, is where a lot of the folks working down here on the waterfront come for lunch. They make some great sandwiches (try the Reuben) and sell them at humane prices. **Full Moon Café,** in the Waterfront Shops in Manteo, 252/473-6666, serves up a beautiful view of Shallowbag Bay and *Elizabeth II*, and unique and constantly changing menu with wraps and quesadillas, baked crab dip, hummus, quiches, and salads. More formal and also delicious in the same plaza is the **1587 Restaurant,** 252/473-1587, website: www.1587.com, serving pricey and smallish dinners from 5–10 P.M. daily. Entrées include spice-rubbed, grilled yellowfin tuna on herb mashed potatoes, with a smoked tomato cream and a Spanish olive salsa.

Weeping Radish Brewery and Bavarian Restaurant, U.S. 64/264 on the way to Nag's Head, 252/473-1157, is an unexpected delight, a bit of Bavaria. It includes the Outer Banks' first and only minibrewery, but also more than that, it serves up great sausages (try the knockwurst, $8.95, served with homemade sauerkraut, mustard, and a pretzel,) and smoked pork loin ($13.95), authentic Bavarian goulash, and both authentic and not-so-authentic German sandwiches (including *Ein fleischfreier Hanseat*—a garden burger). The restaurant and Biergarten sit inside a wooded, villagelike plaza that includes a bakery, memorable toy store, and playground. You'll find other locations (though not quite as charming) in Corolla in the Food Lion Plaza 252/453-8638, and at Milepost 1.5 at Bermuda Green, Kitty Hawk, 252/261-0488. But proprietor Uli Bennewitz, native of Bavaria, is most proud of his beer, which he sells both at the tables ($2.10 for .25 liter) and at the counter by the bottle.

Big Al's Soda Fountain and Grill, 100 Patty Lane (U.S. 64/264), 252/473-5570, plays the nostalgia card, 1950s style, but featuring more than burgers. Big Al's offers the sorts of vintage diner food—pork chops, Reuben sandwiches ($6.95), tuna melts ($6.95), as well as the nod toward the then-exotic chicken parmesan ($10.95)—that you'd actually find on the menu of a real diner, circa 1959. Also served are the regionally appropriate fresh seafood dinners ($9.95–13.95). Of course, the dinners here feature names like "Leader of the Pack" (a quarter-pounder burger with cheese, chili, and slaw, $5.95), and the "Lil' Deuce Scoop" (two chocolate chip cookies sandwiching vanilla ice cream, $2.95). Open 11 A.M.–11 P.M., and featuring a dance floor and a jukebox.

WANCHESE

Wanchese, down on the southern end of Roanoke Island, is named after one of the two Native Americans (with Manteo) taken to England by British explorers in 1584. The Town of Manteo's development and popularity with tourists reflects Manteo's embrace of Christianity and English customs; Wanchese's distrust of, and eventual overt antipathy toward, the English and their culture seems reflected in this fishing village's apparent lack of interest in capitalizing on the region's tourist boom. Its time will probably come, but as for now, this is still mainly a fishing town without guile. Many folks visiting the Banks make a point of driving over to eat some of the fresh seafood at **Fisherman's Wharf,** N.C. 345 S, 252/473-5205. If you'd like to spend the night out here, you might want to book a room at the **Island House of Wanchese Bed & Breakfast,** 104 Old Wharf Rd. 252/473-5619, website: www.bbonline.com/nc/islandhouse, $55–110.

NEW BERN AND THE CENTRAL COAST

Let's start with pronunciation. As the region of the state initially settled by Europeans, a lot of firsts come from this part of the state: North Carolina's first towns, its first state capital, even its first Hall-of-Fame pitcher Jim "Catfish" Hunter come from what was known as the Albemarle District. Maybe this is why when approaching the name of a place, locals generally love to plunge in and get the thrust of their word over right away. Pronounce New Bern as one word, "NEWburn," and Beaufort as "BOUferd."

And yet this rush toward syllabic stress is pretty much where the hurry stops along the Central Coast. The historic Albemarle district,

the "Inner Banks," as it were, are in fact the direct opposite of the strip malls in Jacksonville, in greater Wilmington, or up in Nag's Head. The Albemarle coast is blessed in that its heyday, its time of regional importance and spurting growth, came when the architectural styles had style. So while Nag's Head, largely developed in the 1960s and 1970s, features ugly, car-oriented strips of concrete and neon, towns like Bath, Edenton, Elizabeth City, and New Bern enjoy quiet, narrow, tree-lined streets with classic 18th- and 19th-century homes. Every one of these towns, it seems, you'll enter by crossing a bridge.

NEW BERN AND VICINITY

New Bern (NEWburn, remember) has a lot to brag about. Founded in 1710, it's the second-oldest town in North Carolina, and served as a colonial and early state capital. Unlike most coastal cities, which were settled by the English, New Bern was founded by a combination of Swiss and Germans, giving it a slight alpine feel unique

to the region. In fact New Bern is the world's only daughter-city to Bern, Switzerland. And New Bern is home to the Tryon Palace, a reconstruction of the 18th-century colonial governor's mansion, which draws thousands of visitors a year.

But New Bern's greatest claim to fame is a local invention that gave its name to a generation,

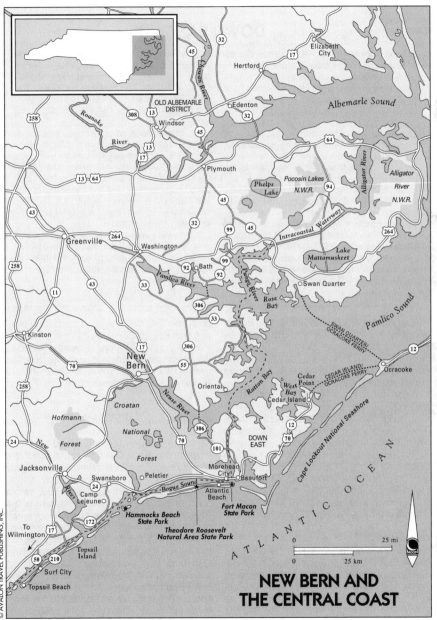

NEW BERN AND
THE CENTRAL COAST

DOWN EAST

Head northeast on U.S. 70/U.S. 12 from Beaufort and you'll find the tourism-based 21st-century Carolina Coast disappears like a fluorescent memory, leaving you amid green fields, seasoned frame buildings, and a compulsion to check the road map. Surely, you think, this can't be the way.

But North Carolina's "Down East" area—running generally from north of Beaufort clear to Cedar Island Bay—*is* the way, if you're looking for authentic, unglamorous maritime culture. If it weren't for the ferry to Ocracoke leaving from Cedar Island, few tourists would ever come through here at all.

Turn south at Otway (named for local pirate-hero, Otway Burns, buried in Beaufort) to get to **Harkers Island.** Harkers is home to a former ship-building village, the most populated area in the region. Down at the southeast corner of Harker's you'll find **Core Sound Waterfowl Museum,** 252/728-1500, worth a stop.

After passing through tiny villages like Davis and Atlantic, toward the northeastern end of the road you'll find the 12,500-acre **Cedar Island National Wildlife Refuge,** largely a salt marsh and home to wild ducks, gulls, geese, ospreys, owls, red-tailed hawks, along with such earthbound critters as deer, otters, minks, and the occasional black bear. The refuge offers a observation area and boat landings. And you can camp there. Call 919/225-2511 for information.

For lodging Down East, check out the inexpensive **Driftwood Motel** in Cedar Island, 252/225-4861, beside the ferry terminal. It's popular with duck hunters and ferry-missers. The **Harkers Island Fishing Center** at 1002 Island Rd., 252/728-3907, also offers twenty rooms. Both it and **Calico Jack's Inn and Marina,** also on Island Road, 252/728-3575, offer efficiencies, fishing access, and ferries to uninhabited Portsmouth Island.

But if you're looking to visit an uninhabited island, **Morris Mariana Kabin Kamps,** 1000 Morris Marina Rd., Atlantic, 252/225-4261, will take you across to Core Banks and set you up in a cabin for $100 a night.

---

challenged all of America, became a John Belushi punch line in the mid-1970s, and, in the 1980s, indirectly caused Michael Jackson's hair to explode into flames. Turn-of-the-century New Bern pharmacist Caleb Bradham called it "Brad's Drink"; you and I call it Pepsi-Cola.

But to New Bern's credit, the city doesn't play the Pepsi card very often. The Bear City (*bern* is German for "bear") had to choose between highlighting its colonial roots—by reconstructing the Tryon Palace—or slapping Pepsi logos all over everything and opening up a small town version of Atlanta's World of Coke. Fortunately, thankfully, they chose the former. You will find a couple of Pepsi sights, but they're integrated into the preservationist tone of things here. The true star of the town is the rebuilt Tryon Palace.

Orientation

New Bern sits at the junction of the Trent and Neuse Rivers; two of its major streets, running in perpendicular directions along different riverfronts, are called Front Street: east/west-running "South Front," and north/south-running "East Front," also called "U.S. 70 Business." Heading north from the Trent river, you'll pass South Front and then Pollock Street, an important street for many of the town's historic attractions (including the Tryon Palace), lodgings, and shopping. The next block up comes Broad St., also U.S. 70 Business/U.S. 17 Business.

HISTORY

New Bern's post-settlement history, like that of much of the North Carolina coast, starts out with the trumpets of colonial pomp, quiets after the snares of the Civil War, and slowly, slowly, begins to build again through the 1900s before flaring into a swing number at the turn of the 21st century, as the town booms with immigrants and their bulging wallets. New Bern was founded in 1710 by Baron Christopher de Graffenried, a Swiss baron leading a group of German Protestants expelled from Catholic Baden and Bavaria. With the blessings of (and £4,000 from) England's Queen Anne, de Graffenried sent out 650 settlers from Gravesend, England, under the direct authority of John Lawson and

Christopher Gale, but storms, sickness, and French ships thinned them out to less than half that number by the time they reached the Chowan River. There the wealthy planter Thomas Pollock, for whom Pollock Street is named, took pity on the survivors and provided them supplies and transportation to the spot where the Trent River meets the Neuse. In September they were joined by de Graffenried himself, leading a large group of Swiss settlers. He bought 10,000 acres from the lords proprietors and John Lawson, who had surveyed the colony. But de Graffenried was smart, and maybe even ethical, so he also paid King Taylor,

the chief of the local Tuscarora Indian tribe, for the land. Lawson laid out the town in the shape of a cross and built fortifications along the transverse road as a defense against Indian uprisings. With the support of his Swiss comrades, de Graffenried named the settlement "New Bern," after the Swiss capital.

And everyone lived happily ever after . . . until the outbreak of the vicious Tuscarora War a year later. At war's end, however, the "Indian threat" was largely gone, and the area prospered. Thomas Pollock oversaw the rebuilding of New Bern. Edenton, Beaufort, Brunswick, and eventually Wilmington were founded. These

NEW BERN

towns and New Bern were showered with trade ships, quickly drawing the curtain on Bath's short reign as North Carolina's primary city. Though Edenton soon became the capital city, and though as late as 1737 visiting Irishman Dr. John Brickell would describe New Bern as having "but a few Houses or Inhabitants in it at present," by 1771 New Bern's centrality along the coast and its expanded population made it the place to be. Because of this Governor William Tryon decided to build a formal, permanent governor's house there. Possibly Tryon guessed that the colonials would respect the Crown more if they saw a little of its grandeur here in the colony, and he built an elaborate governor's mansion in New Bern, considered by most contemporary observers to be the finest government building in America. Local wags called it the "Tryon Palace," as a criticism of the misuse of their taxes. Tryon moved up to New York to become its governor and Josiah Martin moved here until he fled at the beginning of the American Revolution. After the Revolution, the governor of the state of North Carolina was housed here briefly, but by 1798 fire had ravaged the palace and the locals decided they'd always wanted George Street to continue on clear to the river anyway. The building was razed and remained razed for the next 150 years.

New Bern did well as a trading port through antebellum days, but during the war she was quickly captured by Union forces. This worked in her favor since the Union actually needed the town to operate from and thus didn't torch it. The Confederates attempted to retake the town a couple of times but unsuccessfully. After the war the area's economy dipped with that of the region and not until recently has it truly looked up.

Hence the rebuilding of the palace in the 1940s is truly amazing. In the 1940s, money was still very tight for most people in New Bern, and the city hadn't exactly highlighted the phrase "historical preservation" in their community mission statement. (Even as late as 1974 the city redevelopment commission was petitioning to have the 1797 Harvey Mansion bulldozed in the name of "progress.") Nonetheless, having witnessed the popularity of the outdoor historical drama *The Lost Colony* over on Roanoke Island and the increased interest in colonial sites, New Bernians rebuilt the Tryon Palace in painstaking detail, giving the city its future tourist draw. In retrospect New Bern's choice was a miracle of foresight and good taste. Most small American communities in the 1950s, confronting the same choices, would probably have spent their tourism dollars building the world's largest Pepsi bottle.

SIGHTS

Tryon Palace Historic Sites and Gardens

If this imposing structure at 610 Pollock St., 800/767-1560 or 252/514-4900, website: www.tryonpalace.org, seems a bit grandiose for little New Bern, know that that's certainly what New Bernians have always thought. When the imperial Royal Governor William Tryon built the imposing structure in 1770, they protested that their taxes were being used for such extravagance. Later the New Bernians gladly paved it over and pretended it had never been there. The only thing left was the stables.

In the 1940s wealthy Gertrude Carraway began to think about the glory that had been New Bern's for 28 short years. She spearheaded a drive to bring it back. Finally, in the 1950s, the palace was "restored," as the official pamphlet puts it, a fairly massive piece of understatement, since when the "restoration" began, Fords and Chevys used to drive to and from the river through the spot where the Georgian mansion now stands. British understatement aside,

---

ALBEMARLE AND CENTRAL COAST HIGHLIGHTS

- **Bath**
- **Beaufort Waterfront**
- **Croatan National Forest**
- **Edenton**
- **Museum of the Albemarle, Elizabeth City**
- **Hertford**
- **New Bern's Downtown and Pepsi-Cola Museum**
- **Oriental**
- **Sanitary Restaurant,** Morehead City
- **Tryon Palace Historic Sites and Gardens,** New Bern

Tyron Palace

here it is, a tribute to the grandeur of times past. Soon, the Tryon Palace will have stood for twice as many years as the original.

The incredible research and painstaking craftsmanship required to recreate a building and grounds so many years back is really a fascinating story in itself. The rebuilders worked using the house's original blueprints, uncovered in 1939. The house was refurnished based on a detailed inventory of items Tryon and his wife had written out after their new home in New York burned down and they wanted compensation. And the re-creators continue to refine their vision; at first, after the restoration, the gardens were long kept in the British style for lack of specific details about their design. Then in 1991 Tryon Palace researchers, searching at Venezuela's Academia Nacional de la Historia, found the original garden plan—in the collection of 18th-century Venezuelan traveler Francisco de Miranda, who had toured the young United States in 1783. Apparently palace architect John Hawks had drawn up the plans for Miranda himself, and they revealed a definite French influence the original restorers hadn't known about.

Today the Tryon Palace bustles with costumed reenactors and tour guides, also includes fourteen acres of gardens planted to match colonial specifications. Open Mon.–Tues. and Thurs.–Sat. Admission for the guided tour (there are no unguided tours) is fairly steep—about $15 for adults, $6 students in 1st–12th grade. Tickets good for two consecutive days. The costumed guides will show you the palace along with three other historic homes from the 18th and 19th centuries, and the New Bern Academy Museum.

Other Sites

The **Attmore-Oliver House,** 510 Pollock St., 252/638-8558, was built in 1790 by Samuel Chapman. Today it's headquarters for the New Bern Historical Society. You can tour the house, which includes period furnishings, a Civil War room, and doll collection, for free.

Also free is the art museum set in a pre-World War I bank and aptly renamed **Bank of the Arts,** 317 Middle St., 252/638-2787. True, you can no longer cash your check here, but you'll find plenty of change afoot, what with the ever changing exhibitions of Southeast paintings, sculptures, photographs, pottery, and fiber arts available for the viewing.

At 256 Middle St., 252/636-5898, you'll the **Birthplace of Pepsi-Cola,** a small museum and gift shop built to celebrate Pepsi, invented here 100 years ago by Caleb Bradham. This re-creation of an early 1900s drugstore is a nice place to stop in and order a soda. Just don't ask for a "Coke." It's been done.

Christ Episcopal Church, 320 Pollock St., 252/633-2109, built in 1752 for a parish that has existed since 1715, is the third-oldest church in

North Carolina and features a communion ware donated to the church by King George II. The outdoor chapel was built over the site of the first church, which had been built in 1752.

Long listed on the National Register of Historic Places (and saved from the wrecker's ball because of it), the 1797 **Harvey Mansion,** 221 S. Front St., 252/638-3205, offers six rooms of artwork and four archaeological exhibits. It is open for free self-guided tours daily from 10 A.M.–4 P.M. If you really like it here, you can eat dinner, or even rent a room to spend the night. (See "Accommodations," below.)

The **Firemen's Museum,** 408 Hancock St., 252/636-4087, celebrates the history of one of the nation's oldest continually operating fire companies—and fire fighting in general. Here you can see some neat old equipment, including an 1884 horse-drawn steamer. They've even preserved the head of Fred, a valiant firehorse who died pulling a fire-fighting wagon. Ben Gaskill will tell you Fred's story, and will tell you about the great Fire of 1922, which destroyed every third building in New Bern, and no doubt caused some mean puns in neighboring communities. The museum also features a Civil War display. Open Mon.–Sat. 10 A.M.–4:30 P.M. and Sun. 1–5 P.M.

Outside of town the **Bellair Plantation and Restoration,** 1100 Washington Post Rd. (N.C. 43 N), 252/637-3913, was the largest (and is the last remaining) 17th-century country house in North Carolina. The folks at Bellair give one-hour tours by appointment only, so call ahead.

Tours

The **Queen Anne Horse and Carriage Co.,** 252/244-1690, offers tours by horse-drawn carriage and also in an omnibus. **New Bern Trolley,** 333 Middle St., 252/637-7316, operates ninety-minute guided trolley tours of the historic district.

SHOPPING

New Bern has a colonial feel to it, and as in any good colonial village, the best goods are to be found near the riverfront and around the governor's house. Local farmers, canners, bakers, herbalists, and artisans do business down on the waterfront at the **Farmer,** 252/633-0043,

421 S. Front Street. Open Friday, 8 A.M.–5 P.M., Saturday 6 A.M.–2 P.M.

You could do a lot of good shopping without ever leaving Pollock Street. **Bern Bear Gifts,** 301 Pollock St., 252/637-2300, seems like a tourist shop in Switzerland, which is exactly the idea. It features European imports, English teapots, lots and lots of bears, beer steins, and of course, Swiss Army knives. It's one of New Bern's little but undeniable delights. Open Mon., Wed., Fri., and Sat. 10 A.M.–5:30 P.M., Tues. and Thurs. 1–5:30 P.M. At the Tryon Palace, **The Craft and Garden Shop,** 610 Pollock St., 252/514-4927, is a great little garden shop with atmosphere to spare. You can get a pass at the gate that will allow you to visit the shop without having to pay admission if you don't want to visit the palace. The **Museum Store** on the corner of Eden and Pollock Streets offers the best place to get various souvenirs of your visit. Diagonally across from the palace you'll find four converted old residences now branding themselves as the **700 Block of Pollock Street.** They include several stores such as **Kunstlerhaus,** 720 Pollock St., 252/636-1604, which features jewelry, pottery, and so on; and **Backyard Bears,** 718 Pollock St, 252/637-7122, which is literally in the backyard of an old house, and contains bruinous merchandise. Near the Tryon Palace, **Ben's Teeks,** 252/635-1822, is where Ben Rider keeps a good selection of antiques.

Finally, I couldn't describe New Bern's shopping without mentioning **Mitchell Hardware,** 215 Craven St., 252/638-4261, one of those old-fashioned hardware stores packed with everything for the home. It carries some homier items worth a traveler's browsing and is staffed by people who seem to *know* everything, including where to find things amid all the clutter. Founded in 1898.

EVENTS

New Bern is a culturally minded town and is always throwing some sort of event. In January it's the Garden and History Lecture Series at Tryon Palace 800/767-1560; in February it's the **Sunday Jazz Showcase,** down at the Sheraton, 252/638-2577; the **Pepsi Heritage Festival,** 252/636-3812, takes place each June at sites all across town, and includes three stages-worth of entertainment, a sailing regatta, hoedown, battle reenactments, and more. The Fourth of July features fireworks over the water; the late-summer **Rotary Cup Regatta** pits cruising class boats against one another, and the Christmas season includes the **Holiday Tour of Historic Inns,** 252/638-8558; a Christmas parade of boats, 252/5781; **Handel's *Messiah*** over at the Centenary United Methodist Church, Middle and New Streets, 252/638-2577; and more. For information on these and the dozens of other annual events in New Bern, call the **Craven County Convention and Visitors Bureau** at 800/437-5767 or 252/637-9400.

ACCOMMODATIONS

New Bern is the sort of town where you'll want to be able to wake up and stroll somewhere for coffee without having to climb in the car or cross a major highway. Leave New Bern's historic downtown and suddenly you're in a not-so-quaint city that you probably don't want to make a part of your vacation. For this reason, if your budget permits, it's worth it to shell out for one of the historic inns downtown, or one of the riverview hotels. Keep in mind too that if you're looking to spend the night in a less-urban spot after spending the day in New Bern, Oriental and Hertford aren't far away.

As far as the historic old inns go, you won't find many places in America where you can sleep in a house that's over 200 years old, but you can do it at **Harvey Mansion: The Captain's Quarters,** 221 S. Front St., 252/638-3205. The inn and the three-star restaurant downstairs, as well as the basement pub, are owned and operated by Beat Züttel, a Swiss chef who hails from none other than Bern, Switzerland, and his wife Carolyn.

Starting at the intersection of Pollock and U.S. 17 Business and working west, you'll find Ed and Sooki Kirkpatrick's friendly (and child-friendly), 1850 **Harmony House Inn Bed & Breakfast,** 215 Pollock St., 800/636-3113 or 252/636-3810, a comfortable inn set in a large Greek Revival inn decorated with antiques, reproductions, and family mementos. Rates for the ten rooms (each with private baths) run $55–120, and that includes a full breakfast.

Also within walking distance of Tryon Place and the rest of downtown is **Kings Arms: A Colonial Inn** set in an 1848 home. Guided tours are available through the visitors center, and everywhere you wander you will find a piece of history on a house plaque, historic marker, or painted mural. $100 per night for the seven guest rooms. The third floor Mansard Suite, features original beaded board walls and a view of the Neuse River, for $145 per night. Innkeepers Richard and Patricia Gulley will serve you breakfast right to your room by candlelight, along with the morning paper.

New Berne House, 709 Broad St. 800/842-7688 or 252/636-2250, charges around $88 for its seven guest rooms tucked into a 1923 Colonial Revival house beneath magnolia and pecan trees and camellia bushes. All guest rooms feature antique furnishings, as well as their own baths, air-conditioning, and phone. Mystery weekends twice a month, plus full breakfasts. No children or pets. Howard and Marcia, the innkeepers, consider smoking an outdoor occupation. In addition to their fluent English, they speak limited Spanish, French, and German.

Worth a mention on the way out of town on U.S. 70/17 is **Comfort Suites Riverfront Park,** 218 East Front Street, 800/228-5150 or 252/636-0022, which in exchange for being a fairly far walk from downtown offers a fine Neuse riverfront location. It's won its chain's gold Hospitality Award for years. They offer whirlpool suites, a fitness center, and waterfront balconies as well as a complimentary continental breakfast. All rooms have microwaves, refrigerators, coffee makers, and hair dryers. Other stays in less-central locations include **Days Inn,** 925 Broad St., 252/636-0150, **Economy Inn,** 3465 Clarendon Blvd., 252/638-8166), **Hampton Inn,** 200 Hotel Dr. 252/637-2111, and **Sunset Motel,** 4631 U.S. 17 S, New Bern, 252/633-5682.

FOOD

Locals tend to vote **Harvey Mansion,** 221 South Front St., 800/638-3205 or 252/638-3205, email: zuttel@cconnect.net, tops among New Bern restaurants. Owned and run by a Swiss chef who hails from Bern, Switzerland, the restaurant's decor—what with the 11.5-foot ceilings and all—is usually voted tops among decors, and the Harvey Mansion's chef is usually voted New Bern's top chef. So if money's not an issue and you're only eating one meal in New Bern, make it here. Fresh local fish is featured, along with Angus beef, game, and Cajun dishes. Downstairs **The Cellar** features a cheaper, less-formal menu, lots of beers, and a chance to smoke a stogie in public, if the mood hits. Both restaurants are open Tuesday–Saturday, from 5 P.M. only.

The Chelsea: A Restaurant and Publick House, Broad & Middle Streets, features regional and international cuisine, and larger-than-you'd-expect wine and beer lists. It's set in what used to be Caleb (Inventor of Pepsi) Bradham's *second* drug store. Also on the higher end is **Corina's Restaurant,** 415 Broad St., which presents entrées starting around $10.95, and a tasty seafood bisque as an appetizer. Open for lunch and dinner, closed between meals.

Less expensive is the **Pollock Street Restaurant & Delicatessen,** 208 Pollock St., 252/637-2480, which offers full breakfasts in addition to the normal delicatessen items. Eat indoors or out. Right next door you'll find another cheap alternative, **Bagels Plus.** Both of these are great places for picking up a lunch that you can tote around while you explore the town.

Out at 3711 U.S. 17, **Moore's Old Tyme Barbecue,** 252/638-3937, offers both chopped pork and chicken barbecue, and even fries up a little seafood as well.

Coffee and Tea

For coffee and baked goods you won't find a better spot than **Trent River Coffee Company** 208 Craven St., 252/514-2030. Owner Ed Ruiz's place offers sandwiches, espresso, flavored coffees, muffins, and other such coffeehouse favorites. A very good book selection upstairs. Ed is a friendly former Bay Area flight attendant here fulfilling his dream of sharing San Francisco coffee culture with the New Bern area.

For something more in keeping with the city's colonial spirit, there's **Sarah Pocket Tea Room,** 303 Metcalf St., 252/636-3055, open Monday–Saturday, 11 A.M.–3 P.M. with hot tea and light lunches—soups, salads, crepes, quiches, and other things my wife's always trying to get me to eat.

NIGHTLIFE

Captain Ratty's Piano Bar, 330 S. Front St., 252/633-2088, opens at 5 P.M. and offers live entertainment, including a shag party on Thursday nights and jazz on Tuesdays. Over at the Harvey Mansion you'll find an atmospheric exposed-beam, low-ceiling, low-key pub in **The**

New Bern dining

Cellar, 800/638-3205 or 252/638-3205, email: zuttel@cconnect.net, originally the mansion's kitchen. You'll still see the original fireplace and irons down there, right along with the dartboards and TV. **The Chelsea: A Restaurant and Publick House,** 325 Middle St., 252/637-5469, is a popular place for locals to have a drink downtown. If you'd like to look out over the water as you frolic, try the **ProSail Pub,** at the Sheraton Grand, 100 Middle St., 252/638-3585, with an outside deck overlooking the harbor. On the weekends they also open up the **City Side Café** at the Sheraton, a dance club with a DJ and occasional live performers. If pool's your game, try **Mr. Stix Billiards,** 2724 Neuse Blvd, 252/638-2299, or **Mickey Milligan's,** 3411 Trent Rd. 252/637-3711. Milligan's also has a dance floor and bar food.

GETTING THERE

By Car
From I-95, head east on U.S. 70 and you'll come straight into town. From Elizabeth City, Edenton, Windsor, or Washington, just head south on U.S. 17. Or, if you'd like, head east at Washington out on U.S. 264, veer right when it forks onto N.C. 92, and stop over at Bath. Then continue on along N.C. 92 until you come to the Aurora–Bayview Ferry. Ride across the Pamlico River for free (about 20 minutes) and then take the N.C. 306 south to the N.C. 55 and then take the N.C. 55 west to New Bern.

By Airplane
People coming to the Central Coast from out of state normally fly into Norfolk, Virginia, Myrtle Beach, South Carolina, Wilmington, North Carolina, or even Raleigh/Durham, North Carolina, and then rent a car and drive the rest of the way. See the appropriate chapters for details on the Myrtle Beach and Wilmington airports and on local car-rental places in those towns. For information on Norfolk International Airport, call 757/857-3200. For the Raleigh/Durham airport, call 252/840-2123.

By Bus
Carolina Trailways provides bus service to New Bern: 504 Guion Street, 252/633-3100.

GETTING AROUND

New Bern's rental car spots include **Automotive Rentals of New Bern,** 252/633-6089; **Avis,** 800/831-2847 or 252/637-2130; **Enterprise,** 800/325-8007 or 252/514-2575; **Hertz Rent-a-Car,** 800/654-3131 or 252/637-3021; **National Car Rental,** 800/755-1501 or 252/637-5241.

Taxicab companies include **New Taxi Service,** 252/636-9000, **Safeway Taxi Co.,** 252/633-2828, and **Tryon Cab Co.,** 1018 Pollock St., 252/638-8809 or 252/635-1966.

INFORMATION

For more information on the New Bern area, contact the **New Bern Area Chamber of Commerce,** 316 S. Front St., 252/637-3111. Right next door you'll find the **Craven County Convention and Visitors Bureau** at 314 South Front St., New Bern, NC 28563; 800/437-5767 or 252/637-9400; website: www.visitnewbern.com.

NORTH ON U.S. 17

Oriental
If you're looking for Ocracoke-type tranquillity, but don't have an Ocracoke-type budget, consider a stay in Oriental. Oriental's a bit of an odd bird hereabouts; founded in the 1890s, it misses out on all the Historic Albemarle region promotions because it wasn't a colonial-era town. And unlike many of the towns along the Carolina Coast, which take their name from the birthplaces of homesick European founders or from various European leaders and benefactors whose favor the founders hoped to enlist, Oriental's naming legend has a California Gold Rush town's whimsy to it. The wife of the unincorporated town's aspiring first postmaster couldn't really get excited about the prospect of incorporating under the community's matter-of-fact, place-holdername of "Smith's Creek." While visiting a friend in Manteo, she was taken by the huge wooden sign inside the house, which read "ORIENTAL." The sign, her friends explained, had washed ashore from the wreck of the doomed Union steamship, the USS *Oriental.* The helpful wife smiled widely

and told her husband she had good news: not only had she come up with a very exotic-sounding name for their isolated town—"Oriental"—but she knew where she could get a very large name sign for free.

Television and film writer/actor/director/producer Kevin Williamson was raised hereabouts. Today the pragmatically named burg boasts around 1,000 inhabitants and is a popular Sunday-drive-destination from New Bern, twenty minutes away. Folks come to Oriental largely for the fresh seafood. The village has taken to calling itself the "Sailing Capital of North Carolina." It's a popular port-of-call for yachters and sailors using the Intracoastal Waterway.

Pillar-of-the-community **Oriental Marina, Inn & Restaurant,** Hodges St., 252/249-1818, is a destination by itself. The inn features 18 waterfront rooms, a laundromat, and a pool. Rates range from $55 to $89 a night. The **River Neuse Motel,** at the Corner of S. Neuse Dr. and Mildred Street, 252/249-1404, is another dockable, cheap waterfront stay. It features its own private fishing pier.

Of course a town with this much atmosphere is bound to spawn some bed-and-breakfasts. **The Cartwright House,** 301 Freemason St., 888/726-9389 or 252/249-1337, website: www.cartwrighthouse.com, faces the water and offers four bedrooms and one suite. Somehow it seems closer to the town's colonial past by having British hosts, Tina and Glyn, who will make sure your scones and coffee and full breakfast fill you up. **The Inn at Oriental,** 508 Church St., 800/485-7174 or 252/249-1078, is set in an old 1850s teacher rooming house, but the chalk-wielders of yore wouldn't recognize the twelve rooms today, what with their private baths, antiques and reproductions, and (in three rooms) modern kitchenettes. Full American breakfasts here include Belgian waffles and eggs Benedict, if you ask for them.

Since the term "Oriental" has gone out of vogue for describing "Asian" food, this little town may be one of the last places where you can order "Oriental cuisine." A good local favorite is **The Village Restaurant,** Broad St., 252/249-1700, featuring great country cooking and seafood. And it has all of its alcohol permits, an unusual thing to find in a place with comfort food this good. Breakfast, lunch, and dinner, seven days a week. At the

Marina, **The Oriental Marina Restaurant,** Hodges St., 252/249-2204, serves up grilled mahi-mahi, veal marsala, soft shell cozumel, stuffed lobster, and Raccoon Creek mud pie for dessert. Upstairs the **Topside Lounge** provides a nice view to admire while sipping a cold one; some nights feature live music up here—or downstairs at the Tiki Bar.

Washington

If you've ever sipped a "Cup of Joe," thank Washington. And if you can't read the book of Exodus without picturing a Technicolor Edgar G. Robinson in robes, blame Washington. More on this later.

Washington's bigger than Bath or Oriental. Walk its earnest brick business blocks and you feel its regional importance: this is where local farming and fishing families would come weekdays to sell their produce and buy supplies, and then return on Saturday night to window shop and maybe catch a vaudeville act over at the Turnage Theatre. But because it's always taken the Cinderella's share of the regional economic duties, Washington isn't quite as homey or slow-paced as Oriental or even Elizabeth City. In fact Washington's importance as a store for naval supplies brought its ruin in the Civil War. Neither army was going to waste a lot of men or ammunition to win, say, Bath. But the Union and the Confederacy fought hard for control of Washington, and finally the federal troops burned most of antebellum Washington to keep it out of Confederate hands. It burned again in 1900.

Consequently Washington's features a turn-of-the-century, Victorian ambience. In most places in America, that would make it seem old, but in the Albemarle, it makes it seem like the new kid on the block. Nonetheless, Washington's trying hard to capture a bigger slice of the boating and tourist trade in these parts.

Washington was the first town in the United States named after George Washington. The settlement that formed here in the early 1770s initially went by the name "Forks of the Tar," but local settlers (wisely) seized the historic moment and renamed their village after the general in 1776. This was a fairly risky maneuver, since the Revolution was far from won at that point, and the British would have wrecked particular havoc with a town bearing the hated Virginian's name.

Having cast its lot with the patriots, Washington did all it could to make sure they won. When the ports at Savannah, Charles Town, and Wilmington were bottled up by British ships, Washington took on the port duties, pulling in ships from other colonies and France to supply the troops. By doing so, by war's end, Washington found itself established as a regional center of commerce and culture.

Down on the riverfront you'll find the **Washington/Beaufort County Chamber of Commerce,** 800/999-3857 or 252/946-9168, email: wash.beauf@coastalnet.com. Here you can pick up a self-guided tour map of the business area. Take a walk up there and you'll see a lot of renovation; a good bit of local efforts and money is focused on revitalizing the **Turnage Theater,** 146–154 W. Main St., built in 1916. As the only vaudeville stage in Washington, and for a long time the only movie theatre, it saw young Red Skelton and Tex Ritter here tred its floorboards, along with Roy Rogers and Trigger.

Now back to the "Cup of Joe." Josephus Daniels, U.S. secretary of the Navy during World War I and later ambassador to Mexico under FDR, was born in Washington in the early part of the War between the States. His father was a shipbuilder, but by the end of the war, he was, like so many other fathers, a memory.

Nonetheless, the Daniels family persevered; Josephus went on to become a famous Raleigh newspaperman. After being named secretary of Navy under President (and former Wilmington-resident) Woodrow Wilson, Daniels appointed a young Franklin Delano Roosevelt as his assistant secretary. He also stressed discipline and preparedness in his sailors, and this included banning consumption of beer and wine aboard ship. Consequently all through World War I, disgruntled, begrudgingly sober sailors were forced to sip coffee instead of the grog and ale that had heretofore been their right as sailors. Before long they took to calling a cup of coffee a "Cup of Joe" in honor of their commander.

After he become president, FDR repaid Daniels the favor by naming him ambassador to Mexico. When Daniels took office, protesters threw stones at the embassy, but apparently this has no relationship to the phrase, "getting stoned in Mexico."

Cecil B. De Mille, who directed the blockbuster biblical epic, *The Ten Commandments,* hailed from Washington as well. You can see the De Mille family grave on the grounds of St. Peter's Episcopal Church, though both Cecil and filmmaker brother William are themselves buried in Hollywood. On the corner of Bonner and Main Streets, and you'll find a historic plaque celebrating Cecil and his father, playwright Henry C. DeMille.

Washington's also home to the **North Carolina Estuarium,** 223 East Water St., 252/948-8000, an aquarium with over 200 exhibits that focus upon marine life in the state's many, many estuaries, and on human interaction with the sea critters. Open 10 A.M.–4 P.M., Tues.–Sat., more in the summer. Admission runs $3 adult, $2 for K–12, free for kids under five years.

Bath

The oldest city in North Carolina, Bath was founded in 1705, though French Protestant settlements in the area traces back the 1690s. With easy river access and the Ocracoke Inlet to sail through on the way to England, it seemed this seemed like a good location. John Lawson, surveyor and author of the first history of Carolina (published in 1709), lived here and plotted out the original town.

Even before the town's establishment, Carolina's first public library was founded here, consisting of books sent to St. Thomas Parish. Members of the parish established a free school for African-Americans and Native Americans. Bath, though only 50 people lived here in 1708, was the unquestioned social/political center of embryonic North Carolina, and as such it saw much of the history of the region. The yellow fever epidemics of the early 1700s, political clashes, and the severe drought of 1711 all took their toll on the seedling city. When the Tuscarora Indians wrought havoc on Carolinian settlers, the survivors fled to Bath for safety. When piracy bloomed along the North Carolina Coast, no less than Blackbeard was said to live here. The colonial General Assembly met in Bath three times in the 1740s and 1750s, and the town's name came up when Carolinians were trying to decide on a capital city, but Bath lost that contest. In 1776, when Washington was founded fifteen miles up the river and named the seat of Beaufort

County government, Bath was drained of most all of its prestige and trade. Through the rest of the 18th century, and through the 19th and into the 20th, Bath has remained a small, quiet village on the water.

Stop by the **Historic Bath Visitor Center,** Carteret St., 252/923-3971, website: www.pamlico.com/bath, for pamphlets, maps, and a fine 15-minute orientation video. Guided tours of the 1751 Palmer-Marsh House, the 1830 Bonner House, and the 1790 Van Der Meer House, and 1734 St. Thomas Episcopal Church, the oldest church in North Carolina.

If you'd like to stay here, you'll probably want to do it at the popular Bath Marina, 252/923-5711, or at the **Pirate's Den Bed and Breakfast,** 116 S. Main St., 252/923-9571, a newly built (but traditionally styled) home specifically designed to serve as a B&B, run by native Bath residents Lesha and Roger Brooks. Rooms run $65 to $75, which includes a full Southern breakfast.

Plymouth

Turn right on U.S. 64 to visit Plymouth. Civil War buffs know the name of this town well: Plymouth was the site of the largest battle in North Carolina, fought April 17–20. To learn about the naval vessels involved in the fight, be sure to visit the **Port-O-Plymouth Civil War Museum,** 252/793-1377, email: wccc@coastalnet.com.

Windsor

Back on U.S. 17 headed north you'll pass through little Windsor, founded in 1768, featuring many antebellum homes and a nice river boardwalk. If you're traveling with kids, you may want to stop by **Livermon Recreational Park and Mini Zoo,** 101 York St., 252/794-5553, where they can see a buffalo and pet donkeys, llamas, goats, sheep, and about thirty other species of foreign and domestic animals. Here too you'll find the start (and finish) of the **Cashie Wetlands Walk,** which goes through natural wetlands where you'll see cypress and other flora. From the observation deck you should be able to spot a number of species of endangered birds. And if you'd rather paddle than walk, canoes are available at no charge.

North of town, the delectable country cooking at **Heritage House,** 252/794-4567, where you can pick up a great country breakfast, or a good

BBQ sandwich with slaw for $2.85. Even the top-end of the menu (10 oz. ribeye steak) tops out at $10.05. The pecan pie and peach cobbler aren't bad either. And, as with a lot of country restaurants, the folks at Heritage House offer various knickknacks to buy. Last time I was through the wares included "Evange-Cubes." Rubik's Cubes which, when completed correctly, reveal paintings of various scenes from the Bible.

Outside of Windsor, you're welcome to visit the **Hope Plantation,** 252/794-3140, email: hope plantation@coastalnet.com, featuring two different National Register homes: the 1763 King Bazemore House and the 1803 Governor David Stone house. Both feature regional period furnishings. On grounds also is the Roanoke-Chowan Heritage Center, honoring the region's original dwellers. Admission is $6.50 for adults, $2 for students wtih identification.

EDENTON

With its sleepy 19th-century waterfront ambience, Edenton, former colonial capital, reminds a lot of people of Beaufort, S.C. It's a nice place to quiet down for a couple of days and absorb the small town, waterfront tranquillity.

Named after Royal Governor Charles Eden, Edenton, founded 1715, nonetheless has something Edenic about it. This is the sort of slow-paced, scenic Southern town most people imagine when they come to explore the South, but often find difficult to locate in the flesh. Shortly after its founding, Edenton stole the limelight from Bath and became the chief city of the young colony. In the early days when the capital was wherever the governor chose to live, many of the Royal Governors chose Edenton as their home. The town became internationally famous in 1774 when, in the wake of the Boston Tea Party, local women staged a protest against the new Royal taxes and signed a pledge to promise they wouldn't use East India tea. This incident became known as the "Edenton Tea Party," and it not only inspired patriotic zeal among Americans, but the fact that fragile women were taking part in politics outraged the British and proved to them that Americans in general were clearly too uneducated and uncivilized to be taken seriously. Many of them still think this.

Edenton waterfront

Depraved or not, Edenton managed to build an impressive collection of structures during the colonial period, many of which are still standing today. Stop by the Historic Edenton Visitor Center 108 N. Broad St., 252/482-2637, and pick up a guided tour of the distict that will take you through 1736 St. Paul's Church, the 1758 Cupola House, and 1767 Chowan County Courthouse, and the home of early-19th century U.S. Supreme Court Justice James Iredell.

Other than historic buildings, Edenton offers the **Emmrich Theatre Production Company,** which presents a variety of musicals (most with Christian themes) year-round at a variety of locations. Tickets run $13 for adults, $7 for kids. Call 252/482-4621 for information or tickets.

Accommodations
Not quite downtown but a bit more affordable than most of the inns is the 38-room **Coach House Inn,** 823 N. Broad St., 252/482-2107. The **Colonial Motel and Restaurant** is even further out at 1392 N. Broad St., 252/482-8010. You'll find the 66-room **Travel Host Inn** at 501 Virginia Rd., 252/482-2017.

At the top of the list both in style and price comes Arch and Jane Edwards's landmark **The Lords Proprietors' Inn,** 300 N. Broad St., 800/348-8933. Established in 1982, the inn consists of three restored homes on two acres of grounds in the historic district. The Edwards moved down here from Washington, D.C. in 1980, convinced Edenton was the "prettiest little town in the South," and set about founding an inn. The three houses here today range in age from 200 years old to 80-something, but they all share the ambience of a traditional country inn. Most rooms run from $155–190 a night, which includes a full breakfast. One of the new Satterfield Suites will run $225. Each room in the inn features its own private bath with antiques and reproductions spanning from the federal to Victorian era. Along with New Bern's The Harmony House, this is the only Coastal North Carolina inn named as one of "The Fine Inns of North America," and the only hotel in all the North Carolina Coast listed as one of The National Trust for Historic Preservation's Historic Hotels.

If you golf, ask the Edwards about their golf packages. Or they can put together a musical evening, an art gallery viewing, or have an artist come over and teach a class on furniture painting. Tuesday through Saturday you can also enjoy dinner at the inn's **Whedbee House Dining Room and Patio.** Guests pay a "favored" rate of $35 a person. Or you can order à la carte. Salads run about $10. Chef Kevin Yokley's entrées might include Sautéed Scallops and Crabmeat Sabayon Blue Cheese Encrusted Beef Tenderloin, Red Snapper en Papillote, or Smoked Pork Tenderloin, with Apricot and Jerusalem Artichoke Relish (all $25 à la carte); or if a rich dessert is all the

THE EDENTON TEA PARTY

On October 25, 1774, Mrs. Penelope Barker led a tea party at Mrs. Elizabeth King's house in Edenton. There the two women and their forty-nine female guests signed a decree vowing to support the resolutions of the colonies' First Provisional Congress, which had banned, among other things, the importation of British tea.

That, anyway, is the legend—which has traditionally been accepted as fact in Edenton. A bronze teapot even marks the site of Mrs. King's house on the town's Old Courthouse Green.

The downside of the tea party legend is that it probably never happened. While it's near-certain that fifty-one North Carolinian women signed their names to a protest document sent to England, many historians doubt whether they all ever sat down together—at Mrs. King's house, or anywhere else. The best anyone can figure, it's unlikely that the women, who hailed from at least five different counties and represented a number of different social classes, would or could have ever arranged a mass meeting. Nonetheless, in what is considered one of the earliest examples of political involvement by American women, the women did manage to sign the same piece of parchment, which likely was circulated petition style. In part, it declared:

The Provincial Deputies of North Carolina having resolved not to drink any more tea, nor wear any more British cloth & c., many ladies of this Province have determined to give a memorable proof of their patriotism, and have accordingly entered into the following honourable and spirited association. I sent it to you to shew you faire countrywomen, how zealously and faithfully American Ladies follow the laudable example of their husbands, and what opposition your Ministers may expect to receive from a people thus firmly united against them.

This audacious show of feminine resolve shocked British sensibilities, confirming their conception of American men as barbarians who couldn't control their women any better than they could handle their liquor. A London cartoonist pictured the female signers gathered for a decadent tea party complete with snifters and paramours. Apparently when the colonials heard about the alleged incident, they decided to go along with the idea that an actual party had taken place, and before long the story of the Edenton Tea Party had settled into its present-day form.

The odd thing of course is that the tea party story imagines the women sitting around drinking tea, while the whole point of the resolution was that they vowed not to.

---

bookkeeper ordered, try the Frenched Cranberry Bread with Homemade Banana Ice Cream and Butterscotch Sauce or Chocolate Extravaganza (all $10 à la carte). The inn features an open wine service throughout the meal: for $10 a person, they'll keep pouring (even changing wines) as long as you keep drinking within limits, of course. Nonguests can eat here as well, but they must pay $50 and a one-time $25 "membership" fee.

"Captain" Reuel and Marijane Schappel's **Albemarle House,** 204 West Queen Street, 252/482-8204 ($80–125), and Bill and Phyllis Pepper's 1907 **Captains Quarters Inn,** 202 W. Queen Street, 800/482-8945 or 252/482-8945 ($55–95) are also popular stays in town.

Finally you'll find the **Granville Queen Themed Inn,** 108 South Granville Street, 252/482-5296, charges $95–120 per room, with full breakfast. Themes in the nine rooms in-

clude the Egyptian Queen room, with leopardskin bed, a tomb-mural garden tub, and a bust of Queen Nefertiti. A quirky place with friendly people.

For something outside of town, not particularly historic but still rich with atmosphere, consider **Trestle House Inn,** 632 Soundside Road, 800/645-8466 or 252/482-2282. Built in 1972 overlooking a wildlife refuge on a private lake, the inn derives its name from the old railroad trestle beams spanning the interior. Canada geese and other waterfowl frequent the lake. The five rooms run $85–100 a night, which includes a gourmet breakfast overlooking the lake. Be sure to try innkeeper Peter Bogus's "Peter's Piping Hot Pepper Sauce" on your eggs. Children over the age of five are welcome. From Edenton, take N.C. 32 south 1.8 miles, turn right onto Soundside Road, and continue for 2.8 miles to the Trestle House Inn on the right side.

Food

For casual but satisfying eating, head out to **Lane's Family BBQ and Seafood,** East Church St., 252/482-4008, open 11 A.M.–8 P.M., seven days a week, and featuring a drawing of a pig on the menu—always a good sign. The barbecue's very good and reasonably priced ($2.50 for a sandwich), and so is the French silk pie and banana pudding ($2.50 per serving). Fresh fried or grilled fish runs around $9 and comes (as do all the dinners) with two vegetables, hush puppies, corn bread, or rolls. For something a little fancier downtown, there's **Waterman's Grill,** 427 S. Broad St., 252/482-7733, featuring good fish and homemade desserts.

HERTFORD

If you're looking for the flavor of the small-town South, you probably couldn't find a better place to taste it than Hertford. As you enter town you'll see a large mural painted across the side of an old brick building at Church and Grubb Streets. This is a revised version of the mural; as late as 2000 it sported a huge Confederate battle flag, being saluted by a soldier in Confederate gray.

The New York Yankees cap on the mural salutes the late Hall of Fame A's and Yankees pitcher, Jim "Catfish" Hunter, who hailed from the Hertford area. In front of the 1828 **Perquimans County Courthouse,** you'll find a monument to Perquimans County's favorite son, with a detailed listing of his notable professional accomplishments, which started when he leaped from college ball to the major leagues without pitching a single game in the minor leagues, and later included a perfect game and five straight years winning twenty-plus games before arm trouble cut off his career at age 33. Born in 1946, Hunter died in 1999 from Lou Gehrig's Disease. Though the monument in front of the courthouse is far more impressive, you can see Hunter's grave at the Cedarwood Cemetery, Hertford, on the east side of Hyde Park Road.

But of course Hertford goes back a lot longer than Catfish Hunter or even the War between the States. The oldest brick house in North Carolina, the 1730 **Newbold-White House,** Harvey Point Rd., 252/426-7567, is here, available for the viewing. Heck, even Gregory's 5&10 at 119 Church St. 252/426-7659, has been open since 1915. For a handy self-guided walking tour, pick up a tour booklet at the Perquimans County Chamber of Commerce at Hall of Fame Square on Church Street, 252/426-5657, website: www.perquimans.com. You'll also find some good antiquing along Church Street, near the courthouse.

Hertford is the sort of place where you may well want to stay for the night. If so, you've really got two choices: the Colonial Revival **Covent**

1812 on the Perquimans B&B

Garden Inn, at 107 Covent Garden, 252/426-5945; or the 1820 **Eagle and Anchor Inn,** 215 W. Market St. For a very unique, private stay outside of town, try the **Beechtree Inn,** 948 Pender Road, 252/426-7815, email: hobbs@inteliport.com, a big spread. The main house was built in 1710, but you'll be staying in one of four small cottages, each with private bath and fireplace; all fourteen buildings on the property were built before 1840. Innkeepers Ben and Jackie Hobbs charge $55–90 a night, which includes a full breakfast. If you're interested, Ben, a furniture maker by trade, offers classes in furniture making. Stay from Monday through Saturday, attend class every day, and by the end of the week you'll have built, using hand tools, a bedside table with a drawer. To see some of Ben's work online, check out www.hobbsfurniture.com. Children are welcome, and so are pets, for a $5 fee. The Hobbs themselves have a cat and a dog, so allergy sufferers, beware. To get there from Hertford, take U.S. 17 toward Edenton, turn left onto Snug Harbor Road, then turn left at Pender Road, the first road on the left. The Beechtree is the first group of buildings. North of town on the way to Elizabeth City, turn right off 17 onto Great Neck Road and you'll find **1812 on the Perquimans,** Old Neck Rd., 252/426-1812. Rooms in this historic old plantation house run $75–125 a night, which include a full breakfast and full run of five acres of pasture and woodland featuring a private wharf, canoes, fishing, and sailboating.

For decent home cooking in a cozy environment right downtown, try **Frankies Hertford Café,** right downtown at 127 N. Church St., 252/426-5593, or head over to **Tommy's Family Restaurant,** at 720 Edenton Rd., 252/426-5020, for steaks, seafood, and chicken. For pit-cooked barbecue, head south of town on U.S. 17 to **Captain Bob's BBQ & Seafood,** 252/426-1811.

ELIZABETH CITY

Called "The Harbor of Hospitality," and often named one of the best small art towns in America, Elizabeth City features five different historic districts on the National Register. This town, begun in 1757 and formally founded in 1793, is most famous for the Elizabeth City Rose Buddies, a group of Elizabeth City residents who greet visiting boats at the town marina with a rosebud and a champagne reception. The tradition began in 1983 when retired mail-carrier Fred Fearing and his friend Joe Kramer decided to thank the boaters who had chosen to dock at the town's expensive new Mariner's Wharf. Fred got the wine and Joe clipped some rosebuds—one for each of the 17 boats at the wharf—and they held their first reception. It went well: the boaters were delighted and vowed that they'd return to what had heretofore been a rather unremarkable port. Soon afterward, Fred and Joe, sensing they were on to something, threw a reception for the next group of boaters who came to stop in the local slips. Before long word of Elizabeth City's hospitality had spread up and down the Intracoastal Waterway, and the tradition continues today. In exchange for this hospitality, the generally wealthy boaters spend a lot of money at the town's restaurants and shops, which is at least partly what town had had in mind when it built the wharf in the first place. So famous are these receptions that even national television weatherman Willard Scott heard of them; he presented Fearing with a golf cart in which to make his rounds. For information on Elizabeth City, stop by the Chamber of Commerce at the corner of McMorrine St. and E. Ehringhaus, 252/335-4365, website: www.elizcity.com. In keeping with the city's hospitable reputation, the folks there will let you check your email.

The new waterfront home of the **Museum of the Albemarle,** 1116 U.S. 17 S, 252/335-1453, should be open sometime in 2002. Wherever the museum is when you get there, you'll find exhibits interpreting the human stories of the Albemarle, starting with the Native Americans who settled here first, on through the first English colonists, and the subsequent farmers and fishermen.

For places to sleep, consider the English-style **Elizabeth City Bed & Breakfast,** 108 E. Fearing Street, 252/338-2177, $55–85, or **The Culpepper Inn** at 609 W. Main Street, 252/335-1993, which offers 11 rooms, some with fireplaces and king-sized beds. $65–$105.

On the cheaper (around $50) but less-charming side is The **Days Inn,** 308 S. Hughes

St., 252/338-8900, which offers 48 rooms. Next door is the **Comfort Inn,** 306 S. Hughes Blvd., 252/338-8900, with 80 rooms and a pool.

For eats, try to catch a meal at the hip, over-the-water **Mulligan's Grille,** at the Marina, 252/338-2141, which is clearly less a restaurant in a small Southern town than it is a part of the sun-and-fun international boating scene. But still, the prices are reasonable, especially at lunch, where you can get sautéed shrimp over pasta for $7.95, along with the omnipresent $6 hamburger. Also waterfront is **Arena's Bakery and Deli,** 700 E. Main St., 252/335-2114, a good place to pick up breakfast. At 609 C Street you'll find the less-hip but definitely filling **Southern Pig Bar-B-Que,** 252/338-6859.

For a good latte or mocha, see the **Elizabeth City Milling Company,** indoors on the wharf.

SOUTH ON U.S. 70: CROATAN NATIONAL FOREST

Take U.S. 70 south of New Bern and you'll soon be cutting through the 157,000-acre **Croatan National Forest,** a good place to stop for a picnic or to camp. It also has the largest collection of carnivorous plants, including pitcher plants and Venus flytraps, in any national forest. Speaking of carnivorous, this is the northernmost home of the American alligator. This is a great place to camp or hike; for the latter, an easy one to start with is the 1.4-mile **Cedar Point Tideland Trail,** which makes a loop through hardwood and pine-laced estuary and tidal marsh areas. You can hide behind wildlife viewing blinds along the way and take some great nature shots. To get there heading south on U.S. 70, turn right at Roberts Road, left at the T, and the right again at Millis Road. Turn left at the next T on to Whitehouse Forks Road, then merge onto N.C. 58, and turn right on Dudley Road. Look for the signs to Cedar Point Tideland Trail. You can camp out here too. Or you can camp at **Flanner Beach,** a campground further north and closer to (but still well off) U.S. 70.

Morehead City

Morehead City was founded in 1857 by John Motley Morehead, former governor of North Carolina, as a land-development scheme. The population got a boost during the Civil War when the crews of several British ships, unable to leave because of the federal blockade, decided to settle here. It has developed into the state's second largest port. Today Morehead's historically businesslike waterfront has begun sprucing itself up with a handful of good restaurants, but the town gets most of its attention for two of its fall festivals. Most famous is the annual **Bald Is Beautiful Convention** at the end of September, perennially drawing international media coverage. Founded by Morehead City's John Capps in the early 1970s, the convention celebrates "hairfree" living with big dinners, a deep-sea fishing trip, the traditional "Blessing of the Bald Heads," and several contests, along with motivational speeches and workshops. For further information, call John Capps himself, 252/726-1855.

The second festival is less unique but still very enjoyable. Every first weekend in October, the **North Carolina Seafood Festival** draws people from across the state, allegedly to "celebrate seafood culture," but mainly to eat lots and lots of seafood. Various events involving said eating include the Opening Ceremonies Luncheon (public invited, $15) and the very popular Habitat Fish Fry at 5 P.M. on the waterfront. Live bands play, sailing boats compete in a regatta, and fisherfolk compete in fishing contests; carnival rides run all weekend, and some 100 street vendors offer seafood snacks of various sorts. You can usually tour a couple of naval ships and Coast Guard cutters as well. And on Sunday there's the Blessing of the Fleet.

As far as permanent eating spots in Morehead: one day I asked an employee down at the Beaufort waterfront which of the many fish places was her favorite. She pointed at this Beaufort spot and that, but never with much enthusiasm. And then, finally, with a look to either side, she whispered, "But really, the *best* fish is up in Morehead City at the Sanitary."

Since 1938, **Sanitary Fish Market & Restaurant,** 501 Evans St., 252/247-3111, has become a landmark around here, a large unpretentious place with views of the water and boats, with the owner walking around greeting everyone and the front register offering T-shirts and bumper stickers to go. And the seafood—prepared a number of ways but fantastic fried—really is wonderful. The hush puppies may be the best around.

Why "Sanitary Restaurant"? Obviously an earlier generation thought that naming restaurants "sanitary" would make us want to eat there. (A second "Sanitary" lived a long life in Folly Beach, S.C., before closing a few years back.) But to most of us living today, it's kind of like calling a place "Roach-Free Diner." We worry when restaurateurs protesteth too much. Fortunately the Smuckers Effect seems to be in play here: with a name like Sanitary, it has to be good—and it is.

You'll find at least two other eating spots of note on the Morehead City waterfront. First comes the Sanitary's next-door neighbor, **Amos Mosquito's Swampside Cafe** 509 Evans St., 252/247-6222 (apparently shooting for the Smuckers Effect themselves). Dinners feature seafood and creatively cooked meats. A casual place with a great deck overlooking the boats. For coffee, baked goods, and Internet access, **Coffee Affair** is a pleasant, classy coffee place right over the water.

BEAUFORT

First known as Fish Town, Beaufort (BOUferd) is North Carolina's third-oldest city, founded in 1709, though the town wasn't formally laid out until 1722. The local settlers took a lot of grief from the Tuscarora during the Tuscarora War. Blackbeard liked to stay here in Beaufort, and the town even had a certain marital nostalgia for him: he is said to have hung one of his wives here. In 1747 Beaufort residents were booted from their own city by marauding Spanish pirates, though they returned a couple days later with guns and retook the town.

One of the more colorful characters from Beaufort's past would be Captain Otway Burns, a privateer (government-endorsed pirate) for the United States against British ships during the War of 1812. You can see his grave at the Old Town Cemetery. As commander of the *Snap Dragon,* Burns terrorized British merchant ships in both hemispheres and caused the British so much grief that they offered $50,000 reward for his capture. Finally in 1814, the British did capture the *Snapdragon,* only to find that Burns had gone ashore to tend to his rheumatism. He served in the general assembly and Andrew Jackson appointed him as a lighthouse keeper where, according to all accounts, he lived a raucous good time to the end.

Since the late 1800s, Beaufort has been a popular vacation spot. Today with its home prices soaring and its downtown restaurants jammed, the town happily lives off its good looks and storied past.

SIGHTS

The **Mattie King Davis Art Gallery,** at the Old Town Beaufort Restoration Complex, gives local artisans a chance to show their paintings, ceramics, and weavings. Open Mon.–Sat., 10 A.M.–4 P.M. If local history interests you, stop by the **Beaufort Historic Site,** set in the 1825 Josiah Bell House, at 100 Block Turner St., 800/575-7483 or 252/728-5225, website: www.blackbeardthepirate.com. Here you can pick up visitor's information and embark (Apr.–Oct.) on guided tours of Beaufort's historic district via double-decker bus ($5), or on foot. Open Mon.–Sat., 8:30 A.M.–4:30 P.M. One of the houses it passes, the 1698 Hammock House (Beaufort's oldest), once served as an inn and was often host to Edward Teach, aka "Blackbeard." One legend even has it that he hung one of his wives from a branch of the large oak tree outside, and that even today (you guessed it), sometimes, late at night . . .

A tour of homes departing from the Bell house also runs $5 and will take you through the interior of an apothecary shop, courthouse, and jail, as well as various historic homes,

The **North Carolina Maritime Museum,** 315 Front St., 252/728-7317, website: www.ah.dcr.state.nc.us/maritime/default.htm, presents in-depth and hands-on exhibits that give visitors a good sense of the region's maritime history, which is to say, its *history,* since Beaufort's past and the men and women who worked and docked at its waterfront are inextricably linked. Some interesting relics from what appears to be *Queen Anne's Revenge,* Blackbeard's flagship, which sank off Ocracoke. Also fascinating is the sealable floating car used in the 1890s for ferrying victims from shipwrecked or sinking vessels. Across the street in the Watercraft Center, you can watch the shipbuilders constructing and restoring traditional wooden boats. Free.

If you look out across the water to the unpopulated islands that face Beaufort, you're looking at the **Rachel Carson National Estuarine Reserve,** 216 Front St. (office), named for the famous author of *Silent Spring.* Carson based her ecologically groundbreaking book partly on research conducted in the Beaufort area. To get there you'll need to find a boat to take you, but it's worth the trip to explore the marshes and flats that are home to wild horses, 160 species of birds, and various other wildlife. A great place for shelling and clamming. Call 252/728-2170 for information. Volunteers lead field trips to the preserve during the spring and summer.

ACCOMMODATIONS

Motels

On paper the **Inlet Inn,** 601 Front St., 252/728-3600, sounds like another historic B&B, but it's the most modern-looking thing on the waterfront. Still, the location's great, the prices can be reasonable ($65–85 in the low season, though up to $140 in high), and most of the rooms feature a waterfront view. Some of the rooms have a fireplace; some have porches. Breakfast is included in the price of the room.

Historic Inns, Bed-and-Breakfasts

Often named with North Carolina's top inns, Sam and Linda Dark's 250-year-old **Cedars Inn,** 305 Front St., 252/728-7036, stands set back above the waterfront, within easy walking distance of everything. The Cedars offers 12 rooms/suites with private baths, fireplaces, full Southern breakfasts, a wine bar, and bicycles for exploring the boardwalk and historic area. Rates run $95–165 a night. The 1866 **Pecan Tree Inn,** 116 Queen Street, 252/728-6733, stands a half block from the Beaufort water-

front and offers seven rooms; and two suites offer Jacuzzis and king-size canopy beds. Rooms run $65–$140.

A unique new place to stay is **The Carteret County Home Bed and Breakfast,** 299 N.C. 101, 252/728-4611, built in 1914, and one of the East Coast's last-standing county homes, the place where local residents down on their fortunes would live and work. Now you work elsewhere and then pay to stay here. Ah, progress. In return you get double the room; the individual rooms have been combined into two-room suites. Now to lay on the irony thicker, consider that many people who visit Beaufort are retirees drawing Social Security pensions, and it was the advent of Social Security and welfare that made poorhouses like the Carteret County Home go broke in the first place. The home closed in 1944, and reopened only periodically through the years for a variety of uses. Generally its main use was to serve as the local eyesore. Then some folks converted the home into a B&B and got it registered on the National Register of Historic Places. Nowadays owners Terry and Nan O'Pray run the place, and advertise themselves as "the grumpy hosts with the lumpy beds, bad food, and nasty cat," though, they're quick to admit, "we like to think that is really false advertising."

Diving House

If you're in Beaufort to dive, here's a little-known and possibly inexpensive way to stay in Beaufort, especially if you're with a larger group. **Discovery Diving Company,** 414 Orange St., 252/728-2265, offers two dormitory-style diving lodges for its customers and their families. Rates run $11 a person to stay in one of the two lodges; with a minimum of $77 a night for your group. The two lodges are divided up to provide four different lodgings, with beds for eight, 10, 14, or 21. Lodges include kitchens and refrigerators, but you'll need to bring your own linens.

FOOD

The **Beaufort Brewing and Bodacious Eatery,** 118 Craven Street, 252/728-1808, is Beaufort's only microbrewery/restaurant combination in a very hard-to-find spot back off the main strip. Once you find it, you'll think it's worth it, especially for the Sunday brunch. **Loughry's Landing,** 510 Front Street, 252/728-7541 sits on the boardwalk, serving up steamed crab legs, oysters, clams, fish, and other goodies from the sea.

On a side street **Beaufort Grocery Co.,** 117 Queen St., 252/728-3899, offers good regional dishes with a gourmet flair in a quaint former market. Easier to find on Front Street is **Clawson's 1905 Restaurant,** 425 Front Street, 252/728-2133, another old grocery store with an engaging atmosphere and popular seafood, steaks, and more on the menu. **The Dockhouse Seafood Restaurant,** 500 Front Street, 252/728-4872, is usually crowded with sun-tanned, boat-related people drinking beers and eating fried things. A raucous good time, right on the waterfront. The casual **Finz Grill,** 330 Front Street, 252/728-7459, comes with good recommendations. Deck dining on the water.

The **Royal James Cafe,** 117 Turner Street, 252/728-4573, is about as unpretentious as it sounds fancy: a café, poolroom, and bar, all in one. Founded about the same year as the Waffle House chain, the Royal James hasn't quite multiplied in the same way, yet people keep coming back for the simple café food and the good company.

And as much as the patty melts and cue sticks at the Royal James nod to Beaufort's humbler, fishing village past, the clinking carafes and hissing espresso machines at **Montana Wine and Coffee Bar,** 252/504-3479 (complete with an outdoor deck overlooking Taylor's Creek), points to the town's future as a playground for the affluent. **Roland's BBQ,** 815 Cedar Street, 252/728-1953, on the other hand, is timeless. It just keeps on doing what it does best, fortifying the air around Beaufort with vitamins P, I, and G.

For ice cream **The General Store,** 515 Front Street, 252/728-7707, offers 32 flavors, along with souvenirs, gifts, a laundry room, and—like a good general store—a little of everything else.

Nightlife

In addition to the spots mentioned above, add the **BackStreet Pub,** Middle Lane, 252/728-7108, serves no food, but they do offer a wide selection of beer and wines, and often feature live entertainment.

the Sanitary Restaurant in Morehead City

RECREATION AND INFORMATION

Paddling

People like paddling around the Rachel Carson Reserve, Cape Lookout, and the Shackleford Banks; on the boardwalk you'll find both **AB Kayaks,** 252/728-6330, and **Outer Island Kayak Adventures,** 252/222-3420, ready and willing to get you on the water.

Diving

Discovery Diving, 414 Orange Street, 252/728-2265, website: www.discoverydiving.com, charges $75 for a full day with two dives; or $45 for half a day. Dive sites include the World War II German U-352 sub, resting 115 feet underwater, the Proteus Ocean Liner, and many more. Call for more information and available charters.

Boat Tours

Mystery Tours, Beaufort Waterfront, 252/726-6783, sounds like it gives ghost tours, but it doesn't. It does give scenic harbor tours, and occasionally it's overtaken by "pirates"—but they're flesh-and-blood reenactors, not ghosts. *Lookout Express,* also run by Mystery Tours, 252/728-6997, takes up to 149 passengers out to Cape Lookout, or on morning Dolphin Cruises, or Sunset Cruises. Both the *Mystery* and the *Lookout* can be chartered. Call the numbers above, or see their website www.mysteryboattours.com for more information.

Information
For more information about Beaufort, Atlantic City, or Morehead City, stop by the **Carteret County Tourism Development Bureau,** 3409 Arendell Street in Morehead City, 252/726-8148.

ATLANTIC BEACH

Atlantic Beach, with a year-round population of 1,900, has been a popular vacation spot since the 19th century. Promoters built a large pavilion on the sand in 1887, and ever since then it has been *the* place for beach fun on the Bogue Banks. What's here is typical of what you'll find up at Nags Head or down at Wrightsville Beach.

Head seven miles northwest of Atlantic Beach to find the 265-acre **Theodore Roosevelt Natural Area,** featuring nature trails and observation decks. The president's family donated this land to the state in 1972, and it's become a favorite of wildlife photographers and others who come to observe the osprey, snowy egret, not to mention the oysters, crabs, mussels, and clams abundant in this barrier island ecosystem. Free admission. The **North Carolina Aquarium at Pine Knoll Shores** is here, 1 Roosevelt Dr., 252/247-4003, website: www.aquariums.state. nc.-us/aquariums. Civil War buffs will want to visit **Fort Macon State Park,** N.C. 58, 252/726-3775, originally constructed in 1826–1834 and partly designed by a young lieutenant named Robert E. Lee. Later the Confederate army occupied the fort during the first part of the War between the States, but they surrendered it to U.S. Generals John C. Parke and Ambrose Burnside on April 26, 1862. Free admission and museum. Guided tours available during the summer. Also a good spot for picnicking, fishing, hiking, and swimming.

Accommodations
A funky find on the causeway is the **Caribbe Inn,** 309 E. Fort Macon Rd., 252/726-0051, website: www.caribbe-inn.com, which has ten rooms, two efficiencies and one suite on the waterfront, with pier access and a fish-cleaning area, and boat slips if you're coming in by water. Each room is brightly painted with visions of tropical fish. The price runs $42–72 a night for rooms, $53–83 a night for the efficiencies. Weekly rates. Ask them about their special fishing and diving packages. **Atlantic Beach–Days Inn,** 602 W. Ft. Macon Rd.,

Atlantic Beach Pier

BEFORE THE TOURISTS CAME

"Atlantic (685 pop.), on a bluff of a wide peninsula on Core Sound, is a fishing village. Gnarled and stunted water oaks, wind-swept landward, cluster near the highway in the back yards of houses facing the sound. A little wooden church nestles in a grove of moss-grown dwarf oaks. Here and there throughout the village are clumps of myrtle and yaupon."

—Atlantic Beach, as described in
North Carolina: The WPA Guide to the
Old North State, *1939.*

800/972-3297 or 252/247-6400, runs $68–77 in low season, considerably more in the summer. The **Windjammer Inn,** Salter Path Rd., 800/233-6466 or 252/247-7123, charges $51–120 a night for a double room, depending on the room, the day, and the month. Every room faces the ocean front and has a balcony.

Of course, a time-honored way to approach an Atlantic Beach visit is to rent a cottage or condo. Call 800/334-2737 to talk to the people at **Tetterton Management Group.** Or call **Rains Realty and Rentals,** Atlantic Beach Causeway Shopping Center, 252/247-5141, website: www.rainsrealty.com. A house to sleep 6–8 should run between $600–1,000 a week.

Food
Mainly it's burgers and fried shrimpville on the island, but **Channel Marker Restaurant,** at the foot of the bridge, 252/247-2344, boasts a waterfront atrium lounge and a dining room that overlook Bogue Sound. Fresh seafood, full bar. For something completely different, **New York Deli,** in the Causeway Shopping Center, 252/726-0111, serves up good South Philly cheesesteaks, subs and salads, deli meats and cheeses, as well as breakfast items all day.

POINTS SOUTH

Swansboro
West of the Bogue Banks on N.C. 24, tiny Swansboro, founded circa 1730, keeps getting mentioned as a place nobody's heard of, but

based on the number of restaurants and other traveler-oriented businesses opening up there, clearly it's catching on. Still, this is a relatively quiet and certainly pretty little waterfront town right on the White Oak River. It has some interesting places to catch a meal, including **Yana's Ye Olde Drugstore Restaurant,** 119 Front St., 919/326-5501, a 1950s-style diner. Get a burger or a piece of homemade pie and enjoy.

Fort Lejeune
To anyone unaccustomed to military life, it can be sort of ominous driving into Fort Lejeune, what with the signs warning of overhead artillery fire and the little yellow signs reading, "Tank Xing." This is the world's most complete amphibious training base, where men practiced for the Normandy invasion. The Few and the Proud are very proud but not so few hereabouts: you'll find a greater concentration of U.S. marines in Fort Lejeune than anywhere else on the planet—in peacetime. Some 40,000 marines and sailors live and train here. If you'd like to see what they're up to, stop by the **Camp Lejeune Visitors Center** at the main gate, 910/326-4881, and pick up a visitor's day pass and a self-guided tour brochure.

If you visit on the right day, as you approach the base on N.C. 24, you'll see a long stretch of highway where the side fences are draped with sheets made into touching (and not uncommonly frisky) messages to returning spouses and lovers returning from overseas duty via buses that will pass that way.

Peletier
Located on N.C. 58, two miles north of its junction with N.C. 24, this tiny town is home to the 2,100-seat Crystal Coast Amphitheater, 800/662-5969 or 252/393-8373, where local thespians stage the outdoor three-hour musical Christian passion drama, ***Worthy Is the Lamb.*** said to be the only fully orchestrated musical passion production in the United States. The Easter story gets a full-throttle, and even for most cynics, a moving presentation here: musical numbers, elaborate costumes, real horses and chariots, a real river, and even a re-created city of Jerusalem—all out under the stars on the water in a small town in North Carolina. Staged 8:30 P.M. Thurs.–Sat., mid-June–August. September

performances begin 7:30 P.M. Friday and Saturday. $14 adults, $6 children 6–12 years.

Hammocks Beach State Park
The highlight of Hammocks Beach Park is that for a small fee you can camp primitively on undeveloped, 892-acre Bear Island. To get there you'll need to paddle over, take a boat taxi, or take the ferry that runs from Memorial Day to Labor Day, Fri.–Sun., 9:30 A.M.–4:30 P.M. You pick it up 4 miles south of Swansboro on N.C. 24. Call 910/326-4881 for information.

Topsail Island
Even if it is on the opposite coast from the one Jan and Dean were singing about, I still get as kick out of driving into Surf City. Once there, everything takes on a special importance. How can a person *not* stop in at the "Surf City Surf Shop" or take a walk along the "Surf City Pier"?

Surf City is a sun-and-fun, vacation-centered town. I can't tell you about the "two-girls for every boy" thing (I'm married, so some boy apparently got three), but Surf City is otherwise a pretty traditional North Carolina beach with arcade-fortified fishing piers, lots of rental houses, some seafood joints, and a miniature golf course. With the exception of some Hilton Headesque developments, the rest of Topsail (pronounced "TOP-sul") is a lot like Surf City: a great place to rent a beach house with the family or that special fishing rod, and maybe not such a great place if you're looking for historic sites and cultural events. For the fishing angle, you might consider a stay at William and Kay Smith's **Seaview Pier and Motel** in North Topsail, 910/328-3171. They offer a new 1,000-foot pier and twenty rooms around $60 a night. If it's nightlife you crave, drive your woody to Surf City's **The Mermaid,** N.C. 210, 910/328-0781, for bar food, drink specials, an outside deck, and live entertainment on the weekends. For more information on the island, call 800/626-2780, or stop by the Greater Topsail Area Chamber of Commerce and Tourism at 205 S. Topsail Drive, Surf City, website: www.topsailcoc.com.

WILMINGTON AND THE SOUTHERN NORTH CAROLINA COAST

LAND AND CLIMATE

Anchored by culturally minded Wilmington and featuring a flock of popular coastal islands, the Northern Carolina coast from Wrightsville Beach south to the South Carolina border has come increasingly in vogue as the inland cities of North Carolina balloon with hard-working computer wonks who want to hit the beach now and again. The southern border across from Little River, S.C., marks the southern edge of this region, but where the north part of the Southern Coast ends and where the southern part of the Central North Carolina Coast begins is purely arbitrary. For our purposes here I've drawn the line below the southern edge of Topsail Island.

Climate
Climate in the Wilmington area is mild; rarely above the 80s in the summer and normally in the 50s during winter months. It rains here a lot—locals can expect 50 inches of rain; you won't regret bringing an umbrella.

HISTORY

North Carolina's southern coast has blinked in the spotlight of American history at least three times. In 1865, after the fall of Charleston to federal troops, Wilmington remained the one main Confederate port still open along the Atlantic seaboard; blockade runners ducked in and out of Wilmington, hauling cotton and other local produce to the Caribbean and Europe, and bringing back badly-needed supplies for local residents,

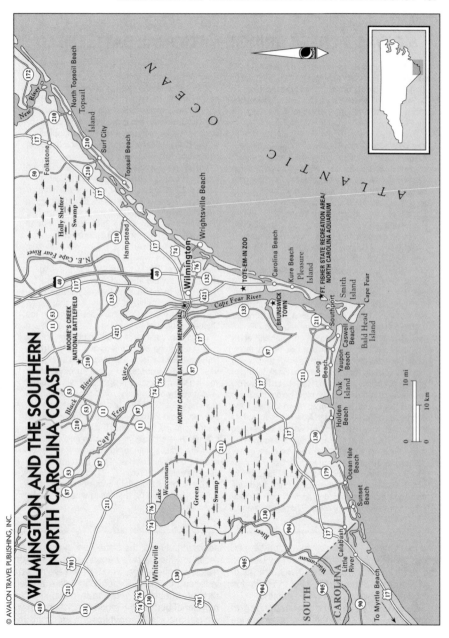

© AVALON TRAVEL PUBLISHING, INC.

WILMINGTON AND THE SOUTHERN
NORTH CAROLINA COAST

MOORE'S CREEK BRIDGE NATIONAL BATTLEFIELD

Though he'd fled the Governor's Palace in New Bern for Fort Johnston, and then fled Fort Johnston for the safety of the British warship *Cruizer,* once safely off shore, Royal Governor Josiah Martin immediately set out to reclaim North Carolina for England.

The Battle for North Carolina

Martin's plan called for Highland Scots to march eastward in February and rendezvous with British General Cornwallis, who would arrive in Wilmington by ship to begin his conquest of the South. Martin also mustered the Black Pioneers, a group composed of free African-Americans and slaves promised their freedom for service to the Crown. These he assigned to the *Scorpion,* a ship ready to assist General Cornwallis when he arrived. Faced with the simultaneous arrival of these two formidable military thrusts, the rebellious colonials would throw down their arms, throw up their hands, and beg to kiss the nearest Union Jack—if all went well.

It didn't. The Scots got there too early; the Brits got there too late. When General Donald MacDonald's 1,600 Highlanders met at Cross Creek (now Fayetteville) and marched toward Wilmington in February 1776, patriot minutemen were waiting for them. They thwarted the Loyalists' attempt to cross at Rockfish Creek, and then moved back to dig in around the bridge at Moore's Creek, about twenty miles east of Wilmington. The night before the Scots arrived there, patriots sneaked down to the bridge and pried off the bottom of it. Now the Highlanders would have to walk across the bridge's slippery log runners. These, the patriots waxed and soaped.

On February 27, 1776, an hour before sunrise, patriot sharpshooters lay in wait across the creek as an advance party of broadsword-brandishing, bagpipe-blowing Highlanders approached the bridge in the cold early morning fog. Most fell from the slippery runners into the icy creek. Those who made it across charged the patriots' earthworks—right into a storm of deadly musket fire.

Within seconds the creek thrashed with wounded and drowning Scotsmen; the others—only about half of them armed—turned kilt, running west. The patriots took chase and captured over half of them, along with guns, wagons, and medical supplies.

The Black Pioneers sat patiently upon the *Scorpion,* wondering where all the action was.

The 30 fallen Highlanders (and single fallen patriot) had been buried for four months when Cornwallis and his 2,000 troops finally managed to stop by Wilmington in June. He sent scouts ashore to size up the situation and learned that the patriots now fully controlled the Lower Cape Fear. Rather than attempt a bloody invasion into hostile territory, Cornwallis decided to head south. Fully disheartened, Governor Martin, who had fought so hard to keep eastern North Carolina, finally gave up the coast. He sought asylum aboard Cornwallis's ship. Together they sailed south to Charles Town and the Battle of Sullivan's Island. (To see how that turned out, see "The Battle of Sullivan's Island" in the Charleston chapter.)

Today the historic site of this important battle is preserved as the 86-acre **Moore's Creek Bridge National Battlefield,** 200 Moores Creek Rd., 910/283-5591, website: www.nps.gov/mocr, where you can see the bridge site and some reconstructed patriot earthworks. The visitors center features a diorama recreation of the bridge as it was on game day, an audio-visual program, and a number of weapons found on the site. The park includes the 0.7-mile History Trail, part of which follows at one point the old colonial-era Negro Head Point Road, and the 0.3-mile Tar Heel Trail. Both trails begin near the visitors center.

To get to the battlefield from Wilmington, take U.S. 421 to N.C. 210; then head west on 210 for five miles.

and for Robert E. Lee's starving, poorly armed troops up in Virginia. Wilmington quickly became the North's primary focus, and with the fall of Fort Fisher on January 15, 1865, Wilmington closed and the war ended within months.

The federal government's occupation of Wilmington, and its attempts to reconfigure the social structure of the Cape Fear region led directly to Wilmington's second appearance on history's center stage. In 1898 white Democrats incensed by black/Republican rule marched through the streets wielding torches, killing a number of blacks who stood up to them, chasing out the white Republican mayor, and re-

THE WILMINGTON TEN

If life under the rule of "separate but equal" was rarely equal, it was *never* cost efficient. All the duplication of public services, from duplicate regional colleges down to the famed dual drinking fountains, burned a hole through the pocket of Carolinians and other Southerners during the already-lean Jim Crow years. When desegregation finally came, this redundancy became doubly apparent. The Wilmington Board of Education, for instance, realized that it now had two high schools within five blocks of one another, and with many white students fleeing to private schools, it had only one campus-worth of students. In 1971 the board decided to demote Williston High School into a junior high, and move Williston's students to New Haven, which was deemed the better facility.

But the African-American students who lived in the Williston neighborhood didn't want to switch. After all, with all the white flight, blacks made up the majority in the new combined student body. So why did *they* have to walk the five blocks to attend the "white kids' school?" Interpreting what was a defensibly logistical move by the board as yet another sign of disrespect, the African-American students began boycotting classes that winter.

The board refused to be coerced by the boycotters, or by their newly arrived out-of-towner coordinator, the Reverend Benjamin Chavis, a Central-Carolina native, but now a professional "field organizer" sent in by the Ohio-based Commission for Racial Justice of the United Church of Christ. Sure enough, roused by Chavis's rhetoric and empowered by his organizing, the students staged protests at school headquarters and city hall. Predictably violence erupted between protesters and white residents.

And then somebody firebombed the white-owned Mike's Grill and Grocery, at 6th and Nun Streets. Fortunately no one was killed, but the blast put Wilmington on the edge of hysteria, open race war, or both. Police quickly arrested Chavis and nine others—six of them high school students, and all but one of them black. Three black witnesses testified that the suspects had conspired to burn the store and then shoot

at responding police and firefighters. Based on this eyewitness testimony, in October of the following year, all 10 were convicted and sent to prison for long terms, the shortest of which was 23 years.

The appeals began—first in the North Carolina Court of Appeals, and then in state Supreme Court. Finally in January of 1976, the appeals of the prisoners reached the U.S. Supreme Court, which turned deaf ears to the case. The Ten had hit the end of the line.

But then something unexpected happened. One of the three key prosecution witnesses, Allen Hall, recanted, signing a sworn affidavit claiming that he'd been coerced to give false testimony in the trial. The following year, the other two main witnesses against the 10 claimed they too had lied to the jury under pressure in 1972—but were now telling the truth.

Those who had always believed in a conspiracy involving a Klansman bomber and an ATF/FBI frame job claimed vindication, and all political heck broke loose. In 1977 poet/author James Baldwin took up the cause, pleading the Ten's case in his widely published "Open Letter to Mr. Carter." The next year Amnesty International declared that the "Wilmington Ten" were now being held purely for political motives, making them the USA's first political prisoners.

Finally in 1979, under not a little pressure himself, Governor Jim Hunt reduced the Ten's sentences, setting most of them free with the five years they'd already served. A year later, based on the witnesses' recanting of their testimonies, a federal appeals court overturned all of the Ten's convictions.

Sprung from his cell, Chavis attacked life with a vengeance. He earned degrees at Duke, UNC Chapel Hill, and Howard University, fathered eight children, penned a number of books, and kept a high profile in the African-American Rights movement through his speaking engagements. In 1993 he was elected the youngest-ever executive director of the NAACP, and in 1995 served as national director of Louis Farrakhan's "Million Man March." In 1997 Chavis converted to Islam and changed his name to Minister Benjamin Muhammad.

placing him with one of their own.

The white Democrats may have recovered power over Wilmington, but Wilmington would not recover its economic momentum for most of

a century. In fact part of the reason Wilmington is such a fine place to visit today is *because* of the Wilmington Riot of 1898. The riot, called by some historians the sole coup d'état in American history,

THE FATE OF THE "BLACK PIONEERS"

After their attempts to assist the British in General Cornwallis's bungled 1776 invasion of Wilmington, the escaped slaves (many of them Coastal Carolinians) of the Loyalist "Black Pioneers" brigade went on to fight for the King elsewhere in the Revolution. In 1783, after the British lost the war, many of the Pioneers moved north (as did many other American Loyalists) to British-held Nova Scotia. There the Pioneers found disappointment at unfair practices by the British government, which awarded black veterans smaller and poorer plots of the rocky land than those awarded to whites. After Thomas Peters visited London to explain the plight of the black Loyalists to sympathetic Brits in 1792, philanthropists in London paid for nearly 1,200 of the black Nova Scotians (as they and their descendants were afterward known) to repatriate to West Africa. The blacks who had fought for their freedom founded a port town called Freetown, Sierra Leone, and with their impeccable English and European dress, enjoyed an elite status in the highly stratified British colony. Sierra Leone became independent in 1961, but sadly, as recent events have shown, the descendents of the Black Pioneers have yet to escape the brutal ghosts of revolution.

disenfranchised the ascending black middle class in the area and sent many of them packing for Northern climes. This drastic draining of area productivity and morale, combined with exterior factors, turned North Carolina's biggest city into something of a backwater. Hence the building booms of the turn of the century in many Southern towns did not affect Wilmington, preserving her colonial ambience. Things began to look up a bit after World War II, but then in 1960 the Atlantic Coastline Railroad stopped running along the Wilmington-Weldon line. This railroad line, along with the shipping lane along the Cape Fear River, had brought Wilmington whatever affluence and influence it had known, and now it was gone. Some four thousand railroad-dependent families transferred down to Jacksonville, Florida, and Wilmington was left financially desolate.

Racial conflicts brought Wilmington international recognition for a third time in 1971, when a firebombing and the subsequent arrest of Civil Rights activist the Rev. Benjamin Chavis and nine others put the fate of the "Wilmington Ten" into headlines worldwide.

Then, as the Jim Crow rope fell in the late 1960s and early 1970s, the town might well have enjoyed some of its share of tourism, but the "Wilmington Ten" made the city's name synonymous with racial division.

But even as the Wilmington Ten were toiling in prison, the town's oldest friend, the Cape Fear River, continued flowing by. And that got some forward-looking people to thinking. As a young Michael Jordan pounded Wilmington's asphalt courts, and up in Oriental, future slasher flick and teenysoaper king Kevin Williamson stood in his crib and practiced his screams, the city managed to get the decaying wharfs and business blocks downtown declared a National Historic District, and business/community groups like the Downtown Area Revitalization Effort encouraged the refurbishing of old buildings and houses. In addition to successfully preserving over 200 acres of historic downtown, the effort bolstered Wilmington's sagging civic pride.

Little by little, the rest of the world began to discover the well-preserved colonial buildings, and suddenly Wilmington found itself named as one of America's fastest-growing areas. Its population grew by some 20 percent during the 1990s, thanks in part to the completion of I-40, which made the city much more accessible to the rest of the Eastern seaboard.

And so, as with Charleston, whose riches came in part from slave trading, Wilmington's clouded past has preserved its gleaming future.

SIGHTS

ORIENTATION

Logistically Wilmington sprawls like a *Smile*-era Brian Wilson recording session; essentially you have Historic Downtown Wilmington, located along the Cape Fear River. When things got ugly and dangerous down on the waterfront, the suburbs began expanding, primarily southeast, toward the beach. Nowadays it's pretty much one big strip between Wilmington and Wrightsville Beach. Now one of the chief issues you'll hear discussed on local talk radio stations is the area's growing traffic problems: there's just too much land to cover for most Wilmington-area residents driving from work to home and back, and there's not enough lanes to prevent gridlock.

Highways U.S. 17 (east-west), N.C. 132, and U.S. 74/76 (north-south) are the big ones around here. You'll use one or more of these to get just about anywhere.

Downtown Wilmington

Historic downtown Wilmington is one of the true gems of North Carolina's Coast. The town rose to power as a shipping port with important, early railroad connections. Later the railroad left, but in the 1980s and 1990s, Hollywood found in Wilmington a friendly, relatively inexpensive place to shoot both interiors and exteriors. Along with the "biz" came money, and with the money came expensive restaurants with international cuisine, a vaguely upscale "underground" tone, and a lot of three-dollar coffees. Though at this writing some of the movie money (and excitement) has left for Vancouver and Toronto, things have reached a critical mass here; expensive condos and gourmet eateries continue to blossom here along the Cape Fear; the riverfront won't be reverting to its 1970s dilapidated state anytime soon.

A main boulevard downtown is Water Street, which fronts the river; a block inland comes the busier and more businesslike **Front Street.** Both of these streets are thriving with cultural and counter-cultural shops and bistros; local thought has it that dining places on Water cater to tourists with money to burn. Anchoring the south end of Water Street is a great little shopping complex called **Chandler's Wharf,** which includes both an indoor market and a five-acre outdoor area with a cobblestone street and the well-established waterfront seafood houses, Elijah's and The Pilot House. At the opposite (north) end of the waterfront you'll find the **Cotton Exchange,** 321 N. Front St., 910/343-9896, website: www.cottonexchange.citysearch.com, a collection of 30 specialty shops and eateries tucked into four historic brick buildings, and featuring a top-notch German restaurant.

Continue north from the Cotton Exchange and you'll come to the Coast Line Convention Center, where folks are trying to make the best of the disappearance of the Atlantic Coast Line railroad, which until 1960 animated this end of town. Over here too is the nifty **Wilmington Railroad Museum.** More on all of these below.

Heading away from the river, after Front comes 2nd Street, and then 3rd Street, a main thoroughfare. Go north here and you'll leave town on the Parsley Street Bridge, or U.S. 117. Or head south on 3rd Street and it becomes Carolina Beach Boulevard, heading to the ocean.

A number of delightful side streets cross Water, Front, and 3rd Street, and dead-end at the river. Just as you'll find down in Charleston, the most important of these is named **Market Street.**

WILMINGTON AND SOUTHERN COAST HIGHLIGHTS

- Calabash
- **Cape Fear Museum,** Wilmington
- **Fort Fisher State Recreation Area,** Kure Beach
- Poplar Grove Plantation
- Southport
- USS *North Carolina* Battleship Memorial
- Wilmington Railroad Museum
- Wilmington Waterfront
- Wrightsville Beach

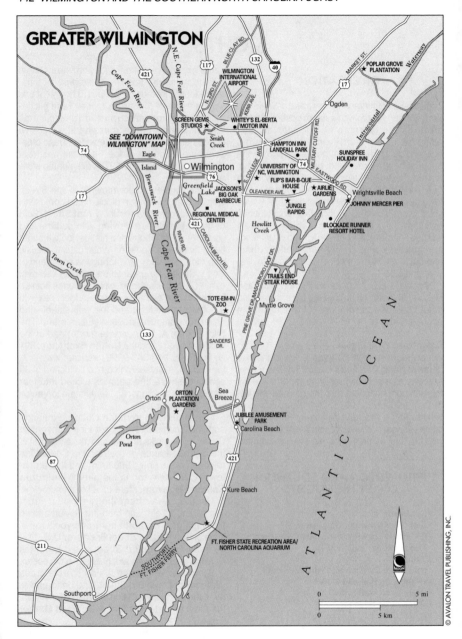

GREATER WILMINGTON

© AVALON TRAVEL PUBLISHING, INC.

If you turn around at the river and head eastward on Market, you'll discover you're also on U.S. 17, the coastal highway of the Carolinas. This will take you deep into the less enchanting parts of Wilmington as you climb the street signs all the way to 16th and 17th Streets, one-way streets that combine to form another important north-south thoroughfare. If you continue on eastward along 3rd, it becomes 74 and carries you straight to Wilmington Beach.

One of the best ways to orient yourself downtown is to take a horse-drawn tour with **Springbrook Farms,** departing from Market Street between Water and Front Streets, 910/251-8889. Owner John Pucci and his period-costumed staff provide a wealth of anecdotes and facts about the many historic buildings in the area.

Suburban Wilmington
The suburbs between Wilmington proper and the Wilmington-area beaches have the sorts of names that roll off of developers' tongues: Long Leaf Acres, College Acres, Winter Park, Windemere, Landfall, and so on. These vary some in age and comeliness, but for most travelers, the only interesting thing they offer are a few restaurants, high-end malls, and moderately priced lodgings between downtown Wilmington and the beaches.

Beaches
Wrightsville is the chief beach of the Wilmington Coast, the most-developed beach, and yet, it's not all *that* different from its sister beaches to the south, Carolina and Kure. **Carolina Beach** used to be one of the hot shagging spots along the Carolina Coasts. It's a pleasure beach, the kind of place where Pinocchio might have run away to. Sure enough, the island that holds all three of these beaches is called Pleasure Island. **Kure** used to have the reputation, as some put it, of being the place where the people you see at drag races go to the beach. This is changing somewhat as the expensive townhouses move in and the trailers move out. But at least around the pier and business district, Kure is still a good place to find people wearing blue jeans at the beach.

Fort Fisher State Recreational Area
South of Kure Beach, just when you begin to despair of sighting natural coastline ever again, you'll discover this pristine area of protected government land. You'll find a lot of history here. The fall of Fort Fisher at the end of the War between the States caused the fall of Wilmington, which shut off the pipeline of goods to Robert E. Lee's armies and effectively ended the war. Today there's enough of the fort left to get a feeling for what transpired here back in 1865. Also here is the **Fort Fisher Aquarium,** a welcome chance to experience the local wildlife, with expert interpretation provided.

Wilmington waterfront

MUSEUMS AND ART

If at all possible, make the **Cape Fear Museum,** 814 Market St., 910/341-4350, your first stop upon arriving in the Wilmington region; it'll give you background for the sites you'll be seeing. This is the kind of lovingly developed mid-sized museum that puts a lot of larger museums to shame with the sheer force of its desire to interpret for visitors. Be sure to catch the scale model of the Wilmington waterfront, circa 1862, as well as the diorama of the battles for Fort Fisher. Kids will enjoy the chance to crawl through a mock beaver's lodge in the Michael Jordan Discovery Gallery. Outside of the gallery you'll find a sprinkling of Michael Jordan paraphernalia, though if that's the only reason you're coming, you may be disappointed. But there's plenty here to entertain adults and kids of all attention spans. Open Tues.–Sat. 9 A.M.–5 P.M., Sundays 1–5 P.M. $2 for adults, less for kids. Free on the first and third Sundays of the month, and on the first day of each month.

The Cape Fear Museum is something new visitors sometimes need pointed out to them: the **USS *North Carolina* Battleship Memorial,** 910/251-5797, website: www.city-info.com/ncbb55.html, is something they can't miss. Located on Battleship Drive on Eagle Island across

from the waterfront, the *North Carolina* stands nine decks high and weighs in at over 35,000 tons. If the Big One ever comes, and the world is reduced to half-savage city-states, Wilmington already has a pretty good head start on its navy. For now though, the USS *North Carolina* is, among other things, the largest museum in the entire state of North Carolina. Boasting nine sixteen-inch guns, it's also the best armed. The big guns can fire 2,700 pound shells 23 statute miles, though I imagine a lot of town statutes forbid the firing of 2,700 pound shells within town limits. A host of workers at the Brooklyn Naval Yard finished the ship in 1941.

A tour of the ship gives you some small sense of appreciation for the life of an average sailor in World War II, taken from a small town or urban ghetto and put in menacing situations in cramped quarters far out to sea with strangers from around the country. The ship itself is dedicated to the 10,000 Tar Heels who died on all fronts during World War II.

After serving over 40 months in combat during World War II and enduring at least one direct torpedo hit, the *North Carolina* lingered in service—a lifer—until 1961, when flock of tugboats dragged the *North Carolina* out of history and wedged it into Cape Fear mud to serve a living history lesson. The battleship arrived, in fact, as part of the first wave of today's tourism industry,

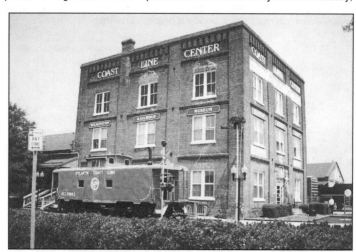

Wilmington Train Museum and Caboose

steaming (okay, being towed) into Wilmington just a year after the Atlantic Coast Line abandoned the town.

Today the most memorable way to get to the ship is to spend a couple bucks a person and take a **Captain J. N. Maffit** water taxi (waterfront, corner of Market and Water Sts., 800/676-0162 or 910/343-1611) from the Wilmington waterfront; to get a full sense of appreciation for the sheer expanse of the vessel, there's nothing like it. But you can also drive to it.

Once there you can tour the ship at your own speed, or pay extra to peek into the engine room, radio center, admiral's cabin, and other interesting rooms. Unfortunately, as you may have guessed, very little of the ship is handicapped accessible. In fact make sure you're in good shape before you start climbing up and down the nine flights of steep steps on a hot August day. Once you're over here on this side of the river, you may decide to make a day of it. If so, take advantage of the picnic grounds and keep an eye out for Old Charlie, the local celebrity gator.

Open 8 A.M.–8 P.M. during the summer, 8 A.M.–5 P.M. the rest of the year. Admission runs $8 for adults, less for children, senior citizens, and (rightfully so) military folks with ID.

The **Bellamy Mansion Museum of History and Design,** 503 Market St., 910/251-3700, serves as a good example of the material beauty and refinement the exploitation of slaves brought to the Wilmington region. Four stories tall and twenty-two rooms large, this 1861 house is Wilmington's best example of (very) late antebellum extravagance. In 1972 someone attempted to burn down this then-vacant Italianate mansion, presumably as a way of getting back at long-dead slave owners (who, if they received the fate the arsonists wished upon them, were already pretty accustomed to flames by then anyway.) Fortunately the building wasn't completely destroyed, and was salvaged and turned into a museum of two sorts; first there is the house and restored gardens themselves. The house features Italianate, neoclassical, and Greek Revival styles. The garden has been replanted the way it was planted when the house was still on its first coat of paint. And the slave quarters—though they were only slave quarters for a short time—should be refurbished by the time you read this, a fitting tribute to the

people who helped keep this large household running. And then there are rotating exhibits and multi-media presentations which spotlight preservation. Forty-five minute tours begin at the quarter and three-quarter marks each hour, Wed.–Sat. 10 A.M.–5 P.M., Sun. 1–5 P.M. Adult admission runs $6.

In late 2001 or early 2002, **St. John's Museum of Art,** 114 Orange St., Wilmington, 910/763-0281, will change its name to the **Louise Wells Cameron Art Museum,** and relocate to South 17th Street. Wherever the museum is when you come to town, it's worth a visit for the extensive collection of Mary Cassatt color prints, and for the work of local artist Minnie Evans (1892–1987). Evans is something like the Howard Finster of Wilmington, a Christian visionary whose folk works reflected her faith in intensely personal fashion. Here you'll also find a fine display of Jugtown Pottery, a unique blending of Asian and traditional Piedmont folk pottery styles, created between 1921 and 1959 by North Carolina craftsman Ben Owen. There are lots of other goodies here, both locally created and not, including the work of acclaimed North Carolina-raised painter Elliott Daingerfield (1859–1932) and Charlotte artist Romare Beardon (1914–1988).

Train fans will need to head over to the **Wilmington Railroad Museum,** 501 Nutt St. (corner of Red Cross and Water Streets), 910/763-2634, where the old freight traffic office now plays home to dozens of displays honoring the area's railroad history and celebrating railroads in general. Outside you'll find a steam engine and caboose for the climbing and viewing, always a favorite with kids. Inside the museum they've got a wonderful, massive model railroad diorama upstairs, which kids and not a few adults will enjoy getting a chance to operate. Downstairs you'll find a re-creation of a railroad depot office and other interactive exhibits that help bring to life the Golden Age of rail travel. The museum store carries a good selection of train-related items, including big wooden whistles that sound just like a real steam whistle. Admission for the museum runs $2 for adults, $1 for ages 6–11 years. April through September, the museum's open daily except for Wednesdays. Call for hours during the winter.

HISTORIC HOMES AND STRUCTURES

The Burgwin-Wright House

At 224 Market St., 910/762-0570, you'll find perhaps the top Revolutionary home tour in Wilmington. When General Cornwallis traveled throughout the colonies, he brought along his own army of red-coated, musket-wielding travel consultants, who had a way of finding the general the best house in town, wherever he might stay. In 1781, though Cornwallis was retreating after the costly victory at Guilford Courthouse, and his military career was on the skids (and about to skid to a stop in Virginia), he still managed to find good digs in Wilmington, choosing the Burgwin-Wright house from the two hundred available for the seizing. Why this house? Cornwallis was a special-needs traveler. He wanted a spot with a nice dungeon underneath for holding prisoners, and wealthy politician John Burgwin's (Bur-GWIN)10-year-old home had been built over the foundations of the old town jail. The house also featured trap doors leading to tunnels leading to the river, so that Cornwallis could make a quick exit to the water if necessary. Or so the story goes.

Today the tiered gardens outside have been restored. You can visit these for free, but the preservation group that could have been named by Frank Sinatra—the Colonial Dames—charges $3 for adults to tour the house, open Tues.–Sat. 10 A.M.–4 P.M.

Brunswick Town State Historic Site

Located on the Cape Fear River, 19 miles south of Wilmington on N.C. 133, 910/371-6613, Brunswick Town is like Charles Towne Landing at Charleston. Both Brunswick and Charles Towne Landing mark the original English settlements in the area, and in both cases, settlements that were abandoned when a second site proved to be safer and more profitable. Unlike Charles Towne, Brunswick Town has not been restored or stocked with buffalo, and this makes the experience all the more ominous. What you will see here are a worthwhile visitors center with exhibits and a slide show to give you some background on what you'll be seeing. You'll also find scores of excavation sites and the earthen remains of the Confederate Fort Anderson, built here in 1862

to help protect the important blockade-running port of Wilmington. Most impressive are the remains of St. Philip's Anglican Church. Open 9 A.M.–5 P.M. Mon.–Sat. and Sun. 1–5 P.M. April 1–Oct. 31; 10 A.M.–4 P.M. Tues.–Sat. and 1–4 P.M. (closed Mon.) Nov. 1–March 31.

The 1999 addition of thirty-eight outdoor exhibit panels along the self-guided tour make it easy to get a handle on what used to be where, and who did what there. Brunswick Town a picturesque walk along the Cape Fear. Archaeologists have dug up some sixty foundations from the old town, and a number of them have been left open for the viewing. Artifacts on display reveal much of what life was like in the colonial port. Open Mon.–Sat. 9 A.M.–5 P.M. Sun. 1–5 P.M. spring–fall; shorter hours the rest of the year. Closed some holidays, so call ahead.

Fort Fisher State Historic Site

Located south of Kure Beach on U.S. 421 (Fort Fisher Blvd.), 910/458-5538, Fort Fisher was site of the most important Civil War battle on North Carolina Coast; once the Union troops seized control of Fisher, Wilmington fell easily. And with Wilmington went the last major port open to the Confederacy. Today you'll find a small visitors center and a nice trail around the remaining earthworks. Be sure to catch the diorama of the battle at the Cape Fear Museum before you come out here; it'll make your visit that much more meaningful. Inside the visitors center you'll find artifacts taken from sunken blockade runners, which used to wait behind the fort until nightfall, when they'd make their mad dashes through the net of Union ships. When the North finally got the courage to launch an amphibious assault on the fort on Christmas Eve 1864, the Confederates repulsed them after two bloody days of fighting. But the North had all the time and manpower in the world, and on January 12 they began using a healthier strategy. For days they literally bombed the sand out of the fort; and on the 15th day they launched a surprise attack around the most weakly defended gate of the fort. Northerner or not, you'll find visiting to be a bit easier today. In high season the center's open from 9 A.M.–5 P.M. everyday except Sunday, when it doesn't open until 1 P.M. But if you get here after the center closes, you can still take a walk around the largest of the remaining berms, with signs that will explain the logistics of the battles and the history of the fort as you go along.

Latimer House

At 126 S. 3rd Street, 810/762-0492, you'll find the carefully preserved late-antebellum (1852) home of prominent Wilmington merchant Zebulon Latimer. You can take a guided tour of the house, which also serves as headquarters of the Lower Cape Fear Historical Society. Walking tours of Wilmington's historical district depart from here Wednesdays and Saturdays at 10 A.M.

North Carolina Aquarium at Fort Fisher

On the other side of Fort Fisher Boulevard, you'll find the aquarium, 910/458-8257, set to reopen in early 2002 after a major renovation and expansion. Long one of North Carolina's modest but informative and state aquariums, the Fort Fisher Aquarium will have tripled in size when it reopens, while retaining its focus on the wildlife found in southern North Carolina waters.

A 20,000-gallon shark tank and its occupants are the stars here, and the alligators are also popular. Judiciously, aquarium curators have included neither of these in the "touch tank," where little folks (and big folks) can touch horseshoe crabs, hermit crabs, and other nonbiting forms of marinelife.

As an example of how dedicated museum curators are to their Cape Fear region focus, even the touch pool is set in a re-creation of the Fort Fisher coquina rock outcropping. Outside you'll find nature trails.

Post-reopening admission prices and hours have not been released at publication, so call the museum for current prices and hours.

Historic Churches

Originally founded in 1729 at old Brunswick Town, the current Gothic Revival home of **St. James Episcopal Church,** 25 S. 3rd St., 910/763-1628, dates from 1839. The second church building (the first structure built after the move to Wilmington) was gutted by the British when they took over Wilmington during the Revolution; the current version used materials from the first, and enjoyed the same treatment courtesy of the U.S. government during the War between the States.

Ironically, as federal troops partook in pew-tossing contests inside the sanctuary, up in Washington D.C., St. James's architect, Thomas U. Walter, was busily completing the addition of the dome atop the U.S. Capitol. Today, fortunately, you'll see that the pews have been put back in place. *Ecce Homo* ("Behold the Man"), the painting of the bound and scourged Jesus that hangs here, was captured from a pirate ship that failed in its attack of Brunswick Town back in 1748.

As with most churches of this vintage, the graveyard is just as interesting as the building itself. Outside of St. James lie a number of colonial figures, including Thomas Godfrey (1736–1763), author of *Prince of Parthia,* the first drama written by a native-born American and professionally produced in the colonies. You're welcome to stop by the grounds anytime during the day, and you can tour the inside of the church any day after 9 A.M. when there are no services underway.

The **First Presbyterian Church,** 121 S. 3rd St., is relatively a new structure—built in the late 1920s—but the congregation itself dates back to 1785. After moving up from a teaching position at Columbia, South Carolina, "Tommy" Woodrow Wilson's pastor father took on the pastorship of this church. A mosaic in the vestibule pays tribute to their Pancho Villa–chasing, League-of-Nations-lobbying former church member. The Neo-Gothic church's bells ring up and down the historic district on the hour, though they no longer play all night on the hour out of respect for their insomniac neighbors.

PLANTATIONS AND GARDENS

Poplar Grove Plantation

Built at the peak of the antebellum period in 1850 and upon the ashes of a former house, the Greek Revival manor house at Poplar Grove Plantation, north of town at 10200 U.S. 17, 910/686-9518, made its money in the underground—growing peanuts. Worked by a team of sixty slaves before the War between the States and by tenant farmers afterward, Poplar Grove bounced back after the Civil War in a jif, remembering that its roots were in the peanut-friendly soil. Today the plantation has been restored as a living memorial to the lives and lifestyles lived out here since the mid-19th century. In the house museum you'll be able to see restored bedrooms, parlor, dining room, and library, as well as displays explaining the agriculture of the area. Craftspersons are generally on hand to demonstrate basket making, blacksmithing, and other crafts. In Poplar Grove's store you can buy some of the crafts produced here.

This is a worthwhile stop if you're hoping to get more than a home tour and really want to understand a bit of what the life was like out here on the plantations. In early 2000 a new Peanut and Agricultural Exhibit Building opened on the grounds, featuring peanut displays and forestry exhibits. Admission to Poplar Grove costs $6 for adults, $3 for children. Open Mon.–Sat. 9 A.M.–5 P.M. and noon–5 Sunday.

Airlie Gardens
Located on Airlie Road, off U.S. 74/76, 910/452-6393, Airlie Gardens are what is left from a large rice plantation whose overseers had green thumbs. The extensive gardens are open from March through October, but get here before May if you want to catch the azaleas in bloom (you do). The gardens include a five-mile drive-through section, so bring the convertible and allergy medicine. Horticultural buffs will be interested to see the Topel tree, a hybrid R. A. Topel created by grafting a yaupon on to a different holly. The bright red berries are three times bigger than regular holly berries (but, importantly, still smaller than Halle Berry). The gardens were owned for generations by the Corbett family, but now New Hanover County owns them, and they're managed by the New Hanover County Cooperative Arboretum. Admission is $5 for adults, less for children.

Orton Plantation Gardens
South of Wilmington off N.C. 133 to Southport, you'll find these gardens, at 9149 Orton Rd. SE, in Winnabow, 910/371-6851. Orton features 20 acres of gardens with a variety of annuals, perennials, huge oaks, azaleas, and camellias. The home here is still standing, but it's a private residence. Though you can't go inside, it certainly adds to the ambience.

AMUSEMENT PARKS AND OTHER ACTIVITIES

The amusement complexes near Wilmington vary between worn beach boardwalks, quaint perma-carnivals, and miniature golf courses on steroids. In the first category you'll find the **Carolina Beach Boardwalk,** though the city's Vision 2005 revitalization plan seeks to re-create it as, the local Convention Visitors Bureau says, a "cluster of oceanfront boutiques, a coffee and ice cream shop, poster galleries, restaurants and juice bars." Carolina Beach has brought in consultants from Virginia, and it looks as though things might be looking up thereabouts.

Jubilee Amusement Park, 1000 N. Lake Park Blvd., Carolina Beach, 910/458-9017, falls into the second group; it's the carnival that arrived sometime in 1953 and never left; a great place for kids and teens with energy and money to burn after a day at the beach. Generations of families and teens have enjoyed summer nights here and Jubilee's survived more storms than the Clinton presidency, so it looks as if it's here to stay.

In the overgrown-miniature-golf course category comes **Jungle Rapids Family Fun Park,**

Lion Head Door, Tote-Em-In Zoo

SIMBA, THE LION KING OF TOTE-EM-IN ZOO

If you had a mind to, you could make a Disney pilgrimage up and down the Carolina Coasts: you'd start out at the Disney resort at Hilton Head, stop by to camp on Hunting Island near Beaufort, S.C., shooting location for the live-action *Jungle Book* of a few years back, and then continue on up to Wilmington and visit the **Tote-Em-In Zoo**, 5811 Carolina Beach Rd., 910/791-0472, to see Simba, the fur-and-blood model for Disney's *The Lion King*. Simba spent his Florida cubhood pouncing about for Disney artists who needed inspiration for the look and movement of the film's singing, talking main character.

Fortunately, unlike that of many child actors, Simba's story has a fairly happy ending. When the Disney gig was over, the cat's Florida owners sold him to Tote-Em-Inn owner Jerry Brewer, who whisked him away from his glitzy movie star lifestyle faster than you can say "Gary Coleman." Consequently Simba's spending his young adult years in Wilmington, instead of sitting in a dark apartment somewhere in the Valley, speedballing catnip, waiting for a call from a casting agent that will never come.

5320 Oleander Dr., 910/791-0666, probably the cleanest and safest—a good bet if you or your kids are looking to kill a roll of quarters (which, of course, must be exchanged for tokens), or if for some reason you'd rather ride chlorine waves instead of the saltwater ones at the beach.

Other Adventures

The **Tote-Em-In Zoo,** 5811 Carolina Beach Rd., 910/791-0472, located ten miles south of Wilmington on U.S. 421, is a throwback to the sort of roadside attraction molded more in the shape of its founder's personality than by an MBA-penciled business plan. After serving in World War II, George Tregembo returned from the Philippines to his home in Maine, bearing a number of artifacts and a newly born interest in tropical wildlife. What George wanted to do was build a zoo to house and display the exotic creatures he'd learned to love, and build a museum to show off his collection of international artifacts. One thing he needed was decent year-round weather. George and his

family moved down their present-day spot on Carolina Beach Road in 1953, bringing along a number of animals he'd already collected. George's Philippine artifacts seeded what would become the uniquely diverse collection of materials in his Museum of Oddities, still an integral part of the Tote-Em-In Zoo (no additional charge).

This Museum of Oddities, with its stream-of-consciousness organization style and hand-written interpretive notes, is like a peek into a young boy's knapsack of found treasures—a monument to an earlier generation's capacity for wonder at the sheer "otherness" of distant places, back before jet planes, satellite television, and the Internet shrank the world. It contains tribal death masks, fossils, foreign currency, World War II relics, arrowheads, mounted animals, weapons, newspaper clippings, and even a fake mummy. Outside, the collection of animals reflects the same kind of whimsical approach; featured are a pair of black leopards, Toby the Mandrill, Clyde the Camel, and a popular pair of Himalayan bears. You'll also find some native turtles and alligators—with all the free food laying around here, you probably couldn't keep them out—but in general the Tote-Em-In is the exact opposite of a museum for local wildlife: it's a collection of exotics.

Running a small zoo requires remembering all the different feeding times and tending to the various illnesses and pregnancies and whatnot, in addition to running the business itself, tending to customers, and keeping the place clean and the gift shop stocked—and working the phones and mailbox to make the trades that would keep his Museum of Oddities fascinating to the increasingly TV-dulled visitors. Through the 1950s, '60s, '70s, and '80s, George and his family kept up their vigil. They didn't take many vacations, but they met thousands of interesting visitors every year, and went to sleep each night to the calls of chimps and leopards.

Jerry Brewer went to sleep listening to the same calls—he was five when George's zoo moved in next door to his parents' home. Brewer grew up "just over a sand hill" from the kinds of species most kids only saw on *Disney's Wonderful World*. As the 1980s drew to a close and George became a little overwhelmed by the task of keeping up the place, he offered it to Jerry and his wife, Sherrie. They've owned it for the past ten years, though George still lives on the property, close to his beloved animals and relics.

Be forewarned: though the Brewers clearly care about and for the animals, this *is* an upgraded version of the kind of old-fashioned, cagey zoo that founders of the new generation of barless, "natural habitat" zoos hope to banish from the earth. If you're an animal lover, this will give you the chance to see your beloved up close. Yet while changes have been slow to come to Tote-em-In, guests have not. Even though they've been open only during summer and early fall, between 40,000 and 50,000 people have visited the zoo each year. With the Brewers' decision to open the zoo year-round, expect that number to increase considerably over the next few years.

Summer hours are 9 A.M.–6 P.M.; after Labor Day 9 A.M.–4 P.M. Admission is $6 for adults, $4 kids under 12.

For a completely different experience with nature, the **Fort Fisher–Southport Ferry,** 800/368-8969, website: www.dot.state.nc.us/transit/ferry, can serve as a scenic, on-the-way-anyway half-hour boat ride for most anyone traveling north or south through the Cape Fear region. It departs about once an hour from the Southport and Fort Fisher terminals, but times vary, so pick up a ferry schedule at your hotel or at the state Welcome Station. Whenever your departure time, be sure to get there a half-hour early to get a space on board. Fare runs $3.00 per car, 50 cents per pedestrian.

Over at 1223 N. 23rd St., **Screen Gems Studios,** 910/675-8479, website: www.screen gemsstudios.com/silverscreentours.html, offers roughly four two-hour guided tours each weekend. You'll need to call ahead to make reservations. Though Screen Gems boasts that it is "the largest and most complete motion picture studio east of California," don't confuse this with the Disney MGM studio tours or Universal Studios. This is a working studio designed to *be* a working studio, with little thought for the tourist trade. Though of course your guides will try to show you all they can, if a film or TV show is in production while you're there, some of the facilities will be closed to you. The films shot here vary in quality but tend (as do the majority of all films produced, to be fair) toward the thumbsdown genre; *King Kong Lives* was shot here; so was *Little Monsters, Exorcist III,* and *Dracula's Widow.* On the upside Screen Gems also saw the making of *Rambling Rose, Road to Wellville, Empire Records, Blue Velvet,* and *Crimes of the Heart.*

For a more sedate and non-movie-related experience, unless you have a *Ghost*-like experience while handling the ceramics, head to 6 Market St. where *Twice Baked Pottery Painting Studio,* 910/343-9886, will let you come in and paint some ceramics, which they'll fire, and which you can then take home. If you live nearby or visit Wilmington a lot, you can even join their Frequent Fire program.

ACCOMMODATIONS

The greater Wilmington area boasts well over 6,000 rooms. As is the case with its restaurants, Wilmington offers an impressive number of memorable stays for a city of its size. There are three fundamental ways to approach a stay in the area: 1) stay downtown on the scenic waterfront, 2) stay on the beach at Wrightsville, Carolina, or Kure Beaches, or 3) stay somewhere in-between. Choices #1 and #2 generally run well upward of $100 a night, particularly in high season, and so a lot of folks end up selecting #3. And this is really not such a bad deal since there are a lot of good choices, and the sprawling nature of the region means that being situated in the middle of it all can save you a

good bit of driving time as you shuttle back and forth between downtown and the beach.

DOWNTOWN WILMINGTON

Coastline Inn, 503 Nutt St., 800/617-7732, 910/763-2800, website: www.coastline-inn.com, anchors the Coast Line Center, the old railroad yards which Wilmington has saved by turning into a convention center. Stay down here and you'll have a room right on the river, be within easy walking distance of the Cotton Exchange, and be just yards away from Grouper Nancy's Restaurant. Rates run $69–121.

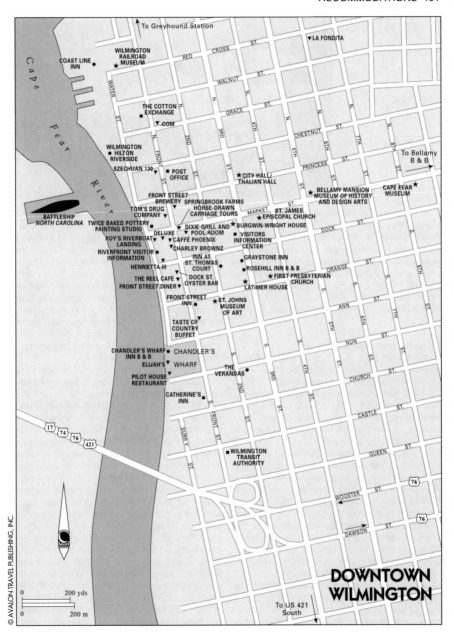

DOWNTOWN
WILMINGTON

Bear Bench at the Graystone Inn Library

You can't miss the nine-story **Wilmington Hilton Riverside,** 301 N. Water St., 910/763-5900, towering over the 19th-century waterfront. The service and amenities are first-rate; it's arguably the city's premier convention facility, and offers some of the best views of the river and the USS *North Carolina,* particularly since the Hilton's are the only views in this stretch of the river that don't have to look *at* the hotel. Rooms are $89–159 a night.

Inns and Bed-and-Breakfasts

American Historic Inns, Inc. recently chose **Graystone Inn,** 100 S. 3rd St., 910/763-2000, website: www.graystoneinn.com, as one of the "Top 10 Most Romantic Inns in the United States." These days Paul & Yolanda Bolda run the huge, atmospheric inn at the corner of S. 3rd and Dock Streets. It offers seven huge rooms (five with fireplaces) atop a grand oak staircase. The inn is the 1906 former home of Elizabeth Haywood Bridgers, widow and heiress by marriage to the fortune of her father-in-law, Robert Rufus Bridgers, former Confederate congressman, founder of the Wilmington/Weldon Railroad, and president of the Atlantic Coast Line Railway. The charms of this establishment are many: the hand-carved staircase and friendly, unpretentious owners; a large sunroom, a baby grand piano, and a wonderful turn-of-the-century mahogany-paneled sportsman's library—the sort of place where Theodore Roosevelt would have felt right at home, and the perfect spot to read in front of the fire on a cold night. The inn is especially romantic at night when you return home

and the huge, illuminated stone front takes on the look of a diplomat's residence; even if you actually spend the night eating wings and watching an Adam Sandler film, you'll feel as if you're an ambassador returning home after a night of high-level chit-chat and intrigue. Each guest room features its own bath with period fixtures; most include a clawfoot tub. Each room features its own phone and a PC data port. The inn also offers a honeymoon suite on the third floor. Golf packages available. Expect to spend from $140–200 a night, which includes breakfast and complimentary drinks in the evening.

To stay in an antebellum home, for about the same price you can stay at the nearby **Rose-Hill Inn Bed and Breakfast,** 114 S. 3rd St., 800/815-0250 or 910/815-0250, website: www.rosehill.com. Innkeepers Laurel Jones and Dennis Fietsch run things in the Neo-classic Revival house. Built in 1848 by Wilmington banker Henry Russel Savage, the house later served as home for Henry Bacon, Jr., architect of the famed Lincoln Memorial in Washington, D.C. While Graystone strives for a period look, RoseHill Inn features a mix of antiques. Each room includes a private bath, and the breakfasts tend toward the gourmet. To be right down on the water, you'll want the 1850 **Chandler's Wharf Inn Bed & Breakfast,** on the cobblestone street at Chandler's Wharf, 2 Ann St., 910/815-3510. Each suite includes a fireplace and personal phone line. Also on the river is **Catherine's Inn,** 410 S. Front St., 800/476-0723 or 910/251-0863, set in the 1888 Italianate Forshee-Sprunt House, and featuring a great two-story screened-in porch for eating breakfast, and wonderful views of the sunset over the Cape Fear River. Each of the five bedrooms features a private bath. The gardens are beautiful too.

The Verandas, 202 Nun St., 910/251-2212, website: www.verandas.com, is set in the 1853 Beery mansion and features four large porches, a screened breakfast patio, and some very large guest rooms. All four rooms are corner rooms, and all four feature a fireplace and a phone with modem jack. Full breakfast. This is the only house in Wilmington with a cupola— you can climb up there and take in a beautiful view of the neighborhood and river below. Finally, the little **Wine House,** 311 Cottage Ln., 910/763-0511, is set in a circa 1863 wine house, a plain, two-room clapboard structure behind a brick-walled courtyard on a small side street in the midst of downtown Wilmington. The two rooms feature heart-pine floors, private baths, and fireplaces. Continental breakfast. Free bikes available for the riding.

Unlike those B&Bs that blossomed inside stately old residences, **The Inn at St. Thomas Court,** 101 S. 2nd St., 800/525-0909 or 910/343-1800, website: www.innatstthomascourt.com, set inside what was a century ago an unremarkable business block, has to try a little harder to be quaint. You can see it in the name (not the "St. Thomas Court Inn," mind you), and in the way the owners pitch the property (it offers "private entrances"—à la Motel 6). But this is quibbling. The St. Thomas succeeds as a combination small inn and upscale lodge, and, really, for longer stays it might be more comfortable (though not much cheaper) than a B&B. The main building is the quaintest, featuring wicker chairs on the porches. Good downtown location too. The various one-bedroom suites feature wooden floors and a variety of themes. Be sure to pick the theme you want. If you're looking for an antebellum experience, for instance, make certain they don't put you into the Southwestern room. Prices run $129–165.

Without a doubt, one of the ways you know that an old hard-nosed downtown has been gentrified is when the meek Salvation Army soup kitchen and flophouse is reborn as a pricey bed-and-breakfast. That's exactly what's happened at the **Front Street Inn,** 215 S. Front Street, 910/762-6442, website: www.frontstreetinn.com.

The Salvation Army used to serve here, providing food and shelter for the destitute; nowadays the current owners will charge you upwards of $100 to spend the night and get a single meal. Though, to be fair, the food is much better. Featuring good second-story views of the river, the Front Street Inn makes for a less-nostalgic, less-distinctively Southern stay than most of Wilmington's B&Bs. But Jay and Stefany Rhodes run a friendly place, popular with business travelers (maybe it's the massage therapist and pool table?) and with weekenders (maybe it's the free bikes to use?). Located close to Chandler's Wharf, the inn features a selection between inn rooms and suites named after various celebrities, from Pearl S. Buck to Molly Brown to Ernest Hemingway (one assumes an extra-large minibar). Prices run $98–$168.

Further from the waterfront, you'll find the oak-canopied **Bellamy Bed and Breakfast,** 1417 Market St., 910/763-3081, with four rooms, a suite, and a shared kitchen.

ON THE BEACH

Resort Hotels

The **Sunspree Holiday Inn, Wrightsville Beach,** 1706 N. Lumina Dr., 910/256-2231, website: www.wrightsville-sunspree.com, feels much more like a resort than any Holiday Inn you might envision. With a great oceanfront location, indoor and outdoor pools, outdoor and indoor dining, even the (good) little gym offers a fine view of the ocean. Thank Fran for this bit of Hilton Head deposited on Wrightsville Beach; the 1996 hurricane destroyed the old Holiday Inn, making room for this welcome, upscale addition.

The huge **Blockade Runner Resort Hotel and Conference Center, Wrightsville Beach,** 275 Waynick Blvd., 800/541-1161 or 910/256-2251, website: www.blockade-runner.com, is something of an institution out on the waterfront at Masonboro Inlet at Wrightsville Beach. This is a full-service resort, with over 150 rooms, activities, kids' programs, and a free breakfast buffet.

Motels

A shell's throw from the Johnny Mercer Pier on Wilmington Beach stands **The Silver Gull Ocean Front Motel,** 20 East Salisbury Ct.,

800/842-8894 or 910/256-3728. Prices for the 32 units run from $90–210 a night, depending on the apartment you want and the room you choose. This is a solid, if not fancy, place for a family that's not really ready to splurge for a beach house, but wants to have the same sort of beach and pier access.

If you're looking for a suite, a spot with its location to recommend it is **One South Lumina**, 1 South Lumina, Wrightsville Beach, 800/421-3255 or 910/256-9100, with daily, weekly, and monthly rates, washers and dryers, fully equipped kitchens, and a pool.

The **Carolina Temple Apartments**, 550 Waynick Blvd., in Wrightsville Beach, 910/256-2773, email: swright168@aol.com, sounds as if it would be a) at Carolina Beach, b) a church, and c) a place for permanent residents. It is none of these: the "Carolina" is used more generally—it's located on the south end of Wrightsville Beach, just up the road from the Blockade Runner, and "Temple" refers to the family that built these two cottages nearly 100 years ago. The "apartments" refers to the fact that the units do include private baths and kitchenettes. This time-honored establishment is a good, relatively inexpensive middle-ground between a hotel and a rental house at Wrightsville Beach. Here you can stay in an early-1900s former trolley station and experience the family vacation spot qualities of Wrightsville that might be lost to you staying at one of the big oceanfronts. You'll find the rooms a bit snug but big enough for beach living; outdoor porches and decks, two and three-room suites with private baths and ceiling fans. During high season (June–Sept.) you'll need to rent by the week, though you may be able to arrange something shorter.

Beach House Rentals

If you know you'll be here for more than a few days, and if you're traveling with a crowd or a family, renting a beach house may well be the best and cheapest way to go. You'll find lots of real estate offices listed in the phone book; some of the more popular ones include **TradeMark Coastal Properties**, 222 Causeway Dr., Wrightsville Beach, 800/529-7653; **Gardner Realty & Management, Inc.** 1009 N. Lake Park Blvd., Carolina Beach, 800/697-7924; and **United Beach Vacations**, 1001 N. Lake Park Blvd., 800/334-5806, website: www.unitedbeach vacations.com.

IN-BETWEEN

For some homegrown, mid-priced lodging, try the Route 66-ish **Whitey's El-Berta Motor Inn,** 4505 Market St., 800/866-9448 or 910/799-1214, featuring 81 rooms, a good restaurant serving up comfort food, and a pool. The **Homestay Inn,** at 245 Eastwood Rd., 800/575-6085 or 910/793-1920, website: www.Homestay-inn.com, is corporate all the way, but offers 108 rooms with kitchen, a pool, laundry. If saving money's important, there's a decent **Motel 6** with a pool at 2828 Market St., 800/466-8356 or 910/762-0120. For something a little more special but still reasonable, the **Hampton Inn, Inn and Suites, Landfall Park,** 1989 Eastwood Rd., 910/256-9600, draws a fair share of beachgoers, business visitors, and movie types; it's a great crossroads stop for anyone who expects to spend time both in city and on the beach, and doesn't necessarily want to plunk down the money for a $200 a night oceanfront or a cute B&B downtown. The main lobby features a huge fireplace and feels more like a well-established lodge than a suburban chain hotel. The pool area has a distinctly resortish feel to it, and the staff is truly first-rate, as though they've all personally committed their corporate mission statement to heart. It's no surprise the inn's been winning awards as one of the best of the Hampton Inn chain. You'll find microwaves and Internet hookups in every room.

A good fall-back is **Best Western Carolinian,** 2916 Market St., 910/763-4653, which charges $65–100 a night.

FOOD

SEAFOOD AND STEAKS

Seafood in a port town? Of course. And where there's surf, there's usually turf. In nature, of course, the two go together like fish and cattle, but in dimly lit restaurants of the credit card variety, the combination claims a certain mystique.

Beginning right on the river over at Chandler's Wharf is the romantic yet semicasual **Pilot House Restaurant,** 2 Ann St., 910/343-0200, serving its nouveau-Southern cuisine by candlelight, both indoors and out. Expect to spend $12–$25 for dinner. Reservations suggested.

Next door on the river is **Elijah's,** 2 Ann St., 910/343-1448, run by the same folks and priced similarly to the Pilot House. It features both an oyster bar (with an outdoor deck) and a dining room with a nautical theme. The crab dip is legendary. Whether observant Jewish diners need to leave an empty chair for Elijah in his own restaurant is one for the theologians.

Note that both the above restaurants close after lunch and don't open again until 5 P.M. for dinner.

A good place to dine outside (or inside) in the midst of things on Water St. is **Water Street Restaurant,** 5 S. Water St., 910/343-0042. Set in an 1835 former peanut warehouse bordered in days of yore by a bawdy riverfront and a bawdier redlight district, the restaurant today keeps a casual tone. Not a bad place to pick up a good sandwich for under $8 even at night. If you're hungrier, they've got full dinners—T-bone steaks, good Mediterranean Scampi for $14–18. Kids menu items run $3–4. Live entertainment.

Another important downtown spot is **Roy's Riverboat Landing,** at 2 Market St., 910/763-7227, right across from the river. Not far from there, the determinedly off-beat **Dock St. Oyster Bar,** 12 Dock St., is an informal place for relatively inexpensive shrimp and other seafood. As you sit drinking your gourmet beer, listening to reggae, and reading the T. S. Eliot quotes on the wall, have them whip you up a Shrimp Florentine, with spinach, mushrooms, shrimp, and alfredo sauce. Stop by for 25-cent oysters Sunday through Thursday.

Out at Lands End on the way to Wrightsville, the B.Y.O.C. (Bring Your Own Cellphone) crowd prefers to eat the fine cuts ($16.95–29.95, much cheaper at lunch) from the **Port City Chop House,** 1981 Eastwood Rd., 910/256-4955.

For another waterfront dining experience, head out on the way to Carolina Beach along the Masonboro Loop Road. **Trails End Steak House,** Trails End Rd., 910/791-2034, has been serving up some of the area's most memorable beef platters for over thirty years; this smallish restaurant overlooks the Intracoastal Waterway. Expect to pay upwards of $35 for dinner. To get there, turn right onto Masonboro Loop Road off Pine Grove Drive, then make a left onto Trails End Road, just over a quarter-mile after the Whiskey Creek bridge.

The Oceanic, 703 Lumina Ave., Wrightsville Beach, provides a great view and some of the best food in the Wilmington area. In fact for a number of years Wilmingtonians voted the Oceanic the overall top restaurant in the area, the best seafood restaurant, and the restau-

Calabash Seafood House

rant with the best water view. For all the hoopla, prepare yourself for a fairly laid-back experience here: historic photos, wood wainscoting, attentive waitfolk in shorts, polo shirts, and ball caps, and some very fresh and thoughtfully prepared seafood. The Shrimp Crab & Scallops Oceanic ($18.95)—fresh shrimp, broiled with backfin crabmeat, scallops, and Monterey Jack in sherry cream sauce—will give you lots of Weightwatchers bonus points, but it sure tastes great.

Out at Kure Beach, **Big Daddy's Seafood Restaurant,** 202 K Ave., 910/458-8622, features quality seafood in a just-growed setting. In whimsical contrast to all the usual nautical paraphernalia on the walls (also here), the owner has hung French poster art. No reason, no marketing strategy—just a quirk of the owner: she went to France, liked the posters, brought them home, and hung them up. Set just a block from the Kure Beach fishing pier, it's perfect for taking a beachfront stroll before or after your meal. Expect to spend about $15 for dinner.

Many people forget about the dinner cruise option, but on Fridays and Saturdays, April through December, taking one of the dinner/dancing cruises aboard the *Henrietta III,* is really a pretty good deal, running $32–35 per person for the complete evening (minus the drinks). Call 800/676-0162 or 910/343-1611 for reservations. The boat leaves at 7:30 on Friday and 7:00 on Sunday, but you'll want to get there early for a good seat.

SOUTHERN

Set in the antebellum W. G. Fowler house, the **Taste of Country Buffet,** 226 S. Front St., 910/343-9888 puts out like a Sunday pig-pickin' seven days a week, offering up an all you can eat buffet of roasted pig, barbecued pork, fried chicken and fish, baked chicken, and other important Southern church potluck staples as chicken and pastry, stewed vegetables, biscuits, hush puppies, banana pudding, and chitterlings. On Friday and Saturday nights, they offer friend shrimp and clams and roast beef; Sunday they cook up a turkey. Prices run $6.50 for lunches Monday–Saturday, $8.23 for dinners and Sunday brunch.

Open Monday–Thurday for lunch (11 A.M.–3 P.M.), Friday and Saturday 11 A.M.–9 P.M., and Sunday 11 A.M.–4 P.M.

The Reel Cafe, 100 S. Front St., 910/251-1832, website: www.thereelcafe.com, celebrates Wilmington filmmaking with a full bar, a rooftop bar, and lots of nifty relics from the Golden Age of Carolina Film . . . which is to say, just a couple of years ago. Specialties include Louisiana Shrimp Pasta, sandwiches, and Blackened Seafood Salad. Prices run from $4.99 for the "'Royalle' with cheese" quarter-pound cheeseburger to nearly $20 for some of the seafood.

Caffe Phoenix, 9 S. Front St., Wilmington, 910/343-1395, offers fine food, an indoor balcony, and the overriding sense that somewhere on the reservations log it reads, *Streisand, Party of Four.* Visiting movie people favor Caffe Phoenix, and so I'm not making a stretch here. It's one of the only places in North Carolina where you can sip a Coppola while sitting *beside* a Coppola. Very pretty at night, more economical during the day. The sandwiches, seafood, and pasta are good anytime. Extensive wine selection.

For sheer ambience . . . or maybe I should say "thick" ambience, it's hard to beat **Alleigh's,** 4925 New Centre Dr., 910/793-0999 with its various theme areas, atmospheric outdoor tiki bar, and so on. Live music. Maybe the food's more fun than good, but good enough if you're looking for fun.

OTHER CUISINES

Italian
I'm not really comfortable with the whole gangster tie-in of **Goodfella's,** 5001 Market St., 910/791-9977; it's not much unlike taking a meal at a place called "Druglord's Colombian Cuisine." But celebration of violent criminals aside (I won't even play the Italian-American stereotype card), Goodfella's offers elegance and some fine pasta and seafood dishes out by the Ramada.

A Italian spot out in downtown Wrightsville Beach, **Clarence Fosters,** 22 N. Lumina Ave., Wrightsville Beach. 910/256-0224, serves good seafood, pasta, steaks, and Italian dishes at moderate prices. **Rialto,** in Wrightsville Beach at 530 Causeway Dr, 910/256-1099, serves up a more uptown version of the same genre.

Mexican

For the best local Mexican food, most folks point to **K-38 Baja Grill,** 5410 Oleander Dr., 910/395-6040, founded by and named after the legendary surf spot by Josh Vach, who surfed the spot and now has found the perfect way to bring up that fact in conversations for the rest of his life. But while Josh's grub is gnarly, and features a lot of innovative variations (tuna rolls, avocado vinaigrettes, multicolored tortillas), **La Fondita,** 604 Red Cross St., 910/762-5211, is far more authentic. The Spanish-speaking staff serves Mexican Coca Cola (even sweeter than the U.S. variety) and knows its way around an enchilada.

Asian

Former Manhattan restaurant owner Joseph Hou runs two popular restaurants now: **Szechuan 130,** 130 N. Front St., 910/762-5782, is the very busy downtown descendant of the beloved **Szechuan 132,** University Landing on College Rd., 910/799-1426. Both offer atmosphere, a good selection of soups, including a nice Velvet Corn Soup. Entrées include the delicious (and awe-inspiring), flaming **Volcano Beef** ($12.95).

The **Wing Chinese Restaurant,** 4002 Oleander Dr., 910/799-8178, features a vast buffet at fair prices. **Hiro Japanese Steakhouse,** 419 S. College Rd., 910/452-3097, offers top-grade steaks and chicken for dinner. Communal seating.

Burgers and Diner Food

As the Mayberry-like ambience of downtown Wilmington works its way from your eyes to your stomach, a chocolate malted or fresh-squeezed lemonade, or even a burger or tuna melt might sound good. If so, look no further than **Hall's Drug Store,** 5th and Castle Streets, 910/762-5265, the sort of counter and booth spot where Norman Rockwell might have come for inspiration.

In the retro-category, **Front Street Diner,** offers breakfast and lunch at 118 S. Front St., 910/772-1311. Open every day but one from 6:30 A.M. to 2:30 P.M. They're closed Tuesdays. Cash only. The **Dixie Grill and Pool Room,** 116 Market St., 910/762-7280, isn't "retro," because that assumes one is going back to a style one has left. The folks at the Dixie Grill are still excited about the paneling

they added in the 1970s. They've been serving up breakfast, lunch, and dinner (including some tasty bean soup) to Wilmingtonians since 1910. Also cash only.

For arguably the best burgers in town, head out to **P.T.'s Grille,** 4544 Fountain Dr., at the south end of the UNCW campus, 910/392-2293. Giant burgers, great fries (with the skin on) keep UNCW students coming back after all these years. Free refills on drinks. For the healthier-minded, try the chicken breast sandwiches.

Brewpubs

First brewery in this part of the state, **Front Street Brewery,** 9 N. Front St., 910/251-1935, nails the brewery thing cold. First, though the brewery only got here in 1995, it's set in an old (1883) building with wood floors, old photos on the walls, fish and chips and pot pies (among more commonly-available seafood and steak dishes,) a friendly crowd, and some unique, top-notch homemade brews, including a memorable raspberry wheat beer. A lot of locals like it because of the $2.25 pints, all day, every day. **Paddy's Hollow,** in The Cotton Exchange, 910/762-4354, features a similarly stellar location and a Victorian Irish theme. Nice location, friendly folks, good chargrilled steaks, 25-cent wings Monday–Thursday 5–7 P.M., a Friday prime rib dinner for $8.95, and many, many beers. The food's better than your average pub, too.

Barbecue

Flip's Bar-B-Que House, 5818 Oleander Dr., 910/799-6350, is a fine, nonself-conscious barbecue place with some great barbecue (you can buy a bottle of the sauce to take home) and a bunch of taxidermied critters all about, including a bear. Closed Sunday. Try some of the Lime Supreme Pie for dessert.

In 1999 **Jackson's Big Oak Barbecue,** 920 S. Kerr Ave., Wilmington, 910/799-1581, was voted the best barbecue in Wilmington by the readers of *Encore* magazine. Good teas, good sides, great barbecue. Closed Sunday. You'll also find good, though not particularly indigenous, ribs at the Wilmington edition of Charleston-based, Memphis-influenced **Sticky Fingers,** 5044 Market St, 910/452-7427. Native or not, these are great ribs.

NIGHTLIFE

The Wilmington downtown scene changes so quickly that it's pointless talking about where's hip to go *today*, since today will be, like, ancient history to trendsetting Wilmingtonians six months from now. When you get to town, hunt up a copy of *Encore, The Outrider,* or one of the other local entertainment freebie mags to find out who is playing where. But here's a general rundown: **The Arena,** 6317 Market St., 910/794-1861, features live music and serves food late night until 2 A.M. Every Sunday night is blues, jazz, or reggae. **Charley Brownz,** 21 S. Front St., 910/245-9499, quickly became an institution downtown, populated by folks in their late twenties and up. You can eat the above-average bar food here as well as drink and watch sports; full menu served until 11 P.M. and "Muncheez" until 2 A.M. The **Paleo-Sun Atomic Bar,** 35 N. Front St., 910/762-7600, website: www.paleoatomic.com, offers (nighttime only) carousing and drinking in a counterculture atmosphere. Costs $2 "Private Membership Fee" to get in. **The Firebelly Lounge,** 265 N. Front St., 910/763-0141, stays open and serves food until 3 A.M. and features live music most nights from Thursday through Saturday. For blues and jazz, head over to the formerly headbanging **Rusty Nail Saloon,** 1310 S. 5th St., 910/251-1888, website: www.grooveright.com/rustynail. Monday is Poetry Open Mic night, and Sunday is an open Jazz Jam, starting at 6 P.M. Hip with the collegiate set is **.com,** 121 Grace St., 910/342-0266, a "Cybar Dance Club," offering a Thursday Ladies/College Nite, and a Sunday Dollar Nite.

ENTERTAINMENT

Theater and Dance Venues
The premier artsy spot in Wilmington is **Thalian Hall Center for the Performing Arts,** 310 Chestnut St., 910/343-3664. The Opera House Theatre Company performs there, along with traveling artists and troupes. The **Sarah Graham Kenan Memorial Auditorium,** 601 S. College Rd., 910/962-3500, also gets many of the traveling companies that come through town. Each summer the **Cape Fear Shakespeare Festival** gets underway at the Greenfield Lake Amphitheater. Call 910/251-9457. Free. During the summer make your way down to the riverfront at dusk for **Sundown Shindig on the River,** a loose collection of street entertainment, arts and crafts, and food vendors.

Movie Theaters
The clean, first-run **Carmike 16** over at 111 Cinema Dr., 910/815-0212, gets most of the "hot" movies first. The **Cinema 6** at 5335 Oleander Dr., 910/799-6666, is another place to check for new releases. **Thalian Hall,** 310 Chestnut St., sometimes shows classic old films on the big screen as part of its popular **Cinematique** series. Call for information. The **Fantail Film Festival** in June features top old Hollywood musicals from the 1940s, shown aboard the USS *North Carolina.* A memorable experience, and only fifty cents to get in. Call 910/251-5797 for information. To get a pulse for what's happening in Wilmington filmmaking, try to catch a **Film Nite** at Mollye's Market. Call 910/509-2890 for information and dates.

SPORTS, RECREATION, AND SHOPPING

Surfing
The 2000 East Coast Wahine Surfing Championships at Wrightsville Beach got some national press when a female surfer from South Carolina broke away from her heat to save the life of a young boy sucked out by a Hurricane Alberto–churned riptide. A photo of the wet-suited heroine towing in the would-be drowning victim appeared in newspapers around the country.

The southern North Carolina Coast enjoys pretty decent surf for this side of the country, and a very active surf scene. East Coast surfers congregate hereabout for surf contests each summer. The best spot in the region is arguably the Crystal Pier, but it's also often the most crowded spot because of this. Good spots include the north end of Wrightsville Beach in front of Shell Island Resort; I've seen some great surf off Fort Fisher, and Carolina Beach and Kure

Beach can be good under the right conditions. So can Bald Head Island, though it's a pain to get there. As anywhere, stop by a surf shop, strike up a conversation with some local surfers, and find out where they're breaking the day you're there.

Check out www.sncsurf.com before you come; it's a great website for planning your Wilmington area surfing.

The area is home to some 12 surf shops, but you'll find that one of the best surf shops is one of the first: **Surf City Surf Shop,** 530 Causeway Dr., 910/256-2265, founded back in 1978 by a couple of surfers, one of whom moved down to North Myrtle Beach to open a couple more stores in the chain, and the other of whom stayed right here. **Sweetwater Surf Shop,** 10 N. Lumina Ave, 910/256-3821, located just as you cross the second bridge in Wrightsville Beach, is even older (founded 1976), and they offer a good selection of new and used boards, including rentals. **Bert's,** U.S. 421, Carolina Beach, **Hot Wax Surf Shop,** 4510 Hoggard Dr., 910/791-9283, and the **Wrightsville Beach Supply Company,** 1 N. Lumina Ave., Wrightsville Beach, 910/256-8821 can also get you in the water.

For **Surf City's Surf Report,** call 910/256-4353.

Cruises

To really appreciate a port town, you have to approach it at least once from the water. The folks at **Cape Fear Riverboats,** waterfront at Dock St., 800/676-0162, offer a good way of doing this with their cruises aboard the *Henrietta III.* Salty Vietnam War veteran Carl Marshburn has run his scenic *Henrietta* cruises up and down the Cape Fear River since 1988, early on in the Wilmington renaissance. He named his dinner and dancing paddlewheeler after the *Henrietta,* the first steam paddleboat built in North Carolina, which ran here safely and profitably for forty years back in the 19th century. After 11 years of service, Carl sold the *Henrietta II,* and then Carl and a skeleton crew flew out to Illinois to his new boat, quickly dubbed the *Henrietta III.* For 16 days of nonstop cruising, the former gambling ship made it down the Ohio and into the Mississippi and then out into the Gulf Coast, around Florida, and up the East Coast until it reached its new home and went, almost immediately, to work. For a long time the inside of the air-conditioned riverboat (not a paddlewheeler) continued to feature a glitzy, Las Vegas motif, but the good captain says he'll have this renovated away by the time you read this.

The *Henrietta III* makes narrated sight-seeing cruises, a lunch cruise, sunset cruises, dinner dance cruises, and moonlight cruises. Call for information. If you take the cruise (you should), Captain Marshburn will likely be piloting, and you ought to try to talk with him, to draw out some of his interesting stories of life here on the Cape Fear River.

One story concerns a friend of his who works coordinating special effects for local filmmakers. The friend lives in a 1790 home along the river, and after filming was completed for TNT's *The Hunley,* the friend installed two of that film's mock cannons outside his home, facing the river as if they were part of Wilmington's 18th-century civil defense system. The Styrofoam cannons looked real, and they could actually fire their fake charges. One afternoon the friend had a party underway, and as Carl and his shipful of visitors cruised by, the friend decided to open fire on Carl's boat. The partying would-be ambushers, not in the clearest of minds, cut the fuse too long and stuffed too much powder into the cannon. Not only did it fire too late, after the boat had passed, but it blew up the cannon, sending Styrofoam flying everywhere. Which goes to show, alcohol and artillery—even Styrofoam mock-19th century artillery—just don't mix. Unless the friend has tried a second attack, you should still be able to see the second cannon in front of the old home today. Carl will probably point it out in his narration.

Bowling

The Sport of the Gods enjoys a first-rate location at the cleverly named **Ten Pin Alley,** Market Place Mall, 127 S. College Rd., 910/452-5455, featuring 24 lanes, pool tables, good food, and enough arcade games and TV screens to send a lit professor into convulsions. Open every night until 2 A.M. Second in the pecking order is **Cardinal Lanes,** 7026 Market St., 910/686-4223.

Shopping

The **Cotton Exchange,** 321 N. Front St., 910/343-9896, website: www. cottonexchange.citysearch. com, features 30 specialty shops and eateries tucked into four historic brick buildings. Much of these are traditional tourist town niche store, but among the stained-glass dolphins and Southwestern handicrafts, you'll find a **Celtic Shop,** 910/763-1990, and the atmospheric **Two Sisters Bookery,** 910/762-4444, with a well-chosen collection of local titles. **Fire and Spice,** 910/762-

3050, offers hundreds of brands of searing hot sauces and salsas, sporting names like "A Woman Scorned" and "Bayou Viagra."

Out at 1956 Carolina Beach Rd., Harriet Torres runs the funky **Funksters,** 910/762-5990, which advertises itself as "Wilmington's One and Only '50s and '60s Store."

INFORMATION AND TRANSPORTATION

Tourist Info
Reach the nice folks over at the **Cape Fear Coast Convention Visitors Bureau** at 14 N. 3rd St., 910/341-4030 or 800/222-4757, fax 910/341-4029, e-mail: info@cape-fear.nc.us.

Emergency Numbers
Call 911 in any emergency on the Cape Fear Coast. If your car breaks down, or if you want to call the State Highway Patrol for any other reason from your cell phone, call *HP.

Hospitals
Hopefully your visit to Wilmington won't require a hospital trip, but if it does, the **New Hanover Regional Medical Center,** 2131 S. 17th St., 910/343-7000, is the largest hospital in the region, and it features five ICUs. The **Cape Fear Memorial Hospital,** 5301 Wrightsville Ave., 910/452-8384, is much smaller, but specializes in women's services.

A cheaper alternative for nonemergency care is to visit one of the many walk-in clinics. Two spots to try are **Doctor's Urgent Care Centre,**

4815 Oleander Dr., 910/452-111, open until 8 P.M. Mon.–Sat., and 12 A.M.–6 P.M. Sunday; and **The Pee Dee Clinic,** 1630 Military Cutoff Rd., 910/256-8087, open 9 A.M.–6 P.M. daily.

Newspapers and Magazines
Owned by the *New York Times,* the *Wilmington Morning Star/Star-News* is the paper of record for Wilmington.

The Outrider is a decent little entertainment freebie you'll see around town, with more ads and charts showing who's playing where than articles. A great barometer of one corner of Carolina culture, this may be the only alternative weekly in existence that carries head shop adverts, a "Bar Babe of the Week" feature, and the NASCAR scoreboard, all within its covers. *Encore* is the more professional entertainment weekly, but either will do if all you want to do is plan your evening. You'll likely also spot the *Wilmington Journal,* in racks around town. Published for and by African-Americans under one name or another since 1927, the *Journal* is a testament to the racial divisions still extant in the region.

Wrightsville Beach

Wilmington Magazine, a glossy, bimonthly publication began appearing on coffee tables throughout Southeastern North Carolina in 1994.

GETTING THERE

By Car
Most people coming to Wilmington get there by private automobile. If you're coming from the west, just take the I-40 until you reach town. If you're heading south or north along the I-95, turn east when you hit the I-40. And if you're taking U.S. 17, just continue north or south on into town.

By Air
With a name that perhaps overstates it a bit, the **Wilmington International Airport,** 1740 Airport Blvd., off 23rd St., two miles north of Market St., 910/341-4125, offers daily flights to and from the major domestic hubs. Airlines serving the airport include Delta-affiliated Atlantic Southeast Airlines, 800/282-3424; Midway Corporate Express Airlines, 800/555-6565; USAir, 800/428-4322; and United Airlines Express, 800/241-6522. It's within ten minutes of downtown Wilmington, fortunately, so even a cab ride won't be too expensive. If you're going to be staying down on the Brunswick Isles, closer to the South Carolina line, try the Myrtle Beach International Airport, listed in the next chapter.

By Bus
Greyhound, 800/231-2222, and **Carolina Trailways,** 910/762-6625, can both get you into Wilmington proper. They'll bring you to the bus terminal at 201 Harnett St.

GETTING AROUND

By Bus
The **Wilmington Transit Authority (WTA),** 110 Castle St., 910/343-0106, provides a low-cost alternative to taxis for carless visitors hoping to explore Wilmington and its suburbs. One-way fare runs 75 cents. A transfer will cost you a dime. The buses run until 7:30 P.M. but not on Sundays or on most state holidays. Your hotel may well have bus schedules; if not, stop by the Visitors Information Center at 24 N. 3rd St. to pick one up.

By Taxi
Lett's Taxi Service, 910/458-3999, **Port City Taxi, Inc.,** 910/762-1165, and **Yellow Cab,** 910/762-3322, can all get you where you want to go in the Wilmington area. Most charge around $1.60 per mile.

VEHICLE RENTALS

The Wilmington area includes all the usual suspects in the rental car business, including **Budget,** 1740 Airport Boulevard, Wilmington, 800/527-0700 or 910/762-8910; and **Enterprise Rentals,** 5601 Market St., 800/736-8222 or 910/799-4042.

SOUTH OF WILMINGTON

SOUTHPORT

Solid little Southport rolled up its sleeves, gritted its teeth, and took the brunt of Hurricane Floyd in 1999. Floyd's gone. Solid Southport remains.

Resting upon the Intracoastal Waterway and protected from Atlantic storms by Oak and Bald Head Islands, Southport was chartered in 1792, but by then, the area already had quite a history. Some argue that the first, ill-fated Spanish explorers bungled through these parts in 1524 and again in 1526. About 200 Native Americans lived in the area in 1715; five years later, none were left. About this time, Stede Bonnet, "The Gentleman Pirate," who admired North Carolina's lax piracy laws (and the state's laxer enforcement of them), operated in the area. He was arrested in the harbor after a fierce battle in 1718. The town itself began forming after the 1748 establishment of the British Fort Johnston.

Just before the Revolution, Josiah Martin, the dogged but not particularly confrontational last royal governor of North Carolina, fled to Fort Johnston hoping for refuge from rebellious colonists, but the horde proved mightier than his men, and he fled on July 18, 1775 to the HMS *Cruizer* offshore. The following night, the colonial patriots burned the fort to the ground.

After the Revolution, fishermen and river pilots began building homes near the fort's ruins. Wealthy city dwellers also built second (and third and fourth) homes here to take advantage of the coastal breezes during Wilmington's hot summers.

One of the first plots of land planned by the community was "The Grove," now known as Franklin Square Park. The Grove was set aside for public use, and now over two centuries later it is still being used by the public. Within the park is Franklin Square Gallery, which displays the works of local artists. Fort Johnston itself was rebuilt by the Army and the "new" officers' quarters, which overlook the river, were constructed in 1805. Fort Johnston has seen more action than a Hollywood divorce lawyer; it has served in some way in every American conflict since 1805.

The victorious Americans built a new fort on the site after 1794; Confederates seized it from the Federals at the start of the war, and along with other forts in the area, it protected Wilmington's valuable blockade runners. Today it's occupied by the commanding officer of the Sunny Point Military Ocean Terminal.

During all these years, the town went by the name of Smithville, named after Revolutionary General Benjamin Smith. In 1887 the town's fathers changed the name to the more place-specific Southport.

In turn-of-the-21st-century Southport, hurricane-tested oak trees still shade Victorian homes, but with 45,000 snowbirds (15,000 permanent residents) living out in the bedroom communities on Oak Island and Bald Head Island, the little town of 2,500 bustles a bit but in a very laid-back way, boasting 15 antique shops, a handful of seafood restaurants and historic sites, the small Southport Maritime Museum, and ample lodgings to make this a nice weekend getaway.

Rand McNally recently named Southport one of the best places in America to retire. It has that kind of pace to it. Today Southport continues to face the Atlantic, even if a couple of islands do somewhat block the view, and so it's fitting that **Waterfront Park** is the most popular spot in town for just sitting and watching life—and mammoth,

ocean-going vessels—go by. From here you can also see Bald Head Light (1817), 109 feet tall, and the oldest in the state. **Oak Island Light** was built in 1958, stands 168 feet tall, and can be seen 24 miles away. By some estimates it's the brightest light in all of the United States, though there is a pawn shop off the I-26 north of Charleston that gives it a run for its money.

Information
At the **Southport/Oak Island Chamber of Commerce,** at 4848 Longbeach Rd. SE, 910/457-5787, you'll find maps, pamphlets galore, and self-guided walking tours.

Accommodations
For most people, Southport's a B&B kind of town. If you want to motel it, try the literally-named **Riverside Motel,** which is clean and simple and may remind you of the place where Gere and Winger used to cavort in *An Officer and a Gentleman.* Or if you're planning to bring in your own fish and need somewhere to cook them, the **Sea Captain Motor Lodge,** 608 W. West St., 910/457-5263, website: www.ncbrunswick.com, offers 12 efficiencies among its 84 rooms.

Brunswick Inn Bed & Breakfast, 301 E. Bay St., 910/457-5278, website: www.ncbrunswick.com; **Cape Fear Inn,** 317 W. Bay St., 910/457-5989, website: www.ncbrunswick.com, offers 12 rooms, right on the waterfront.

Lois Jane's Riverview Inn, 106 W. Bay St., 800/457-1152 or 910/457-6701, is across the street from the waterfont and offers four rooms and a nice fireplace.

Food
Down beside the yacht basin, **Port Charlie's,** 317 W. Bay St., 910/457-0801, is a rustic on-the-water sort of place where you can boat in or walk in. Great views of the harbor and very fresh, and not necessarily fried, seafood, along with good steaks, pasta, and so on. The **Marker One Lounge,** in the same building, has a jukebox and dart boards; you'll expect Jimmy Buffett to stumble in at any moment. A good place to start or finish up the evening.

Sights and Activities
The little **North Carolina Maritime Museum at Southport** aka the Southport Maritime Muse-

um, 116 N. Howe St., 910/457-0003, is a good place to stop in when you first get to town. It tells the Cape Fear region's story with exhibits on the colonial era, pirates, steamboating, fishing, and shipwrecks. You can see a fragment from a 2,000 year old Native American canoe, a 200-pound pile torpedo pulled from the Cape Fear River, and relics from the shipwrecked *City Of Houston*. Admission runs $2 for adults, $1 for senior citizens. Children under 16 years are free. Open Tues.–Sat., 10 A.M. to 4 P.M.

But really the best thing about Southport is the strolling. Head off some evening (morning will do in a pinch) along Howe and Moore or one of the many residential streets in this historic town. Watch the boats passing by along the Southport **Riverwalk** and just melt into the 19th-century ambience of the town. As you might guess, the locals pull out all the stops for the annual **North Carolina 4th of July Festival.**

Diving

Wayne Strickland at **Scuba South Diving Company,** 222 South River Drive, 910/457-5201, takes his 52-foot boat (certified for 24 passengers) up to 100 miles offshore to dive sites off Cape Fear's Frying Pan Shoals, including the *City of Houston* steamship and various Civil War wrecks (blockade runners, freighters, and many more). Fortunately Cape Fear has been more than generous in supplying wreck sites for the pleasure of Captain Strickland's clientele. He leaves most mornings at 7 A.M. Walk-ons are welcome if there's room, but call ahead for reservations if possible.

BALD HEAD ISLAND

Bald Head Island advertises itself as "A Breath of Fresh Sea Air," and "An Exclusive Sanctuary" which it is. Of course, whether or not the wealthy really need *another* sanctuary is debatable . . . but never mind. The advertisements also point to the island's "Low Key Charm," but of course, nobody needs to be ostentatious here to let others know they're loaded—just being here on the island attests to *that*. The island offers a Hilton Head for people who think Hilton Head is for the commoners. You'll find very few short-term stays available; likely you won't be staying here un-

less you know somebody or are ready to pay for a week's rental at a very expensive home; you can, however, go over on the ferry (no cars) and spend the day on the fairly undeveloped (though not fairly developed)island. If you get over there, stop by the **Bald Head Light** (1817), 109 feet tall, and the oldest in the state. Call the Bald Head Island Information Center at 800/234-2441 for information.

OAK ISLAND

You can get to Oak Island, on the other hand, merely by crossing a bridge. Oak Island has been developed in all the usual ways, with golf, miniature golf, tennis, gift shops, seafood restaurants, and many, many rental houses.

THE SOUTH BRUNSWICK ISLES

Between the sprouting fingers of Wilmington and Myrtle Beach lie the South Brunswick Isles, where you can still sense the recent rural past of southern Tar Heel coast as yet uncovered with asphalt and stucco—but you'd best hurry. True, the islands have long been developed in beach-shabby style, here-until-the-next-storm sort of way, but as beachfront land becomes more scarce, the realtors and bulldozers seem to have shifted into high gear.

As opposed to the Outer Banks, which has drawn visitors from the North for generations, Holden Beach, Ocean Isle Beach, and Sunset Beach have drawn mostly Carolinian visitors. They've historically functioned as a laid-back, sand-road, regional vacation spot. Carolinians disinterested in the glitz—and higher prices—of Myrtle Beach and the Wilmington beaches would rent a home here each year. But as upstate Carolinians have grown wealthier, more and more of them meander this way looking for condos and summer houses. Prices are rising, and so are the crowds, though this is still a great place for a low-key family getaway.

Holden Beach, developed in the 1930s, comes first as you head south from Wilmington on US17. Because it sets at just the right portion of land as the coastline sweeps northeasterly to Cape Fear, Holden faces due south; this means you can catch both the sunrise and sunset here without once moving your towel.

Heading south, **Ocean Isle Beach** comes along next. Though it was developed in the 1950s, Ocean Isle Beach was a planned community. Odell Williamson returned from World War II with dreams of creating a perfect beach community, with a small commercial quarter and lots of room for family homes. And that's pretty much what Ocean Isle Beach is, even today. You might blink a bit as you cross the causeway and see the **Ocean Isle Beach Water Slide,** 3 2nd Street, 910/579-9678, but kids won't complain, and that's really about as far as the Myrtlesque developments go on the island. Ocean Isle is also home to the very worthwhile **Museum of Coastal Carolina,** 21 E. 2nd Street, 910/579-1016, which features extensive exhibits on both the natural and human history of the Carolina Coasts. If you're coming to the isles for a few days, stop by here early in your trip to pick up the background information that will make your shell-hunting and tide-watching all the more intriguing.

Little three-mile-long **Sunset Beach** was developed after the other two islands, by Odell Williamson's former partner, Manlon Gore. Sunset feels more remote than the other islands—maybe it's the old-fashioned swing bridge you have to cross to get there—with just a dash of commercialism. Stop by **Bill's Seafood Market,** 310 Sunset Boulevard, 910/579-6372 to stock up for the grill.

Accommodations

If you'd like to stay overnight at Holden Beach you'll find the traditional beachy **Gray Gull Motel** at 3263 Holden Beach Road SW, 910/842-6775. Or try the **Crescent Moon Inn,** 965 Sabbath Home Road SW, 877/727-1866 or 910/842-1190, which offers two rooms and two suites. The **Yardarm Inn,** at 167 Ocean Boulevard W, 910/842-8074, website: www.sirius.com/~ova tion/brothers, is really a pair of rental houses, one on the oceanfront, one on the second row.

Contact **Alan Holden Vacations,** 128 Ocean Boulevard W, 800/720-2200 or 910/842-6061, website: www.holden-beach.com, for information on the Yardarm Inn. Alan Holden can also connect you with a variety of local rental houses on all three of the islands, which is the way most people experience the Brunswick Isles. **Brunswickland Realty,** 123 Ocean Boulevard W, 800/842-6949 or 910/842-6949, website: www.weblync.com/brunswickland, is considered another of the more dependable rental outfits.

For shorter stays, a new and very clean beachfront alternative on Ocean Isle is **The Islander Inn,** 57 W. 1st Street, 888/325-4753, website: www.islanderinn.com. Hard-by is the similar **Ocean Isle Inn,** 37 W. 1st Street, 800/352-5988, website: www.oceanisleinn.com. Down on Sunset you'll find the **Sunset Beach Motel,** at 6 Main Street, 910/579-7093, and **Continental Motel & Apartments,** at 431 S. Sunset Boulevard, 910/579-6772.

Food

For eats at Ocean Isle Beach, try **Sharky's,** 81 Causeway Drive, 910/579-9177, at the island end of the Ocean Isle Causeway, where you'll discover a great deck (boaters can tie up here) and top-quality beach food: seafood, pizza, and steaks. At Holden Beach, try the venerable **Captain Willie's Restaurant,** on Causeway Drive, 910/842-9383 for Calabash seafood at its crunchiest (though they can grill it as well). Located upstairs from Bill's Seafood Market at Sunset Beach is **Crabby Oddwaters,** 310 Sunset Boulevard, 910/579-6372, which serves (as you might guess) seafood as well, and enjoys a lot of popularity. Crabby's is a nice place to sip an adult beverage and enjoy the view, but if you're looking for live music, **Steamers II,** 8 2nd Street, 910/575-9009, at Ocean Isle Beach offers some of the best nightlife on the Southern Brunswick Isles. Weekends bring live bands, which play the kinds of music most popular hereabouts, from beach music to rock and country.

MYRTLE BEACH AND THE GRAND STRAND

The 60-mile stretch of coast running from Georgetown to the northern border of South Carolina is often called the Grand Strand, but the term more aptly describes the area between Murrells Inlet to the south and Little River to the north. The city of Myrtle Beach, named for the many wax myrtles once found along the shore, is today the centerpiece of a region that draws more visitors than any other single South Carolina destination.

But unfortunately, Myrtle Beach suffers from its reputation. Imagine New Yorkers without the wherewithal to drive to Miami. Imagine the Dukes of Hazzard at the beach. Now imagine a pleasure land custom-built for these constituencies. You get the idea. We're talking miles of chain restaurants, cartoonish miniature golf courses, and beachwear shops specializing in genitalia-joke T-shirts.

This is the reputation. It's also one real, regrettable side of the truth. But the Grand Strand didn't become the state's top destination by accident: the local white sand beaches *are* gorgeous; Barefoot Landing, a marketplace built on stilts amid a scenic salt marsh, *is* a memorable shopping experience (and enjoyed the distinction of being the state's No. 1 tourist attraction for much of the 1990s); and such venues as the Carolina Opry, Alabama (owned by the famous country rock band of the same name), and Gatlin Brothers Theatre justify promoters' claims that Myrtle Beach is now the country-and-western music capital of the Deep South.

The Grand Strand is also an international destination for golfers and tennis players. In a state with seemingly more space allotted to fairways than to roadways, the Greater Myrtle Beach area alone boasts more than 100 golf courses. You could almost tee off at a different Grand Strand hole every morning for two and a half years and never play the same hole twice.

In fact the allure of Myrtle Beach is such that today the city claims rank as the second-fastest-growing metropolitan area in the United States. You'll see a lot of former Northerners and land-locked Southerners here in tennis whites, sunglasses, and perfect tans—folks who vacationed in Myrtle Beach for years before finally sinking

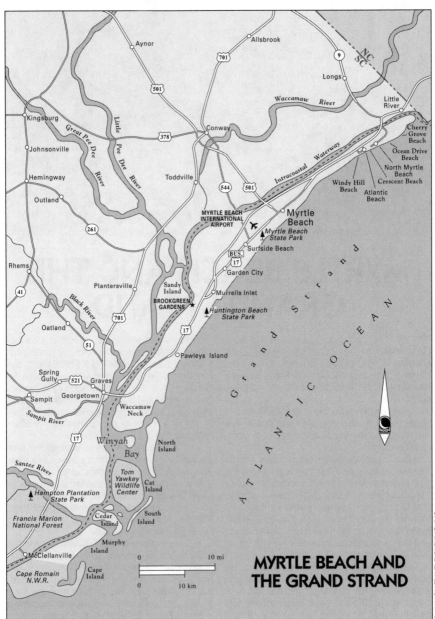

MYRTLE BEACH AND THE GRAND STRAND

permanent roots into the region's fine white sand. In addition to the retirees, many younger folk of less patient generations have moved here to profit off the boom—and to enjoy the sun and fun now, not later.

This immigration is both a blessing and a curse to the Strand. On the positive side, the local economy continues to thrive—even after the devastating 1992 closure of the Myrtle Beach Air Force Base. But while people who readily leave behind family and friends for warm weather and a laid-back lifestyle tend to be very friendly, they don't normally become dedicated environmentalists or historical preservationists once they arrive. Tellingly, the city's most important city festival doesn't honor the area's Revolutionary War heroes or founding families. Instead, just as Salley celebrates chitlins, and Pageland honors watermelons, Myrtle Beach celebrates its own most famous product—sunbaked hedonism—with the annual Sun-Fun Festival.

Head north or south of Myrtle Beach to enjoy fresh seafood in the quaint fishing villages of Little River and Murrells Inlet. Or drive north to the 1950s beach-town ambience of Ocean Drive Beach, longtime mecca for shaggers and beach music aficionados from around the world. **Huntington Beach State Park,** just south of town, provides picnicking and camping on some of the most pristine marshland and beachfront on the Carolina coast, and right across U.S. 17 from Huntington stand the gates to **Brookgreen Gardens,** the world's largest outdoor sculpture garden and one of the most beautiful places in the entire South. Farther south on U.S. 17 lie the "arrogantly shabby" vacation town of Pawleys Island; Georgetown, one of the state's most historic and scenic riverfront towns; the beautiful and historic Hopsewee and Hampton plantations; and the quaint fishing village of McClellanville, head of the state's new Palmetto Trail.

The majority of Myrtle Beach's vacationers have always been South Carolinians. Generations of spring breakers and summer vacationers have trekked to the myriad hotels and motels and cruised the Strand to see and be seen. For some 60 years, young Carolinians have taken their dates to ride the rickety Swamp Fox roller coaster; dine on fried shrimp, slaw burgers, and elephant ears chased with sweet tea; and then head over to the Pavilion in their Weejuns to

---

NOT THE GRANDEST, MAYBE—BUT STILL PRETTY GRAND

A recent survey of the top "urban beaches" in America ranked Myrtle Beach's Grand Strand sixth in the nation, right between Newport Beach, California (#5), and San Padre Island, Texas (#7), and beating out Main Beach Santa Cruz (Calif.), Wrightsville Beach (N.C.), Daytona Beach (Fla.), Cape May (N.J.), and Laguna Beach (Calif.), among others. Myrtle Beach was cited for its plethora of coastal golfing opportunities, and (obviously by nonsurfers) for its "warm, calm waters."

---

shag on the sand or on the sandy, sagging wood floor of The Pad, to beach music by bands like the Tams, the Drifters, and Maurice Williams and the Zodiacs. The shagging subculture is an important part of 20th-century Carolina. What Lafayette is to Cajun music, Myrtle Beach is to Carolina's own unique beach, or shagging, music.

Yes, Myrtle Beach's primary function is as a vacation town. But if you want to understand a people, you really need to understand how it lets its hair down. And anyway, perhaps providing relaxation and family memories is a noble enough function for any community.

LAND

Starting at Little River near the North Carolina state line, a thin sliver of land between the Atlantic Ocean and the Waccamaw River runs on down to Winyah Bay at Georgetown. This sliver is known as Waccamaw Neck. Horry County encompasses this region and beyond, continuing west to the Little Pee Dee River. In today's world of drained swamps and hardly-notice-it concrete bridges, it's easy to underestimate how isolated Horry County was just 100 years ago. Folks liked to speak of "The Independent Republic of Horry County"; the rugged farmers and woodsmen who lived in the woods and swamps got along pretty much on their own.

Horry is South Carolina's largest county, larger than the state of Rhode Island in area. Most of this land is rural farmland, though the massive development of the county's oceanfront strip has rewritten the coast into a different story. But no matter what you might think of the Strand's prostituting its natural resources, Horry is pronounced with a silent "h," as in "O-ree." South of the Strand (and Horry County) proper is Georgetown County.

Here's something to keep in mind: the Strand proper is 60 miles long. If your show starts at 8 P.M. at Barefoot Landing in North Myrtle Beach, and you've made dinner reservations at 6 P.M. down at Murrells Inlet, you may have planned out a pretty breakneck night for yourself, particularly on a busy weekend, when both U.S. 17 and the U.S. 17 Bypass promise bumper-to-bumper traffic.

CLIMATE

January temperatures see an average high of 59°F and a low of 40°F; July and August see highs of 89°F and lows of 74°F. Rainfall during January averages just 4.03 inches; July, the rainiest month, sees an average of 6.41 inches. When I was here one June, it was raining and 95°F. Humidity was up around 85 percent. So if you're expecting cold coastal breezes, you may have another thing coming.

HISTORY

Though many historians suspect that Lucas Vasquez de Ayllon's short-lived 16th-century colony of San Miguel, the first European settlement in continental North America, was set somewhere in the present-day Hobcaw Barony north of Georgetown, this is only speculation. What's certain is that Georgetown was the third permanent city founded in South Carolina—after Charleston and Beaufort—and named after the German-born Prince George II. After its founding in 1735, Georgetown and the surrounding area became a hotbed for rice and later indigo, and grew into one of the richest cities in colonial America.

During the Civil War, the Confederates established a fort up by Cherry Grove, surrounded by a ditch 10 feet wide and five feet deep. In January 1863, U.S. Navy Lieutenant William B. Cushing and 25 men captured the fort to use as an overlook while searching for Confederate boats attempting to run the Union blockade. Cushing and his men held the fort only briefly; before long they ran out of ammunition and made a hasty retreat.

After the Civil War broke most of the plantation owners, the land was bought up by members of Northern industrialist families with names like Ford, Vanderbilt, and Huntington, for summer retreats. In 1893 the region weathered a deadly hurricane.

To see an eerie reminder of the storm's handiwork, head out at low tide to where 42nd Avenue reaches the ocean. You can make out the wreck of the *Freeda A. Wyley,* a 507-ton ship carrying pine lumber from Mississippi to New York when she was caught in the storm and hit by lightning. The ship caught fire and burned clear down to the waterline before sinking, but amazingly the crew was able to escape to shore.

At the time of the hurricane, the present-day town of Myrtle Beach consisted of two things: myrtle and beach. But in the last decade of the 19th century, Conway's F. G. Burroughs cut a swath from Conway to the sea, laying tracks as he went and building a lumber mill three-quarters of the way at Pine Island. He timbered the land between Conway and the ocean and used his new railroad, The Conway Seashore, to move this lumber to Conway where it could be loaded on barges and floated down the Waccamaw to Georgetown. He founded a new town at the ocean end of the railroad and, in a momentary lack of imagination, called it New Town. By 1900 he'd changed the name to Myrtle Beach. Local families got into the habit of riding the lumber trains down to the ocean, and by 1901 Burroughs had built an inn for the visitors.

For quite a while, though, the place didn't really catch on with anyone but the locals. In 1926, Greenville businessman John T. Woodside bought up a lot of the area around town and laid out streets. He built a major hotel, the Ocean Forest Hotel, and began advertising the beaches around Myrtle Beach as "America's Grandest Strand." The following years made Myrtle Beach a respectable player in the East Coast beach-town parade, but since Myrtle had little to offer that wasn't already available in Miami, Virginia

Beach, or even Atlantic City, most of the people it drew continued to be locals: pleasure-seeking folks from the Midlands, Upcountry, and North Carolina. It wasn't until the late 1960s that a local businessman built two golf courses and invented the "golf package," which allowed visiting golfers to receive special deals and preferences on lodging and golf by paying for them together as one "package." Before long, tourists wearing plaid pants and funny hats had begun to linger far beyond the summer months.

In fact over the past 20 years, an alarming number of duffers and others have chosen to linger till death do them part. Development after development, faux plantation after plantation goes up, and retiree after retiree, tan entrepreneurial young couple after tan entrepreneurial young couple move down to feast on the good life they once tasted for only a week a year.

In 1992 as government officials downscaled the U.S. military, the Myrtle Beach Air Force Base was closed, leaving unemployed the largest body of workers in the county. What the county should do with the former base immediately became, and remains, a matter of some debate. Various business and community leaders have proposed a theme park, an expanded airport, and an industrial complex. At this writing negotiations between the city and the North Carolina-based Landex Development Corporation looked promising. Plans would call for a 122-acre natural park in the midst of the 900-acre, $500–700 million development, to be called "Centre Pointe," though Landex was balking at the city's desire for a "mixed use" plan. The plan, if adopted, would require the new development to be built more along the lines of traditional, pre–World War II American cities, where its residents could walk from home to work or to the store. Landex claimed that this sort of building, despite its success in "new traditional" neighborhoods across the country, is economically unfeasible. They're arguing instead for more of the same sort of development that has plagued Myrtle Beach, leading to pedestrian-hostile, high-speed traffic arteries and strip malls separated from the sidewalk by acres of blacktop and parked cars.

Meanwhile the arrival of the massive shopping/entertainment complex Barefoot Landing signaled a positive change in the quality and tone of construction in the area; for the first time in a long time, something had been built here that contained an extended concept, a larger vision. And the public responded very positively, quickly turning Barefoot Landing into the state's top attraction, bar none. If other Myrtle Beach building followed suit, the "beachy" bric-a-brac street fronts could be on the way out, and an era of buildings more worthy of their location might be on its way in. Myrtle Beach might begin to attract more of the aesthetically sensitive visitors repelled by the gaudy tack.

But it was not to be. The addition of the even more massive shopping/entertainment complex Broadway at the Beach in the early 1990s seemed, at first, to signal another step in the right direction, with its coherent, classic theme. But then came the chain tourist town eyesores: Hard Rock Café built a pyramid—a *pyramid*—at the Beach's Celebrity Square. And then, worst of all (so far), Planet Hollywood built its worthy-of-Vegas globe building, stuck right out on the U.S. 17 Bypass where you can't miss it, no matter how hard you may try.

SIGHTS

ORIENTATION

Murrells Inlet

This is mainly a strip of restaurants along the inlet named for a pirate (Captain Murrell) who made this his home base. Over the past decades, this fishing town with a 3,300 population has increasingly become a tourist draw, almost entirely for the fresh seafood and water sports along the inlet. Crime novelist Mickey "Mike Hammer" Spillane lives here. Pick up the local paper and you may see the name of his wife, Jane Spillane, an Inlet native who's active in area politics.

Downtown Myrtle Beach (The Pavilion Area)

This describes most everything near the Pavilion at 9th Avenue, for about 20 blocks in either direction. On the south side of 1st Avenue, the

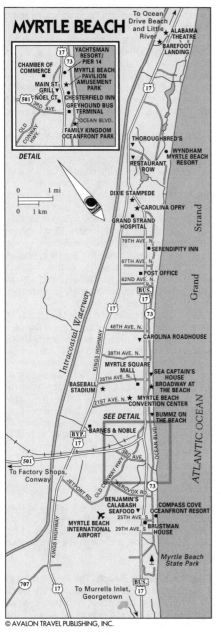

MYRTLE BEACH

DETAIL

YACHTSMAN
RESORT/
PIER 14
CHAMBER OF
COMMERCE
MAIN ST.
GRILL
NOEL CT.
MYRTLE BEACH
PAVILION
AMUSEMENT
PARK
CHESTERFIELD INN
GREYHOUND BUS
TERMINAL
FAMILY KINGDOM
OCEANFRONT PARK
OCEAN BLVD.

0   1 mi
0   1 km

To Ocean
Drive Beach
and Little
River
ALABAMA
THEATRE
BAREFOOT
LANDING

THOROUGHBRED'S
WYNDHAM
MYRTLE BEACH
RESORT
RESTAURANT
ROW

DIXIE STAMPEDE
CAROLINA OPRY
GRAND STRAND
HOSPITAL
79TH AVE. N.
SERENDIPITY INN
67TH AVE. N.
POST OFFICE
62ND AVE. N.

48TH AVE. N.
CAROLINA ROADHOUSE
38TH AVE. N.
MYRTLE SQUARE
MALL
SEA CAPTAIN'S
HOUSE
28TH AVE. N.
BROADWAY AT
THE BEACH
BASEBALL
STADIUM
21ST AVE. N.
MYRTLE BEACH
CONVENTION CENTER
SEE DETAIL
BUMMZ ON
THE BEACH
BARNES & NOBLE

3RD AVE.

To Factory Shops,
Conway

AEROVOX RD.

BENJAMIN'S
CALABASH
SEAFOOD
25TH AVE. S
COMPASS COVE
OCEANFRONT RESORT
MYRTLE BEACH
INTERNATIONAL
AIRPORT
29TH AVE. S
BRUSTMAN
HOUSE

Myrtle Beach
State Park

To Murrells Inlet,
Georgetown

Intracoastal Waterway

KINGS HIGHWAY

Strand

Grand

ATLANTIC OCEAN

JETPORT RD.   OLD CONWAY HWY.

streets intersecting U.S. 17 and Ocean Boulevard contain an "S" in their names, as in "19th Avenue S." North of 1st Avenue, they receive an "N," as in 12th Avenue N. The downtown area encompasses the famed Pavilion area, center of spring break activities and the teenage cruise scene, and home to two mid-size amusement parks and myriad miniature golf courses.

Broadway at the Beach
With the huge success of Barefoot Landing, that tastefully designed 100-acre complex north of town, it didn't take long for the next Big Thing to come to town. Broadway at the Beach opened in the early 1990s between 21st Avenue N and 29th Avenue N, southeast of U.S. 17 Bypass, and takes up 350 acres, featuring a park, a 23-acre lake, theaters, nightclubs, 16 restaurants, and 100 specialty shops. The design is admirable, and it includes the worthwhile Ripley's Aquarium, but BATB has also attracted such garish Vegas-esque tourist-town inescapables as Bullwinkle's, Hard Rock Café, and Planet Hollywood. For better and worse, this is the new heart of Myrtle Beach. For information, call 800/386-4662 or 843/444-3200, or see the website at www.broadwayatthebeach.com.

Restaurant Row
Sometime in the 1970s, folks began building restaurants up here just beyond where U.S. 17 and the U.S. 17 Bypass rejoin north of town, and ending somewhere around the Briarcliffe Mall. Today you'll still find many fine restaurants up here, including Thoroughbred's and Garcia's, but with the hip new restaurants at Barefoot Landing and Broadway at the Beach, this is no longer the only place to eat in Myrtle Beach.

Barefoot Landing
This 100-acre complex, built along the Intracoastal Waterway and around a 27-acre freshwater lake, is perennially named South Carolina's single-most popular attraction, entertaining over seven million people annually with its 100 specialty and retail shops, 15 waterfront restaurants, and 14 factory outlet stores. The area also includes the Barefoot Princess side-paddle-

GRAND STRAND HIGHLIGHTS

Alligator Adventure
This is not your father's alligator farm. Instead it's got a professional, eco-friendly demeanor and under-stated natural wood architecture, but it still offers plenty of chances to get close to more alligators than you can count.

Barefoot Landing
The classiest modern shopping experience in South Carolina, with a number of interesting restaurants; repeatedly voted the state's No. 1 tourist attraction.

Broadway at the Beach
Okay, okay, okay. This complex has grown so massive and contains so many attractions that I can't keep it off this list any longer. Kids like the water park, the miniature golf, and the kiddie rides at Carousel Park, not to mention the NASCAR Speedway, Ripley's Aquarium, and the Imax Theatre, and the nightly fireworks and laser show. And . . . okay. I like them too. Over 100 specialty shops, five restaurants, a brew pub, nine nightclubs, and a 16-screen cineplex. BATB may be garish and carnivalesque, but it's packed with entertainment choices.

Brookgreen Gardens/Huntington Beach
Either of these would make the list by themselves, but considering that they're just across U.S. 17 from each other and share a common history, there's no reason to only visit one. Brookgreen contains a wonderful set of aviaries in addition to its exquisitely landscaped gardens, accented by the world's largest outdoor sculpture collection.

Huntington Beach is one of the most pristine coastal stretches in South Carolina—great for shelling, solitary walks, and wildlife viewing. The Huntingtons' Spanish Moorish home, Atalaya, is worth a tour as well.

Carolina Opry
Calvin Gilmore and the gang put on a show worthy of Nashville; of the region's many showcases, this is the one to catch.

Conway
This charming riverfront town is worth the drive inland from Myrtle Beach.

Georgetown's Harborwalk
South Carolina's second-oldest city offers a slow-paced and scenic downtown, lots of historic B&Bs, and waterfront dining.

Murrells Inlet
More good seafood places (including standout Oliver's Lodge) than you can shake a shell-cracker at, and enough residual authenticity to make this a welcome change from Myrtle Beach.

Ocean Drive Beach
Both the Holy Land and ground zero for the shag explosion. Pop into one of the many shagging clubs for an eyeful—and a chance to join the slow-motion jitterbug.

The Pavilion
The bass-pumping, cat-calling heart of Myrtle Beach; if you're 16, you'll be in heaven; if you're not, this may be worth a quick visit just to remember how it felt. And if you're a cheesy T-shirt vendor, you're probably already here.

Pawleys Island and the Pawleys Island Shops
Ever-serene Pawleys Island itself is worth a visit, but don't dismiss the shops. A Pawleys Island hammock will make a perfect souvenir or gift.

You also won't want to miss:
- Hampton Plantation
- The Swamp Fox section of the Palmetto Trail (Mc Clellanville)
- Sea Captain's House restaurant

---

wheeler, the Alligator Adventure Live Reptile Zoo, the Alabama Theatre, and Dan Aykroyd's blues club, House of Blues. For information, call 800/272-2320 or 843/272-8349, fax 843/272-1052, or visit the Barefoot Landing website at www.bflanding.com.

Ocean Drive
"Old O.D.," as beach music icons the Embers called it, is one of the northernmost beaches on the Strand. It was up here in little hangouts like The Pad that the whole shagging/beach music subculture was born, and it's here shaggers

near The Pavilion,
Myrtle Beach

return each year for various contests and festivals. The sidewalk on the north side of Main Street contains the Shagger's Walk of Fame, which has honored famous shag dancers, beach musicians, disc jockeys, and other shag-related personalities since the 1980s. Judy's House of Oldies, also on Main Street, is arguably the best place in the world to pick up beach music or shagging instructional tapes.

Little River

The quaint fishing village of Little River is a good place to get away from the crowds of the Grand Strand. The town draws a lot of people who come for the deep-sea fishing charters that depart from here. Others come for the annual Blue Crab Festival.

The Outlets and Fantasy Harbour

Up U.S. 501 on the way west to Conway you'll

"The Beach was a sexual gold rush town. Males competed for female attention in all quarters and by various methods. Young lotharios from surrounding farm communities and military bases gathered on summer weekends to prospect. The nightclubs where the Shag was danced were the richest claims to jump."

—Bo Bryan, describing Myrtle Beach in the
1950s, *Shag: The Legendary Dance
of the South*, 1995.

---

come across the Myrtle Beach Outlet Mall and the Waccamaw Pottery Shops, good places to look for new merchandise at good prices. Fantasy Harbour contains some of the newer entertainment houses in the area, including the Crook and Chase Theatre.

Conway

This is probably the best inland day trip from the Strand; head inland on U.S. 501 to reach the well-preserved river town of Conway, with antique shops and a number of good restaurants.

MUSEUMS AND GARDENS

Brookgreen Gardens

This preserve, on U.S. 17 three miles south of Murrells Inlet, 843/235-6000, is Myrtle Beach's one must-see attraction. It's America's largest outdoor sculpture display, 9,127 acres in all, including the beautiful gardens shaded by gigantic oaks, a wildlife park, two aviaries, and indoor art galleries.

The history of Brookgreen is an interesting one. What is now called Brookgreen Gardens was once four different plantations. George Washington spent the night at the Brookgreen plantation on his southern tour in 1791, the guest of Dr. Henry Collins Flagg, a surgeon during the Revolution, and his wife, Rachel Moore Allston Flagg. Joseph Alston, who inherited the plantation next, married Theodosia Burr, daugh-

> *A Southern river at night is a haunting thing, with great stars hanging like spangles in the dark pines and the ancient water oaks fringing the river shores. Wider flows the dim stream as it moves through the last reaches of the immense coastal plain. Baffling to navigate by broad daylight, the Santee at night is mysterious . . . a huge river that seems to be wandering toward eternity.*
>
> —Archibald Rutledge, *Peace in the Heart*, 1923

ter of Vice President Aaron Burr, and generally considered one of the most educated women of her era. In 1812, after her husband's election as governor of South Carolina, Theodosia sailed from Georgetown on the schooner *Patriot* to visit her father in New York. The ship disappeared forever off the North Carolina coast during a terrific storm.

Early in the 1900s, Archer Huntington—son of 19th-century railroad magnate (and one of California's "Big Four" robber barons) Collis Huntington—having grown up in mansions and riches, and assured of a life of ease, was not quite as motivated a capitalist as his father. He didn't want to take over the family business and instead became a poet. In his middle age, he met middle-aged Anna Hyatt, by this time a self-supporting artist.

Huntington bought a huge plot of land made up of the four former Waccamaw Neck plantations and built a huge summer home styled as a Moorish castle. As Anna continued with her sculptures, she needed a place to show her work, and she wanted to support the work of other artists as well. Hence Brookgreen Gardens was born. Later additions include a 50-acre wildlife park and 90-foot-high aviary, and excursions on the Waccamaw River. Open daily 9:30 A.M.–4:45 P.M., longer hours in summer. Admission runs $8.50 for adults, $4 for children 6–12, and the best thing is that the tickets are good for seven days, so you can come back as often as you like for morning or afternoon strolls through the gardens. Best time to go is in April when everything seems to be abloom, but as long as you avoid the hotter months of summer—when you just won't feel like enjoying the swamp trails—any time is a good time to visit. Closed Christmas.

Southern Living readers named this one of the South's five favorite public gardens a few years back, and the magazine went on to build a ***Southern Living*** Showcase Home here, which you can tour for an additional $6.00.

Vereen Memorial Historical Gardens
Up north of Myrtle Beach, on U.S. 17 just 1.4 miles before you reach Little River, you'll see a sign for Vereen Memorial Historical Gardens, named after one of the founding families in the area. Here you'll find a 115-acre natural park with a 1.25-mile self-guided nature trail that winds past the Vereen farmhouse and a Revolutionary War cemetery.

Ripley's Aquarium
When I first heard that Ripley's—of "Believe It Or Not!" fame—and the "Believe It Or Not!" museum chain opened a $37 million aquarium, I was a little concerned: I kept imagining two-headed sea bass and flounder with ping pong balls crammed in their mouths. But Ripley's Aquarium, at Broadway at the Beach, 1110 Celebrity Circle, 800/734-8888 or 843/916-0888, achieves an admirable balance of science and show business. It offers visitors the chance to stand face-to-face with deep-sea life that they were probably never even supposed to know about.

The 74,000-square-foot aquarium, the first of seven that Ripley's plans to open worldwide over the next few years, is designed so that the path taken by the visitor replicates the experience of submerging in the water to the ocean's depths, then reemerging. You start out at a display called Rio Amazon, where you get a look at a cross section of a simulated Amazon River, featuring various indigenous fish, including piranhas. From Rio Amazon you move down a winding ramp "below the surface" to Rainbow Rock, which features more than 119 colorful species of fish from the Indo-Pacific region in a 10-by-40-foot viewing window. As you continue down "underwater," you actually end up literally underwater at Dangerous Reef, the world's longest clear acrylic underwater tunnel, the best of its type that I've seen. Normally these tunnels are never as impressive as I think they'll be, perhaps because you're carted through the tunnel on a conveyor belt, which helps with the traffic flow but always makes me feel as if I'm being given the bum's rush. To stand still on these other belts, I need to sidestep those being pulled toward me. Fortunately the Ripley's conveyor moves very slowly through the 310-foot-long tunnel. Best of all, staying on the moving belt is optional—at any time, you're free to take a step to the right and stand on carpet firma, giving yourself more time to commune with the shark, fish, eel, or ray of your choice.

As you ascend up out of Dangerous Reef, the nearby crashing waterfall is meant to suggest to you the feeling of surfacing from the deep—nice touch. On your way up and out you'll see the Monterey Wharf exhibit, featuring rockfishes and starfish. The jellyfish displays and living coral are enough to make you want to rent some scuba equipment and head out for some diving. Up here on the surface you'll find Ray Bay.

And speaking of rays, one thing you may notice if you've visited aquariums in other states is that Ripley's has no mammals—no dolphins, no whales, no seals, no walruses. That is to say, it has none of the cute, cuddly, money-making critters that places like California's Monterey Aquarium depend upon to generate plush toy sales, otter book bags, and the like. This is no oversight on Ripley's part: it's actually against the law to keep an aquatic mammal in captivity in South Carolina. What the marketing folks here have done in their stead, you'll notice, is start a campaign to change the public image of the ray family. Though many of us have grown up afraid of being stung by stingrays, the folks at Ripley's point out that only a handful of the roughly 100 species of rays can harm humans. Caribbean-island-themed Ray Bay is an interactive spot where guests can pet rays (the Southern stingrays have had their stingers removed). In the gift shop you'll find plush stingrays for the kids.

The kids will probably also enjoy the Sea-for-Yourself Discovery Center, where you and they can learn more about the creatures they've been gawking at. And finally, you'll find the Feeding Frenzy fast-food restaurant upstairs, where you can pick up a veggie burger—you probably won't feel much like a fish sandwich.

Why did Ripley's decide to build the aquarium here in Myrtle Beach? It's not because it was close to the ocean. After all, the second Ripley's Aquarium opened in 1999 in Gatlinburg, Tennessee. No, Myrtle Beach's unique year-round tourist-based economy attracted Ripley's to the Grand Strand, and they knew it well, through the company's Believe It Or Not Museum down by the Pavilion, which has done strong business for over 20 years.

But there's a difference between luring sun-dizzy tourists into a modern-day freak show like the Believe It Or Not Museum and enticing them into—no matter how it's packaged—an educational experience like the aquarium. Sure, Ripley's has built it, but will people come?

Consider this: The aquarium opened in June 1997. On April 24, 1998, Gerald Pomery from Maryland stepped through the turnstiles to become the aquarium's millionth visitor.

Enjoy your visit. And be sure to pet one of those cute stingrays for me. Open 9 A.M.–9 P.M. Admission runs $13.50 for adults, $7.95 ages 5–11, $2.95 ages 2–4.

South Carolina Hall of Fame
In the lobby of the Myrtle Beach Convention Center, 21st Avenue N and Oak Street, this small museum adds members each year, normally one living member and one who has passed on. Members include John C. Calhoun; Apollo 10, 13, and 16 astronaut Charles M. Duke; Andrew Jackson; Federal architect Robert Mills; General William Westmoreland; Dizzy Gillespie; presidential advisor and college founder Mary McLeod Bethune; Cardinal Joseph Bernardin; and Pulitzer Prize–winning novelist Julia Mood Peterkin. Hours are Mon.–Fri. 9 A.M.–5 P.M. Admission free.

AMUSEMENT PARKS AND OTHER ADVENTURES

Myrtle Beach Pavilion Amusement Park and Family Kingdom
Myrtle Beach suffers for its vast wealth of small amusement centers; down by the Pavilion, it seems you can't drive three blocks without seeing a Ferris wheel or concrete volcano. In sheer terms of size or originality, those used to the Disney or Six Flags parks will find neither of the Pavilion area's two main amusement parks—

the Myrtle Beach Pavilion Amusement Park, Ocean Blvd. and 9th Ave. N., 843/448-6456, website: www.mbpavilion.com; and Family Kingdom Amusement Park, Ocean Blvd. and 3rd Ave. S, 843/626-3447—anything to write home to Mom about (unless Mom happens to be a retired carny).

You've seen it all before: the barkers, the cotton candy, the skee ball, the shirt-screening places. But there really is nothing quite like clicking to the top of a seaside roller coaster and looking over at the huge ocean, feeling the coastal breeze in your hair, smelling the salt air, and wondering about the corrosive effects of salt on wood and metal.

Admission to both parks is free; you can purchase all-day unlimited ride passes at the 11-acre, 40-ride Pavilion for $12 and for $14.95 at Family Kingdom (somewhat cheaper rates for children), but unless you're 13 years old and cruising for girls/boys, there's really not much to keep you here all day.

Of course, since Disney is currently building a mock seaside amusement park at its new California Adventure Park in Anaheim, California, the Pavilion and Family Kingdom are not only good representatives of amusement parks past but of the future as well.

At **Family Kingdom Oceanfront Water Park,** 3rd Ave. S, 843/916-0400, which stands right across from Family Kingdom Amusement Park, the big news is the new old-fashioned beachfront wooden roller coaster, aptly named The Hurricane, which features a 110-foot drop at a 53-degree angle. The only oceanfront water park in town, Family Kingdom also features a 60-foot free-fall slide and a number of different flumes and tubes. You can choose between paying for a one-day pass (adults $13.55, $12.55 older kids, $10.95 for children under 48 inches) and buying a "Ride and Slide Combo Pass," which allows admission into both Family Kingdom parks, for $25.26 per person. If you're interested, look for a coupon-heavy Family Kingdom pamphlet in the racks of your motel/hotel lobby. It'll save you $3 off an all-day pass.

Myrtle Waves Water Park

This is the granddaddy of South Carolina water parks, 20 acres in size and offering more than 30 rides and attractions including water slides and a wave pool, where the surf is often bigger than that of the actual ocean hereabouts. Open June–Aug. 10 A.M.–7 P.M., mid-May–May 31 and Sept. 1–mid-Sept. 10 A.M.–5 P.M. Closed the rest of the year. Admission is $17.99 per adult for an all-day pass; senior/child discounts available. Discount admissions after 3 P.M. Allow about four hours to get your fill.

Alligator Adventure

This place out on U.S. 17 at Barefoot Landing, 843/361-0789, surprised me with its quality and cleanliness. Next to House of Blues at Barefoot Landing, the park is attractively staged with wooden boardwalks, shade areas, and Africa-inspired buildings. I was also surprised by the sheer number of gators here; on the swamp boardwalk I saw perhaps 50 or 60 lying on the ground or swimming in the "river" just a few feet below the boardwalk. All told you're sharing Alligator Adventure's 15 acres with more than 800 alligators, not to mention the snakes and Komodo dragons. You can view rare albino alligators and, in the spirit of "compare-and-contrast," a collection of crocodiles at the park's south end.

Periodic gator feedings and venomous snake demonstrations on alternating hours let you see the often lethargic animals in action and help you learn about these feared but also beautiful and fascinating creatures. You'll also find some giraffes and tropical birds here, blessedly oblivious to the park's demographics. Give yourself a couple of hours to see it all. Do I need to tell you that kids love it? Just be sure *not* to—for obvious reasons—sit them on the guardrails or put them on your shoulders while viewing the gators.

When you've seen all the critters you care to, head out the South Gate entrance, take the boardwalk to Barefoot Landing, and get yourself something to eat at Mad Boar Restaurant and Brewery. Open 9 A.M.–8 P.M. $11.95 for ages 13 and above, $7.95 for ages 4–12.

Carolina Safari Jeep Tours

Here's a different way to get off the paved road and experience the history and natural environment of the Waccamaw Neck region. These 3.5 hour tours pick you up at your hotel and promise to take you through three different ecosystems

SHAG: THE DANCE

The shag is best performed on a hot summer night, on a wooden dance floor sparkling and gritty with beach sand. The humidity needs to be eighty percent or above. The crowd should be thick, the temperature near the jukebox, almost insufferable. The dancers need to feel fully justified in sweating.
—Bo Bryan, *Shag: The Legendary Dance of the South*

South Carolina has an official state dance, and it's not the Charleston. In the years just after World War II, a uniquely Southern phenomenon evolved along the Carolina coast. As author Bo Bryan explains it, as the rest of the nation worked off its postwar exuberance doing a violent, provocative dance called the "flying jitterbug," Southern couples on the Grand Strand moved a bit slower, and a bit more conservatively. The women—young Southern ladies, after all—were not quite so willing to have their thighs (and underwear) exposed as they flew over their partner's shoulders or wrapped their legs around his torso. And the young men on the dance floor, young Southern gentlemen that they were, could not ask their partners to do it. And besides, it was hotter than Hades in Grand Strand dance clubs in the middle of summer: slower tempos and more intricate, subtle movements only made sense.

And thus was born the "subtle wildness" called the shag. Most South Carolinians will tell you that the dance developed in the late 1940s in Myrtle Beach. Some North Carolinians argue that the whole "shag scene" first appeared in Carolina Beach, near Wilm-

ington, and moved down to the Grand Strand only after the Carolina Beach police department cracked down on the rowdy dancers. A third theory has the "birth" of the shag (i.e., the moment that the Northern jitterbug met South Carolinian understatement) taking place at the old Folly Beach Pavilion near conservative Charleston.

Wherever it began, the shag has been *the* dance of coastal Carolina for more than 50 years, and increasingly of the lower South as a whole. The music the first shaggers danced to was "race music," or blues and soul, of a certain tempo—approximately 120 beats a minute, to be precise. The Dominoes' 1951 R&B hit "Sixty Minute Man," Maurice Williams and the Zodiacs' "Stay," and the Drifters' "Under the Boardwalk" all had the right feel, and all became classic examples of what was called, from the 1940s onward, "beach music." Though not played on white radio stations, records by black R&B artists filled beach jukeboxes throughout the 1940s and early 1950s.

If the birthplace of the shag is disputed, nobody debates the historic headquarters: Ocean Drive Beach north of Myrtle Beach (now a part of North Myrtle Beach) became the mecca of shaggers from 1954 on—after Hurricane Hazel leveled a number of popular Myrtle Beach dance spots and left standing a dumpy old Ocean Drive house that was converted into "The Pad," the Strand's dive of dives and the holy of holies for shaggers. The floor was dirt at first and then later an uneven plank floor, and the walls and bare rafters were covered with shagger

and show you alligators, bald eagles, a barrier island, slave cabins, an 18th-century church, antebellum rice fields, and the grave of *Deliverance* author and poet James Dickey. Call 843/497-5330 for details—pickup is available from most Myrtle Beach hotels. $34 for adults, $15 for kids 12 and under.

BEACHES

For a city, being named "North Myrtle Beach" must be a lot like being known as "Joe's kid brother." South San Francisco, East St. Louis, North Charleston, North Augusta—none of them grow their own identities; all too often

they become or ever remain incomplete towns, towns without centers, because they are in truth a mere addendum to the town with the famous name.

With this in mind, I can't see why the towns of **Cherry Grove Beach, Ocean Drive Beach, Crescent Beach,** and **Windy Hill** allowed anyone to staple them together to form a single nine-mile-long beach city under the polyester banner of "North Myrtle Beach." Ocean Drive Beach, in particular, had enjoyed regional notoriety as birthplace and capital city of the shagging world.

Determinedly ducking this civic group-hug was **Atlantic Beach,** five miles south of the new city's border. Known during segregation days

shagging at Fat Harold's

The whole Bohemian ambience of the place was not something in which proper Southern girls immersed themselves in the late 1950s and early 1960s. And, as one fiftysomething shagger told me, it certainly wasn't something you told your father about beforehand. As this Pad alumna puts it, there was something "naughty" about The Pad and the whole shagging scene that made it especially attractive to white Southerners of the pre-Vietnam era. It was the chance to break free from social taboos, dance to "race" music—often with sexually provocative lyrics ("Sixty Minute Man," for example, is little else but a sexual boast with a great beat)—drink too much beer, and generally do all the things they'd feel terrible about in church come Sunday morning.

In the late 1970s, some of the now-middle-aged former shaggers began to talk about getting the old crowd back together. Thus was born the first Society of Shaggers festival in Ocean Drive. The SOS continues to meet several times each year, during which time the rooms book up at Ocean Drive and the floors at Fat Harold's, Ducks, Ducks Too, and the Spanish Galleon pack out. You'll find a shaggers' Walk of Fame on Main Street in Ocean Drive in front of Fat Harold's—and across the street, there's even a store specializing in shag-themed art. In 1984 Governor Dick Riley signed a bill declaring the shag the official South Carolina state dance.

For a superficial but accurate peek into shag culture, circa 1963, check out the 1989 movie *Shag,* with Bridget Fonda and Phoebe Cates. Or head online to www.shagger.com for more information or to order beach music and shag "how-to" videos.

graffiti. But from the 1950s through the early 1990s, when it was regrettably torn down,The Pad was the center of action, and a kind of rite of passage for "Bos" and "Sugs" (as in "Sugar").

as one of the top African-American beaches on the East Coast, Atlantic Beach even today shows no interest in changing the status quo.

Ocean Drive Beach

This little beach, just south of Cherry Grove Beach on Ocean Boulevard S, is where, by some accounts, the whole shagging subculture began. It's also a nice little beach, though some shortsighted planning is allowing highrises to be built right on the beach, somewhat altering the ambience of the place, and certainly robbing the ocean views from a number of the small beach houses that have long been the bread and butter of the region. A necessary shrine any shag pilgrim must stop to see is

Judy's House of Oldies, 300 Main St., North Myrtle Beach, 843/249-8649, website: www.judyshouseofoldies.com, a small record store with perhaps the best selection of beach music in the world, run by Judy Collins (no relation), a top DJ at shagger's dances, and occasionally by the knowledgeable Mr. Rufus Oates and Miss Esther.

Huntington Beach State Park

Huntington, 16148 U.S. 17, three miles south of Murrells Inlet, 843/237-4440, website: www.southcarolinaparks.com, is one of the most beautiful coastal parks in the state, with three miles of virgin, beachcombing sand, untold acres of coastal marsh for crabbing and gator- or

SHAGGERS BOUND FOR GLORY RIDE DUCKS' OVERHEAD RAILROAD

Step inside Ducks, at 229 Main Street ("Old O.D."), and you'll find more than a vintage shaggers' club. Look overhead and you'll notice a small model train circling the dance floor. The trains that run these tracks bear the ashes of veteran shaggers Lee Huggins and Dewey "Tinker" Kennedy, who asked in their wills to be allowed to spend the hereafter chugging along above the dancers. Other shaggers have lined up to request berths when they, too, reach an ashen state. Owner Norfleet Jones says he'll extend the tracks if he needs to in order to accommodate additional glory-bound shaggers.

bird-watching, and Archer and Anna Hyatt Huntington's intriguing Moorish castle, Atalaya, to tour. This was the coastal section of the Huntingtons' massive landholdings in the area—Brookgreen Gardens, directly across U.S. 17, made up the rest.

Surf and jetty fishing may net spottail bass, flounder, croakers, and whiting; if you're without tackle, stop by the park office and borrow a rod and reel. The park has two campgrounds.

The critter-watching here is excellent. Besides the ever-present alligators, more than 280 bird species have been recorded here, making it one of the premier birding spots on the entire East Coast. Favorites include whistling swans, bald eagles, and various sandpipers. Call ahead and ask about the various ranger-led programs, ranging from alligator classes to evening "ghost tours" of Atalaya.

In tune with the Huntingtons' artistic spirit, a prestigious juried arts and crafts show attracts thousands of visitors to the park each September. Call for information.

You can also camp here at one of the park's 184 campsites. Call for reservations.

Myrtle Beach State Park

This beach, at 4401 U.S. 17 south of Myrtle Beach, 843/238-5325, website: www.south carolinaparks.com, offers 312 acres of Grand Strand in near-mint condition, with a 700-foot post-Hugo fishing pier, a freshwater swimming pool, a nature trail, picnic areas, and 350 campsites. Some sites ($17.60–22) are first come, first served, but some you can reserve ahead of time by calling.

ACCOMMODATIONS

For a complete list of accommodations, call the South Carolina Division of Tourism at 843/734-0122.

RESORTS

Ocean Drive Beach and Golf Resort

This newish ocean-eclipser, 98 N. Ocean Blvd., 800/438-9590 or 843/249-1436, fax 843/249-1437, email: odresort@sccoast.net, advertises itself as "A New Resort of Distinction in Ocean Drive," which seems to miss the laid-back, unpretentious nature of Ocean Drive altogether. Nonetheless, the golf packages and reasonable room rates so far away from the crowds of Myrtle Beach will doubtless fill the ODBGR's beds, particularly during local shaggers' conventions. $60–190 a night.

Kingston Plantation, Featuring anEmbassy Suites

The 145-acre Kingston Plantation, 9800 Lake Dr., 800/876-0010 or 843/449-0006, fax 843/497-1110, website: www.kingstonplantation.com, a right turn off U.S. 17 just before it rejoins the bypass north of town, will remind you of Hilton Head. Unfortunately the private beachfront resort looks little like a true plantation, what with its three towers looming over the Atlantic, but I suppose this is where a modern-day Scarlett O'Hara would choose to stay while in town. If the towers don't interest you, consider the one- to three-room villas offering lakefront, wooded, tennis court, and poolside views. Amenities include a private beach, sport and health club (including clay and hard surface tennis courts), a pool complex, and children's programs. You can still hop in the car and head over to rub elbows with the

Myrtle Beach masses if you like, but you could also easily spend all of your trip right here. Suites range from $139–239.

Wyndham Myrtle Beach Resort

Nine miles north of Myrtle Beach on U.S. 17, at 10000 Beach Club Dr., 877/887-9549 or 843/449-5000, you'll find this 15-story building. All of the 255 suites in the towers have balconies. Amenities include lighted tennis courts, a rooftop lounge, and the Arcadian Shores Golf Club on-site; suites and golf packages are available. $72–149.

Compass Cove Oceanfront Resort

Formerly the Swamp Fox, this revitalized juggernaut of a resort at S. 2311 Ocean Blvd., 800/228-9894 or 843/448-8373, fax 843/448-5444, website: www.compasscove.com, offers oceanfront efficiencies and tower suites, two indoor and five outdoor pools, whirlpools, and a Lazy River, as well as a steam sauna and an on-site restaurant. Golf packages available. Rates vary from $49–200.

Chesterfield Inn

When you first see the solidly Georgian-style Chesterfield Inn, you get the impression that if everything in downtown Myrtle Beach were washed away in the next hurricane, the Chesterfield alone would remain, its front porch rocking chairs creaking softly in the retreating winds. Located a coin toss away from the Pavilion at 700 N. Ocean Blvd., 800/392-3869 or 843/448-3177, this 1946 brick inn sits nobly placid amid downtown's squalor like a New Hampshire schoolmarm at a love-in. The Chesterfield features a lobby with a fireplace and a warm, informal dining room with wood-paneled walls, a terra-cotta tile floor, and an unbelievable ocean view. Rooms are decorated in early American, and the complex contains a pool and shuffleboard court. The inn offers a number of different plans, including the popular Modified American Plan, which includes breakfast and evening dinner with the room rate. The menu changes daily, always offers a choice of entrées, fruits and vegetables, and homemade desserts. Given the wealth of dining opportunities in the area, I'd recommend the less expensive European Plan. The wings of motel rooms added in the 1960s allow more rooms with private balconies over-looking the ocean. Golf packages available. No elevators. The time of your visit greatly affects your room rate—a room that costs $34 in November will cost you $107 in July. Closed mid-December through the third week in February.

Yachtsman Resort

At 1400 N. Ocean Blvd., 800/868-8886 or 843/448-1441, fax 843/626-6261, this all-suite, front-row establishment is a favorite with families. Two shorter towers sit to either side of a 20-story third. All rooms have kitchens and whirlpool baths, and nearly all have full or partial ocean views, though the "city view" rooms do not. Within walking distance of the Pavilion, and with Pier 14 right at its base, this is the kind of place where you might just park for the duration of your stay. Studios, efficiencies, one- and two-bedroom apartments are available. Amenities include indoor and outdoor whirlpools, sauna, weight room, shuffleboard, minigolf, all on grounds. One tip: The only downside of being in the middle of it all is that you're, well, in the middle of it all. During warm weather months, Ocean Blvd. carries a nightly cruise scene with a nearly dusk-till-dawn orchestra of thumping bass, honking horns, and hooting adolescents. Try to get an oceanfront room or one high in the central tower. Golf packages, smoke-free rooms available on request. $59–200 for an oceanfront room with a fully equipped kitchen and two-person Jacuzzi bath.

Hampton Inn: Broadway at the Beach

Think what you want about the huge doings of Broadway at the Beach, but as hotel amenities, they'd be hard to beat—especially for a family. Within easy walking distance of your room you'll find all the restaurants, night clubs, shops, and other attractions (two theaters, miniature golf, arcades, the Ripley's Aquarium,) of this massive complex. Since the main attractions here are not seasonal, the prices here don't dip quite as sharply as those of the beachfronts, but low season two-person rooms do go for as low as $80. High season can run $249.

MOTELS

Catherine and Robert Marlowe own and run the homey **Noel Court and Apartments,** 306 N.

6th Ave., 843/448-6855, much more like staying in a beach house than staying in a motel. $30–58 for a double room, but they also offer houses with up to four bedrooms for $65–198 a night. The **Blake Motel,** 209–211 N. Ocean Blvd., 843/448-5916, is a funky old place with one- and two-room apartments and a heated pool smack dab between the Pavilion and the Swamp Fox roller coaster. Depending on who else is staying there when you are, it could be a nice, cheap, quiet stay. Up in Cherry Grove, you'll find the **Inlet Motel,** 5409 N. Ocean Blvd., 800/968-7975 or 843/249-1853, fax 843/249-8661. Nothing special to look at, but it offers a nice, relatively quiet location up there near the Intracoastal Waterway, right across Ocean Boulevard from the ocean, and you're not far from the fishing at the Cherry Grove Pier. Extras include refrigerators in every room, kitchens, tennis courts, and golf privileges. Efficiencies (sleep four) from $35–76; rooms from $30–65.

GUEST AND RENTAL HOUSES AND BED-AND-BREAKFASTS

Cozy **Stella's Guest Home,** Little River, S.C., 843/249-1871, email: Stella@scarolina.com, is owned by one of the sweetest women you'll ever meet—Miss Stella, of course—who will make you feel as if you'd simply forgotten you had a favorite Southern aunt living in Little River. Though

it's located on busy U.S. 17, Stella's single-story brick ranch home, decorated in antique reproductions, is a homey spot to return to after a long day of fishing or a night at the theater, clubs, and Restaurant Row. Unfortunately the golf course behind Stella's recently built some condos that cut off the view of the golf course back there, but you can still walk to it from here. All the rooms have private baths, private entrances, and color cable TV. You'll see it on the left as you head north on U.S. 17. Just $35–55 a night.

If you're looking for something comfortable and low-key, consider Kate and Phil Mullins's **Serendipity Inn,** 71st Ave. N, 843/449-5268, a motel converted into a Spanish-style bed-and-breakfast inn on a lazy side street, just a block and a half from the sand. With your window open, you can hear the traffic from Kings Highway, but you can't see it. The courtyard includes several fountains, and the breakfast room boasts a fireplace, which can make for a cozy winter's morning. Theme-decorated rooms and suites are complemented by a breakfast buffet with fresh fruit, breads, and so on. Amenities include a heated pool and whirlpool, and you can use a grill on the grounds to grill up whatever fish you've caught during the day, or whatever meat you've found at the Piggly Wiggly. Children welcome. $55–149.

Of the bed-and-breakfasts on the Grand Strand, perhaps the most traditional is Dr. Wendell Brustman's **Brustman House,** 400 25th

Stella's Guest Home in Little River

Ave. S, 843/448-7699, a quiet two-story on a wooded lot not far from downtown. All three rooms have private baths with two-seater whirlpool tubs. Homemade breakfasts feature 10-grain pancakes. Smoke-free. Children allowed on case-by-case basis. A two-bedroom suite with kitchen is available for $110 and up.

Condo and beach-house rentals are a popular way to go here, especially for families and large groups. For a great, restful weekend or week, pick a spot in Ocean Drive or Cherry Grove, where you'll find a number of small places to eat, dance, and shop. You'll want to reserve far ahead, however, especially during peak season. Fortunately, since most of the area real estate companies work on a multiple listing service, contacting one will give you access to most every rental on the Strand. You might start by calling **Booe Realty,** 7728 N. Kings Hwy., 800/845-0647 or 843/449-4477; **Elliott Realty,** 401 Sea Mountain Hwy., N. Myrtle Beach, 888/669-7853 or 843/249-1406, website: www.we-can.com/elliott; or **Sea Breeze Realty,** 1210 N. Waccamaw Dr., 800/446-4010 or 843/651-1929, website: www.sea-breeze-realty.com.

CAMPGROUNDS

Unfortunately there are no hostels on the Grand Strand, but fortunately, with more than 10,000 sites in the area, camping is always a budget option at Myrtle Beach. Keep in mind, though, that when the weather gets hot, even an occasional coastal breeze isn't going to make you forget that your tent is not an air-conditioned room. Also keep in mind that many people see Myrtle Beach camping more as a way to save beer money than as a chance to commune with nature; pick the wrong neighbors and the campground can get rather loud.

But this is not to say there isn't some fine camping on the Grand Strand. For pristine, or relatively pristine, land and the cheapest rates go with the public campgrounds at **Myrtle Beach State Park** and **Huntington Beach State Park** (see above). Beyond this, you'll find no less than seven privately owned camper's havens in Myrtle Beach. All are overly geared toward RV campers, which means, in some cases, that you'll find very few shade trees around.

Two of the top choices are the **Apache Family Campground,** 9700 Kings Rd., 800/553-1749 or 843/449-7323, on the oceanfront in the Restaurant Row area, which offers the East Coast's longest fishing pier, a restaurant, trading post, and complete hookups (including cable TV). **Barefoot Camping Resort,** 4825 U.S. 17 S, 800/272-1790 or 843/272-1790, is probably the cream of the crop, with oceanfront sites, mobile home rentals, a sauna and a fitness center, as well as indoor and outdoor pools.

For more information on Myrtle Beach's camping options, contact the **Myrtle Beach Family Campground Association,** P.O. Box 2158, Myrtle Beach, SC 29578-2158.

FOOD

If you're staying somewhere with a kitchen, think about heading over to any of the numerous local grocery stores to stock up on food. This is really a good way to save money so that when you *do* go out, you can afford to hit one of the area's finer restaurants. You'll find a lot of Food Lions and Piggly Wigglies in this region, so don't think you have to shop at one of the overpriced small corner beach markets if you don't want to.

Looking for a restaurant in Myrtle Beach is like looking for sand at the beach. Two local television stations, which you'll likely find on your motel/hotel television, do nothing but advertise area restaurants and interview the owners, 24 hours a day. One way to pick a place to eat is to simply flip on the station and watch until something makes you hungry.

Another way to go is to look for where the locals eat. Of course since a busy week brings 10 tourists to Myrtle Beach for every resident, finding a true locals' hangout can be a challenge indeed, especially since so many of the bars and restaurants advertise themselves as just this. In general you'll find three types of restaurants in Myrtle Beach: 1) Tourist-oriented theme restaurants frequented almost solely by out-of-towners; 2) tourist restaurants revered by out-of-towners and locals alike; and 3) places frequented primarily by locals. Now, in my book, since Myrtle Beach is, and was born as, essentially a vacationers' village, there's no shame in frequenting the first group. The downside is that the prices are geared toward those who've come to town to dispense with their discretionary income. Locals generally stay away from most of the restaurants on Restaurant Row, at Barefoot Landing, and at Broadway at the Beach for precisely this reason. But many of these restaurants nonetheless have become traditional spots for families to visit on their annual pilgrimage to the sea. In this group you'll also find the chain theme restaurants lately unloaded at the new complexes, including the House of Blues, Hard Rock Café, and Planet Hollywood.

Seafood and Steaks

Most places in the area—no matter what their theme—serve seafood; these are just ones that make it their specialty.

A cheap way to go in Murrells Inlet is the **Seven Seas Fish Market,** U.S. 17 Business, 843/651-1666, where you can pick up a shrimp dinner with fries, slaw, and hush puppies for around $7.

Oliver's Lodge, 4204 U.S. 17 Business, 843/651-2963, is the one you should not miss; open since 1910, it has a big screened back porch where you'll want to sit to watch the boats along the waterway. Plan on spending $15–20 for a hearty seafood dinner. Oliver's is simply the kind of been-there-forever place that most of the other places are trying to be.

Nance's Creek Front Restaurant & Original Oyster Roast, U.S. 17 Business, 843/651-2696, website: www.the-strand.com/nances, combines a nice view with happy hours and an early-bird special wherein you can buy one dinner at full price and receive a second one for half price, 4–5 P.M. daily. Nance's features Alaskan snow crab legs, steak, and fried chicken, in addition to local seafood: oysters, scallops, deviled crab, and so on.

Pier 14, 1304 N. Ocean Blvd., Myrtle Beach, 843/448-4314, website: www.the-strand.com/pier14, is a relaxed restaurant located (surprise) on a pier on 14th Street, directly behind the Yachtsman Resort. Great views, live entertainment nightly March–October. Large outdoor deck, happy hour 4–6 P.M., early-bird specials,

fresh fish seafood, and all variety of steaks, poultry, and lamb from $13.95–21.95—and a friendly Canadian expatriate owner.

Readers of the Myrtle Beach *Sun News* have voted **Benjamin's Calabash Seafood,** 2290 S. Kings Hwy., 843/448-9787 the "Best All-You-Can-Eat Restaurant" and the best "Calabash-style Restaurant" on the Grand Strand. North on the same road, not far from the Pavilion is **Sir John's Sea Food,** 411 N. Kings Hwy., 843/626-7896, featuring a salad bar, prime rib, and of course seafood—especially crab legs.

The Sea Captain's House, 3002 N. Ocean Blvd., 843/448-8082, was built in the 1930s as a private family beach house and opened as a restaurant in 1962. It's something of an institution here with its nice location, just at the northern end of the commercial district blocks as you head north on N. Ocean Drive. Breakfast features brie and bacon omelettes, blueberry pancakes. Late in the day you'll find sautéed crab cakes, avocado and roast beef sandwiches, Carolina shrimp, or Inlet oyster stew. Lots of original specials. Gives the feeling of the kind of place people return to year after year after year with their families. Also it's one of the only places with a nice view of the water from just about every spot in the place; the restaurant is actually built on pylons over the sand. The food includes innovative variations of local seafood plates; I had a nice crab au gratin for $15. It wasn't overly filling, but where quantity is lacking, quality abounds. If you arrive really hungry, just eat a lot of the hush puppies that come with your meal.

Perhaps the very best time to eat here is in the winter, on a cold foggy day when they've got a fire going in the fireplace. I recommend this place. The food's good, more creative than you might expect; it was voted No. 1 seafood restaurant by *Southern Living* magazine.

Thoroughbred's, 9706 U.S. 17 N, 843/497-2636, website: www.thoroughbredsrest.com, is perhaps the premier restaurant in Myrtle Beach. The people here just take their jobs seriously. Locals have voted it the most romantic restaurant in the area, with its candlelit tables, fine linen tablecloths, and dark paneled walls made to resemble the ambience of a horse breeder's den, complete with paintings of famous horses on the walls.

The waiters here wear long-sleeved white shirts with ties, which is about as formal as you'll get on the Strand; nonetheless, this doesn't mean that the patrons dress very formally, though everyone I saw was wearing their long Duck Heads rather than their shorts, and at least their very best Izod shirt.

This is a place to dine, not just eat. The bread and herbed butter just about became my main course, I ate so much of it. The appetizers ("The Starting Gate") include some intriguing items, as well as traditionals like shrimp and grits ($9.95). I had the herb-seared ostrich, a nice-sized cut for an appetizer ($7.95), and it was fabulous. And for those who are wondering, no, it didn't taste like chicken.

As for salads, be sure to go ahead and let your waiter talk you into the house dressing, a fine poppyseed blend. The meat cuts are the specialty, but the seafood's fine as well; I ordered the seafood platter, which, at the then-current market price, came out as a high-ticket item at $24.95. The food was excellent and plentiful. Try the Kentucky Derby pie for dessert. Thoroughbred's is working hard to gain the reputation as Myrtle Beach's finest dining experience, and the warm, attentive service shows it. Even if spending $50 or so for dinner and wine stretches your budget a bit, I'd recommend cutting back on a couple of the all-you-can-eat Calabash seafood lunches to save up for this fine experience. As you'd expect, Thoroughbred's carries an extensive wine list.

Giving Thoroughbred's a run for its money is the relatively venerable **The Library,** 1212 N. Kings Hwy., Myrtle Beach, 843/448-4527 or 843/448-9242, founded way back in 1974. European and continental cuisine. A hushed atmosphere. If you're going to The Library to check things out, be sure to bring your (credit) card. Reservations preferred.

Set in a rebuilt 1885 Methodist church, with stained-glass windows imported from a Baptist church in Mullins, **Parson's Table,** U.S. 17, Little River, 843/249-3701, website: www.the-strand.com/parsons, keeps quietly winning awards up in Little River. Ed and Nancy Murray's beef and seafood place has been ranked as one of the top 50 best overall restaurants in the United States by the industry, and as the No. 1 historic restaurant in South Carolina. With a semiformal atmosphere, straight ladder-back chairs, and wood paneling, it specializes in veal, prime rib, steaks, poultry, and seafood. Open for dinner Mon.–Sat. (Sun., too, in summer). Ask about the early-bird/pre-theater specials. Reservations suggested. Expect to spend around $20 a meal.

American

Olympic Flame Waffle House, 14th Ave. N and Ocean Blvd., 843/448-2746, offers—if you lean the right way and peer between the towers of the Yachtsman Resort—a view of the beach along with its stellar pancakes, waffles, and other breakfasts. The pecan pancakes are excellent. Breakfast and lunch only.

The **Main Street Grill,** 746 Main St., 843/946-6149, a couple blocks from and within sight of the Pavilion, is a true locals' spot, with basic Southern cooking and an authentic home-grown atmosphere. Great basic lunches here cost $4.40; try the two tasty pork chops with three sides and cookies thrown in to boot. A great spot to head to if you're tired of spending $12.95 for all you can eat, or if you're simply tired of the tourist culture. Good spot for simple breakfasts as well.

For a raucous time—and possibly a raucous *good* time—I'd recommend **Dick's Last Resort,** 4700 U.S. 17 S, at Barefoot Landing, 843/272-7794. The food's pretty good (shrimp, ribs, so on), but that's not what draws people. They come for the 74 different kinds of beer and for the atmosphere, which is—to put it delicately—abusive. Waiters and waitresses are instructed to act surly. Imagine that John Belushi had lived to retire at the beach and open a restaurant, and that's pretty much what you have here. And it's an interesting study; when you know that they're *supposed* to be mean, being mistreated by a rude waitperson can actually be kind of fun. Did I mention it's over the water? You can see alligators and ducks during the day.

Maybe it's not the place for a romantic date, but it is a lot of fun with a crowd. Would this be the great job for a cocky young teenager or what? Live rhythm and blues. Open seven days a week, noon till late.

Carolina Roadhouse is one place, 4617 N. Kings Hwy., 843/497-9911, you will certainly find locals; it's with-it, owned by the same folks who did so well with California Dreaming. Already locally famous for its tender baby-back ribs and seafood platters. Also strong on salads, steaks, chicken, and the "Killer Dog." Happy hour 4–7 P.M. Open for lunch and dinner seven days. Phone ahead or be prepared to wait.

House of Blues, at Barefoot Landing, 4640 U.S. 17 S, 843/272-3000, website: www.hob.com, features the ambience and menu of an old Southern Delta home, with such Southern-inspired fare as jambalaya, barbecued chicken, étouffée, and catfish bites. While the "Southern Breakfast Buffet" Monday–Saturday dips down into the affordable range ($5.95, with two-for-one offers you'll want to ask your server about), the rest of the time, Dan Aykroyd's scrupulously themed chain restaurant honors the culture of poor Southern blacks while its prices keep them away. Sunday, it features a $16.95 gospel brunch ($8.50 for children 6–12 years old) that includes a Southern-style buffet and a live gospel choir. Hours 11 A.M.–2 A.M. A separate concert hall features various types of music—recent guests ranged from Brian Setzer to Rick Springfield to King X to Sister Hazel. On Friday nights during the summer, the House holds a "Summer Deck Party," featuring classic and new beach music stars. Stop by the information booth among the shops at Barefoot Landing.

Italian

Rossi's Fine Italian Cuisine, located in the Galleria shopping center at 9636 N. Kings Hwy., 843/449-0481, fax 843/626-4578, website: www.the-strand.com/rossis, offers serious Italian seafood, veal, beef, and pasta plates. Cozy little **Mancuso's Italian Restaurant,** 4700 U.S. 17 Bypass S, 843/293-3193, focuses on well-prepared southern Italian entrées, with fresh seafood, pasta, and other meats. Casual dress here, dinner only, 5–10 P.M. Expect to spend around $13 a plate. **Angelo's Steak and Pasta,** 2011 S. Kings Hwy., 843/626-2800, features Italian food and steaks in a casual atmosphere. Early-bird specials. Closed for much of December and January. Dinner only, 4–9:30 P.M. Features a magician some nights. No cover.

Mexican

Rosa Linda's, 4713 U.S. 17 S, 843/272-6823, serves up the best Mexican food in Myrtle Beach, which is, believe it or not, saying something. Featuring early-bird specials and a cocktail lounge, Rosa Linda's specializes in Mexican, Italian, and casual American. **Garcia's,** 9600 N. Kings Hwy., 843/449-4435, specializes in fajitas and serves up some pretty good authentic northern Mexican cuisine to boot. You'll find it behind the Galleria Mall on Restaurant Row.

Asian

Yamato at Broadway at the Beach, 843/448-1959, prides itself on its Japanese seafood, sushi, steaks, and showmanship. Columbians constantly vote it the best restaurant—all genres included—on the Strand.

Nakato Japanese Steak House, Seafood and Sushi Bar, 9912 N. Kings Hwy., 843/449-3344, has prices starting at about $11. Open seven days a week 5–10 P.M.

Burgers

There are dozens of good places to pick up a hearty $6 burger on the Strand. Two that come to mind are **Hamburger Joe's,** 810 Conway St., 843/272-6834, and the **River City Café** over at 404 21st Ave. N, 843/448-1990. Of course either of the town's **Sonic Drive-Ins,** located at 1930 10th Avenue N and 200 N. Kings Highway, will do in a pinch.

Brewpubs

Mad Boar Restaurant & Brewery, Barefoot Landing, 4706 U.S. 17 S, 843/272-7000, website: www.pubbrew.com/mbbb.html, offers six hand-crafted beers on tap and a happy hour 4–7 P.M. every day. Sure, its location at Barefoot Landing makes all the polished wood and olde-style furnishings seem a little forced, but after a couple of pints, you won't notice.

Liberty Steakhouse Brewery, Broadway at the Beach, 843/626-4677, offers eight different beers, changing weekly. The brewery also features steaks and your standard brew food. I prefer the Mad Boar over at Barefoot Landing for atmosphere; both are prefabricated olde neighborhood pubs, but Mad Boar's friendlier. But heck, if you're at Broadway at the Beach and you feel like a beer, and the smarm level is tolerable, go ahead and order the Waccamaw Blonde.

Dinner Theaters

Dolly Parton's **Dixie Stampede,** junction of U.S.17 and U.S. 17 Bypass, 843/497-9700, modeled on Parton's Pigeon Forge, Tennessee, complex, features a fun, horse-riding, gun-shootin' spectacular to watch as you dine on vegetable soup, roasted chicken, hickory smoked ribs, corn on the cob, herb-basted potatoes, homemade Dixie bread, dessert, and bottomless nonalcoholic drinks. It sure beats dinner in front of the motel tube, and at $23.99 ($16.99 ages 4–11), it's actually a bargain over some of the show-only theaters. Shows are at 6 and 8 P.M. nightly. Reservations suggested.

Medieval Times Dinner and Tournament, 2904 Fantasy Way, 800/436-4386 or 843/236-8080, is part of a tourist-town chain that features hearty dinners in a replica castle, eaten while Arthurian jousts and various other contests of skill and strength take place. Cost is $37.35 per adult, $19.35 ages 3–12. Reservations required.

NIGHTLIFE

CLUBS AND PUBS

In Ocean Drive Beach you'll find a handful of classic shagging spots, great places to practice the state's official dance or just sit with a cold one watching others tear up the floor. The best thing is, most of these spots are within walking distance of one another: **Ducks and Ducks Too,** 229 Main St., N. Myrtle, 843/249-3858, no cover; **Fat Harold's Beach Club,** 212 Main St., 843/249-5779, no cover; **Spanish Galleon,** Main St., 843/249-1047, no cover Sun.–Thurs., $7 Friday (ladies free), $10 Saturday. **Pirate's Cove Lounge,** 205 Main St., 843/249-8942, no cover 8 P.M.–closing, has featured Joe Turner, Martha Reeves and the Vandellas, and Clyde McPhatter over the years. Ducks, Fat Harold's, and Pirate's Cove all offer shag lessons at different times during the week; call for details.

For $6–10 cover charge, **2001,** Restaurant Row, 843/449-9434, offers one of the hipper places to dance and mingle, featuring beach music in its Razzie's Beach Club area and "dance" music in its Pulsations Dance Club. **Studebakers,** 21st Ave. N on U.S. 17, 843/448-9747, features a mythic 1950s' theme and one of the largest dance floors on the Strand. Open daily 8 P.M.–2 A.M.

At Broadway at the Beach's Celebrity Square, the New Orleans–style nightclub district offers nine different clubs all within staggering distance of one another: **Celebrations** combines three different themed nightspots in one; **Froggy Bottomz Blues and Beach Music** is important because it contains the Beach Music Hall of Fame and features some good live and recorded music. **Malibu's Surf Bar** is top 40, and **Club Boca** reminds me of a Latin discotheque, with Latin/European cuts mixed in with the top 40. Of course by the time you get there, one or more of these themes is almost sure to have changed. Next door at **Revolutions Retro Dance Club** the theme, tragically, is disco. Across the way you'll find **Crocodile Rock's Dueling Piano Bar,** 1320 Celebrity Circle, 843/444-2096, home to a fun and funny dueling pianos act. It's lively, rowdy, and features some good music. When they play "stump the piano players," you're welcome to come up with a song they don't know. One of the pianists is the son of Kate and Phil Mullins, owners of Serendipity Inn. Cover charge.

True local's favorite **Bummz on the Beach,** 2002 N. Ocean Blvd, 843/916-9111, features a nightly happy hour, burgers, beer-steamed shrimp, and a beachfront patio.

Local country fans tend to mosey on over to **Beach Wagon,** 906 S. Kings Hwy., 843/448-5918, but any serious country-rock fans will want to take a pilgrimage to **The Bowery,** 110 9th Ave. N, 843/626-3445, which offers live music for a $2–5 cover charge. This classic hole-in-the-wall has served them up cold since 1944. But the Bowery became truly famous when its longtime house band, Wildcountry, which played here for tips from 1973 to 1979, changed its name to Alabama and went on to country-rock fame and fortune with such megahits as "Mountain Music," "40 Hour Week," and "Cheap Seats." In 1997 the band saluted its

Myrtle Beach roots with the song "Dancin', Shaggin' on the Boulevard."

THEATER AND DANCE VENUES

Okay, granted, my corn tolerance is perhaps higher than most people's, but I think the **Carolina Opry,** the original theater at Myrtle Beach at the junction of U.S. 17 and U.S. 17 Bypass, is a hoot. They do mostly country music, but with dalliances into everything from Broadway show tunes to gospel and an oldies medley, broken up with some good, family-oriented humor. It helps to have some knowledge of roots country, but if you don't, this might make it all the more exotic for you. The cost is $28.95 a pop, but most area lodging spots can offer you some kind of cut on the price. Most of the performers hail from South Carolina, making this a nice showcase for the state's vocal and dancing talent. If you can swing it, it's a nice place to enjoy an old-style variety show; you'll be wondering why these seasoned performers aren't in Nashville. Locals have voted it the best live show on the Strand, as well as the best place to take out-of-town visitors. Reserve your seats ahead of time: 800/843-6779 or 843/913-4000, website: www.cgp.net.

Since the venue's owned by country-rock icons Alabama, you might come to the show at the Alabama Theatre, 4750 U.S. 17 S, 800/342-2262 or 843/272-1111, website: www.alabama-theatre.com, expecting country music, but the focus here is on variety—Broadway, pop, and oldies (as well as country)—and on big, flashy dance numbers. $26. If you're heading to just one showcase during your stay at Myrtle Beach, make it Carolina Opry. The Alabama Theatre *does* host some major entertainers (including the theater's owners), and if you're here when someone you want to see is performing, by all means get a ticket—this is a fine, intimate place to catch an old favorite.

Up U.S. 501 at Fantasy Harbour, the **Crook and Chase Theatre,** 800/681-5209 or 843/236-8500, website: www.fantasyharbour.com, is owned by Leann Crook and Charlie Chase, the joint Casey Kasems of country music. The shows vary, but one popular one has been the **Summer of '66,** a musical-comedy look at the local shagging culture, told through the story of "The Villagers," a real-life local band that played at Myrtle Beach Pavilion. It's a good chance to hear old shagging tunes played well. Crook and Chase also have a Christmas show. Call for showtimes.

Upstart *From Nashville to Broadway,* the show at the **All American Music Theatre,** Fantasy Harbour, 800/236-8500 or 843/236-8500, offers two hours of country, big band, and show tunes, with a 23-member cast. Rounding out the show scene is the **Eddie Miles Theatre,** 701 Main St., N. Myrtle Beach, 843/280-6999, featuring Eddie himself imitating Elvis Presley. The Strand's surrogate King appears Tuesday–Saturday at 8 P.M. during the summer; hours vary during the off season. And if that's not enough for you, the Myrtle Beach location of **Legends in Concert,** 301 U.S. 17 Business S, 800/960-7469 or 843/236-7827, offers Elvis, along with Marilyn Monroe, Buddy Holly, and a host of other late-greats who, if they were still alive, would probably be playing lounge venues exactly like this. They're joined by an imitation Dolly Parton, Bette Midler, Neil Diamond, Garth Brooks, Michael Jackson, Jerry Lee Lewis, and so on.

Most any time you're in town, Broadway at the Beach's **Palace Theatre,** 1420 Celebrity Circle, 800/905-4228 or 843/448-0588, website: www.palacestars.com, will have a beloved old Broadway show up and running. The casts often resemble a veritable Who-Was-Who of American pop culture: heartthrob Rex "You Take My Breath Away" Smith played Jesus in a past production of *Godspell;* Barbara "I Dream of Jeannie" Eden starred in *Gentlemen Prefer Blondes,* and Sheena "Morning Train" Easton played the female lead in *Man of La Mancha.* The Palace also hosts other major and second-rung acts; performers in past seasons have included the Bolshoi Ballet, B. B. King, Travis Tritt, Liza Minnelli, Clint Black, The Temptations and Four Tops, and a *Dukes of Hazzard* reunion. The theater seats 2,700.

The Palace's summertime entertainment revue, *Pizzazz,* features an orchestra, trained

---

Myrtle Beach ranks as the nation's second most popular destination for bus tours, behind only Nashville—and just ahead of Branson, Missouri.

lions and chimps, former Broadway dancers and singers, fireworks, and lasers. Tickets for all shows run $30–38 adults, $18–38 children.

MOVIE THEATERS

At Broadway at the Beach, you'll find the area's largest—so far—movie theater, the **Carmike Broadway Cinema 16,** 843/445-1616. It's a top-of-the-line theater, with THX auditoriums and digital sound systems. But while the Carmike has more screens than any other theater in Myrtle Beach, the **IMAX Discovery Theater,** 843/448-4629, has more *screen*—six stories tall, to be specific—along with an appropriately gargantuan sound system. The specially photographed films vary in topic from the undersea world to the Rolling Stones. Call ahead for movies and times.

SPORTS, RECREATION, AND SHOPPING

ON THE WATER

Surfing
Between 20th Avenue N and 20th Avenue S, you'll find the best surf Myrtle Beach has to offer, which normally isn't much. But this has not kept a full-blown surf culture from blossoming on the Grand Strand. Some surf shops at which to pick up tips for where the big ones—or, here, moderate ones—are breaking and/or rent a board or wet suit from include **Surf City Surfboards,** with three locations: 1103 N. Kings Hwy., 843/626-7919; Myrtle Square Mall, 843/626-5412; and N. Myrtle Beach, 843/272-1090. **Village Surf Shoppe,** 30 years old and an institution on the Strand, offers rentals from two locations: 500 Atlantic Ave., Garden City, 843/651-6396, and 2016 N. Kings Hwy., Myrtle Beach, 843/626-8176. Finally, **Xtreme Surf and Skateboard Co.,** over at 515 E. U.S. 501, 843/626-2262, makes custom surf and skateboards, and also rents sticks to the visiting gremmies.

When you hit the surf, make sure you wear your leash and stay at least 400 feet away from all piers—in Horry County, it's the law.

Windsurfing and Catamaran Sailing
Downwind Sails, located on the beach beside Damons at 29th Ave. S, 843/448-7245, offers rentals, rides, and lessons on sailboats, personal watercrafts, windsurfers, catamarans, and kayaks April–September. Or check **Surf City Surfboards,** with three locations: 1103 N. Kings Hwy., 843/626-7919; Myrtle Square Mall, 843/626-5412; and N. Myrtle Beach, 843/272-1090, for windsurfer/catamaran rentals.

Parasailing
Parasailing is something of a staple in Myrtle Beach. Two outfits specialize in getting you up above the sea: **Captain Dick's Marina,** Murrells Inlet, 843/651-3676; and **Marlin Quay Marina,** 1318 S. Waccamaw Dr., Murrells Inlet, 843/651-4444. Cost at either place is $45 per person; your actual flying time is about 12–15 minutes, but the boat ride out and back (with as many as six people in the boat, each of whom also takes a turn in the harness) lasts up to two hours.

Diving
The folks at **Coastal Scuba,** 1626 U.S. 17 S, N. Myrtle Beach, 843/361-3323, advertise the area's largest, most comfortable dive boat, offering dive charters to Civil War and World War II wrecks, along with rentals, repair, and instruction. **Mermaid Diving Adventures,** 4123 U.S. 17 Business, Murrells Inlet, 843/357-3483, and **The Scuba Syndrome,** 515-A U.S. 501, 843/626-3483, Myrtle Beach, also provide diving instruction, equipment rentals, and charters.

Boat Rentals
Whether you're looking for a jet boat, pontoon boat, personal watercraft, or even just a lowly kayak, you'll find them at **Barefoot Watersports,** 4898 U.S. 17 S, at the Barefoot Landing Docks, 843/272-2255, and at the North Myrtle Beach Marina, 843/280-0080. **Downwind Sails,** on the beach at 29th Ave. S, 843/448-7245, offers rentals, rides, and lessons on sailboats, personal watercrafts, windsurfers, and kayaks April–September. Finally, **Myrtle Beach Water Sports,** 843/497-8848, guarantees its rates as best on the beach for personal watercraft, pontoon boat,

kayak, and canoe rentals, plus jet boats, island trips, and morning nature tours.

Cruises
Taking a nice cruise before or after dinner can be a great way to unwind from the hectic pace of having a good time; try **The Great American Riverboat Company,** located at Barefoot Landing, 843/272-7743. For something a little faster, hop aboard the hydroplaning **Sea Screamer of Myrtle Beach,** 1 Harbor Place N, 843/249-0870. Or call **Captain Dick's Explorer Adventures** in Murrells Inlet at 800/344-3474 or 843/651-3676.

Fishing Charters
With the Gulf Stream surging by just a few miles off the Carolina coast, a lot of deep-sea fisherfolk find their casting wrists twitching every time they look out to sea. Chartering a boat is very expensive, but if you get five or six other people to go in on it with you, you can usually get it down to around $200 a person, which, for the true angler, is well worth the chance to drop a line into the Gulf Stream. The Grand Strand abounds in charter outfits. **Marlin Quay Marina,** 1398 S. Waccamaw Dr., Garden Beach, 843/651-4444, fax 843/651-7795, email: marlinquay@marlin quay.com, website: www.marlinquay.com, offers sportfishing charters for half day, three-quarter day, or full day, as well as overnights.

ON LAND

Golfing
The Grand Strand is arguably the very best golf destination in the world, with several courses perennially among *Golf Digest's* top 50 in the United States. In a state with seemingly more space allotted to fairways than to roadways, the Greater Myrtle Beach area alone boasts—by one count—more than 100 golf courses. You could tee off at a different Grand Strand hole every Saturday for two years and never play the same course twice.

Some of these courses are must-plays for avid golfers. If this describes you, be sure to call up the desired course before you make your hotel reservations and ask them which hotel's golf packages will enable you to play your Links of Dreams. Then call up one of the hotels and

Miniature golf is serious business along the Grand Strand.

make a reservation there.

To get up to speed on the Grand Strand golfing scene, pick up a free copy of *Myrtle Beach Golf* at an area pro shop, or subscribe by sending $12 for 12 issues to Myrtle Beach Golf, P.O. Box 406, Myrtle Beach, SC 29578-0406. The paper is owned by the *Sun News,* which has a website at www.myrtlebeachaccess.com.

Tennis
The Grand Strand claims more than 200 tennis courts. Call the Myrtle Beach Parks and Recreation Department at 843/918-2280 for a list of public courts. A few privately owned ones where visitors can play for a fee include the **Litchfield Country Club–Racquet Club,** 843/448-3331; the **Myrtle Beach Tennis and Swim Club,** U.S. 17 Bypass, 843/449-4486; the **Riverfront Tennis Center,** 7 Elm St., 843/248-1710; and the **Sport and Health Club at Kingston Plantation,** 843/497-2444.

Volleyball

There are few more pleasant ways to spend a day than sitting on the sand with a loved one and a cooler, watching a beach-volleyball tournament. If you're interested in a game yourself, you'll find pickup beach volleyball games all along the Strand. Two good spots to hunt down a game are down on 29th Ave. S at the public nets at Downwind Sails and at the Radisson in Kingston Plantation.

Miniature Golf

The Grand Strand is the Pebble Beach of miniature golf, hosting over 40 courses, more than many U.S. states have. Some people call it puttputt; others call it miniature golf. Yet others call it "championship golf," which seems a little extreme to me. One of the best in town is **Mount Atlanticus,** 707 N. Kings Hwy., 843/444-1008. You have to see this course—it's set on a manmade mountain that rises above Kings Highway like a . . . well, like a mountain. In September **Hawaiian Rumble Golf,** 4201 U.S. 17 N, 843/449-5555, and **Hawaiian Caverns,** 33rd Ave. S and U.S. 17, 843/272-7812, both owned by Bob Getweiller, are home to the Masters of Miniature Golf, which began in 1997 and was covered by both ESPN and *Golf* magazine. Hawaiian Rumble was featured in the 1992 Dennis Hopper flop *Chasers.* You'll see a montage of photos from the shooting inside the office and across the street at the Baskin-Robbins.

If you're interested in joining the international group of putters playing the Masters of Miniature Golf, contact either course, or write Masters Miniature Golf, 4201 N. Kings Hwy., Myrtle Beach, SC 29577. Entry fee is $100; first prize is $5,000.

Myrtle Beach Braves (Baseball)

The Atlanta Braves' single-A affiliate began playing in Myrtle Beach for the 1999 Carolina League season. The stadium cost $12 million and seats over 5,000, humongous for a single-A ballpark.

The team plays 70 home games over the summer; besides the many between-inning contests that are a staple of minor league baseball, for every home run the Braves hit, Dinger the Homerun Dog—a Labrador retriever—is let loose. (For every double play they hit into, is he swatted with a rolled-up newspaper?) Call 843/946-7557 for ticket information.

SHOPPING

There are so many malls, so many specialty stores, so many outlet shops, and so many tourist beachwear boutiques that you'd think all people do here is shop. Both Broadway at the Beach and Barefoot Landing offer over a hundred specialty stores. You should pretty much avoid the tourist chains like **Eagles, Wings,** and **Bargain Beachwear,** 843/249-7215, out of general principle—they're eyesores on the outside, and on the inside they're the visual equivalent of too much caffeine. At Ocean Drive, **Beach Memories,** 209 Main St., sells shag-related art.

Outlet Stores

Myrtle Beach Factory Stores, 4635 U.S. 501, 843/236-5100, is home to 85 outlet stores, including Harriet & David, Off Fifth Saks Fifth Avenue Outlet, Coach, Nine West, and Lillian Vernon. Most importantly it offers a **Duck Head Outlet,** where you can buy some true Southern fashions for a reasonable price. Get some shorts, get some shirts. Now you'll fit in at the next shag contest.

The **Waccamaw Factory Shoppes,** U.S. 501 at the Intracoastal Waterway, 800/444-8258, is so large it actually comprises four separate malls, connected by shuttles you can pick up outside. It offers stores like Waccamaw Pottery (advertising "Over 3 Football Fields of Unique Items for Your Home!"), Black and Decker, London Fog, Bugle Boy, and American Tourister.

BEST BOOKSTORES

New

You'll find a **Barnes and Noble** at 1145 Seaboard St., 843/444-4046. Out at the Outlet Park Mall you'll find a spotty but bargain collection at **Book Warehouse,** Outlet Park Mall III, 843/236-0800. **Readers Outlet** offers a similar selection at Outlet Park II, 843/236-1571. Those so inclined will find a large collection of Christian and inspirational reading at the earnestly named **Faith Bible Mart,** 1910 U.S. 17 N, in Surfside Beach, 843/238-5912.

Used
The Bookstall, 843/272-2607, tucked away on the left between Briarcliffe Mall and Barefoot Landing as you head north up Kings Highway, carries over 50,000 books, many bought from estate sales: paperbacks, hardbacks, children's books, fiction, and nonfiction. Hours tend to vary; call ahead.

INFORMATION AND TRANSPORTATION

INFORMATION AND SERVICES

Tourist Offices, Chamber of Commerce
You'll find all the pamphlets, coupon books, and area maps you can carry at **The Greater Myrtle Beach Chamber of Commerce** at 1200 Oak St., 843/626-7444. The **Little River Chamber of Commerce** is over at 1569 U.S. 17, 843/249-6604. Or check online at www.myrtle-beachaccess.com.

Hospitals and Police
The **Grand Strand Regional Medical Center,** 809 82nd Pkwy., 843/692-1000, is the place you want to get to in a medical emergency. If it's not life-threatening, see the folks at **Care Express,** 843/692-1770, a walk-in clinic. Or head to **Atlantic Medical Care,** 1410 S. Kings Hwy., just north of 6th Ave., 843/626-4420, which is open extended hours in the summertime.

If you're down in Georgetown, **Georgetown Memorial Hospital,** 843/527-7461, would be the place to call.

Public Libraries
On the hottest day of summer, on the craziest day of Sun Fun weekend, you'll find air-conditioning, quiet, and clean public restrooms just waiting for you at the **Myrtle Beach City Library** at 400 14th Ave. N, 843/918-1275, and at branches of the **Horry County Library** at 799 2nd Ave. N, in North Myrtle Beach, 843/249-4164, and 410 Surfside Dr., Surfside Beach, 843/238-0122.

Newspapers
The *Sun News* is the paper of record in Myrtle Beach; you'll find it in newsstands all around town. Weekly, it publishes *Kicks!,* where you'll find all the entertainment news you need, including movie listings, special events, and a long list of who's-playing-where in the area. *Alter-*

natives is the local free arty paper. Look for it in record stores, surf shops, and anywhere else nose rings and tattoos can be found.

GETTING THERE

By Car
Most people who visit Myrtle Beach come by car. From Washington, D.C. and coastal points north, take I-95 south to U.S. 301 at Dillon. Take U.S. 301 to S.C. 576 E; this will lead to U.S. 501 W. Take this on in through Conway and into Myrtle Beach. From Columbia, take U.S. 378 east through Sumter and Lake City to Conway, where you'll turn onto U.S. 501 E to Myrtle Beach. From Charleston and Georgetown, just head north on U.S. 17. Look for the billboards.

By Air
The **Myrtle Beach International Airport,** 1100 Jetport Rd., 843/448-1589, fax 843/626-9096, operates a 125,000-square-foot terminal with four gates and one runway.

By Bus
Greyhound Bus Lines serves the Myrtle Beach terminal at 511 7th Ave. N in Myrtle Beach, 800/231-2222 or 843/448-2471.

GETTING AROUND

By Bus
The **Coastal Rapid Public Transit Authority,** 1418 3rd Ave., 843/248-7277 or 843/626-9138, provides regular local bus service up and down the Strand. Call for schedule and information.

By Taxi
What with all the space between attractions, it's no wonder Myrtle Beach is home to over two dozen cab companies. Some of the more dependable are **Yellow Cab,** 843/448-5555;

Coastal Cab, 843/448-4444; and Broadway Taxi, 843/448-9999. All three offer 24-hour service. A cheaper way to go (sometimes) can be the Magic Bus, 843/361-2467, offering a special $15 multiple-pickup "ride-all-night" deal Thursday–Saturday operating from U.S. 501 in Myrtle Beach to Cherry Grove in North Myrtle and along U.S. 17 and the U.S. 17 Bypass. Buses are radio dispatched.

By Car

You'll find plenty of rental cars available in the area, and given the logistics of the place, if you want to do some sightseeing, you'll probably want to take advantage of one if you're here without a car. You'll find full listings in the local Yellow Pages, but some places to start with include Budget, 1100 Jetport Rd., 800/527-0700 or 843/448-1586, and Enterprise Rent-a-Car, 1377 U.S. 501, 843/626-4277, or 3108 Terminal Rd., N. Myrtle Beach, 843/361-0418, toll-free for both locations 800/736-8222.

By Bicycle

The flat terrain of the Grand Strand makes it top-notch biking territory for even the novice biker. If you can't bring your own bike along, you can find one to rent at Bicycles-N-Gear, 515 U.S. 501, 843/626-2453; The Bike Shop, 715 Broadway, 843/448-5335; and Full Circle Cycles, down in Garden City Beach at 2450 U.S. 17 S, 843/651-2659.

GEORGETOWN AND VICINITY

The first thing many people (especially those coming up from Charleston) notice about Georgetown is the huge paper mill billowing smoke into the sky. But don't let the smoke fool you—this is one of the friendliest, most historic, most attractive towns in the state. And if you don't believe me, just ask Norman Crampton, whose last two editions of *The Best Small Towns in America* list this slow-paced river town of 9,500 as one of his anointed burgs.

One of the best times to be in Georgetown is during its annual Harborwalk Festival held in late June or early July, when you'll find live music, a shag dance contest, a boat show, a road race, street dance, arts and crafts, and lots of good food available on Front Street and around the Harborwalk, the 1,000-foot walkway that's become the centerpiece (if not, for obvious reasons, the physical center) of Georgetown's newfound tourist district. For more information, contact Peggy Wayne at 843/546-1511.

In 1965 Grammy-award-winning comedian Chris Rock was born here at Georgetown Memorial Hospital when Rose Rock, who was raised in Andrews, was in town visiting an ailing grandmother. After the surprisingly quick delivery, she spent two weeks recovering from the birth and then took Chris back up to New York, where she and her husband raised him in Brooklyn. He was eventually discovered by Eddie Murphy. Rose Rock moved back down to South Carolina in 1992, after the death of her husband, and owns and runs the First Steps Daycare on South Island Road.

Chris occasionally comes to town to visit his mother. His visits are major local news. He's been spotted walking over to the Wendy's for a hamburger.

HISTORY

The story of the six or seven Native American tribes who dwelt in the Georgetown area before the arrival of Europeans is murky, since by the early 1700s illness and war had shrunk the tribes and caused them to either disappear or combine with others. The main Native American legacy in the area is, as it is in so many areas in the United States, the region's place-names: the Sampit, Pee Dee, Santee, and Waccamaw Rivers, for instance.

Georgetown is undoubtedly the third-oldest city in South Carolina—after Charleston and Beaufort—but some historians claim that European-American history actually began in Georgetown County, on what's now called the Hobcaw Barony, just north of Georgetown on U.S. 17. Lucas Vasquez de Ayllon gathered up about 500 men, women, and children for the colonization effort, establishing San Miguel in

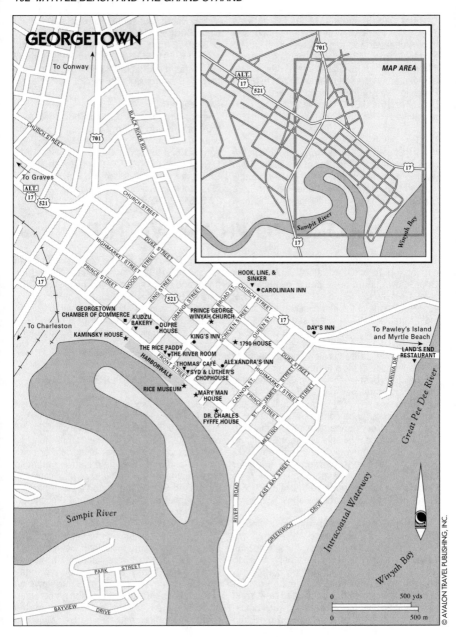

GEORGETOWN

To Conway

CHURCH STREET
701

To Graves
ALT.
17 521

CHURCH STREET

BLACK RIVER RD.

MAP AREA

701

ALT.
17 521

Sampit River

Winyah Bay

17

© AVALON TRAVEL PUBLISHING, INC.

HIGHMARKET STREET
PRINCE STREET
DUKE STREET
WOOD STREET
KING STREET
ORANGE STREET
521
17

To Charleston

GEORGETOWN
CHAMBER OF COMMERCE
KUDZU
BAKERY
DUPRE
HOUSE

KAMINSKY HOUSE

HOOK, LINE, &
SINKER
CAROLINIAN INN

BROAD ST.
CHURCH STREET

PRINCE GEORGE
WINYAH CHURCH

SCREVEN STREET
QUEEN ST.

17

DAY'S INN

To Pawley's Island
and Myrtle Beach

LAND'S END
RESTAURANT

MARINA DR.

KING'S INN

1790 HOUSE

THE RICE PADDY
THE RIVER ROOM
HARBORWALK
FRONT STREET
THOMAS' CAFÉ
SYD & LUTHER'S
CHOPHOUSE

ALEXANDRA'S INN

DUKE STREET

HIGHMARKET STREET
ST. JAMES STREET

RICE MUSEUM

MARY MAN
HOUSE

CANNON ST.

PRINCE STREET

DR. CHARLES
FYFFE HOUSE

ST.
JAMES
STREET

MEETING

Great Pee Dee River

Sampit River

RIVER
ROAD

EAST BAY STREET

GREENWICH DRIVE

Intracoastal Waterway

Winyah Bay

PARK STREET

BAYVIEW DRIVE

0   500 yds
0   500 m

MOON

1526, the first European settlement in what would become the United States of America.

No one knows precisely where San Miguel was located, but many suspect it may have been in Winyah Bay. Wherever it was, one thing's for sure—San Miguel was no eternal city. The settlers' Native American guide, Francisco Chicorana, abandoned them as soon as they landed, and before three months were up, Ayllon was dead. By the end of that winter, only three in 10 colonists were still alive. Leaving behind little but regret and a lot of graves, the survivors sailed back to Santo Domingo.

Over a century later, after the settlement of Charles Town, the British residents began hankering for new, tillable lands fairly quickly. The area where Georgetown stands today was granted to John and Edward Perrie as early as 1705, and a few hardy souls did leave Charles Town to begin working the land here. In 1721 the royal government granted the designation of a new parish to those who had settled here: "Prince George, Winyah Parish on Black River." But it wasn't until the bloodshed of the Yamassee War had passed in 1729, that the new community of Georgetown was laid out. With the importation of African slaves to clear the swamps and work the crops, indigo and rice soon became fiercely profitable for parish planters. Three years later Georgetown became an official port of entry, allowing local planters to cut out Charles Town as a middleman and thus reap even bigger profits. In 1757 the first public school between Charles Town and Wilmington, North Carolina, was opened in Georgetown by the wealthy members of the Winyah Indigo Society.

Wealth brought power to the city and its inhabitants; area planters Thomas Lynch, Sr. and Thomas Lynch, Jr. both represented the state, and the latter signed the Declaration of Independence. When the Revolution ruined the indigo trade, rice became the main crop in the area; soon the Georgetown District supplied nearly 50 percent of the young country's rice crop. The slave population rose to 85 percent of the area's total population. During and after the Civil War, however, the emancipation of the slaves and hurricanes harmed the rice crops; the area never regained its supremacy in rice.

Georgetown eventually turned to lumber for its chief industry, and this did the region well until the Depression hit. In 1936 the International Paper Company opened what would later become the largest mill in the world here. Later a steel mill opened here as well. More recently tourists have become a staple crop cultivated by local merchants, innkeepers, and restaurant owners.

SIGHTS

Rice Museum

This museum at 633 Front Street, 843/546-7423, website: www.ricemuseum.com, is far more interesting than it sounds. Yes, it's about rice cultivation, but since the story of rice cultivation is the background to nearly everything that's happened to Georgetown in the past 200 years, it's an interesting story. Here you'll find maps, dioramas, historical artifacts, and original boats used in the rice fields by slaves and other workers. The museum is in the Old Market Building (1842), which in turn is home to the Town Clock, a four-sided timepiece set atop a tower added to the main building in 1845. A slave market operated here in antebellum days. Federal troops attempting to take over Georgetown during the Civil War landed on the dock behind the building. Open Mon.–Sat. 10 A.M.–4:30 P.M.; closed Sunday and major holidays. Admission is $2 adults, students free, military personnel in uniform 50 cents. If you're lucky, Zella Wilt will be volunteering at the information/entrance desk; she's a transplant from up north, but she's helpful and knows her stuff. In June of 2000, the museum opened up a Maritime History Gallery, with a separate charge of $5 for adults and $2 for students.

This is a good place to begin a tour of Georgetown's historic district. Pick up a self-guided tour in the Rice Museum annex downstairs in the 1842 **Kaminski Building,** one of the first new Front Street business buildings erected—in brick—after a devastating 1841 fire that wiped out most of the business district. The cast-iron front was created by Daniel Badger of New York. But the Polish-born Kaminski didn't purchase the building until 1869, when he opened a hardware store there.

If the annex is closed, or you're in a hurry, I'll give you an abbreviated tour that will show you some of the oldest and most historic structures in town:

Georgetown's Rice Museum is housed in the 1824 Old Market Building, which is also home to the 1845 Town Clock tower.

A Brief Walking Tour

From the Kaminski building, continue southeast down Front Street to the corner of Queen and Front. On the northeast corner you'll see the circa 1775 **Mary Man House,** a Georgian two-story double house with paired interior chimneys. Mary Man's father owned the Mansfield Plantation outside town; Mary had the home built using her father's timber and slaves.

Continue in the same direction along Church and turn right at Cannon. Here you'll see on your right the circa 1765 **Dr. Charles Fyffe House.** Fyffe was a Scottish doctor forced to flee the country because of the intolerance of his pro-independence neighbors, who resented his loyalty to the royalty. Fyffe returned to Georgetown after the war and repurchased another house, but this one was lost to him forever. Across the street you'll see the late-18th-century **Red Store Warehouse,** from which one of the state's most

educated women, Theodosia Burr Alston (Aaron Burr's daughter and Governor Joseph Alston's wife), boarded the good ship *Patriot,* which promptly disappeared at sea during a storm off the North Carolina coast.

Now head back up to Front, turn right, and walk to the corner of Front and St. James. On the right hand corner nearest you, you'll see the circa 1737 **John and Mary Cleland House,** one of the earliest remaining homes in Georgetown. Turn left on Saint James and walk up two blocks, passing by the circa 1790 **Thomas Hutchinson House,** which originally looked identical to the **Savage Smith House** next door, until federal soldiers and freed slaves stripped the building during the Civil War.

Turn left on Prince and you'll pass a number of antebellum homes on either side of the street. When you get to the corner of Screven and Prince, you'll see the site of the Masonic Lodge on the northeast corner. George Washington, a Mason himself, visited this lodge on his 1791 Southern tour. Continue across Screven. The circa 1824 **Georgetown County Courthouse** on your left was designed by Robert Mills, the South Carolinian who also designed the Washington Monument. Just beyond the courthouse is the circa 1734 **Thomas Bolem House,** which historians believe was a pre-Revolutionary tavern run by Mr. Bolem himself.

Turn right on Broad and walk a full block until you reach the corner of Highmarket and Broad. On the near right-hand corner stands the circa 1825 **Benjamin King House,** now the King's Inn B&B. Across the street on the right is one of the town's most beautiful and historic buildings, the circa 1747 **Prince George Winyah Church,** 300 Broad St. at Highmarket St., 843/546-4358. This was the first major building in Georgetown, a government building as well as a church building during the time when the Church of England was the official religion of the colony of South Carolina. The steeple is a "new" addition, having been added in 1824. The local Episcopal congregation still uses the building weekly for services, making them the envy of other Episcopalians for miles around. The graveyard contains graves dating back to the colonial period. Open for viewing Mar.–Oct. Mon.–Fri. 11:30 A.M.–4:30 P.M. No admission fee.

Now head back southwest on Broad until you come back to Prince, and turn right. Continue until you've crossed Orange and are nearly to King Street. On your left you'll see the circa 1760 **Joseph Hayne Rainey House,** the home of Rainey, the first African-American member of the U.S. Congress. Rainey lived here during the Civil War.

The next house on the left is the circa 1740 **John Arthur House,** unique because it looks like something you'd see up in New England. Today this serves as the DuPre House B&B.

Now turn left on King and walk back to Front Street, and head into the Park area. The circa 1769 waterfront **Harold Kaminski House Museum,** 1003 Front St., 843/546-7706, was owned originally by the prominent colonial businessman Paul Trapier II, known locally as "The King of Georgetown." Harold Kaminski's widow gave it to the city in 1972.

While you're here, you really ought to tour the home—it contains one of the best collections of antiques in the American Southeast, and the guides here can answer just about any question you might think to ask. Tours given on the hour Mon.–Sat. 10 A.M.–4 P.M., Sunday 1–4 P.M. Admission runs $4 for adults, $2 for kids 6–12.

Also at the park is the circa 1750 **Robert Steward House,** a two-and-a-half-story Georgian on the river, where President George Washington spent the night while in Georgetown in 1792.

Now work your way back down Front Street, eating, drinking, and shopping as you go.

ACCOMMODATIONS

Motels
Carolinian Inn, 706 Church St., 843/546-5191, is a nice, clean, cheap place to stay. You can walk to dinner at the on-site **Hook, Line, and Sinker,** or across the street to breakfast at **Lafayette Restaurant.** $65–75.

Days Inn, 210 Church St., 843/546-8441, offers continental breakfast, an outdoor pool, and an on-site grill and lounge. It's one of the better bargains in town. $49–58.

Bed-and-Breakfasts
Winyah Bay Inn, at 3030 S. Island Rd., 843/546-0464, is a two-story, plantation-style inn two miles south of the U.S. 17 and U.S. 17A intersection. The manor offers four rooms and a full breakfast on a large screened porch overlooking a lake. Look out in the lake and you may see the resident alligator. No smoking. No pets. $65–75.

The **1790 House,** 630 Highmarket St., 800/890-7432 or 843/546-4821, offers six luxurious guest rooms with private baths, wraparound porches, beautiful gardens, and full breakfasts. There's also a romantic cottage with a Jacuzzi. Smoke free. $95–135 a night—lower rates for longer stays.

For about the same rates you'll find innkeeper Marshall Wile's **DuPre House,** 921 Prince St., 800/921-3877 or 843/546-0298, website: www.virtualcities.com/sc/dupre.htm, built in 1740 by John Arthur. This tastefully decorated three-story home offers five bedrooms with private baths. Three rooms offer tubs; the rest offer showers only. Two rooms offer fireplaces. Wile serves a full breakfast and afternoon refreshments. Swimming pool, hot tub. Smoking outdoors only.

Also in the same price range is **King's Inn at Georgetown,** 230 Broad St., 843/527-6937, With so many vintage 18th-century homes around, don't let the "newness" of this 1825 inn cause you to overlook it. After all this seven-room, two-story inn, with its original moldings, floors, and chandeliers, was a few years back ranked one of the top 12 inns in the country by *Country Inns.* Private baths, lap pool, no smoking.

Rob and Sandy "Alexandra" Kempe's **Alexandra's Inn,** 620 Prince St., 888/557-0233 or 843/527-0233, fax 843/520-0718, website: www.alexandrasinn.com, is set in an 1880 home originally built as an overflow for guests of the Winyah Inn, now the Masonic Lodge. Alexandra's offers five rooms, all with 11-foot ceilings and fireplaces, and each named and themed after a character from *Gone with the Wind.* Scarlett's Room features a hot tub (just like in the movie?), three bay windows, and a four-poster bed. Rhett's Room features a king-size sleigh bed and a red velvet settee, with a double hot tub and a separate corner shower. When Sandy's not around, maybe you could slip Rob a bill and ask him about "Belle's Room."

Alexandra's carriage house sleeps six and features a full kitchen. Discount rates available for extended stays. No young children allowed inside the main house—not even in Bonnie's Room. Smoke-free except on the porches. Gardens, swimming pool.

For a vintage Lowcountry plantation experience, drive 3.5 miles outside of town on U.S. 701 where you'll see the magnificent avenue of oaks leading to Sally and Jim Cahalan's **Mansfield Plantation,** 1776 Mansfield Road, 800/355-3223 or 843/546-6961, website: www.bbonline.com/sc/mansfield. Set on 900 acres of marsh and forest, Mansfield was used as Charlotte's house in Mel Gibson's *The Patriot,* but its history goes back much, much further than that—to 1800 or so—and who better to tell you about that history than Sally, whose father owned Mansfield before she did. Born in Columbia but a longtime resident of the North, Sally left her position as historical director at the James Buchanan Birthplace to return south and take over the family plantation. Amenities include access to the Black River for boating, and golfing next door ($25, includes cart). The shops and restaurants of Georgetown are only a short drive away. Pets are welcomed and usually quite happy here; a travel book for pet owners recently awarded Mansfield the coveted Five-Paw rating. Children are welcome too, though you'll need to pay an extra charge for them. Smokers will be given the chance to spend some private time outdoors. $95–135 a room.

FOOD

At 1 Marina Dr., 843/527-1376, website: www.the-strand.com/landsend, **Land's End Restaurant** offers great views of the Marina, the Intracoastal Waterway, and some tasty seafood, chicken, and prime rib. Dine indoors or outside on the covered deck.

Yum's Barbecue, 843/237-9052, said to be one of best, if not *the* best barbecue joint in the state, hides in its cinder-block shell on the left-hand side of U.S. 17 north of town. Located on the boardwalk is the **River Room,** 801 Front St., 843/527-4110. Strong seafood menu; open Mon.–Sat. 11 A.M.–2:30 P.M. and 5–10 P.M. **Rice**

Paddy, 819 Front St., Georgetown, 843/546-2021 is another old favorite. Nearby, the new, casual, family-style **Syd and Luther's Chophouse,** 713 Front St., 843/527-3106 (open Sunday—a rarity in town), has attracted a local following. **Hook, Line, and Sinker,** 706 Church St., 843/546-5191, specializes in seafood, steaks, sausages, pasta, chicken, and more. Located at the Carolinian Inn. **Thomas' Café,** 703 Front St., 843/546-7776, is a good low-key, informal spot for a basic meal.

A lot of travelers secretly believe that our bodies do not store fat and calories consumed while fifty or more miles from home. If you subscribe to this theory, then hustle on over to **Kudzu Bakery,** 120 King St., 843/546-1847, where buttery pies and red velvet cakes with fresh cream cheese frosting await after the reasonably priced lunches, which you can eat on the outdoor terrace if you like.

ACTIVITIES

Antiquing
Georgetown contains a number of fascinating antique stores. Stop in at **Augustus & Carolina,** 830 Front St., 843/545-9000, to take a look at some of the high-end imported French and English antiques. **Aunt Maggie's,** 1032 Front St., 843/545-5024, usually has some interesting items to browse, as do **Emma Marie's Antique Shoppe,** 827 Church St., 843/545-8030, and **Tosh Antiques,** 802 Church St., 843/527-8537. Over on Highmarket St., poke your head into **Grandma's Attic,** 2106 Highmarket St., 843/546-2607, and **Hill's Used Furniture and Antiques,** 4161 Highmarket St., 843/546-6610.

Paddling
If you're looking to get onto the river, Winyah Bay, or the Intracoastal Waterway, you need to talk to the folks over at **Black River Expeditions,** 21 Garden Ave., U.S. 701, three miles north of Georgetown, 843/546-4840, website: www.blackriveroutdoors.com. They'll rent you a canoe or kayak if that's all you need. They also lead day and evening tours of blackwater cypress swamps, rice plantation creeks, saltwater tidal marshes, wildlife refuges, and/or around

historic Georgetown Harbor itself. Bring your (waterproof) camera. Half-day guided tours are $40 a person, children under 13 years old $20.

INFORMATION

Visit the **Georgetown County Chamber of Commerce** at Front and King Streets when you first get to town. The folks there will load you up with pamphlets and maps, and they have some good local history books for sale as well. Or call before you leave home at 800/777-7705 or 843/546-8436 and ask them to send you a travel guide.

Tours

To really get into the spirit of things, you might want to take a walking tour with **Miss Nell's Tours,** 308 Front St., 843/546-3975. Miss Nell Cribb, a native Georgetonian, leads tours starting and ending at the Mark Twain Store at 723 Front Street. Departure times are Tues.–Thurs. 10:30 A.M. and 2:30 P.M., all other times by appointment. A 30-minute tour runs $5, one hour runs $7, and the full 90-minute tour runs $9. Children under 12 years of age accompanying adults get to come along for free, as long as they don't pay attention.

If all that walking sounds a bit too pedestrian, you might consider covering much of the same ground with **Swamp Fox Tours II,** 3525 Choppee Rd., 843/527-6469, website: www.georgetown-sc.com, a 20-year-old outfit recognizable by the blue and white tram the tour operators drive around. Geraldine Jayroe and her cohorts offer tours Mon.–Fri. 10 A.M.–4 P.M. on the hour, departing from 1001 Front St., the Georgetown County Chamber of Commerce Visitor's Center. Cost is $7.50 for adults, children $4.

But if riding around in a tram pulled by a gas engine ruins the 19th-century ambience for you, you may want to consider taking a ride with Ashley Cooper Carriage Co., located on Front St., 843/546-8727. These horse-drawn carriage tours, offered Mon.–Fri. 10 A.M.–4 P.M. and Saturday 10 A.M.–2 P.M., are one hour long and fully narrated.

Yet another possibility is the two-hour historic sailing boat tour with the crew of the **Jolly Rover,** 735 Front St., 843/546-8822, open Mon.–Sat.

Bookstores

Harborwalk Books, 723 Front St., 843/546-8212, with a good collection of local-interest books, is one of the places where I've always got to stop in when I visit Georgetown. The **Mark Twain Store,** 723 Front St., 843/546-8212, features books on local history as well, along with local art. **Goat Island Mercantile,** 911 Front St., 843/527-8538, also carries new and used books and unique local gifts. **The Olive Branch,** 829-A Front St., 843/546-9630, features Christian and inspirational books.

NORTH OF GEORGETOWN: PAWLEYS ISLAND

Pawleys Island, just north of town on U.S. 17, has been a resort for over 200 years; it's where planters would come during the warm weather to get away from the fevers and mosquitoes, and to take advantage of the beach breezes. Before Hugo the local bumper stickers proclaiming the town as "Arrogantly Shabby" perfectly described the weatherworn, air-conditioning-free, antebellum houses with their open windows flanked by beaten shutters and sagging porches crisscrossed by the now-famous Pawleys Island hammocks. But by the early 1980s, people started moving in who just didn't "get it." Up went the big new houses. In 1989 Hugo slammed through here, leaving a new inlet, flattening nearly a hundred houses, and paving the way for a host of new air-conditioned beach homes with six- and seven-figure prices. Still, a week on noncommercial Pawleys Island can unknot even the tightest shoulder muscles, and the sight of the remaining old tin-roofed classic Pawleys houses is a delight not to be missed.

Accommodations

On the island itself you'll find 18 airy rooms at the venerable **Sea View Inn,** 843/237-4253, $190–250. Out on U.S. 17, you'll find a friendly and nicer-than-average **Ramada Inn,** U.S. 17 S, 800/553-7008 or 843/237-4261, fax 843/237-9703. Golf packages available. $39–89.

Litchfield Plantation, King's River Rd., 800/869-1410 or 843/237-9322, fax 843/237-8558, offers a unique chance to stay in the real thing—an authentic 1750 plantation. Once you've entered the 600-acre property, follow the avenue of live oaks up to the Georgian mansion. You'll choose from four suites with views of either the oaks or the old rice fields. Swimming pool, tennis courts, golf, oceanfront beach clubhouse. A private restaurant is located on the property. Rooms run $148–186 (and on up into the $600s if you're really interested in nourishing the local tourism industry), but include all meals. Poet James Dickey had a special affection for this place. He bought a house here, which he named "Root-Light," in the early 1970s with the money he made off of *Deliverance.* He's buried not far away.

A lot of duffers like to stay at the pricey **Pawleys Plantation Country Club Villas,** U.S. 17, 843/237-6100, which is not right on the island, but is right on a golf course. Most units have a fireplace and sleep up to six people.

To stay on Pawleys itself means you're probably going to need to rent a house. Call **James W. Smith Real Estate,** 1336 U.S. 17, 800/476-5651 or 843/237-4246, or **Pawleys Island Realty,** on Pawleys Island, 800/937-7352 or 843/237-4257. Or pick up a phone book and start calling.

Food

You won't find any restaurants on the island itself. On the highway, **Frank's Restaurant and Bar,** 10434 Ocean Hwy., 843/237-3030, website: www.the-strand.com/franks, is an upscale standard in this area, known for its gourmet seafood and extensive wine list. Expect to spend more than $25 a plate. Behind the restaurant you'll find the more casual and less expensive **Frank's Outback,** 10458 Ocean Hwy., 843/237-1777. Open Tues.–Sat. 6–10 P.M. If the weather's good, eat outside under the oaks.

TO THE WEST: THE CHUBBY CHECKER BIRTHPLACE

Ernest Evans, aka Chubby Checker, was raised a country boy just down U.S. 521 in **Spring Gully.** Although his mother now lives in Walterboro, he returns occasionally to visit his aunt and old friends in Spring Gully. Checker (who got his game-piece stage name after Dick Clark's wife remarked that he looked like a younger, thinner Fats Domino) attended Great Pleasant

Church on U.S. 521 as a boy, and he has ancestors in the graveyard outside dating back to the 1850s. He also attended the decaying schoolhouse next door. His family moved to Philadelphia when he was just eight, and after high school, when he was toiling as a chicken-plucker, already-discovered schoolmates Frankie Avalon and Fabian brought him into the studio to jump-start his career. There he met Dick Clark, who was looking for someone to rerecord a Hank Ballard dance song called "The Twist." It became one of the biggest hits in rock history—the only single ever to rise to No. 1 on the *Billboard* charts, disappear, and then rocket back to the top again the following summer. Chubby also churned out numerous other hit dance tunes, including "Let's Twist Again," "Slow Twisting," "Pony Time," and "Limbo Rock."

Every year local boy Chubby performs for the home crowd at nearby Andrews' **Good Ole Days Festival** in May.

POINTS SOUTH

Hopsewee Plantation

Hopsewee Plantation, 494 Hopsewee Rd., U.S. 17, 12 miles south of Georgetown, 843/546-7891, overlooks the Santee River. It's one of the oldest plantation homes still standing, having been built in the 1730s by Thomas Lynch, who attended the Continental Congress. His son, Thomas, Jr., signed the Declaration of Independence. This restored home features period furnishings. Open Mar.–Oct. Tues.–Fri. 10 A.M.–4 P.M. Getting on the grounds, which allows you to see the outside of the house and hike a short nature trail, costs $3 a vehicle. Touring the house costs $6 for adults, $2 for kids 5–17.

Hampton Plantation State Park

Turn off U.S. 17 (a left if you're headed north) and visit this important plantation home at 1950 Rutledge Rd., built circa 1730 and long the chief building on this former rice plantation. When George Washington visited here, he learned that a small young oak in front of the house was soon to be cut down; he convinced the owner to spare the tree, and today the Washington Oak still stands before the house—blocking the view exactly as the building's

Pawley's Island

owner had said it would. Archibald Rutledge, South Carolina's first poet laureate, returned here to his ancestral home after retiring from a career in teaching and devoted himself to his writing and to the restoration of the Hampton Plantation. No admission for grounds, open Thurs.–Mon.; $2 admission for house, open Thurs.–Mon. 1–4 P.M.

McClellanville

McClellanville is a quaint, largely unself-conscious antebellum fishing village between Myrtle Beach and Charleston. It gets little coverage in travel literature, but because of a number of movies filmed there (including Don Johnson and Melanie Griffith's 1992 film *Paradise*), a small number of travelers have begun to trickle in. A good place to stay is Cheri and Matthew George's one-room **Village Bed-and-Breakfast,** 843/887-3266, where you can simply relax. Be sure to stop in at the ancient **Buster Brown's The Country Store** on Pinckney St., 843/877-3331, where you'll find everything from clothing to tackle to food. The Browns also serve good home-cooked meals here out on the screened porch.

McClellanville is also the easternmost head of the Palmetto Trail, a 240-mile hiking path reaching from the small coastal town all the way across to the mountainous Oconee State Park near the Georgia border.

A very, very off-the-beaten-path place to stay here is the moderately-priced **Laurel Hill Plantation,** 888/887-3708 or 843/887-3708, a post-Hugo B&B reconstruction of an old two-story Lowcountry home with wraparound porches overlooking the Cape Romain Wildlife Refuge's salt marshes and creeks, and the Atlantic Ocean. Look for the entrance opposite St. James Santee School out on U.S. 17 four miles south of McClellanville, then turn east and follow the dirt road just over a half mile through the trees until you see the house. There's plenty of bird-watching to do here. Pontoon boat rides, conversation, and lots of porch sitting will make up the rest of your day. Hosts Jackie and Lee Morrison also operate an antique shop on site. Children are allowed at the Morrisons' discretion. Call ahead for a reservation, because once you see the place, you're going to want to move your bags in and stay a spell.

© JOHN ELK III

CHARLESTON AND VICINITY

Travel writer John Milton Mackie puts his finger on one of Charleston's greatest charms: "It was pleasant to find an American city not wearing the appearance of having all been built yesterday," he writes. "The whole town looks picturesquely dingy, and the greater number of buildings have assumed something of the appearance of European antiquity." Few who have visited here would disagree. What makes Mackie's opinion interesting is that he wrote these words 140 years ago, in 1864. Even then Charleston was already closing in on its bicentennial. Founded in 1670, this is about as old an American city as you'll find.

Charleston's nickname, the "Holy City," refers to the number of cathedral peaks that tower over its streets, not to any especial piety in the populace. The city functions as the Austin, Texas, or the San Francisco of South Carolina: it's where the quiet, creative kid at Pickens High disappears to after graduation, to return a year later with tattoos and an independent record deal. It's where interracial couples kiss on the street.

Charleston is a noted player on the international arts scene: the annual Spoleto Festival draws hundreds of thousands of art enthusiasts from around the world. Charleston also overflows with culture of the more organic variety: African, Greek, and Irish-American festivals (among others), Gullah basketweaver stands, Civil War reenactments, black-tie only debutante balls for the daughters of SOBs (wealthy Charlestonians living South of Broad Street), and shrimp boils held by fifth-generation shrimpers. And Charleston has the Citadel Military College, perhaps the most distinctively Southern—and South Carolinian—place left on the planet.

Charleston's history is as worthy of veneration as that of any American city: the first decisive American victory of the Revolutionary War was won over at Sullivan's Island in 1776; the first shot of the Civil War was fired here. A lot of people through the years have chided Charleston as a city that worships the past. But all of Charleston's careful primping and long-sighted preservation has paid off. In 1997 *Travel and*

Leisure named Charleston the 24th-best city in the world and sixth-best in the United States, handily besting such traveler's favorites as Seattle, Portland, Miami, Las Vegas, Austin, Atlanta, Savannah, Washington, D.C., Philadelphia, and Los Angeles. Of other Southern cities, only New Orleans made the top 25. In 2000 the magazine named Charleston one of the world's Top Ten cities for value.

Readers of *Southern Living* have named Charleston the "Premier Shopping Area," "Most Romantic Getaway," and "Most Historic Travel Destination in the South." *Condé Nast Traveler* readers have named it a top 10 domestic destination for years. In 2000 they ranked it #3, following only San Francisco and New Orleans. And *Family Fun* magazine named Charleston the second-most popular city in the Southeast for family vacations—and this before the aquarium opened.

Perhaps most telling is the compliment given Charlestonians by Marjabelle Young Stewart, nationally renowned etiquette expert. Over the past 20 years, Charleston has never failed to make her list of the United State's most polite cities. And in seven recent years, Charleston has ranked number one.

If you're looking for the Old South, you won't find a better urban expression of it than Charleston.

CHARLESTON AREA HIGHLIGHTS

- African-American National Heritage Museum
- The Battery and White Point Gardens
- College of Charleston
- Charleston Museum
- The Citadel
- Fort Sumter National Monument/Fort Moultrie
- Hyman's Seafood
- Magnolia Plantation and Gardens
- Old City Market
- Old Exchange Building and Provost Dungeon
- Patriots Point Naval and Maritime Museum (Mount Pleasant)
- Seewee Restaurant (Awendaw)
- St. Michael's Episcopal Church

LAND

Charleston stands on a peninsula lying between the Ashley and the Cooper Rivers, a tongue of land pointed at the Old World. Here, Charlestonians like to say, the Ashley and Cooper Rivers meet to form the Atlantic Ocean.

At the southernmost point of the peninsula stands White Point Gardens and the Battery, where pirates were left hanging in the coastal breezes to scare off their scurvy brethren, and where guns fired upon British ships during the War of 1812.

Though the peninsula points southeast, Charlestonians have traditionally seen their city as the center of the world and thus have decided that the area above old Charleston is north; northeast of the Cooper, by Mount Pleasant, becomes "East Cooper"; the islands to the other side are "West Ashley"; and southwest of the Battery is "South." And White Point Gardens is due south.

Thus the region to the northeast of the Cooper River is called simply "East Cooper," and this encompasses the major town of Mount Pleasant as well as the buffer Sea Islands of Sullivan's Island and Isle of Palms. The area southwest of the peninsula, on the other side of the Ashley, encompassing James Island, John's Island (where slaves composed the hymn that would become the Civil Rights anthem "We Shall Overcome"), and Folly Beach is called simply "West Ashley." The Charleston Neck region and further northwest are now called "North Charleston."

CLIMATE

Weather on the Charleston coast tends to be mild, with average lows in January still well above freezing at 40°F and average midsummer highs below 90°F. That, however, doesn't mean things can't get quite sticky in July and August in Charleston, especially downtown, where the standing water from the frequent rain showers adds to the humidity. Things are most always a bit better right on the beach on one of the surrounding islands, when a breeze is blowing.

Hurricane season rolls in from July to October.

HISTORY

History is as palpable in Charleston as the scent of the wood pulp factories, locally called "bread and butter." In 1855 back before most other American cities had even *begun* their histories, Charleston's elites decided to form the South Carolina Historical Society, which today maintains a collection of books, letters, plantation histories, and genealogical records. A number of the local TV and radio stations even start off their newscasts with, "And now, from America's *most historic city.*"

Colonial Powerhouse

Charles-town is, in the north, what Lima is in the south; both are Capitals of the richest provinces of their respective hemispheres.
—Hector St. John de Crévecoeur, *Letters from an American Farmer,* 1782

South Carolina's first permanent European settlement, Charleston was founded at its current peninsular site only after the original colonists changed their minds twice. Their first choice was Port Royal, site of the former failed French and Spanish colonies and thus the best-documented site for 17th-century European travelers. But when the English colonists under Governor William Sayle arrived at Port Royal on March 15, 1670, they were greeted by Spanish-speaking Indians—a disheartening reminder that the Spanish still considered Carolina their land and that the Spaniards' base in St. Augustine was not all that far away. Neither did it help that the colonists kept running across the overgrown remains of Spanish forts on Santa Elena Island; they knew well that the Spaniards had massacred French Huguenot settlers in the past, and that this low-lying site, surrounded on three sides by woods, was hard to defend. All this made the British wary. To top it off the local Edisto Indians weren't really showing them much Southern hospitality (it hadn't been invented yet).

Fortunately, soon after they had landed, the leader of the Kiawah Indians, based north in the present-day Charleston region, sent word that the English would be very welcome in the Kiawah land farther north: they could help the Ki-

awah fight against the hated Spanish and the Westo Indians, the latter of whom the Kiawah described as "a ranging sort of people reputed to be man-eaters." Joined by a number of Edisto Indians and led by the cassique, the settlers sailed for the region now called West Ashley, just south of Charleston Peninsula. There, in early April, on the shores of the Ashley at Albemarle Point—site of present-day Charles Towne Landing—they founded Charles Town, named after their king.

As rice and, later, indigo became important local crops, and as Barbadians and Europeans, drawn by the reports drifting back from Carolina of cheap land and high profits, sailed into Charles Town Harbor, the city grew and prospered. By 1700 Charles Town had become inarguably the crown jewel of England's North American colonies.

The bulk of Europeans who emigrated to South Carolina in the early colonial period came as indentured servants or slaves to work for those already in the colony. With so much land, and a rice economy that required a great amount of labor, indentured servants and slaves soon poured by the boatload into Charles Town to be bought by planters who were building plantations among the coastal Sea Islands and up the rivers.

By 1680 the settlers had decided that the Albemarle Point spot was too unhealthy and hard to defend; some settlers began moving over to Oyster Point, site of the present-day Charleston Battery. The white-shell-covered point at the end of a narrow-necked peninsula was much easier to defend—there was no question about which direction a ground attack might come from—and planters both north and south of the port city could easily transport their goods from plantation to town using the natural currents of tidal creeks. In May of 1680 the lords proprietors formally instructed the governor and his council to resettle Charles Town at Oyster Point.

Meanwhile, the English-African-Indian mix was becoming even more diverse. French Huguenot Protestants began arriving in Charles

HERMAN MELVILLE AND THE "STONE FLEET"

In December 1861, at the start of the Civil War, the U.S. government sent sixteen old ships, loaded with granite ballast, up from newly-captured Port Royal to the blockade line outside Charleston Harbor. There the old ships were sunk to block the harbor from below. One Northern newspaper account crowed, "Before two days are past it will have made Charleston an inland city."

Some Northerners called the move heartless on humanitarian grounds. To *Moby Dick* author Herman Melville of New York, it was a waste of good sea vessels. In "The Stone Fleet: An Old Sailor's Lament," he bemoans in particular the sinking of the *Tenemos,* a whaler in which he had as a young man sailed around Cape Horn. He calls the ships' scuttling "a pirate deed," and chides those in charge for the deed's futility, since ultimately it had no effect on Southern blockade running.

And all for naught. The waters pass—
Currents will have their way;
Nature is nobody's ally; 'tis well;
The harbor is bettered—will stay.
A failure, and complete,
Was your Old Stone Fleet.

Town by the boatfuls in 1680. French King Louis XIV's 1685 repeal of religious freedoms for non-Catholics accelerated this process. European Jews, enticed by the colony's tolerant policies on religious freedom, poured in as well; by the end of the 18th century, Charleston had the second-largest Jewish population in the country.

In 1686, though they had resigned themselves to the idea of a English settlement at Charles Town, the Spanish forbade further encroachment to the south. Nonetheless, the increased population of Charles Town required planters to move out away from the city to find enough land for their plantations.

By 1690 the gradual movement of Charles Town to Oyster Point was officially completed. By now the city's population was estimated at around 1,200 people, making Charles Town the fifth-biggest city in all North America. By 1695

Charles Town citizens (or rather, their slaves) had built thick stone walls and six bastions, making the city into an armed fortress.

In 1700 the city established a tax-supported free library, possibly the first in America. On September 2, 1706, joint French and Spanish units attacked Charles Town during Queen Anne's War, but the Carolinian forces captured a French vessel and sent the Papists packing. The Powder Magazine at 79 Cumberland St. and the Pink House Tavern at 17 Chalmers were built in 1710, and the Rhett Mansion went up at 54 Hasell St. in 1712. The city served as a refuge for survivors of the initial Yamasee attacks in Beaufort and the Lowcountry plantations, and in the years leading up to the American Revolution, Charles Town served as the Southern center of patriot sentiment.

Though it held off the British Navy at the Battle of Sullivan's Island in 1776, the city was captured by the British in 1780 and remained in British hands until they withdrew at war's end. Charleston (residents changed the name because "Charles Town" sounded "too British") was the state's capital until 1788 and served as one of the nation's most important ports, exporting Southern cotton and rice in the early part of the 19th century until protective tariffs ended the trade. In 1830, to compete with Savannah, which received produce from eastern Carolinian farmers who floated their goods down the Savannah River, a group of Charlestonians built America's first commercial railroad, stretching from Charleston to the newborn Savannah River town of Hamburg (near modern-day North Augusta). When the "Best Friend of Charleston" began taking this run, it was the longest railroad in the world.

The War between the States

In 1860, after being chased out of Columbia by an epidemic, South Carolina leaders passed their Ordinance of Secession here, a major step toward the beginning of the Civil War. The first armed conflict of the war began here the following April with the Confederates firing upon the Union garrison holed up inside Fort Sumter.

During the War between the States, Charleston saw little action after Fort Sumter, though Union boats quickly sealed off the port to all but the most stealthy blockade runners. Union

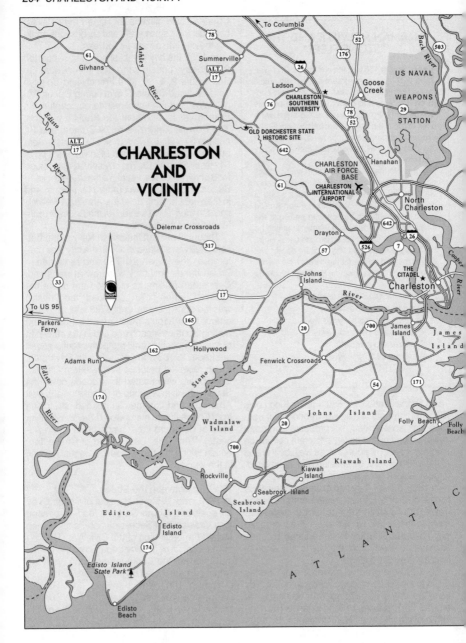

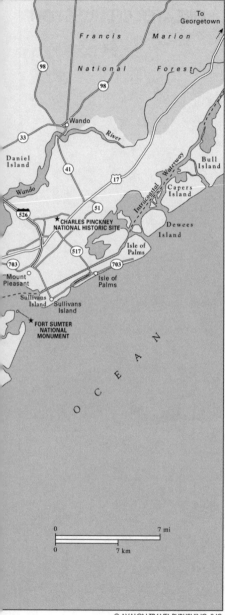

forces, including the famed African-American 54th Massachusetts, attempted to take Fort Wagner to the south of the city, but Confederate forces successfully defended it. The world's first "successful" military submarine, the CSS *Hunley,* sailed out from Breach Inlet between Sullivan's Island and Long Island (Isle of Palms) and sank the USS *Housatonic* before sinking itself, with all hands. The war in Charleston ended as Confederate troops fled and the black 55th Massachusetts marched through the streets, shocking white citizens and bringing emancipation to the city's black slaves.

After the War

> *If ever there was a place that rejected the New South, it was the port city.*
> —Walter Edgar, *South Carolina: A History*

The city had been ravaged by long-term bombardment, and it took a long time to recover. The discovery of nearby phosphate deposits brought some life back into the local economy, but the severe "shake" of 1886—an earthquake of an estimated 7.7 on the Richter scale—left 60–92 dead and caused an estimated $23 million damage.

By dredging Charleston Harbor to make room for large trans-Atlantic freighters, the city improved its shipping activity.

Around this time, a number of savvy Charlestonians began to think that perhaps all the postwar poverty had actually been a blessing in disguise, since by impoverishing Gilded Age business interests, it had prevented them from initiating new projects, for which the city's historic buildings would have been torn down. In the early 1920s Charleston devoted itself to expanding its tourism industry, leading to the building of both the Fort Sumter Hotel—now the Fort Sumter House—and the newly revitalized Francis Marion Hotel. With its harbor, and with the construction of the Charleston Naval Yard (spearheaded by North Charleston–raised Chief of the U.S. Armed Services Committee Mendel Rivers), Charleston became an important military installation during both world wars. Though many places shut their doors with the base closures at the end of the Cold War, by then tourism had become the city's chief

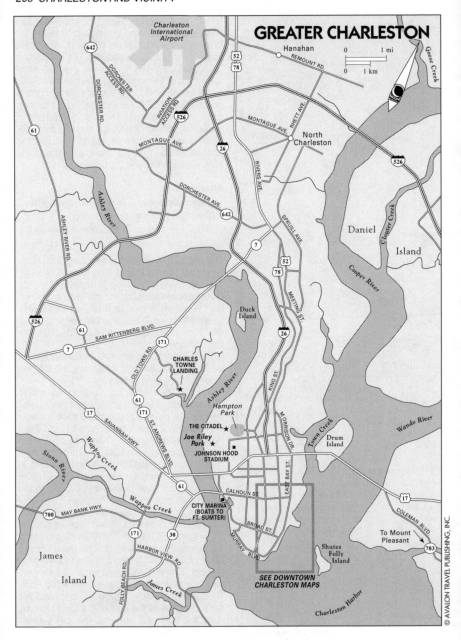

A TURN FOR THE WORSE: THE COSTLY SANTEE-COOPER DIVERSION

We humans have a way of playing with nature's rules. In the 1930s, to help generate more electrical power along the outer coastal plain, Santee waters were diverted to the Cooper River to increase its flow. This increased flow did generate more electricity, but it also enabled the Cooper to carry more sediment, with which it dutifully began to fill Charleston Harbor, the state's premier shipping port.

A costly rediversion built in 1985 carries about 80 percent of the Santee's water back to the Santee after it has done its job of generating electricity.

He spearheaded the annexation of Daniel Island and numerous other areas so that Charleston's physical size—and thus the size of its tax base—has exploded from 16.7 square miles in 1975 to nearly 90 square miles by the turn of millennium. The River Dogs' new classy riverfront baseball stadium—lovingly named Joseph P. Riley, Jr. Stadium (or "The Joe") in the mayor's honor—is one of Riley's more recent accomplishments, along with the forward-looking, pedestrian-friendly development of Daniel Island and the new South Carolina Aquarium, placed amid what has been until recently a fairly ugly and certainly not tourist-friendly part of town.

Avid fans or foes of planned developments will want to see Daniel Island off I-526 North. Long an agricultural island farmed by poor blacks, Daniel Island is now being reborn as Riley's dream city, a re-creation of the classic Charleston neighborhoods of yesteryear. Charleston's popular soccer team, the Charleston Battery, now plays here at a new stadium.

The biggest trial the city has faced lately was Washington's 1992 announcement that it was shutting down Charleston's base and naval shipyard, which employed some 19 percent of Charleston's workforce. Fortunately city leaders worked together to find industries to fill the projected shortfall, and by 1995 some $1.2 billion in capital investment had created more than 8,000 new jobs.

industry. Today tourism complements the city's production of paper and wood pulp, asbestos, clothing, cigars, rubber products, fertilizer, and other items.

One of the best things that's happened to Charleston over the past quarter century has been the reign of Citadel graduate Joseph P. Riley as mayor. First elected in 1975, Riley has focused on stimulating new development and restoration of historic downtown Charleston, starting by planting high-end projects—1986's Charleston Place, for instance—in run-down neighborhoods, and then watching as the adjacent neighborhoods rejuvenated themselves.

SIGHTS

ORIENTATION

Our houses are flirts. Lined up all along the streets, they are approachable and alluring, without the vast front lawns or privacy fencing with which suburban houses shield themselves. These houses are touchable, right from the sidewalk, yet at the same time they are very clearly private.
—Josephine Humphreys, *Travel Holiday*

To understand Charleston's logistics, think "parallels." Parallel rivers—the Ashley to the west and the Cooper to the east—separate the peninsula from the mainland. The primarily suburban area west of the Ashley is called **West Ashley,** and this includes **James Island, Folly Beach, Johns Island, Kiawah Island,** and **Seabrook Island.** East of the Cooper is called **East Cooper,** which includes **Mount Pleasant, Sullivan's Island,** and the **Isle of Palms.** And the area immediately north of Charleston is called **North Charleston.** Who needs Rand McNally? Farther north lie the booming suburbs of **Hanahan, Ladson, Goose Creek,** and **Summerville.**

Parallel U.S. 78 (King St.) and U.S. 52 (Meeting St.) thread the peninsular spine one block apart from each other. A couple blocks east of Meeting, East Bay St. (U.S. 52 Spur) follows the southward plunge, turning to East Battery Street after Broad. Over toward the Ashley side of the peninsula, Ashley and Rutledge Streets provide the main artery for traffic, and similarly end up at the south end of the peninsula.

Being as Charles Town was founded from the tip of the peninsula and spread its way up, you'll find the very oldest and most historic sections in the southern half of the peninsula. The visitors center on Meeting Street is a good starting point for southbound walking tours, though the Citadel and a few other historic sites north of this point are certainly worth viewing. But if you see nothing else in the area, see downtown Charleston. First off, there are some things you'll want to notice. For instance

The 186-foot steeple atop St. Michael's Episcopal Church—built in 1751, the oldest church building in South Carolina—is visible for blocks.

© JOHN ELK III

you'll see a few streets still paved with stones, but there just aren't a whole lot of stones sitting around in the Charleston soil. In fact most of the stones in the streets were imported as ballast from English ships.

Various Charleston promoters have broken up the historic district itself into various subdistricts, but in practice all you need to know to successfully navigate downtown Charleston is a handful of landmarks. First of all, know that **The Battery** (aka White Point Gardens) perches on the very tip of the land tongue that is Charleston Peninsula, and the term in general use refers to the area south of **Broad Street,** which bisects the peninsula partway up. Nearly any route you take between White Point Gardens and Broad Street will take you by some incredible old homes. **St. Michael's Episcopal Church** is another handy landmark, since you can see its steeple for many blocks. It stands at the intersection of Broad and Meeting Streets, also known (and made famous in *Ripley's Believe It or Not!*) as the **Four Corners of Law.** Almost due east of the Four Corners you'll find **Waterfront Park,** a beautiful modern facility with swings, fountains, and lots of lawn to nap upon. Just north of here, back toward the center of the peninsula on Meeting Street between North and South Meeting Streets, you'll find the **Old City Market,** or "the Market" in local jargon. If downtown Charleston has a nucleus, this is it; many popular clubs, restaurants, and shops orbit around, including a recently opened Saks Fifth Avenue and **Charleston Place,** the hotel whose opening kick-started the revival of Old Charleston. The Market is also the place from which many tours leave.

Within a couple blocks north of the Market, the tourist-centered economy thins out and the area can even look a bit dicey, though this is improving. At **Calhoun Street** you'll come across **Francis Marion Square,** which sits right between King Street and Meeting, and is home to many of the city's public events, including the Farmers' Market held every Saturday from April 18 to October 31. Just north of here you'll find the **Charleston Visitors Center.** You'll pass this on your left coming south on Meeting Street; stop in and grab all the pamphlets and coupons you can carry.

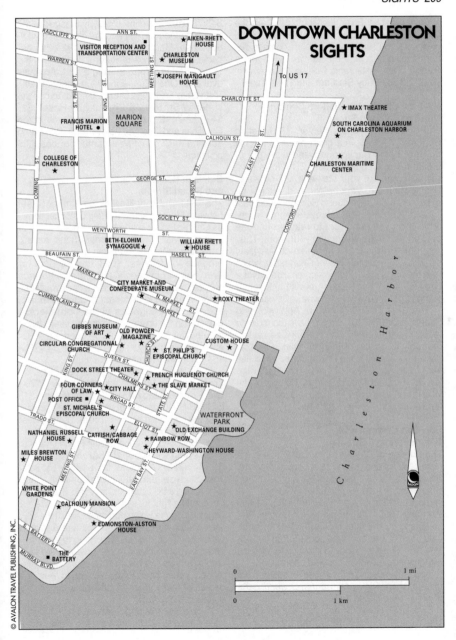

DOWNTOWN CHARLESTON SIGHTS

RADCLIFFE ST.
ANN ST.
★ AIKEN-RHETT HOUSE
VISITOR RECEPTION AND TRANSPORTATION CENTER ■
WARREN ST.
CHARLESTON MUSEUM ★
★ JOSEPH MANIGAULT HOUSE
To US 17
CHARLOTTE ST.
★ IMAX THEATRE
FRANCIS MARION HOTEL ●
MARION SQUARE
SOUTH CAROLINA AQUARIUM ON CHARLESTON HARBOR
CALHOUN ST.
EAST BAY
ST.
COLLEGE OF CHARLESTON ★
CHARLESTON MARITIME CENTER ★
COMING ST.
GEORGE ST.
ANSON ST.
CONCORD ST.
LAUREN ST.
SOCIETY ST.
ST.
WENTWORTH ST.
BETH-ELOHIM SYNAGOGUE ★
WILLIAM RHETT ★ HOUSE
BEAUFAIN ST.
HASELL ST.
MARKET ST.
CITY MARKET AND CONFEDERATE MUSEUM
CUMBERLAND ST.
★
N. MARKET ST.
★ ROXY THEATER
S. MARKET ST.
GIBBES MUSEUM OF ART ★
OLD POWDER MAGAZINE
CIRCULAR CONGREGATIONAL CHURCH
★ CUSTOM HOUSE
KING ST.
QUEEN ST.
★ ST. PHILIP'S EPISCOPAL CHURCH
DOCK STREET THEATER ★
CHURCH ST.
CHALMERS ST.
★ FRENCH HUGUENOT CHURCH
FOUR CORNERS OF LAW ★ ★ CITY HALL
★ THE SLAVE MARKET
POST OFFICE ■ ★
BROAD ST.
STATE ST.
ST. MICHAEL'S EPISCOPAL CHURCH
TRADD ST.
ELLIOT ST.
WATERFRONT PARK
NATHANIEL RUSSELL HOUSE ★
CATFISH/CABBAGE ROW
★ OLD EXCHANGE BUILDING
MILES BREWTON ★ HOUSE
★ RAINBOW ROW
MEETING ST.
★ HEYWARD-WASHINGTON HOUSE
EAST BAY ST.
WHITE POINT GARDENS
Charleston Harbor
CALHOUN MANSION
S. BATTERY ST.
★ EDMONSTON-ALSTON HOUSE
MOON
THE BATTERY ■
MURRAY BLVD.

0   1 mi
0   1 km

© AVALON TRAVEL PUBLISHING, INC.

On the Ashley River, just south of where the **U.S. 17 Alternate** cuts across the neck of the peninsula, you'll find the *Charleston,* home to dinner/dancing cruises, Fort Sumter tours, and a number of fine restaurants. North of the Alternate, you'll find **Joe Riley Stadium** and **The Citadel.**

Near the Charleston Visitors Center: North of Calhoun Street

The Charleston Visitors Center, 375 Meeting St., 843/723-5225, is a great place to stop in and get some background and a bagful of brochures and coupon books. The folks here will also plan out your stay and call hotels to find you a room. Very helpful and, except on extremely busy days during Spoleto, good, fast service. A bookstore also provides some worthwhile titles you may want to read around the pool or out on the balcony of your room. They also offer tickets for an in-house audio-visual show, the 24-minute *Forever Charleston,* which tells the city's story. Admission charged. Not a bad first step if this is your first visit and you're trying to get an overview of what-all's here.

The **Best Friend Museum,** Ann and King Streets, 843/973-7269, doesn't have too much to recommend it, other than the full-size replica (but only a replica) of the first train in regular passenger service in the United States, which left from Charleston. Most of the rest of what's here is a gift shop, but if you're going to be over by the visitors center anyway, or if you're a train nut, it's right around the corner, and free.

Between Calhoun and Beaufain/Hasell Streets

The **College of Charleston** is simply one of the most beautiful and historic campuses in America. Situated as it is near the bright lights of downtown Charleston, it's no surprise that COC has long had a reputation as a party school; even back in the early 1800s, famed pioneer, Mexican War commander, and later U.S. presidential candidate John C. Frémont was booted from the college rolls for his tendency to show up for classes with a hangover—if he showed up at all.

You may recognize the school buildings from the Alexandra Ripley miniseries, *Scarlett,* parts of which were filmed here.

Over at 90 Hasell Street you'll find the large, 1840 Greek Revival **Beth Elohim Synagogue,** 843/723-1090, second-oldest synagogue in the nation (founded 1749) and the oldest in continuous use. More importantly, in 1824 this became the birthplace of Reform Judaism in the United States. Worth making a visit. Archives available. Open Sun.–Fri. 10 A.M.–noon. Free.

If you're feeling ecumenical, head across the street to **St. Mary's Church,** 89 Hasell St., 843/722-7696, the first Catholic church in the Carolinas and Georgia. Built in 1839, the church building itself contains a number of beautiful paintings.

Between Beaufain/Hasell and Broad Streets

The 1841 **Old City Market,** on Market Street between Meeting and East Bay, continues today as Charleston's beating heart. A good place to start your visit, it features small shops, restaurants, and a flea market with everything from produce to antiques. You'll find vendors for everything from special homegrown hot rice recipes ("So good you'll double-smack your lips!" brags one sign) to professional photographs of the city. The **Daughters of the Confederacy Museum** in the upstairs building has been closed for renovation, but it should be open again upstairs by the time you get here. Call 843/723-1541 before noon for information.

In the wake of Indian attacks, early Charles Town residents built the square, low-lying 1703 **Old Powder Magazine,** 23 Cumberland St., 843/805-6730, as part of the city's fortifications near the northwest bastion. Today it's the oldest remaining public building in Charleston. Open Mon.–Sat., Sun. afternoons. Admission charged.

St. Philip's Episcopal Church, 142 Church St., 843/722-7734, was built 1835–1838 by Joseph Hyde, though Edward Brickell White later added a tall octagonal steeple. The steeple once held a light for seamen, but this made it a target during the Union bombardment of the city. This church congregation is the first Anglican parish south of Virginia. According to local legends, barristers questioned Reverend White's credibility, since he had in 1682 drunkenly christened a young bear. White went on to remain a pastor for many years, but the bear apparently drifted from the faith.

If you'd like to attend a service in this magnificent structure—and many traveling visitors do—

Sunday services are held in the mornings at 7:45, 8:45, and 11; Wednesday services are 10 A.M. and 5:30 P.M. No bears allowed.

Declaration of Independence–signer Edward Rutledge and John C. Calhoun lie buried out in the church's graveyards, along with Colonel William Rhett, capturer of pirate Stede Bonnet. Both Christopher Gadsden, the maverick Revolutionist, and Charles Pinckney, four-time governor and drafter and signer of the federal Constitution, are also said to be buried here in unmarked graves.

Though the current Gothic **Huguenot Church** at 44 Queen St., 843/722-4385, is "only" 150-plus years old, it was built on the walls of its predecessor. French Huguenots have worshiped on this site since as early as 1687. Until the early 1900s, the service was conducted in French on certain Sundays, but now it's English only.

The **Circular Congregational Church,** 138 Meeting St., 843/577-6400, a huge brick Romanesque building, was built in 1891 for a congregation founded way back in 1681. The church began with a group of non-Anglican Calvinists from a number of nationalities and was originally known as the Church of Dissenters. Architects designed the present church in the aftermath of the 1886 earthquake, using circular logic. Dr. David Ramsay (1749–1815), author of the definitive early South Carolina history, *History of South Carolina* (1789), and an important early biography of George Washington, is buried among others in the churchyard. Today the church building continues in use for the local congregation of the United Church of Christ.

The historic **Dock Street Theater** at 135 Church Street, 843/720-3968, is a reconstruction of the 1736 Dock Street Theater—the first building in American designed for purely theatrical purposes—and the 1809 Planters Hotel. The Dock Street Theater (on Dock St., which was later renamed Queen St., near Church) opened on February 12, 1736, with a performance of *The Recruiting Officer* by George Farquhar. After a few successful seasons, the theater burned. But Charles Town had caught footlight fever, and a second theater opened on the same site on October 7, 1754. Theater became wildly popular with the powdered wig set before the Revolution, so much so that the proprietors built a new, grander theater to replace this second

theater on nearly the same site, opening in 1773. Unfortunately, though the theater miraculously survived the heavy bombardments during the Revolution, it burned to the ground shortly thereafter.

In the last decades of the 18th century, theater productions were later banned in Charleston under a particularly harsh blue law, as thespians were officially condemned as antithetical to decent, upright living. But this era was short-lived, and shortly thereafter productions were taking place in various spots around Charleston, though the Dock Street Theater still lay in ruins. In 1809 a business concern built the **Planters Hotel** around the ruins of the theater. In 1835, to meet popular demand, the hotel was remodeled to include a theater, so that by the theater's centennial, the Dock Street Theater was again up and running. Though the theater was closed by the Civil War, the WPA during the Depression got the theater refurbished and open in time for its bicentennial on February 12, 1936.

Charleston-born actor Thomas Gibson ("Greg" of TV's *Dharma and Greg*) performed here with the long-running Footlight Players in the 1970s before the Players moved full-time to their own workshop on Queen Street, and Gibson moved on to the College of Charleston, and later Julliard, *Chicago Hope,* and Gregdom. Today the Dock Street Theater continues to offer first-rate theatrical performances through the Charleston Stage Company, the state's largest theater company, producing over 120 performances a year. If you just want to poke your head inside to take a look around this historic building, stop by during business hours. To speak with folks in the box office, call 800/454-7093 or 843/965-4032 Mon.–Fri. 9 A.M.–5 P.M. Shows are held Thursday, Friday, and Saturday at 8 P.M., Sunday at 3 P.M.

The Slave Market, 6-8 Chalmers Street, is one of the many places where slaves were sold during the days of the slave trade in town.

The intersection of Broad and Meeting Streets is known as the **Four Corners of Law,** because the buildings on each corner represent a different sort of law. On the northeast corner stands City Hall, circa 1801 (Meeting and Broad Streets), representing city law. The Charleston County Courthouse, representing legal law, stands on the northwest corner. On the southwest corner, the U.S. Courthouse and Post Office represent federal law. Directly across Broad you'll find St. Michael's Episcopal Church holding down the southeast corner, representing divine law. On most days, the traffic on Meeting Street represents the law of perpetual motion.

Charleston City Hall, on Meeting and Broad Streets, open Mon.–Fri., free admission, was built circa 1801; the City Council Chamber contains valuable works of art, including the John Trumbull portrait of George Washington, dated 1791. The tower above is topped by an Indian weathervane; the Indian is supposed to be King Haigler, a Catawba chief, and savior of the Camden Quakers in 1753. He fought with the Carolinians against the Cherokee in 1759, but was killed by a Swanee ambush in 1765. The town bell was cast in Philadelphia in 1824. It used to ring out every night at nine o'clock, marking the beginning of curfew hours for slaves.

South of Broad Street

St. Michael's Episcopal Church, 1751, is the oldest church building in South Carolina. During colonial days, this was the second Anglican church built south of Virginia. The clock toward the top of the 186-foot tower/steeple has kept time for Charlestonians since 1764. Inside the church is grand, with box pews; wealthy Charlestonians would rent these to assure themselves the best—and hence the most prestigious—seats possible on Sundays. How they reconciled this kind of privilege with the teachings of a peasant rabbi who spent most of his time around the downtrodden is beyond me. The graveyard beside the church is worth visiting for its many ornate and affecting tombstones. The bells overhead were stolen by the British during the Revolution and carried back to England in

> *The mansions South of Broad Street form a magnificent archipelago of exclusion. It was not a matter of money that assured access to the charmed region; it was a matter of blood. . . . If you were crass, lowborn, or socially offensive, it would have made no difference to the proud inhabitants South of Broad that you owned France; they would not invite you to their homes.*
>
> —Pat Conroy, *The Lords of Discipline,* 1980

1784, though they came back to Charleston. In 1862 they were shipped to Columbia for safekeeping from Federal shells and stored in a shed on the grounds of the State House—as if that wasn't a target. When the State House was burned in 1865 by Sherman's troops, the bells were partially destroyed. Preservation-minded folks sent the fragments that remained to England in 1866, and they were recast in the original molds. Then the bells made their fifth trip across the Atlantic, landing in Charleston in 1867.

St. Michael's stands on the corner of Broad and Meeting Streets, where St. Philip's, the first church in Charles Town, was built in 1681–1682. When the growing parish was divided in 1751, the lower half was named St. Michael's. George Washington and Lafayette both worshiped here, and here the first vested boys' choirs in the country began. During the Revolutionary period, the Reverend Robert Cooper was forced out of the pulpit—and out of the country—for offering prayers for the king of England. Since the church's steeple provided the highest viewpoint in Charles Town, Peter Timothy, editor of the *Charles Town Gazette,* climbed up there with a spyglass to watch the approaching British troops before the American loss of the town in 1780. Timothy had taken over the paper from his mother, the first woman publisher in the United States and a business partner of Benjamin Franklin. To make the steeple less of a target for British guns, Continental Commodore Abram Whipple proposed that someone should paint it black to make it less obvious to the eye. But once it was painted black, against the blue sky, it stuck out far more than before. Hours are Mon.–Fri. 9 A.M.–5 P.M., Saturday 9 A.M.–noon. Donations accepted. Call 843/723-0603 for more information. Sunday services are at 8 A.M. and 10:30 A.M.

The **Old Exchange and Provost Dungeon,** 122 E. Bay St., 843/727-2165, stands on the site of the original British Court of Guards, built in 1680. In 1767 the current exchange and customs house was built right on top of the old building, preserving the basement down below. Admission is $4 for adults.

Today you can visit the basement dungeon, where Stede Bonnet, the pirate, was imprisoned in 1718. The building itself once stored the tea taken during Charles Town's version of the

PORGY IN EXILE

Though based upon a novel written by Charleston's own Dubose Heyward, and set in the city, the classic American opera *Porgy and Bess* was not performed in Charleston until 1970. The interracial cast required to stage the show would have violated segregationist city codes.

Boston Tea Party. When the British had the Carolinians bottled up in the city in 1780, General William Moultrie hid 10,000 pounds of gunpowder in a secret room behind a false wall down in the basement. Though the British moved in and took over the city and the building, they never did find the hidden powder.

In 1791 George Washington stood on the steps of this building to watch a parade given in his honor. That night Washington tripped the light fantastic at a ball and governor's dinner up in the Exchange Hall.

You'll come to **Cabbage/Catfish Row** at 89–91 Church Street, the model for DuBose Heyward's Catfish Row in his novel *Porgy,* the basis for George Gershwin's opera *Porgy and Bess.* Vendors once peddled produce along the street here (hence the name Cabbage Row). In the novel Heyward relocated *his* row over to E. Bay St. to place it closer to the waterfront (hence Catfish—not that you'll find many catfish in Charleston Harbor).

Farther south along Church Street you'll come to the **Heyward-Washington House,** circa 1772, 87 Church St., 843/722-0354, which was the home of Thomas Heyward, Jr., whose name you may remember from the bottom portion of the Declaration of Independence. George Washington lived here awhile in 1791. The original kitchen building is still there, as well as Charlestonian furniture and a formal garden abloom with plants available in Charleston in the 18th century. Open daily 9 A.M.–5 P.M. Admission is $6 adults, $3 children. This home is owned by the Charleston Museum.

The **Nathaniel Russell House,** built for a local prosperous merchant in 1808, the year before Abraham Lincoln was born, stands yet at 51 Meeting Street, 843/724-8481, amid a large garden. A great example of the Federal style popular after the Revolution, this is a rectangular three-story mansion with a three-story octagonal bay on one side, a free-standing spiral staircase, and ornate moldings. Adams-style furnishings. Guided tours Mon.–Sat. 10 A.M.–5 P.M., Sunday 2–5 P.M. Last tour begins 4:40. Closed Thanksgiving, Christmas Eve, Christmas. Admission $6, under 6 free. It's possible to buy a combination ticket for Drayton Hall, Edmondston-Alston House, Gibbes Museum of Art, Middleton Place, and the Nathaniel Russell House, all for $29, or $19 for those under 12.

If you're only going to take one home tour, you may want to make it the circa 1828 **Edmondston-Alston House,** 21 East Battery, 843/722-7171. For one thing, this is one of those beautiful mansions on the Battery that overlook the harbor. It's also a great example of the "golden era" for Charleston antebellum society. Originally built for Charles Edmondston, a wealthy Scottish-born merchant and owner of a lucrative wharf, the home has been owned by Alston family members since 1838. Because members of the Alston family still live here, your 30-minute guided tour ($7, under 6 years old free) will cover only the lower two floors of this stately three-floor Greek Revival. Open Tues.–Sat. 10 A.M.–5 P.M., Sunday and Monday 1–5 P.M.; the last 30-minute tour starts at 4:30 P.M. You can buy a combination ticket for Drayton Hall, Edmondston-Alston House, Gibbes Museum of Art, Middleton Place, and the Nathaniel Russell House, all for $29, or $19 for those under 12.

Calhoun Mansion, 16 Meeting St., 843/722-8205, a 24,000-square-foot Victorian baronial manor house, circa 1876, features a 75-foot domed ceiling with stairwell. John C. Calhoun never lived here, but a kinsman did. Hours are Wed.–Sun. 10 A.M.–4 P.M. (closed January); admission $10 adults, $5 children.

Colonists came to call **The Battery** "White Point" after the oyster shells, which you'll still find on the ground; today it's still called **White Point Gardens.**

Later, a lot of pirates used to hang around here—literally. In 1718 Stede "The Gentleman Pirate" Bonnet and 21 of his men were allowed to hang for quite a while, so that their corpses' ghastly presence could send a message to other would-be pirates.

JFK AND THE SPY WHO . . . UM . . . LOVED HIM

FBI files released in 1998 revealed that in 1942, when John Fitzgerald Kennedy was a 24-year-old naval lieutenant living in the Atlantic fleet's intelligence office at 29 East Battery, Charleston, he enjoyed two visits from tall, blonde Inga Arvad Fejos, a former Miss Denmark. But Fejos was also a Nazi sympathizer with ties to Hitler, Goebbels, and Goering.

President Franklin Delano Roosevelt's attorney general was aware of Fejos's background and had set the FBI on her case. When she rented a room at the Fort Sumter Hotel, the FBI promptly bugged it. Apparently the lovers set the bug wires aglow with their passionate carryings on. In between, Kennedy was recorded spilling the beans to Fejos about his future military assignments. Kennedy would have been of interest to the Nazis because of his intimacy with his father, former ambassador to England, Joseph Kennedy.

Instead of taking the evidence to the navy, which would probably have resulted in JFK's receiving an assignment swabbing decks, the attorney general unaccountably took it to Joseph Kennedy himself. The elder Kennedy, to save his son's political future, had him shipped off to PT boat duty in the Pacific theater.

The rest of the story is, as they say, history: Kennedy captained PT-109, which was rammed and sunk, but he saved his crew, which made him a hero back home, igniting his political career and eventually leading to the White House.

So there it is—incontrovertible evidence that Charleston's romantic ambience led to JFK's election as president.

But the city long ago cleaned up all the bodies, so don't let this keep you from visiting. However, to keep the same general demeanor of tension in the place, the city has neglected to put any bathrooms here, so plan ahead.

This area got its nickname when it housed guns protecting Charleston Harbor during the War of 1812. The northeast side of the Battery is also called "High Battery." While no one's been executed here in many years, a lot of couples take advantage of the natural beauty here and get married on the gazebo.

In 1923 the city donated land on the Battery for the Fort Sumter Hotel (now the Fort Sumter House, the condo building at 1 Meeting St.). John F. Kennedy and a Danish woman who was probably a Nazi spy spent some passionate nights here back in February 1942.

PLANTATIONS, GARDENS, AND PARKS

Most South Carolinians, even at the height of antebellum society, never owned a slave. Only a relative handful owned, much less lived on plantations. In fact more African-Americans lived on plantations than European-Americans ever did—and they lived as slaves. This means, of course, that the vast majority of people who lived on the famed Southern plantations, with their stately buildings that nearly every new house built in South Carolina seems to emulate, did so unwillingly.

Still most non-Southerners don't really feel that they've visited the "real" South until they tour a plantation. And if it's antebellum excess you're seeking, you'll come to the right place in South Carolina. Coastal South Carolina in particular was one of the wealthiest plantation areas in antebellum times, and Charleston was the hub of antebellum Carolinian life—as it is today in many ways—so you'll find many old plantations here, a number of them open to the public.

Drayton Hall

Drayton Hall, 3380 Ashley River Road (S.C. 61) in North Charleston, 843/766-0188, is a red-brick Georgian-Palladian, one of the finest examples of early Georgian architecture in the United States. It was the home of John Drayton, who was not the nicest guy, but then neither was William Randolph Hearst. Drayton was a rich man, the owner of 500 slaves at his death.

Completed in 1742, Drayton Hall was used as a smallpox hospital during the War between the States, which allowed it to be the only authentically colonial structure along the Ashley to survive Shermanization. Just keep in mind that this was the—ahem—"smaller" house of the Draytons. There's no furniture here, which makes it easier to appreciate the architecture, moldings, and flooring. Prices run $10.00; youth (12–18) $8.00; children (6–11) $6.00; 5 and under free. Grounds only $3.00.

Magnolia Plantation and Gardens

Of all the Charleston plantations, Magnolia is my personal favorite—and that's saying something. John Drayton, son of one of the original Barbadian immigrant planters who arrived with John Yeamans in 1671, built this behemoth in 1738, before Thomoas Jefferson had even drawn breath. It's the oldest remaining example of the sort of Georgian Palladian architecture in the South.

Wealthy as he was, Drayton wasn't known as a particularly nice man. Fortunately for the house, Drayton's great-great-grandson, the Reverend Dr. John Drayton, apparently was. He treated his slaves quite well, educating them in reading, writing, and math skills—all illegal— while providing them with religious instruction. Sherman and Co. Remodelers burned the Magnolia Plantation house to the ground and strung up Adam Bennett, the top-ranking slave, from a nearby (still standing) tree, because he refused to tell them where he'd buried the family treasure. Fortunately the Boys in Blue remembered at the last moment that they were, after all, supposed to be "God's Truth Marching On," and cut poor Bennett down. After the war was over, Bennett traveled 250 miles on foot to Flat Rock, North Carolina, where Reverend Drayton was hiding out in one of the Draytons' summer homes, having heard that the freed slaves had seized control of the plantation and had "taken [it] for their own." Bennett told Drayton everything was ready for his return. Drayton later disassembled his Summerville house and floated it downriver to the plantation, where it stands today on the foundation of the Shermanized house.

The good reverend planted his informal gardens in the 1840s and opened them to the public in 1870 as a way of paying for the upkeep of the plantation; the magnificent gardens today include the **Biblical Garden,** featuring most of the plant species you grew to love in the Old and New Testaments (unfortunately, the Tree of Eternal Life from Genesis is missing); an herb garden; a Barbados tropical garden; a wildlife refuge; and a petting zoo.

If you feel that your own family tree could stand a little thinning, you might be interested in the quarter-mile *Camellia sasanquas* **maze.** Perhaps most impressive is Magnolia's latest addition, the 60-acre **Audubon Swamp Garden.** For $5 an adult, you can take the "Nature Train"—a tram car, to be more accurate—for an interesting tour of the grounds, but you should take the Swampwalk (also $5) as well. If you were at the drive-ins in the late 1970s, you saw these swamps featured in the Adrienne Barbeau epic *The Swamp Thing.* Many years before Barbeau slogged these waters, trailing a residue of acting greatness, no less a personage than John J. Audubon, the famed ornithological artist, wandered the same area, sketchbook in hand, as a guest of the Reverend Dr. Drayton.

picture-perfect bridge at sumptuous Magnolia Gardens

mansions at Magnolia Gardens

Magnolia Plantation and Gardens, S.C. 61, 843/571-1266 email: magnolia@internetx.net, website: www.magnoliaplantation.com, is open 8 A.M.–5 P.M. Mon.–Sat.; prices vary according to which of Magnolia's attractions you want to tour, but plan on spending from a minimum of $10 up to about $25 for adults, about half that for children. Senior citizens save a dollar on most admissions. A number of the trails are paved and wheelchair accessible.

Middleton Place

Here you get an idea of Charleston's abundance of floral beauty. Drop Middleton Place into the middle of nearly any other region in the country and it would attract visitors from hundreds of miles away. But then I suppose Middleton Place does that already, and it's just four miles past Magnolia Plantation on Ashley River Road (S.C. 61), 800/782-3608 or 843/556-6020, website: www.middletonplace.org. Open daily 9 A.M.–5 P.M. Admission is $14 adults, $7 children.

And well they *should* come, for Middleton Place holds the nation's oldest landscaped gardens, begun back in the 1740s. Arthur Middleton, signer of the Declaration of Independence, grew up here. A lot of locals prefer Middleton for its lack of hype; a visit here is more like visiting an actual plantation than is a visit to, say, Magnolia, which has been opened for, and shaped by, the demands of paying customers since Recon struction. Though only a staircase and foundation

remain of the main house, for a couple of bucks extra you can tour the "flanker" house, where the Middletons lived after the war. Don't even think about taking a camera inside: the folks at Middleton have gone so far as to construct a row of lockers on the house's front porch, where you may (must) leave your camera before en tering the house. Mel Gibson and company were treated a little differently. They used Middleton Place as the location for Lord Corwallis's party in the 2000 film *The Patriot.* Then again, I suspect Mel paid more than $14 for the privilege.

Remarkable gardens here as well, of a more formal, French variety. Unlike Magnolia, these aren't particularly impressive outside of spring— go in June and you'll be mainly touring rows of shrubs. You can also take a tour of the authen tically appointed guest (now main) house, walk amid a small slave graveyard, or visit an au thentic working stable yard.

You'll also find the good Southern-style **Mid dleton Place Restaurant** here (open Friday and Saturday only) with impeccable atmosphere and surprisingly moderate prices. Lunch is es pecially affordable (Middleton Roast Chicken, with homemade corn pudding, vegetables, and cornbread, $6.95), but dinner—especially ro mantic—isn't bad either (Panned Quail with a country ham julienne, and spoon bread, $15.95).

You'll also find the **Middleton Inn,** a flagrantly "modern" design that won the coveted American Institute of Architects (AIA) Honor Award in (shudder) 1975. Yeah, I've read the *Fountainhead* too, but with all the colonial splendor about—which is, after all, what draws tourists out here—the architects might have just *gone* with the theme. Instead what we have is what the inn's marketing folks, thirty years later, assure us is an "exciting counterpoint" to the traditional architecture of Middleton Place. From the inside, however, the inn's not bad-looking. If you'd like to stay out here, call the inn at 800/543-4774 or 843/556-0500, website: www.middletoninn.com, and ask about their Middleton Inn Restaurant package deals. These include dinner for two with your room charges, which start at $210 a night.

Cypress Gardens

Up north along the Cooper River, in Moncks Corner, you'll find 163 acres of azaleas, dogwoods, daffodils, wisteria, and dark waterways. Two nature trails offer you good chances to look for wildlife: river otter, woodpeckers, owls, and, of course, our friend the alligator. Springtime's bloom time, and fall is also quite pretty. Summertime is pretty too—pretty hot, and a pretty good time to bring repellent. Take the glass-bottom boat ride, or canoe yourself and a significant other around. From Charleston, head north on I-26 to Exit 208; follow U.S. 52 north and look for the signs to Cypress Gardens, 3030 Cypress Gardens Rd., Moncks Corner, 843/443-0515. Open Mon.–Sat. 8 A.M.–5 P.M. Admission is adults $6, children 6–12 $2, under 6 years admitted free Feb.–Apr.; May–Jan. the price drops to adults $4.

Boone Hall Plantation

Closest to downtown Charleston is Boone Hall Plantation, lying along the Wando River near Mount Pleasant. Though its main plantation house is a 1935 reconstruction of the original, Boone Hall is worth visiting because 1) it allows you to see what a plantation looked like when it was relatively new; 2) it contains nine original slave cabins, which tell more about slave conditions than all the interpretive exhibits in the world; 3) if you're looking for the type of plantation you may have seen in the TV miniseries *North and South,* Boone Hall Plantation *is* where that miniseries and several others were filmed; and 4) rumor has it that Margaret Mitchell's Tara—her *Gone with the Wind* was published in 1936, a

year after Boone Hall's renaissance—is modeled after the place, down to the gauntlet of moss-dripping oaks at the entrance. Battle reenactments are performed here in the summer, filling the grounds and mansion with period-dressed soldiers and belles (nobody seems to want to come dressed as a slave). For the Civil War buff, there's nothing like it. Boone Hall Plantation is off U.S. 17, 843/884-4371, website: www.boonehallplantation.com. Open all year 8 A.M.–5 P.M. Admission is $7.50 adults, $5 for senior citizens, $3 for children 6–12. Under 6 admitted free.

Angel Oak Park

Over on John's Island you'll find Angel Oak, 3688 Angel Oak Road, 843/559-3496, a massive live oak *(Quercus virginiana)* tree just 65 feet tall but 25.5 feet in circumference and providing some 17,000 square feet of shade. Because live oaks tend toward heart rot, making core samples useless in determining age, nobody knows for sure how old the Angel Oak is, though some estimates—based on the large limbs stretching out up to 89 feet from the trunk and measuring 11.25 feet around—indicate that the tree may possibly be 1,400 years old.

Incidentally, though some have waxed poetic about the way the Angel Oak spreads its angelic, "winglike" branches to the ground, the name actually comes from Justis Angel, who owned the tree and its land in the early 1800s. The South Carolina Agricultural Society rented the tree for $1 a year from the Mutual Land and Development Corporation 1959–1964, until another private owner bought the tree and surrounding site. He opened the land to the public, but vandalism and other problems forced him to build a fence around it and start charging a viewing fee.

In 1991 the City of Charleston acquired the Angel Oak and the surrounding property, and opened Angel Oak Park to the public on September 23, 1991. People meet here for picnics, family reunions, weddings, and other special events. Permits are required for large events and for the use of alcoholic beverages.

Charles Towne Landing State Historic Site

At 1500 Old Towne Road, off S.C. 171 about three miles northwest of downtown Charles Town, 843/852-4200, this peculiar park rests on the original site of Charleston—the spot the founding folk abandoned when they decided it was safer and healthier to move over to White Point. You can take a guided tram tour of the original 1670 fortification, explore seven miles of pathways through the gigantic shade oaks and lagoons of English Park gardens, and walk through the Animal Forest, where you'll see the same animals the settlers would have seen in 1670, including bison, pumas, bears, wolves, alligators, and bobcats. You're also free to participate in activities in the Settler's Life area, a re-creation of an early South Carolina village. Perhaps most interesting is the full-scale replica of a 17th-century trading vessel moored in Old Towne Creek. Unlike the original Charles Town settlement, most everything here's wheelchair accessible. Admission: $5 (15 and older), $2.50 (children 6–14), South Carolina senior citizens free. Open daily 8:30 A.M.–5 P.M.

James Island County Park

This park, at 871 Riverland Drive, is a 640-acre facility with boardwalks, bike and hiking trails, a fishing/crabbing dock, lagoons, a playground for the kids, picnic sites, a campground, rental cabins, and the **Splash Zone** water park, featuring a 200-foot slide, a lazy river, and other attractions.

Palmetto Islands County Park

This is a beautiful facility on Long Point Road in Mount Pleasant, featuring marsh boardwalks, trails, a mile-long canoe trail, a playground, an observation tower, bicycle paths, and fishing docks.

Folly Beach County Park

A neat beach-access park, Folly Beach, on W. Ashley Avenue in Folly Beach, offers 4,000 feet of oceanfront beach and 2,000 feet of riverfront beach. Lifeguards are on duty during the high season. Plenty of parking, dressing areas, showers, public restrooms, and picnic tables.

Francis Marion National Forest

Francis Marion comprises 250,000 acres of forest north of Charleston, offering picnicking and camping sites; boat ramps; fishing; and horseback, bicycle, and motorcycle trails. Head north on U.S.17 and look for the signs.

THE GARDENIA: NAMESAKE OF DR. ALEXANDER GARDEN

The fragrant white gardenia is named after South Carolinian Dr. Alexander Garden. Born in Scotland around 1730, Garden settled into Charles Town and worked as a physician. But it was in his dedicated dabblings as a naturalist that Garden became most noted. To most of Europe, America was still very much a "new world," and to his many scientist correspondents in distant Old World universities—including the Swedish naturalist Linnaeus—Garden served as a "man in the field," slogging through South Carolina's swamps in search of new species. Garden was welcomed into numerous scientific societies on both sides of the Atlantic and is formally credited with discovering several species, including the congo snake and the mud eel. It was Linnaeus who complimented Garden by naming one of his new plant discoveries the gardenia.

Garden died in London in 1791.

Seewee Visitor and Environmental Education Center

This center, at U.S. 17 N, Awendaw, 843/928-3368, is open Tues.–Sun. 9 A.M.–5 P.M. The center focuses on the natural history of the Lowcountry, featuring hands-on displays, a live birds-of-prey area, and a red wolf education area.

MUSEUMS, HISTORICAL SIGHTS, AND ART

Charleston Museum

You can't miss this museum, at 360 Meeting St., 843/722-2996, fax 843/722-1784, as you head south toward the Market and Battery off U.S. 17 or I-26 along Meeting Street. It's on the east side of the street, a modern-looking brick building fronted by a large model of the CSS *Hunley*. The oldest museum in all North America, this is one of the best, first places to stop and get a handle on Lowcountry culture and history. Kids will enjoy the interactive "Discover Me" room upstairs, and history buffs will enjoy the collection of small-press historical books in the gift shop downstairs. The museum also operates the historic Heyward-Washington and Joseph Manigault Houses. No flash photography. Open Mon.–Sat. 9 A.M.–5 P.M., Sunday 1–5 P.M. Admission to any one of the museum's sites (the museum or either house) is $7 adults, $4 ages 3–12; admission to two sites is $12 adults, $8 children; admission to all three is $18 adults, $12 children.

Joseph Manigault House
As long as you're here, you might as well head across John Street to this house at 350 Meeting Street, 843/723-2926, a national historical landmark also owned by the Charleston Museum. Many consider this house, built in 1803 by amateur architect Gabriel Manigault, the premier example of Adams-style architecture in the country. Open daily, $6 if visited individually, $3 children.

Aiken-Rhett House
And while you're over *there,* why not take in the Aiken-Rhett House, 48 Elizabeth Street, 843/723-1159, begun in 1817. The former home of Governor William Aiken, Jr., this unique three-story home also served as headquarters for C.S.A. General P. G. T. Beauregard during the war. This house has been preserved pretty much as it was during the Aiken-Rhett days, with the original wallpaper, paint colors, and many of the original furnishings still there. Ask the staff at the museum for directions to the house. Admission to the Aiken-Rhett House is $7 adults, free for children; admission to the Aiken-Rhett and the Samuel Russell House (as well as the Powder Magazine) is $12 adults. Open Mon.–Sat. 10 A.M.–5 P.M. (last 40-minute tour starts at 4:15), Sunday 2–5 P.M. (last tour at 4:15).

African-American National Heritage Museum
This is actually a collection of sites in the Charleston area, with its hub at the **Slave Mart Museum** on Chalmers Street. Fittingly, given the city's prominent role in slave importation, this is one of the nation's premier museums exploring the origins and contributions of African-American culture in the United States. Other museum properties include the reconstructed **McLeod Plantation,** 843/723-1623, where you can find a complex of antebellum home, farm structures, and slave dwellings. Open by advance appointment only, so call ahead.

Daughters of the Confederacy Museum
For the other side of the story, visit this facility, upstairs above the Old City Market. It has been closed for renovation, but it should be open again by the time you get here. Call 843/723-1541 before noon for information.

Museum on the Common
This is one of my favorite smaller museums. It features the "Hurricane Hugo Revisited" exhibit. Find it at 217 Lucas Street, Shem Creek Village, Mount Pleasant, 843/849-9000.

Gibbes Museum of Art
This museum, at 135 Meeting Street, 843/722-2706, has presented outstanding collections of American art to the public since 1905, with an emphasis on portraits relating to Southern history. Artists represented include Benjamin West, Thomas Sully, and Rembrandt. The museum also includes Japanese woodblock prints and one of the world's best collections of miniatures, with over 7,000 pieces to view. Each year the Gibbes presents dozens of exhibitions by regional, national, and internationally known artists.

If you come for nothing else, come for the local artwork; Alice Ravenel Huger Smith, Anna Heyward Taylor, and other Lowcountry artists have created an impressive body of work focused on the Holy City.

The museum also offers films, lectures, videos, talks, and symposia on the works and on the arts in general. Art classes for all ages are also held here quarterly, in case viewing all this fine work makes your palette hand twitch.

Allow yourself time to browse the museum shop as well. The building itself was erected as a memorial to James Shoolbred Gibbes; it's Charleston's best example of Beaux Arts architecture. Open Tues.–Sat. 10 A.M.–5 P.M., Sunday 1–5 P.M. Admission $5 adults, $3 children, $4 seniors. Find parking on nearby Queen and Cumberland Streets. For a guided tour, call ahead and ask for the Education Department. Photography prohibited. Handicapped accessible.

Avery Research Center for African-American History and Culture
Even if the College of Charleston (125 Bull St.) wasn't one of the most beautiful college

campuses in America, the Avery Research Center, 843/727-2009, website: www.cofc.edu/library/avery/avery.html, would make it worth a visit. The research center, set in the restored 1868 Avery Normal School for freedpersons, is a research center for documenting and preserving the history and culture of Lowcountry African-Americans. Includes the John's Island Collection of historical photographs and taped gospel music. Reading room and archives. Open Mon.–Sat. noon–5 P.M. Walk-in tours are offered Mon.–Fri. 2–4 and Sunday noon–5 P.M. Donation requested.

American Military Museum

Here at 40 Pinckney Street, 843/723-9620, you'll find uniforms and other artifacts from every U.S. war and from every branch of the service.

Patriots Point Naval and Maritime Museum

Among the exhibits here, 843/884-2727, across the harbor from the city, you'll find a little thing called the aircraft carrier **USS *Yorktown.*** Those fascinated by things nautical, or easily bullied by those who are, can also tour a submarine, a destroyer, and a re-creation of a Vietnam naval support base.

Clanging your way around these ships can be fascinating, though you should note that most of the tours are inaccessible to the wheelchair-bound, and anyone may find the climbing from deck to deck something of a challenge, especially on a hot day. Also, claustrophobes should think twice before descending into the *Clagamore* submarine.

On the hangar deck of the USS *Yorktown,* you'll find the **Congressional Medal of Honor Museum,** 40 Patriots Point Road, 843/884-8862, headquarters of the Congressional Medal of Honor Society. The Medal of Honor, of course, is the highest award for valor in action that the U.S.A. awards to servicemen and servicewomen. The museum divides up into the eight eras of U.S. military history: the Civil War, Indian Campaigns, Wars of American Expansion, Peacetime, World War I, World War II, Korea, and Vietnam. Some of the recipients' names you'll probably recognize—Audie Murphy, Sergeant Alvin York—while others you may not, such as Marcario Garcia, who single-handedly assaulted two German machine-gun emplacements during

World War II, and Brent Woods, one of the African-American Indian fighters dubbed "buffalo soldiers" by their foes. Admission: $10 adults, $5 children. Open daily.

Fort Sumter National Monument

Set on a man-made island begun in 1829, this fort had only recently been completed when U.S. Major Robert Anderson withdrew all the federal troops from Sumter's hard-to-defend mainland sister forts (including Fort Moultrie on Sullivan's Island) and holed up out here in the middle of Charleston Harbor, awaiting relief from the North. When word came that Lincoln was sending a flotilla to supply the soldiers, the Southerners who had taken over the mainland forts fired the first shots of the Civil War. After getting bombed for 34 hours straight—a feat not duplicated until some Citadel upperclassmen on weekend leave did it in 1959—Anderson surrendered. Just two years later, Union troops working their way north from the landing at Hilton Head took over the Morris Island guns and returned the favor, bombarded Fort for two years—one of the longest sieges on the books. The Confederates finally evacuated in February 1865, and Charleston fell immediately afterward. Today to go out and visit this important American landmark you'll need to take a boat either from Patriots Point or the City Marina. Either way, call **Fort Sumter Tours** at 205 King Street, 800/789-3678 or 843/722-2628, website: www.spiritlinecruises.com. The trip will take you a little over two hours, round-trip, with a stopover to tour the island. $11 adults, $6 for ages 6–11.

Charles Pinckney National Historic Site

Take U.S. 17 north through Mount Pleasant proper, past the Isle of Palms connector, and you'll come to the point where Long Point Road tees onto U.S. 17 at Christ Church, a colonial-era, still-active Episcopal church. Turn left, following the brown National Park Service signs, go up a mile or so, and you'll arrive at Charles Pinckney National Historic Site, 1254 Long Point Road, 843/881-5516, a 28-acre spot preserved from the former 715-acre Snee Farm, a plantation owned by Charles Pinckney (1757–1824), framer of the U.S. Constitution, four-time South Carolina governor, and U.S. ambassador to

ELIZA LUCAS PINCKNEY

When Charleston's Eliza Lucas Pinckney died of cancer in Philadelphia in 1793, President George Washington, at his own request, served as one of her pallbearers. This was a fitting finale to the life of one of America's most accomplished 18th-century women.

Born in the West Indies around 1722, Eliza came to Carolina with her family in 1738, at the age of fifteen. Her father, Major George Lucas, owned a large plantation overlooking Wappoo Creek "seventeen miles by land and six by water" from Charles Town. The Lucases owned other plantations around the colony. In 1739 the political conflicts between Spain and England required the elder Lucas to return to his military post in Antigua. With her brothers schooling in England and her mother an invalid, Eliza was left to supervise the 600-acre Wappoo plantation (including its 20 slaves) and to maintain correspondence with the overseers who managed the plantations on the Combahee and Waccamaw.

Since many of the rice markets were unavailable now that they were at war with Spain, at her father's suggestion Eliza began methodically experimenting with raising indigo. In 1740, 1741, and on through 1744 she experimented with raising a promising grade of indigo. By the end of 1744 she had impressed the British government, which wanted the dark blue dye for its uniforms.

By 1745 the Lucases were making a large income from the crop. The sales saved the family's Wappoo plantation. In 1744 she married Charles Pinckney, South Carolina's first native lawyer, a widower more than twice her age. He built her a home in Charles Town overlooking the harbor, and they also lived on the Belmont Plantation on the Cooper River. Eliza bore four children, three of whom lived to adulthood; her daughter, Harriet, ended up marrying into the Horry family of Hampton Plantation and competently managed that plantation after her husband died. Eliza's two sons, Charles Cotesworth and

Thomas, became important American leaders during the Revolutionary period. After spending five years living in England, the family returned to the colonies in 1758, whereupon the elder Charles immediately was stuck with malaria. He died in Mount Pleasant and is buried in St. Philip's churchyard.

Eliza survived her grief and went on to take care of the family's long-neglected Belmont Plantation, along with the islands they owned near Hilton Head (today known as Pinckney Island), the Pinckney Plains Plantation west of the upper Ashley, the 1,000-acre Auckland tract on the Ashepoo River, and several others. She also oversaw two homes on East Bay Street in Charles Town.

During the Revolution, Eliza's slaves deserted the plantation for the British camps, where they were promised freedom, though smallpox immediately broke out there and many died. Charles Cotesworth Pinckney became a brigadier general by war's end and was elected to the General Assembly in 1782. He was named one of South Carolina's delegates to the national Constitutional Convention in 1787. That same year Thomas had been elected governor of the state, and the following year he presided at the state convention that ratified the Constitution. Both men were national candidates for the Federalist party; when President Washington made a tour of the South in 1791, he stopped at Hampton Plantation for breakfast with the Pinckneys and Horrys.

Just a year later, Eliza journeyed to Philadelphia to consult a doctor famous for cancer cures. She died there on May 26, 1793, and was buried the next day, with President Washington as one of her pallbearers. She was 70 years old.

The Letterbook of Eliza Lucas Pinckney includes a fascinating collection of letters, most from her indigo-experimenting years, but spanning in all 1739–1762. You can pick up a copy in most any South Carolina library, as well as from Sandlapper Publishing.

Spain under President Jefferson, 1801–1805. Pinckney is one of those guys in the background of all the famous historical paintings like Louis S. Glanzman's *Signing of the Constitution,* where you can see Pinckney rubbing elbows with George Washington, James Madison, and other varsity squad Founding Fathers.

One of the things about historic sites like this one, and Fort Moultrie across the marshes over on Sullivan's Island, is that they are not nearly as imposing as most NPS properties tend to be. It's a good spot to spend a couple of hours, though—George Washington did so back in 1791, while making his triumphant presidential tour of the South. Though no standing structures remain from the Pinckney era, the folks in the National Park Service have turned a circa-1820 Lowcountry home into a nice visitors center and museum. It includes a display of the archaeological work going on here (more than 150,000 artifacts have been recovered thus far), as well as exhibits showing the efforts of the African-American slaves (and, later, sharecroppers) who made Snee Farm a successful farm.

South Carolina Aquarium

Opened after many delays in 2000, this 93,000-square-foot marvel, 100 Aquarium Wharf, 843/720-1990, website: www.scaquarium.org, features some 10,000 living organisms, representing some 500 species indigenous to the state. The aquarium's more than 60 exhibits focus on the state's water life, beginning with the Blue Ridge ecosystems of the northeast, then moving on to include life forms found in the state's rivers, swamps, and salt marshes, and off its shores. The aquarium actually sticks some 200 feet out over the Cooper River, reinforcing the aquatic theme and giving guests the chance to spot the dolphins who frequent the waters.

Built in a former industrial area—part of it a federal Superfund site—the aquarium is the centerpiece of Joe Riley's master plan for this part of the Cooper River. That plan will also eventually include, among other things, a new departure marina for the boats to Fort Sumter. The total improvement to the area cost well over $100 million (the aquarium itself cost $47 million), but the project has boosted Charleston's already high ratings as a desirable vacation and relocation destination.

Admission prices run $14 for adults, $12 for students (13–17 years), $7 for kids 4–12, and free for kids 3 and under. The aquarium's open seven days a week: July–Aug. 9 A.M.–7 P.M., Sept.–Oct. and Mar.–June 9 A.M.–5 P.M., and Nov.–Feb. 10 A.M.–5 P.M.

While you're down here, you might want to see what the current offering is next door at **Charleston Imax Theatre,** 360 Concord Street, 843/725-4629, website: www.Charleston imax.com. Shops and restaurants and a new landing for Fort Sumter boats are underway at publication.

The Citadel: The Military College of South Carolina

Located at 171 Moultrie Street, 800/868-3294 (800/868-DAWG) or 843/953-6726, the Citadel Military College moved over here across from Charles Town Landing back in 1922, after 80 years at Marion Square in the Old Citadel. The Old Citadel building was originally built in 1822, after the Vesey conspiracy was uncovered, as a place for whites to hole up in the event of another slave uprising. Though originally this first building kept a standing army of professional soldiers—as did the Arsenal, now the Governor's House, in Columbia—Governor Peter Richardson suggested in 1842 that it would be cheaper and smarter to replace the professional soldiers with young men who could both provide protection and receive military and "practical" training. By 1861 the two schools merged into the single South Carolina Military Academy.

On January 9, 1861, Citadel cadets stationed on Morris Island fired the first shot of the War for Southern Independence, firing on the Union steamer *Star of the West* as it attempted to reprovision the Union soldiers garrisoned at Fort Sumter. After the war Union soldiers occupied the old campus until 1881, after which the South Carolina Military Academy reopened under the state's jurisdiction and quickly became the training ground for the

> When cadet Pat Conroy attended the Citadel in the late 1960s, he spent most of his time in Capers Hall (home of the English Department), named for one of the most distinguished graduates of the Citadel, Confederate general, Episcopal bishop, and Sewanee chancellor Ellison Capers, class of 1857.
>
> Apparently Capers was always a man of deep spiritual devotion. The following prayer is attributed to him while he was a cadet here. Tom Law, one of Capers' fellow cadets, recorded the prayer thus:
>
> > Lord of love
> > Look from above
> > Upon this tainted ham;
> > And give us meat
> > That's fit to eat
> > For this ain't worth a damn.

state's business and political leaders. In 1919 the City of Charleston donated the present 200-acre site to the college, which was in need of expansion.

When you get there, just tell the cadet at the gate to direct you to the museum. You'll find **The Citadel Museum,** 171 Moultrie Street, 843/953-6846, on the third floor of the Daniel Library, the first building to your right inside the main gate. The museum features the history of the Citadel, with photographs highlighting exhibits that attempt to document the military, academic, social, and athletic aspects of cadet life. Open Sun.–Fri. 2–5, Saturday noon–5. No admission. Closed when the college is.

Next to the library is the Summerall Chapel. If you go inside, walk quietly; the poor harassed first-year cadets ("knobs") sometimes sneak in here to take a nap on a pew. If it's Christmastime, ask around and see when they've scheduled the candlelight service, a memorable spectacle that you'll want to catch, if possible.

Of course, the most famous Citadel graduate of the past 40 years is novelist Pat Conroy, who drew upon his experiences here to write two of his earliest books: 1970's *The Boo,* a nonfiction biography of Thomas Nugent "The Boo" Courvoisie, the commandant of cadets during Conroy's time there, and 1980's fictional *The Lords of Discipline,* also set at the Citadel. In *Lords,* Conroy changes the school's name to "The Institute," and changes The Boo's name to "The Bear."

Folks at the Citadel don't generally take to the latter book, which revolves around corruption in the ranks of the cadets and the school administration. In fact when *Lords* was made into a movie, the filmmakers had to film the campus scenes at an institute up north.

Continue along to Mark Clark Hall, where you'll find a canteen and gift shop, both open to civilians. To find out about Citadel events, including Bulldogs games, call 800/868-DAWGS or 843/953-6726.

MOUNT PLEASANT

The East Cooper area includes beautiful antebellum Mount Pleasant, fun-and-sun Isle of Palms, and historic Sullivan's Island. Mount Pleasant is a subtly beautiful Lowcountry town founded in 1680. Erase the cars parked on the sides of the narrow streets in the historic district, and you can well imagine that it's 1859 here. Not surprisingly, even many island dwellers consider a move inland to Mount Pleasant a move "up." Novelists Bret Lott and Josephine Humphries and former Milwaukee Brewers star Gorman Thomas all call the town home.

Other than the Patriots Point Naval and Maritime Museum, Hurricane Hugo Museum, and Boone Hall Plantation (see above), one of the best things to do in Mount Pleasant is to walk around the Old Village.

Development has taken its toll, particularly north of town, but the Mount Pleasant Commercial Design Review Board has had some effect on curtailing the madness. Credit them with the walkable Mount Pleasant Towne Centre (on 17, just south of the Isle of Palms Connector), which features a Farmers' Market during the summer.

ISLE OF PALMS AND SULLIVAN'S ISLAND

On the north lip of Charleston Harbor, Sullivan's Island is a beautiful southern beach retreat, home of Fort Moultrie, which was the site of a famous Revolutionary battle, the burial place of great Seminole chief Osceola (who died while incarcerated here), and sometime home of Edgar Allan Poe (who, while stationed here, found the settings for such famous stories as "The Gold Bug," and, some argue, "Fall of the House of Usher") and Lieutenant (later General) William Tecumseh Sherman. Along with Fort Wagner on the southern side of the harbor, Fort Moultrie was designed to work in unison with Fort Sumter in providing protection for Charleston Harbor. Hence it's doubly ironic that Moultrie's guns were used for firing upon the Union-held Sumter at the start of the Civil War.

Today, besides some pretty good surfing, Sullivan's Island is best known for its unpretentious but expensive homes (some built in former military bunkers), a handful of nice seafood restaurants, and Fort Moultrie, now part of Fort Sumter National Monument. The

THE BATTLE OF SULLIVAN'S ISLAND

With war erupting in and around Boston, the British decided their best strategy was to take advantage of the strong Loyalist support in the Southern colonies. They planned to begin a military drive from the Carolina Coast, at either Wilmington or Charles Town, that might sweep through the South Carolina Upcountry, gathering men, and then on through North Carolina and Virginia to sandwich Washington in the north.

Realizing this, the Continentals sent English professional soldier General Charles Lee down to Charles Town to oversee the defense of the town. After inspecting the palmetto log fort at the southern tip of Sullivan's Island, protecting the mouth of the harbor, and after noting that its isolation left its defenders no avenue of retreat, he declared it a "slaughterhouse" and ordered it closed. The stubborn Colonel William Moultrie said he and his men could hold the fort, even if the British guns blasted away the earthworks and the Americans had to hide behind the piles of rubble to await the landing party. Therefore South Carolina President Rutledge refused to evacuate it. And so it was that on June 18, 1776, as

British troop ships sailed to Charles Town, prepared to first seize Sullivan's Island and then the town, they found the fort expertly manned by Colonel William Moultrie and a garrison of men who fought as though their lives depended on it.

Having found Wilmington firmly in patriot hands, Sir Henry Clinton continued south and landed 2,000-3,000 men on Long Island (now Isle of Palms), just a narrow inlet to the north of Sullivan's. The plan was that at the same moment the nine British ships began shelling the fort, these trained soldiers would rush across the shallow Breach Inlet, overtake the Americans guarding the opposite shore, and proceed southward down the island to overtake the fort.

Unfortunately for the plan, the Breach Inlet was five feet deeper than British intelligence had said it was. The Brits could not "rush" across, but would have to be ferried across by longboat. The extra time it would take to row instead of wade would slow down the process considerably, since there were only boats enough for 600 redcoats to cross at once, and since 780 Americans under Colonel William

---

Sullivan's Island Lighthouse, at Station 18 1/2 on Middle Street, is the most modern lighthouse in the United States. Built in 1962, it's 140-feet tall, shines a light that can be seen 26 miles out to sea, and features an elevator. It's closed to the public.

Isle of Palms was developed relatively recently—around the turn of the century—and for a long time was accessible only by ferry. In the early 1900s it became a tourist destination, with a giant pavilion and the second-largest Ferris wheel in the world spinning high overhead. Hurricanes inspired renovation of the town's layout, and today the Isle of Palms, while still a tourist destination, largely serves as the beach for East Cooper residents and a favorite dinner destination for Charlestonians. The north part of the island, untouched jungle until the 1970s, is now the home of the Wild Dunes Resort, a megaplex of jungle condos, bungalows, and golf courses. Wild Dunes is a popular destination for people boating the East Coast along the Intracoastal Waterway.

History

The Breach Inlet between Isle of Palms and Sullivan's Island has made the history books twice. First, during the American Revolution, British General Cornwallis landed a regiment of troops on Isle of Palms and tried to sneak them south across the shallow inlet and onto the north end of Sullivan's Island. They hoped to rear-surprise the Americans holding down the palmetto-log fortress on Sullivan's southern tip, but unfortunately for Cornwallis, the inlet proved treacherous. While attempting to march across its swift currents, dozens of his men drowned or were picked off midstream by American sharpshooters. The British retreated.

In the 1860s Confederate soldiers launched the *Hunley,* claimed by some as the world's first successful submarine, from Breach Inlet's shore. Pedaled by one man and steered by another, the sub slipped southward around Sullivan's Island and successfully planted and exploded a bomb on one of the Union ships blockading Charleston Harbor, but sank itself (with all

Thomson had dug into reinforcements on the opposite shore to prevent just such an attack.

Communication broke down. The infantry on Long Island were as surprised as the Americans when the British ships swooped in closer and opened fire. Uncertain as to what exactly the navy had in mind, and facing severe losses if they tried the assault, the infantry decided to wait until the ships had silenced the Carolinian guns before attempting the crossing. A captain of the British 37th regiment assigned to Long Island wrote, "Very fortunately for us it was not attempted, for in the opinion of all present, from what we have since learned, the first embarkations must have fallen a sacrifice."

Around 11 A.M. the British ships continued on to a point 300 yards (900 yards, according to one British source) from shore, dropped anchor, and opened fire. Moultrie and his 400-plus South Carolinians had little powder and had to ration their shots, but to everyone's surprise, including the relieved Carolinians', the spongy palmetto logs absorbed the British salvos. Still, some shots got through, eventually killing 11 Carolinians and wounding 50.

"I never experienced a hotter fire," General Charles Lee, who visited the fort midbattle, later wrote General Washington. But his description reveals that despite 12 hours of this unrelenting barrage, Moultrie's men held out with typical Carolinian obstinance:

The noble fellows who were mortally wounded conjured their brethren never to abandon the standard of liberty. Those who lost their limbs deserted not their posts.

Upon the whole, they acted like Romans in the 3rd century.

No one's quite sure why the British decided they needed to overtake Sullivan's Island first before taking Charles Town; possibly they feared entering the harbor and thus exposing themselves to both the guns set up on the southern side of the harbor as well as Moultrie's. Presumably, had they won Sullivan's Island, they would have established a base of operations on the relatively secure site, from which they might begin the taking of Charles Town.

When the British troops on Long Island awoke the next day, they saw that their British boats had disappeared. In truth, the British ships had lost hundreds of men. A few weeks later, complaining that "The heat of the weather now is almost become intolerable," the sweltering Brits were picked up by British naval vessels and taken north to other perils.

This key victory caused the British to rethink their strategy and abandon the South for nearly three years.

---

hands) in the process. The wreck of this pioneer sub was finally discovered in 1995 by a team headed by popular novelist Clive Cussler. It turned out to be much smaller than historians had believed. After much debate over whether or not the ship should be raised, it was—in the summer of 2000, right about the time the Confederate battle flag came down from the capitol in Columbia.

Sights

Fort Moultrie, 1214 Middle St., Sullivan's Island, 843/883-3123, website: www.nps.gov/fomo is officially a part (the larger part) of Fort Sumter National Monument, featuring a visitors center where you should take time to watch the short but worthwhile film giving the history of the fort. The present-day Fort Moultrie is in a sense the third fort to occupy the south end of Sullivan's. The first was the palmetto-log fort that took a beating but held during a fierce June 28, 1776, battle against nine British warships. The current fort, its 15-foot walls encompassing 1.5 acres, was completed in 1809, though improvements (including radar) continued on through World War II. During the Civil War, Fort Moultrie held some 40 guns and 500 Confederate soldiers, who weathered a 20-month siege that began in 1863. In 1947, when new technological advances made the fort obsolete, Fort Moultrie was deactivated, after 171 years of service. Since its adoption as a National Park site in 1961, the interior of the fort has been restored with various weapons and fortifications spanning from the 1820s through World War II.

Private Edgar Allan Poe pulled sentry duty on these walls in the 1820s. Ten years later, Lieutenant William T. Sherman served here as well, developing an affection for the city that would serve it well at the end of the Civil War.

Out in front of the fort on Middle Street, you'll see the small, fenced grave of Osceola, leader of the Seminole resistance to President Andrew Jackson's relocation of all Native American tribes to the west side of the Mississippi.

U.S. troops caught Osceola in 1837 and brought him north to Fort Moultrie, where he was by most accounts given reasonable freedoms (for a prisoner) and treated with respect by his captors. Famed American artist George Catlin hurried here and captured Osceola on canvas, finding him "ready to die . . . cursing the white man . . . to the end of his breath." That end came shortly thereafter; Osceola died here in 1838, far from his beloved Florida homeland.

A major outcry arose here in 1999 when, while nobody was looking, a developer threw up a row of condos an arm's length from Fort Moultrie. Fortunately The Trust for Public Lands, a private, nonprofit organization from Washington, D.C. stepped in to buy the land, demolish the house, and preserve the views.

Fort Moultrie is open daily 9 A.M.–5 P.M. with extended hours in summer. No fee to tour the visitors center, but a small fee, usually $2, is charged to enter the fort. Closed Christmas Day. Partially wheelchair accessible.

Stella Maris Catholic Church, near the fort, is an interesting old church, which, rather than featuring a large crucifix above the altar, features a statue of Mary holding the baby Jesus. Every October the local parishioners hold a Halloween carnival that's worth stopping by for the village ambience.

One other thing to see before you leave the island: down on I'On Street (yup, the spelling is correct) you'll see some interesting homes, but by far the most interesting ones are those built in the old bunkers. To see one of these, head over to Middleton Street. It's private property, so be sure to stay out on the street.

BEACHES

My favorite beach in this region is Isle of Palms—but then, I never pack a lunch, so being close to a number of good lunch spots is important to me. If you're looking for a beach-beach, meaning bikini shops, hamburger stands, and board rentals, then you'll want to hit either Isle of Palms—right around the Isle of Palms County Park at the end of the Isle of Palms Connector—or Folly Beach.

Isle of Palms

One of the reasons that Isle of Palms is now so easy to reach—via the 1994 Isle of Palms Connector—is the owner of the Windjammer bar campaigned to get the road built with tax dollars, and then immediately began broadcasting to all the young party animals of Charleston how easy it was to get out to Isle of Palms. When he was the first person mugged by unsavory youth drawn by the "easy access" and good times, a lot of people had a hard time feeling sorry for him. But all that aside, Charleston County has built a nice recreational facility on the water at Isle of Palms. This is for the loud, tan, bikini-and-bathing-suit crowd; it's a great place to join a pickup game of volleyball or watch one of the recurring tournaments.

Isle of Palms is really a great little beachy sort of beach, with its hamburger shops and beach bars right there on the water, although the arrival of a new hotel may change things a bit.

Pencil-thin for protection from winds, this lighthouse stands on Sullivan's Island.

Sullivan's Island

Named for Captain Florence O'Sullivan, captain of the *Carolina*, Sullivan's today has some of the better surf in the area, right down by 21st Street. This area has become one of the pricier addresses in the Charleston area; if you can't afford to buy on The Battery, you might just have to settle for oceanfront on Sullivan's. The challenge of going to the beach here is the lack of a parking lot; just park on a residential street, but make sure no signs forbid it. At the south end of the island (down by Fort Moultrie), swimming is prohibited. And a good thing, too—it's dangerous there. But don't let that stop you from heading down after a day at the beach to visit Fort Moultrie and walk along the beach where you'll have a great view of Fort Sumter and, if you're fortunate, a huge ship that passes by like a city block on water.

Folly Beach

Folly Beach has always had great bumper stickers. It calls itself "The Edge of America." After Hugo, when most of the beach's famed white sands were swept away, a new bumper sticker began to appear: "Where's the Beach?" Now with beach renourishment programs, the beach is back, though no one thinks it will be here very long. Better see it while you can.

Folly Beach has served many roles in its history: from Civil War killing field to Southern Coney Island, from archaeological excavation site to countercultural refuge, and, increasingly, to upscale Charleston oceanfront suburb.

The island first appears on history's radar during the Civil War, when Union troops stationed at Hilton Head waded through waist-high water onto the south end of Folly Beach as part of their attempt to capture Fort Wagner, the nearly impregnable Confederate fort on Morris Island, north of Folly Beach. In the 1930s and 1940s, the Folly Pavilion provided great dancing; an amusement park drew the kids. Ira Gershwin stayed down here to pick up local flavor while working on the libretto and lyrics to *Porgy and Bess*. But tide, time, and storms have taken all of those away from Folly, though in the last few years a new fishing pier has opened, and the Holiday Inn has become a favorite place for local shaggers.

If Hurricane Hugo (1989) had a good side, it is that in passing through it ripped open the sands enough to expose some long-hidden archaeological remnants from the Union encampments on Folly Island. Five months after the storm, a number of Folly residents and beachcombers called to report that they'd found bones on the beaten-up island. Archaeologists raced out and quickly identified the bones as cattle bones. Big deal.

Fortunately Rod O'Conner, a former Folly Beach policeman, shortly thereafter notified the Charleston Museum that he'd found not just bones but leather remnants. Local members of the Underwater Archaeological Division, South Carolina Institute of Archaeology and Anthropology, headed out to the scene, collected what they could, and got the U.S. Coast Guard, which controlled the land, to allow a dig to take place immediately. Time was running out: the sand in which the artifacts lay was daily being lost to the ocean.

From April 24 through November, archaeologists removed as many artifacts as they could, while the ocean ate away at the dig site. By November the remaining land yielded little. The site was officially closed.

Fortunately, two years later, when the Coast Guard prepared to relinquish control of the property, federal laws required them to commission an archaeological survey of the entire area. A private archaeological firm located remnants of the assault batteries and other important occupation-era features on the island. They recommended that the land be preserved as an historic park, and most of it has been acquired by the Department of Parks, Recreation, and Tourism with plans to preserve it as a park.

Partly because it had had some of the tackiest pre-Hugo buildings, Folly took one of the worst hits from the storm, and took the longest to recover. You could walk here for years after Hugo and find telephones and food processors still buried in the Folly sand. But when the buildings finally went back up, they began reflecting the increased value of the oceanfront property. As *Post and Courier* reporter Linda L. Meggett reported, prices had begun to climb significantly by early 1998. A vacant lot assessed for $45,400 in 1993, for example, sold for $100,000 in March 1996. The starting sale price of the villas in the new 96-unit complex on West Arctic Avenue opened at $169,000 in 1997. By early 1998 it had climbed to $240,000. For a villa, mind you—essentially a condo.

The dreadlocks seem to be headed out and the dread Yuppies are on their way in, paying too much for houses and thus pushing up everyone's assessments and, thus, their property taxes.

Kiawah's Beachwalker Park

This is the only public beach on Kiawah Island; it's a beautiful stretch of beach—about 300 feet worth—with restrooms, dressing areas, outdoor showers, a snack bar, picnic area, and parking. It's on Beachwalker Drive, at the west end of the island, 843/762-2172. Unfortunately the rest of the island is privately owned.

COLLEGES

With nearly 11,000 students, the **College of Charleston,** aka University of Charleston, is the largest in the area, offering both B.A. and M.A. degrees. It has something of a reputation as a creative school, and as a party school. It's also one of the most beautiful campuses in America. It was used in the filming of TV's *Scarlett,* the alleged sequel to *Gone with the Wind—* but don't hold that against it. Founded in 1770, chartered in 1785, opened in 1790, and made a municipal college in 1837, this is the oldest municipal college in America. Attendance used to be free to Charleston students; it was considered a natural extension of the K–12 free education. It's a wonderful place to walk around, though the area can get a little dicey at night.

The College of Charleston's **Robert Scott Small Library** is open for varying hours throughout the year. **The Avery Research Center for African–American History and Culture,** 843/953-7609, is open Mon.–Sat. noon–5, closed Sunday. Open before noon by appointment only.

Charleston Southern University is a private Baptist school lodged deep in North Charleston. Its campus is modern but still reasonably attractive, and the basketball team is top-notch.

ACCOMMODATIONS

Charleston is full of charming places to stay, from quaint B&Bs to world-class hotels, from seaside cottages to beautiful campsites overlooking the undulating golden salt marshes. And there are also a number of cheaper, more practical motels for those who would rather spend their money at the restaurants and clubs than at the hotel desk.

My listings here are necessarily incomplete; I've given you a sampling of the different types of lodgings available, but feel free to stop into the visitors center on the way into town and browse the racks of pamphlets by the many different businesses offering a place to sleep in the Holy City. If you stumble upon a really first-rate place I've failed to mention, drop me a line about it so we can tip off other folks who would appreciate the things it has to offer. This way you can be more certain it will still be around next time you come to town.

There are a couple different ways you might approach lodging in Charleston. One is to find somewhere quiet off in the wilderness not 25 minutes away from the downtown historic district. Another approach is to grab a room at one of the local beaches, making daily or nightly trips into the Holy City for sight-seeing and entertainment.

Approach number three is to find a cheaper place on the outskirts, in Summerville or North Charleston, or maybe over in West Ashley. The upside of this is that you can save some money. The downside is that you probably won't save *that* much money from the better-value downtown spots, and you'll be spending your evenings staring at the glare of a Shoney's or Waffle House sign rather than the quaint flickering gaslights of the historic district.

This brings me to approach number four, which is to stay downtown as cheaply as possible. This is usually my strategy. There's just nothing like waking up early and strolling down Market or King until the smell from some coffeehouse or bakery yanks me in off the street. And if it's possible to fall in love with a city, I can pinpoint the moment I fell in love with Charleston for the first time: it was 7 A.M. and I stumbled

DOWNTOWN CHARLESTON ACCOMMODATIONS

RADCLIFFE ST.
ANN ST.
WARREN ST.
VISITOR RECEPTION AND TRANSPORTATION CENTER
CHAPEL ST.
HAMPTON INN
EMBASSY SUITES
CHARLOTTE ST.
FRANCIS MARION HOTEL
MARION SQUARE
KING ST.
ST. PHILIP ST.
COMING ST.
CALHOUN ST.
EAST BAY ST.
GEORGE ST.
BARKSDALE HOUSE INN
ANSON ST.
LAUREN ST.
CONCORD ST.
1837 BED & BREAKFAST
SOCIETY ST.
WENTWORTH ST.
BEST WESTERN KING CHARLES INN
BEAUFAIN ST.
HASELL ST.
INDIGO INN
MARKET ST.
CHARLESTON PLACE
PINCKNEY ST.
CUMBERLAND ST.
PLANTERS INN
MEETING ST. INN
N. MARKET ST.
DAYS INN
S. MARKET ST.
KING'S COURTYARD INN
ELLIOTT HOUSE
CHURCH ST.
MILLS HOUSE
QUEEN ST.
JOHN RUTLEDGE HOUSE INN
CHALMERS ST.
STATE ST.
HARBOUR VIEW INN
VENDUE INN
BROAD ST.
ELLIOT ST.
WATERFRONT PARK
TRADD ST.
KING ST.
MEETING ST.
EAST BAY ST.
36 MEETING STREET
BATTERY CARRIAGE HOUSE INN
S. BATTERY ST.
TWO MEETING STREET INN
THE BATTERY
MURRAY BLVD.

Charleston Harbor

0   1 mi
0   1 km

© AVALON TRAVEL PUBLISHING, INC.

downstairs from the King Charles Inn and sat out in front of Fulford and Egan (since moved) on Meeting Street, sipping a mocha as the dawn stretched over the weathered storefronts and wet, deserted streets.

Approach number five is paying whatever it costs to stay wherever you want in the quaint spots downtown. This isn't normally an option for me, but if it's an option for you, skip ahead to the "Luxury" section below.

One note: High seasons for many Charleston lodging spots are spring and fall, meaning that you'll find low season (with rate reductions of up to 50 percent) in the heat of summer—after Spoleto—as well as in the chill of winter. And winter is not always that chilly either. December temperatures often sneak up into the 70s.

HISTORIC DISTRICT

Moderate ($60–85)
I like the **Best Western King Charles Inn,** right downtown at 237 Meeting St., 843/723-7451. Sure, your balcony (if you get one) probably doesn't look out over much, but it's an excellent base to head out from and return to each day, and the rooms are spacious and reasonably priced. Since a lot of business travelers stay here, you can sometimes get pretty good rates on the weekends. Recently the inn underwent a major renovation, with the entire eastern facade replaced with a stucco surface, a secondary lobby added, and the guest rooms enlarged. Now it fits into the neighborhood even better than before.

The new-on-the-block **Hampton Inn: Historic District,** 345 Meeting St., 800/426-7866 or 843/723-4000, fax 843/722-3725, sits beside the Charleston Visitors Center, in itself a reasonable walk from the Market area, though you can take one of the Visitors Center trams, which are always heading down into the historic district. Though it's relatively new, this place seems like it's been here forever; it features antique reproductions in the rooms and lobby. Offers a nice, gated pool and an exercise room. This might be perfect for you if you don't mind not being right on top of things, location-wise.

When I'm not feeling particularly wealthy or adventurous, I usually find Days Inns to be a safe bet. If you're looking for a clean bed and decent service downtown, you might want to head over to **Days Inn: Historic District,** 155 Meeting St., 843/722-8411. Call 800/DAYS INN to get the central reservations number, or go online to www.daysinn.com. The facility here looks like a revamped motel, but you can't beat the location, right next door to the Meeting Street Inn.

For my money—or, for that matter, for your money—**Meeting Street Inn,** 173 Meeting St., 800/842-8022 or 843/723-1882, fax 843/577-0851, is one of the most romantic spots to stay in the city. It features a very nice courtyard with a number of fountains and tables, and large, beautiful rooms with wallpaper, West Indian architecture, four-poster rice beds (in most rooms), armoires, and wood shutters on the windows. Ask for a room on the ground floor so your view will look out into the courtyard and not over the courtyard wall and into the Days Inn parking lot. If no first-floor rooms are available, then ask for a room on an upper floor (there are four) in the high numbers—you'll be able to step out onto your back balcony and see the main entrance to Charleston Place, beautifully lit at night. There's a stellar staff here, and room rates include continental breakfast and an afternoon wine-and-cheese reception.

Premium ($100–150)
One of the most intimate spots in Charleston is the **Elliott House,** 78 Queen St., 843/723-1855, with a charming, fully enclosed courtyard, built on the site of original buildings designed by Robert Mills. If you call, ask about the packages—the "Get Away" includes three nights in a queen room with parking, a horse-drawn tour for two, and a tour of Sumter, all for $383. Summer and winter "low-season" rates run about $94. Expect to pay about 50 percent more for high season. Room rates here include use of the hotel's many bikes—perfect for exploring the nooks and crannies of the historic district.

A nice spot right up by the College of Charleston is **Barksdale House Inn,** 27 George St., 843/577-4800. Only 14 rooms here, so the feeling is intimate. Nice floral prints on the walls, armoires, four-poster beds. You'll discover a bottle of wine or champagne in the room every night, teas and sherry on the back porch in the afternoon. Located right in the midst of the historic district. $69–150 single or double. Children 7 and older only.

Battery Carriage House Inn is right down on the Battery, 843/727-3100 or 800/775-5575, fax 843/727-3130, with 11 rooms featuring four-poster beds, hardwood floors, quilted bedspreads, and so on. Continental breakfast only, unfortunately—down here on the Battery, it's not like you can walk around the corner and get shrimp and grits.

Rooms at the **Indigo Inn,** 1 Maiden Ln., 843/577-5900 or 800/845-7639, fax 843/577-0378 face an interior courtyard with a fountain.

The four-story circa 1844 **Planters Inn,** Market at Meeting St., 843/722-2345 or 800/845-7082, fax 843/577-2125, offers 62 rooms and a number of suites with fireplaces and whirlpool baths.

Farther up the peninsula, at Citadel Square you'll find the **Francis Marion Hotel,** 387 King

Hit hard by Hurricane Hugo, the lovely 1924 Francis Marion Hotel has undergone a $12 million renovation.

St., 843/722-0600, built in 1924 as part of a push to turn Charleston into a tourism center. The Francis Marion was hit hard by Hugo and underwent a major $12 million renovation by the Westin Company in the 1990s as part of Mayor Joe Riley's effort to bring a renaissance to this stretch of King Street.

Luxury ($150 and up)

And the waterfront was darkness, and the spirit of the South Bronx ran too and fro across the face of the peninsula.

This is how things were before the Omni, renamed **Charleston Place,** corner of King and Meeting Streets, 843/722-4900 or 800/611-5545, opened up in 1986. Today it's owned by the same folks who own and run the famous Orient Express. A couple years back *Travel and Leisure* rated Charleston Place the 54th best hotel in *the world,* placing it above such also-rans as New York's Ritz-Carlton (72), London's The Ritz (81), Los Angeles's Hotel Bel-Air (87), and the Four Seasons hotels in Boston (76), New York (97), and London (100). Of hotels in the continental United States, Charleston Place ranked 20th. *Condé Nast Traveler* ranked it as one of the U.S.A.'s top 10.

While the Francis Marion Hotel was under refurbishment during the 1990s, another exceptional renovation took place about the same time across Calhoun Square at the original Citadel Building. After months of work, the **Embassy Suites,** 337 Meeting St., 800/362-2779 or 843/723-6900, emerged, offering elegant two-room units, 12 rooms with whirlpools, and a complimentary full breakfast.

The **Mills House,** 115 Meeting St., is a fine reconstruction of a famed antebellum inn, right downtown at the corner of Queen and Meeting, 800/874-9600 or 843/577-2400. Robert E. Lee and Teddy Roosevelt both raved about it.

Of course, if Bob and Teddy aren't big enough names, you might want to head over to the **John Rutledge House Inn,** 116 Broad St., 843/723-7999, where no less than George Washington once sat down to breakfast. And traveling writers take note: the former owner, John Rutledge, brainstormed on a little thing called the U.S. Constitution in one of the inn's rooms. Wine and sherry are offered each evening in the ballroom.

A new spot down in the nighttime quiet by Waterfront Park is the appropriately named **Harbour View Inn,** 2 Vendue Range, 800/853-8439 or 843/853-8439. A little farther back up the street is the very romantic 18th-century **Vendue Inn,** 19 Vendue Range, 800/845-7900 or 843/577-7970. Fireplaces in some rooms, a beautiful restaurant, and a rooftop bar. This building was once home to a print shop financed by Benjamin Franklin; when the printer, Lewis Timothy, died, his widow took over and capably managed the business, becoming the first female publisher in the United States. She later handed over the business to her son, Peter Timothy, who daringly used to climb up into the bell tower of St. Michael's and spy on the British troops camped over at James Island.

BED-AND-BREAKFASTS

Charleston overflows with historic B&Bs. When you stop by the visitors center, be sure to pick up the booklet *Historic Charleston Bed and Breakfasts* to get the full selection. Below I've listed some of the more interesting and diverse options.

If you'd like to stay in an authentic Charleston Single House, the **1837 Bed and Breakfast,** 126 Wentworth St., 843/723-7166, gives you just that opportunity—and for under $100 a night (sometimes much under), which includes a full breakfast. This is a bit off the beaten path but still in the old, historic part of Charleston. Eight rooms in all, including some in the carriage house.

Two Meeting Street Inn is a favorite, a pretty Queen Anne Victorian down on the Battery, at 2 Meeting St., 843/723-7322, facing White Point Gardens, Charleston Harbor, Fort Sumter, and, if your eyes are really good, western England. Afternoon tea and sherry; continental breakfasts.

Built back in 1734, **36 Meeting Street** is at (sensing a pattern?) 36 Meeting St., 843/722-1034. The lodging offers a private walled garden, authentic Lowcountry rice beds, and kitchenettes.

King's Courtyard Inn, 198 King St., 843/723-7000, is a very private, very inviting place to stay. Beautiful courtyard, elegant rooms. Best of all, step outside the courtyard and you're right on King St., with a multitude of great places to eat and intriguing antique stores to explore.

THE CHARLESTON SINGLE HOUSE

In the narrow lots of Charleston, the Charleston Single House sits far to one side of the lot for maximum outdoor living space—much of it found on the large veranda and balconies located on one side of the house. The Single house was known as such because it ran only one room wide. Unlike most homes which run lengthwise so that their widest side parallels the street, the Single House's façade is short, and the long sides of the structure run from front to back on the lot. The veranda and balconies sheltered doors to the rooms that could thus be left open on hot afternoons, and even in sticky summer rain storms. Windows located at the far end of these breezeways, on the opposite long wall, allowed for cross ventilation.

Over in the Old Village section of Mount Pleasant, **Guilds Inn Bed and Breakfast,** 101 Pitt St., 800/331-0510 or 843/881-0510, is set in an 1888 home with six large rooms/suites with private whirlpool baths, telephones, TVs, and continental breakfast. Next door is the fine Captain Guild's Cafe.

EAST COOPER

Moderate ($60–85)

Before my wife and I moved out to Isle of Palms, we used to stay at the **Ocean Inn,** 1100 Pavilion Blvd., 843/886-4687, website: www.awod.com/oceaninn, just a block off the ocean. It's a small place with a laid-back ambience and a little pathway running back to the convenience store out on Palm where you can get late-night munchies. Reasonable rates, especially in the off season, as well as weekly rates. Some rooms feature kitchenettes, which, with all the shrimp you're going to catch while here, would be a good idea.

Last time I was out on the island they were just opening up the 51-room **Seaside Inn,** 1004 Ocean Blvd., 888/999-6516 or 843/886-7000, right on the waterfront, amid the bars and beach traffic, but also right on the sand. No pool, but the inn does have a hot tub. You'll find a microwave and refrigerator in every room, and a free "grab and go" breakfast downstairs. Free parking here, which will mean something to you if you're coming during the busy warm-weather months. $89–175.

Another, catacomby way to go is to rent one of the **Sea Cabins** right beside the county park. These are small and not exactly private, but staying here *does* give you access to private tennis courts, a pool, and a fishing pier. They also (unlike the condos down at Wild Dunes) put you within walking distance of the island's restaurants and shops. Choose between one- or two-bedroom villas. Call Island Realty at 800/707-6429 or 843/886-8144 in the U.S., or Canada 800/876-8144 to get a nice, thick brochure.

Days Inn: Charleston Patriots Point is at 261 Johnnie Dodds Blvd., Georgetown Exit, Mount Pleasant, 800/329-7466 or 843/881-1800, website: www.daysinn.com.

Holiday Inn: Mt. Pleasant is at 250 Johnnie Dodds Blvd., Mount Pleasant, 843/884-6000.

Premium ($100–150)

If a little bit of city bustle goes a long way with you, consider staying at the **Charleston Harbor Hilton Resort Patriots Point,** 20 Patriots Point Rd., Mount Pleasant, 843/856-0028, which is a new, deluxe resort offering a great across-the-harbor view of Charleston's steepled skyline and blinking lights. Though swimming in the harbor is forbidden (not to mention a bad idea) because of harbor mouth currents, the resort has pools and a nice sand beach to relax on. When I was there they were building some waterside cottages perfect for families; call and ask for rates. You're also a cart-ride away from the Patriots Point Golf Course. The best thing about this place is the hotel-front water taxi that takes you right over to Waterfront Park and the heart of Charleston's historic district actually makes you closer, time-wise, at the Hilton than you would be at some of the drive-to hotels in West Ashley and East Cooper, especially if you consider the time you won't have to spend looking for parking.

One more additional plus: you can watch the big freight ships pass by your window, something like watching a New York City street slide by.

Or head farther east to the north end of Isle of Palms to **The Boardwalk Inn** at Wild Dunes, 5757 Palm Blvd., 800/845-8880, ext. 1, or 843/886-2260, fax 800/665-0190, website: www.wilddunes.com. They've painted these pastel colors in an imitation of Rainbow Row. If you want to golf while in Charleston, this is the place to stay, since it includes the world-ranked Wild Dunes Links, as well as the Harbor Course.

There's also the seaside Grand Pavilion, a mock turn-of-the-century boardwalk without the rides and carnies. Really, it's a charming place, nicer and cleaner than it could be if it were open to the general public, which I guess is the point.

About as close as you can be to the Isle of Palms without actually being *on* the Isle of Palms is **Hampton Inn & Suites** right at the foot of the Isle of Palms Connector on U.S. 17 in Mount Pleasant, 843/856-3900. Sometimes a double room goes for as low as $79, but plan to spend over $110. It sports a tropical, sugarcane-plantation look, with Bermuda shutters; Canary Island date palms; hardwood, stone or woven matted floors; and teak, mahogany, and rattan furniture. Forty of the 121 rooms are two-room suites including a full kitchen.

WEST ASHLEY

Moderate ($60–85)

Holiday Inn: On the Beach, 1 Center St., at Folly Beach, 843/588-6464, website: www.holiday-inn.com, is one of several nice Holiday Inn locations. Another is up on the Savannah Highway—**Holiday Inn: Riverview,** 301 Savannah Hwy., 843/556-7100—and a third is over in Mount Pleasant.

RENTAL HOMES

You'll find rental houses a-plenty in the beach cities. You might call **Ravenel Associates** for a free 28-page guide on one of the Charleston area's many beach resorts, offering information on lodging rates, golf packages, tours, and more. Call for information on rentals on Isle of Palms, 800/365-6114; Kiawah Island, 800/845-3911; Wild Dunes, 800/346-0606; Seabrook Island,

800/845-2233; or Sullivan's Island, 800/247-5050. For more historic establishments in Charleston itself, call **Carriage House Vacation Accommodations,** 11 New Orleans Rd., 800/845-6132.

If you're thinking about staying on Folly Beach, consider calling **Fred Holland Realty,** 843/588-2325; **Seashell Realty,** 34 Center St., Folly Beach, 843/588-2932; or **Sellers Shelters,** 104 W. Ashley Ave., Folly Beach, 843/588-2269, ext. 9.

For Kiawah Island rentals, one major player is **Beachwalker Rentals, Inc.** 3690 Bohicket Rd., Suite 4-D, 800/334-6308 or 843/768-1777, website: www.aesir.com/Beachwalker.

Good places to find a rental on the Isle of Palms or Sullivan's Island are **Carroll Realty, Inc.,** 103 Palm Blvd., Isle of Palms, 800/845-7718 or 843/886-9600; **Dunes Properties of Charleston,** 1400 Palm Blvd., 888/843-2322 or 843/886-5600; and **Island Realty,** 1304 Palm Blvd., 800/707-6430 or 843/886-8144.

CAMPGROUNDS

Unlike most major cities, Charleston offers a number of fine campgrounds within 20 minutes of downtown. As long as it's not high summer, so that you won't be essentially camping in a bug-infested sauna, if you're trying to save your money for the restaurants rather than for your bed, you might want to give it a try. Of area campgrounds, **The Campground at James Island County Park** certainly bears the most inflated name. For Pete's sake, we're talking about a *campground* here. What's next? "The Convenience Store at Isle of Palms"?

But I digress. TCAJICP is a neat campground at a nice park, with 125 RV sites, full hookups, 24-hour security, an activity center, the **Splash Zone** water park for the kids, and a round-trip shuttle service to the historic district and Folly Beach. Reservations recommended. Rates are $24 for sites with full hookup, $22 for water and electricity, $18 for tent sites. TCAJICP, 871 Riverland Dr., James Island, 843/795-7275 (795-PARK), also offers 10 modern vacation cottages overlooking the Stono River marsh. Each sleeps up to eight and includes a kitchen, TV, and telephone. Rates for the cottages are $99.50 a night, $557 a week. There's a two-night minimum and a two-week maximum stay, and Memorial Day through Labor Day they rent only by the week. (Prices do not include tax.)

In East Cooper, right around the northernmost (so far) tract developments of Mount Pleasant along U.S. 17, the newish **KOA Mt. Pleasant–Charleston,** 3157 N. U.S. 17, Mount Pleasant, 843/849-5177, is a beautiful spot surrounded by pines, set on a pond, and next door to a golf course. Of course, like most KOAs, it's managed to mow down every semblance of a shade tree in the midst of the campground itself, but this one's definitely better than most, while still offering the KOA standard features that have made them so popular: a swimming pool, playground, boat rentals, and so on. A cute little campstore there will keep you from having to run into town for hot cocoa and such. It also has little air-conditioned Kamping Kabins if you forgot to bring your tent, or if it's just too dang-blasted hot to camp properly. Not a bad choice if you just want out of the urbane. Sites and Kamping Kabins (for two) run about $25–35.

There's another **KOA** up U.S. 78 (just off I-26) in Ladson, south of Summerville, at 9494 U.S. 78, 843/797-1045 or 800/489-4293—not a bad place to stop if you're coming into the area late in the day and don't feel up to taking on Charleston quite yet; it offers pretty much what the Mt. Pleasant one offers. Sites and Kamping Kabins (for two) both run about $20–25.

FOOD

CHARLESTON PROPER

Charleston is one of the best restaurant cities in the United States; to avoid overwhelming you, I've listed 25 or so here that are personal favorites. You won't go wrong if you eat from one of the places on this list, but if you find a spot that's not mentioned here, and it looks good, go ahead and give it a whirl.

Seafood/Lowcountry Cuisine

Hyman's Seafood, 215 Meeting Street, 843/723-6000, is my favorite place for seafood. It's warm, with bright wood paneling and wooden floors, a friendly staff, hot boiled peanuts at your table, healthy meal choices, reasonable prices, and fresh fish daily.

Unfortunately we made the mistake of telling a few friends, and they apparently told a few friends, and so on, and so on. Now this place is a serious institution: in 1997, *Southern Living* readers from 18 states (from Delaware to Texas) voted on the best seafood houses in all of the American South; Hyman's was named No. 2 overall and No. 1 in all of South Carolina. The Hyman family owned the building that was renovated to make the Omni Hotel (now Charleston Place), and they had the foresight to hang onto the two streetfront properties that now comprise Hyman's and **Aaron's Deli,** right next door to Hyman's, and one of our favorite places for breakfast. This place is usually *packed,* with waits that can easily last an hour or more. It doesn't take reservations, so the best you can do is put your name in with the staff person outside on Meeting Street when you first start sensing that you might be starting to think about getting hungry—then go sightsee or shop some more until you reach the time your name should come up.

Better yet, if you're a local, be sure to ask your waiter for a VIP card, which will enable you to slip past the hordes of out-of-towners next time.

For a true locals' haunt, visit the **Blind Tiger Pub/Four Corners Cafe,** at 38 Broad St., 843/577-0088. Live music and Lowcountry cooking.

Another place to grab some reasonably priced seafood is up King Street, just past where it starts looking dicey. At 467 King Street is **The Bubble Room,** a simply appointed restaurant with occasional live music and outrageous specials like a whole Maine lobster dinner for $8.95 on Monday, and all-you-can-eat snow crab legs for $10.95.

Like Hilton Head's Salty Dog Cafe, **Poogan's Porch** is named after a dog—in this case, the pooch that once graced its porch. Founded in 1976, praised in *Gourmet, Bon Appétit,* and *Cuisine,* Poogan's, 72 Queen St., 843/577-2337, is set in an old house on a side street and boasts "authentic Southern Cooking."

Hyman's Seafood, a deserved Charleston institution, was voted best seafood restaurant in South Carolina in 1997 (and second-best in 18 southern states).

DOWNTOWN CHARLESTON FOOD

RADCLIFFE ST.
ANN ST.
WARREN ST.

VISITOR RECEPTION AND TRANSPORTATION CENTER

▼ ARIZONA BAR & GRILL

CHAPEL ST.

BOOKSTORE CAFÉ

CHARLOTTE ST.

BUBBLE ROOM

MARION SQUARE

JUANITA ▼ GREENBERG'S

KING ST.

CALHOUN ST.

EAST BAY ST.

HORSE AND CART CAFÉ

ST. PHILIP ST.

COMING ST.

GEORGE ST.

JACK'S CAFÉ

ANSON ST.

LAUREN ST.

CONCORD ST.

MIKE CALDER'S PUB ▼

SOCIETY ST.

▼ OLD COLONY BAKERY

WENTWORTH ST.

▼ HARRIS TEETER

BEAUFAIN ST.

STICKY FINGERS ▼

HASELL ST.

VICKERY'S ▼

▼ LOUIS'S RESTAURANT

MARKET ST.

HYMAN'S ▼

▼ PINCKNEY CAFÉ

MICKEY'S ▼

T-BONZ/ ▼ KAMINSKY'S

PINCKNEY ST.

CUMBERLAND ST.

CITY MARKET ▼

N. MARKET

▼ ANSON

▼ FULTON FIVE

S. MARKET

TOMMY CONDON'S ▼

BOCCI'S ▼

▼ A.W. SHUCKS

82 QUEEN ▼

POOGAN'S PORCH ▼

CHURCH ST.

▼ WET WILLIE'S

QUEEN ST.

▼ SLIGHTLY NORTH OF BROAD

FAST & FRENCH GAULART & MALICLET FRENCH CAFÉ

MAGNOLIA'S ▼

▼ CHARLESTON CHOPS

WIRED & FIRED ■ ▼ SOUTHEND BREWERY

FOUR CORNERS/ BLIND TIGER ▼

STATE ST.

TRADD ST.

BROAD ST.

WATERFRONT PARK

★ CATFISH/CABBAGE ROW

KING ST.

MEETING ST.

EAST BAY ST.

Charleston Harbor

THE BATTERY ■

MURRAY BLVD.

0   1 mi

0   1 km

© AVALON TRAVEL PUBLISHING, INC.

Lunch 11:30 A.M.–2:30 P.M., dinner 5:30–10:30 P.M. Be sure to try the triple-layer chocolate cake, fried Carolina alligator, Charleston chicken, and anything with shrimp in it. During the warm weather they throw open the windows and you can sit out on the porch; during the winter, they light fires in the fireplaces and the restaurant takes on an intimate, romantic feel. Dress is casual. Reservations are a good idea. About $15 an entrée for dinner.

Anson, 12 Anson Street, 843/577-0551, tucked back off Meeting St. facing one of the public parking lots, with Orleans railings and torches flickering outside, is one of the prettiest and most expensive restaurants in Charleston, a very romantic spot serving up regional recipes, heavy on the seafood. Open for dinner only, seven days a week. Dinner will cost you about $15 an entrée.

Over in an old house at 18 Pinckney Street, you'll find **Pinckney Cafe & Expresso,** owned by a husband and wife who live upstairs. A versatile spot: bright and cheery in the morning (you can eat out on the porch), casual at lunch, romantic at night, with full wait service. You'll find creative menu items including some tasty pasta fritters. The espresso and cappuccino are first-rate. And two other important words here: smoke free. Dinners cost around $12 an entrée, but lunch is considerably cheaper, and you don't need to leave a tip. Open Tues.–Sat. Lunch is served 11:30 A.M.–2:30 P.M., dinner 6–10 P.M.

Slightly North of Broad, 192 East Bay St., 843/723-3424, is one you'll remember; it offers relatively healthy items, plenty of creative seafood and meat entrées. Nice atmosphere; dinner should run you about $15 a plate.

Another good spot for seafood downtown is **A. W. Shucks,** 35 Market St., just off East Bay, 843/723-1151. Casual; a good place for families or large groups. Open Sun.–Thurs. 11:30 A.M.–11 P.M.; open at noon Friday and Saturday. Dinner will run you anywhere from $6 or $7 on up to over $15.

When Bradley O'Leary wrote his *Dining By Candlelight: America's 200 Most Romantic Restaurants,* he named **Louis's Charleston Grill at Charleston Place** South Carolina's most romantic restaurant. And it is a beautiful, formal spot, looking out on Charleston Place's courtyard. Dinner entrées average around $17, but

the price is worth it if you're tired of conventional Lowcountry fare. You'll find Charleston Place at 139 Market St., 843/577-4572. It recently won a Mobil Four Star rating. Chef Louis Osteen himself is not there anymore, however he and wife, Marlene, have opened their own place, **Louis's Restaurant,** atop the NationsBank building right across from Charleston Place, 843/722-6274. You won't go wrong at either place.

Magnolia's 185 East Bay St., 843/577-7771, describes itself as "Uptown, Down South," and I can't think of a better way to put it. It's located at the site of the original Customs House, overlooking Lodge Alley. Lunch can be downright cheap; dinner easily runs upward of $15 a plate. Reservations are suggested. Open daily 11:30 A.M.–11 P.M. and until midnight on Friday and Saturday. A good place to find some worthy Lowcountry dining late at night. Did I mention that it's an entirely nonsmoking restaurant?

Easy-to-miss local favorite **Vickery's Bar and Grill,** 15 Beaufain St., 843/577-5300, sits between King and Archdale Streets, where it serves up fine Cuban/Lowcountry cuisine. The interior is Havana, circa 1959; at any moment, you'll expect Ricky Ricardo and the boys to break into "Babalu." The jerk-roasted chicken with black beans and rice is a favorite. Appropriately the martinis here are widely considered tops in town. Lots of light meals, black beans, and salads; Charlestonians like the relaxed outdoor patio seating. Open every day except Christmas and July 4, 11:30 A.M.–1 A.M.

One final spot I can't *not* mention: **82 Queen,** 82 Queen St., 843/723-7591, website: www. 82queen.com, is a wonderfully romantic spot right between King and Meeting Streets. The She Crab Soup is widely praised; the entrées include everything from crab cakes to Southern Comfort BBQ Shrimp and Grits to a mixed grill of filet mignon, lamb loin, and Carolina quail. Bring a good appetite, nicer casual clothes (no jacket required, though one certainly wouldn't look out of place), and by all means, the plastic. *Southern Living* readers recently voted this the "Best City Restaurant" in the entire South.

Continental

Long considered one of, if not *the* finest dining experience in Charleston, **Robert's of Charleston,** 183 East Bay St., 843/577-7565, closed down in the early 1990s so that owner/chef Robert Dickson could take a break. He reopened in 1998 to a very grateful public. Dickson sings as well as he cooks, and so you'll be treated to operatic selections and songs from Broadway musicals as you dine on the prix fixe; expect to pay $65 a person, not including tax and tip. You needn't worry about what to order; Robert will decide that for you. As you might guess, you'll need reservations.

Fast & French Gaulart & Maliclet French Cafe, 98 Broad St., 843/577-9797, is a very unique, very *narrow* restaurant that feels like a quick trip to the Continent. A good place for lunch.

Italian

If you've been bustling about the historic district all day and can use a little tranquillity, head on over to **Fulton Five** at 5 Fulton St., 843/853-5555. Here's one of the most intimate restaurants in town. Tucked back off King Street south of Market, Fulton Five offers very fine Northern Italian cuisine. You can dine outside if the weather's nice, or inside. Either way, the ambience is impeccable. Dinners run around $15. Reservations suggested. Open Sun.–Thurs. 5:30–10:30 P.M. and until 11 P.M. Friday and Saturday. The owners close the place sometime in mid-August when it gets too hot and open again in early September.

You'll find **Bocci's,** another slightly off-the-beaten-path Italian joint, over at 158 Church St., 843/720-2121. It serves lunch and dinner daily, but for ambience, come at night, when the soft lighting looks nice on the darkened street.

Steak and Ribs

Sticky Fingers, begun just in 1992, is constantly voted Charleston's "Best Ribs, Barbecue, and Family Dining" joint. Find it at 235 Meeting, at the Market, 843/853-7427.

The small regional chain, **TBonz Gill and Grill,** is famous for its grilled steaks. The Charleston location is 80 N. Market Street, right on the Market, 843/577-2511. Opens daily at 11 A.M. and food is served late here. Afterward, head next door to the connected Kaminsky's for a rich dessert.

Charleston Chops, 188 E. Bay St., 843/937-9300, knows how to put out a wonderful piece of meat, including 21-day aged Angus beef. Ex-

pect to pay for the high quality—toward or upward of $20 a plate. Nice candlelit ambience; piano music, chandeliers, fountains.

Barbecue (Beyond Charleston—But Worth the Travel)

For a true barbecue joint you'll need to leave the peninsula. One of the oldest (1946) and most revered greater area spots is **Bessinger's Barbecue,** 1124 Sam Rittenberg Blvd., 843/763-0339, run by Thomas Bessinger and featuring his mustard-based sauce. Hours are Mon.–Wed. 11 A.M.–7 P.M. and Thurs.–Sat. until 8 P.M. You'll find another location in West Ashley at 1602 Savannah Hwy., 843/556-1354.

You'll also find **Melvin's Barbecue,** owned by Thomas Bessinger's brother Melvin, at 538 Folly Rd., right on the way to Folly Beach, 843/762-0511.

In East Cooper you'll find another **Melvin's,** at 925 Houston Northcutt Blvd., 843/881-0549. This is probably my favorite barbecue spot in the Charleston area; it's been down here for some 50 years. Much to the surprise of everyone here, in 1999 *Playboy* Magazine voted Melvin's *hamburgers* the best in all the United States. But I'd still go for the barbecue—it's that good.

I have friends who swear by newcomer hole-in-the-wall **Momma Brown's Barbecue,** 1471 Ben Sawyer Blvd., 843/849-8802. Momma's features a North Carolina-like pepper and vinegar sauce (Melvin's excels with its South Carolina hickory mustard and hickory red sauces). They'll sell it to you by the sandwich, the plate, or the pound. Also, Momma opens at 6 A.M. and serves breakfast.

Mexican/Southwestern

Arizona's, set over at 14 Chapel St., 843/577-5090, is off the beaten path, toward the north end of the peninsula, and really too far to walk from the Market. Nonetheless, it's the city's oldest Mexican restaurant, famous for quesadillas, ribs, and other spicy meals. Features live music.

For more casual surroundings, head up King St. to **Juanita Greenberg's Burrito Palace,** 75 1/2 Wentworth St., Charleston, 843/577-2877, and another location at 439 King St., 843/723-6224, both great places to shake off the formality of Charlestonian living and the glaze of tourist life.

Pub Grub

Right down on the Market, at 36 N. Market St., 843/722-9464, you'll find one of my favorite places to catch a USC game: **Wild Wing Cafe,** which features Chernobyl Wings. They're actually quite delicious. The only downside, of course, is that years after you eat these, your kids will be sterile. But who needs grandkids when you can eat wings like these? In fact, isn't there an old saying about giving your children wings?

Tommy Condon's, on the other hand, is one of my favorite places to catch a Notre Dame game. It's an essential Charleston eating place, at 160 Market Street, 843/577-3818, owned by the pillarlike (and verifiably Irish) Condon family. This is the kind of neighborly place that Applebee's tries to make you believe you're in. Come to hear live Irish music Wed.–Sun. nights. The food, featuring local seafood, is good, but maybe the main reason to eat here is that this is, after all, *Tommy Condon's.* Tell Charlestonians you ate there and they won't have to ask, "Where's that?" Family friendly.

At 288 King St., 843/577-0123, on the way toward the College of Charleston, **Mike Calder's Pub** is one of those dark places that seems to have been around forever: a good place for cheap fish and chips, fried shrimp, wings, bangers and mash, and steaks. Not to mention beers, Bloody Marys, and other libations.

Diner Food

Mickey's used to be *Fannie's* Diner before it was sold. Call it what you will, this 1950s' throwback at 137 Market St., 843/723-7121, is important as one of the only 24-hour food joints in the downtown district. You can order breakfast all day, and, most important, there is a jukebox. Lots of seafood and sandwiches. Try the shrimp and grits ($6.45) or the Beach Boy Po'Boy ($5.95). Definitely one of the more reasonably priced spots in the Market area.

A classic locals' breakfast spot in town is **Jack's Cafe,** 41 George St., 843/723-5237, featuring top-notch waffles, grits, home fries, decent coffee, eggs, and of course, Jack himself behind the grill, as he has been since around 1973.

At the City Marina

One of the best possible ways to spend a night in Charleston is to take a dinner and dancing cruise on the **Spirit of Charleston** at the marina, 843/722-1691. Tickets run around $35 each for an excellent prime rib dinner. When you think about what you'd pay for dinner at a waterfront restaurant and cover to get into a club with dancing, this really is a great deal.

OUTLYING AREAS

West Ashley

California Dreaming, 1 Ashley Pointe Dr., 843/766-1644, has one of the best waterfront views in the whole Charleston area, right at the Ripley Light Marina. Set in a replica of an old Civil War fort on the Ashley River, this is a very good-looking branch of the small Carolinian chain; if you can forgive the name of the place (who comes to Charleston to dream about California?), you'll probably have a good time here. Pricier than it needs to be, and the portions won't require you to purge before dessert, but by and large a nice location with tasty (if all-too-precious) food. Try the babyback ribs. The various salads provide a (here's the Californian influence) healthy alternative to the good but cardiac-arresting alternatives in most of the local restaurants.

The Charleston Crab House is one of my favorite places in West Ashley to enjoy a relaxed dinner with friends. At the foot of the Wappoo Creek Bridge at 145 Wappoo Creek Dr., 843/795-1963, this is a place where you can pull the boat up to the dock, tie up, and come inside to eat. Good food—the crab's excellent and plentiful, and the shrimp's fresh and flowing.

Also on the way out to Folly Beach is **Bowen's Landing,** over on Bowen's Island at 1870 Bowen Island Rd., 843/795-2757. Actually the place, a slightly dolled-up hut of sorts, isn't all that hard to believe, since the Lowcountry is full of such hovels. What's hard to believe is that this is one of the best spots in the Lowcountry to eat authentic South Carolina seafood.

On the beach at the foot of the Folly Beach Pier is the **Starfish Grille,** 101 E. Arctic Ave., 843/588-2518, featuring indoor and outdoor seating, creatively prepared seafood, and an unbeatable view. The **Sea Shell Restaurant** is a cute place at the end of the drive into Folly—across from McKevlin's Surf Shop and the Holiday Inn.

Shem Creek

Locals normally avoid most of the restaurants at Shem Creek (on U.S. 17), feeling that the prices have been hiked up for the tourists. That said, there's some very good eating to be done out here on the creek. My favorite is the casual, creekside **Shem Creek Bar and Grill** at 508 Mill St., 843/884-8102. Local restaurant icon John Avenger and company make some mean milk shakes, as in Dreamsicle (vanilla ice cream, orange juice, amaretto) and the Oreo (vanilla ice cream, Oreo cookies, kahlua), for $5.95. But the true star here is the seafood; every day brings new specials, but you won't go wrong with the basic shrimp dinner ($12.99) or Carolina Deviled Seafood, a baked casserole with crab, clams, and shrimp, topped with Swiss cheese. All dinners are served with creek shrimp and vegetables. Good place for a cheap lunch too. At night you can have a drink down on the dockside bar. Great place for sunsets. Arrive by boat if you like. Next door you'll find **John's Oyster Bar,** 508 Mill St., 843/884-8103, also owned by Avenger, but a little less casual.

Back in 1999, **Vickery's**—they of downtown fame—opened a Shem Creek location at 1313 Shrimpboat Ln., 843/884-4440. With the double martinis seafood and Cuban theme, they've become just as popular here.

If even the Shem Creek Bar and Grill's not casual enough for you, try out **The Wreck (of the Richard and Charlene),** 106 Haddell St., 843/884-0052. This truly used to be a place that no one but a handful of locals knew about, but once everybody heard about this great undiscovered place in a rundown ice house with big portions and reasonable prices, The Wreck became, well, *discovered.* But that doesn't mean it's not still good. Deep-fried shrimp and fish are the specialties. Expect to pay $12 for dinner.

Mount Pleasant

Captain Guild's Cafe is one of the quaintest places in East Cooper, in the midst of old Mount Pleasant at 101 Pitt St., 843/884-7009. Dinner here will run you around $10, though specials can go higher. Creative menu with "New Cuisine" touches. Closed Monday.

Though it doesn't look like much from the street, **Locklear's,** 427 W. Coleman Blvd., 843/884-3346, has been a favorite seafood spot with East Cooper locals for some time now. Sample authentic Lowcountry eats at **Gullah Cuisine,** 1717 U.S. 17 N, 864/881-9076, with entrées for $8–11.95. **The Mustard Seed** is a friendly, heartfelt hole-in-the-strip mall that you might well miss if you aren't looking for it. Good vegetarian and American food with a twist, for $5–8.

You'll find the best, and best-priced, Mexican food in East Cooper at the unassuming-looking **Chili Peppers,** 426 Coleman Ave., 843/884-5779, closed Sunday. Another choice is **La Hacienda,** 1035 Johnny Dodds Blvd., which features a happy hour 4–8 P.M. How authentic is the food? Last time I visited, the restaurant was temporarily closed after a raid by Immigration.

Over at 341 Johnnie Dodds Blvd., you'll find the original **Sticky Fingers Restaurant and Bar,** 843/856-9840. Open Mon.–Thurs. 11 A.M.–10 P.M., Fri.–Sat. till 10:30 P.M., Sunday 11 A.M.–9:30 P.M. Closed Thanksgiving, Christmas Eve, and Christmas. Loud, hip, fun. You can order out as well as eat there. Memphis and Texas wet and dry ribs, as well as Carolina sweet ribs. Reservations accepted.

For a better-than-average country breakfast, try **Billy's Back Home** at 1275 Ben Sawyer Blvd., 843/881-3333.

Sullivan's Island

Gibson Café, on Middle Street, 843/883-3536, has replaced Sully's, long a favorite place to head to after a day at the beach. Used to be you'd get here late in the afternoon on a day in July and you'll find lots of sunburned, salty families catching a good meal before hitting the road home. Big wood tables, paneled walls. This place—despite having been shut down for a year a while back after a fire—has been around forever, doing simple things in the right way. The folks who reopened this place as Gibson Café have retained much of the original innocence of the place. They've kept the prices moderate too.

Station 22 has also been around for years, at 2205 Middle St., 843/883-3355, serving soft shell crabs and local grouper. Eat here and you feel as if you've come to know something vital about Sullivan's Island.

Atlanticville Restaurant and Cafe, 2063 Middle St., 843/883-9452, is set in and above what used to be a fairly unassuming produce stand here on the island. The restaurant is upstairs, complete with piano music and a deck, serving "contemporary American" cuisine. Downstairs you'll find a café with coffee and sandwiches. It's all gourmet, for people who insist on the best for themselves and don't mind paying for it.

Bert's Bar and Grill, 2209 Middle St., 843/883-4924, is everybody's favorite secret place on Sullivan's Island. It's more an enigma than a secret, really—it's a *dive,* is what it is. And we're all darned glad to have a dive out here among the pricey restaurants and multi-million-dollar homes. This is a place where if you came often enough, everybody really would know your name.

Dunleavy's Pub, 2213 Middle St., 843/883-9646, is a great place to eat fairly cheaply out on the island. The hot dogs are stellar. I believe they may serve some beer as well. A great place to watch the game.

Isle of Palms

When I lived on the Isle of Palms, our favorite place to go was **Banana Cabana,** 1130 Ocean Blvd., 843/886-4361. Even if you don't hear it playing while you're here, you'll leave singing Jimmy Buffet. The bar area itself, when you first walk in, is small and friendly, but walk on through to the enclosed porch and outside patio, where you'll find good seating and wonderful ocean views. Order the chicken nachos, the drink of your choice, and enjoy. Owned by John Avenger, of Shem Creek Bar and Grill fame.

Right upstairs from the Cabana, you'll find the pricier **One-Eyed Parrot,** 843/886-4360. Fresh seafood, Caribbean style.

The other great restaurant on IOP is **The Sea Biscuit Cafe,** 21 J. C. Long Blvd., 843/886-4079, which has great grits, great biscuits, and an exemplary collection of hot sauces. Another of those great secret places that everybody knows about; if you get here late for breakfast on the weekend, bring or buy a paper, sit down outside, and prepare for a (worthwhile) wait. Another great place for breakfast or lunch is the low-key **Hearts of Palm Cafe,** 843/886-9661, in the red-roofed pavilion facing the beach. Tables outside, and occasional live acoustic music to accompany your eggs.

Finally, I always have to blink to think that the former greasy spoon that attracted bikers and boat-livers and looked and smelled like an old boathouse over at Breach Inlet has been revitalized into a fancy restaurant called **The Boathouse at Breach Inlet,** 101 Palm Blvd., 843/886-8000. Apparently Charlestonians have become accustomed to the face of this culinary Eliza Doolittle: in 1999, *Post and Courier* readers voted the Boathouse Charleston's "Best Waterfront Dining."

Farther North

A wonderfully authentic place out on U.S. 17 N is **Seewee Restaurant,** 4808 U.S. 17 N in Awendaw, 843/928-3609. A great homey, tasty spot, set in a circa 1920s general store. Owner Mary Rancourt opened it up as a restaurant in 1993, but didn't—thank goodness—remove the red tin roof, old shelving, worn flooring, and tongue and groove paneling. Most dinners include a fish, three sides, and hush puppies. The fried fish is excellent. The roast pork loin is great as well, and if you've been saving up your fat intake, now is the time to splurge and get the country fried steak—you won't find better. Make sure one of your sides is the spicy fried green tomatoes. If you've never tried them, you won't find a better example.

The seafood is wonderfully (and simply) prepared. Each piece of fish is so fresh that its next of kin have yet to be notified. It's as casual as the house of a country uncle (a popular country uncle—it gets very crowded most nights, so you might want to head out there for a late lunch or early dinner). The lunch buffet, open 11 A.M.–3 P.M., usually runs about $5. For dessert try the pineapple cake or the peanut butter pie.

Unfortunately the front steps aren't particularly amenable to wheelchairs, and there's no ramp. But call ahead and maybe Miss Mary can work something out for you—even if it's just a carryout.

SUPERMARKETS

If I have a favorite chain supermarket in the world, **Harris Teeter** has got to be it. Set in an old warehouse on East Bay St., this is the way supermarkets should look—brick on the outside, brick on the inside. Over in East Cooper you'll find a **Publix** in Mount Pleasant, containing a first-rate seafood section.

ENTERTAINMENT AND EVENTS

The *Post and Courier Preview* is the weekly entertainment guide of note, featuring movie listings and reviews, as well as previews and reviews of Charleston area theater.

FESTIVALS

Historic Charleston Foundation's **Annual Festival of Houses and Gardens,** mid-March to mid-April, gives you the chance to visit privately owned historic sites during its festival. The monthlong program includes afternoon and evening walking tours and special programs and events. Call 843/723-1623 for reservations. Or visit the foundation at 108 Meeting Street.

The Preservation Society of Charleston, founded way back in 1920, runs the **Annual Fall Candlelight Tours of Homes and Gardens,** which are much like the Annual Festival of Houses and Gardens tours, only darker. Visit the society at 147 King St., 843/722-4630.

Spoleto Festival U.S.A.
This world-famous international arts festival—originally established in historic, aesthetically blessed Spoleto, Italy—chose Charleston when establishing its America-based festival back in 1977. For two weeks in late May and early June each year, the streets and parks of Charleston fill with experimental and traditional works by artisans from as far away as Kingston and as near as King Street. The festival's producers pack more than 100 dance, music, and theater performances into these exhilarating weeks, usually 10 or more events per day—enough to satisfy even the most Faustian traveler.

For information on the Spoleto Festival, call 864/722-2764.

Piccolo Spoleto Festival
For folks on a budget, the good news is that Piccolo Spoleto runs concurrently with Spoleto, offering local and regional talent at lower admission prices (most performances are free) and generally appealing to a broader audience than the Spoleto events proper. Call the City of Charleston Office of Cultural Affairs, 843/724-7305, for a schedule of acts and exhibits.

MOJA Arts Festival
Talk about taking a lemon and making lemonade: Charleston served as the port of entry for a majority of the slaves imported to the United States; from this grim historical fact each fall aris-

A dance band enlivens dinner cruises of Charleston Harbor.

es this joyous festival focusing on the area's rich African-American and Caribbean heritages. The festival's events are mostly free, but some require tickets. For information call the Charleston Office of Cultural Affairs, 843/724-7305.

CONCERT VENUES

The 13,000-seat **North Charleston Coliseum,** 5001 Coliseum Dr. N, 800/529-5010 or 843/529-5050, catches most of the big rock and country acts these days, as well as ice shows and various other events. Tickets to Coliseum events are available at the Coliseum Ticket Office and at all SCAT outlets. Be sure to visit the South Carolina Entertainer's Hall of Fame on the premises. It honors world-famous celebrities with a South Carolina connection, including Spring Gully's Ernest Evans (Chubby Checker). See the Hall of Fame online at www.members.tripod. com/SCME_Hall_of_Fame. Charge tickets by phone at 843/577-4500.

The **Music Farm,** 32-C Ann St., 843/853-3276 (concert line) or 843/722-8904 (business office), is legendary in the area for giving local bands a place to open for traveling college-circuit bands, and for attracting nationally known acts. **Cumberland's** and **Windjammer** over on Isle of Palms are other major places to find live acts, though they're certainly not the only ones. Check the *Post and Courier*'s *Preview* insert (or one of the free entertainment weeklies in newsstands) to find out who's playing where.

CLUBS AND BARS

Clubs

One of the best places to catch live acts in town is also the oldest: small and smoky **Cumberland's Bar & Grill,** 26 Cumberland St., 843/577-9469. Monday is open-mike night; the first Saturday of the month at 10 P.M. Cumberland's hosts the Lowcountry Blues Society Monthly Blues Jam emceed by DJ Shrimp City Slim. For information send them an email at emusic@mind spring.com.

Love the nightlife? Got to boogie? A place with a reputation as a college-age pick-up joint on the Market is **Level 2,** 36 N. Market St. (be-

tween Mesa Grill and Wild Wings), 843/577-4454, blasting everything from oldies to the latest dance mixes over the ever-present hum of come-on lines. Also rumoured to earn a significant percentage of its income from its condom dispensers is **Wet Willie's,** a neon daiquiri bar at 209 E. Bay St., 843/853-5650.

But if luck deserts and you're still unaccompanied (or hungry) when the disco balls stop spinning, stumble over to small, smoky, offbeat late-night Charleston standard **AC's Bar and Grill,** 338 King St., 843/577-6742. Or head upstairs over Clef & Clef for raw local blues at **Red, Hot and Blues,** 102 N. Market St., 843/722-0732. **Mistral Restaurant,** 99 S. Market St., 843/722-5708, features live blues on Tuesday nights and Dixieland jazz on Thursday, Friday, and Saturday.

After closing for a few weeks back in 1998, the legendary Charleston showcase **Music Farm,** 32-C Ann St., 843/853-3276 (concert line) or 843/722-8904 (business office), reopened under new owners Craig Comer and Yates Dew, who vowed not to change anything major, other than adding bluegrass, jazz, and swing to the club's repertoire, and considering weeknight shows with earlier start times, stage and sound improvements, and a high-quality menu. Ticket prices vary but range as low as $5 for over 21 and $7 for under 21. They are available at the club ticket window at 32-C Ann Street. The **Blind Tiger Pub,** 38 Broad St., 843/577-0088, draws a slightly more mature crowd attracted to its secluded ambience and beautiful deck.

Finally, a time-honored hangout for Citadel cadets is **Your Place,** 6 Market St., 843/722-8360.

Over on the Isle of Palms, **Coconut Joe's,** 1120 Ocean Blvd., 843/886-0046, is a great place to sit up top and listen to reggae on the roof with the crashing of waves in the background. At **Windjammer,** 1008 Ocean Blvd., 843/886-8596, also right on the beach, it's always spring break. Downstairs there's a fenced-in outdoor area with volleyball courts, where various professional volleyball tournaments are held. Live music here most nights—Hootie and the Blowfish have been known to try out new music here, and sometimes the club even hosts local theater.

In West Ashley, **J. B. Pivot's Beach Club,** Savannah Hwy., 843/571-3668 (just behind

Shoney's), offers a Shag Night on Tuesdays, with free beginner's shagging lessons. Thursday night is ballroom night and Saturday usually features live entertainment.

A Bit Dressy

One hates to make any claims in advance about the hipness of a place—these things change so quickly—but at press time, one of the hippest spots in Charleston was along the same brick way as Houlihan's at 39 John St. up by the visitors center. **Tango** is owner Leo Chakeris's three-story, atrium-themed club, which has been drawing the notice of the city's dress-to-impress crowd, though the dress code is technically fairly lax—no T-shirts, ball caps, or flip-flops. Women get in for free; men hoping to have access to these women must pay between $5 and $10. Open Thurs.–Sat. 9 P.M.–3 A.M.

If you're old enough to remember looking *forward* to the American Bicentennial, you're old enough to enjoy **Fannigan's,** 159 E. Bay St., 843/722-6916, a fine place to see (or participate in) shagging, or to just get out there and shake your groove thing. DJ most nights. Open Tues.–Thurs. 5 P.M.–2 A.M., Friday 5 P.M.–4 A.M., Saturday 8 P.M.–2 A.M. Minimal cover charge.

Along with Pusser's, two of the cocktail spots with the most romantic ambience in town are Clef & Clef and The Library at Vendue. **Clef & Clef,** 102 N. Market St., 843/722-0732, is a very elegant club on the market, featuring live jazz. A wonderful place to stop for late drinks or dessert. **The Library at Vendue,** 23 Vendue Range, 843/723-0485, features a rooftop bar that provides a wonderful view across Charleston Harbor.

Pubs

McGrady's Tavern, established in 1778, is the oldest tavern in Charleston. Bartender Steve is as friendly and knowledgeable a host as you're likely to meet. McGrady's is a great place to come to on a rainy or foggy day. It's a warm, friendly place, with a long history.

Mike Calder's Pub at 288 King St., 843/577-0123, is the kind of dark, friendly neighborhood place that Applebee's and Co. pretend to be. **Tommy Condon's,** 160 Market Street, 843/577-

3818, features live Irish music five days a week.

One of the hippest (and smokiest) spots to get a cocktail near the Market is **Club Habana,** 177 Meeting St., 843/853-5008, upstairs from the Tinder Box cigar shop. Photos of famous carcinogen-blowers grace the walls.

Gay and Lesbian

Gays generally feel welcome at most clubs in the Charleston area, but gay-specific spots include **Dudley's,** 346 King St., 843/723-2784, downtown (a private club, so call ahead for information); **The Arcade,** 5 Liberty St., 843/722-5656; and **Deja Vu II,** 335 Savannah Hwy., 843/556-5588.

Brewpubs

Southend Brewery and Smokehouse, 161 East Bay St., 843/853-4677, features handcrafted microbrewed beers, smoked ribs and chicken, and a third-floor cigar lounge, with billiard tables. I never pass up a chance to ride in a glass elevator, so up I went to the third floor, tracing the brass path of the steam vent of one of the brewing tanks as we rose. Up on the third floor they've got TVs tuned to sporting events and a nice view of the entire restaurant. It's really a wonderful location, and a good place to watch the game. Expect to spend $7–18 for some worthy burgers, pizza, pasta, and "brew-b-que." Southend has become so popular that today you can find sister locations up in North Carolina in Charlotte, Raleigh, and Lake Norman, as well as Jacksonville, Florida, and Atlanta, Georgia.

Sure, Charleston is chic, but can these people really be South Carolinians? This is what runs through my mind sometimes while visiting **Zebo,** 275 King St., 843/577-7600. It seems like somewhere Michael J. Fox might have partied in *Bright Lights, Big City*—hip and slick. These are pretty much the types of adjectives a lot of us seek out brewpubs to avoid, but Zebo *is* technically a brewpub, meaning that it features its own brews, including a pretty decent American Pale Ale. Good pasta and wood-fired pizza. Maybe best is the jazz/gospel brunch it has started up on Sunday.

The small regional chain, **TBonz Gill and Grill,** 80 N. Market St., right on the Market, 843/577-2511, already locally famous for its grilled steaks, has savvily started up its own TBonz Homegrown Ale to cash in on the brew boom. Food is served late here, so if Dave Letterman gives you a hankering for a rib eye, you may be in luck.

What to Do if You Find Yourself Headed for a Chain Restaurant

Yes, the Applebee's in downtown Charleston is warm and cozy. But the very sort of thing—a warm, been-there-forever sort of neighborhood bar—that Applebee's (and TGIFs and Ruby Tuesdays) attempts to re-create is the very sort of place Charleston has in abundance. So if you find yourself walking across East Bay toward Applebee's, turn around and head back to at the very least a smaller chain, TBonz or Wild Wing Cafe—or, better yet, to Tommy Condon's. You bought this book to avoid the Applebee's and the Shoney's of the world.

THEATER AND DANCE VENUES

The **Charleston Stage Company,** the state's largest theater company, offers first-rate theatrical performances at the historic Dock Street Theater, producing over 120 performances a year. For the box office, call 800/454-7093 or 843/965-4032 Mon.–Fri. 9 A.M.–5 P.M. Shows are held Thursday, Friday, and Saturday at 8 P.M., Sunday at 3 P.M.

The Have Nots! comedy improv company plays at the ACME downtown at 5 Faber St., 843/853-6687. All shows 8 P.M. Admission is $8 per adult, $6 for seniors and students.

The **Footlight Players Theatre,** 20 Queen St., 843/722-7521 (office) or 843/722-4487 (box office), has box office hours Mon.–Fri. 10 A.M.–5 P.M. or till curtain on performance days.

MOVIE THEATERS

Calling the **Charleston Imax Theatre,** 360 Concord Street, 843/725-4629, website: www. Charlestonimax.com, a "cinema" is a bit like calling Charlestonians a tad nostalgic, but it does show films, of the five-story-high, and often 3-D variety. The **American Theater Cinema Grill,** 446 King St., 843/722-3456, allows you to eat while you enjoy your choice of two first-run films. A virtual reality game center on the premises allows you to play games along with surfing the Internet or checking your email. A fine "art" theater is **The Roxy,** 245 E. Bay St., 843/853-7699. For a nice clean suburban theater, head over to Mount Pleasant and attend **Movies at Mt. Pleasant,** 963 Houston Northcutt Blvd., 843/884-4900, or the even nicer **Palmetto Grande 16** at 1319 Theatre Dr., 843/216-8696. And for one of the cleanest, finest second-run theaters you'll ever find, head up into North Charleston and get off at the Northwoods Mall; head over to the **Regal North Charleston 10,** at 2055 Eagle Landing Blvd., 843/553-0005. So reasonable, you can even afford popcorn.

COFFEE SHOPS AND CAFÉS

The **Horse and Cart Café,** 347 Kings St., 843/722-0797, is run by Ken Newman, an escaped New Yorker who is very glad to be down here. How glad? He puts his testimony on every menu, encouraging others to likewise "Follow Your Dream." What's obvious about this place is Ken's very self-conscious attempts—the board games, the shelf of used books, the low prices—to create a warm, human place where a community of regulars would naturally take root.-In other words, he wanted to create a café rather than just another place to pick up a bagel and coffee. He's succeeded wonderfully, and no doubt for a lot of folks the 113 different kinds of beers don't hurt. Menu items range from a bagel ($1.17) to a $2.54 refillable bowl of soup to sandwiches (around $4.50) and lasagna for about $6.50. Note, too, how the menus list not only the proprietor, but the chef, cook, waitresses, and bartender. Drumming on Monday at 8:30 P.M., Irish folk jam on Tuesday at 8:30 A.M., poetry readings on Wednesday, and live music Thursday–Sunday. Open 9 A.M.–2 A.M. A light brunch is served here on Sunday 10 A.M.–1 P.M. for $3.74.

Kaminsky's Most Excellent Cafe, on the Market, is constantly voted the best place to get dessert in Charleston. And if you have the money to spend and the time to wait out the usual line outside, it is. Beautiful dark wood paneling, incredibly indulgent desserts, wide selection of wine. Open seven days, afternoons till 2 A.M. If you're going to go off your diet, you may as well do it here.

Mirabel, on East Bay St., 843/853-9800, is something like a quieter version of Kaminsky's.

wired & fired: a pottery playhouse, 159 East Bay St., 843/579-0999, fax 843/579-0311, email: wiredchas@mindspring.com, is the result of a great idea that's starting to appear in various artsy towns around the United States. It's a coffee house/pottery studio, where you pay $8 an hour for studio time, $2–50 for the pottery you want to paint, $3 a piece for the paint, supplies, glazing, and firing. And yes, you have to pay for the coffee too. A perfect, unique place for a date. Of course, you'll need to leave your pottery for a couple days for the firing, so if you're only in town for a few days, try to hit this toward the beginning of your stay.

Port City Java is a small chain of coffee-houses with two Charleston locations: one at Saks 5th Avenue and one at the Francis Marion Hotel at 387 King St., 843/853-5282. In addition to the coffee made from beans roasted on the premises (good but not spectacular), Port City offers a juice and smoothie bar—a very healthy, tasty way to go. Interesting coffeehouse cuisine includes the usual baked goods, hot crab dip crostini ($6.95), wraps ($6.50), and salads ($4.25–8.95).

Old Colony Bakery, 280 King St., 843/722-2147, puts on no airs, but the scents it puts *into* the air—pastries, muffins, cookies—will yank you in off the street like a stage hook. Old Colony also bakes benne wafers, an authentic Charleston food derived from West Africa and named after the Bantu word for sesame seeds, from which the wafers are made.

Bakers Café, at 214 King St. offers a variety of coffees; **Coffee Gallery,** 169B King St., allows you to view (and, if you desire, purchase) local art while high on caffeine purchased on the premises. Finally, **The Bookstore Café,** 412 King, 843/720-8843, fax 843/853-9446, email: cater@mindspring.com, combines a bookstore and a coffeehouse, just a block north of the Francis Marion and around the corner from the Hampton Inn. An upscale, clean, well-lit place serving breakfast and lunch (try the roasted pork and fried green tomato sandwich for lunch), along with scones, croissants, and other caffeine-den favorites. Open for breakfast and lunch only, seven days a week.

Like every other American town with a stoplight, Charleston now has its share of **Starbucks.** Both downtown locations, in fact—one on King St. and one on a side street down by College of Charleston—are uniquely situated inside pre-existing buildings.

MORE PLACES TO MEET PEOPLE

Charleston is such an active city that there are plenty of ways to meet local people who share your interests. The best place to look for a comprehensive menu of what's going on is in the *Post and Courier*'s Thursday *Preview* insert, but here's a quick overview of some groups.

Special Interest Groups
Books-a-Million locations in West Ashley and Northwoods Mall hold singles nights on the second Thursday of each month 7–10 P.M. featuring discounts, giveaways, live music, and (I suspect) lots of awkward pickup lines. Call 843/556-9232 for more information.

The local **Sierra Club** gets together to explore, enjoy, and protect what's left of the world the way we found it. Meetings held on the first Thursday of every month. Call Pat Luck at 843/559-2568 for more information.

Or take the Village People's advice and give the **YMCA** a call at 843/723-6473 to hear more about their tai chi, seniors' exercise, massage therapy, hatha yoga, bridge, bingo, modern dance, and swimming programs.

Of course, one of the best ways to use your free time, and to meet people who share your values, can be to spend it helping someone else. **Charleston Habitat for Humanity** builds homes to eliminate poverty housing. If you can pound a nail or even carry water to those who do, call 843/747-9090.

Recovery Groups
Smokers Anonymous (843/762-6505) meets every Monday at Roper North at 7:30 P.M.

SPORTS, RECREATION, AND SHOPPING

ON THE WATER

Surfing

The single best, most dependable surf spot in the Charleston area, if not in the entire state, is **The Washout** at the end of East Ashley Avenue in Folly Beach. If the waves are small everywhere else, they may still be decent here. If they're good everywhere else, they'll be pounding here. Of course, if the swell's good, it's also going to be *crowded* here, and while the localism among area surfers isn't as bad as it is down in Florida or out in California, you might want to let the tube-starved locals enjoy themselves and head to another beach.

Another popular spot at Folly is **10th Street,** where you can count on smaller but often cleaner—and less-crowded—waves than you'll find up at the Washout. Beside the Holiday Inn at East Atlantic Avenue, the **Folly Beach Pier** sometimes offers cleaner waves and longer rides than the Washout, but you'll need to keep an eye out for The Law: though not always enforced, it's illegal to surf within 200 feet of the pier.

Over in East Cooper, a lot of folks like surfing at the **Sea Cabins Pier,** right at 21st and Palm Boulevard. If the wind's blowing out of the northeast, you may want to head over here, or to **Bert's** at Station 22, Sullivan's Island. Named in honor of the venerable nearby bar, this is one of the best places to surf at low tide.

McKevlin's Surf Shop's 24-hour surf report, 843/588-2261, is updated several times throughout the day. The Charleston *Post and Courier* offers its own **InfoLine Surf Report,** updated a minimum of three times a day, 843/937-6000, ext. 7873.

Founded in 1965, McKevlin's are fine surf shops in both Folly (8 Center Street) and Isle of Palms (1101-B Ocean Boulevard). Both of owner Tim McKevlin's locations sell and rent both new and used boards and body boards. They also feature the most knowledgeable and courteous counter folk in the area. **Pura Vida,** 1419 Ben Sawyer Blvd., Mount Pleasant, also rents boards.

Water-Skiing

The **Bohicket Boat Adventure and Tour Company,** 1880 Andell Bluff Blvd., 843/768-7294, offers water-skiing, knee boarding, and tubing trips along the backwater creeks of West Ashley. **Tidal Wave Runners, Ltd.** has two locations, one at the Wild Dunes Yacht Harbor on 41st Ave., Isle of Palms, 843/886-8456, the other at the Charleston City Marina, 17 Lockwood Dr., 843/853-4386, offering water-skiing trips as well as water-ski school. They also rent powerboats.

Sailing

The **Bohicket Boat Adventure and Tour Company,** 1880 Andell Bluff Blvd., 843/768-7294, offers sailing trips and rentals both inland and out on the ocean.

Personal Watercraft Riding and Parasailing

Tidal Wave Runners, Ltd. has two locations, one at 69 41st Ave. Isle of Palms, 843/886-8456, and another at the Charleston City Marina, 17 Lockwood Dr., 843/853-4386. Personal watercraft rental costs $55 an hour single, $15 per passenger; more for high performance models.

Parasailing runs $50 for a 10-minute ride at 600 feet. If you'd like to go higher, they'll take you up to 1,200 feet for 10–14 minutes for $70.

Kayaking and Canoeing

The **Bohicket Boat Adventure and Tour Company,** 1880 Andell Bluff Blvd., 843/768-7294, offers a three-hour guided kayak tour along the remote salt marsh adjoining the North Edisto River. They'll also take you by boat out among the dolphins and onto remote sea islands. Once there, you can either decide to relax on the beach, or head out for more explorations via kayak. Rates for both excursions runs about $40.

Over in East Cooper, **Coastal Expeditions,** 514-B Mill St., 943/884-7684, next to the Shem Creek Bar and Grill at the Shem Creek Maritime Center in Mount Pleasant, 843/884-7684, is the best place to rent a kayak or canoe, or to sign up for a guided tour of the Lowcountry's barrier islands, the cypress swamp, and Charleston Harbor. Since you'll be paddling a sea kayak, larger and much more stable than other kayaks, you don't need prior training for most of these trips. Half-day trips cost $45 in Shem Creek and Morgan Creek behind Isle of Palms. If you do want lessons, call to book a class or find out when one's scheduled. Full-day tours are 5–10 miles long and cost $85; one is a trip to undeveloped Capers Island, accessible only by boat. Overnight trips to Capers Island State Wildlife Refuge are also available. One unusual option is the Edisto River Treehouse Trip, where you'll get to sleep in a treehouse on a 130-acre nature preserve.

If you'd like to get over to Bull Island in the Cape Romain National Wildlife Refuge, Coastal Expeditions sends a ferry over there that you can catch. Call for rates and schedule. If you don't need no stinking tour leader, rent a single kayak for $25 half day, $35 full day. Double kayak rental: $35 half day, $50 for a full day. Store hours are Feb. 15–Oct. 31 daily 9 A.M.–6 P.M.; Nov. 1–Dec. 23 closed Mon.; Dec. 24–Feb. 14 by appointment only. **Tidal Wave Runners, Ltd.** with two locations, one at the Wild Dunes Yacht Harbor on 41st Ave., Isle of Palms, 843/886-8456, another at the Charleston City Marina, 17 Lockwood Dr., 843/853-4386, rents kayaks.

Boat Rentals
The **Bohicket Boat Adventure and Tour Company,** 1880 Andell Bluff Blvd., 843/768-7294, offers everything from little johnboats to speedboats, 15-foot Boston whalers, and 22-foot Catalina sailboats. Rental for a full-size boat runs around $100–200 a half day, $150–350 for a full day. Open year-round except for January and February. **Tidal Wave Runners, Ltd.** with two locations, at the Wild Dunes Yacht Harbor on 41st Ave., Isle of Palms, 843/886-8456, and at the Charleston City Marina, 17 Lockwood Dr., 843/853-4386, rents powerboats and leads guided personal watercraft tours.

Diving
With history comes shipwrecks; off the coast you'll find great wreck diving. If you're here in the winter, beware that rough, cold waters can make offshore diving here pretty inhospitable between October and April or May. But people dive in the historic rivers year-round; one Lowcountry favorite is the Cooper River, filled with fossilized giant shark teeth, bones, mammal teeth, as well as colonial and prehistoric artifacts. Expect water temps in the 50s.

Contact **Charleston Scuba,** 335 Savannah Hwy., 843/763-3483, website: www.charleston-scuba.com, or the **Wet Shop,** 5121 Rivers Ave., 843/744-5641.

Cruises
One of the best possible ways to spend a night in Charleston is to take a dinner and dancing cruise on the *Spirit of Charleston,* 205 King Street, 843/722-1691. Tickets run around $35 each for an excellent prime rib dinner; the night we went, the alternative plate was chicken cordon bleu, which, along with the She Crab Soup that proceeded it, was some of the best food I've ever eaten.

Over in West Ashley, the **Bohicket Boat Adventure and Tour Company,** 1880 Andell Bluff Blvd., 843/768-7294, offers dolphin watching and sunset cruises, water-skiing trips, eco tours, shelling shuttles, and tours of the ACE Basin National Wildlife Refuge. Open Mar.–Dec.

Gray Line Water Tours, 196 Concord St., 843/722-1112, behind the Customs House, offers gourmet dinner cruises, harbor tours, and private charters aboard a paddlewheeler. Dinner tours include live music.

Fishing
What if you get to South Carolina and realize you forgot to bring your yacht? Don't panic—it happens to all of us. Fortunately a number of companies specialize in getting fisherfolk out to where the deep-sea fish are biting. Most will also rent you the tackle you left back home on the yacht as well. Out in the Gulf Stream you can fish for marlin, sailfish, tuna, dolphin, and wahoo. Closer in, you can still hope to land mackerel, blackfin tuna, cobia, and shark. The **Bohicket Boat Adventure and Tour Company,** 1880 Andell Bluff Blvd., 843/768-7294, offers inshore fishing trips and offshore fishing trips on a fleet of six passenger boats, running from 25 feet to 55 feet in size. Open Mar.–Dec.

For tackle, try **Captain Ed's Fly Fishing Shop,** 47 John St., 843/723-0860, website: www.atlantic-boating.com, open Mon.–Fri. 9

A.M.–5 P.M. and Saturday 9 A.M.–1 P.M., or **Silver Dolphin Fishing,** 1311 Gilmore Rd., 843/556-3526, open 7 A.M.–5 P.M. daily.

Shrimping and Crabbing

The **Bohicket Boat Adventure and Tour Company,** 1880 Andell Bluff Blvd., 843/768-7294, offers crabbing and shrimping outings. Open Mar.–Dec.

Water Parks

Splash Island in Palmetto Island County Park in Mount Pleasant and **Splash Zone** in James Island County Park are open every weekend in the summer 10 A.M.–6 P.M. Cost is about $8 for Charleston County residents, $10 for non-county residents. These fees are in addition to the $1 park entrance fee. Call 843/795-4386 for information.

ON LAND

Hikes

Just north of Steed Creek Road in Awendaw at U.S. 17, you'll find the trailhead for the 27-mile **Swamp Fox Passage of the Palmetto Trail,** 843/336-3248, fax 843/771-0590. It connects with the **Lake Moultrie Passage** up at Moncks Corner, 843/761-8000. Bring insect repellent. Believe it or not, you could have walked through some parts of this area just after Hurricane Hugo and been the tallest thing in the forest. Today you'll find lots of pine trees, some Carolina bays, the famous insect-gulping pitcher plant, and cypress swamp. Pack a lot of water, since the primitive campgrounds along the way won't provide any. Don't do this hike in the summer, unless as some type of penance; the humidity, heat, and insects will take most of the fun out of the excursion. Bikers use this trail as well, but most of the time you should have the trail to yourself. Three primitive campsites along the way. Bring a hand trowel.

Biking

If you want to bike around downtown Charleston, check out **Mike's Bikes** at the corner of St. Philips and Wentworth, 843/723-8025. Rates run $4 hourly, $12 daily, $25 for three days, and just $35 for an entire week.

Of course, no one says you have to keep your rental bike confined to downtown. One of the joys of Carolina beaches is that the flat landscape allows the ocean to creep up quite a ways along the beach, leaving a cement-hard, flat surface behind, perfect for long bike rides on the beach. It's possible to park on Isle of Palms at the county park and ride all the way to the north end of the island, giving you a look at the Wild Dunes boardwalk and Rainbow Row. Or you can head south, take the bridge across Breach Inlet to Sullivan's Island, and check out some of unique houses there. Stop at Dunleavy's or Sullivan's for lunch, and turn back.

You can also mountain bike the 27-mile **Swamp Fox Trail.**

Golf

The South Carolina coast played home to the first golf course in America—that's no surprise. Way back in 1786, when the manufacture of white polyester was only a pipe dream, Charlestonians created Harleston Green and organized the South Carolina Golf Club—also the nation's first. Through the years, Charlestonians have continued to golf with style. In 1998 *Links* magazine named Kiawah Island Resort and Wild Dunes as two of the top 100 golf resorts in North America.

The first thing a duffer will want to do is stop in at the Charleston Visitors Center and pick up a *Charleston Area Golf Guide,* an annual publication by **Charleston Golf, Inc.,** a nonprofit organization dedicated to promoting the Charleston area as a golf destination. Call these people at 800/774-4444 (get it?), and they'll help you arrange your golfing on your next visit. This will give you a listing and ranking of every course in the area.

Charleston boasts courses by Pete Dye, Tom Fazio, Arthur Hills, Jack Nicklaus, Rees Jones, and Robert Trent Jones, Sr., among others. Dye's **The Ocean Course** at Kiawah Island has been ranked by *Golf* magazine as one of the top 100 courses in America, and *Golf Digest* has dubbed it "America's Toughest Resort Course," as well as one of its "100 Greatest Courses." Taking up more than two miles of oceanfront beach dunes, this is one of the most beautiful courses in the world. Local hotels offering golf packages include Charleston Harbor Hilton Resort, Dunes Properties, Francis Marion Hotel, Hampton Inn,

Holiday Inn: Riverview, Island Realty, Kiawah Island Resort, the Mills House, Kiawah Island Villa Rentals, Seabrook Island Resort, Wild Dunes Resort. See accommodations listings for address and phone numbers.

Tennis

If you're looking for tennis lessons, try the **Charleston Tennis Center,** 19 Farmfield Rd., 843/724-7402; **Wild Dunes Resort,** 800/845-8880 or 843/886-2113; or **Kiawah Island Resort,** 800/845-2471 or 843/768-2121, which offers tennis clinics for adults and kids in two tennis complexes with 23 clay courts, three hard courts in all.

More Recreation

You can shoot pool at Southend Brewery, or head over to **Salty Mike's** at the Marina, where you can challenge any Citadel candidates who come in.

Sand Dollar Mini Golf, 1405 Ben Sawyer Blvd., Mount Pleasant, 843/884-0320, seems to have been there on the way to Sullivan's Island forever. This is humble compared to Myrtle Beach's towers of stucco, but with its lighthouse and Willie the Whale, and especially with the souvenir shop, Carolina Gifts and Sea Shells, on premises, this is one of those quaint, time-past spots that will give you an idea of what the area was like before the world discovered the Lowcountry.

In 1998 a **bowling** alley, **Twin River Lanes,** opened up at 613 Johnnie Dodds Boulevard, Mount Pleasant, 843/884-7735.

PROFESSIONAL SPORTS

Baseball

Charleston has long hosted some estimable minor league ball teams, dating back to the Southern League's Charleston Seagulls, who first took the field back in 1886. Later, major league brothers Sandy Alomar, Jr. and Roberto Alomar played minor league ball in Charleston before making the bigs, as did Carlos Baerga, Kevin Seitzer, Willie Randolph, Pascual Perez, Danny Jackson, David Cone, and John Candelaria. Nowadays the Riverdogs are affiliated with the Tampa Bay Devil Rays.

But they haven't been called the Riverdogs for all that long. In the late 1980s and early '90s, the team played as the Charleston Rainbows, a name that not only featured some pretty goofy-looking logos but also made it rather hard to cheer with conviction as the team battled tough-sounding squads like the Hickory Crawdads or Capital City Bombers. It just never felt right, bolting you your feet in a tense late inning, raising a beer, and yelling, "Go *Rainbows!*"

Today the mercifully renamed **Riverdogs** play Class A ball at the 1997 Joseph P. Riley Park, named for the city's innovative and generally beloved mayor.

If you want to see a game at this fine, old-timey-styled stadium, designed by the same folks who created Baltimore's famed Camden Yards, call 843/577-3647, check online at www.riverdogs.com, or head down to "the Joe," 360 Fishburne Street, and buy tickets in person. They run $4–8. The great thing about parks this small is that there really aren't any bad seats; 10 or so rows may be the only difference between high-end and low-end tickets. The highest-priced seats feature wait service, which could be helpful if you're physically disabled. Most games start at 7:05 P.M.

If you can't make the game, Jim Lucas and Don Wardlow provide the play-by-play on WQNT 1450-AM. Color-commentator Wardlow is blind. He and Lucas have worked as a team since they were college students in 1983. After years of honing their craft, they sent out demo tapes to over a hundred minor league baseball owners aross the country. Fortunately one of the tapes made it into the hands of owner Mike Veeck, son of famed baseball showman Bill Veeck—most known for such publicity stunts as fielding a dwarf, Eddie Gaedel, to pinch hit; breaking the American League color line with (South Carolinian) outfielder Larry Doby, bringing 50-year-old Satchel Paige to the majors, and holding the disastrous Disco Demolition Night in 1979. Wardlow, born without eyes, became the first blind sports announcer in history when he and Lucas called a game for a Florida team Veeck owned. They've been professional announcers ever since. The two were working for a team in Minnesota when, in 1999, Veeck's 8-year-old daughter was diagnosed with retinitis pigmentosa. He decided to move the family to Charleston and—

partly out of desire to have his daughter close to the inspirational Wardlow—asked Lucas and Wardlow if they'd consider moving their families there and taking over duties for the Riverdogs. They did and they have, and Charleston is the richer for it.

Hockey

The **South Carolina Stingrays,** 3107 Firestone Rd., 843/744-2248, play Oct.–May in the North Charleston Coliseum as members of the East Coast Ice Hockey League. They won the 1996–1997 Kelly Cup and have posted winning records every season since their inception in the mid-1990s. They also average over 7,500 fans a game. If you haven't ever caught a live hockey game, give it a try. A fun time, even if you haven't watched a hockey game since the 1980 Winter Olympics. You'll find Stingrays games on the radio at 98.9 FM.

Soccer

The **Charleston Battery,** who play at Daniel Island stadium over on Daniel Island (right off I-526), 843/740-7787, do battle April–September in the U.S. International Soccer League.

SHOPPING

King Street is the single best shopping street, especially if you include the back entrance to the Shops at Charleston Place, which opens out onto the street. The shops down here include most tourist town standards—the Audubon Shop, Banana Republic, Liz Claiborne, Victoria's Secret, the Gap, and so forth—but they also include some unique locally owned shops much worth visiting.

To sample or take home some local music, visit **Millennium Music,** 269 King St., 843/853-1999, a very worthwhile, locally owned (franchise) music store featuring lots of listening stations, at least one of which always contains releases by local artists. Also a good place to find out who's playing where while you're in town.

Chili Chompers is a fun little shop at 333 King St., 888/853-4144, fax 843/853-4146, within easy walking distance of the visitors center. What's for sale? Basically anything that will singe your palate. Owner Chesta Tiedemann's exten-

sive hot sauce collection covers an entire set of shelves and includes at least two brands that require customers to sign a written waiver before purchasing a bottle. Here too you'll find the spicy Blenheim Ginger Ale and Ginger Beer (nonalcoholic).

Artists' Galleries

Showcasing the work of more than 50 local craftspersons, **Charleston Crafts,** 38 Queen St., 843/723-2938, is a fun place to browse for baskets, clay, glasswork, jewelry, paper, photos, wood, and more. Open Mon.–Sat. 10 A.M.–5 P.M., Sunday 1–5 P.M. Inside Charleston Place you'll find **Rhett Gallery,** 843/722-1144, featuring the watercolors of Nancy Ricker Rhett, along with a wide collection of antique prints. **Gallery Chuma/African American Art Gallery,** 43 John St., 843/722-7568, website: Chuman@gallery Chuma.com, features—you guessed it—works created by African-American artists. Occupying both floors of a historic building, covering a total of some 2,900 square feet, Chuma claims to be the largest African-American gallery in the South. Gullah artist Jonathan Green's works are a permanent fixture, as are those of several other renowned artists. Open Mon.–Sat. 10 A.M.–6 P.M. or by appointment. **Gullah Tours** of Charleston leave from the gallery daily. Call for information. Finally, with all the great birding in the area, it's only proper that you'll find **The Audubon Shop and Gallery** over on 245 King St., 800/453-2473 or 843/723-6171, offering exhibits of wildlife art by regional artists, and featuring the work of Vernon Washington, as well as prints by Old Man Audubon—no stranger to Charleston—himself. You'll also find handcrafted birdhouses and feeders, binoculars and telescopes, and old decoys for sale here.

Farmers' Market

Charleston's Farmers' Market is held every Saturday at the Maritime Center on Concord Street, down by the South Carolina Aquarium, April 18–October 31.

Antiques

Charleston is so old that people throw away as "too modern" items that would be antiques anywhere else in the country. Between 152 King St. (152 A.D. Antiques) and 311 King St. (Wilson

& Gates Antiques), you'll find no less than 33 antique shops, specializing in everything from venerable old rugs to rare maps.

For cheaper prices, folks head out to the suburbs to **Page's Thieves Market,** 1460 Ben Sawyer, Mount Pleasant, 843/884-9672, or the **Hungryneck Antique Mall** at 401 Johnnie Dodds in Mount Pleasant, 843/849-1733.

Great Bookstores

For new books, try **Chapter Two** 249 Meeting St., in downtown Charleston, 843/722-4238. It's a good place to pick up a copy of *Sandlapper,* the best magazine available on South Carolina.

For used books, **Atlantic Books'** two locations—310 King St., 843/723-4751, and 191 East Bay St., 843/723-7654—are the best places in town. If, however, all you want is a paperback for beach reading, you might be interested in **Trade-a-Book,** 1303 Ben Sawyer Blvd., 843/884-8611.

Pawn Shops

If you drive into Charleston from Columbia on I-26, at U.S. 17A in Summerville, you'll pass the garish **Money Man Pawn** on your left, 843/851-7296. But this is only one in a chain; you'll find another in Mount Pleasant, at 1104 Johnnie Dodds Blvd., 843/971-0000.

TRANSPORTATION AND INFORMATION

GETTING THERE

By Air

Continental Airlines flies into Charleston International Airport. Delta Airlines' **US Airways** has a city ticket office at 135 King St., 800/428-4322, 800/221-1212, or 843/577-0755. Open Mon.–Fri. 9 A.M.–5 P.M., closed daily for lunch 1:30–2:30 P.M.

GETTING AROUND

One Word of Advice: Walk

My motto for enjoying downtown Charleston is to PASAP: Park As Soon As Possible. Rain or no rain, you don't want to drive around downtown Charleston any longer than you have to, especially if you're a first-time visitor. Charleston was designed to be walked, not driven.

The city has a number of public and private parking lots. Most are reasonably priced. A good place to stop on your way downtown is the **Charleston Visitors Center** at 375 Meeting St., right across from the Charleston Museum. Here, ask the person at the information window for a *Visitors' Guide Map,* which labels quite clearly the places where you can legally park your car. If you want to play it really safe, just leave your car there at the center and take one of the tourist trolleys farther down the peninsula.

DASH

The Downtown Area Shuttle (DASH) is just one segment of the City of Charleston's public transportation system. DASH buses look like trolleys, and they're really pretty nice ways to get from one end of the peninsula to another. Fare is 75 cents, exact change required. A one-day DASH pass costs $2, and the perfect-for-a-weekend-visit three-day pass costs $5. Purchase passes and DASH schedules at the Visitor Reception and Transportation Center and all city-owned downtown parking garages. Seniors and riders with disabilities pay just 25 cents during the week 9 A.M.–3:30 P.M., after 6 P.M., and all day Saturday and Sunday. DASH does not operate on New Year's Day, July 4, Labor Day, Thanksgiving Day, or Christmas Day. You'll notice DASH shelters, benches, and trolley stop signs located throughout the city. These are the only places you'll be able to get on or off a trolley—DASH drivers aren't allowed to make any special stops.

After you pay your fare and climb on board, don't sit in the seats directly behind the driver unless you are a senior or a passenger with a physical disability. For more information, call 843/724-7420.

You'll also find DASH stops at the Folly Island, North Charleston, and Mt. Pleasant/Isle of Palms visitors centers.

Another way to get around is by rickshaw: the **Charleston Rickshaw Company,** 843/723-5685, provides human-powered service

Mon.–Thurs. 6 P.M.–midnight, Fri.–Sat. 6 P.M.–2 A.M., and Sunday 5–11 P.M. The cost is $3 per 10 minutes per person, or $32 per hour per bike. A great, cheap way to see downtown without having to hunt for parking. Call ahead for reservations if you'd like.

By Boat
The **Harbor Intra-Transit System,** 843/209-2469 (843/209-AHOY), offers an intriguing alternative to land travel. For $8–12 round-trip, you can take a boat from any dock to any dock. It's cheaper, generally faster, and, depending on how much drinking you're doing, safer than driving yourself.

ORGANIZED TOURS

Walking Tours
Charleston Strolls, 843/766-2080, website: www.ccharlie.com, and **Civil War Walking Tours,** 17 Archdale St., 843/722-7033, website: civilwartours.com, both offer organized walking tours, for about $15 a person. The folks from *The History Channel* got a kick out of the **The Pirates of Charleston** tour from the folks at **Tour Charleston,** 800/854-1670, website: www.tour charleston.com; tours focused on Charleston's parrot-endowed visitors from days of olde leave twice a day (10 A.M. and 4 P.M.) from the waterfront at the end of Vendue Range. Tickets run $14 for adults, $8 for 12 and under.

Carriage Tours
One fun way to learn the history of the historic buildings of Old Charleston without having to walk around, nose-in-book, is to take one of the city's many carriage tours. And here's a tip: the folks who run these tours love to know they have customers lined up in advance, so all the ones mentioned here will give you a lower price for reserving spots ahead of time; prices range $15–20 per adult. **Palmetto Carriage,** 40 N. Market St., 843/723-8145, offers one-hour tours daily from 9 A.M. Kids will appreciate the small petting zoo at the Red Barn.

Charleston Carriage Company, 14 Hayne St., 843/577-0042 or 843/723-8687, has been at this longer than anyone, and offers hour-long tours by well-trained guides.

Finally, offering similar services and more unnecessary e's than any other company in town is **Olde Towne Carriage Company,** over on Anson St., 843/722-1315. **Old South Carriage Tours** is nearby at 14 Anson St., 843/723-9712.

Minibus Tours
For all the romance of the horse-drawn carriage, there are days in Charleston when you feel the town is best seen from the inside of an air-conditioned vehicle. **Talk of the Towne,** 843/795-8199, boasts of being able to take you past 250 historic buildings in just two hours. And that's not including all the nonhistoric buildings thrown in as gimmes. All tours leave from the Visitors Center. The tour

U.S. Custom House, Charleston

company offers complimentary pickup at downtown hotels, inns, and the Market. The two-hour tour includes a visit to either the 1808 Nathaniel Russell House or the 1828 Edmondston-Alston House. Fares run $21 adults, $14 for children. Fares for the shorter, 75-minute tour run $13 for adults, $8 for children 12 and under.

Harbor Tours

For a memorable tour of Charleston Harbor, contact **Gray Line Water Tours,** 17 Lockwood Dr. S, 800/344-4483 or 843/722-1112. The daytime 90-minute 20-mile Charleston Harbor Tour departs from the City Marina at 2 P.M. daily year-round, plus additional cruises at 9:45 A.M. and 3:45 P.M. March–November. Fares are $8 adult, children 6–11 $4. For another few bucks you can have a meal while you motor past Fort Sumter and the houses on the Battery. The two-and-a-quarter hour, 30-mile Charleston Harbor of History and Cooper River Tour departs from the marina at 11:30 daily year-round. Cost is $10 adults, $5 children 6–11. Lunch onboard for just a few dollars more. Or take the Harborlites Dinner Cruise. You'll cruise 7:30–9:45 P.M., eat a fine dinner while you go, and then dance it off to live music afterward. If you're here in the summer, you'll still be able to sightsee around the peninsula as you go. Adults $25, children 6–11 $18, 5 and under $14. Reservations required.

INFORMATION AND SERVICES

Tourist Offices and Visitors Centers

The **Charleston Visitors Center,** 375 Meeting St., 843/723-5225, is a great place to stop in and get some background and a bagful of brochures and coupon books. Or check the **Charleston Area Convention and Visitors Bureau,** 81 Mary St., 800/868-8118 or 843/853-8000, fax 843/853-0444, website: www.charlestoncvb.com. For golf tee times and info, call 800/744-4444.

Kiawah Island visitors will want to call the **Kiawah Island Visitor Center,** 22 Beachwalker Dr., Kiawah Island.

You'll find **Mt. Pleasant/Isle of Palms Visitor Center** at U.S. 17 N, at McGrath Darby Boulevard in Mount Pleasant.

Hospitals, Police, Emergencies

The top hospital in the region is the **Medical University of South Carolina Hospital** on the peninsula, 843/792-2300, but you should be in good hands at **Roper Hospital,** 843/724-2000, or **Charleston Memorial Hospital,** 843/577-0600. In North Charleston, call **Trident Regional Medical Center,** 843/797-7000. In East Cooper, call 843/881-0100, and in West Ashley, call **Bon Secours St. Francis Xavier,** 843/402-1000.

In an emergency, reach the police, fire department, and ambulances by dialing 911. The **Poison Control Center 24-Hr. Help Line** is 800/922-1117.

To reach the police for a nonemergency, call the **Office of Tourism Services** at 843/720-3892.

Child Care

The Charleston Nanny, 1045-F Provincial Circle, Mount Pleasant, 843/856-9008 or 843/813-6717, email: tmorris.413@aol.com, offers professionally trained, CPR-certified, insured and bonded babysitters who will watch the kids while you enjoy a day or night on the town.

Post Office

You'll find the main post office downtown at 83 Broad St., 843/577-0690, and another at 557 E. Bay St., 843/722-3624.

Public Libraries

The **Charleston Public Library**'s main branch does business at 68 Calhoun St., 843/805-6802. You'll find the **Edgar Allan Poe Library,** 1921 I'On St., Sullivan's Island, 843/883-3914—the coolest little branch library in the state—on Middle Street on Sullivan's Island, built into an old defense bunker.

Newspapers

Post and Courier is the paper of record in Charleston, as it has been for many years. Every Thursday it includes an insert called the *Preview,* which provides pretty much all the current movie, play, and music listings you could need.

The Upwith Herald is a freebie you'll find around downtown, providing pretty much the same information as the *Preview,* as does *Charleston Free Times.*

The Charleston Weekly actually comes out only two times a month, runs two pages long, and features listings only—no articles or full reviews in this other freebie.

Radio Stations

96 WAVE is the big "alternative" station here; you'll see its bumper stickers stuck to everything that's not tied down around here, including traffic signs. A good place to hear local rock. **WBBA—"THE BIG BUBBA,"** is one of the better country stations in the state, featuring some very corny jingles. **WSCI FM 89.3** is the local NPR affiliate. Saturday at 9 P.M. listen for "Vintage Country," with Roger Bellow. If it's talk you want, listen to **WTMA 1250 AM** in the mornings for Dan Moon, a local celebrity and a Charleston institution, to get a sense of the workings of the city, as he broadcasts live from store openings, flea markets, and just about any event with room for a mobile unit. Libertarian Scott Caysen hosts a local call-in talk show 3–5 P.M. that occasionally touches on local issues. Midday is filled with the normal syndicated talk shows.

BEYOND CHARLESTON

NORTHWEST ON I-26

Summerville

Summerville's quiet, old-resort-like feel, with its meandering azalea- and pine-shaded streets, is no accident: this burg of 22,000 used to be a place where Lowcountry planters and Charleston residents would hide from the summer fevers. Apparently the distance from the coast and the "high" elevation (75 feet) kept down the mosquitoes.

Summerville is home to author Effie Wilder, whose manuscript was discovered in the slush piles of Peachtree Press. This long-time resident of Presbyterian Home of Summerville became a first-time novelist at age 85 in 1995 with *Out to Pasture: But Not Over the Hill,* and tossed out two other novels (*Over What Hill: Notes from the Pasture,* and *Older But Wilder: More Notes from the Pasture—My Final Short Novel)* before she was 89. She's retired again. For now.

One good place to stay here is the **Bed & Breakfast of Summerville,** 304 S. Hampton St., 843/871-5275, set in a one-room cottage in a garden behind the 1865 **Blake Washington House,** on S. Hampton Street. Emmagene and Dusty Rhodes's place features a pool, grill, bicycles for touring the town, and a greenhouse. This place is privacy incarnate. Infants okay, pets are not. Around $50 without breakfast, $60 with. Reservations a must.

While in town, you may want to visit the **Summerville Dorchester Museum,** 100 E. Doty Ave., 843/875-9666, which features exhibits on Dorchester County and Summerville history, with an emphasis on medical, natural, and plantation history. Open Wed.–Fri. 10 A.M.–2 P.M. and Saturday 2–5 P.M. Admission. And just a couple blocks from the downtown district, you'll find the **Azalea Park and Bird Sanctuary.**

At **Old Dorchester State Historic Site,** on S.C. 642 (Dorchester Rd.) about a quarter mile north of Old Trolley Road Road and six miles south of Summerville, 843/873-1740, you'll find the spot where, in 1697, Massachusetts Congregationalists founded a bluff-top town overlooking the Ashley River. Most of them moved on to the town of Midway, Georgia, by the 1750s, but the British soldiers retreating after their evacuation of Charles Town took out their wrath on what remained of Dorchester in the 1780s. Today you'll still find the bell tower of St. George's Church and the tabby walls of the old town fort. Open Thurs.–Mon. 9 A.M.–6 P.M. with free tours on the weekends at 2 P.M. On-site archaeological excavation every Thursday and the first and third Saturdays of the month.

SOUTHWEST ON U.S. 17

Charleston Tea Plantation

On Wadmalaw Island at 6617 Maybank Highway, 800/443-5987 or 843/559-0383, fax 843/559-3049, this is the only tea plantation in America, home to American Classic Tea. Here you can learn about the process of tea making. Generally the plantation is open to visitors only on the first Saturday of the month May–October

10 A.M.–1:30 P.M. Free walking tours begin on the half hour starting at 10 A.M. with the last tour at 1:30 P.M. At present the plantation offers group tours on weekdays by appointment. So if you have a minimum of 19 friends who would like to join you for a tour, for $5 a person you can get a one-hour tour in which you learn about the world of tea production and take a short walk to see the tea fields and the plantation's unique tea harvester in action—something not seen by the folks who show up for the Saturday open houses. You can stock up on tea bargains or special gift baskets not available in stores. And of course, lots of tea sampling, along with Charleston benne wafers and the plantation's unusual line of tea jellies.

Call for information. Fully accessible.

Kiawah Island

This 10,000-acre island, 800/992-9666, features some 10 miles of beautiful beach (though only the area at Beachwalker County Park is accessible to those not staying in one of the island's resort villages).

The island features four championship golf courses and is also popular with the tennis crowd. Ice skaters like it, too, apparently: not long after the 1998 Winter Games, Olympic gold medalist Tara Lipinsky and her family announced that they were buying a house here on the island.

Seabrook

Seabrook, 1001 Landfall Way, 843/768-0880, is located 23 miles south of Charleston off U.S. 17. It's all villas and a beach club with swimming pools, restaurants, lounges, tennis courts, two golf courses, an equestrian center, trails, fishing gear, sailboats, and bicycles.

EDISTO ISLAND

In 1861, as South Carolina's statesmen gathered in Charleston to debate whether to secede from the Union immediately or wait for other Southern states to come along, the delegate from Edisto Island leapt to his feet and shouted that if South Carolina didn't vote to secede from the Union immediately, then by God, Edisto Island would secede by itself.

NO CATS WERE HARMED IN THE MAKING

Many of the first buildings made in Carolina by European settlers were "tabby," made from a mixture of lime, and two things the Carolinians had in abundance: sand and oyster shells.

This gives you a little insight into the independent, the-hell-with-y'all feel of this little Sea Island. Coming out here for a vacation stay is a little bit like seceding from the rest of the world.

Archaeologists have found numerous sites used by Edisto Indians in the centuries before the Europeans arrived. In 1674 the British bought the island from the tribe for a few tools, cloth, and some really neat trinkets. Indigo and Sea Island cotton plantations covered the island for quite a while, but after the boll weevil plague in 1920, the land was reduced to mostly small farming and, near the water, tourism.

The island could call itself "The Last Unresort." It remains largely resortless, and most of the locals seem committed to keeping it that way. The Edisto Island Historical Preservation Society opened up the Edisto Island Museum (see below) in 1991 to combat encroachment.

Edisto is a great spot to rent a beach house or camp and just relax. The waves can be pretty decent; the handful of restaurants are perfectly decent and sometimes quite good, and the people are friendly.

Sights

On your way into town, keep a sharp eye out on your right for the **Edisto Island Museum,** S.C. 174, Edisto Island, 843/869-1954. They've done a wonderful job there with a small building, presenting a number of exhibits interpreting the unique ingredients of Sea Island life. A few books and old posters here for sale, and very helpful workers. Admission is $2 for adults, free for kids under 10.

The oldest home still standing on the island was built around 1735, but most seem to have been built in the 1950s, '60s, and '70s, before land prices raced upwards. The **Zion Baptist Church,** which you pass on your left as you enter Edisto Beach, was founded in 1810 by Hepzibah Jenkins, a strong-willed woman raised by her family's slaves after her mother died and her father was imprisoned during the American Revolution. So grateful was she to these people that she built this church for them in 1810.

Edisto Island State Park

Edisto State Park, S.C. 174, 843/538-8206, may just be the best shelling beach in South Carolina. My wife and I once scored about a dozen conch (here pronounced "conk") shells in a 20-minute walk. However, the no-see-ums are equally legendary here: bring Skin-So-Soft and Deep Woods OFF! and you should be okay. Better yet, pick up one of those screened-in tents to put around the picnic table. Of course, if you're at one of the sites that faces the ocean and not the marshes, you'll be better off. But these are usually reserved in advance, so call ahead.

The number of shells in the sand at Edisto is incredible. But look a little closer and you might

camping on Edisto Island

realize that some of them are actually fossils; their presence in this area is attributed by some to the theory that this area was once under the Atlantic Ocean. Back then, Upcountry rivers and streams poured directly into the ocean, depositing the shark teeth, horse, and mastodon bones found here today.

Events

Every July the **Edisto Summer Fest** celebrates the warm weather with a raft race, shag contest, street dance, music concert, boat poker run, and lots of food. Call 843/869-3867 for information.

On the second Saturday in October, the Edisto Island Historical Preservation Society's **Tour of Historic Plantation Houses, Churches, and Sites** is held. Call 843/869-1954 for tour information.

When the weather gets colder in November, folks all gather for the **Edisto Oyster Roast,** a one-day festival featuring live entertainment, games, and the namesake shellfish, along with other seafood. Call 843/869-3867 for information.

Accommodations

If you're not camping, see if you can't reserve one of the five air-conditioned cabins at Edisto Beach State Park. Generally you'll need to get one months and months in advance, but you might get lucky. Call 843/869-2156 or 843/869-2756. $61 a night. During the summer, they rent by the week only. Otherwise, the traditional place to stay on Edisto Island (practically the only way, given the determined lack of hotels and motels) is one of the hundreds of beach houses lining the shore.

A number of rental companies service the island. Here are a few: **The Lyons Company,** 440 S.C. 174, 800/945-9667 or 843/869-2516; **Edisto Sales and Rentals Realty,** 1405 Palmetto Blvd., 800/868-5398; or **Fairfield Ocean Ridge,** 1 King Cotton Rd., 800/845-8500 or 843/869-2561.

One warning: Rent a house too far south on the island and the water nearest your house will contain inlet currents that make it unsafe to enter. This means you'll need to hop in the car every time you want to go swimming—not everyone's idea of a relaxed week at the beach.

The reason I say "practically the only way" is because Edisto Island features the two-unit **Seaside Plantation,** 400 S.C. 174, 843/869-0971. $85–95 a night.

Food

After a long while dormant, the **Old Edisto Post Office,** 843/869-2339, reopened out on S.C. 174 a couple years back, much to the delight of residents and annual visitors, many of whom had made a dinner at the "New Lowcountry" restaurant a tradition. The fish, grits, and sausages, are what people talk about here. And the soup's not bad either. Out on the water, **Pavillion** restaurant at the corner of S.C. 174 and Palmetto Drive is said to be a decent place to catch a meal, especially if you order the all-you-can-eat shrimp. On the other side of the island, facing the marshes, you'll find **Dockside Restaurant,** 3730 Duck Site Rd., 843/869-2695, featuring fresh shrimp, hush puppies, crab, shrimp, and shrimp. Moderately priced.

There's a gas station across from the Pavillion. Inside you'll find a sandwich counter. The sandwiches are good deli food. If you're looking to cut corners, this is a good place to do it.

Shops and Rentals

Right at the point where S.C. 174 bends at the BP station and becomes Palmetto Boulevard, you'll find **Island Rentals,** 101 Palmetto Blvd., 843/869-1321, renting four-wheel bikes, Island Cruisers, Waverunners, SeaDoos, 17-foot rental boats, and all the umbrellas, beach chairs, crab traps, fishing rods, rafts, tubes, strollers, and pull carts you'll ever need for a good time on the beach. You can rent by the hour, by the half day, full day, three days, and by the week. Reserve ahead if you can. The young entrepreneur owner, Tony Spainhour, says he'll deliver too.

You'll come across Karen Carter's **The Edisto Bookstore** at 547 S.C. 174, 843/869-1885 or 843/869-2598, on the right on your way into town. Karen's a friendly, helpful person who keeps her shelves well-stocked with both new and used books.

Information

For more information on this unique little island, contact the **Edisto Chamber of Commerce** at P.O. Box 206, Edisto Beach, SC 29438, 843/869-3867.

BEAUFORT AND THE LOWCOUNTRY

To understand the just-growed feeling of the South Carolina Lowcountry today, consider what the area was like just a couple of decades ago. Residents of the Sea Islands used to have an arduous time traveling around from island to island, much less from island to mainland. To

LOWCOUNTRY HIGHLIGHTS

- **Beaufort Historic District**
- **Edisto River Canoe and Kayak Trail**
- **Gullah House Restaurant** (St. Helena Island)
- **Harbour Town** (Hilton Head Island)
- **Hunting Island State Park**
- **Laurel Hill Wildlife Drive** (Savannah National Wildlife Refuge)
- **Pinckney Island National Wildlife Refuge**
- **Sheldon Church ruins** (Sheldon)
- **Shrimp Shack** (St. Helena Island)
- **South Carolina's Artisan's Center** (Walterboro)

get from Beaufort to Savannah, a 45-minute trip today, used to require a drive from Beaufort to Sheldon, Sheldon to Ridgeland, Ridgeland to Garden City, Georgia, and then on to Savannah, which took up the good part of a day. Add this to the fact that not many Sea Islanders owned a car in the first place, and it's no wonder that many people in Beaufort never set foot in Savannah, and vice versa. People living on the smaller islands traveled even less, and some part of nearly any trip they *did* take was sure to involve a boat. In the late 1960s when Pat Conroy taught there, Daufuskie Island was so isolated from the mainland that the Gullah children Conroy took across on Halloween to trick or treat in Port Royal came away believing that on the mainland, all one had to do to get candy was knock on a door.

Today, in the world of satellite television, car phones and pagers, you'd be hard-pressed to find anyone that innocent down here. But while the modern world of air-conditioning and cappuccino has found the Sea Islands, their

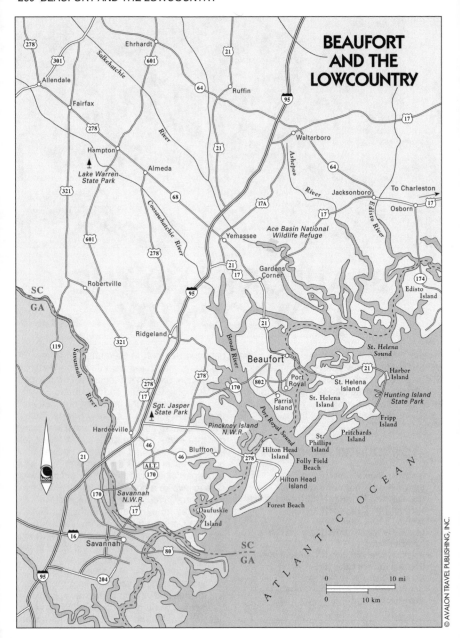

BEAUFORT
AND THE
LOWCOUNTRY

© AVALON TRAVEL PUBLISHING, INC.

character is imbedded enough that it will never wash away entirely—at least not until the last shrimp boat has been beaten into a golf cart.

Despite the bridges that connect most of the islands now, the Lowcountry is still a land where, what with all the shrimping, crabbing, and fishing to be done, boats are considered essential equipment. As Jackie Washington of the little village of Broad River puts it, "If you don't own a boat around here, you're living half a life."

BEAUFORT AND VICINITY

A scene in *The Big Chill* captures Beaufort beautifully: Kevin Kline and William Hurt jog-walk down Bay Street in the early morning fog, long-time friends reunited after years, middle-aged men in T-shirts drenched with the humidity and with their efforts to remain potent into old age. Old business blocks lean over the men's shoulders like kindly merchants of a 1950s childhood. Dawn gleams from the dewy asphalt of the narrow street. The scene's visuals perfectly illustrate the film's thematic issues: the post-war generation's search for renewed hope and vital community.

And it is these things that seem to draw baby boomers to Beaufort, even today.

Beaufort is a quiet, romantic poem of a town, a town best absorbed, rather than "done." It's a historic town—second oldest in the state, founded in 1710, only 20 years after Charles Town. And because it sits far from the heavily trafficked path beaten flat by the 20th century, Beaufort remains a town where many of the differences between 1840 and the present seem trivial somehow, and the visitor immediately feels either desperately out of place or home at last.

Orientation
You'll probably want to stop in the visitor information center at 1006 Bay St., 843/524-3163, for tour maps, information on lodging and dining, and plenty of brochures. But here's a general overview of the town.

Some 65 islands make up Beaufort County. Named after one of Carolina's lords proprietors, Henry, Duke of Beaufort, the town of Beaufort (pronounced "BYOO-fort") is the county seat, its 12,000 residents making it the biggest town on Port Royal, one of the biggest islands in the county. The historic downtown district is called "Old Point." The reason you see so many old buildings still standing here is that Union troops occupied this region early in the Civil War, meaning that it was already Union-held for more than three years by the time Bill Sherman and his 8,000-man incineration squad came to the Carolina coast.

HISTORY

Six flags—or eight, counting the flagless Westoes' and Yamasees' earlier claims to the land—have flown over the people living their lives out in this location: the French, Spanish, English, Scottish, American, and Confederate flags have all waved overhead. Though the French and Spanish both failed to successfully settle the area, Scottish subjects pouring into already-crowded Charles Town in the late 1600s asked the lords proprietors if they could try to settle the bad-luck

---

LUKE 9:23–25 IN GULLAH

:23. Jedus tell um all say, "Ef anybody want fa folla me, e mus don't do jes wa e want fa do no mo. E mus cyah e cross an be ready fa suffa an die cause ob me, ebry day. 24. Anybody wa da try fa sabe e life, e gwine loss e true life. Bot anybody wa loss e life cause ob me, e gwine habe de true life. 25. Wa good e do a man ef e own ebryting een de whole wol an gone ta hell wen e ded? E done loss e true life, ainty?" 23. And he said to them all, "If any one will come after me, let him deny himself, and take up his cross daily, and follow me. 24. For whosoever will save his life shall lose it: but whoever will lose his life for my sake, the same shall save it. 25. For what is a man advantaged, if he gain the whole world, and lose himself, or be cast away?"

—From *De Good Nyews Bout Jedus Christ Wa Luke Write*, 1995

region and were given permission. Thus in 1684 Lord Cardross founded the city as a haven for Scottish immigrants. Two years later Cardross and his fellow settlers were all dead, murdered by an army of Spaniards and Westoes.

The Yamasee

As early as 1684 the Yamasee Indians of Georgia, who had had trouble getting along with the Spanish, asked for asylum in Carolina. The Carolinian settlers granted the Yamasees' request, figuring that it couldn't hurt to have this warlike tribe who hated the Spanish between St. Augustine and themselves. In the next decades, 10 different Yamasee towns were founded between the Savannah River and Charleston. In 1711 Yamasee warriors joined with British troops under Colonel Barnwell in aiding North Carolinian settlers in their fight against the Tuscarora Indians.

But by this time the Spanish threat had fairly subsided, and the town of Beaufort had already been laid out in 1710. It became home to a number of seasoned Barbadian planters, along with other immigrants who had arrived in Charles Town to find all of the best land there already purchased. Unfortunately the new settlers' homesteads infringed on the lands granted earlier to the Yamasee, and, worse, some of the British Indian traders cheated the Native Americans and allowed them to run up oppressive amounts of credit that gave them every reason to want to do whatever it took to be free from their debts.

Thus it was that when Beaufort was just five years old, Yamasee Indians wiped out most everybody in the town—most everybody south of Charles Town, in fact. But after the Yamasee and other hostile tribes were chased away and killed (many ran south and joined the defiant Seminole confederation in Florida), settlers came back to the old Second City and began settling here again. The British conquered and occupied the town during the Revolution.

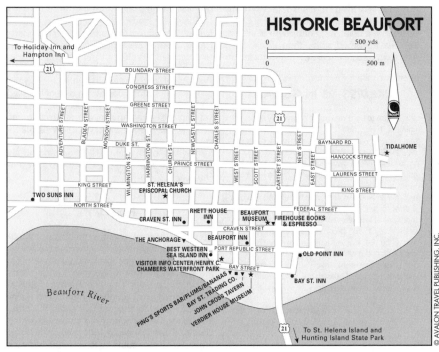

HISTORIC BEAUFORT

To Holiday Inn and Hampton Inn

BOUNDARY STREET
CONGRESS STREET
GREENE STREET
WASHINGTON STREET
DUKE ST.
PRINCE STREET
KING STREET
NORTH STREET

ADVENTURE STREET
BLADEN STREET
MONSON STREET
WILMINGTON ST.
HARRINGTON ST.
CHURCH ST.
NEWCASTLE STREET
CHARLES STREET
WEST STREET
SCOTT STREET
CARTERET STREET
NEW STREET
EAST STREET

BAYNARD RD.
HANCOCK STREET
LAURENS STREET
KING STREET

TIDALHOME

TWO SUNS INN
ST. HELENA'S EPISCOPAL CHURCH
CRAVEN ST. INN
RHETT HOUSE INN
BEAUFORT MUSEUM
FIREHOUSE BOOKS & ESPRESSO
FEDERAL STREET
CRAVEN STREET
THE ANCHORAGE
BEAUFORT INN
BEST WESTERN SEA ISLAND INN
PORT REPUBLIC STREET
OLD POINT INN
VISITOR INFO CENTER/HENRY C. CHAMBERS WATERFRONT PARK
BAY STREET
BAY ST. INN
PING'S SPORTS BAR/PLUMS/BANANAS
BAY ST. TRADING CO.
JOHN CROSS TAVERN
VERDIER HOUSE MUSEUM

Beaufort River

To St. Helena Island and Hunting Island State Park

0   500 yds
0   500 m

ROBERT SMALLS, BEAUFORT'S SAVIOR SLAVE AND UNION WAR HERO

In 1862 Confederates dismantled an old fort on the southern end of Folly Island to take the guns to another fort that needed them. They loaded the Confederate guns onto the CSS *Planter,* piloted by African-American slave Robert Smalls. That night while the others slept ashore, Smalls loaded his family and a group of other slaves aboard and slipped the Confederate ship past rebel guns, through the mines he and his crewmates had helped place, and delivered the boat to the Union soldiers in Charleston.

Smalls's heroism made him an instant cause célèbre for the North. He was given a reward for "capturing" an enemy craft and sneaking it through the mined harbor. He was then sent north to meet with President Lincoln and Secretary of State Edwin Stanton, where he pleaded for the arming of black troops. Upon his return to the South he continued to serve aboard the *Planter.* In 1863, while plying the waters of Folly River, the ship came under such heavy fire from Confederate guns that the ship's captain abandoned the wheelhouse and hid in the coal storage. Smalls, who faced certain death as a traitor if captured, took over the ship and sailed her clear of the enemy's guns. For this he was named captain of the *Planter.* He served the Union forces for the duration of the war, providing the Federals with invaluable information about the Lowcountry coast. His service also included a stint with the Beaufort Light Infantry, during which he was stationed in the Beaufort Arsenal (now the Beaufort Museum).

After the war the Union honored Smalls by asking him to take part in the ceremonies at the re-raising of the Union flag over Fort Sumter. He was later voted the United States's first African-American congressman, and he purchased the home of his former owner.

Smalls served in the South Carolina house of representatives, the state senate, and eventually the U.S. Congress. Though convicted of taking a bribe and removed from office, Smalls was later pardoned by Governor Wade Hampton III.

He was appointed collector of the Port of Beaufort by the Republicans and served almost continuously in this position from 1889 through 1913. In 1895 he served as a delegate at the South Carolina Constitutional Convention, where he attempted (unsuccessfully) to stop the disenfranchisement of African-Americans. Here, in response to the charge that he was a Confederate deserter, Smalls testified:

I stand here the equal of any man. I started out in the war with the Confederates; they threatened to punish me and I left them. I went to the Union army. I fought in 17 battles to make glorious and perpetuate the flag that some of you trampled under your feet.

Until his death in 1915, Smalls lived in his former master's home in Beaufort. The Robert Smalls Parkway and Beaufort's Robert Smalls Junior High School are both named for this remarkable man.

The War between the States

In the War of 1812 English gunboats sailed into range but found the port city too strongly fortified to attack. Fifty years later, during the Civil War, the Union Army was not so intimidated. And they had little reason to be, since most of Beaufort's fighting men had already left town to join the Confederate Army elsewhere. The Yankees attacked the Sea Islands in early November 1861, beginning with an amphibious landing at Hilton Head; they took Beaufort, the wealthy planters' town, on November 7.

The women and children, horrified at the rapacious Northern men bursting into their homes, fled the city, leaving only one white citizen of Beaufort—a pro-Union Northerner who'd moved down just before the war. Though some slaves left with their white owners' families, thousands upon thousands of field hands were left behind. Some acquired plots of land subdivided by the Northern Army for farming; some acquired the huge empty houses in town. The Penn School was opened on Saint Helena Island by Quaker missionaries from Pennsylvania to educate the former slaves.

After the War

When the railroad came to town, Beaufortians insisted it be built a mile away from downtown, to reduce the noise and soot. As the 19th

THE YAMASSEE WAR

The Carolina settlers had suffered from animosities with the indigenous peoples as early as 1671, when they declared open war on the Kussoes, a Lowcountry tribe who had been stealing corn from the settlers' public holds and whom they believed to be in league with the Spanish conspiring against the English settlement. But by and large, Carolina's Indians and settlers got along in an interdependent fashion, as Charles Town merchants sold and shipped the furs that traders acquired farther upstate. Unfortunately the men who lived among and traded with the various indigenous tribes, as one settler admitted, "were not (generally) men of the best morals." Many tended to cheat the Indians in financial dealings and were known to seduce Indian women and use violence against the men. Against the pleas of the village chiefs, they continued to sell whiskey to the men of the tribe. And worst perhaps was the fact that traders—against the wisdom of most other Carolinians—liked to extend credit to the Indians, allowing them to run up cumulative tabs as high, some estimate, as 50,000 pounds sterling. Hence even if they forgave the Europeans' other harassments, the Indians now had a strong financial motive for throwing off the strangling yoke of the English.

On top of all this, some of the Lowcountry tribes were concerned about squatters who had begun encroaching on land they hadn't first purchased from the Indians. So universal in fact was Indian resentment against them that one tribe—some suspect the Upcountry Creek, though most believe it to have been the Lowcountry Yamasee—went about spreading word of an upcoming intertribal massacre of the traders and the rest of the non-Indians in Carolina. Odds are also that the Spanish, always trying to present themselves as the Indians' true friend, egged on the violence.

Initial Violence

In 1715 a number of settlers in the Port Royal area heard from Indian friends that such a plot was taking shape, especially among the local Yamasees, a tribe who had moved up from the Spanish-held Georgia coast with the Carolinians' permission in the 1680s and settled on and near Coosawhatchie Island. The planters were well aware of the unscrupulousness of many traders—they were something like the used car salesmen of the colonial era—and promptly sent a delegation to the Yamasee town of Pocotaligo to promise redress of their grievances and let them know that the governor himself was on the way to negotiate treaties with them. On April 14 the Yamasee welcomed the Carolina diplomats, received their message, fed them dinner, and then, the following dawn, murdered most of them. A few were taken prisoner. Among these were Indian agent Thomas Nairne, whom they subsequently burned at the stake in a prolonged torture that took several days.

All told, the Yamasee killed somewhere around 90 settlers who were living with them at Pocotaligo. Then they moved on to Port Royal, where they killed 100 more whites and Africans.

The First Stage

South Carolina Governor Charles Craven was en route to the Yamasee negotiations when word of the slaughter reached him. He immediately called out the meager state militia and, leading the troops himself, attacked in retaliation. He stopped them at the Stono River, and while they faced off, Craven sent a company of riflemen up by water to Port Royal, from where they sailed up the river to Pocotaligo and destroyed the town.

When Craven had sent the delegation to Pocotaligo, he'd also dispatched messengers to each of the other tribes supposedly involved in the conspiracy, sending conciliatory messages, along with pleas for help in standing against the Yamasee. One by one, each of Craven's messengers drifted back into camp with grim news: their assigned tribe had massacred every or nearly every white man, woman, and child among them.

Though an estimated 16 Indian nations, reaching as far as present-day Alabama, began the war as part of a coalition with the Yamasee and Creeks, most of these tribes were more concerned with exacting vengeance on the scurrilous traders than with wholesale genocide. Given the overwhelming ratio of Native Americans to Europeans and Africans, only the humanity of these reluctant warriors spared the Carolinians from complete annihilation.

After the first wave of killing, frightened settlers came fleeing to the walled city of Charleston. One thing Carolina had on its side was a shrewd governor. Craven realized quickly that this was not going to be a brief campaign. He also knew well that once the initial excitement had died down and the most obvious threat had passed, his untrained militiamen were going to want to head back home—and that this was just what the Indians would be waiting for. To prevent this, he declared martial law and ordered militia deserters put to death. He also sent messengers to the other colonies, and to England, pleading for assistance.

By June 6, Craven and an army of 250 Carolinian militiamen and Native Americans, in cooperation with another party of men led by Colonel Robert Barnwell (who sailed south past Beaufort and approached from the rear), decisively defeated the Yamasee at Pocotaligo, at the head of the Cumbahee (Salkehatchie) River.

The Second Stage

Now the Cheraws and Creeks grew more aggressive in the north, marching southeast toward Charles Town. North Carolina's Colonel Maurice Moore headed down with a small army to help, and Craven and his militia marched north to join them. But no sooner had Craven and his now 700-man militia crossed the Santee River than a party of 700 Native Americans attacked European settlements from the south, pouring across the Edisto River and burning and slaying their way up the coast until only a few miles stood between them and the cowering city of Charles Town. Fortunately for the Holy City, when word came that Craven was returning, the Indians retreated.

In fact, the number of men who could legally take up arms to defend the colony—white men, free blacks, and loyal Native Americans—stood at only 1,400–1,500, and men not yet burned out of their homes were understandably torn between staying to support and defend their houses and families and joining the militia to battle the aggressors directly elsewhere. The Indians numbered an estimated 15,000. The Colonial Assembly voted to raise a "standing army" of 1,200 men, to include 600 white Carolinians, 100 Virginian mercenaries, 100 loyal Indians, and (here you can hear the collective "gulp!" of Lowcountry planters) 400 African-Americans or other slaves. The move to arm the African-American slaves—who, their advocates noted, were after all just as concerned about their families' safety as anyone else—was a wise one, though it understandably made a lot of slave owners nervous.

Craven sent agents to Virginia, New York, and Boston to get men, guns, and ammunition. Virginia, by far the strongest colony and most able to help, was making a fortune while South Carolina was preoccupied and unable to trade with the Indians. Finally Virginia Governor Alexander Spotswood convinced his stingy burgesses to send 130 men. The burgesses agreed but demanded that South Carolina send up 130 African-American slave women to take these men's places at their jobs.

Virginia dragged its gutters to come up with its 130 men, many of them derelicts and malcontents whom they were just as glad to get out of the state. South Carolina knew it shouldn't look a gift horse in the mouth, but it also realized that to take the 130 women Virginia wanted away from their slave husbands for a prolonged period was a good way to start a slave insurrection. Wisely South Carolina never made good its part of the deal.

Up in New York, the governor of New York and New Jersey attempted to get the Seneca Indians to come down and help fight on the side of the English, but they proved unwilling. Most colonies were hesitant to send along their best fighting men when, for all they knew, a riot might break out among Indians in their own region. To forestall this eventuality, the British government sent along 1,000 muskets, 600 pistols, 2,000 grenades, and 201 barrels of gunpowder, but no soldiers.

The lords proprietors (in some cases the heirs of the original grantee) helped very little at all. They provided some money but weren't able to ship any arms or ammunition. The British Parliament told them to hand over the province if they couldn't defend it; the lords told the king he could buy the property if he wanted, but that they would never give it up without getting paid the fair price. Just what the "fair price" for a colony full of butchered colonists and their slaves was, the lords did not say. So, while the Carolinians sweated and looked longingly eastward for their deliverance, a debate arose in England about what the proper price of South Carolina should be, and about whether or not England really needed a colony in Carolina after all.

The Cherokee to the Rescue

Fortunately for the Carolinians, their salvation didn't depend upon the actions in England. In truth it rested in another nation, just a few hundred miles away. North Carolina's Colonel Maurice Moore took 300

(continues on next page)

THE YAMASSEE WAR

(continued)

men up the eastern side of the Savannah River and into the homeland of the Lower Cherokee peoples. The Cherokee were old trading partners with the British, and aside from murdering a few corrupt traders, they had taken no part in the violence thus far. They wavered back and forth between remaining neutral and joining the British to help them defeat the other tribes. If the Cherokee helped the English and the English won, the Cherokee would be in a great position to demand land rights they coveted. And if they did *not* help the English and the Creek and Yamasee, the Cherokee's longtime adversaries, won, the Cherokee would probably be the coalition's next target. In fact though, this was true whether or not the Cherokee helped the English. So it was ultimately in the Cherokee's best interest to protect their trading partners.

Finally an incident between the Cherokee and the envoys sent by the nearby Creeks, who wanted to murder the English in the woods on the way back to Charleston, decided the issue. On January 27, 1716, the red "war stick" was sent throughout the Cherokee villages to announce that the Cherokee would fight on the side of the English.

A Hostile Peace

This Cherokee/Carolinian combination was unstoppable, and the other tribes knew it. Most of them quickly made peace upon the Cherokee's arrival.

The Lower Creeks bolted from their Georgia homes and fled clear to the Chattahoochee. The Cherokee also put an end to the Cheraws' bartering for guns with Virginia traders.

Knowing the war was essentially won, Craven sailed that April for the mother country, leaving Colonel Robert Daniel to serve as governor in his stead. Isolated killings of settlers continued for another year or so, but by the summer of 1717 even these had tapered off to a prewar level. All told, 400 settlers had been killed during battle, many of them in the initial ambushes. History doesn't record how many Native Americans died, but the number was horrendous. The once-great Yamasee tribe was devastated, and its members drifted south, eventually becoming part of the hodgepodge Seminole people.

South Carolina, which had generally tried to help the "loyal" tribes get along, was now confronted with the threat of a united Indian coalition attacking them. From now on the Carolinians' theory was divide and rule.

Perhaps the most profound result of the Yamassee War was the way it proved the lords proprietors' inability, or unwillingness, to protect the lives and livelihoods of those to whose labor they owed much of their wealth. When the colonists had come to them for help, the proprietors had passed the sixpence. It was something the Carolinians would not forget.

---

century wound down, the strong Northern presence in the area refused to fade. By 1940 one-third of the taxable land of Beaufort County had been purchased by Northerners for hunting preserves. Today in new "Old South" developments like Newpoint on Saint Helena Island, many of the residents are emigrated Northerners, many living in large mock plantation homes modeled after those owned by the slaveholders their ancestors came to undermine during the Civil War.

In the 1960s and '70s, Beaufort gained a bit of renown as the hometown of Smokin' Joe Frazier, heavyweight boxing champion of the world. And then Beaufort native Pat Conroy started broadcasting the town's beauties, foibles, and sins to the world via such novels as

The Great Santini, The Prince of Tides, and *Beach Music.*

Southern Archetype

Today Beaufort is a beautiful antebellum town, something of an archetype for Southern splendor, given the town's high profile in a host of recent movies set in the South, including film versions of Conroy's novels and *The Big Chill, Forrest Gump,* and *Something to Talk About.* In fact *The Big Chill's* Tom Berenger liked it so much here he bought a home on the Okatie River for himself and his family.

Many South Carolinians come here to visit Hunting Island State Park, preserved for decades by a hunters' collective and later grabbed by the state and reserved for public use. Here you'll see subtropical flora at its best. Speaking of Hollywood, Hunting Island was recently used (along with Fripp Island) as the location for Disney's recent live-action version of *The Jungle Book.*

SIGHTS

Beaufort Museum

The brick and tabby arsenal building at 713 Craven St., 843/525-7077, looks like a small-town satellite campus of the Citadel. The two brass guns outside were captured from the British in 1779 and seized by Union soldiers after the fall of Fort Walker in 1861. They were returned to Beaufort in 1880. This 1798 building—rebuilt in 1852—makes a great place for a museum. This is a nice, small museum. Granted, the sheer amount of history in the town seems to deserve a grander reckoning, but the museum does a good job of documenting day-to-day life in the early days of the Sea Islands. In the film version of *The Prince of Tides,* starring Barbra Streisand, this building doubled as a Greenwich Village loft for the dinner party scene.

Open Mon.–Tues. and Thurs.–Sat. 10 A.M.–5 P.M. Admission is about $2.

St. Helena's Episcopal Church

Founded in 1712 and built in 1724, this church at 505 Church St., 843/522-1712, has seen a lot of history. It survived the Yamassee War in 1715, the Revolution in the 1770s and '80s, and even the Civil War when army doctors performed surgeries using the churchyard's flat tombstones as operating tables. Stop by and pay a visit Sept.–May 10 A.M.–4 P.M., June–Sept. 10 A.M.–1 P.M.

National Cemetery

Right on U.S. 21 in Beaufort, you'll come upon the National Cemetery, established by Abraham Lincoln in 1863 for burying the Northern Army's victims of its war against the South. Some 9,000 Union boys lie here, along with 122 Southerners who died defending their homeland from the Northern invaders. Relatively recently, in 1989,

THE STONO UPRISING

Just as the fruits of leisure began to bloom in Charles Town, adversity struck again. Ever trying to weaken the English colony in Carolina, Spain sent out operatives who made it known that the country offered freedom to any Carolinian slaves who could reach St. Augustine.

On September 9, 1739 at Stono Creek, a large number of African-American slaves broke open a store from which they took weapons. They killed 21 whites, including women and children, and marched southward, killing every white in their path, encouraging other slaves to come with them, and burning numerous houses along the road. At 11 the next morning, Governor William Bull, riding back to Charles Town from Granville County with four other men, saw this fireball of human rage barreling down the road. Fortunately for him, he spotted them far enough away that he was able to hide until they had passed.

It's unfortunate for the slaves that they hadn't stolen horses as well as guns. Bull rode to give notice to the Charles Town militia, which rode after the walking mob, catching up with them by four o'clock and shooting and hanging 44 of them. The surviving rebels escaped into the dense woods but were hunted down over the following weeks.

The uprising understandably frightened white Carolinians. "If such an attempt is made in a time of peace," Bull wondered, "what might be expected if an enemy should appear upon our frontier with a design to invade us?"

Over the next year, a number of minor insurrections arose across the colony and were put down. Numerous other plots for rebellion were uncovered, and no doubt many slaves and free blacks were unjustly implicated and tried for plans dreamed up only in the minds of anxious slave owners. Eventually a law was passed requiring white men to go armed to church, in preparation for slave uprisings.

The slave code became stricter after the Stono uprising, but—talk about your thin silver linings—so did laws against the brutal maltreatment of slaves, which white Charlestonians saw as a factor in the rebellion.

19 Union soldiers from the African-American Massachusetts 54th Infantry were reburied here after having been discovered on Folly Island in the wake of Hurricane Hugo.

John Mark Verdier House Museum

Over at 801 Bay St., 843/524-6334, John Mark Verdier, a wealthy merchant, built this Federal-style home in the 1790s. In 1825, when the Marquis de Lafayette visited town on his triumphant return tour of the United States, he was welcomed here as a house guest. Union soldiers received a less cordial welcome, but nonetheless, they made this home their headquarters during the Northern occupation of Beaufort during the Civil War. Who can blame them? Each of the eight guest rooms has its own fireplace. Open for viewing Mon.–Sat. 11 A.M.–4 P.M. Admission charged.

Henry C. Chambers Waterfront Park

Concerts take place all the time on the outdoor stage, and weekdays find mothers and nannies sitting on the porch swings while their children play on the mock-Victorian jungle gym. A pleasant place to bring a snack and have an impromptu picnic.

Tidalholm

Sam and Sarah Cooper (Kevin Kline and Glenn Close) lived in this 1856 home in *The Big Chill;* apparently they bought it from the Santini family after Bull Meachum (Robert Duvall) crashed his plane off the coast at the end of *The Great Santini.* The real-life, current owners have signs up to remind you that Bull, Sam, and Sarah can't come out to play—this is a private home. But for fans of these films, it can be fun to peer through the gates to see where Kline, Jeff Goldblum, Tom Berenger, and Meg Tilly played football during half-time for the Michigan game, or the porch where Duvall sat reading the paper and cussing out Fidel Castro.

Tidalholm actually carries with it a wonderful story. James Fripp owned the house at the outbreak of the Civil War. When he returned from battle at war's end he found it occupied by a Frenchman and in the process of being auctioned off to pay his estate's back taxes. Fripp watched as the French stranger outbid the others and purchased the home. Then the Frenchman, who had dwelled in the abandoned home during the war, walked over to Fripp, kissed him on both cheeks, handed him the deed to the house, and walked away forever.

Tours

Carriage Tours of Beaufort, 843/521-1651, leave from the visitors center at Henry C. Chambers Waterfront Park on the Intracoastal Waterway, providing you with a narrated history of the city. Prices run $15 and up. For tours focused specifically on the Gullah culture, call **Gullah-n-Geechie Mahn Tours,** 843/838-7516 or 843/838-3758.

The privately owned 1856 Tidalholm house was the primary setting for the film The Big Chill *and the home of the title family in* The Great Santini.

BEAUFORT

The Northman comes no longer there,
With soft address and measured phrase,
With bated breath, and sainted air,
And simulated praise.

He comes a vulture to his prey;
A wolf to raven in your streets;
Around on shining stream and bay
Gather his bandit fleets.

. . . .

But, ready with avenging hand,
By wood and fen, in ambush lie
Your sons, a stern, determined band,
Intent to do or die.

—W. J. Grayson (1864)

Shopping

I can never stop into Beaufort without having to browse through **Bay Street Trading Co./The Book Shop,** 808 Bay St., 843/524-2000, which offers plenty of rare, locally written books and wonderful souvenirs. **Fordham Hardware** is a fun place to poke around in as well.

EVENTS

On an early spring weekend, St. Helena's Episcopal Church offers its self-guided **Spring Tours** of the city's gorgeous colonial homes and plantation estates, a tradition since the 1950s. Call the church at 843/524-0363 for information. In May the annual **Gullah Festival** features dances, live music, storytelling, and art displays in an all-out celebration of the Sea Island's unique African-American culture. Call Rosalie Pazant at 843/525-0628 for dates and information. If you missed the Spring Tours, then maybe you can make the late-October **Beaufort Fall Festival of Homes and History,** sponsored by the Historic Beaufort Foundation and featuring home tours, lectures, and special events. Give Isabella Reeves a call at 843/524-6334 for more information, or stop in and see her at 801 Bay Street. Over on St.

Helena Island, November brings the annual **Heritage Days Celebration,** a three-day festival celebrating African-American Sea Island culture. Call 843/838-8563 for information.

ACCOMMODATIONS

Motels and Hotels

The **Best Western Sea Island Inn** at 1015 Bay St., 843/522-2090, $79–119, enjoys a great location downtown across from the water. Most other chains cluster out along Boundary Street, including a **Holiday Inn** at 2001 Boundary St., 843/524-2144, $67–89. You'll also find a very nice **Hampton Inn** at 2342 Boundary St., 843/986-0600, $78–96. Over by Port Royal, worth a look is the 20-room **Battery Creek Marina and Inn,** 19 Marina Village Ln., 843/521-1441. Rooms rent for $86 a night.

On St. Helena Island, the **Royal Frogmore Inn,** at 864 Sea Island Pkwy., 843/838-5400, offers 50 units for $64.80, double occupancy.

Inns and Bed-and-Breakfasts

You just know a cute town immortalized in the baby boomer classic *The Big Chill* is going to have its share of B&Bs.

Named by *American Historic Inns* as one of the "Top Ten Inns in the Country," the **Beaufort Inn,** 809 Port Republic St., 843/521-9000, website: www.beaufortinn.com, offers 13 units, all handicapped accessible, $125–225 a room, breakfast included. Private balconies, private baths. Rooms with small Jacuzzis are available. Even if you're staying elsewhere, try to poke your head in to see the unique atrium wrapped by a curving stairway. In fact, if you're not staying here, you ought to consider eating there at the restaurant, named by *Country Inns Magazine* as one of the top 10 restaurants in the country. Dinner or Sunday brunch only.

At 601 Bay St., the **Bay Street Inn,** 800/256-9285 or 843/522-0050, also enjoys a lot of popularity, partly because the eight-room former Civil War hospital faces the river and partly because the inn was featured prominently in the motion picture version of *The Prince of Tides* and in *Forrest Gump.* All but one of the guest rooms has its own fireplace. Private baths, antique furnishings. $125–195.

Beaufort's Bay Street Inn, a former Civil War hospital, featured prominently in the films Prince of Tides and Forrest Gump.

The **Rhett House Inn,** at 1009 Craven St., 843/524-9030, offers 10 rooms, each featuring its own minilibrary to complement a larger one downstairs. It's here that "fire-eater" Robert Barnwell Rhett is said to have written up a draft of the Ordinance of Secession, which led to the Civil War. Nick Nolte and champion of the underprivileged Barbra Streisand stayed here in these regal furnishings during the filming of The Prince of Tides. Owners Stephen and Marianne Harrison hail from Manhattan originally, so perhaps it's understandable why Babs felt at home here. $100–275.

Other B&Bs include the five-unit **Craven St. Inn,** at 1103 Craven St., 843/522-9000, $115–225; the six-unit 200-year-old **Cuthbert House Inn,** 1203 Bay St., 800/327-9275 or 843/521-1315, where General Sherman once stayed, $125–195; the **Old Point Inn,** 212 New St., 843/524-3177, $75.00–125.00; and the **Scheper House,** at 915 Port Republic St., 843/770-0600, $90–165.

At the fully accessible, five-room 1917 **Two Suns Inn Bed & Breakfast,** 1705 Bay St., 800/532-4344 or 843/522-1122, each room features a view of the bay and salt marsh. $95–155.

Camping

The place to camp in the Beaufort area is **Hunting Island State Park,** 2555 Sea Island Pkwy., 843/838-2011, but you'll also find two campsites over at **Coosaw Plantation** on U.S. 21 N, 843/ 846-8225, and another 15 at **Kobuch's Campground,** about two miles from the Parris Island Gate on S.C. 802, 843/525-0653.

FOOD

Coffee

For coffee and baked goods, you won't find a better spot than **Firehouse Books and Espresso Bar,** 706 Craven St., 843/522-2665, set, as you might guess, in an old firehouse. Offers sandwiches, espresso, flavored coffees, muffins, and other such coffeehouse favorites. A very good book selection upstairs. At 703 Congress Street, **Magnolia Bakery Café** specializes in light lunches and fresh-baked desserts, in addition to providing caffeine to the masses. Outdoor sipping available. At Waterfront Park **Common Ground,** 102 West St., 843/524-2326, offers smoothies as well as espresso.

Casual Eats

Banana's, at 910 Bay St., 843/522-0910, is right on the waterfront, offering sandwiches, the famous Banana's Burgers, fresh shrimp, and hot dogs. Gimmicky enough to draw the tourists, but tasty enough to draw the locals. A good place for late-night eats. **Plum's,** 843/525-1946, facing the park, is a casual café serving up giant salads, omelettes, sandwiches, stir-fries, shrimp rolls, and pancakes, along with meats and pasta for dinner. Live blues, Motown, groove, funk, and reggae music on Thursday, Friday, and Saturday nights, beginning at 10 P.M.

A true locals' hangout is **Boundary Street Clubhouse,** 2317 Boundary St., 843/522-2115, featuring a sporty atmosphere—TVs on the wall show sporting events—and reasonably priced seafood, chicken, ribs, and steak. Open for lunch and dinner, till 11 P.M. on Friday and Saturday, till 10 P.M. on weekdays. Nice Sunday brunch here as well 10 A.M.–2 P.M. Outdoor dining available.

Lowcountry

Along U.S. 21 on St. Helena Island, you'll run across the famous **Shrimp Shack,** 843/838-2962, a place that keeps getting written up in major national magazines, but somehow manages to retain its casual-meal-on-the-back-porch charm. Fried shrimp is king of the menu, but they've got shrimp cooked other ways, and other types of seafood, chicken, and steaks that contain no shrimp whatsoever.

But when in the Shrimp Shack, eat shrimp. My favorite is the shrimp burger.

Gadsby Restaurant, 822 Bay St., 843/525-1800, offers one of the prettier views in town, overlooking the park and the river, and featuring soups, salads, and sandwiches, including a grouper melt you won't believe. Scenes from the Julia Roberts/Dennis Quaid film *Something to Talk About* were shot here in the mid-1990s.

The **Beaufort Inn,** 809 Port Republic St., 843/521-9000, named one of the United States's top 10 restaurants by *Country Inns* magazine, continues to draw the crowds and the accolades. The *Atlanta Constitution* pronounced it a "a MUST dining experience"; AAA gave it Four Diamonds, and still, the dress style is only "nice casual." Beaufort's like that. People like to come here for the elegant atmosphere, fine wine list, and fresh seafood. It'll cost you quite a bit to eat here, but you won't forget the experience anytime soon. Open for dinner only, and Sunday brunch.

For another true Southern experience, take the bridge from Beaufort to Lady's Island, take the first sharp right at Whitehall Drive, and turn right into the grounds of the **Whitehall Plantation Inn Restaurant,** 843/521-1700. This old plantation was owned by Colonel John Barnwell, who now resides yonder in the burial grounds of the St. Helena's Anglican Church. Set on the waterfront, amid pecan trees, camellia bushes, live oaks and cedars, and a gardenful of flowers, Whitehall serves up authentic Southern dishes—crab cakes, She Crab Soup, and the Shrimp Beaufort (baked in sweet butter, shallots, garlic, herbs, spices, lemon and sherry), which would be a good place to start, though you'll also find Maine lobster, lamb, and veal here. Try to time it so you're here at sunset—the view is spectacular. Expect to spend around $20 a dinner, less at lunch. Kids' prices available. Open Tues.–Sat. 11:30 A.M.–2:30 P.M. for lunch, 5:30–9:30 P.M. for dinner, closed Sunday and Monday.

Over at 1103 Bay St. you'll find **The Anchorage,** 843/524-9392, offering seafood and steaks, mostly for under $20.

Steamer's Restaurant on U.S. 21, 843/522-0210, is another pricey but tasty place for seafood. Rumor has it that Nick Nolte favored this place while filming *The Prince of Tides* here in town.

Over on St. Helena, you'll find the **Gullah House Restaurant,** 843/838-2402, next door to Red Piano Too art gallery (see below). Breakfast here features a $4.95 buffet—a wonderful place to stop on your way to points west. Lunches and dinners are about what you'd expect from a Lowcountry restaurant next door to an art studio—items like "Hot Ya Mout Swimps," and "Uncle Woolie's Crab Cake Dinner," along with meat dishes. Live jazz on the weekends. Featured in *Southern Living* a while back.

Mexican

Some of the best (and only) Mexican food you'll find in the area is **La Posada Mexican Food,** an outdoors restaurant at the intersection at Frogmore. Open 8 A.M.–11 P.M. Food is served in terra-cotta bowls. I ate outside under an awning. How down-home Mexican style is this? I ordered a Gatorade and they handed me a bottle of Gatorade and a cup with ice in it. This place had just opened up when I was there, but hopefully it will do well and be there for you to try when you visit.

Fast Food

If you're in a hurry or low on cash and you're tempted to eat fast food, at *least* head over to the **Sonic Drive-In** over at 340 Robert Smalls Pkwy., 843/522-8378, in the Wal-Mart Shopping Center.

Be sure to get the cheese-covered tater tots instead of the fries.

If you want to cook your own shrimp, go even farther on U.S. 21 toward Fripp Island and you'll come across **Gay Fish Incorporated,** owned by a guy named Charlie Gay, who will sell you fresh shrimp by the pound.

Barbecue

In this part of the state, it seems like the best barbecue joint in just about every town is a Duke's. This **Duke's** is at 3531 Trask Pkwy., 843/524-1128, and features a large buffet and a half-mustard, half-tomato-based sauce. An all-you-can-eat buffet. Open Fridays and Saturdays only, 11 A.M.–9 P.M. You'll see it on your left if you're headed down U.S. 21 into Beaufort.

NIGHTLIFE

By and large, this is a casual town where there are lots of places to have a couple drinks with friends, and not many places to boogie down and get rowdy. That said, **Plum's** and **Banana's** are two of the warmer spots at night: both fruits have live music on the weekends; Banana's tends toward the more laid-back Jimmy Buffett 1970s middle-of-the-road crowd; Plum's offers live blues, Motown, groove, funk, and reggae music on Thursday, Friday, and Saturday nights, beginning at 10 P.M. Over at the **Days Inn** on Boundary Street, they whir up the karaoke machine in the evenings for a sing-along.

John Cross Tavern, upstairs above Harry's at 812 Bay St., 843/524-3993, has served spirits on the waterfront since about 1720. Fortunately they've been washing their glasses all along, so it's quite safe. They serve dinners here as well, but the lounge is a real treat. It's not often you can quaff a glass of ale in a place old enough to have carded George Washington (it didn't, but it could have). Enter from the side of the building.

Ping's Sportsbar & Grill at 917 Bay St., 843/521-2545, is a good sports bar. Popular happy hour, decent pizza. The **Boundary Street Clubhouse,** 843/522-2115, offers large-screen satellite sports in every room, as well as good prime rib, ribs, seafood, and chicken. A real locals' hangout.

Movie Theater

One of the last around, the **Hiway 21 Drive-In,** 55 Parker Dr., 843/846-4500, still shows movies out under the stars. Call to hear what's showing.

INFORMATION

For more information on the Beaufort area, contact the **Greater Beaufort Chamber of Commerce** at P.O. Box 910, Beaufort, SC 29901, 843/524-3163.

ST. HELENA ISLAND

Frogmore

Frogmore is a tiny town—officially part of St. Helena—intersected by Rt. 21. You can't miss it if you're headed in from Beaufort. Also unavoidable is the **Red Piano Too,** 843/838-2241, an old wooden grocery store on the National Register of Historic Places that has reopened as an art gallery for African-American artists. A great place to pick up a one-of-a-kind (literally) souvenir, including painted furniture, mobiles, regional landscapes, and books written in Gullah. Be sure to stop in at the Pat Conroy Room, where you can pick up an autographed book by Beaufort's most famous native son. You'll also notice the **Gullah House Restaurant** next door.

If shopping's got ahold of you, head across the intersection over on the left across from the park and see what they're selling today over at the vendors' booths, a roadside stand that offers some unique Africa-themed clothing and knickknacks. In the late 1980s, islanders voted to restore the old Spanish name "St. Helena" to the island, though the island had been called "Frogmore"—after a former plantation owner—for years. It was a controversial, politically motivated attempt to refocus the history of the island, and some locals disagreed vehemently: for a time, islanders' produce was refused at mainland farmers' markets, and a noose was even hung at the park outside the Penn Center as a warning. But now the St. Helena name seems to have grown (back) on folks.

"WE PAPA" ("OUR FATHER"): THE LORD'S PRAYER IN GULLAH

Jedus tell um say, "Wen oona pray, mus say:
And he said unto them, When ye pray, say:

We Papa een heaben,
Our Father which art in heaven,

leh ebrybody hona you nyame
cause you da holy.
Hallowed be thy name.

We pray dat soon you gwine
rule oba all ob we.
Thy kingdom come,

Wasoneba ting you da want,
leh um be een dis wol,
Thy will be done,

same like e be dey een heaben.
On earth as it is in heaven.

Gee we de food wa we need dis day
yah an ebry day.
Give us this day our daily bread,

Fagibe we fa de bad ting we da do.
And forgive us our sins

Cause we da fagibe dem people
was do bad ta we.
As we forgive those who sin against us.

Leh we don't have haad test
wen Satan try we.
And lead us not into temptation,

Keep we from e ebil.
but deliver us from evil.

Translation from *De Good Nyews*
Bout Jedus Christ Wa Luke Write,
prepared by the Sea Island Translation
and Literacy Team, 1995.

Penn Center Historic District

Here on Martin Luther King Drive stands one of the first schools established for the recently freed slaves of the South. The Penn School was founded by two white Quaker women, Laura Towne and Ellen Murray, and supported by the Freedman's Society in Philadelphia, Pennsylvania. Later that year (1862), African-American educator Charlotte Forten joined the team. Her struggles and victories on the island were reenacted in the 1984 television-movie, *Charlotte Forten's Mission,* starry Mary Alice and Ned Beatty. In the early 1900s Penn began to serve as a normal (teachers'), agricultural, and industrial school. The school graduated its last class in 1953.

Every January from 1963 to 1967, Dr. Martin Luther King met here with the biracial Southern Christian Leadership Conference to plan strategies for overturning segregation and Jim Crow laws. The **Retreat House,** which still stands at the end of a dirt road on the waterfront, was built for Dr. King in 1968, but he was assassinated before he could stay there. For years the Peace Corps trained many of its tropics-bound volunteers here. Angela Brown, an East Los Angeles schoolteacher who trained here in 1987 before heading off to Cameroon, says the similarities between Gullah and the pidgin English she heard in Cameroon were striking.

Today the 49-acre, 16-building center continues as something of a spiritual homeland for those devoted to civil rights in general and the betterment of African-Americans in particular. Its mission statement states that the Penn Center's purpose is to "preserve the Sea Island's history, culture, and environment." Ironically the school built for the movement of Gullah blacks into mainstream American society has become something of a shrine to the unique African-American culture the original Northern teachers came down here to "educate" the freed persons out of.

The center, deemed a national historic landmark district in 1974, consists of some 19 buildings. The first one to visit is the **York W. Bailey Museum,** 843/838-8562, on the right side of Land's End Road as you come in from U.S. 21. Admission runs $2. This is one of the world's centers of information on the Gullah culture and the connections between West Africa and the Sea Islands. Be sure to peek into the book shop, where you'll find a number of hard-to-find books,

> *When war come, Missus take me and two more niggers, put we and chillun in two wagon, and go to Barnwell. My mother been one of the nigger. We stay in Barnwell all during the war. My father, he been with the Rebel. . . . When Freedom come, Missus didn't say nothing; she just cry. But she give we a wagon and we press [stole] a horse and us come back to St. Helena Island. It take three day to get home.*
>
> *When we get home, we find the rest of the nigger here been have Freedom four year before we. . . .*
>
> *My father come back and buy twenty acre of land, and we all live together.*
>
> —Former Fripp family slave Sam Polite, a resident of St. Helena Island, interviewed in the 1940s by the WPA

including a couple penned by Penn Center alumni. You'll also find recordings by the **Hallelujah Singers,** the gospel group featured in *Forrest Gump* and renowned throughout the country for their powerful vocal harmonies. The singers are based here at Penn Center and perform frequently in the area.

Ms. Lola Holmes, an alumna (class of 1939) of Penn Center School and author of *An Island's Treasure,* says plans are underway to move the museum to a bigger, climate-controlled building where its treasures can be better preserved. Museum hours run Tues.–Fri. 11 A.M.–4 P.M. and Saturday 10 A.M.–4 P.M.

If you can make it here in November you may get to take part in the **Heritage Days Celebration,** a three-day festival celebrating African-American Sea Island culture. Call 843/838-8563 for information.

Newpoint

If the shiny new shopping centers on the Sea Island Expressway are making you feel a bit queasy, it may help a bit to take a walk through the Newpoint development on Sam's Point Road. When you see the quality craftsmanship on the old-style homes, with their front porches within conversation's distance of the sidewalk, you'll swear that the neighborhood comes from

the 1820s, but these homes are generally less than 10 years old.

Interestingly the folks in the real estate office here say that only about one-fifth of Newpoint's population is native South Carolinian. The rest are people looking for the South of their imaginations, who have found that it's easier (and cheaper) to re-create it than to buy into The Point in Beaufort itself. The riverbank here, though fronted by huge multimillion-dollar homes, is a public waterfront, open to all.

The strength of a place like this is that when people move here they are signing on to a code of conduct, to a view of life, and promising to share a set of values—neighborliness, respect for others' property and privacy—with the rest of their neighbors. The downside? The homes here run $207,000–364,000 and on up to $1.4 million. A lot of others who would love to live in a place with this sort of lifestyle simply can't afford to buy a home here.

Nonetheless, to see a new development done right, head over to St. Helena Island, turn left on the first light onto Sams Point Road (S.C. 802), and drive for a mile and a half until you see the brick columns on the left, heralding Newpoint's entrance.

HARBOR ISLAND

This 1,700-acre island is the latest to receive developers' dehydrating, blood-powdering touch. Homes and villas rent out here; call Harbor Island Rentals at 800/553-0251 or 843/838-5800 for information. Or call **Harbor Island Sales and Accommodations,** 800/845-4100 or 843/838-2410.

HUNTING ISLAND STATE PARK

Take U.S. 21 east of Beaufort for 16 miles and you'll finally reach the ocean at Hunting Island State Park, 843/838-2011. Native tribes used to hunt here, and after Europeans moved in, hunters purchased the land and ran the island as a hunting club. To reward them for their preservation efforts, the government snatched up the land and turned it into a park.

And what a park it is. This is a subtropical forest. Tell the kids they're going camping where the exteriors for Disney's recent live-action remake of *The Jungle Book* were shot.

The 1875 140-foot **Hunting Island Lighthouse** provides a dramatic view—and a mild aerobic workout, getting to the top. Here on the island, you can camp or rent a cabin—though unless you get lucky you'll need a lot of advance notice for the latter. Then just spend your days shelling or fishing from the **Paradise Fishing Pier**, 843/838-7437, the East Coast's longest freestanding pier.

If you're just here for the day, it'll cost you $3 to park your car within the park. It wouldn't be too hard to find parking outside the park, but this is the sort of place where you'll want to make a contribution, even if you're only staying an hour or so. If you want one of the 200 campsites, it'll cost you around $15 a night, but this includes electric and water hookups. The park's facilities include showers, and two of the sites are modified for the physically challenged. Call ahead to reserve one.

FRIPP ISLAND

Captain Johannes Fripp, hero in the British battles against the Spanish, purchased this coastal island between Hunting Island and Pritchard's from the Yamasee Indians, who had come to settle here in the last part of the 1600s. Nowadays it's a developed resort island with controlled access. Very few automobiles get over here, but more than 300 homes and villas are for rent. For lodging, golf, or tennis information, call 800/845-4100 or 843/838-3535, or check online at www.FrippIslandResort.com.

The **Fripp Island Marina** is a popular place to hook up with charter fishing boats.

Things are changing here quickly. How quickly? Remember the Vietnam sequence in *Forrest Gump*? It was filmed here in 1993. Today "Vietnam" is a golf course.

PARRIS ISLAND

Stop by the gate when you reach Parris Island Marine Base. If you don't, you may be shot. But seriously (and I was serious), be sure to ask the guard there to tell you how to get to the Douglas Visitor's Center, or call the center ahead of time (843/525-2650) and get directions. But stop at the gate anyway.

Over a million men and women have trained here before being shipped off to do battle elsewhere. During World War II alone, more than 204,000 Marines were prepared for battle on this island—as many as 20,000 at a time. At the visitors center you can pick up maps and brochures, and tour the remains of some of the earliest European settlements in North America.

Charles Fort, Fort San Felipe, Santa Elena, and San Marcos

Here in 1564 French settlers under Jean Ribaut attempted to create a settlement they called Charles Fort on the shore of what is today called Parris Island. But after Ribaut was imprisoned during political intrigues on a trip back to France, the suffering Frenchmen left in Charles Fort were miserable, thinking they'd been forgotten. After surviving awhile upon the good graces of the local Native Americans, they built a boat—the first ever built in North America for trans-Atlantic travel—and sailed it back to France, and that was the end of French Carolina. In 1566 the Spaniards built Fort San Felipe and the village of Santa Elena on the exact same site. Indians destroyed the village in 1576 after the Spaniards fled from their hostility, but a year or so later the

> *Having cast anchor, the captain with his soldiers went on shore, and he himself went first on land; where he found the place as pleasant as was possible, for it was all covered with mighty, high oaks and infinite stores of cedars . . . smelling so sweetly, that the very fragrant odor made the place seem exceedingly pleasant. As we passed through these woods we saw nothing but turkey cocks flying through the forests; partridges, gray and red, little diferent from ours, but chiefly in bigness. We heard also within the woods the voices of stags, bears, lusernes [lynx], leopards, and divers other sorts of beasts unknown to us.*
>
> —René Goulaine de Laudonnière, a French colonizer who accompanied Jean Ribaut on the first French expedition to Spanish "Florida" in 1562, describing Port Royal

LOWCOUNTRY SPIRITUALS

The Lowcountry has produced some of America's most popular spirituals. "We Shall Overcome," the anthem of the 1960s' Civil Rights movement, began as a Johns Island folk song. The even better known (and much-recorded) "Michael Row the Boat Ashore" had its beginnings in Beaufort. Northern teachers and missionaries present in Beaufort during the Civil War heard the song belted out by African Americans as they rowed the ferry boats from the landing at the foot of Beaufort's Carteret Street across the Beaufort River to the opposite shore of Lady's Island, now known as Whitehall Landing. Some of the missionaries wrote down the words and music, and the song appeared for the first time in the 1867 book *Slave Songs of the United States:*

Michael Row the Boat Ashore
Michael row the boat ashore, hallelujah,
Michael boat a Gospel boat, hallelujah.

Michael boat a music boat, hallelujah,
Gabriel blow the trumpet horn, hallelujah.

O you mind your boastin' talk, hallelujah,
Boastin' talk will sink your soul, hallelujah.

Jordan stream is wide and deep, hallelujah,
Jesus stand on th' other side, hallelujah.

Common wisdom has it that the "Michael" of the song is the archangel mentioned in the Bible. Whether he ever worked in the Beaufort area as a boatman is unknown. Why Michael has to row while Gabriel gets to play his horn is also unknown.

Spaniards rebuilt the town, protected by a new, larger fort they called San Marcos. For centuries the exact location of the Charles Fort site was a mystery—until archaeologists realized that some of the artifacts they were finding at San Felipe were French, not Spanish. Those crazy Spaniards had built right on top of the French foundations, more or less. Over behind the clubhouse for the base golf course (a sign in front of the old home says: "Golfer's Dream House"),

you'll find the oldest European-style pottery kiln ever found on the continent. Inside the clubhouse itself, you'll find a pretty decent cheese sandwich.

Stop by the visitors center before you come out here to get a driving map.

Parris Island Museum

If you are a fan of things military, you'll need a cold shower after visiting here. Located at Building No. 111, the War Memorial Building, this museum, 843/525-2951, celebrates the long history of military life on Parris Island, which I suppose is what you'd expect. One exhibit celebrates women Marines, who have served here since 1943 when they arrived as reservists, filling in jobs vacated by men needed in the Pacific. Another room attempts to help visitors understand the grueling regime of a Marine Corps recruit here at Parris Island. One display allows you to push a button and get an earful of abuse (minus the obscenities) from a mannequin drill instructor. But perhaps most interesting for civilians are the display cases interpreting local history going all the way back to 1564, when Huguenot pioneer Jean Ribaut arrived with settlers to establish an ill-fated French colony in North America. You'll see some neat artifacts from the 500-person 16th-century Spanish town of Santa Elena, built atop—or so researchers discovered just a couple years back—the former French settlement of Charles Fort. The upper echelon Spaniards ate off imported Ming dynasty china, shards of which have been recovered in the soil near the 14th green of the Parris Island Golf Course. Open 1000–1630 hours (10 A.M.–4:30 P.M.) seven days a week.

PORT ROYAL

This relatively undiscovered town of 3,000 gives you an idea of what Beaufort was like before *Santini*. Here you can view one of the new but old-looking neighborhoods, along the lines of Newpoint on Saint Helena.

A fine seafood spot is **11th Street Dockside Restaurant,** 1699 11th St., 843/524-7433, one of those waterfront restaurants with open-beam ceilings, wooden tables and chairs, and tanned waitstaff running around in shorts and aprons, with the name of the restaurant emblazoned on their polo shirts. It is, in fact, what many of the places up in Murrells Inlet and Shem Creek started out as, and still pretend to be. Good seafood and a relaxed, great atmosphere with a view of the boats out on the river.

The restaurant has been around for years, though new owners bought it in 1995 or so. It draws a lot of visiting parents who come to see their gun-toting children graduate from Parris Island on Fridays. For this reason, you'll want to get here early if you're here on a Thursday night.

Keep heading south along S.C. 281 and you'll come across a quaint location of **Plum's,** a nice place to pick up an ice cream while strolling around town on a warm summer's night toward the sands, which is where the young folk of Port Royal hang out and play volleyball and such. Here you'll find a boardwalk leading to an observation tower, which provides a great view of the harbor and the docks of the port authority, where the hurricane scene from *Forrest Gump* was filmed.

DAUFUSKIE ISLAND

Hilton Head is a creature unto itself (see below). But hop over it and you'd land here, on Daufuskie. After over a century of virtual obscurity as a home for freed slaves who shrimped and farmed on the small island, Daufuskie gained fame as the setting for Pat Conroy's 1972 novel *The Water is Wide,* which later became the Jon Voight movie *Conrack.* Still accessible only by boat, this island remains partially authentic Lowcountry and part generic Golfland, in the form of the Daufuskie Island Club and Resort.

The island is a nice little half-day trip; you can walk or drive a golf cart around the small village and see the 1912 **Daufuskie Island Elementary School.** Over on the south end, you'll find the old 1880 **First Union Baptist Church,** with two front doors, one for women worshippers, and one for men. Down at the end of the dirt road here is the old **Mary Dunn Cemetery,** with tombstones dating back to the late 18th century.

Check with the marinas in Hilton Head for scheduled ferries and tour boats. One, the *Adventure,* sails out of Shelter Cove Harbor's Dock C, 843/785-4558. For $15 adults, $7.50 children (3–12 years), you get a narrated cruise to Daufuskie's Freeport Marina and a guided bus nature tour, with stops at spots made famous by *The Water is Wide.*

If you'd like to stay in one of the resort's 191 units, call 800/648-6778 or 843/842-2000.

HILTON HEAD

In his sequel to *Less Than Zero,* Brett Easton Ellis sends one of his overstimulated-kid-with-too-much-money characters to Hilton Head for the weekend. This alone is a good proof of the island's emergence as a domestic jet-setter paradise.

"Planned communities" of this sort remind me of short haircuts—they never look all that bad, but then, they never look all that great, either. However Hilton Head still has its attractions.

Annually about 500,000 people visit 42-square-mile Hilton Head Island, the largest Sea Island between New Jersey and Florida. One of the first communities in the United States to bury its phone lines, hence preserving its 19th-century motif, this planned community is conceptually head and shoulders above the Irvines of the world.

The annual Renaissance Gathering is held here, made famous by regular attendee, ex-president Bill Clinton.

Most come to stay in one of four main resort communities—Palmetto Dunes, Port Royal Resort, Sea Pines, and Shipyard Plantation—to play the area's 40-plus championship golf courses, play tennis on one of the island's 300-plus courts, and relax on its 12 miles of white-sand beaches.

Orientation
Stop by the **Hilton Head Island Chamber of Commerce Welcome Center** at 100 William Hilton Parkway for information on the island. You can book a room or a tee time there as well. Open daily 9 A.M.–6 P.M.

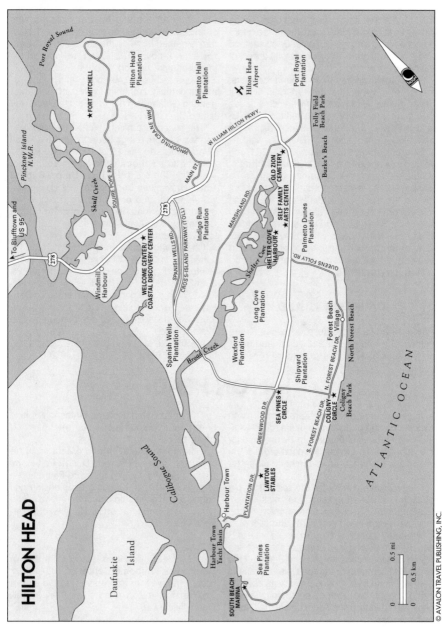

HILTON HEAD

Port Royal Sound

Pinckney Island N.W.R.

To Bluffton and US 95

Daufuskie Island

Calibogue Sound

ATLANTIC OCEAN

★ FORT MITCHELL

Hilton Head Plantation

Palmetto Hall Plantation

✈ Hilton Head Airport

Port Royal Plantation

Folly Field Beach Park

Burke's Beach

Skull Creek

SQUIRE POPE RD.

WHOOPING CRANE WAY

W. WILLIAM HILTON PKWY.

MAIN ST.

MARSHLAND RD.

OLD ZION CEMETERY ★

SELF FAMILY ARTS CENTER ★

SHELTER COVE HARBOUR ★

Palmetto Dunes Plantation

QUEENS FOLLY RD.

Windmill Harbour ○

WELCOME CENTER/ COASTAL DISCOVERY CENTER ★

278

SPANISH WELLS RD.

CROSS-ISLAND PARKWAY (TOLL)

Indigo Run Plantation

Shelter Cove

Long Cove Plantation

Spanish Wells Plantation

Broad Creek

Wexford Plantation

Shipyard Plantation

Forest Beach Village

N. FOREST BEACH DR.

North Forest Beach

GREENWOOD DR.

SEA PINES CIRCLE ★

COLIGNY CIRCLE ★

S. FOREST BEACH DR.

Coligny Beach Park

PLANTATION DR.

LAWTON STABLES ★

Harbour Town ○

Harbour Town Yacht Basin

SOUTH BEACH MARINA ▲

Sea Pines Plantation

0   0.5 mi

0   0.5 km

© AVALON TRAVEL PUBLISHING, INC.

HISTORY

Hilton Head Island contains two ancient Native American shell rings, one located in the Sea Pines Forest Preserve and the other on Squire Pope Road. Nobody knows quite what they were used for, but their presence here argues for the existence of a people who lived here before the Yamasee, and even before the earlier Ewascus Indians. British captain William Hilton spotted this island in 1663 while scouting for good sugar and indigo-growing land for his Barbadian employers and advertised in London for settlers, though since no one in London knew what a "golf villa" was, he didn't get any takers. Nonetheless, the island did eventually develop as an agricultural area, becoming the home of several large plantations in the colonial period and on up to the Civil War.

During the Civil War, this was the site of an amphibious landing of 13,000 Union troops in November 1861—he largest U.S. amphibious landing until World War II. However, despite its use during the Civil War as a major control center and supply base for the Union navy's blockade of Charleston and Savannah, once the Yanks were gone, Hilton Head returned to its old, sleepy ways. It remained isolated from the mainland until 1956, when a bridge was built connecting the 12-mile-long island to the mainland.

People didn't catch on immediately. As late as 1961 Hilton Head was home to just 1,000 African-Americans and about 50 whites. The only businesses were a liquor store and a gas station. But Hilton Head landowner Charles Fraser had a vision: a Southerner's utopia, where golf courses, coastal breezes, and casual lodgings went side by side. Fraser built and opened **Sea Pines Plantation,** the island's first resort complex, in the 1960s. **Palmetto Dunes, Shipyard, Forest Beach, Hilton Head Plantation,** and **Port Royal** followed over the years. All have things to recommend them, but stick with Sea Pines, Shipyard, Palmetto Dunes, or Port Royal if you want to be on the ocean.

Hilton Head's a unique place with unique problems, the most inescapable of which is traffic. Nearly all of the different massive "plantations" are de facto large cul-de-sacs, traffic-wise, so all traffic eventually spills onto one of the two main through-roads on the island U.S. 278 (the William Hilton Pkwy.) and the new four-lane Cross Island Expressway ($1 toll), which cuts from U.S. 278 near Spanish Wells Road to Sea Pines Circle on the south end of the island.

Today the island offers 3,000 hotel rooms and 6,000 apartments and villas, hosting as many as 55,000 people during a busy spell.

> *The lands are laden with large tall oaks, walnut and bays, except facing on the sea, it is most pines tall and good. . . . The Indians plant in the worst land because they cannot cut down the timber on the best, and yet have plenty of corn, pompions, water-melons, and musk-melons . . . two or three crops of corn a year as the Indians themselves inform us. The country abounds with grapes, large figs, and peaches; the woods with dear, conies, turkeys, quails, curlews, plovers, teal, herons; and as the Indians say, in winter with swans, geese, cranes, duck and mallard, and innumerable other waterfowls, whose names we know not, which lie in the rivers, marshes, and on the sands. There are oysters in abundance, with a great store of mussels; a sort of fair crabs, and a round shell-fish called horse-feet. The rivers are stored plentifuly with fish that we saw leap and play.*
>
> —William Hilton, *A True Relation of a Voyage Upon Discovery of Part of the Coast of Florida,* 1664

SIGHTS

The island of Hilton Head is divided up into various private and public complexes. **Harbour Pointe Village** is an odd mix of New England seafront, Mediterranean chateau, and 1970s condo tack. Here's where you'll find the famed **Harbour Town Lighthouse.** Developer Charles Fraser built the lighthouse in 1970. Though folks laughed at him at the time, he was building the lighthouse not to help lead ships into port, but rather to lead golfers into real estate offices—he knew that camera operators covering the MCI Classic across the water on the Harbour Town Golf Links would naturally focus in on this red and white lighthouse, perched poetically at the

THE BATTLES FOR FORT WAGNER

Folly Island first appears on history's radar during the Civil War, when Union troops stationed at Hilton Head waded through waist-high water onto the south end of Folly Beach as part of their attempt to capture Fort Wagner, the nearly impregnable Confederate fort on Morris Island, north of Folly Beach. Once it captured Fort Wagner, the Union planned to turn the fort's guns on Fort Sumter, the island fortress in the midst of Charleston Harbor—the disabling of which Northerners saw as the key to capturing Charleston. Capturing Charleston, in turn, was the key to crippling Southern importation and shipment of arms and supplies to its armies throughout the South.

First, however, the Yanks had to capture the southern end of Morris Island, just across Lighthouse Inlet from them. From April 7, 1863 until July 6, 1863, the Union soldiers spent their time building up earthworks to protect their gun batteries and constructing barges for an amphibious assault. When the battle actually began, the hard-pressed Confederates holding down the south end of the island eventually ran for the safety of Fort Wagner, leaving 17 dead, 112 wounded, and 67 missing. The Union, though it suffered similar losses, had won the south end of the island.

The next day the Union assaulted Fort Wagner and suffered terrible casualties. A week later, as immortalized in the movie *Glory,* the black 54th Massachusetts Volunteer Infantry, led by Colonel Robert Shaw, attempted to take the fort and was bloodily repulsed, costing 40 percent of the 54th's lives. Over 1,500 men were lost in both attacks. The fort was never taken. However, the men stayed on Little Folly Island, and the black 55th Massachusetts and 1st North Carolina landed on Folly on August 3rd. The Northern army believed, apparently, that the African-Americans could naturally work better than whites in the extreme heat and humidity. Unfortunately nature had no such preconceptions, and the men started dropping like flies as they dug trenches, cut timber, built wharves, loaded and unloaded goods, and hauled heavy guns to the front on Morris Island. Most of this work was done under heavy Confederate fire. As if this weren't enough, the Northern whites took advantage of their black cohorts, using them to police and lay out the white camps. In the first seven weeks on Folly, 12 members of the 55th Massachusetts died; 23 had perished by December.

Eventually the Southerners withdrew from Wagner to defend Charleston itself, and the Northerners quickly moved in and turned their guns onto Sumter, which nonetheless hung in there until reduced to rubble. Eventually the surviving members of the 55th Massachusetts would get the honor of marching into Charleston to bring the Day of Jubilee to the African-Americans of Charleston.

---

entrance to Harbour Town like a Statue of Liberty for the world's affluent:

Bring me your sires, your well-born,
Your coddled masses yearning to tan
deep . . .

And of course he was right. The zoom lenses haven't yet pried themselves from the giant candy-cane lighthouse: it's become the internationally recognized symbol of Hilton Head.

As you ascend the lighthouse to a gift shop and overlook at the top (free, but not wheelchair accessible), you'll find photos and descriptions of each of the 12 other lighthouses on the East Coast.

South Beach is another quaint spot on the island that plays on the New England-seaside-village-with-exceptionally-warm-weather theme.

Last time I was here it was almost 105°F—everyone sat around in the chairs and along the seaside bar drinking and talking. A visit to the **Salty Dog Cafe** is a must, something like the Hussong's of South Carolina, where people who don't even eat there feel compelled to purchase a T-shirt in the gift shop. **Captain John's Gallery** is a decent seafood place that's affiliated with the Salty Dog, featuring a good view and the sort of inflated prices you'd expect from a place famous for its T-shirts.

If you get weary of the island's calculated charms, the **Audubon Newhall Preserve,** 843/785-5775, on your left just before you reach the cross-island tollway, is a wonderful place to disappear into awhile. Here you'll see what the island looked like in its natural sublimity, before it was improved.

Just after you come down onto the island on U.S. 278 from the bridge, look to your right and you'll see the antebellum **Old Zion Cemetery** and the **Zion Chapel of Ease,** one of a number of chapels serving St. Luke's Parish, established in these parts in 1767, back in the days when the Church of England was the state religion and the state was divided into Anglican parishes rather than counties.

Self Family Arts Center
Over at 15 Shelter Cove Lane stands this $10 million complex, 843/842-2787, featuring an art gallery and a theater for the Hilton Head Playhouse. Open Mon.–Sat. 10 A.M.–4 P.M. No admission charged to view the art gallery.

The Coastal Discovery Museum on Hilton Head Island
You'll find this natural history museum on the second floor of the Hilton Head Welcome Center, 100 William Hilton Parkway, 843/689-6767. The museum also features displays on Hilton Head's roles in the American Revolution and the War between the States. Stop in and see if the folks there have planned any of their historic or environmental tours or beach walks. Open Mon.–Sat. 10 A.M.–5 P.M., Sunday noon–4 P.M. No admission charged.

The neatest thing about the museum is all the tours and events it sponsors, including a Marine Life and Dolphin Study Cruise, Pinckney Island Tour, History of Hilton's Headland Tour, African Americans on the Sea Islands, and Fort Mitchel Tour with Civil War Overview. Call the museum for dates, times, fees, and reservations.

Pinckney Island National Wildlife Refuge
On U.S. 278, just a half mile west of Hilton Head Island, you'll come across the entrance to the Pinckney Island National Wildlife Refuge, which was named after the land's former owners, U.S. Chief Justice and Constitution-framer Charles Pinckney and Declaration of Independence signateur Charles Cotesworth Pinckney. Here you'll find over 4,000 acres of salt marsh and small islands, 14 miles of trails to walk or bike, and not a single car beyond the parking lot. Take the 2.9-mile–round-trip **Osprey Pond Trail,** or, if you really want to experience the refuge's flora

and fauna, and have a day to do it in, take the 7.9-mile–round-trip **White Point Trail.** No charge, closed dusk to dawn.

Waddell Mariculture Research and Development Center
On Sawmill Creek Road about three miles west of Hilton Head, near the intersection of U.S. 278 and S.C. 46, you'll find both the Waddell Center, 843/837-3795, and the Victoria Bluff Heritage Preserve. The center researches the cultivation of marketable marine life, and you can tour this facility and ponds to see what they're up to over here. By appointment only. Open weekdays, no charge.

Internationally recognized as the symbol of Hilton Head, the Harbour Town Lighthouse was constructed by developer Charles Fraser in 1970 to attract attention and publicity to the harbor community.

TOURS

Based at Shelter Cove, **Adventure Cruises,** 843/785-4558, offers dinner and sightseeing cruises, dolphin-watching tours, and even "Murder" cruises. **Discover Hilton Head,** 843/842-9217, brings to life the history of the island.

The **Coastal Discovery Museum** sponsors numerous tours and events, including the Marine Life and Dolphin Study Cruise, Pinckney Island Tour, African Americans on the Sea Islands presentation, Native Plants and Lowcountry Gardens, a Nature Cruise, and the Fort Mitchel Tour with Civil War Overview. Call the museum for dates, times, fees, and reservations. **Hilton Head Parasail H20 Sports Center,** Harbour Town Marina, Sea Pines, 843/671-4386, offers "Enviro Tours" in a USCG-certified Zodiac inflatable, specializing in up-close dolphin encounters and bird-watching. Finally, **Outside Hilton Head,** 843/686-6996, offers two-hour dolphin nature tours leaving from a number of different locations, which run $35 adults, $17.50 for children under 12 when accompanied by adult. A full-day kayak excursion runs $48–60 adults.

SPORTS AND RECREATION

Beaches
At **Coligny Beach Park** on Coligny Circle, **Driessen's Beach Park** on Bradley Beach Road, **Folly Field Beach** on Folly Field Road, and down at **Forest Beach,** you'll find parking and public access to some of the most beautiful, pristine white beaches in North America.

Not much in the way of waves though. But bring your bike and you can ride for miles along the hard-packed sand.

Golf
Hilton Head is well-known as home to the annual MCI Classic, The Heritage of Golf, held on Pete Dye's Harbour Town Golf Links at Sea Pines Plantation the weekend after the Masters Tournament in Augusta. But the island is also known for the renowned Robert Trent Jones, George Fazio, and Arthur Hills courses inside Palmetto Dunes. Call 800/827-3006 or 843/785-1138 for information on any of these courses, as well as

information on the Arthur Hills II and Robert Cupp courses. For information on the **Pete Dye Harbour Town Golf Links,** call 800/845-6131 or 843/363-4485. For any of the other courses in the Sea Pines Plantation, call the same 800 number or 843/845-6131.

The best thing to do is pick up a free *South Carolina Golf Guide* before you visit or see the website www.travelsc.com for information on the state's public golf courses. Call 800/2-FIND-18 or 800/689-GOLF to find out about any of the courses at Shipyard Plantation.

Tennis
With some 300 courts, including clay, hard, and grass surfaces, Hilton Head is as much a tennis mecca as it is a holy land for golfers; for more than a quarter century, the Family Circle Magazine Cup has hosted such women's tennis stars as Chris Evert, Martina Navratilova, and Steffi Graf. Stan Smith, Jimmy Connors, and Bjorn Borg have all appeared between the lines here too.

In 1997 Sea Pines was named the "Top Tennis Resort in the United States," by no less than *Tennis* magazine, and a number of other island resorts regularly make the magazine's top 50.

The number for the **Sea Pines Racquet Club** is 800/732-7463 or 843/363-4495. The **Palmetto Dunes Tennis Center** contains 23 clay, two hard, and eight lighted courts, 800/972-0257 or 843/785-1152. For tennis **lessons,** ask at any racquet club; many offer them. Or call the **Van der Meer Tennis University,** 800/845-6138 or 843/785-8388.

Horseback Riding
Unfortunately **Sea Horse Farms** doesn't really raise sea horses. But the ones they do keep there are fun to ride on terra firma. Call 843/681-7746. **Lawton Stables,** 843/671-2586, is another place where you can saddle up.

Biking
With the growing traffic on Hilton Head, and with the many fine trails laid out across the island, biking is a good idea on Hilton Head. Though the designated paths won't take you far into Hilton Head Plantation or Sea Pines Resort, you can get almost anywhere else in the island by bike. To rent, you might call **AAA Riding Tigers Bike Rentals,** 843/686-5833; **Fish Creek Land-**

ing, 843/785-2021; or **South Beach Cycles,** 843/671-2453.

Diving

In Hilton Head, the folks at **Island Scuba Dive and Travel,** 130 Matthews Dr., 843/689-3244, offer local river diving, classes, and eco-river tours. In Beaufort call **Outfar Diving Charters,** 843/522-0151, to arrange a trip.

Paddling

For on-the-island canoe rentals, you'll want to talk to **Outside Hilton Head,** 843/838-2008, website: www.outsidehiltonhead.com; **Moore Canoeing Center,** 843/681-5986; or **Island Water Sports of Hilton Head,** 843/671-7007.

If you're thinking about venturing off the island, you'll find canoe and kayak rentals, as well as guided paddling tours of the ACE Basin National Wildlife Refuge (see below), barrier islands, coastal marshes, and the Edisto River canoe trails, offered at **Carolina Heritage Outfitters** in Canadys, 800/563-5053 or 843/563-5051; **The Kayak Farm** on St. Helena Island, 843/828-2008; and **Tullifinny Joe's** in Coosawhatchie, 800/228-8420 or 843/726-4545.

If at all possible, bring your own kayak, since rentals aren't cheap. Outside Hilton Head, for example, charges $15 an hour, $45 a day for a single kayak. You could rent a Ford Escort for that (though they've been known to bog down in the marshes).

Boating

You'll find several places willing to help you out: **Island Watersports of Hilton Head, Inc.,** 843/671-7007; **Hilton Head Parasail H20 Sports Center,** Harbour Town Marina, Sea Pines, 843/671-4386; **Lowcountry Water Sports, Inc.,** 843/785-7368; and **Outside Hilton Head,** 843/686-6996, website: www.outsidehiltonhead.com.

Parasailing

If you want to be dragged by a speedboat through the Lowcountry sky, **Hilton Head Parasail H20 Sports Center,** Harbour Town Marina, Sea Pines, 843/671-4386, will do it.

Fishing Charters

With the Gulf Stream so close by, no doubt the true anglers will want to get out and truly angle

for something big enough to cover a wall in the den. **Adventure Cruises,** 843/785-4558; **Drifter Excursions,** 843/363-2900; and **Seawolf Charters,** 843/525-1174, can get you started.

ACCOMMODATIONS

Hunting for the best possible room in Hilton Head is like hunting for a bullet casing on Normandy Beach on D-Day plus one—it's easy to become overwhelmed. Most people choose their room based on what they hope to be doing while on the island. You probably ought to contact **Hilton Head Central Reservations** at 800/845-7018 or 843/785-9050, website: www.hiltonheadcentral.com, and tell them what you're looking for. Open Mon.–Sat. 9 A.M.–6 P.M. Or call **Hilton Head Oceanfront Rentals Company,** 800/845-6132, website: www.oceanfrontrentals.com. Ask for the free literature they'll be glad to send you.

As far as specific resorts go, you might consider **Palmetto Dunes,** a 2,000-acre resort with the aforementioned world-class golfing, a tennis center, and miles of white-sand beach. Check into the Palmetto Dunes Hilton and immediately your biggest worry is choosing where to eat that night—the folks here will take care of everything else. $80–370. Get a room through Central Reservations, or call 843/785-1138 if you'd like to speak with the folks at Palmetto Dunes directly.

Sheraton Four Points, 800/535-3248 or 843/842-3100, has a luxurious lobby, with five floors in the main building providing scenic views of the island. Several amenities including a complimentary beach shuttle, pools, and a fitness center. A stay here entitles you to a complimentary membership to Coligny Beach Club. Rooms come with cable, video games, iron, full-sized ironing board, and hair dryer. $59–209.

Disney's Hilton Head Island Resort, 22 Harborside Lane, 800/453-4911 or 843/341-4100, claims to offer special activities for kids, but other than that, it's hard to imagine how even Walt's minions can improve upon the natural beauty already here. The intricate illusions of nature that seem impressive in downtown Anaheim or Orlando feel a bit unnecessary here, but you might give them a call to hear Mickey's side of it. $99–550.

On the U.S. 278 drag, between Shipyard Plantation and Palmetto Dunes, you'll find the humble two-story **Red Roof Inn–Hilton Head,** 5 Regency Parkway, 843/686-6808, with 111 rooms that run from $47–87 a night. Along the same "we're-only-going-to-sleep-there-anyway" lines is Hilton Head's **Motel 6,** 830 William Hilton Parkway, 800/466-8356 or 843/785-2700.

Inn

Bed-and-breakfasts seem to have a hard time of it on Hilton Head, but in a world of massive resorts, the **Main Street Inn,** 2200 Main St., 800/471-3001 or 843/681-3001, seems relatively intimate, offering 34 units, many of which are wheelchair accessible. Nice gardens here, and a continental breakfast comes with the price of the room, which will run you $148–275 a night.

FOOD

Southern and Seafood

The **Old Fort Pub,** 843/681-2386, stands in Hilton Head Plantation beside Skull Creek. Crouched beneath tremendous live oaks draped with Spanish moss, this historic old house once served (briefly) as Confederate headquarters and later (not so briefly) as headquarters for the Union. Beautiful views of the Intracoastal Waterway, marshes, harbor, sunset, and sailboats from the dining room, lounge, or deck. This same view inspires some of the most uniquely delicious Lowcountry cuisine. Some of the items include blackened salmon with tomato coulis, red rice, crab cakes, and grilled prawns, or triggerfish with crab, zucchini cakes, and sweet potato crepes. If you choose to dine outside don't worry about the mosquitoes: an army of citronella tiki torches, along with the citronella candle and a bottle of insect repellent at each table, will protect you. Great wine list. Could well be the culinary highlight of your visit.

Over in Harbour Town is **Crazy Crab,** 843/363-2722, which as you might guess is famous for its crab boil and other seafood dishes. Dinner only. Expect to pay toward $20 for dinner.

Despite some tough competition, the family-owned **Abe's Native Shrimp House,** 650 William Hilton Pkwy., 843/785-3675, which

began in 1968 as a convenience store on the then-dirt road U.S. 278, has operated as a full-service seafood restaurant since 1975, which is, in Hilton Head restaurant terms, forever ago. Open daily for dinner only at 5 P.M. A Lowcountry Shrimp Boil will cost you $11.95; get there early for the early-bird buffet, offered Mon.–Sat. 5–7 P.M. and Sunday 5–9 P.M. For something light, try a bowl of the fine seafood gumbo and a salad for about $6. For something heavy, go in with someone else on the Charlie Mae's Chaplin Plantation Dinner, which features fried shrimp, fried chicken, and country ham, served with rice and red-eye gravy, green beans, corn, hush puppies, and dessert. It runs $23 for two people, $43 for four. Of course, you'll need nitroglycerin pills afterward, but if you're only going to eat one big, authentic Lowcountry meal on your trip, this'd be a good place to do it.

Barbecued Italian

If you want real South Carolina barbecue, you'll have to head off the island and over to Beaufort to eat at Duke's. But if good barbecue ribs will do you, then head over to Shelter Cove for the schizophrenic seafood/Italian **Kingfisher-La Pola,** 18 Shelter Cove Harbor, 843/785-4442. Deck dining available with a nice view of the water, good tomato-based rib sauce, good Italian dishes, good Angus steaks. Open for dinner only, daily 5–10 P.M. They serve a pretty good three-course early-bird dinner here for a reasonable $13.50 from 5–6 P.M., which gives you plenty of time afterward to walk the Harbor shops. The restaurant's Harbour Lounge and South Deck feature happy hour with $1.25 drafts, $2.50 wine and well drinks, 25-cent shrimp, 40-cent oysters, and $7.95 crab legs from 5 to 7 P.M.

Great Plains, 36 Palmetto Bay Rd., 843/842-8540, includes pork ribs and seafood.

Italian

In addition to La Pola (above), Hilton Head has **Di Vino's,** 5 Northridge Plaza, 843/681-7700. Set in an uninspiring shopping plaza, Di Vino's has a sign out front:

No Pizza
No Iced Tea
No French Fries

In other words, when you head into this cozy (14-table) restaurant, expect to meet with some serious Italian food. Shrimp and fettuccine pesto, seafood, chicken, pasta. Expect to spend about $7 for an appetizer, $17 and up for dinner. **Antonio's Restaurant,** at G-2, The Village at Wexford, also offers some authentic Italian in a nice setting.

Rita's Italian Ice, in the heart of Hilton Head, is the local link of a Northern-based chain well situated to serve all the Yankee resorters. This is the best Italian ice I have ever had (yes, even better than the Sons of Italy booth at the fair). Rita's also serves frozen custard and, for the best of both worlds, "gelati" (Italian ice with frozen custard on the bottom and top). Try the lemon ice with chocolate custard.

French

A casually chichi place right beneath the Harbour Town lighthouse is **Cafe Europa,** 843/671-2299, where you'll spend upward of $20–30 for a full dinner and maybe less for lunch. The café doesn't serve between 2:30 and 5:30 when it's cleaning up after lunch and preparing for dinner. Fancier is the **Rendez-Vous Café,** 843/785-5707, where an honest-to-DeGaulle Paris-trained French chef whips up pâté, onion soup, oysters Provençale, steamed mussels, bouillabaisse, cassoulet, along with homemade fruit tarts, chocolate mousse or crème brulée.

Mexican

Aunt Chilada's Easy Street Café, 69 Pope Ave., 843/785-7100, features both Mexican and Italian meals, along with seafood and steaks. Open every day, but on Sunday they only serve a brunch. **San Miguel's Mexican Café,** 843/842-4555, offers another south-of-the border choice for a good price, with a bueno view of Shelter Cove Marina. For authentic food on paper plates (and lower prices), try **Amigo's,** 70 Pope Avenue, Circle Center, 843/785-8226.

Breakfast

Cheap spots to enjoy cheap breakfasts on the island include the **Palmetto Dunes General Store,** which has a little kitchen in back where you can buy a basic breakfast for real world (i.e., *not* Hilton Head) prices. One of my favorites, especially since it's open 24 hours, is the **Hilton Head Diner,** where you'll find not only the predictable hamburgers, fries, and shakes, but (oddly) a full bar. So if you've always thought your patty melt would taste better with a screwdriver, here's your chance. Bring change for the jukebox; there's a box at each table.

Of course the **Huddle House** offers you lots of ways to eat hash browns. You'll also find fast-food chains on the island, including what must be the world's most aesthetically pleasing Hardee's, but if you're going there, please don't let anyone see you carrying this book inside.

Brewpubs

When it opened up a few years back, the **Hilton Head Brewing Company,** over at Hilton Head Plaza, 7-C Greenwood Dr., 843/785-2739, became the state's first brewpub or microbrewery to operate (legally) in South Carolina since Prohibition. The menu features some good brew favorites: babyback ribs, pizza, seafood, steak, and even bratwurst.

In the Northridge Plaza, **Mickey's,** 843/689-9952, re-creates an old-time pub feel. Open from 11:30 A.M. Mon.–Sat., with happy hour 4–8 P.M. Good solid pub menu, televisions blaring sports . . . the usual. A place where actual locals head to escape the tourists.

Vegetarian

You'll find vegetarian items on most Hilton Head menus nowadays. Spots with extended vegetarian menus include the **Main St. Pizza and Bistro,** 843/689-9100, and **Starfire Bistro and Wine Bar and Grill,** 843/785-3434.

ENTERTAINMENT AND EVENTS

Hilton Head is a resort, meaning that a lot of people here, especially the retirees, have a lot of free time on their hands. It's no surprise then that some of that free time gets turned toward the planning of various festivals. The **Winter Carnival,** a monthlong festival beginning in mid-January, combines a celebration of Italian culture, Gullah culture, and jazz music. If you're a Gullah jazz saxophonist with a taste for lasagna, this is really a must. The third weekend of March brings on **Wine Fest,** billed as the East Coast's largest tented public wine-tasting event, complete with a silent auction. Call 843/686-4944 for information.

During March, the Hospitality Association puts on **Springfest,** a monthlong event celebrating sports, arts, and food. If you're going to be on the island in March, call 800/424-3387 for information on events. Later in the month, the **Family Circle Magazine Cup,** the nation's top women's professional tennis tournament, features female superstar racketeers. Call 800/677-2293 for information on getting tickets.

In April the Harbour Town Golf Links are the site of the **MCI Classic Golf Tournament,** wherein 120 of the world's top duffers battle over $1.4 million in prize money. Call 843/234-1107 for information on getting in.

Come October, **Bubba's Beaufort Shrimp Festival** barrels into town for a one-day orgy of things crustacean. Tour marine exhibits, check out shrimpboats, listen to music, and eat, eat, eat. Call 843/986-5400 for information.

usurp. The daughters and sons of Sam do business on Pembrook Drive.

On the island, you'll find two notable bookstores: one is the **Authors Bookstore,** D-4 Village at Wexford, 843/686-5020, connected with the **Authors Caffé Espresso,** 843/686-5021. Unfortunately the bookstore is only open till 6 P.M. The other bookstore of note is the **Port Royal Bookstore** at Port Royal Plaza, 843/522-1315.

The Hilton Head Factory Stores, on U.S. 278 at the Gateway to Hilton Head Island, 888/746-7333 or 843/837-4339, are divided up into two separate malls, but all told, they offer scores of stores, including **Nike, The Gap, Book Warehouse, Mikasa, Oshkosh B'Gosh, Geoffrey Beene, Eddie Bauer, J. Crew, Laura Ashley, Oneida, Samsonite,** a frightening-sounding store called **Toy Liquidators,** and a crazy little joint called **Perfumania** ("Smellorama" was apparently already taken). It's like a monthful of shopping catalogs come to life. Enter at your own risk.

SHOPPING

With up to 55,000 folks penned onto an island with discretionary income and lots of leisure time on their hands, you can just see the merchants' register fingers twitching, can't you? There are a number of shopping centers on the island, including **The Mall at Shelter Cove,** 24 Shelter Cove Ln., anchored by **Belk** and **Saks Fifth Avenue,** but also including **Banana Republic,** a **Talbot's** and **The Polo Store,** among many others. Not a bad place to go during a torrential downpour. **The Plaza at Shelter Cove,** also on Shelter Cove Lane, is the requisite parasite strip plaza near the mall, featuring a **T. J. Maxx** and **Outside Hilton Head,** a good sporting-goods store.

Other options include **The Village at Wexford,** 1000 William Hilton Pkwy.; **Harbour Town,** on Lighthouse Rd. in Sea Pines Resort; **Northridge Plaza,** 435 William Hilton Pkwy.; **Pineland Station,** also on William Hilton Pkwy.; **Port Royal Plaza,** 95 Mathews Dr., which offers a **Sam's Wholesale Club;** and **Shoppes on the Parkway,** 890 William Hilton Parkway.

You'll find a **Wal-Mart** here—perhaps one of the few you needn't feel guilty about visiting, since there was no cute old downtown for it to

SERVICES

Information
For more information on Hilton Head Island, stop by the **Hilton Head Island Chamber of Commerce Welcome Center,** at 100 William Hilton Parkway, 843/689-6767, website: www.info@hiltonheadisland.org. You can book a room or a tee time there as well. Open daily 9 A.M.–6 P.M.

Child Care
A number of the resorts offer child care and children's programs. But if you're in an independent villa or hotel and aren't willing to risk taking baby out to a nicer restaurant, you may want to call **Amazing Creations Child Care, Inc.** 843/837-5439; **Companions, Nurses & Nannies,** 843/681-5011; or **EF Aupair,** 843/342-2044.

GETTING THERE

By Car
Most people drive to Hilton Head, plummeting down from the north on I-95 before hanging a left at U.S. 278 or the newly expanded S.C. 46 and arcing over the large bridge that leaves from

South Carolina and touches down in Hilton Head. From anywhere on the South Carolina coast, you'll want to drive down U.S. 17 to get here. From almost anywhere else in the state, you'll want to cut over to I-95; from most spots in the Upcountry, you'll want to find I-26 first, then head south on I-95 when you reach it.

By Air

People coming from out of state normally fly into Charleston or Savannah, Georgia, and then rent a car and drive the rest of the way. See the Charleston chapter for details on the airport and on local car-rental places in that town. For information on the Savannah Airport, call the **Savannah Airport Commission,** 912/964-0514.

USAir Express, 800/428-4322, does offer daily commuter flights direct to the Hilton Head Island Airport. You'll find taxi service at the Hilton Head airport to get you to your hotel or villa.

By Train

Oh yeah, right—like they're going to allow a noisy train chugging its way onto the island. You can, however, take **Amtrak** to Savannah, Georgia, just 45 miles away, and then take a shuttle from there. Call Amtrak for information.

GETTING AROUND

Because so many of the island's highlights are spread far apart on this large island, unless you're just planning to hole up in a specific complex, you'll want to consider either biking (see above) or renting a car. Local rental car spots include **Avis**, 843/681-4216; **Budget**, 843/689-4040; and **Enterprise Rent-A-Car**, 843/689-9919.

Taxicab companies include **Yellow Cab**, 843/686-6666, and **Palmetto Coach**, 843/726-8000.

ACROSS THE BRIDGE TO BLUFFTON

Once, when I was 20, I spent a week at Disney World in Florida. About halfway through the week, my friends and I grew so tired of the manicured lawns, overpriced meals, and carefully constructed walkways, spiels, and smiles that we exploded out of Disney airspace just to find a burger joint, talk to the locals, and say we'd actually seen a bit of central Florida.

This same sort of reaction against cultural vacuousness is what seems to propel many Hilton Head guests over the bridge and into Bluffton. This tiny antebellum town, founded in 1825, has become something of a day trip for people staying at Hilton Head. Initially established as a summer resort for Lowcountry planters escaping the fevers in the rice fields and swamps, Bluffton was home to poet Henry Timrod, "poet laureate of the Confederacy," when he taught here briefly in the 1860s. And lest we forget, Simons Everson Manigault, Holden-Caulfield-on-Sweet-Tea hero of Padgett Powell's *Edisto,* attends school in Bluffton.

Truth be told, there isn't all that much to see here, but at least you know that the old Gothic 1854 **Church of the Cross,** Calhoun St., 843/757-2661, was built by South Carolinians in a style 19th-century Blufftonians felt was appropriate, not one that the marketing department in New York told them would maximize profits. During the Northern invasion, Union gunboat bombardment nearly leveled the town, and the church would have burned down if small detachments of boys in gray hadn't arrived to put out the fires in time.

Visit Bluffton and you've at least touched the face of the South, though I'd recommend you head over to Beaufort or on up to Charleston to see what Lowcountry South Carolina is really about.

BEYOND BEAUFORT

SHELDON CHURCH RUINS

Between Gardens Corner and the town of Yemasee on Route S-7-21, you'll pass the ruins of this church. The Sheldon Church was first built in 1753, but the British burned it in 1779. It was rebuilt, but in 1865 William Tecumseh Sherman came through and burned it again.

In the dark days of Reconstruction nobody around here had the money to rebuild the church again. The ruins remain ruins even today, an indictment of the violence of the Northern armies of 1865. Memorial services are held here under the open sky and moss-draped oaks on the second Sunday after Easter.

ACE BASIN NATIONAL WILDLIFE REFUGE

Named for the three rivers draining the basin—the Ashepoo, Combahee, and Edisto—this refuge serves as home to American alligators, the shortnose sturgeon, wood stork, loggerhead sea turtle, blue-winged teals, and southern bald eagle, along with a number of other endangered or threatened species. Call 843/889-3084 or 843/549-9595 for information. If you'd like to tour the area in a 38-passenger pontoon boat, call **ACE Basin Tours** in Port Royal, 843/549-9595.

The best way to experience the ACE, however, is in a canoe or kayak. For rentals and/or guided tours, call **Carolina Heritage Outfitters** in Canadys, 800/563-5053 or 843/563-5051; **The Kayak Farm** on St. Helena Island, 843/828-2008; **Outside Hilton Head,** on Hilton Head, 843/838-2008, website: www.outsidehilton head.com; or **Tullifinny Joe's** in Coosawhatchie, 800/228-8420 or 843/726-4545.

YEMASEE

This town is farther off I-95 than the others on this list, but it's close enough. The main thing it offers—that some of the other highway stops don't—is campsites. **Point South KOA,** U.S. 17, 800/KOA-2948 or 843/726-5733, offers 53 sites. **The Oaks,** Rt. 1, 843/726-5728, has 80 more. In fact Yemasee is the headquarters for the South Carolina Campground Owners Association.

Evocative ruins today, the Sheldon Church was built in 1753, burned by the British in 1779, rebuilt, and burned again, by William Tecumseh Sherman, in 1865.

Outside of town and closed to the public stands **Auld Brass,** the one and only plantation ever designed by Frank Lloyd Wright. It's owned today by Wright aficionado and Hollywood producer Joel Silver, of *Die Hard* and *Lethal Weapon* fame.

WALTERBORO

Here's a good-looking town with some vision. With just under 6,000 residents and more a-coming, the Colleton County county seat knows it's got enough beautiful old homes and history to draw some bulging pocketbooks on their way down to Hilton Head. Wisely it recently lobbied for and got the right to open South Carolina's official Artisan's Center here, showcasing (and selling) the best handicrafts from Palmetto State craftspersons.

The story goes that Walterboro's name comes from a tree-felling contest. The rice town, founded in the early 18th century, was first named Ireland Creek, but two prominent citizens, a Mr. Walter and a Mr. Smith, each believed the burg should be renamed after himself, and a tree-felling contest was used to settle the matter. In truth there were two Walters, Paul and Jacob Walter, Lowcountry planters who carved out a retreat up here just far enough away from the mosquitoes and sand fleas.

Another local legend says that the 1879 tornado that tore through town only knocked over the churches, leaving all the bars standing.

A lot of people like to walk or drive **Hampton Street** for its old houses, the earliest of which were built in 1824. Another site is the (private) **Jones-McDaniel-Hiott House,** 418 Wichman St., where the most famous person who ever lived in the house somehow managed to not be a Jones, McDaniel, or Hiott. Instead it was Elizabeth Ann Horry Dent, widow of the commander of the USS *Constitution* during 1804's Battle of Tripoli, which later worked its way into the nation's consciousness through the Marine Corps Hymn:

From the halls of Montezuma
to the shores of Tripoli,
We fight our country's battles
In the air, on land and sea.

The **South Carolina's Artisan's Center** at 334 Wichman St., 843/549-0011, features original handcrafted jewelry, pottery, baskets, furniture, and more, all made here in South Carolina, and most of it for sale. Getting this state center located in Walterboro was a major boon for the plucky little city, and finding it is your own boon. Open Mon.–Sat. 10 A.M.–7 P.M., Sunday 1–6 P.M. No admission charged, but bring money.

The **Colleton Museum,** Jefferies Blvd. at Benson St., 843/549-2303, is set in a restored 1855 jail. Pop inside—no admission—to check out some of the artifacts reflecting the area's importance during colonial days as a rice-growing region, along with other displays detailing life in this region. Open Thurs.–Fri. 9 A.M.–5 P.M. (closed 1–2 P.M. for lunch), Saturday 10 A.M.–2 P.M., Sunday 2–4 P.M.

The **Colleton County Courthouse,** on Hampton St. in Walterboro, 843/549-5791, is the site where Robert Barnwell Rhett, the fiery states' rights politician, demanded that South Carolina secede from the United States—way back in 1828, during the Nullification Crisis.

West of town, on the other side of I-95 on U.S. 64, you'll run across **Mt. Carmel Herb Farm,** 843/538-3505, where you'll find just about everything with an herbal essence, from books to seasonings.

Events

Come to Walterboro on one of the 18 Saturdays each year when it hosts the **Handmade Series,** wherein you can watch artisans creating their works right before your eyes (let's hope no one's making sausage). Call 843/549-0011 for information and to find out dates. The last weekend of April brings out the **Colleton County Rice Festival,** featuring the world's largest pot of rice and a rice-cooking contest. Call 843/549-1079 for information.

Accommodations and Food

Walterboro offers a number of chain hotels up on the interstate. Me, I'd recommend the **Walterboro Inn,** 904 Jeffries Blvd., 843/549-2581, or the two-unit **Mt. Carmel Farm B&B,** Mt. Carmel Rd., 843/538-5770; or the four-unit **Old Academy Bed and Breakfast,** 904 Hampton St., 843/549-2541.

If you've brought along a tent or have an RV, **Green Acres RV Park,** 330 Campground Rd., 800/474-3450 or 843/538-3450, and **Lakeside Campground,** Brunson Ln., 843/538-5382, offer nearly 170 sites between them.

As far as eating goes, the **Washington Street Cafe,** at 242 Washington St., 843/549-1889, is an inexpensive place for excellent Italian. **Duke's Barbecue,** 725 Robertson Blvd., 843/549-1446, uses a mustard-based sauce that has made them a very popular outfit. Open Thurs.–Sat. only, 11 A.M.–9 P.M. Head west of Walterboro on U.S. 15, then take a right on Robertson to get there.

Information

For more information on Walterboro, call the **Walterboro-Colleton Chamber of Commerce** at 843/549-9595, or fax 843/549-5775.

COLLETON STATE PARK/EDISTO RIVER CANOE AND KAYAK TRAIL

If you go left on U.S. 17 at Walterboro, you'll end up on U.S. 15. Before long you'll come to the park, hidden among the live oaks growing along Edisto River, flowing black and silent like Waffle House coffee (and tasting much the same). This is the headquarters for the Edisto River Canoe and Kayak Trail, which covers 56 miles of blackwater. Stop by or call **Carolina Heritage Outfitters** in Canadys, 800/563-5053 or 843/563-5051, to rent a canoe or kayak, or to sign up for a guided tour along the trail. Call the park at 843/538-8206 between 11 A.M. and noon to catch the rangers in the office and ask them whatever questions you might have.

There are 25 campsites here at the park. It's a good place to sleep before slipping off down the river in the morning.

SAVANNAH NATIONAL WILDLIFE REFUGE

Along the South Carolina shore of the Savannah River, 26,295 acres have been set aside as a sanctuary for migratory waterfowl and other birds, as well as other Lowcountry creatures. With all these tasty morsels around, its no won-

der that this is also a good place to see alligators. Open dawn to dusk only; no charge. Off I-95, take Exit 5; off U.S. 17 S, take S.C. 170.

You'll want to take the **Laurel Hill Wildlife Drive,** where you're likely to spot some gators— and possibly quite a few. Bring a camera, but don't get too close: they may look like logs with legs, but when they're motivated, for short distances they can move much faster than a human being. Now you've probably heard someone say that the muscles an alligator has to open his mouth with are very weak, so if necessary you can wait until the gator has his mouth closed and then clamp the mouth shut with your hands. This is true. But if you get to the point where you find yourself holding a whipping, writhing six-foot alligator by the mouth, then you have probably gotten too close in the first place.

Be sure to check out the small plantation cemetery, marked by a millstone that once belonged to a nearby mill. The Laurel Hill Plantation, where most of the cemetery's current residents once spent their vertical days, is no more.

Something else many people like is to hike or bike along the miles of dikes. Bring insect repellent.

SAVANNAH, GEORGIA

If you've come this far down the state, you might as well zip across the border and see Savannah. Then, if nothing else, when you get home and your friends ask you about *Midnight in the Garden of Good and Evil,* you can say, "Oh, Savannah was fine . . . but I *prefer* Charleston." For independent travelers, Kap Stann's *Moon Handbooks: Georgia* is the best book available on the state.

HARDEEVILLE

From the Georgia line, turn back north and head up I-95 to reach this little town, which has nearly as many rooms for rent (1,500) as it does residents (1,740). It offers 18 restaurants. But the state is busily expanding S.C. 46 to make the drive to Hilton Head faster and safer, and because it sits at the intersection of these two roads, Hardeeville is set to take off. Also exciting is the arrival of a Disney property—a shopping, food, and hotel complex located adjacent to I-95—which is supposed to feature a few Disney stores, chain restaurants, and a Disney-run/leased hotel.

You'll find about a dozen different chains here, but you may want to try out the **Carolina Inn Express,** 843/784-3155.

SERGEANT JASPER STATE PARK

This relatively new state park on Exit 8 off I-95 north of Hardeeville serves as both a recreational park for local residents and a deluxe rest stop for folks barreling down the interstate to Florida or up to New York. Call 843/784-5130 for information. The park's name honors the man who raised the Palmetto flag after it was shot down during the battle of Fort Moultrie; he was killed later in the Revolutionary War.

RIDGELAND

Ridgeland used to be known as something like the Las Vegas of South Carolina—not for its gambling, but for the goggle-eyed Georgians who used to sneak over here and take advantage of South Carolina's relatively lax marriage requirements. Today Ridgeland is home to the **Pratt Memorial Library** and **Webel Museum,** at 123-A and -B Wilson St., 843/726-7744, where you'll find 250 rare books on Lowcountry history and culture, Native American artifacts, and other historical displays reflecting life in this part of the world. You'll also find a number of chain motels, along with the **Plantation Inn,** U.S. 17 N, 843/726-5510, and the **Lakewood Plantation B&B,** 800/228-8420 or 843/726-5141, with just four units. **Duke's Barbecue,** U.S. 17 S, 843/726-3882, offers a large buffet with vegetables and fried chicken, and Duke's fine mustard-based sauce. Open Wed.–Sat. only, 11 A.M.–9 P.M. Call for directions.

ROBERTVILLE

This little town, a short jog northwest along arcing S.C. 652, gets its name from the family of Henry Martyn Robert (1837–1923). The town is proud to claim Robert, who wrote *Robert's Rules of Order,* the world's most popular handbook on parliamentary procedure. (This in spite of the fact that he, a well-known military engineer, made the social faux pas of fighting for the Union during the war.) So if you've ever "had the floor" or "seconded a motion," you may want to tip your hat to the master as you pass through town.

BOOKS AND FILMS

BOOKS

Battaile, Andrew Chandler, Arthur W. Bergernon Jr., et al. *Black Southerners in Gray: Essays on Afro-Americans in Confederate Armies.* Edited by Richard Rollins. Redondo Beach, CA: Rank and File, 1994. Fascinating studies on this little-known minority group in the Civil War.

Bodie, Idella. *South Carolina Women.* Orangeburg, S.C.: Sandlapper Publishing, 1991.

Bryan, Bo. *Shag: The Legendary Dance of the South.* Beaufort, S.C.: Foundation Books, 1995. The single best reference on the dance and the surrounding subculture.

Chesnut, Mary Boykin. *The Civil War Diary of Mary Boykin Chesnut.* This sharp-quilled woman was there, backstage, in the Confederate circles of power during the Civil War. Fascinating reading.

Conroy, Pat. *The Boo.* 1970. Conroy's first book, written shortly after he left the Citadel, about the man called "The Bear" in The Lords of Discipline. When I taught at the Citadel, I found this book much more accurate in its descriptions and tone than that other Conroy epic. It's more accurate and less sensationalistic than Lords.

———*The Prince of Tides.* 1986. A lumbering novel set in both Lowcountry South Carolina and in New York City about the American South in the modern world. Perhaps the single best book about the Southerner in the post-Faulknerian era.

DeForest, John William. *Miss Ravenel's Conversion from Secession to Loyalty.* 1867. One of Hemingway's favorites; the one great war novel published by a participant in the Civil War. Fascinating for its Northerner view of South Carolinians.

Dickey, Christopher. *Summer of Deliverance: A Memoir of Father and Son.* New York: Simon and Schuster, 1998. A heart-wrenching and insightful look at the rough-edged career of the late James Dickey—poet, novelist, screenwriter, critic, and longtime USC professor.

Edgar, Walter. *South Carolina: A History.* Columbia: USC Press, 1998. A long-needed 700-page comprehensive history by a longtime Carolina scholar.

Federal Works Project, *North Carolina: The WPA Guide to the Old North State,* 1939. The definitive old-time guide, created during the WPA years.

———. *South Carolina: A Guide to the Palmetto State,* 1941. Ditto.

Gale, Jack. *Same Time, Same Station.* Palm City, FL: Gala Pub., 1999. Great anecdotes of the days of early rock and roll radio in the Carolinas.

Godwin, John L. *Black Wilmington and the North Carolina Way: Portrait of a Community in the Era of Civil Rights Protest.* 2000. The definitive resource on the story of Benjamin Chavis, the Wilmington Ten, and the birth of the 20th-century Civil Rights movement in North Carolina.

Heyward, Dubose. *Porgy.* 1925. The novel on which Dubose based his Pulitzer Prize-winning play, *Porgy and Bess,* later made into the opera by George Gershwin.

Hudson, Charles, and Carmen Chaves Tesser, eds. *Forgotten Centuries: The Indians and Europeans in the American South, 1521–1704,* Athens, GA: UGA Press, 1994.

Humphries, Josephine. *Rich in Love.* 1989. Set in Mount Pleasant, Humphries' book gives you one of the best portrayals of real-world, shopping-mall-and-public-school modern-day

South Carolina. If the book has a weakness, it may be in that it tries to be so strident in asserting its "modern" viewpoint that it becomes a bit sappy and moralistic. Still, the book's loaded with memorable Lowcountry characters, and full of human warmth.

Hurmence, Belinda, ed. *My Folks Don't Want Me to Talk About Slavery, Before Freedom, When I Can Just Remember: Twenty-seven Oral Histories of Former South Carolina Slaves.* Winston-Salem: John F. Blair, 1997. Fascinating compilations of WPA narratives from (respectively) North Carolina and South Carolinian ex-slaves.

Johnson, Michael P., and James L. Roark. *Black Masters: A Free Family of Color in the Old South.* New York: Norton, 1984. Details the experiences of William Ellison, African-American cotton-gin builder in Stateburg before the Civil War.

Jones-Jackson, Patricia. *When Roots Die: Endangered Traditions on the Sea Islands.* Athens, GA: UGA, 1987.

Kovacik, Charles F., and John J. Winberry. *South Carolina: A Geography.* Boulder, CO: Westview Press, 1987. Reprinted by USC Press in 1989 as *South Carolina: The Making of a Landscape.* The definitive look at the various geographies of the state.

Lippy, Charles H., ed. *Religion in South Carolina,* Columbia, S.C.: USC Press, 1993. Fourteen essays shed light on the tangle of denominations that make up organized religion in South Carolina.

Martin, Floride Milner. *A Chronological Survey of South Carolina Literature.* Self-published. A representative sampling of the state's literature, from early explorer records to present-day Carolinian authors.

McCloud, Barry. *Definitive Country: The Ultimate Encyclopedia of Country Music and Its Performers,* New York: Berkley, 1995. A wonderful reference for the student of country music.

Naylor, Gloria. *Mama Day.* 1989. A Lowcountry resident herself, Gloria Naylor's fictional island of Willow Springs is home to a small group of black families who have lived there since the time of Sapphira Wade, a 'true conjure woman' who may or may not, as legend has it, have murdered the white landowner who was first her owner and then her husband. A good insight into Gullah culture, set on the South Carolina–Georgia border.

Peterkin, Julia. *Scarlet Sister Mary.* 1928. The Pulitzer Prize–winning novel about the life of a Gullah woman. Peterkin's husband worked as a plantation manager in the Waccamaw Neck region near Myrtle Beach, allowing her some insight into the daily lives of the Gullah people.

Pinckney, Elise, ed. *Letterbook of Eliza Lucas Pinckney, 1739–1762.* Chapel Hill: UNC, 1972. Along with Mary Chesnut, the indigo pioneer Pinckney is one of South Carolina's most interesting women.

Powers, Bernard E., Jr. *Black Charlestonians: A Social History: 1822–1885.* Fayetteville: University of Arkansas, 1994. A much-needed account of the important contributions of the black citizens, slave and free, to one of the most important Southern cities of the 19th century.

Rhyne, Nancy. *Carolina Seashells,* Orangeburg, S.C.: Sandlapper Publishing, 1989. Learn to know your conch from your limpet.

Simms, William Gilmore. *The Yemassee.* 1835. The greatest of Simm's historical romances, which earned him the title "The Southern Cooper." Strong in its account of the true-life Colonial-era Yamassee War. In this early novel, you'll notice Simms' already playing the apologist for slavery, but even this is fascinating and informative for those who have always wondered how the sensitive, well-educated Southern mind was able to live with itself.

Simpson, Lewis P. *Mind and the American Civil War,* Baton Rouge: LSU, 1989. Studies American history's foremost conflict in terms of the collision of two distinct philosophies and the cultures that spawned from them.

Smith, Reed. *Gullah.* Edisto Island, S.C.: Edisto Island Historical Preservation Society, 1926. Reprinted 1993.

Starobin, Robert S., ed. *Denmark Vesey: The Slave Conspiracy of 1822,* Englewood Cliffs: Prentice-Hall, 1970. A collection of essays and original documents pertaining to the aborted revolt.

Stick, David, ed. *An Outer Banks Reader.* Edited by David Stick. Chapel Hill: UNC, 1998. Concise, compelling first-person accounts of the Outer Banks, written by an assortment of explorers, sailors, soldiers, scientists, and plain-old civilians—from 1524 through today. Compiled by David Stick, legendary Banks historian.

Wallace, David Duncan. *South Carolina: A Short History 1520–1948.* UNC, 1951. Until Walter Edgar's book, this was the most recent large work on the entire state. Still worth reading for its compelling storytelling.

Woodward, C. Vann, ed. *Mary Chesnut's Civil War.* New Haven, CT: Yale, 1982. The Pulitzer Prize–winning collection of letters by a witty, shrewd eyewitness to the inner workings of the Confederacy.

FILMS

The Apostle. 1998. Though set in Texas and Louisiana, this is worth seeing for the unique insight it provides. It's one of the only literate studies of the highly influential Christian Fundamentalist/Pentecostal subculture of South Carolina and other Southern states.

Conrack. 1971. Jon Voight in Pat Conroy's autobiographical recounting of his time spent on St. Helena Island teaching English to Gullah children.

Glory. 1989. The powerful dramatization of the story of the 54th Massachusetts, the first black regiment to see combat in the Civil War. Most of the battles the regiment engages in take place in South Carolina; the climactic Battle of Fort Wagner was fought on Morris Island, just south of Charleston and north of Folly Beach.

Gone With the Wind. 1939. Sure it all takes place in Georgia, but this romantic epic belongs to all of the South and is essential for grasping the white South's romantic understanding of its past. And Rhett Butler, you'll remember, hails from the wickedly worldly city of Charleston.

The Great Santini. 1985. Set in Beaufort, based largely on author Pat Conroy's childhood there. Some great shots of Beaufort. The same waterfront house later doubled as Harold and Sarah Cooper's house in The Big Chill.

Paradise. 1991. Then-married Don Johnson and Melanie Griffith (now real-world divorced) play a couple whose wounded marriage heals with the visit of a sensitive young boy (Elijah Wood). Okay, so maybe nobody in the film bothered to sit down with a voice coach (Johnson apparently figured his Missouri twang was close enough to a Lowcountry lilt), but the film does capture some great shots of the shrimping culture around McClellanville. Actually a remake of a European film, the English-language script was originally set in a Washington state fishing village before the South Carolina Film Commission lured the filmmakers to McClellanville.

Prince of Tides. 1988. At least she didn't make it a musical. See this only if you don't let it keep you from reading Pat Conroy's novel, since director Barbra Streisand's script favors the New York–based subplot of the story. Still, some good performances, realistic accents, and nice location footage shot in and around Beaufort.

Rich In Love. 1990. In this movie, based upon Josephine Humphrey's novel, Albert Finney makes this movie, with his on-the-money portrayal of a Mount Pleasant man struggling to his feet after his wife abandons his family. A little heavy-handed in its philosophizing, but not a bad first hour and a half.

Shag—The Movie. 1991. In the summer of 1963, four recent high school graduates head from their homes in Spartanburg for a weekend of romance, drinking, and shagging at Myrtle Beach. Okay, so it's not *Citizen Kane,* but it's not *Beach Blanket Bingo,* either. Notably accurate in overall tone and cultural nuances. Great soundtrack, realistic accents, and fine shagging! Fiftysomethings who were cruising Ocean Boulevard back in '63 tell me the filmmakers get it right. South Carolina shagging czar Barry Thigpen makes a guest appearance as the emcee of the big dance contest at the end.

INDEX

AQUARIUMS

BREWERIES

CARRIAGE RIDES

GARDENS

MARITIME HISTORY

ABOUT THE AUTHOR

Mike Sigalas is the author of *South Carolina Handbook*. A graduate of the University of South Carolina and former resident of Columbia, Isle of Palms, and Orangeburg, S.C., Sigalas currently writes from a small town in the Appalachian foothills.

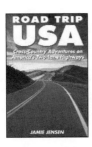

U.S.~METRIC CONVERSION

1 inch = 2.54 centimeters (cm)
1 foot = .304 meters (m)
1 yard = 0.914 meters
1 mile = 1.6093 kilometers (km)
1 km = .6214 miles
1 fathom = 1.8288 m
1 chain = 20.1168 m
1 furlong = 201.168 m
1 acre = .4047 hectares
1 sq km = 100 hectares
1 sq mile = 2.59 square km
1 ounce = 28.35 grams
1 pound = .4536 kilograms
1 short ton = .90718 metric ton
1 short ton = 2000 pounds
1 long ton = 1.016 metric tons
1 long ton = 2240 pounds
1 metric ton = 1000 kilograms
1 quart = .94635 liters
1 US gallon = 3.7854 liters
1 Imperial gallon = 4.5459 liters
1 nautical mile = 1.852 km

To compute celsius temperatures, subtract 32 from Fahrenheit and divide by 1.8. To go the other way, multiply celsius by 1.8 and add 32.

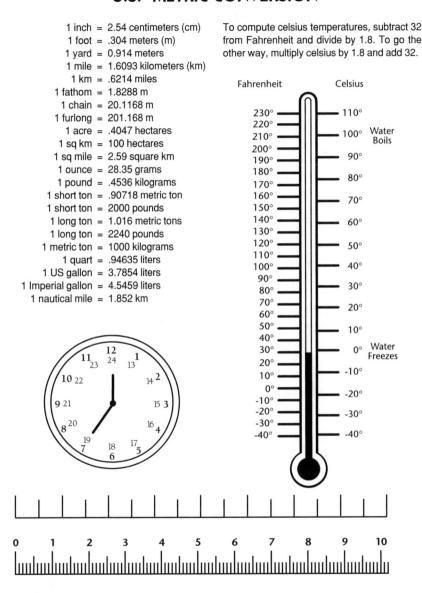